Microsoft Office Inside Out: 2013 Edition

Ed Bott
Carl Siechert

ISBN: 978-0-7356-6906-2

Second Printing: September 2014

Printed and bound in the United States of America.

Microsoft Press books are available through booksellers and distributors worldwide. If you need support related to this book, email Microsoft Press Book Support at *mspinput@microsoft.com*. Please tell us what you think of this book at *http://www.microsoft.com/learning/booksurvey*.

Microsoft and the trademarks listed at *http://www.microsoft.com/about/legal/en/us/IntellectualProperty/ Trademarks/EN-US.aspx* are trademarks of the Microsoft group of companies. All other marks are property of their respective owners.

The example companies, organizations, products, domain names, email addresses, logos, people, places, and events depicted herein are fictitious. No association with any real company, organization, product, domain name, email address, logo, person, place, or event is intended or should be inferred.

This book expresses the authors' views and opinions. The information contained in this book is provided without any express, statutory, or implied warranties. Neither the authors, Microsoft Corporation, nor its resellers or distributors will be held liable for any damages caused or alleged to be caused either directly or indirectly by this book.

Acquisitions and Developmental Editor: Kenyon Brown
Production Editor: Kristen Borg
Editorial Production: Curtis Philips
Technical Reviewer and Copyeditor: John Pierce
Indexer: Lucie Haskins
Cover Design: Twist Creative • Seattle
Cover Composition: Karen Montgomery

To Claudette Moore, "The Hammer"

Contents at a glance

Part 8: Other Office programs

Table of contents

Part 1: Office fundamentals

What do you think of this book? We want to hear from you!

Microsoft is interested in hearing your feedback so we can continually improve our books and learning resources for you. To participate in a brief online survey, please visit:

microsoft.com/learning/booksurvey

Part 4: Excel

Part 5: Outlook

Part 6: PowerPoint

Part 7: OneNote

What do you think of this book? We want to hear from you!

Microsoft is interested in hearing your feedback so we can continually improve our books and learning resources for you. To participate in a brief online survey, please visit:

microsoft.com/learning/booksurvey

Introduction

MICROSOFT OFFICE is the most popular collection of application software ever, and for good reason. The programs in the Office family allow you to perform just about any task that involves words, numbers, charts and graphs, slide decks, email, and more.

With Office 2013, Microsoft has polished the entire collection and introduced tight connections to cloud-based services, which allow you to sync settings between multiple devices just by signing in with an Office account and using the SkyDrive and SkyDrive Pro services from Microsoft.

Office 2013 introduces one new wrinkle that might confuse some longtime Office veterans. In addition to the conventional one-copy-per-PC license, Office 2013 is available as a subscription product, which includes the rights to install and use the full suite of Office software on multiple devices. We encourage you to read Chapter 1 carefully for a full overview of what's new and changed in this version.

Who this book is for

We wrote this book with a broad audience in mind: students, small business owners, professionals, information workers, and anyone else who's interested in maximizing their productivity at home or at work. Our goal is to help you become productive with the core applications in Office 2013—Word, Excel, Outlook, PowerPoint, and OneNote. In addition, we provide thorough introductions to three additional Office programs—Access, Publisher, and Lync.

Assumptions about you

We assume that most of our readers have already used at least one previous version of Office and are proficient (or at least comfortable) in one or two Office programs. For each program, we provide a quick overview that helps you understand its core concepts, and we concentrate on explaining the similarities between the products so that you can transfer skills you learn in one Office program to another.

This book does not cover advanced topics of interest to IT professionals and developers, so you won't find detailed discussions of deployment and macros.

How this book is organized

This book gives you a comprehensive look at features that are common to all the Office programs and then moves through each of the individual programs for a more detailed examination.

Part 1, "Office fundamentals," describes the various Office editions and explains how to install the program. After that, we explain features and procedures that are common to all Office programs: the ribbon and other user interface components, working with text, and working with pictures and other graphics.

Part 2, "Office on the desktop and in the cloud," shows you how to manage your Office files, whether you store them on a local hard drive, on a network drive, or in the cloud. We then show how Office integrates with SkyDrive and other online services, and how to get the most out of an Office 365 subscription.

Part 3, "Word," begins our detailed looks at individual Office programs. In this part, we cover essential Word information and then dive deeper into topics such as working with long documents, using templates and themes, using tables, tracking changes and review comments, creating blog posts, and combining documents and data with mail merge.

Part 4, "Excel," shows how to navigate around a worksheet and how to perform calculations. But it's not just numbers on a grid: we explain how to create compelling charts and how to use tables, PivotTables, slicers, and the new Quick Analysis tool to view numeric data in new and useful ways.

Part 5, "Outlook," describes the program that some people spend most of their day using. Outlook sends and receives email, manages your contacts database, maintains a calendar of meetings and other activities, and keeps track of your tasks and other to-do list items. We explain how to use each of these features to the fullest.

Part 6, "PowerPoint," explains how to create captivating slide presentations. We describe the various views in PowerPoint and explain how to use slides to show pictures, videos, animations, transitions, and other objects as well as tried-and-true bulleted lists. We show how to present a slide show on a single computer, with a second monitor or projector, or over the Internet.

Part 7, "OneNote," describes the underappreciated program for collecting all manner of notes in a freeform (yet easily searchable and retrievable) style. We show how to fill a notebook with information, tag it, and search for it. We explain how to integrate OneNote and

Outlook for managing messages, contacts, meetings, and tasks. We also show how to use shared notebooks stored in the cloud, an incredibly useful capability whether you're sharing with others or with your various devices.

Part 8, "Other Office programs," introduces three other programs included with Office 2013. First up is Publisher, a desktop publishing program for creating brochures, catalogs, and other printed materials. Then we take a look at Lync, a unified communications program with which you can connect to others via instant messages, audio and video messaging, and shared desktops. We wrap up with an overview of Access, the database program that now creates Access web apps.

Acknowledgments

Producing a book of this size requires teamwork and coordination, and meeting our quality standards takes time and concentration. For this edition, we were fortunate to work with a familiar team made up of total pros.

We were delighted when the publishers told us we could work with our longtime collaborator Curtis Philips of Publishing.com, who performed the production and layout tasks for this book. He and his team of experts, including technical reviewer and copy editor John Pierce and proofreader Andrea Fox, made invaluable improvements to the manuscript.

Our good friend and literary agent Claudette Moore did her usual magic with contracts and bookkeeping. Thanks to her efforts, we were able to concentrate on the content without being distracted by business details.

Carl's colleagues at LittleMachineShop.com endured his extended absences and grouchier-than-usual demeanor. Their support, along with that of our long-suffering wives, made it possible to bring you this book and keep a bit of our sanity.

A big thank you to the Microsoft Office team for producing a new version that was solid enough for us to use in writing this book. And we tip our hat to the team responsible for SkyDrive, which we used to share files and notes throughout the production process.

Most importantly, thanks to you for buying this book. We're grateful for your support.

—*Ed Bott and Carl Siechert, April 2013*

Support and feedback

The following sections provide information on errata, book support, feedback, and contact information.

Errata & support

We've made every effort to ensure the accuracy of this book and its companion content. Any errors that have been reported since this book was published are listed on our Microsoft Press site at

http://aka.ms/Office2013InsideOut/errata

If you find an error that is not already listed, you can report it to us through the same page.

If you need additional support, email Microsoft Press Book Support at *mspinput@microsoft.com.*

Please note that product support for Microsoft software is not offered through the addresses above.

We want to hear from you

At Microsoft Press, your satisfaction is our top priority and your feedback our most valuable asset. Please tell us what you think of this book at

http://www.aka.ms/tellpress

The survey is short, and we read every one of your comments and ideas. Thanks in advance for your input!

Stay in touch

Let's keep the conversation going! We're on Twitter: *http://twitter.com/MicrosoftPress*

CHAPTER 1

Inside Office 2013

MICROSOFT OFFICE is, without question, the single most widely used piece of productivity software in the world today. More than 1 billion (that's billion with a b) people actively use one of the many versions of Office that Microsoft has released in the past two decades.

If you're one of those longtime Office users, you'll find that Office 2013 feels new and greatly improved but without feeling dramatically different. That's both reassuring and somewhat puzzling.

At first glance, Office 2013 looks slightly different, with a flatter user interface than in previous editions. Also, most actions in individual programs are accompanied by subtle animations. Beyond that, you'll find little that's obviously new. There are no new desktop programs or web apps—Word, Excel, PowerPoint, Outlook, OneNote, and the rest of the Office family are still around. File formats have changed in only minor ways between Office 2010 and 2013. A few rarely used utilities have been retired and will not be missed.

The most important new feature, which seamlessly connects you to online file storage, builds on the familiar SkyDrive and SharePoint products. The utility that syncs local and cloud-based files is a retooled version of the venerable Groove utility, rebranded as SkyDrive Pro. Microsoft's well-established App-V and Click-to-Run technologies power the web-based installer that is at the heart of the new subscription-based Office.

And yet...

With Office 2013, Microsoft has taken its cloud services, desktop programs, and browser-based apps and fused them into a product that feels unified and natural. Small but significant improvements are scattered through the individual Office programs. Collectively, they add up to a greatly improved experience, all without altering the fundamental character of Office.

The basic challenge of Office 2013 remains, however. Depending on which edition you purchase, you have at your fingertips as many as eight full-featured programs with a sweeping range of capabilities. You have to use both sides of your brain (the analytical and the artistic), sometimes in the same program at the same time. And you're expected to remember the ins and outs of a program you might use only once every few weeks or months.

It's little wonder that most of us are comfortable with one or two Office programs and flail around in frustration when we need to use one of the others. When you're using a program that's less familiar to you, you're so busy trying to figure out how to accomplish basic tasks that you don't even think about time-saving strategies and advanced features and capabilities.

That's where we come in. Our goal in this book is to deliver exactly what you need to become productive with the core applications in Office 2013—Word, Excel, Outlook, PowerPoint, and OneNote. We provide a cram course in each program, covering the essential features and technologies and suggesting productivity-enhancing expert tips to help you work smarter. We cover three additional Office programs—Publisher, Lync, and Access—in fewer pages, but with enough detail, we hope, to propel you firmly ahead on the road to productivity.

We're confident that most of our readers have at least a passing familiarity with Office, so we won't waste your time with trivial details. In this introductory chapter, we offer a whirlwind tour of what's new and what's changed from your previous Office edition, along with a basic road map to this book.

What's new? What's changed?

The single biggest change in Office 2013 involves the decision you must make when you upgrade: will you opt for a traditional perpetual license, which allows you to pay a single price and install the software on a single device? Or will you choose a more flexible Office 365 annual subscription, which allows you to use the same Office 2013 programs on up to five devices and includes additional cloud-based services?

The economics and logistics of that decision are not obvious, which is why we break the decision down in as much detail as possible in "Choosing an Office edition" in Chapter 2, "Installing and updating Office 2013."

Although the installation and update processes are different in the subscription and installer-based Office 2013 versions, the programs themselves are functionally identical.

In this release, the Office ribbon continues its evolution. This interface element was intro-duced in Office 2007 (for every program except Outlook). It was refined (and added to Outlook) in Office 2010 and is now a part of every program in the Office family, with the exception of the difficult-to-categorize Lync communications suite.

The ribbon replaces the drop-down menus and icon-laden toolbars in earlier Office edi-tions with tabs that stretch horizontally across the top of the program window. Each tab contains commands that are organized into groups. Figure 1-1, for example, shows the Home tab in Word 2013.

Figure 1-1 The ribbon interface combines menus and toolbars into a single horizontal arrangement.

Two other elements in Figure 1-1 are worth calling out. The Quick Access Toolbar, above the ribbon at the left, is a row of shortcuts that you can customize easily. At the right of the tab headings is the name of the currently signed-in user, which lets you know at a glance which SkyDrive accounts and other Office-connected services you'll see when you click File to open or save a document.

Other additions to the Office interface allow you to choose formatting options from a gal-lery and preview their effect on your live data before committing to a change.

In all Office programs, paste options allow you to adjust formatting on the fly rather than using Undo in a series of trial-and-error attempts.

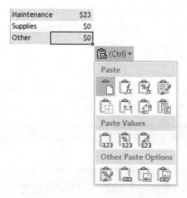

If you skipped Office 2010, you'll notice significant improvements in the ribbon. For start-ers, it's customizable. Using the dialog box shown in Figure 1-2, you can remove command groups from the ribbon, create your own custom command groups and tabs, rename exist-ing groups and tabs, and export your custom settings for reuse on a different Office 2013 installation.

Figure 1-2 If you don't like the default ribbon in an Office program, change it by adding, removing, and rearranging tabs and individual commands.

With one exception, clicking a heading on the ribbon displays the tab of the same name, a horizontal strip of commands and options related to that task. The exception is File, which always appears in the first position on the left side and is distinguished by a color back-ground that matches the color of the program's icon.

In Office 2013, clicking File opens the Office Backstage view, which occupies the entire pro-gram window and consolidates multiple tasks into a single location without forcing you to open multiple dialog boxes. This feature was introduced in Office 2010 and is significantly enhanced in Office 2013.

Click any of the options that appear, menu-style, along the left side of the window to fill Backstage view with the details for that task. Figure 1-3, for example, shows the Share tab in PowerPoint 2013, with options to share a slide show by attaching it to an email message, by creating a link to a SkyDrive folder, or by posting it to a social network that you've connected to your Office account (Facebook, in this example).

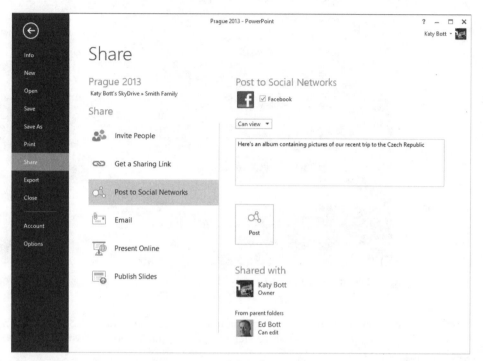

Figure 1-3 Clicking the File heading opens Backstage view, which consolidates common options and previews in a single location using the entire Office window.

For a detailed look at the Office 2013 ribbon, Backstage view, Live Preview, and other interface elements, see Chapter 3, "Using and customizing the Office interface."

All of the Office programs we cover in this edition (with the exception of OneNote) include significant improvements for inserting and editing graphics and online videos. The picture-editing tools are noteworthy, especially for anyone who skipped over Office 2010. You can use them to crop a photo, remove distracting background elements, and add artistic effects without having to leave the document window. Figure 1-4 shows an original photograph transformed by applying the Light Screen effect.

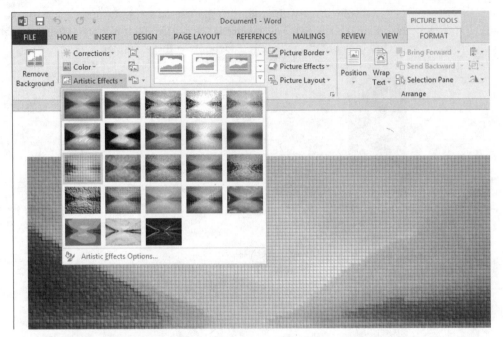

Figure 1-4 Image-editing tools available throughout Office 2013 allow you to crop and transform pictures without leaving the document window.

You'll find comprehensive instructions on how to insert and edit photos, screen shots, Smart-Art graphics, and other visual elements in Chapter 5, "Working with graphics and pictures."

Using Office Web Apps

Some (but not all) of the programs in Office 2013 have corresponding online versions that allow you to create, save, view, share, and collaborate on documents, workbooks, presentations, and notebooks.

You don't need to own Office 2013 or have an Office 365 subscription to use these Office Web Apps; all you have to do is sign in with a free SkyDrive account. You can create, view, and edit files in the default formats associated with document-centric programs in Office 2013—Word, Excel, PowerPoint, and OneNote. You can do simple edits using the web app associated with a document format; the option to open the file in the full program works easily if Office 2013 is already installed; you can "stream" the program to run on any computer running Windows 7 or Windows 8 without permanently installing it. Figure 1-5 shows the two editing options for a PowerPoint presentation stored in a SkyDrive folder.

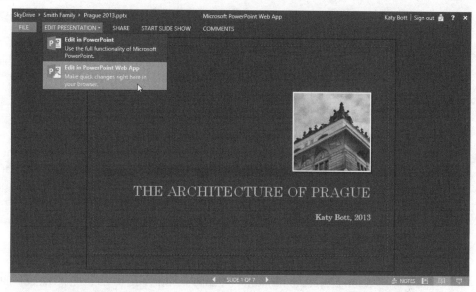

Figure 1-5 Documents stored in a SkyDrive folder can be opened for editing directly in the browser or in the associated Office program, if it's installed.

Two or more users can edit documents simultaneously when those files are stored on Sky-Drive or a SharePoint server; this capability is also available with SkyDrive Pro when used with an Office 365 Small Business Premium subscription.

You'll find more details about these tools and techniques in Chapters 7 and 8, which document the SkyDrive and SkyDrive Pro/SharePoint options, respectively.

A field guide to Office 2013 editions

If you want to install Office on a new PC or upgrade an earlier Office version on an existing PC, you have an impressive—and potentially confusing—array of options. The prices, licensing terms, and features for each edition vary significantly. Making the right choice is more complicated than simply selecting a retail box.

Subscription editions

Subscribing to Office 365 provides access to the following Office 2013 desktop applications: Word, Excel, PowerPoint, OneNote, Outlook, Access, and Publisher, as well as Lync in business editions. These programs, which are available in their desktop versions on Windows 7 and Windows 8, are installed and updated online but run from your local hard disk, with or without an Internet connection, exactly like the Office desktop programs you use today.

The biggest difference between Office 365 and the traditional installer-based versions of Office 2013 is that the subscription-based Office programs are licensed on a per-user basis rather than on a per-device basis. That's an important distinction in a world where you are likely to use multiple computing devices: a desktop PC, a notebook, a tablet, and a smartphone.

Office 365 is available in two new editions intended for consumers and small businesses:

- **Office 365 Home Premium** is intended for use by families. A single annual subscription payment covers all family members. The primary user manages the subscription and can assign Office 2013 rights to up to five devices (Windows PCs or Macs). Those devices can then be used by any family member who signs in with his or her individual Microsoft account to install and run Office 2013 programs. The primary user also gets an additional 20 GB of SkyDrive storage and 60 minutes of worldwide Skype calling.

- **Office 365 Small Business Premium** is intended for use by businesses with up to 10 employees (although it actually supports up to 25 users). The annual subscription payment covers a single user, who in turn is allowed to install and run Office 2013 programs on up to five PCs or Macs. The subscription also includes a 25 GB mailbox (on a Microsoft-hosted server running Microsoft Exchange), shared file storage of 10 GB (plus 500 MB per user), and online communications using Lync.

Businesses with more than 10 employees can acquire Office 2013 Professional Plus as part of enterprise-class Office 365 subscriptions. Students, faculty, and staff at universities can get Office 365 University, which is identical to Home Premium but allows installation on only two devices.

For a full list of features and pricing for all available Office 365 plans, see *http://bit.ly/ Office365plans*.

Retail editions

Through traditional retail distribution channels (in brick-and-mortar stores or online), you can choose from three editions:

- **Office Home and Student 2013** includes Word, Excel, OneNote, and PowerPoint. The license agreement allows you to install and activate a retail copy of this edition on a single PC. (That's a significant change from this edition of Office 2010, which included the right to install the software on up to three PCs.) The license agreement specifically prohibits using this edition "for commercial, nonprofit or revenue-generating activities."

- **Office Home and Business 2013** includes all the programs from the Home and Student edition and adds Outlook. Here, too, licensing options allow installation on a single PC.

- **Office Professional 2013** is the top-of-the-line retail Office edition, intended for consumers and small businesses. It includes the programs in the Home and Business edition and adds Publisher and Access.

For instructions on how to install and activate a retail copy of Office 2013, see Chapter 2.

Any of the preceding editions may also be sold by a PC manufacturer and preinstalled on a new computer.

What's happened to Office Starter Edition?

With Office 2010, Microsoft experimented with a free Starter Edition, available only with new PCs. This edition was considerably more limited than any retail Office edition and included only two ad-supported, limited-feature programs, Word Starter and Excel Starter. This edition was unceremoniously dumped with the introduction of Office 2013.

Volume-license editions

Businesses that have volume-license agreements with Microsoft can choose from two available Office editions:

- **Office Standard** includes Word, Excel, OneNote, PowerPoint, Outlook, and Publisher.

- **Office Professional Plus** is the high-end enterprise offering, containing the same set of programs as Office Standard and adding Access and Lync.

INSIDE OUT
How to check which Office edition is installed on a Windows PC

If you're not certain which Office edition is installed on your PC, here's how to check.

Open any Office program (this example uses Microsoft Word, but the steps are identical for other programs). Click File, and then click Account. At the right side of the window you'll see a block of information like the one shown here.

Product Information

Product Activated

Microsoft Office Professional Plus 2013
This product contains

About Word
Learn more about Word, Support, Product ID, and Copyright information.

In addition to information about your edition and the programs in it, this display also allows you to see whether your installation has been activated. Click the About *Program Name* button to see more detailed information about the program you're currently using, including the full version number and whether you're running a 32-bit or 64-bit copy. This dialog box also includes links to support resources and allows you to read the license agreement associated with your edition.

Note

In this book we do not cover stand-alone programs such as Microsoft Project and Microsoft Visio, which are part of the Office family but aren't included in any packaged Office edition. We also do not cover the enterprise-only InfoPath program.

Word 2013

Word is arguably misnamed. Yes, after all these years it still processes words with alacrity, allowing you to enter and edit blocks of text and check your spelling and grammar as you go. But modern versions of Word include design and page-layout tools that make it suitable for medium-strength desktop publishing and web design jobs. We cover the full range of Word features in the three chapters devoted to Word in this book.

The Navigation pane, an optional interface element that appears at the left side of the Word editing window when enabled, continues to evolve. As in previous versions, you can use headings in your document to quickly move between sections. The search box at the top of the Navigation pane allows you to find words and phrases easily, especially in long documents. Figure 1-6 shows search results using the page browser; an alternate view allows you to see the same results organized as snippets of text so that you can see them in context.

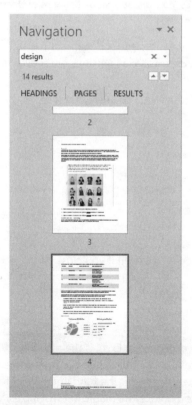

Figure 1-6 When you use the Navigation pane to search for a word or phrase, you can view the results as thumbnail pages (shown here) or as text snippets.

The most significant change in Word 2013 is the new Design tab on the ribbon, which consolidates colors, fonts, and document formatting options in a single location. The most welcome addition, shown in Figure 1-7, is the Set As Default button, which allows you to save a group of options for use with all new documents you create.

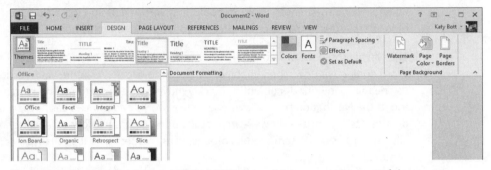

Figure 1-7 The Design tab, new in Word 2013, consolidates an assortment of document formatting options and allows to save them for reuse.

Like its Office-mates, Word also includes an assortment of document recovery features that allow you to roll back to one of five previous AutoSaved versions or recover from an unexpected crash.

You can also restore a draft version of a document even if you close Word without saving it.

Excel 2013

Shockingly, many Office users have no idea that Excel can be used for many things other than budgets and simple lists. If your only exposure to Excel is the monthly ritual of adding your department's numbers to the corporate budget template, we have some surprises for you. In the three chapters we devote to Excel, we cover the fundamentals of formulas, formatting, and filtering data; we also help you unlock the magic of PivotTables, which sound intimidating but are easy to master and incredibly useful once you learn how they work.

The most obvious improvement in Excel 2013 is a Quick Analysis tool that allows you to quickly choose data analysis and presentation options for a selection. You can apply conditional formatting, create charts, or use visualizations to add a graphic dimension to an otherwise impenetrable mass of raw numbers. Figure 1-8 shows this tool in action.

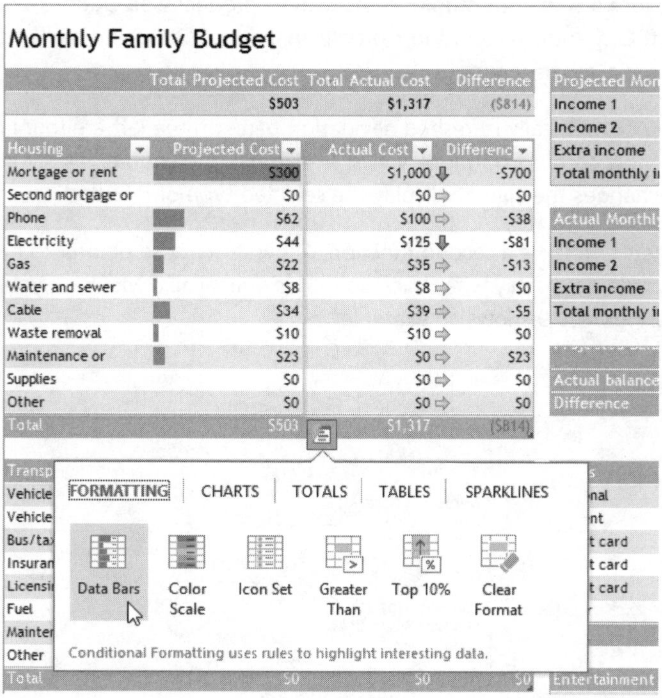

Figure 1-8 Clicking the Quick Analysis icon in the lower-right corner of a selection allows you to instantly preview and apply any of these analytical options.

For cutting large data sets into manageable workloads, Excel 2013 offers several useful tools: use PivotTables, for example, to quickly and easily create crosstabs and summaries of even very large data sets with just a few clicks. In traditional lists or PivotTables, you can create search filters to help find relevant items.

Outlook 2013

For many Office users (especially those in corporations that live and die by email), Outlook is the first program they open in the morning and the last one they shut down at night. In between, Outlook helps you juggle email, meetings, appointments, tasks, and contact information for friends, family, clients, coworkers, and anyone else. In this release, Outlook is significantly less cluttered than its predecessors. The comparison is especially striking if you've skipped over Outlook 2010.

First and foremost, Outlook is an email client program that helps you compose, send, receive, and manage messages using most standard email protocols. You can combine multiple accounts into a single set of folders. As with its predecessor, Outlook 2013 supports up to 15 Microsoft Exchange accounts in a profile; in Outlook 2007 and earlier, each Exchange account required a separate profile.

Beneath the typographically refreshed navigation pane on the left are four large labels representing the most common Outlook views: Mail, Calendar, People, Tasks. Clicking any of those targets changes the view to display the selected type of information.

But those targets also have a second function. Allow the mouse pointer to hover over Calendar, for example, to display what Microsoft's designers call a "peek" at your upcoming appointments. Figure 1-9 shows an example.

Figure 1-9 Allowing the mouse pointer to hover over Calendar displays this "peek," where you can scroll through upcoming appointments without leaving Mail.

You can scroll through the calendar, looking at events for individual days, and open any event for editing without leaving your email window. The People peek lets you pin favorite contacts to the peek list, so you can look up an address or compose an email with a click or two. The peek goes away shortly after you move the mouse away, although you can dock any or all of the three panes to the right of the Outlook window.

Outlook 2013 includes some refinement on the conversation view that debuted in Outlook 2010, most notably the animations that create a sliding effect when threaded conversations open and close. Use the Ignore button to automatically delete conversations (including future responses) in which you're an uninterested bystander trapped on the Cc line.

To manage the deluge of email, you can create rules that fire automatically when a new incoming message meets certain conditions. We'll also explain how to create Quick Steps, which automate repetitive message-handling tasks. These "macros" appear by default as buttons on the Message tab and can also be assigned to keyboard shortcuts, as shown in Figure 1-10.

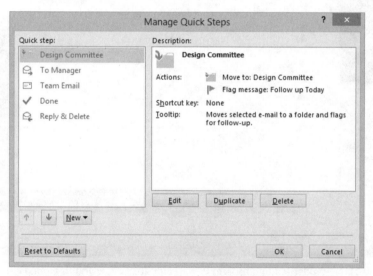

Figure 1-10 Quick Steps are an effective way of taking the drudgery out of routine message-management tasks.

Outlook 2013 also recognizes the increasing importance of keeping track of interactions with friends, family, and coworkers over time. The People pane at the bottom of every email message and contact displays a complete message history for the message sender or contact, along with connections to social networking sites, RSS feeds, status updates, meetings, and so on.

PowerPoint 2013

Most audiences groan when they realize you're about to launch into a PowerPoint presentation. But slide shows don't have to be deadly or dull—in fact, as we demonstrate, they don't even have to be slide shows, in the traditional sense. Using PowerPoint 2013, you can create photo albums and web-based presentations that don't include a single bullet point.

PowerPoint 2013 contains a new set of tools that allow you to find video clips online or in your SkyDrive account and embed them into a slide. Figure 1-11 shows these tools in action.

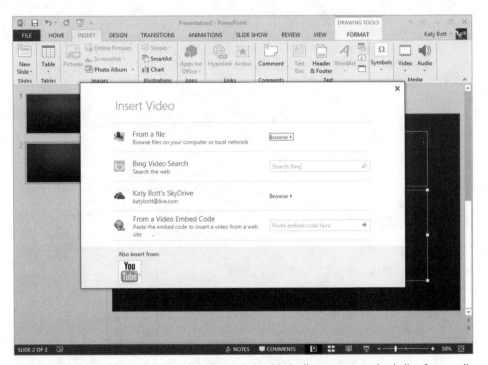

Figure 1-11 New video-editing tools in PowerPoint 2013 allow you to embed clips from online storage, including your SkyDrive account.

If you already have a solid background in building presentations with PowerPoint, we'll show you the subtle (and, in some cases, dramatic) changes in familiar tools. You can now open multiple presentations in separate windows, for example, making it easier to copy slides in one presentation for use in another. You can also divide complex presentations into sections for easier management. We'll also demonstrate how to use animations and slide transitions to best effect.

OneNote 2013

Although OneNote has been a part of Office since the 2003 release, many experienced Office users are unlikely to have spent even a minute with it. That's because for its first seven years, OneNote was included only with the Home and Student and Ultimate editions of Office. Beginning with Office 2010, OneNote was reassigned as one of the core programs installed with every retail and enterprise Office edition.

If you've never seen OneNote, we strongly recommend that you spend some time with this incredibly useful and versatile free-form note-taking program. If you're already familiar with OneNote, you'll want to pay special attention to its connections with SkyDrive. When you open a notebook from SkyDrive, OneNote syncs its contents automatically to your PC so that changes you make on one device are available on every other device you use.

Figure 1-12 shows a group of notebooks open from SkyDrive with the option to share a notebook readily available.

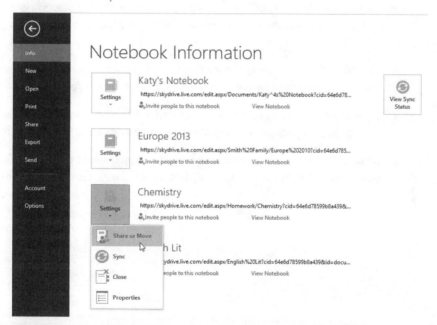

Figure 1-12 Storing a notebook on SkyDrive gives you fail-safe backups as well as the ability to share a notebook with others.

And yes, to use a bit of Microsoft jargon, we eat our own dog food. The authors and editors who worked on this book kept notes, ideas, links to outside websites, reference information, formatting instructions, and more in a shared notebook stored on SkyDrive.

Your familiarity with Word pays off in OneNote as well: you can apply formatting for headings and body text in OneNote by using the same keyboard shortcuts that work in Word. OneNote also offers excellent tools for searching and organizing information in your notebooks. That capability is invaluable when your collection of notebooks becomes too big for you to find random bits of information simply by flipping through pages.

In this book, we devote three chapters to OneNote. If you're new to the program, we recommend that you start at the beginning and read all the way through to learn some of the subtleties of this unusual but powerful program.

Other Office 2013 programs

Planning this book involves some trade-offs. Our emphasis is on the four core applications that are common to all Office editions, as well as Outlook, which is in all of the business editions.

That leaves three "lesser" applications fighting for attention. Our solution is to devote a chapter to each of these three programs, with enough information to help you get started with each one:

- **Publisher 2013** is a design tool that's specialized for creating things that don't fit neatly into Word's page-based model: invitations, brochures, flyers, cards, and so on.

- **Lync 2013** allows you to communicate with coworkers using voice, video, and messaging, with the option to share screens and collaborate on projects in real time.

- **Access 2013** manages data, big and small, in applications that keep simple lists as well as front ends to large Microsoft SQL Server databases on server farms.

Installing and updating Office 2013

NSTALLING Office 2013 is practically painless. There are few options to choose from, and if you use one of the subscription-based Office 365 options, you can actually begin working within minutes after you begin setup. The most difficult part, in fact, is deciding which Office edition is right for you. In this chapter, we guide you through that decision-making process and help you install and configure Office for problem-free performance.

Choosing an Office edition

It used to be so simple: you figured out which Office programs you needed, matched that list against the contents of Microsoft's many Office editions, picked the best match, ran a setup program, and got to work.

With Office 2013, the buying decision is more complicated, primarily as a result of the addition of new subscription options to the traditional mix of licenses.

Instead of poring over the fine print on the back of software boxes, you need to first ask a series of questions to narrow down your options:

Are you a student, teacher, or faculty member at an accredited college or university?   As a member of the academic community, you have access to subscription offerings that include just about every program in the Office family, at a price that is a tiny fraction of retail alternatives. If you skip these options, give yourself a failing grade.

Do you plan to use Office for commercial or revenue-generating activities or in a non-profit organization?   Two of the most economical Office options contain license terms that specifically prohibit commercial use. There's no technical restriction to prevent you from using these products for occasional work-related activities, but a business of any size that tries to game the system by using one of these editions risks a potentially expensive audit, with expensive consequences.

Which apps do you need?   A core of Office programs are in every edition of Office, but you still have to check the roster for each one to ensure that it has the capabilities you need. If you demand Outlook, for example, the retail version of Office Home & Student 2013 is a nonstarter for you.

Do you want a perpetual license or are you willing to pay a monthly/annual subscription?   This is the single biggest change in Office 2013. In our experience, longtime Office users have a knee-jerk reaction against the idea of paying a monthly or annual fee for software; they prefer a so-called perpetual license, which allows you to "Pay once, use indefinitely." But if you can get past that prejudice and do the math (using Excel can help you break down the costs quickly), you might find that a subscription will cost less in the long run.

How many devices (PCs, Macs, tablets) do you plan to install Office on?   The answer to this question is directly related to the previous question about subscriptions versus perpetual licenses.

Does your organization have a volume license for Office 2013?   Many large corporations buy Office licenses in bulk. If so, you might be entitled to a benefit that allows you to use Office at home for a pittance. You'll find the details later in this section.

If you've answered all those questions, then follow along as we break down each type of Office offering by category.

Subscription editions

Historically, Microsoft Office has been the very embodiment of traditional software, sold in shrink-wrapped boxes and delivered on shiny discs.

With the addition of subscription-based pricing for Office 2013, Microsoft is aggressively breaking free of that traditional software business. Instead of you paying a single flat price for the right to install Office on a single PC, the new subscription-based offerings ask you to pay a monthly or annual subscription fee.

These new Office 365 subscriptions include the same Office 2013 applications as their traditional counterparts, but they allow you to install and use the software on multiple devices (the exact number varies by plan). In addition, subscribing to Office 365 typically entitles you to additional online benefits, such as increased SkyDrive storage and Skype world minutes (for consumer plans) or Exchange-based mail accounts and SharePoint storage (for business plans). Finally, all of the plans allow you to "stream" Office applications for temporary use on a device where the full Office program isn't installed.

The single most important (and potentially confusing) difference between subscription-based Office plans involves the licensing terms for consumer and business plans.

- Consumer plans are licensed on a *per-device basis, with a limited number of concurrent installations*. As the account holder, you may install Office on as many devices as the plan permits, and any member of your household may use any of those devices, simply by signing in with a Microsoft account.

- Business plans are licensed on a *per-user basis, with a limited number of concurrent installations*. As the account owner, you assign a license to an individual (typically yourself or an employee), who may then install Office on as many devices as the plan permits, but only for his or her own use.

INSIDE OUT   Say goodbye to product keys

The single biggest advantage of subscription-based plans is that they don't require you to enter a product key and go through the activation process when you install Office on a new device. As the account owner, you visit your administrative dashboard, sign in with your Microsoft account, and begin setup from the web, without having to download a bulky installer. If you've reached the maximum number of installations for your account, you can deauthorize a device to make room for the new one. We discuss the details of this Click-to-Run setup process later in this chapter.

Here's what you'll find in each of the subscription-based Office plans:

- **Office 365 Home Premium**   This plan, intended for use in a single household, includes the core Office programs (Word, Excel, PowerPoint, and OneNote), plus Outlook, Publisher, and Access. It includes the right to install the most recent version of Office on up to five PCs or Macs. It also includes an additional 20 GB of SkyDrive storage for the primary account holder and 60 Skype world minutes per month. Note that this plan specifically prohibits using the software for commercial use.

- **Office 365 University**   To sign up for this plan, you must be currently enrolled as a full-time or part-time student in an accredited university or college or be employed as a faculty or staff member at an eligible educational institution. You must provide proof of eligibility at the time you enroll. The Office programs, license limitation, and additional benefits for this plan are identical to Office 365 Home Premium, with two exceptions: a single payment provides four years of coverage (compared to one year for Home Premium), and Office may be installed only on two devices (PCs or Macs) rather than five.

- **Office 365 Small Business Premium** This is the most basic of the business-oriented Office 365 subscriptions, designed for businesses with up to 10 employees and available for purchase in quantities as low as a single license. It includes the same Office programs as Office 365 Home Premium and adds Lync and InfoPath. Each subscription is assigned to a single user, who in turn may install the software on up to five PCs or Macs. Small Business Premium customers get a hosted Exchange account through Office 365, with a 25-GB mailbox for each licensed user and shared calendars, and a total of 10 GB of SharePoint storage for the organization, plus an additional 500 MB of SharePoint storage per user. The Lync software also allows free HD video conferencing and screen sharing.

- **Office 365 Midsize Business** This offering is similar to the Small Business Premium package, except that it includes the full-featured management dashboard of the Enterprise edition and is suitable for businesses with as many as 250 employees.

- **Office 365 ProPlus** Think of this plan as the online equivalent of the stand-alone Professional Plus edition of Office 2013, which is available only to Volume Licensing customers. It includes all of the programs in that package (which we describe in detail at the end of this section). Unlike the other business-oriented subscriptions, a subscription does not include Exchange, SharePoint, Lync, or other online services.

- **Office 365 Enterprise** Features in this edition are specifically designed for large businesses with substantial existing investments in Exchange and SharePoint deployments. It includes the same features as Office 365 Midsize Business with additional capabilities suited for large businesses that are subject to government regulation, including archiving and legal hold features. Its SharePoint Online and Lync Online features allow meetings and extended collaboration scenarios.

Retail perpetual license editions

Three editions of Office are available for purchase through retail outlets. These editions are licensed to run on a single PC or device and require activation with a product key. (Some of these packages might also be included for purchase with a new PC, typically as a card key that unlocks a trial version installed on the PC.) The license does not expire, and no additional payments are required beyond the initial purchase.

CAUTION !

Microsoft does not offer an easy or inexpensive upgrade path that would, for example, let you purchase Office Home and Business and then later upgrade to Office Professional for the difference in price. (You can purchase Office programs individually, but that turns out to be an expensive way to upgrade.) Therefore, you should evaluate your requirements carefully and decide exactly which programs you need before you select an Office edition.

If you read the license agreement for a perpetual-license edition, you might notice language that specifically prohibits transferring the software to another computer after it is installed and activated. That restriction was part of the initial release of Office 2013, but Microsoft changed those terms shortly afterward. You may indeed reassign a license to a different device after removing it from the original device. For details, see *http://w7io.com/20265*.

Each edition in this group includes what Microsoft calls the "core Office applications": Word, Excel, PowerPoint, and OneNote.

- **Office Home & Student 2013** includes only the core Office applications (note that this edition does not include Outlook). Its license agreement specifically prohibits "commercial, non-profit, or revenue-generating activity."

- **Office Home & Business 2013** includes the core Office programs plus Outlook. Its license agreement does not include any restrictions on commercial use.

- **Office Professional 2013** includes the core Office programs plus Outlook, Access, and Publisher. It too is licensed for commercial use by businesses and nonprofit organizations.

The one-PC-per-installation restriction is new in Office 2013. Some (but not all) previous editions of Office allowed multiple installations of a single purchased copy. For example, the Home and Student edition previously included the rights to install on up to three PCs in a single household. That product is no longer available. Likewise, the license agreement for some business editions included the right to install on a primary PC and on a secondary portable PC. That option too is no longer available.

If you believe you will need to install Office on more than one PC, you should look carefully at the subscription options and see whether one of them will be a better deal. That's especially true if you value the subscription-based right to upgrade automatically to subsequent Office releases without having to purchase a new license.

Volume license editions

Office 2013 is available to corporations, government agencies, and educational institutions through Volume Licensing (VL) programs. Volume licensing requires a minimum purchase of five or more licenses and offers a handful of benefits that are not available in retail or subscription editions.

For example, an organization that purchases a volume-licensed copy of Office 2013 Professional Plus can purchase Software Assurance as well. That add-on includes home-use rights for employees, who can then visit a Microsoft-run website, download a fully licensed copy of the latest Office version for Windows or OS X for a nominal fee (approximately $10 in the United States), and install it on a single device for business and personal use. (For details, see *http://microsofthup.com*.)

Two VL editions of Office 2013 are available for purchase. Both of them contain a full selection of Office apps that are useful in enterprise settings, as well as a selection of features intended for use with enterprise networks:

- **Office Standard 2013** includes Word, Excel, PowerPoint, OneNote, Outlook with Business Contact Manager, Publisher, Access, and the Office Web Apps. It also supports Group Policy, volume activation, access via Terminal service, and a feature called App Telemetry, which allows administrators to monitor the status of Office deployments. Some additional enterprise features, including Information Rights Management and voice features, are supported in a limited fashion.

- **Office Professional Plus 2013** includes all of the applications in Office Standard, plus Access, InfoPath, and Lync. It also includes a lengthy list of fully supported enterprise features.

For a full comparison of the two VL editions, see *w7io.com/10282*. For more information about the intricacies of Volume Licensing programs, visit the Microsoft Volume Licensing home page at *w7io.com/10202*. (Be prepared to spend some serious time there—it's a complicated topic.)

Setting up Office

As with any software installation, you should check system requirements before you get started.

For Office 2013, the full list of system requirements is here: *w7io.com/10283*. The list is long, primarily because it has to cover legal disclosures, but most of the salient details can be summarized in this abbreviated list:

- A PC with a modern CPU with an SSE2 instruction set. This seemingly esoteric requirement rules out some older processors. For details, see *en.wikipedia.org/wiki/SSE2*.

- At least 1 GB of RAM (32-bit) or 2 GB (64-bit). These values should be considered absolute minimums.

- Windows 7, Windows 8, or Windows Server 2008 R2 or later, with .NET 3.5

- 3 GB of free disk space

- A DirectX10 graphics card and a minimum of 1366x768 resolution; if this requirement is not met, Office will run without graphics hardware acceleration and some features will be unavailable or their performance will be degraded.

INSIDE OUT   Check for DirectX compatibility

Windows includes a diagnostic program that tells you at a glance which version of DirectX your GPU is using. To use it, press Windows key+R to open the Run dialog box, type **dxdiag,** and then press Enter. On the System tab, the DirectX Diagnostic Tool shows the DirectX version in use.

Should you choose 32-bit or 64-bit Office?

Office 2013 is available in 32-bit and 64-bit editions. If the underlying operating system is 32-bit, your only option is to install a 32-bit version of Office. If you are running 64-bit Windows, you can choose either 32-bit or 64-bit.

Most new PCs sold today run 64-bit Windows, but Microsoft strongly recommends that you install the 32-bit version of Office. What's the difference?

The 64-bit version of Office offers some distinct advantages for extreme usage scenarios. Most importantly, it enables access to much more memory than its 32-bit counterpart, which allows you to work with extremely large files (for example, Excel files larger than 2 GB).

However, there is little to be gained if your files are not humongous, and the 64-bit version has its own limitations. Many add-ins for Office are not compatible with the 64-bit version, and you're more likely to encounter other compatibility problems, such as issues with Visual Basic for Applications (VBA) macros and with certain ActiveX controls in Internet Explorer. Furthermore, with some hardware configurations, graphics rendering can be slower on the 64-bit version. It is for these reasons that Microsoft recommends the 32-bit version for most users, and that version is the one most likely to be installed as a trial on a new Windows PC.

For a technical discussion of the issues surrounding 64-bit versions of Office, see the TechNet article at *w7io.com/10281.*

Assuming you pass those hurdles, setting up Office is generally a straightforward process that requires little input from you and in which you're aided by plenty of on-screen guidance. In this section we describe three methods for procuring and installing Office:

- Using the web-based Click-to-Run installer. This is your only option for retail versions and for Office 365 installations: You click an Install button (like the one shown in Figure 2-1) that downloads and runs a small bootstrapper program; that program in turn automatically downloads the required Office installation files and allows you to begin using Office programs almost immediately.

- For Office Professional Plus and for Office Standard (available for Volume Licensing customers only), you can use Windows Installer (MSI) files, typically downloaded from Microsoft-operated services such as the Volume Licensing Service Center, TechNet, and MSDN. (The latter two services allow subscribers to download Microsoft software, including certain Office editions, for evaluation purposes.)

- Activating a trial Office edition that's included on many new computers.

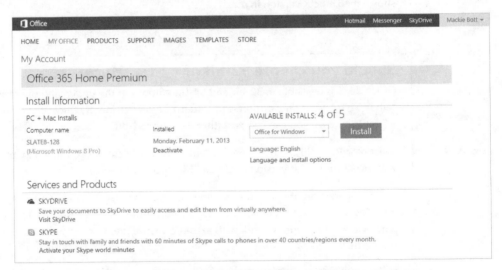

Figure 2-1 Clicking the Install button on the Office 365 account management page automatically begins the Click-to-Run Office setup process.

It's worth noting that installing Office 2013 doesn't require that you abandon your previous version. Multiple Office versions can coexist on the same PC. You can even run older versions of the programs in the Office family at the same time as current ones, so you can open one document in Word 2010 and another in Word 2013. The only exception to this rule is Outlook, which allows you to install multiple versions side by side but run only one at a time.

INSIDE OUT   Install Office throughout your organization

Microsoft provides tools and information that make it easier to install multiple copies of Office. You can push customized versions of Office to computers over the network, for example. The Microsoft Office 2013 Resource Kit provides deployment resources at *w7io.com/10285*. Note that much of the information pertains primarily to use of volume-licensed editions of Office. For step-by-step instructions for deploying Office 2013 in volume, see "Deployment methods for Office 2013," at *w7io.com/12177*.

Using the Click-to-Run Office installer

When you install a retail version of Office 2013 or one you acquire as part of an Office 365 subscription, the web-based installer uses Click-to-Run technology to download and install Office. Purchasing a retail version of Office online gets you a product key as your end of the transaction; retail boxed versions contain a product key card. In either case, you visit the Office setup website (*office.com/setup*) where you enter the key to associate the subscription with your Microsoft account and begin the Click-to-Run setup process.

> **Note**
>
> The product key you enter determines which edition will be installed. For the three retail editions (Home & Student, Home & Business, and Professional), the installation files are identical. The Office setup website adjusts its setup behavior to match the product whose key you enter.

The Click-to-Run method uses virtualization in a way that allows you to begin using Office programs almost immediately as they are streamed to your computer. During this process, you need to remain connected to the Internet to download the Office installation files, but upon completion Office is fully installed and you can use it offline.

Click-to-Run offers other advantages over traditional online program delivery: you get the most up-to-date version of Office, and you don't need to download or install patches immediately following installation.

This technology isn't new. Some editions of Office 2010 (especially Starter edition) pioneered the technology, but did so with sometimes less-than-graceful results. (If you remember having to wrestle with a phantom Q drive, you know what we're talking about.) The Click-to-Run installer in Office 2013 is remarkably more polished than its predecessors.

> **Note**
>
> A Click-to-Run Office installation is subtly different from one that is installed using the Windows Installer. Both types of installations can run Office programs after the download is complete without requiring an Internet connection. The Click-to-Run installation keeps a program called IntegratedOffice.exe running continuously; it periodically uses your Internet connection to check for updates, download them, and install them automatically. By contrast, a conventional Windows Installer–based version of Office uses Microsoft Update to deliver security updates and service packs.
>
> For Click-to-Run installations, the Microsoft Office service must run at all times. When an individual Office program is running, you'll see its executable file in Task Manager—Winword.exe for Microsoft Word, for example. But if you check the location of that file, you'll find it in a different place depending on the mode of installation. For a conventional installation of 32-bit Office 2013 from a Windows Installer file, the program files will be located in C:\Program Files (x86)\Microsoft Office\Office15. The

corresponding files for a Click-to-Run installation on a 64-bit Windows 8 machine will be in C:\Program Files\Microsoft Office 15\root\office15.

None of these details should matter in day-to-day use. In fact we recommend strongly against poking around in these locations, much less trying to tinker with these files manually. But the details are worth knowing about if you're puzzled when program files aren't where you expect them. (If you really must know the ins and outs of the technology, see *w7io.com/10286*.)

We discuss the mechanics of installing Office from an Office 365 dashboard in more detail in Chapter 8, "Using Office 2013 with an Office 365 subscription." For now, you should be aware of the following characteristics of the Click-to-Run installation method:

- Click-to-Run allows you to choose between 32-bit and 64-bit versions of Office 2013. The default is 32-bit. Before installation, Click-to-Run checks for current Office installations (including previous versions). If you have a 64-bit version of Office installed, you will be blocked from running the 32-bit installer, and vice-versa. You must install a Click-to-Run version that matches the "bitness" of currently installed Office versions or uninstall those versions before you can proceed.

- Click-to-Run does not allow you to pick and choose which Office programs to install as part of setup. Your installation includes all of the programs that are part of your Office 365 plan. You can hide or remove shortcuts and Start screen tiles, but you cannot remove individual Office programs.

- Click-to-Run does not upgrade existing Office programs but instead exists alongside them. You can remove the older Office versions before or after installing the Click-to-Run version of Office 2013.

- Microsoft says you cannot have a Click-to-Run version and a Windows Installer version of Office 2013 on the same PC. You may encounter an error message if you try to create this configuration.

To install using Click-to-Run, you must be a member of the Administrators group. After you click OK in the User Account Control dialog box (providing your Administrator credentials if necessary), the Microsoft Office Click-to-Run program begins. You must accept the license

Chapter 2

agreement and choose a theme, but after that, installation is automatic, with a window that notifies you of the installer's progress and reminds you to remain connected.

The actual time to complete installation depends on the speed of your Internet connection. Click-to-Run is optimized for broadband connections, and initial setup will take much longer on a slower connection.

You'll find shortcuts for all the new Office programs on the Start screen (or Start menu, if you're running Windows 7). Although it might take considerable time—hours, if your connection is slow—to finish downloading the entire Office package, you can go ahead and run any of these programs immediately; code needed for programs and features you use jumps to the head of the queue.

Although it's wise to wait until the setup files are downloaded and cached, you won't break anything if you need to disconnect prematurely. The Click-to-Run setup program picks up where it left off the next time you connect to the Internet.

Installing from physical media or an installer file

Installing a full version of Office 2013 from a physical disc (or its electronic equivalent, an ISO file) is possible for volume-licensed editions of Office 2013 only (Professional Plus and Standard editions.) It works much as it did with previous versions of Office and other programs.

Start the installation by running the Setup program on the installation DVD (or by running the downloaded installation file). We assume you've probably set up Office and other

Windows programs before and can follow the prompts, so in this section we'll focus only on the details where you're likely to encounter important choices.

The initial setup dialog box offers two choices. If no version of Office is currently installed, you see the two large buttons shown in Figure 2-2. Click Install Now and most of the rest of setup is automatic.

Figure 2-2 If an earlier version of Office is already installed on your computer, the top choice in this dialog box is Upgrade.

Clicking Install Now allows you to proceed with a nearly fully automated installation.

If a previous Office installation is available, an Upgrade option appears in place of Install Now. Click that option and all previous Office versions will be removed automatically, after which Setup will install Office 2013.

In either case, you can bypass the default settings by clicking Customize. Doing so allows you to be selective about which Office components you install, to determine which (if any) Office programs you want to retain from a previous version, and to specify where the program files will be stored.

The dialog box that appears when you click Customize has either three or four tabs. If an earlier version of Office is installed, the Upgrade tab is first in the lineup, as shown in Figure 2-3.

Figure 2-3 By default, an upgrade using the Windows Installer version attempts to remove all previous Office versions; it retains settings and data files.

By changing the option on the Upgrade tab, you can keep all previous versions or remove selected applications. The latter configuration might be useful if you want to continue using Outlook 2010 to connect to an Exchange 2003 server (a configuration not supported by Outlook 2013) while discarding other members of the 2010 family.

The Installation Options tab (shown in Figure 2-4) shows a hierarchically organized list of Office components. Click the plus sign next to an item to see a list of that item's subcomponents. When you click a component's name, a brief description of the component appears near the bottom of the dialog box.

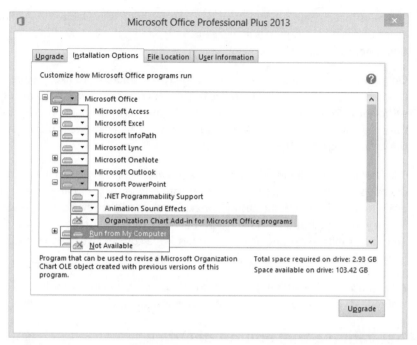

Figure 2-4 Each program gets its own option in this portion of a custom installation using a volume-license version of Office 2013.

A button with a white background indicates that all subcomponents are set the same way as the displayed component; a gray background indicates that one or more subcomponents have an installation setting that's different from the displayed component. For each component, you can select one of as many as four settings by clicking the arrow next to the component's name:

- **Run From My Computer**   Select this option to install the component (but not any of its subcomponents) on your computer's local drive.

- **Run All From My Computer**   This option installs the component and all of its subcomponents on your computer's local drive.

- **Installed On First Use**   If you select this option, the component won't be installed on your computer until you attempt to use the component. At that time, Office will need access to your Office DVD or the installation file from which you ran Setup.

- **Not Available**   Select this option for each component you don't plan to use or install.

For items that contain subcomponents, a fourth option is available: Run All From My Computer. Choosing this option is equivalent to expanding the item and selecting Run From My Computer for each subcomponent.

On the File Location tab, you can specify the folder where you'd like to store the Office program files. Unless you have unique requirements, it's best to use the default location—a subfolder of Program Files or Program Files (x86)—because it inherits appropriate protections that allow access by all users while preventing inadvertent (or malicious) changes to the Office program files.

The User Information tab provides a place to enter your name, your initials, and the name of your organization. Office uses this information to enter your name in a document's properties (to identify you as the author, for example), to tag review comments with your initials, to put your organization's name in a predefined header or footer in printed documents, and other similar purposes. If you don't perform a custom installation, Office asks for this information the first time you run an Office program.

After you've made your settings on each tab of this dialog box, click Install Now (or Upgrade if you have an earlier Office version installed) to complete the process.

Activating a trial edition of Office

If a trial version of Office 2013 is already installed on your new computer, you can enter your product key when you first run Office. If you decide to use Office 2013 in trial mode, you'll be prompted to enter a product key when the trial expires, or you can look on the Account Information page in Backstage view for an activation link.

Activating your Office installation

In the new, mostly Click-to-Run world of Office 2013, a product activation dialog box is a rare sight. With Office 365, you assign Office licenses to new computers and deactivate existing licenses by signing in to the management page using your Microsoft account. (We discuss this in more detail in Chapter 8.)

When installing a perpetual license version of Office 2013, you enter the product key as the first step in the web-based Click-to-Run setup program. You can use the same product key when you reinstall the software (on the same device) if you need to reinstall Office because of a disk crash or other disaster.

If you have a trial version of Office 2013, you have the option to activate it using an Office 365 account or a product key. The activation dialog box, available from the Account page in Office Backstage view, looks like this:

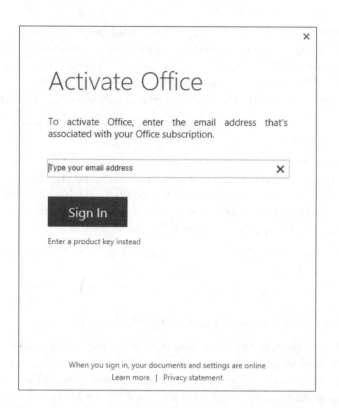

As you can see, the default setting in this dialog box assumes you will enter an email address and sign in to an active Office 365 subscription. If you have a product key and want to use that to install Office 2013 on a single PC, click Enter A Product Key Instead. That leads to the dialog box shown here.

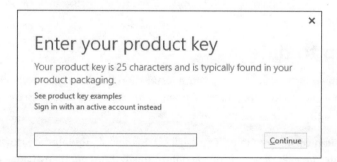

If you allow an Office 365 subscription to lapse, your Office programs remain installed but enter "reduced functionality" mode. Your data files are unchanged, and if you have another device running an activated version of Office you can work with them there or on SkyDrive, using the free Office Web Apps. You can still open and view data files using nonactivated Office programs, but you cannot create new files or edit existing ones using that software.

> ### Note
>
> The activation process for volume-licensed editions of Office is not the same as the process described in this book for retail copies. Volume activation can be done using either of two methods: Multiple Activation Key (MAK) or Key Management Service (KMS). For details about these methods, see "Volume Activation of Office 2013" in Microsoft's TechNet Library (*http://w7io.com/10287*).

INSIDE OUT   Which version is installed, 32-bit or 64-bit?

Part of keeping Office up to date is installing and maintaining current versions of Office add-ins. Because most add-ins run on either 32-bit Office or 64-bit Office (but not both), you need to know which you have before you download add-in files. Once Office is installed, it's not easy to tell whether you're using the 32-bit or 64-bit version because the outward differences are few. The foolproof way to tell? Click File in any Office program and then click Account; click About *Program Name* to see the full version number of the program and Office, with either "(32-bit)" or "(64-bit)" appended to the end of that version string.

Keeping Office up to date

As they say, nothing lasts forever. Every Office installation needs regular updates to address security vulnerabilities, to update junk mail filtering rules, to fix a newly discovered bug, or to add new features.

With a Click-to-Run version of Office, you're all set. By default, updates are downloaded and installed automatically. If you want to confirm this setting, open any Office program, click File, and then click Account (Office Account in Outlook). The Product Information section displays the currently installed version number. Clicking Update Options reveals a menu that allows you to disable updates (we recommend you don't do that) as well as a

View Updates option that takes you to a webpage where you can confirm that you have the latest Click-to-Run release installed.

In non–Click-to-Run versions of Office, updates are delivered through Windows Update—the standard part of Windows that manages the download and installation of updates to Windows and Microsoft applications, including Office.

You'll find Windows Update in Control Panel (hint: the easier route is to use search from the Windows 8 Start screen or the Windows 7 Start menu search box). In Windows Update, click Change Settings to review your current update settings. We concur with Microsoft's recommendation: select Install Updates Automatically (Recommended). Also ensure that the check box beneath the Microsoft Update heading is selected. With those settings in place, important updates are downloaded and installed for Office automatically. Optional updates—ones that might add features or functionality but are not critical to your computer's security—are installed only at your specific direction. You do that by opening Windows Update, clicking the optional updates link if it appears, selecting the updates to install and clicking OK, and then clicking Install Updates.

Customizing Office with add-ins and apps

Office 2013, like its predecessors, supports the use of add-ins. These are supplemental programs, often created by a developer other than Microsoft, that plug into Office programs to add features or capabilities. In addition, Office 2013 adds support for a new class of apps, which are available from the Office Store and can significantly enhance the capabilities of Office programs.

A number of legacy add-ins are included with Office 2013. To see the full list, click File, Options, and then click Add-Ins. As shown here, Office displays a list of installed add-ins, including those that are installed but not currently active.

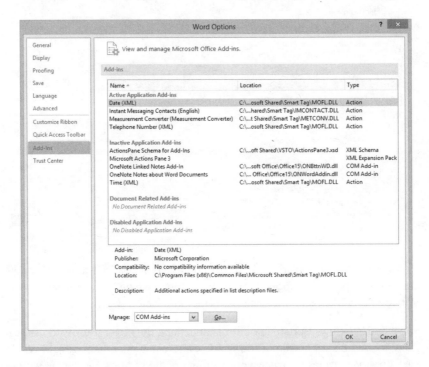

In addition, third-party programs you install might include add-ins for Office.

To remove or disable an installed add-in, in the Manage box select COM Add-Ins and click Go to display the COM Add-Ins dialog box, shown in Figure 2-5.

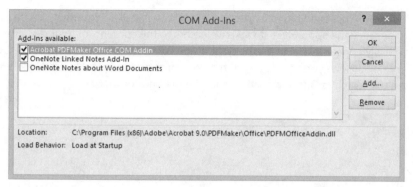

Figure 2-5 Clear a check box to unload an active add-in.

The new Office 2013 apps are available in the Office Store, which you can visit from within any Office 2013 program by clicking Apps For Office (on the Insert tab) and then clicking See All. That opens a dialog box like the one shown in Figure 2-6, where you can browse and search for both free and paid apps.

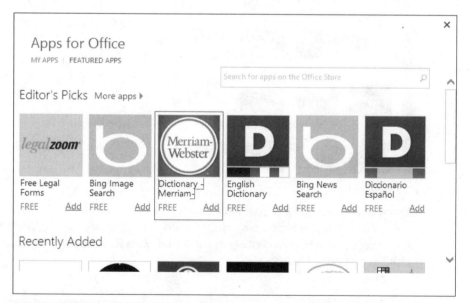

Figure 2-6 To add apps to an Office program, visit the Office Store. Note the search box in the upper-right corner, where you can narrow the selection.

The list displayed in this dialog box includes only apps that are compatible with the program you're currently using.

Chapter 2

When you locate an interesting app, click Add to install it. Note that you might be required to approve the app before it can have access to the contents of your document. Office apps typically appear in a pane to the right of the current workspace. Bing Image Search, for example, allows you to select text in a document and then locate matching images, displaying the search results in a results pane, like the one shown here.

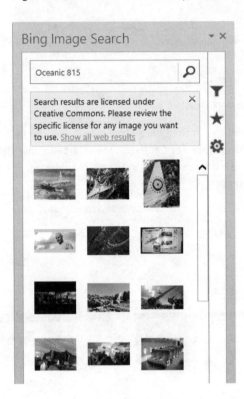

To manage apps, visit *office.com*, sign in with your Office account, and click Store. (You'll find a shortcut to this page from any Office program. Click Apps for Office on the Insert tab, click See All, and then click My Apps. The resulting dialog box shows installed apps and includes a Manage My Apps link.)

Uninstalling Office

When you no longer need your older Office version—or if you deactivate an Office 365 subscription license from a device and want to remove the Office 2013 programs you installed via Click-to-Run—you can uninstall either one. In Control Panel, open Programs And Features, select the Office version you want to remove, and then click Uninstall.

This process, alas, is not always foolproof. Some bits of Office detritus can remain behind. That's especially true with preview versions. If you encounter uninstall issues, it's helpful to haul out more specialized tools. The following are available from Microsoft's support pages:

- For Office 365 and Office 2013, you can use a downloadable Microsoft Fix It tool from support article 2739501, "Uninstall Microsoft Office 2013 or Office 365," available at *w7io.com/2739501*. The same article includes manual removal instructions.

- For Office 2010 and earlier versions, see support article 290301, "How to uninstall or remove Microsoft Office 2010 suites," available at *w7io.com/290301*. This article includes four separate steps for Office 2010, which you should try in order. It also includes links to corresponding articles for Office 2007 and Office 2003 for Windows and Microsoft Office for Mac (2011 and 2008).

Chapter 2

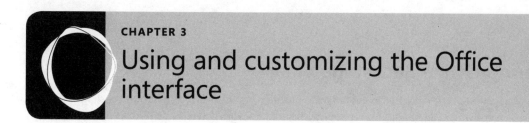

CHAPTER 3

Using and customizing the Office interface

SEVEN of the eight programs in the Office 2013 family share a common, ribbon-based layout, with a set of interface elements and a typographic design that are strikingly similar. (The exception is Lync, which we will ignore for the balance of this chapter.)

Thanks to this common layout, you can find the same elements in the same positions, regardless of which Office program you're using. A ribbon filled with commands appears at the top of the window, occupying the window's full width; a much smaller Quick Access Toolbar is just above the ribbon. Clicking File (located just to the left of the ribbon headings in every program) takes you to Backstage view, where you can perform file management tasks and adjust program and Office account settings.

The guiding principle behind this consistency, of course, is to make it easier for you to switch between programs. When you learn that the Spelling command is on the Review tab in Word, you can reasonably (and correctly) assume that the corresponding command will be on the Review tab in Excel, PowerPoint, and Publisher—and in the same position in Outlook when you're composing a new message.

When you dig deeper into each program, you'll see other common elements. A customizable status bar appears at the bottom of most program windows. Most formatting tasks can be accomplished using the Mini toolbar that floats over a selection. Galleries of design and formatting tools allow you to instantly preview the effects of making changes, such as altering the default font in a document, worksheet, presentation, or project.

The similarities are most pronounced among the four document-oriented programs—Word, Excel, PowerPoint, and Publisher. Even here, however, you'll spot obvious differences as you gain more experience with each program. Although the access point is the same, options for checking spelling and grammar in a Word document are much more robust than the simpler spelling tools in PowerPoint and Excel, for example.

Our goal in this chapter is to introduce the interface elements that are common to all Office programs and explain how to use each one. We also describe the best ways to customize and personalize the Office interface. Our starting point is Backstage view.

Mastering Office Backstage view

Just below the title bar in every Office program, to the left of the ribbon headings, you'll see a white File heading on a brightly colored background. This can't-miss target is available in every Office program.

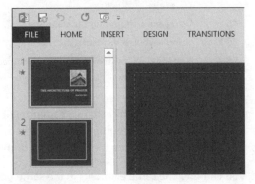

Clicking File causes the program window and the ribbon and Quick Access Toolbar to disappear temporarily. The contents of the program window are replaced with Backstage view. Options on the left of that view let you flip between available actions, with each option displaying its own pane, such as the Export pane shown in Figure 3-1.

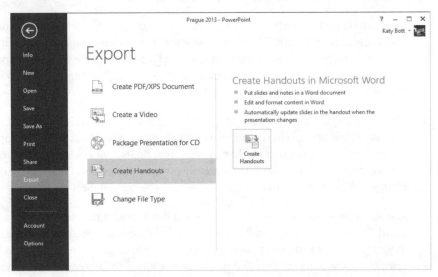

Figure 3-1 Click File to open Office Backstage view, which consolidates information and tasks related to the current file or project.

The basic arrangement of Office Backstage view is similar in each of the seven programs we cover in this chapter and is refined considerably compared to Office 2010. The choices available in the navigation pane on the left vary slightly, depending on the program.

INSIDE OUT

Changing the appearance of Office 2013 with themes and color-coding

Office 2013 offers a choice of three themes: White (the default), Light Gray, and Dark Gray. Regardless of which theme you choose, every tab heading in every Office program is identified with black text on a white or gray background. The nonconformist is the File heading, which sits at the left of the ribbon and stands out with white type on a bold-colored background.

Each Office program has its own designated color: Word is blue, Excel green, OneNote purple, PowerPoint orange, and so on. That color scheme is consistent throughout a program's design. The green Excel icon on the Windows taskbar and the Start screen matches the green logo in the program's title bar. The orange background behind the options in Backstage view for PowerPoint matches the program icon.

If those nearly fluorescent background colors are too much to take, you can tone them down by switching to the Dark Gray theme. In any Office program, click File to open Backstage view, click Account, and then select Dark Gray from the Office Theme list, as shown here. (The Office Background option just above it controls whether you see a faint decorative pattern in the space above the ribbon.)

Changing your theme takes effect in all Office programs immediately. The Dark Gray theme reverses the color coding in the navigation pane in Backstage view: Options appear in white type on a black background, with only the highlighted option appearing in the program's color. (Note that you can also change the Office Background and Office Theme settings using the General tab of the Options dialog box in any Office program.)

Viewing document properties in the Info pane

The Info option sits at the top of the navigation pane in all seven Office programs. In document-oriented programs, clicking Info displays details about the current document in two columns. Figure 3-2 shows the Info pane for a typical Word document.

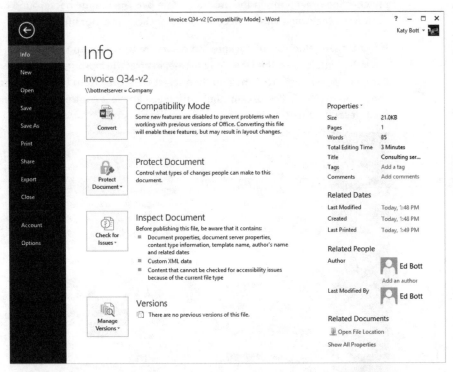

Figure 3-2 Details in the Info pane depend on the contents of the document. The Convert button shown here is visible only with documents created with an older version of Word and displayed in Compatibility Mode.

Atop the left column is the name of the document and its location. Below those details are command buttons that allow you to inspect the document's contents for confidential information, manage versions, and restrict who can view or edit the file. In the right column are properties such as file size, the dates the document was created and last modified, and any tags added by the program itself (author name, for example) or by a person who worked on the file.

For an in-depth discussion of how to create and save files and view or change their properties using Office programs, see Chapter 6, "Managing Office files."

Creating, editing, and saving files in Backstage view

As the successor to the venerable File menu, Backstage view plays a crucial part in the process of creating new files, saving those files locally or on SkyDrive, and reopening saved files for viewing or further editing. Most of the commands described in this section are identical across Office programs (the notable exception is Outlook).

Creating a new document

Clicking New fills the right side of Backstage view with a selection of templates. Use the search box at the top of the list to filter the results, after which you can refine the results further using the list of categories along the right side of the results pane, as shown in Figure 3-3.

Figure 3-3 Use the Category list on the right to refine the results for a template search. Matching templates are also shown for other Office programs.

The thumbnail image that appears in the list of templates typically represents a template that is available on Microsoft's servers, not one that's stored locally. Click the thumbnail to display a pop-up box showing more details about the selected template, or right-click the thumbnail to display the list of options shown next.

Chapter 3

Photo album

If you're certain this is the template you want to use, click Create to download the template (if you haven't previously used it) and open a new file based on that template. If you plan to reuse the template, click the Pin To List option to ensure that it's available for future projects.

For a full discussion of how to find, use, and manage Office templates, see "Using templates to streamline document creation" in Chapter 6.

Opening, saving, and closing files

Four options in the navigation pane in Backstage view—Open, Save, Save As, and Close—allow you to perform core file-management tasks for the current document. We discuss the Open and Save As options in more detail in Chapter 6.

In the main Outlook window, Backstage view includes an Open & Export tab that provides basic tools for opening calendars and data files and for importing and exporting files and settings. This option is not available in the Info pane for a window containing an Outlook item.

OneNote includes New and Open options that are designed to handle the program's unique file-management challenges, which can't be handled in the Windows Open and Save As dialog boxes. Figure 3-4 shows the Open tab, with a selection of notebooks available on SkyDrive for the signed-in user.

Clicking the Close option in Backstage view doesn't display anything in the pane to its right. Instead, it immediately closes the current file or item, prompting you to save it if you've made changes since the last time you saved.

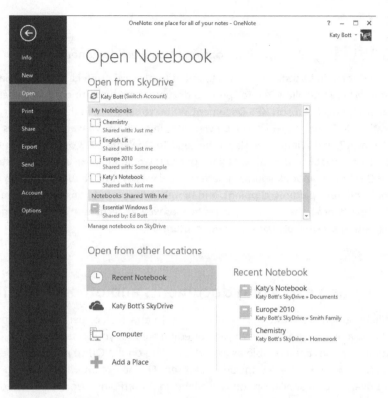

Figure 3-4 Click Open to choose an existing notebook from SkyDrive and begin syncing it to the current device.

Printing from Backstage view

Click Print to preview the current document, presentation, worksheet, or Outlook item and then send it to a local or network printer. From this information-rich tab, you can select a printer, adjust printer settings, and adjust options for the current print job, such as the number of copies to be printed. You'll notice some subtle per-program differences in available options; you have direct access to headers and footers in PowerPoint, for example, but must click Page Setup to reach the equivalent settings in Word and Excel.

Print options for individual Outlook items are dramatically simpler than in the four document-centric programs, and OneNote print options are downright spartan, with only two buttons, Print and Print Preview, on the tab.

INSIDE OUT   Use the Print option to convert documents, too

The Print tab in Backstage view isn't limited to physical printers. You'll also find virtual printers here that allow you to "print" a document without using a single sheet of paper. Use the Microsoft XPS Document Writer to save files in the XML Paper Specification (XPS) format, which can be viewed using the XPS Viewer in Windows Vista, Windows 7, and Windows 8. Using the Send To OneNote 2013 option on the Printer list creates a resizable image of what your printout would look like and then pastes it into the OneNote notebook you designate (a topic we cover more fully in "Filling a notebook with text, pictures, clippings, and more" in Chapter 21, "Inside OneNote 2013"). Third-party programs can add entries here as well, as TechSmith's SnagIt program does in creating a virtual printer for screen captures.

Sharing and exporting documents and other Office items

The Share option in Backstage view allows you to attach all or part of a document to an email message or invite people to view or edit a file that you've saved in a SkyDrive folder. Additional options are available as well, depending on the Office program. The Share pane in Word, shown in Figure 3-5, includes a Present Online option, which lets you share a document over Lync. (A similar option is available in PowerPoint.) Word also includes an option to post a document to a blog.

In Word and Excel, the Export option includes only two choices. You can save the current document as a PDF or XPS file, or click Change File Type to choose an alternative format. PowerPoint and Publisher offer additional options, including the capability to save a slide deck as a video file or to package a Publisher project for output by a commercial printer, as shown in Figure 3-6.

For a more detailed discussion of options included in the Export pane, see Chapter 6.

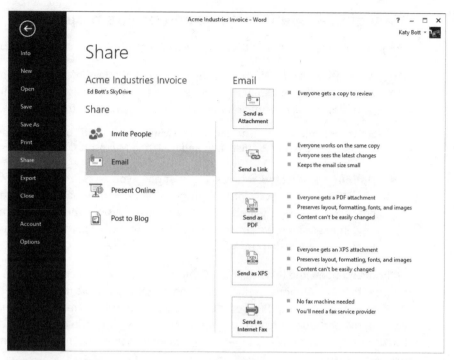

Figure 3-5 Options on the Share tab in Office Backstage view allow you to send documents via email as attachments or share them using SkyDrive links.

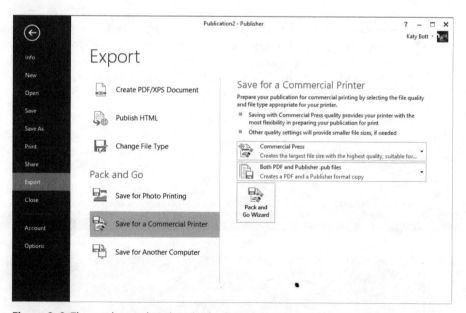

Figure 3-6 These advanced options in the Export pane are unique to Publisher.

Managing account settings and program options

The final two options in Office Backstage view are available in every Office program.

- **Account** (shown as Office Account in Outlook) displays information about the user who is currently signed in and any services to which that account is connected. This pane also shows information about the product and its activation status.

  For the ins and outs of installing and activating Office and configuring your Office account, see Chapter 2, "Installing and updating Microsoft Office 2013."

- **Options** opens a tabbed dialog box that gives you access to a sometimes over-whelming set of options for that program. Many of the options are program-specific, but others represent shared features or similar ways of handling the same general task. In this section, we concentrate on the most useful common features you're likely to find in these dialog boxes.

Without exception, the first tab in the Options dialog box for each program is General. In the User Interface Options section, you'll find options to disable the Mini toolbar and Live Preview—although we find these features generally useful, you're free to disable them if you find the pop-ups more distracting than helpful. You can also change the display of ScreenTips, the descriptive tips that appear when you allow the mouse pointer to hover over a command.

> **Note**
>
> Any changes you make in the User Interface Options section apply to the current program only. If you want to change these settings for multiple programs, you need to visit the Options dialog box in each program. However, any changes you make in one program to the Office Background, Office Theme, or User Name fields apply immediately to other Office programs as well.

The General tab is also where you set the default font for Excel workbooks (shown in Figure 3-7) and OneNote documents.

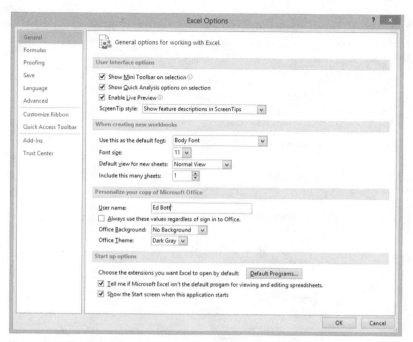

Figure 3-7 For Excel (shown here) and OneNote, use the font options to change the appearance of new workbooks or notebooks.

At the bottom of the General tab, the Start Up Options group provides access to the Windows Default Programs feature, where you can change file associations for the current program. In Word, Excel, PowerPoint, and Publisher you can clear a check box to bypass the list of available templates when you open the program for the first time; with the Show The Start Screen When This Application Starts check box cleared, you go directly to a new document using the default template.

The Proofing tab (see Figure 3-8) contains settings for the spelling checker used throughout Office programs; it also allows you to adjust program-specific spelling in Word, Excel, OneNote, and PowerPoint. (To find the Proofing tab in Outlook, select the Mail tab and click Editor Options.) This tab is also where you'll find settings that control how AutoCorrect works. Although this feature is most commonly associated with Word, the core features are actually available in Excel, PowerPoint, Publisher, OneNote, Access, and Outlook's Mail Editor as well.

For an explanation of how AutoCorrect can save you time and keystrokes and how to use it in Word and elsewhere, see "Entering boilerplate and other oft-used text" in Chapter 4, "Entering, editing, and formatting text."

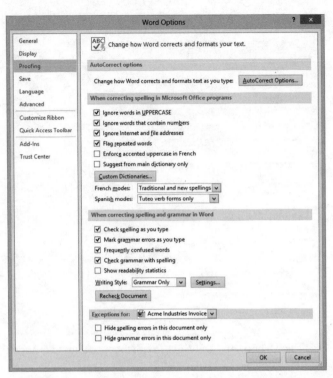

Figure 3-8 Word has the most extensive set of spelling and grammar options of all Office programs. Most of these settings are shared with Outlook's Mail Editor as well.

For any program you use regularly, you should be sure to visit the Save tab at least once. In Word, Excel, and PowerPoint, this is where you assign a default document format, configure how often the program should automatically save your work, and specify default locations for your files and for AutoRecover files. Publisher has a smaller set of options. In OneNote, the tab is called Save & Backup, and the backup procedures are much different but still worth paying close attention to.

For more information on how to configure AutoRecover and why it can help you breathe a sigh of relief, see "Backup and recovery options" in Chapter 6, "Managing Office files." For details on how to configure OneNote's automated backup options, see "Backing up and recovering notebooks" in Chapter 22, "Tagging, organizing, and finding information."

Finally, every program has an Advanced tab in its Options dialog box. There, you'll find a mix of essential and esoteric settings, most of them specific to the current program. We discuss these options in more detail in the chapters dedicated to each program.

Using and customizing the ribbon

An archeologist looking at the evolution of Microsoft Office would no doubt divide its timeline neatly into two eras: The Menu-Toolbar Era lasted from the early 1990s through Office 2003. The emergence of Office 2007 marked the dawn of the Ribbon Era.

If you've used Office 2010 for any length of time, the workings of the ribbon will be familiar, even if the ribbon's visual treatment is strikingly different in Office 2013. In this section, we explain how to use the ribbon, with a special emphasis on galleries and live previews. We also describe the best ways to customize and personalize the ribbon.

Using the ribbon

Without question, the ribbon marked a radical change in appearance for the Office interface. If your time with Office began in 2006 or earlier, you learned how to navigate through Office programs by using drop-down menus that were essentially lists of commands under a group of headings: File, Edit, View, and so on. Some widely available competitors to Microsoft Office still use these traditional menus.

Despite the visual differences between the ribbon and the old-style menus, their basic functionality isn't all that different. Tabs on the ribbon function in much the same way as the top-level menu choices do, and commands are arranged into groupings in a manner that's like cascading menus. One benefit of this big switch was that it created an opportunity to reorganize the overall menu structure into a more modern arrangement. For example, many of the commands on the Edit and Format menus in Office 2003 and earlier are consolidated, logically, on the Home tab in Office 2013.

The key to using the ribbon effectively is to understand how it's organized and learn how it works. As we noted earlier, the ribbon is divided into tabs, each with its own heading. Every program contains a default set of tabs that are available at all times. Figure 3-9 shows the References tab from Word 2013, which contains roughly 20 visible commands organized into six groups.

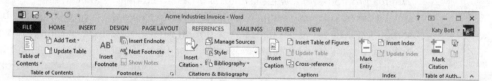

Figure 3-9 This tab is divided into six groups, each labeled along the bottom and separated from other groups by vertical dividers.

INSIDE OUT   Auto-hide the ribbon

When you want to use as much screen real estate as possible for your document, the ribbon can feel like a space hog. For those occasions, the solution is simple: click the small, upward-facing arrow at the far right of the ribbon, on the same level as the names of the command groups. (You can also right-click any part of the ribbon and then click Collapse The Ribbon on the shortcut menu, double-click the heading for the active tab, or press Ctrl+F1 to achieve the same effect.) Collapsing the ribbon hides its contents, leaving only the tab names behind in an arrangement that looks surprisingly like the old-style Office menu bar. Click any tab name to show the contents of that tab so that you can use its groups of commands. Click anywhere in the document to hide the ribbon again. Click the downward-facing arrow or double-click any tab name to expand the ribbon to its full height and keep tabs visible even when you click away.

If you *really* find the ribbon to be distracting (and you don't mind maximizing your Office window), click Ribbon Display Options, one of the icons in the upper-right corner of each window (shown next). Choose Auto-Hide Ribbon, and the ribbon, the tab names, and the Quick Access Toolbar disappear altogether as your window fills the screen. Click anywhere in the slim remaining bar to view the ribbon.

When a program window is maximized on a large monitor, you can see a mix of large icons, small icons, and labels designed to make it easier to see these groupings at a glance. But something interesting happens to the ribbon when you resize a program window. The order of groups (and of commands within each group) remains the same, but the labels alongside some commands disappear, and some commands are moved to drop-down menus to accommodate the horizontal space available.

In addition to the default tabs, context-sensitive tabs appear at the right side of the ribbon when needed. If you click within a table in a Word document, a pair of distinctively color-coded tabs appear under the Table Tools heading at the end of the ribbon, as in Figure 3-10.

Figure 3-10 Context-sensitive tabs, such as these Design and Layout options for Word tables, appear only when needed and always at the right side of the ribbon.

For details on how to create custom tabs or change the layout of built-in tabs, see "Personalizing the ribbon" later in this chapter.

In the lower-right corner of some command groups, you might see a button that looks like a tiny arrow pointing down and to the right. These launchers enable access to settings that aren't available through the ribbon itself. In some cases, clicking the launcher opens a dialog box—that's the case with the Font and Paragraph options on the Home tab in Word.

Other launchers open a pane on the right side of the document containing task-specific tools. Figure 3-11, for example, shows the Format Picture tools in Word. To make this pane appear, select a picture in a Word document or PowerPoint slide and then click the launcher in the lower right of the Picture Styles command group on the Format tab.

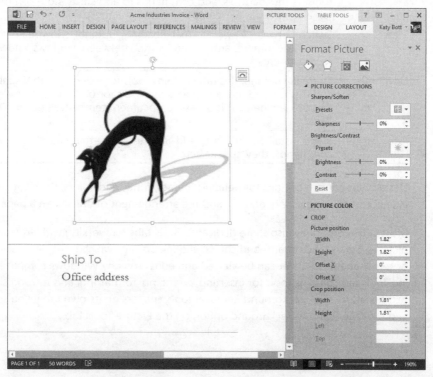

Figure 3-11 Formatting tools such as those in the pane at the right of this document appear when you click a launcher on the Picture Tools or Drawing Tools tabs.

> **Note**
>
> In one of the increasingly rare minor inconsistencies between Office programs, clicking this launcher in Publisher opens the old-style Format Picture dialog box.

Every Office program includes an enormous selection of tabs, most of them dedicated to groups of features that are specific to that program. A handful of default main tabs are available in multiple programs and are described in Table 3-1.

TABLE 3-1 Features, tools, and commands available on common ribbon tabs

Tab name	Contents
Home	Basic editing and formatting tools, as well as the Clipboard and find/replace functions. Outlook has seven task-specific Home tabs to cover individual item types (email messages, contacts, appointments, and so on).
Insert	Insert and edit tables, charts, shapes, text boxes, and all types of images. This tab also provides access to tools for inserting symbols and creating and editing hyperlinks.
Review	Basic proofing (spelling, grammar) and reference (dictionary, thesaurus) tools, language tools, and commands to add sticky-note comments. This tab also includes file-comparison and change-tracking options.
View	Switch between views (Normal, Reading, Outline), show rulers and gridlines, zoom a document, arrange and switch between windows, and view or record macros.
Developer	Normally hidden, this tab contains tools for working with Visual Basic code and macros and managing add-ins. Tools for building custom forms in Outlook are here, as is access to document templates and the Document Panel.
Add-Ins	If you install a third-party add-in or template that creates its own custom commands, they appear here.

Design tabs contain options for defining themes, fonts, and colors; Page Layout tabs provide access to margins, orientation, and the arrangement of objects on a page.

Most Office programs also share dedicated Tools tabs for working with equations, tables, pictures, SmartArt diagrams and charts, and ink objects (which must be created on a tablet or touch-enabled PC but can be viewed and edited on any Windows computer). The Drawing Tools tab contains tools for inserting, arranging, formatting, and resizing shapes and text boxes. A set of Background Removal tools appears on its own tab if you select a picture and click the Remove Background option on the Picture Tools tab.

Galleries and live previews

If the ribbon were merely menus turned on their side, it would be mildly interesting but not worth more than a few seconds' thought. What makes the ribbon much more interesting in everyday use is its ability to help you pick from collections of defined formatting options called galleries and see the effects of those changes on your document using Live Preview.

Some live previews are supremely simple. The Fonts list in all Office programs, for example, displays each font name in the font it represents; when you hover the mouse pointer over a font name, the current text selection changes to that font. Move the mouse away, and the font returns to its current setting; click the font name to apply it. The same is true of font attributes, colors (for fonts or backgrounds), tables (in Excel), styles (in Word and Excel), and transitions in PowerPoint, among other elements.

After inserting a picture into a document, you can use the Quick Styles gallery on the Picture Tools tab to apply a preset border and shadow to it. As you move the mouse pointer over an effect, the image in the document previews that effect, as in the example in Figure 3-12. Click to select the effect, or move the mouse away to return to the document without making a change.

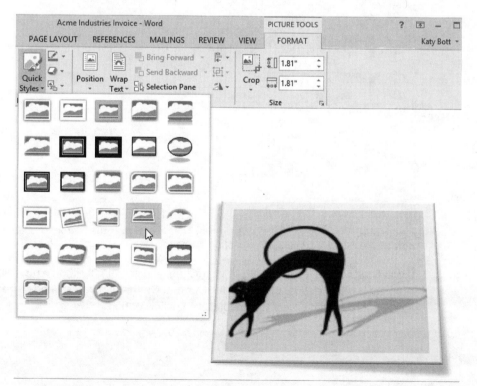

Figure 3-12 Pointing to an option in the Quick Styles gallery allows you to preview borders, rotation, and shadow effects.

For a complete discussion of the many options available for manipulating pictures and graphics in Office programs, see Chapter 5, "Working with graphics and pictures."

You can see a similarly compelling effect using the galleries that apply themes (collections of colors, fonts, and effects) to an entire document, workbook, or presentation. The Themes gallery is on the Page Layout tab in Excel and on the Design tab in Word and PowerPoint.

In some (but not all) galleries, you can tweak an existing entry or create a new one from scratch and save the result as a custom entry in the list. If this option is available, you see a Save option in the gallery itself, and any custom items you create appear in a separate section of the gallery. Figure 3-13 shows a custom theme saved to the Word Themes gallery.

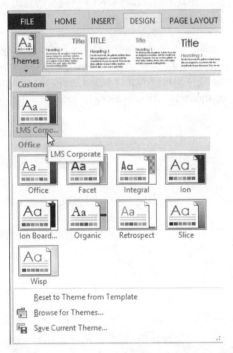

Figure 3-13 When you use the Save Current Theme option at the bottom of this gallery, your new theme is saved in the Custom section at the top.

If you find Live Preview annoying or distracting, you can turn it off on a program-by-program basis. Click File, and then click Options. On the General tab, under the User Interface Options heading, clear the Enable Live Preview option.

INSIDE OUT   Add a gallery to the Quick Access Toolbar

Although the most obvious use of the Quick Access Toolbar is to save shortcuts to individual commands, you can also use this slim strip of screen real estate to save shortcuts to entire galleries. The gallery appears on the Quick Access Toolbar as an icon with a small black arrow to its right; click the icon to display the gallery's contents in a visual list, just as they would appear had you switched to the appropriate tab and unfurled the gallery directly. To add a gallery to the Quick Access Toolbar, right-click the main command button for the gallery, and then click Add To Quick Access Toolbar. If you right-click within the gallery itself, the command is Add Gallery To Quick Access Toolbar. The effect is the same either way.

Personalizing the ribbon

One of the most vociferous complaints about the ribbon when it first appeared in Office 2007 was its inflexibility. Customization options required specialized tools and a programmer's skills. Microsoft added a robust customization option for the ribbon in Office 2010, and its workings are essentially the same in Office 2013.

The starting point for all ribbon customizations is the dialog box shown in Figure 3-14. Right-click any empty space on the ribbon, and then click Customize The Ribbon on the shortcut menu. You can also click File, Options, and then select the Customize Ribbon tab. This example is taken from Word, but the overall appearance and general operation of the Customize Ribbon page are the same in all seven Office programs we cover in this chapter.

The Choose Commands From list above the left column allows you to control which items are shown in the list beneath it. You can show a filtered list (select Popular Commands), show all commands, or restrict the display to commands that are not available on any default tab. Use one of the tabs options (All Tabs, Main Tabs, Tool Tabs, and so on) if you want to copy an existing tab or group.

The Customize The Ribbon list on the right allows you to pick which tab or group you want to work with. You can filter the choices shown here by selecting All Tabs, Main Tabs, or Tool Tabs.

Commands list ⌐   Show or hide a tab   ⌐Tabs list

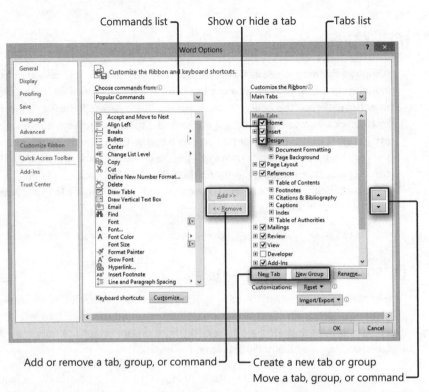

Add or remove a tab, group, or command ⌐   └ Create a new tab or group

Move a tab, group, or command ⌐

Figure 3-14 Use the customization options to create new tabs and hide existing ones, organize commands into new groups, and otherwise personalize the ribbon.

Here's what you can and can't do with the ribbon in all Office programs:

- You can change the left-to-right order in which default and custom tabs appear on the ribbon. (You cannot, however, move context-sensitive tabs such as Background Removal.) If you want to move PowerPoint's Slide Show tab to the third position, after Home and Insert but before Design, you can do that. To move a tab, select its entry in the Tabs list and drag it up or down; alternatively, you can use the Move Up and Move Down arrows to the right of the list, or right-click and then click Move Up or Move Down on the shortcut menu, as shown next.

- You can hide individual tabs. The Developer tab is hidden as part of the initial configuration in all programs. You can banish any other tab as well by clearing its check box in the Tabs list. If you're confident that you will never use Word's Mail Merge feature, you can banish the Mailings tab. A hidden tab is not deleted, and it can be restored at any time.

- You can change the order of groups within any tab, including default and contextual tabs. You can, for example, move the Themes group from the left side of the Design tab in Word or PowerPoint to the far right or to any position in the middle. To do so, select the group and use the Move Up or Move Down button, or right-click and use the equivalent choices on the shortcut menu.

- You can remove groups from any tab, including built-in tabs. Right-click the group and click Remove. You can also move groups from one tab to another by using the Move Up and Move Down buttons.

- You cannot remove commands from a default group, nor can you rearrange the order of commands within such a group. (Commands in a default group appear dimmed and are unavailable for editing on the Customize Ribbon page.)

● You can create one or more custom tabs for each program. Each new custom tab starts with one new custom group, which you can fill with individual commands. You can also add groups from any existing tab to a custom tab. Figure 3-15 shows the settings for a custom tab in Word, assembled from existing groups and individual commands. Figure 3-16 shows the resulting custom tab in Word.

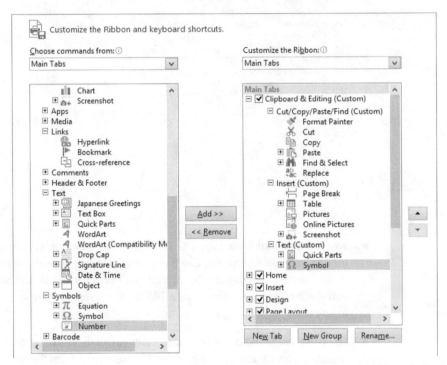

Figure 3-15 The custom tab at the top of the list on the right is assembled from individual commands picked from the list on the left.

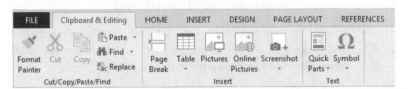

Figure 3-16 This custom tab is the result of the settings shown in Figure 3-15.

● You can add one or more custom groups to any tab, including default, custom, and contextual tabs. You can then fill those groups with any commands available in the current program and position the custom group anywhere on the tab. Use the New Group button to create a group; click Rename to change the default label that appears beneath the group.

- You can rename any default tab or group. The new name can contain punctuation and other special characters, and can be any length. Select the item from the Tabs list, and then click the Rename button to enter its new name.

- You cannot change the name of a command in a default group, nor can you change the icon associated with a command.

- You can rename a command within a custom group. The Rename dialog box also gives you the option to choose an alternative icon for the command.

- You can use small icons without labels for all commands within a custom group. To do so, right-click the group name in the Tabs list and select Hide Command Labels.

INSIDE OUT   A roundabout way to rearrange commands

As we note here, the option to rearrange commands is not available within default groups on a built-in tab. But you can accomplish the same goal if you're willing to make it a multistep process. Start by creating a custom tab using the same name as the one you want to clone (your copy is identified by the Custom label after it). Rename the default custom group that's created to match the name of the first group you want the tab to contain. Next, select All Tabs from the list above the left column. In that list, select the first command from the first group on the tab you want to clone, and then click Add. Continue clicking Add until you've created a clone of the existing group. Repeat this process for each additional group and tab, and then use the basic customization tools to remove unwanted commands and adjust the order of other commands. Hide or remove the built-in tab or group and move your custom clone to its position.

If you find that you've made a mess of the ribbon and you want to start over, click the Reset button beneath the Tabs list. The two options here allow you to reset changes for a single tab or remove all customizations. Beware, though: the latter option resets the Quick Access Toolbar as well!

And one final word on the subject: Just because you can tweak the ribbon doesn't mean you should. Using a nonstandard, heavily customized layout means that you're likely to be unproductive, at least briefly, whenever you sit down to work with a PC that uses an unmodified ribbon. You'll also have to remember to save your customizations in a safe place so that you can apply them if you replace your PC or reinstall Office.

INSIDE OUT   Saving and reusing custom ribbon and toolbar settings

The right customizations can have a positive effect on your productivity and on your aching muscles. Arranging commonly used commands in a convenient location can help you eliminate unnecessary mouse movements and clicks. If you invest more than a few minutes customizing a layout, save your settings in a backup location. Later, you can use that settings file to restore your custom ribbon and Quick Access Toolbar arrangements on a new PC or after reinstalling Office. You can also share the saved settings with other people.

You'll find the Import/Export button at the bottom of the customization dialog boxes for the ribbon and the Quick Access Toolbar. The available options and results are the same in either place.

Click Export All Customizations to save an XML file containing details about all additions and modifications to the ribbon and the Quick Access Toolbar. You'll be prompted to save the file in your Documents folder using the Exported Office UI File format (with the .exportedUI file name extension). The default file name is *ProgramName* Customizations, where *ProgramName* is the program you're currently using: Word, Excel, and so on.

To replace the settings on another Office installation with the settings you saved in the Exported Office UI file, open either the Quick Access Toolbar or ribbon customization dialog box, click Import/Export, select Import Customization File, and browse to the file you saved previously. Note that the saved settings eliminate any existing customizations you made to the ribbon or Quick Access Toolbar; you can't use the Import/Export feature to merge settings from two machines.

Customizing the Quick Access Toolbar

The Quick Access Toolbar consists of a single row of small icons, with no labels allowed. In its default configuration, it includes only a few shortcuts (Save, Undo, and Redo for Word, Excel, PowerPoint, Access, and Publisher, with slightly different options for OneNote and Outlook), but you can add as many more as you like, with each icon associated with a single command.

INSIDE OUT   Make the Quick Access Toolbar go away

There's no check box or button to hide the Quick Access Toolbar, but you can achieve almost the same result by leaving it in its default position above the ribbon and removing all commands. With no commands assigned to the Quick Access Toolbar, you'll see a tiny separator line and arrow to the right of the program icon in the title bar. It's almost, but not quite, invisible.

By default, this tiny toolbar is located on the title bar, just to the right of the program icon and above the ribbon. If you plan to add more than a few shortcuts to the Quick Access Toolbar, we recommend that you exercise your option to move it below the ribbon. (Click the arrow to the right of the Quick Access Toolbar to see the Show Below The Ribbon option at the bottom of a list of frequently used commands.) In that configuration, the commands are easier to see and are less likely to crowd out the title of the current window.

Note

Any commands you add to the Quick Access Toolbar are reflected in the current program window only. If you want the same arrangement of shortcuts on the Quick Access Toolbar in different programs, you must make those changes in each Office program individually. Likewise, the setting to position the Quick Access Toolbar above or below the ribbon must be applied separately in each program.

Personalization options for the Quick Access Toolbar are severely limited. You can add separator lines to arrange commands into groups, and you can move commands to suit your fancy, but that's about it. You can't resize the toolbar itself or the icons on it; you can't add text labels; and you can't add a second row or create submenus. If you add more icons than will fit in the width of the program window, you need to click the double-headed arrow at the end of the toolbar to see the overflow.

The simplest customization option for the Quick Access Toolbar is to choose from a short list of 10 to 12 popular commands, as picked by the designers of Office. To expose this list, click the arrow to the right of the Quick Access Toolbar. A check mark indicates that the corresponding command is on the toolbar already. Click the command to toggle the selection, as in the list of commands from Excel shown next.

Chapter 3

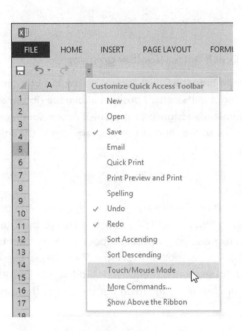

You can also add individual commands directly to the Quick Access Toolbar by right-click-ing any command on the ribbon and selecting Add To Quick Access Toolbar. If you use this option or the short list, the new command appears at the end of the Quick Access Toolbar.

To add commands that aren't readily available, or to rearrange the order of commands, you need to open the dialog box shown in Figure 3-17. Right-click the Quick Access Toolbar or the ribbon, and then click Customize Quick Access Toolbar. Or click the arrow to the right of the Quick Access Toolbar and select More Commands. (You can also reach this location from Office Backstage view: click File, click Options, and then select the Quick Access Tool-bar tab.)

You work with items in this dialog box using the same tools and techniques as for personal-izing the ribbon, except with fewer options. Filter the list of commands on the left to locate those you want to add. Use the Move Up and Move Down buttons to change the order of commands, and use the Separator item as needed to arrange commands in groups that are easier to remember and locate.

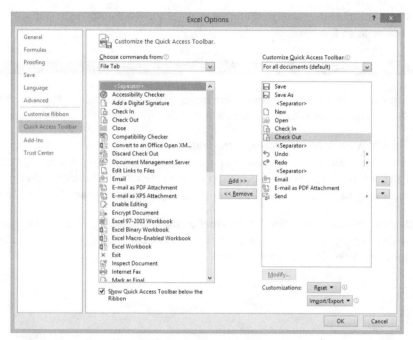

Figure 3-17 Pick commands from the list on the left and add them to the Quick Access Toolbar. Separators help group related commands together.

To remove all your customizations and start fresh, click the Reset button at the bottom of the dialog box, and then click Reset Only Quick Access Toolbar. As for the second option, Reset All Customizations, we offer the same caution here as we did with respect to the ribbon. This option is an all-or-nothing choice, resetting every change you've made to both the ribbon and Quick Access Toolbar. If you're experimenting, you'll want to back up your settings regularly so that you can restore them easily after a full reset.

Using and customizing the status bar

On any list of common interface elements in Office, it's easy to miss the status bar that runs along the bottom of the program window in Word, Excel, PowerPoint, Publisher, Access, and Outlook (but not in OneNote). That's understandable. After all, this thin strip of screen real estate is a mere 22 pixels high. By default, the status bar displays information about the current document on its left side: page number and word counts in Word, slide number in PowerPoint, number of items and number of unread items in the current Outlook folder, and so on.

On the right side of the status bar you'll find controls that allow you to interact with the current document. The Zoom slider at the right side of the status bar allows you to make the contents of the current editing window (or the Reading pane in Outlook) larger or smaller, as shown here.

Just to the left of the slide control are buttons that let you change the view: from Normal to Slide Sorter in PowerPoint, for example, or from Print Layout to Web Layout view in Word.

The status bar is actually more interesting and useful than it first appears, for two reasons. First, many options on the status bar are clickable. In Word, for example, you can click the Page indicator to open the Navigation pane, or click Words to open a dialog box containing additional statistics, such as the number of paragraphs, characters, and lines.

Second, you can customize the information displayed there by right-clicking the status bar and clearing or selecting items on the list of available options. Figure 3-18 shows the customization options available for Excel.

Figure 3-18 In the Customize Status Bar menu, the check marks indicate items that are currently available for display on the status bar.

Using keyboard shortcuts

Most Windows shortcuts work equally well in Office programs, both for managing windows and for text editing. In Word, Excel, PowerPoint, and Publisher, for example, you can press Ctrl+N to start a new blank document, workbook, presentation, or publication. Ctrl+F6 switches between open windows in the current program. Ctrl+B, Ctrl+I, and Ctrl+U apply bold, italic, and underline formatting to the current selection.

For a list of keyboard shortcuts associated with text formatting, see "Applying text formatting" in Chapter 4.

You can find the keyboard shortcuts for some commands by using the ScreenTip that appears when you allow the mouse pointer to hover over a command on the ribbon or Quick Access Toolbar. In most Office programs, those shortcuts are fixed and cannot be changed, nor can you add custom keyboard shortcuts.

The single exception to this rule is Word, which allows you to attach keyboard shortcuts to any command. On the Customize Ribbon tab of the Word Options dialog box (shown earlier in Figure 3-14), click Customize. A dialog box opens in which you can select commands and assign keyboard shortcuts.

If you're an Office veteran and a fast touch typist, you're likely to miss the old-style menus, which made it possible to use the Alt key to pull down menus and make selections without having to move your hands off the keyboard. The good news is that those accelerators are still available in Office 2013. Virtually every object in the Office 2013 user interface is accessible via a keyboard sequence. Tap the Alt key to see which keys are attached to each on-screen object, as shown in Figure 3-19.

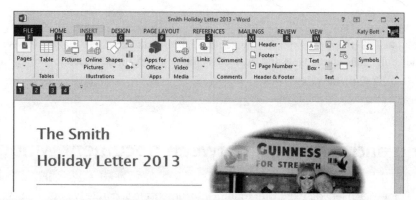

Figure 3-19 Tap Alt to display keyboard shortcuts associated with objects on the ribbon and Quick Access Toolbar. Tapping H, for example, shows shortcut keys for the Home tab.

Chapter 3

In some cases, the keyboard shortcut for a command might require multiple keystrokes in sequence. If you tap Alt, then H, then F in Word, you'll see the options shown here:

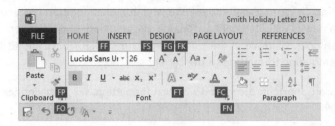

Press F to move to the Fonts list, S to select a font size, G or K to make the current selection larger or smaller, and so on.

INSIDE OUT Many old keyboard shortcuts still work

If your muscle memory is hard-wired with ancient menu sequences from Office 2003 and earlier versions, you're in for a pleasant surprise. Many of those old sequences still work. If you're editing a document in Word 2013 and press Alt+E, for example, Word recognizes that as the accelerator key for the Edit menu in Word 2003 and displays the ScreenTip shown here:

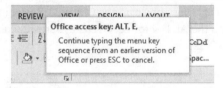

Press E (the accelerator for the Replace option on the old Edit menu), and Word dutifully pulls up the Find And Replace dialog box with the Replace tab highlighted, just as your muscles remember.

Arranging and switching between document windows

The document-centric programs in the Office family—Word, Excel, Publisher, and Power-Point—each let you work with multiple documents in separate windows. In Word, Excel, and PowerPoint, you can also open a single document, worksheet, or presentation in multiple windows; this technique is especially useful with long documents, when you want to compare content in widely separated parts of the same file.

To facilitate the process of managing multiple windows, the View tab is stocked with window-oriented commands. New Window (not available in Publisher) opens the current document in a new window, appending a window number to the document's name in the title bar, with the original document identified as Document:1 and the new window labeled Document:2. The Arrange All command tiles all open document windows for the current program on the main monitor. Use the Switch Windows option to select from the list of open windows.

Word and Excel have an additional set of window controls on the View menu specifically intended to make it easier to compare the contents of multiple windows. If two and only two windows are open in the current program, you can click View Side By Side to automatically arrange them for comparison. If more than two windows are open, Word or Excel asks which document you want to compare with the current one. Synchronous scrolling is enabled by default when you view two windows side by side; with this option on, you can use the mouse wheel or scroll bars to move through both documents at the same pace.

Chapter 3

Entering, editing, and formatting text

S ERIOUSLY? An entire chapter about entering and editing text? Don't you just click in a document and type? At its most basic level, yes. You can enter and edit text in Office 2013 programs in much the same way you would in the simplest text editor, such as Notepad. But as you would expect, Office offers much more, including various shortcuts to expedite text entry and rich formatting capabilities. In this chapter, we describe the features and techniques common to all Office programs for entering and editing text, using fonts, and formatting text.

Entering, selecting, and deleting text

You might assume that as the core functionality of word processors and other productivity programs like the ones in Office 2013, features for entering, selecting, and editing text have fully matured and that there's nothing new in this area. Although that's largely true, with each new version Office incorporates a number of small but meaningful enhancements to the genre. And many of the less well-known techniques that are not new to Office might be new to you.

First, let's take a brief look at some basic procedures. These techniques apply not only to all Office programs, but also to most dialog boxes and other programs in which you enter or edit text.

To enter text, place the insertion point where you want the text, and then start typing. (The *insertion point* is a flashing vertical line that indicates where the text you type will be inserted. Don't confuse it with the *mouse pointer*, a nonflashing cursor that takes on different shapes as you point at different objects, which indicates where your next mouse action will occur.) To position the insertion point, move the mouse pointer to the place you want to enter text and then click. With a touch screen, simply tap where you want to enter text.

Alternatively, you can move the insertion point by using the keyboard shortcuts shown in Table 4-1.

TABLE 4-1 Keyboard shortcuts for moving the insertion point

Action	Keyboard shortcut
Move one character left or right	Left Arrow or Right Arrow
Move one word left or right	Ctrl+Left Arrow or Ctrl+Right Arrow
Move up or down one line	Up Arrow or Down Arrow
Move to beginning of previous or next paragraph	Ctrl+Up Arrow or Ctrl+Down Arrow
Move to beginning or end of current line	Home or End
Move up or down one screen	Page Up or Page Down
Move to top of previous or next page	Ctrl+Page Up or Ctrl+Page Down
Move to beginning or end of a document	Ctrl+Home or Ctrl+End

To perform other tasks with text, you must first select it. When text is selected, the insertion point disappears and the selected text is highlighted with a colored background. Your editing now affects the selection; for example, you can apply text formatting to the selection or copy the selection to the Clipboard. If you type, your typing replaces the selection.

Select text by holding down Shift and using the keyboard shortcuts shown in Table 4-1 to extend the selection. To select text using the mouse, click where you want to begin the selection, and then drag to the end of your selection. With a touch screen, tap to place the insertion point, and then drag a selection handle (the circle below the insertion point or selection) to extend or contract the selection. You can also employ a couple of mouse shortcuts: double-click to select an entire word, or triple-click to select an entire paragraph. If you don't release the mouse button after the final click, you can drag to extend the selection by words or paragraphs. (Word offers additional keyboard and mouse shortcuts for selecting text. For details, see "Use Word tricks for selecting text" in Chapter 9, "Inside Word 2013.")

The final topic in our tour of text editing basics is deleting text. With the keyboard, it's easy: use any of the keyboard shortcuts in Table 4-2, and your text is gone. (If you change your mind, you can restore the deleted text; for details see "Using Undo, Redo, and Repeat" later in this chapter.)

To remove text using the mouse, select the text to delete, right-click, and choose Cut. Note that doing so moves the text to the Clipboard, enabling you to subsequently paste the text elsewhere. Unless you're using the Office Clipboard, the text you delete replaces the current Clipboard contents. The Backspace and Delete keys do not move text to the Clipboard. For details about Clipboard operations, see "Using the Clipboard with Office programs" later in this chapter.

INSIDE OUT   Enable precise selection

When you select text in Word or PowerPoint with the mouse, once you drag beyond a word boundary, the selection extends by a word at a time. For most routine editing tasks in ordinary text, that's a handy feature that forgives a little sloppiness in your mouse handling. Some users find this behavior annoying, however, and you might encounter situations where it's undesirable.

To configure Word or PowerPoint so that selections begin and end precisely where you drag instead of observing word boundaries, click File, Options, Advanced. Under Editing Options, clear When Selecting, Automatically Select Entire Word.

TABLE 4-2 Keyboard shortcuts for deleting text

Action	Keyboard shortcut
Delete one character to the left of the insertion point	Backspace
Delete one word to the left of the insertion point or selection	Ctrl+Backspace*
Delete the selection or one character to the right of the insertion point	Delete
Delete one word to the right of the insertion point	Ctrl+Delete*

* Does not work in Excel

What about speech input?

Versions of Office earlier than Office 2007 included rudimentary speech recognition capabilities that you could use to dictate text and edit documents. This feature is no longer included in Office because speech recognition is now part of Windows. Windows 7 and Windows 8 both include speech recognition capabilities that use your spoken words to work with all programs—not just Office. You can use this feature to dictate text, to issue commands, to switch between applications (making it easier to bring in text from other programs), and to perform nearly any computer task without touching your keyboard or mouse. To learn about speech recognition capabilities in Windows, see *w7io.com/10501*.

Chapter 4

Entering symbols and other special characters

Not all of the text characters you need to insert in a document are represented by a key on the keyboard. This is often the case for letters used in languages other than your own, math symbols, unusual punctuation marks, and many more situations. You can enter such characters in any of the following ways:

- **Insert Symbol**   On the Insert tab of any Office program, click Symbol.

- **AutoCorrect**   Type a character sequence associated with an AutoCorrect entry.

- **Character code**   If you know the ASCII character code or the Unicode character code, use a keyboard shortcut to convert those values to a character.

Each of these methods is described in detail next.

> **Note**
>
> Word offers additional ways to enter certain symbols with little or no effort, including inserting fraction characters and dashes, and lets you define your own shortcut keys for symbols you use often. For details, see "Inserting special characters" in Chapter 9.

Entering characters with Insert Symbol

A simple visual way to find and insert nonkeyboard characters is with Insert Symbol. Click the Insert tab, and then click Symbol. In Word, OneNote, and Outlook, a gallery of recently used symbols appears, as shown next.

If the symbol you want is in the gallery, simply click it, and Office "types" it at the insertion point. If you need a different symbol, click More Symbols, which takes you to a Symbol dialog box similar to the one shown in Figure 4-1. (Clicking Symbol in Excel or PowerPoint takes you directly to this dialog box, bypassing the gallery view.)

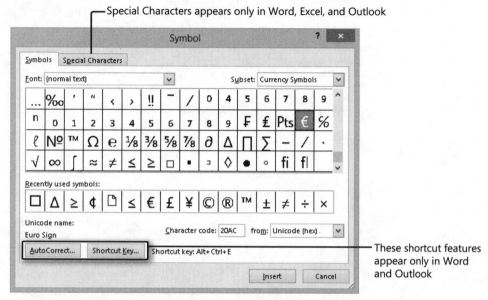

Figure 4-1 The Symbol dialog box from Word, shown here, includes some elements that are not available in all Office programs.

Hundreds of characters are available in the Symbol dialog box. Although you can scroll through the entire list, you can save some time by selecting a subset from the list in the upper-right corner. In Word, Excel, and Outlook, the Special Characters tab offers a short list of symbols commonly used in typesetting applications, such as dashes, fixed-width spaces, and "curly" quotation marks.

Leaving Normal Text in the Font box inserts a character without any formatting; it inherits the formatting of the paragraph, word, or cell in which you insert the character. Select a font if you want the selected character to appear in a font that's different from the target area or if you need symbols from a special symbol font, such as Webdings or Wingdings.

Once you find the character you want, click to select it, and then click Insert. The dialog box remains open so that you can insert additional characters; click Close when you finish.

Additional Symbol dialog box features in Word and Outlook make future entry of a particular character easier:

- **AutoCorrect**   To define an AutoCorrect string that Office automatically changes to the selected character whenever you type the string, click AutoCorrect. For more information, see the next section.

Chapter 4

- **Shortcut Key**   If a shortcut key for the selected character has been defined, it appears near the bottom of the Symbol dialog box. Within a document you can press the shortcut key (or key sequence) to insert the character without visiting the Symbol dialog box. To define or change the shortcut key for the selected character, click Shortcut Key, which opens a dialog box like the one shown next.

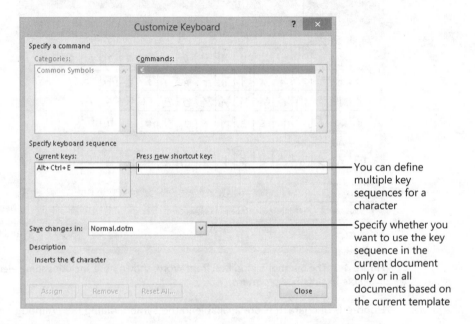

You can define multiple key sequences for a character

Specify whether you want to use the key sequence in the current document only or in all documents based on the current template

Entering characters with AutoCorrect

AutoCorrect is a feature that automatically replaces a character sequence that you type with another sequence you specify. The replacement occurs as you type. The feature was initially introduced to Word as a tool for automatically correcting common typing errors, such as typing **teh** for "the." But it's also a convenient way to enter commonly used characters and symbols that would otherwise require a visit to the Symbol dialog box; you type a mnemonic character sequence, and Office automatically replaces it with a character.

Many common symbols already have AutoCorrect definitions. For example, typing **-->** changes to a right arrow symbol (➔), and typing **(tm)** changes to a trademark sign (™). From the Symbol dialog box in Word or Outlook, you can select a character and then click AutoCorrect to open an AutoCorrect dialog box in which you can specify the mnemonic sequence you want to use to invoke the selected character. With other Office applications, you get to the AutoCorrect dialog box by clicking File, Options, Proofing, AutoCorrect Options.

INSIDE OUT
See which keys are already assigned as symbol shortcuts in Word

In Word (but not Outlook), click File, Options, Customize Ribbon. Click the Customize button (next to Keyboard Shortcuts). In the Categories list in the Customize Keyboard dialog box, scroll down and select Common Symbols. Then select items in the Common Symbols box to see the shortcut keys, if any, assigned to each symbol.

While you have the AutoCorrect dialog box open, scroll through the list on the AutoCorrect tab to see which characters already have definitions.

For details about AutoCorrect, see "Entering boilerplate and other oft-used text" later in this chapter.

Entering characters with character codes

You might've noticed the Character Code box in the Symbol dialog box. (See Figure 4-1.) Each character and symbol is identified by a unique numeric code called a *Unicode character code*. Each of the most common letters and symbols—essentially the ones that have been in every Western-language font since the dawn of the computer age—can alternatively be identified by its *ASCII character code*. (ASCII, which stands for American Standard Code for Information Interchange, is an older character-encoding system that uses a single byte to represent each character. That provides for a maximum of 256 characters, a limitation that led to the development of the Unicode system, which supports thousands of unique characters.)

Once you know the code for a character, you can use that knowledge to insert the character using the keyboard. Simply use the key combinations shown in Table 4-3.

TABLE 4-3 Key combinations for entering symbols and other characters

Action	Keys	Notes
Insert a character using its ASCII character code	Alt+0 *code*	Hold down Alt as you type a zero followed by the code as a decimal value (up to three digits) on the numeric keypad.
Insert a character using its Unicode character code*	*code*, Alt+X	
Replace the character to the left of the insertion point with its Unicode character code*	Alt+X	Use this to learn a character's code without opening the Symbol dialog box.

* Does not work in Excel or PowerPoint

Chapter 4

> ### Inserting a character: an example
>
> As you've seen in this section, Office offers several methods for entering symbols and characters. You'll undoubtedly use different methods depending on how often you use a particular character and which method you find easiest to use. For example, to enter a copyright symbol (©), you could use any of these techniques:
>
> - Choose Insert, Symbol. Scroll until you find © on the Symbols tab, select it, and click Insert.
>
> - Choose Insert, Symbol. Scroll until you find © on the Special Characters tab, select it, and click Insert.
>
> - Type **(c)**. A predefined AutoCorrect entry changes this sequence to a copyright symbol.
>
> - In Word or Outlook (but not Excel, OneNote, or PowerPoint), press Ctrl+Alt+C, the predefined shortcut key for the copyright symbol.
>
> - Hold down the Alt key and, on the numeric keypad, type **0169**, the decimal ASCII character code for the copyright symbol.
>
> - In Word, OneNote, or Outlook, type **a9** (the Unicode character code for the copyright symbol), and then press Alt+X.

Expert text-editing techniques

In the following sections, we describe some features that can make it faster and easier to produce letter-perfect text. Some, such as the undo and redo features, are used by practically everyone—but even those familiar features have some capabilities you might not be aware of. Other features, such as the ability to enter mathematical equations, are used by few people, but because they make quick work of complex tasks, they're good to know about for those rare occasions when you do need them.

Using Undo, Redo, and Repeat

As in most Windows-based programs, if you make an error in an Office program you can undo your last edit by pressing Ctrl+Z. (Table 4-4 shows the keyboard shortcuts for undo, redo, and repeat operations.) But Office goes further; while you work in an Office program, it retains a history of each edit you make. You can view this history by clicking the arrow next to the Undo button, a default resident of the Quick Access Toolbar, as shown next.

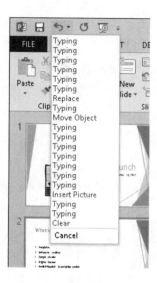

To undo one or more edits, click the earliest edit you want to undo. Office undoes that edit and all subsequent edits (you can't selectively undo a single edit except for the most recent one), reverting your document to the state it was in when you made that edit. If you go too far (or if you change your mind again), you can restore the undone edits by pressing Ctrl+Y or clicking the Redo button, which appears by default to the right of the Undo button on the Quick Access Toolbar.

If you don't have any undone edits, in Word and Outlook you can use the alternate function of the Redo button and keyboard shortcut: Repeat. The Repeat command performs the same edit again, but the edit is applied to the current selection or at the current location of the insertion point. For example, you could type a word, move the insertion point to a different place, and then press Ctrl+Y to type the word again. Similarly, you could format some selected text (italicize it, for example), select some different text, and click Repeat to italicize the new selection.

TABLE 4-4 **Keyboard shortcuts for Undo, Redo, and Repeat**

Action	Keyboard shortcut
Undo the last edit	Ctrl+Z
Redo or repeat an edit	Ctrl+Y*

* In Word, you can use F4 as an alternative for Ctrl+Y.

Entering boilerplate and other oft-used text

Earlier in this chapter, we explained how to use AutoCorrect to insert a symbol or other character. AutoCorrect, of course, can handle more demanding tasks. One of these tasks is to replace a short mnemonic character sequence with a bigger chunk of text, such as boilerplate text for a proposal or contract, or even a commonly used phrase, such as "To whom it may concern:". Follow these steps to define an AutoCorrect entry:

1. Enter the text you want to be able to reuse, and then select it. If you're using Excel, PowerPoint, or OneNote, press Ctrl+C to copy the selection.

2. Click File and then, in Backstage view, click Options.

3. In Outlook (but not other Office 2013 programs), click Mail and then click Spelling And Autocorrect.

4. Click Proofing, and then click AutoCorrect Options to display a dialog box similar to the one shown in Figure 4-2.

Figure 4-2 In Word (shown here) and Outlook, you can preserve formatting as part of the AutoCorrect entry.

5. In the Replace box, type the mnemonic text you want to use as an abbreviation for the full text.

6. If you're using Excel, PowerPoint, or OneNote, paste your boilerplate text into the With box.

7. If you're using Word or Outlook, select Plain Text or Formatted Text, depending on whether you want the text to inherit the formatting from the place where you use it or to always retain its current formatting.

8. Click Add.

While you're in the AutoCorrect dialog box, review the other options on the AutoCorrect tab; these options vary a bit between Office programs.

To use AutoCorrect in your document, simply type the mnemonic text you specified. The moment you follow that text with a space or punctuation mark, or you press Enter, Office replaces the mnemonic text with the full text.

If you then move the mouse pointer or the insertion point to someplace within or immediately after the corrected text, a small bar appears below the beginning of the inserted text. Click the bar or press Shift+Alt+F10 to display the AutoCorrect Options menu, shown next. There's always an option to undo the AutoCorrect action; other menu options vary depending on the type of replacement that's made.

AutoCorrect entries that you create in Excel, OneNote, or PowerPoint are available in all Office programs. Plain text AutoCorrect entries that you make in Word or Outlook are also available in all programs, but formatted entries you make in Word are available only in Word, and formatted entries you make in Outlook are available only in Outlook.

Word and the message editor in Outlook offer another feature for inserting frequently used elements. Called AutoText, this feature provides additional capabilities for storing formatting, page breaks, graphics, and other elements as part of a building block. For details, see "Using building blocks" in Chapter 11, "Word 2013 inside out."

Entering hyperlinks

On the web, everyone is familiar with *hyperlinks*—text or graphics that open another webpage when you click them. But hyperlinks don't exist only on webpages, and they don't link only to other webpages. You can insert hyperlinks in any Office document, and the links' targets can be files or documents stored on your computer as well as webpages.

Chapter 4

To insert a hyperlink, select the text or graphic you want to use as a clickable region. Then, on the Insert tab, click Hyperlink. Alternatively, use the keyboard shortcut for Insert Hyperlink, Ctrl+K. The Insert Hyperlink dialog box appears.

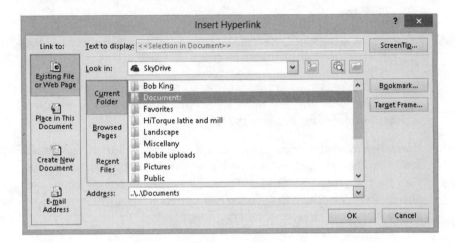

This small dialog box is packed with options and features. Start by making a selection under Link To:

- **Existing File Or Web Page**   Click to create a link to another document, file, or webpage. Then, under Look In, click Current Folder (to link to a file on your computer), Browsed Pages (to link to a webpage that you visited recently), or Recent Files (to link to a file you recently used).

    Alternatively, you can browse to a file location by using the File Explorer–like controls to the right of Look In. Or you can browse to a web location by clicking the Browse The Web button, which opens your web browser. When you find the page you want, switch back to the Insert Hyperlink dialog box without closing your browser; the page's URL appears in the Address box.

- **Place In This Document**   Click to link to a heading or bookmark (Word), cell or range (Excel), or slide (PowerPoint) in the current document.

- **Create New Document**   Click to create a new document and link to it.

- **E-Mail Address**   Click to create a hyperlink that opens a new, preaddressed message window in your default mail program.

The Insert Hyperlink dialog box includes other options you might want to customize:

- **Text To Display**   If you select text or graphics before you open the Insert Hyperlink dialog box, it appears here. Otherwise, Office suggests the text that forms the clickable link in your document; you can override that suggestion by typing your own text.

- **ScreenTip**   ScreenTip text appears when you hover the mouse pointer over the hyperlink in the document; you can use the ScreenTip to provide a description of the link destination or other assistive text.

- **Bookmark**   To specify a location within the targeted webpage or document, click Bookmark and choose a heading, bookmark, cell, or slide.

- **Target Frame**   In Word, you can specify what kind of window the linked page or document will appear in.

To edit a hyperlink in a document, right-click it. The shortcut menu includes options to open, edit, or remove the hyperlink.

> **Note**
>
> In place of the Hyperlink command, OneNote has a Link command, which provides comparable capabilities. The dialog box is not at all like the Insert Hyperlink dialog box in other Office programs, however. For details about links in OneNote, see "Using links for quick connections" in Chapter 22, "Tagging, organizing, and finding information."

Entering mathematical equations

Although Office cannot solve the world's complex mathematical problems, it can present them in an eye-pleasing fashion. Office includes a powerful equation editor that supports the use of symbols and layouts that'll make you look like a genius.

To insert an equation in your document, click the Insert tab. If you then click the arrow next to Equation, you'll see a gallery of common equations that you can use as is, or you can use them as a starting point for building an equation of your own. Click an equation in the gallery, or (in Word only) click More Equations From Office.com to see additional predefined options.

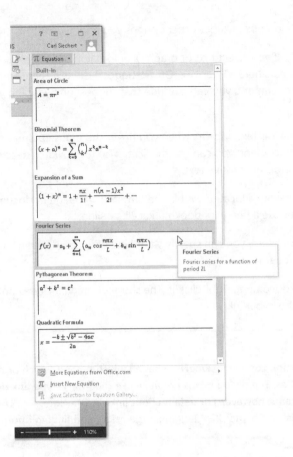

If you prefer to start with a clean slate, click Insert New Equation or, more simply, click directly on Equation on the Insert tab instead of clicking the arrow next to it.

When you have inserted an equation—using one from the equation gallery or by starting fresh—you can click anywhere within it to select the equation or a part of it. The ribbon then sprouts an Equation Tools tab, as shown in Figure 4-3.

The Tools group on the Equation Tools Design tab shown in Figure 4-3 has commands for inserting a new equation (it can be inserted within an existing equation or it can replace the existing equation, depending on the selection) and formatting it. Click the arrow button in the lower-right corner of the Tools group to open the Equation Options dialog box.

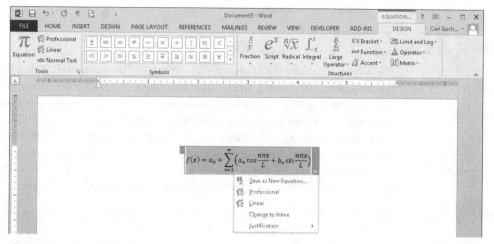

Figure 4-3 A shortcut menu for equations appears when you click the arrow to the right of the equation (Word and Outlook only) or right-click the equation.

The Symbols group provides a gallery of math symbols to insert in your equation. Click the arrow below the scroll bar to expand the size of the symbols gallery; you can then click the title bar of the expanded gallery to switch to different subsets of symbols, as shown next.

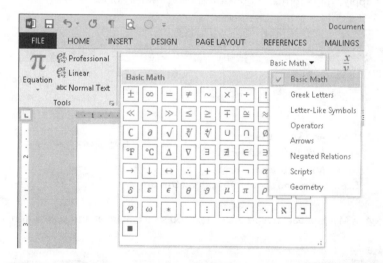

Lastly, the Structures group on the Equation Tools Design tab shown in Figure 4-3 provides galleries of components to insert into an equation, such as integrals, fractions, radicals, and so on.

INSIDE OUT   Use AutoCorrect in equations

You might've noticed the Math AutoCorrect tab in the AutoCorrect dialog box shown earlier in Figure 4-2. Math AutoCorrect provides similar functionality within a math region (the frame that encompasses an equation). Type a mnemonic character sequence, and Office automatically replaces it with the associated symbol or word. For example, type **\le**, and Office changes it to ≤, the symbol for less than or equal to. You can review the predefined mnemonic sequences and add your own by opening AutoCorrect (for details about how to do this, see the steps in "Entering boilerplate and other oft-used text" earlier in this chapter) and clicking Math AutoCorrect.

Applying text formatting

One of the most essential feature sets for enhancing the appearance of your documents—the ability to format text—is also among the easiest to understand and implement. In short, you select the text you want to format and then choose one of several readily accessible tools for applying the format. Figure 4-4 shows how it's done.

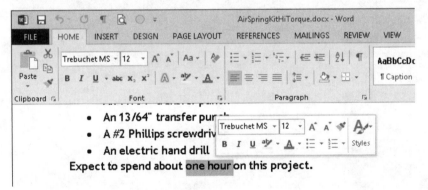

Figure 4-4 A Mini toolbar appears above text you select; point at it to keep it from fading away.

> **Note**
>
> As an alternative to applying formatting directly to selected text, *styles* provide a way to apply multiple attributes simultaneously. (They also make it easier to maintain a consistent look throughout your documents.) The style galleries appear in the Styles group on the Home tab in Word and Excel. For details about styles in Word, see "Giving your documents a consistent appearance" in Chapter 9. For Excel, see "Formatting cells and ranges" in Chapter 12, "Inside Excel 2013."

Applying character formatting

After you select text (for details, see "Entering and selecting text" earlier in this chapter), you can apply formatting such as font (typeface), size, bold, italic, underline, highlighting, and text color by clicking options on the Mini toolbar that appears or in the Font group (in Outlook and OneNote, look for the Basic Text group) on the Home tab (Message tab in Outlook). If you prefer to use the keyboard, Table 4-5 shows shortcuts for common formatting tasks.

TABLE 4-5 Keyboard shortcuts for formatting

Action	Keyboard shortcut
Make text bold	Ctrl+B
Make text italic	Ctrl+I
Make text underlined	Ctrl+U
Decrease text size*	Ctrl+Shift+<
Increase text size*	Ctrl+Shift+>
Decrease text size by 1 point**	Ctrl+[
Increase text size by 1 point**	Ctrl+]
Remove character formatting**	Ctrl+Spacebar

* Does not work in Excel
** Does not work in Excel or OneNote

INSIDE OUT   Apply formatting to part of an Excel cell

In Excel, formats normally apply to all content in the selected cell. You can selectively format text within a cell by selecting the part you want to format in the formula bar.

Additional text formatting options are available in the Font dialog box, which you can open by clicking the Font dialog box launcher (the arrow in the lower-right corner of the Font group on the Home tab) or by pressing its keyboard shortcut, Ctrl+Shift+F.

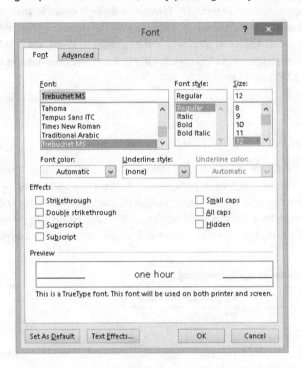

Not surprisingly, Word offers the most options for text formatting. For information about the advanced, Word-only features (such as ligatures and other features of OpenType typography), see "Applying advanced text-formatting capabilities" in Chapter 11.

Applying paragraph formatting

To apply formats that control layout, such as alignment (left aligned, centered, indented, and so on) or line spacing, you use options in the Paragraph group on the Home tab. (Comparable functions are found in the Alignment group on the Home tab in Excel and in the Basic Text group in OneNote and Outlook.) Commands for rotating text and for setting up bulleted lists or numbered lists are here too.

Table 4-6 shows keyboard shortcuts for common paragraph alignment tasks. Note that none of these shortcuts work in Excel.

TABLE 4-6 Keyboard shortcuts for aligning paragraph text

Action	Keyboard shortcut
Left align	Ctrl+L
Center*	Ctrl+E
Right align	Ctrl+R
Justify (align left and right)**	Ctrl+J
Increase left indent***	Ctrl+M
Decrease left indent***	Ctrl+Shift+M

* Does not work in OneNote

** Does not work in OneNote or Outlook

*** Does not work in OneNote or PowerPoint

Using and managing fonts

Office shows a sample of each font when you open the Font list on the Home tab or the Mini toolbar, as shown in Figure 4-5.

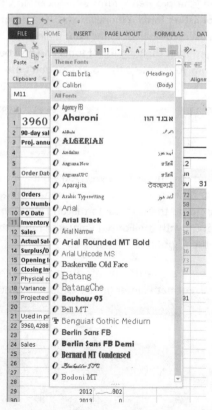

Figure 4-5 Fonts in the current theme are grouped at the top of the fonts list.

Modern computers are likely to have scores of fonts installed, which makes for a long list to choose from when you want to specify a font. You can ease the selection process by focusing on the fonts at the top of the list, under the Theme Fonts heading. Among other elements, a *theme* incorporates a pair of fonts (one for headings and one for body text) that work well together.

To select theme fonts, open the Design tab (in Word or PowerPoint), Page Layout tab (Excel), or Options tab (Outlook). Then click Fonts. (In PowerPoint, the Fonts command appears when you open the gallery in the Variants group.) Select one of the existing themes or create your own.

The new theme fonts you select immediately apply to all text in your document except that which has had explicit nontheme formatting applied. For more information, see "Using Office themes" in Chapter 5, "Working with graphics and pictures."

> **Note**
>
> In Windows 7 and Windows 8, Fonts in Control Panel has an option to hide a font. A font that's hidden does not appear in your programs' fonts list—except in Office programs. Office uses its own control for listing fonts. Whenever an Office program lists fonts, whether on the ribbon, on the Mini toolbar, or in the Font dialog box, the list includes all fonts installed on your system. If the long list of fonts annoys you, the only way to shorten the list is to delete from your system the fonts you don't use; to delete fonts, visit Fonts in Control Panel.

Copying formatting

After you get one part of your document looking just the way you want it to, you'll often find it easier to copy its formatting to another place in your document (or in another document in the same Office program) than to go through the formatting steps again. In Office programs, you can copy and paste formats with the Format Painter in much the same way that you copy and paste content with the Clipboard.

To copy text formatting, begin by placing the insertion point within the text that has the format you want to reuse. Then click Format Painter (in the Clipboard group on the Home tab).

To apply the formatting, click the text that you want to "paint." (If you want to apply the formatting to more than one word, drag across the text you want to reformat.)

The Format Painter ordinarily works only for the first click or drag after you click Format Painter. The mouse then returns to its normal function. If you want to copy formatting from one bit of text to several places, double-click the Format Painter button. The Format Painter then applies the format to each place you subsequently click, until you click Format Painter again or press Esc.

You can also copy formatting by using the keyboard. Position the insertion point or selection in the text with the format you want to copy, and then press Ctrl+Shift+C, the keyboard shortcut for copying formatting. To apply the copied formatting, position the insertion point or selection in the text you want to change, and then press Ctrl+Shift+V.

The formatting copied with Ctrl+Shift+C remains available for pasting until you copy a different format. It's not a one-shot deal (like the Format Painter), and although this feature works much like the Clipboard, the copied formatting is not displaced when you copy something to the Clipboard.

Using the Clipboard with Office programs

The Clipboard—an intermediate storage location that facilitates copying and moving text and other objects—has been a part of Windows since the earliest days. It continues to work in Office programs the same way it works throughout Windows:

- To copy, you select the item to copy, use the Copy command (or its keyboard shortcut, Ctrl+C) to copy to the Clipboard, and then use the Paste command (or press Ctrl+V) to insert the item in a new location. (Table 4-7 shows Clipboard-related keyboard shortcuts.)

TABLE 4-7 Keyboard shortcuts for copying and moving text and formatting

Action	Keyboard shortcut
Copy the selection	Ctrl+C
Cut the selection	Ctrl+X
Paste the Clipboard contents	Ctrl+V
Display Paste Special dialog box to select format for pasted item*	Ctrl+Alt+V
Copy formatting only	Ctrl+Shift+C
Paste formatting only	Ctrl+Shift+V

* Does not work in OneNote

Chapter 4

- To move, use the Cut command (or press Ctrl+X) to remove the item from your document and place it on the Clipboard, and then use the Paste command to insert the item elsewhere.

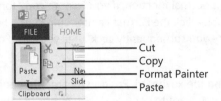

The Clipboard in Windows holds only a single item. When you copy or cut something to the Clipboard, it remains there until you copy or cut something else; the original content is then lost. By default, Office programs rely on the Windows Clipboard, but Office also includes the more capacious Office Clipboard. For details, see "Managing multiple clippings with the Office Clipboard" later in this chapter.

INSIDE OUT   Move and copy without using the Clipboard

Word (and Outlook, which borrows Word's engine for its message-editing features) has some additional tricks that make it easy to copy or move selected text and graphics. These are one-time actions that do not affect the Clipboard, unlike normal copy, cut, and paste operations.

- To move the selected item, press F2, place the insertion point at the target location, and press Enter. This is comparable to the standard mouse technique of dragging the selection to a new place.

- To copy the selected item, press Shift+F2, place the insertion point at the target location, and press Enter. You can do the same thing with the mouse by holding the Shift key as you drag the selection to the new location.

You might find these shortcut keys easier to manage than the standard Ctrl key shortcuts. And because these methods don't use the Clipboard, the previous Clipboard contents remain in place, ready to be pasted again. Remember, however, that these techniques work only in Word and in Outlook messages.

Using Paste Options

Studies of Office users have shown that the most common action that users perform after pasting something from the Clipboard is to immediately choose Undo. For a variety of reasons, more often than not the paste operation produced results other than what the user wanted or expected. Office 2013 addresses this problem through the use of Paste Options, which uses Live Preview to show the paste results and lets you select other paste options without first using Undo.

To use Paste Options, select the document matter you want to replace with the Clipboard content or place the insertion point where you want the content to be inserted. Then do any of the following:

- On the Home tab, click the arrow below the Paste button (in the Clipboard group) to display Paste Options, as shown in Figure 4-6.

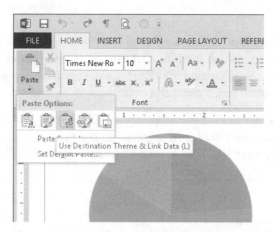

Figure 4-6 Available paste options depend on Clipboard content.

- Right-click the selection or where you want the content to be inserted. Paste Options similar to those shown in Figure 4-6 appear as part of the shortcut menu.

- Press Alt, H, V to display Paste Options.

Regardless of how you get there, as you hover over each of the options (or use the Left Arrow or Right Arrow key to move the highlight between options), Office displays the Clipboard content in the document exactly as it will appear when you complete the paste operation by clicking an option or pressing Enter. Options vary depending on the content on the Clipboard and the capabilities of the target location; the choices can be numerous, as you can see in the Excel example shown next.

Options typically include Use Destination Theme and Use Destination Styles (options that paste text but pick up formatting from the destination document), Keep Source Formatting (an option that retains the formatting from the original copy location), and Keep Text Only (which pastes unformatted text, making this option essentially the same as typing the text).

After you paste—whether you use Paste Options or just press Ctrl+V—if you're not pleased with the result you have another chance to correct it. The Paste Options button appears near the end of your pasted text. Click it, press Ctrl, or press Alt+Shift+F10 to open the Paste Options menu with choices as before.

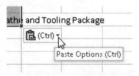

If the Paste Options button is in your way, press Esc to make it disappear.

INSIDE OUT   Setting default paste options in Word

For each of several different paste scenarios, Word maintains a default action for paste operations. The default action takes place if you simply click the Paste button or press Ctrl+V. You can specify the default action by clicking the arrow below the Paste button on the Home tab and then clicking Set Default Paste. Scroll to the Cut, Copy, And Paste section to see the options for controlling paste behavior, shown next.

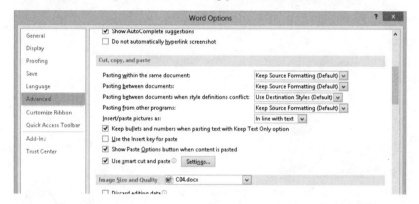

The Clipboard-related options for Word are so numerous that some are tucked away in a dialog box that appears when you click Settings.

Managing multiple clippings with the Office Clipboard

The Clipboard in Windows holds a single item. When you copy or cut something, the current Clipboard content is discarded and replaced with the new content. Office programs include the Office Clipboard, which can store up to 24 items that you copy or cut. You can select any of these 24 items and paste it into your document.

To enable the Office Clipboard, click the arrow in the lower-right corner of the Clipboard group on the Home tab or press Alt, H, F, O to display the Clipboard task pane. Figure 4-7 shows the task pane after several items have been copied to it.

Chapter 4

Figure 4-7 To paste an item from the Office Clipboard, click it. Alternatively, point to the item, click the arrow next to it, and click Paste.

By default, the Office Clipboard collects items you copy only while the Clipboard task pane is shown. (You can change this behavior with an options setting.) While your Office program is running and the task pane is open, it collects items you copy from any program—not just Office programs. After you copy or cut 24 items to the Office Clipboard, the oldest item is discarded. You can also delete individual items; as shown in Figure 4-7, click the item's menu arrow and then click Delete.

> ### Note
>
> Paste Options uses only the most recently added Clipboard content. Pasting any other item from the Office Clipboard uses the simple Paste command. (In most cases, that's equivalent to selecting Keep Source Formatting in Paste Options.)
>
> If that doesn't produce the result you want, simply press the Ctrl key or click the Mini toolbar that appears after you paste. Paste Options then appears, and you can try different options with Live Preview to correct the problem.

You can modify how the Office Clipboard works with a few settings, which you access by clicking Options at the bottom of the Clipboard task pane.

> **Note**
>
> The Office Clipboard retains all the clipped items between Office sessions, but these items are accessible (and new items are added) only when an Office program is running. In addition, the Clipboard task pane must be open in at least one Office program or the Collect Without Showing Office Clipboard option must be selected.

Finding and replacing text and formatting

Searching for text in a document is a basic function in all Office programs, whether you're trying to locate a particular passage in a lengthy report or you need to find all occurrences of a newly obsolete product name. A related feature allows you to replace occurrences of one text string with another, either en masse or one at a time as you review each occurrence.

The implementation of the Find command in each Office program is slightly different:

- **Word** Press Ctrl+F or, in the Editing group on the Home tab, click Find, which opens the Search tab in the Navigation pane. (If you prefer to use the traditional Find dialog box, click the arrow next to Find and choose Advanced Find.)

- **Excel** Press Ctrl+F or, in the Editing group on the Home tab, click Find & Select, Find.

- **OneNote** Press Ctrl+E or click in the search box. (To limit your search to the current page, press Ctrl+F.)

- **PowerPoint** Press Ctrl+F or, in the Editing group on the Home tab, click Find.

- **Outlook** In a message window, click the Format Text tab, and then, in the Editing group, click Find.

In each case, your initial search options are fairly simple, as suggested by the Find dialog box from PowerPoint shown in Figure 4-8. Type the text you want to find, specify any search options, and click Find Next.

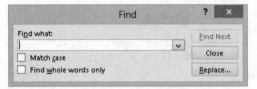

Figure 4-8 To search again for a term you previously used, click the arrow in the Find What box.

The Find dialog box remains open until you click Close, so you can click Find Next repeatedly to search through your entire document. Even with the dialog box open, you can continue to work in your document—something you can't do with many other dialog boxes in Office programs. If the Find dialog box gets in your way, close it. You can continue your search without it; simply press Shift+F4 to repeat the last search.

To find text and replace it with different text, the process is similar: Press Ctrl+H or, in the Editing group (on the Home tab in Word, Excel, and PowerPoint; on the Format Text tab in Outlook), click Replace. (In Excel, you click Find & Select, Replace.) The dialog box that appears is similar to the one shown in Figure 4-8, with a few additions, as shown in the following example from Word.

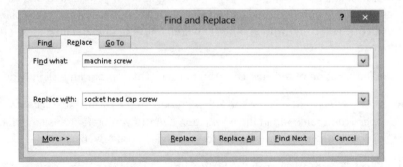

Click Find Next to locate the next occurrence of your search text. Then click Replace to replace that occurrence, or click Find Next to skip to the next one without making a change. If you're certain that you want to change all occurrences, click Replace All, which quickly does the deed with no further review. (Remember that, as with all edits, you can use Undo if you take this action in error.)

Table 4-8 shows the keyboard shortcuts for finding and replacing text.

TABLE 4-8 Keyboard shortcuts for finding and replacing text

Action	Keyboard shortcut
Open the Find tool	Ctrl+F
Repeat find	Shift+F4
Find and replace text and formatting	Ctrl+H

Word (Figure 4-9) and Excel (Figure 4-10) also have the ability to search for text that's formatted a certain way and to (optionally) replace that formatting with new formatting. For details about the additional find and replace features in Word, see "Searching within a document" in Chapter 9. For more information about similar capabilities in Excel, see "Finding, editing, moving, and copying data" in Chapter 12, "Inside Excel 2013."

Figure 4-9 Word has additional options for searching and replacing text that are exposed when you click More. The Format button leads to options for finding and replacing text formats.

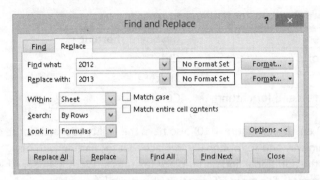

Figure 4-10 In Excel, click Options to customize how searches operate and to search for formatting information.

Checking spelling

While the appearance of your document is important, spelling errors can make your document (and you) look bad no matter how attractive it is in other ways. To avoid such errors, each Office program includes a feature to check the spelling of each word in a document. You can use this feature to check the spelling of individual words, or you can check the entire document, perhaps as part of your final review.

Correcting a single word

By default, in Word, OneNote, PowerPoint, and Outlook (but not Excel), the spelling checker works as you type to identify words that might be misspelled. Office programs indicate potential spelling errors with a squiggly red underline. You don't need to act on it right away; the underline remains in place until you fix the error or tell Office to ignore it. (Don't worry; the red underlines don't appear when you print your documents.)

To review a word that has a squiggly red underline, right-click the word. At the top of the shortcut menu, Office offers its best guesses at what you meant to type, as shown in Figure 4-11.

33. Replace the M6 socket head cap

34. Using a 6.5 mm or ¼" drill bit, er
    mouting holes on the belt cover.

35. Replace ⎡ mooting ⎤ y install
      ⎢ mounting ⎥
36. Replace ⎢ mouthing ⎥ stalling t
      ⎢ muting ⎥
      ⎣ moating ⎦

      Ignore All
      Add to Dictionary
Installing th 🌐 Hyperlink...
            🗔 New Comment

Figure 4-11 Spelling suggestions and options appear at the top of the shortcut menu when you right-click a word that has a squiggly red underline.

To replace the misspelled word, simply click the correct word from the choices presented. (If the correct choice doesn't appear, click outside the menu to close it, and then make the correction manually.) In some cases, Office flags a word that isn't really wrong; this happens often with proper names, for example. When that happens, you have two choices:

- **Ignore All**   Choose this option, and Office deems correct all occurrences of the word in this document.

- **Add To Dictionary**   Office adds the word you typed to its spelling dictionary, which means it won't be marked as wrong in this document or any other. Be sure you're right before you choose this option. (You can edit the dictionary if necessary. For details, see "Using custom dictionaries" later in this chapter.)

Correcting spelling throughout a document

To review spelling throughout your document, click the Review tab. In the Proofing group (Spelling in OneNote), click Spelling (Spelling & Grammar in Word and Outlook). Or, more simply, press F7. Office begins scanning your document from the beginning, and when the first error is found, a Spelling pane similar to the one shown in Figure 4-12 appears. (In Excel, similar options appear in a dialog box.)

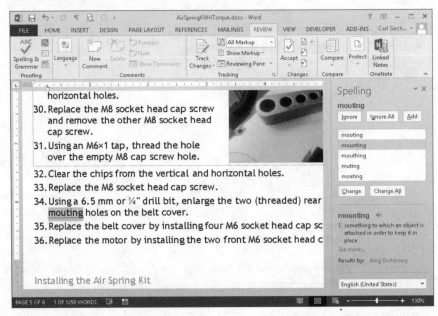

Figure 4-12 Office highlights the misspelled word. The Spelling pane suggests alternatives, provides definitions of the selected alternative, and has a button that says the word aloud when clicked.

To make a correction, select a replacement from the suggestions and click Change (or click Change All to correct all occurrences in the document). If the correct word doesn't appear in the suggestions list, type the correction directly in the document, and then click Resume. Office then continues its search for the next misspelled word.

As part of its spelling review, Word also checks the grammar in your document. For information about the additional options for checking spelling in Word, see "Checking grammar and spelling" in Chapter 9.

Setting options for spelling correction

You might find that Office is too aggressive in finding errors in the type of documents you produce or that it misses some errors. You can set options to control how the spelling checker works. In any Office program, click File to open Backstage view, click Options, and then click Proofing. A dialog box like the one shown in Figure 4-13 appears.

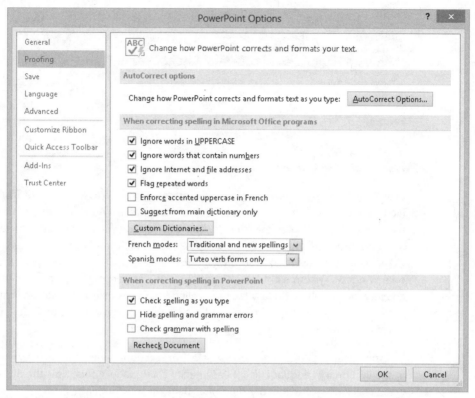

Figure 4-13 Options in the center of this dialog box affect all Office programs. Options near the bottom affect only the program in which you open this dialog box.

Using custom dictionaries

The standard dictionary included with Office includes hundreds of thousands of standard words, plus proper names for many well-known companies, products, and people. But your documents undoubtedly include words that are correctly spelled but not included in the standard dictionary. These words might include specialized terms used in your business (medical terms, for example) or uncommon proper names (Bott and Siechert come to mind).

For these terms, Office uses custom dictionaries. Some custom dictionaries, such as for industry-specific terms, are available from third-party suppliers. But you can also build your own. In fact, when you choose Add during a spelling review, you're adding the word to a custom dictionary, not to the standard dictionary for your language.

To work with custom dictionaries, open the Options dialog box and click Proofing, as shown in Figure 4-13. Then click Custom Dictionaries to open the dialog box shown next.

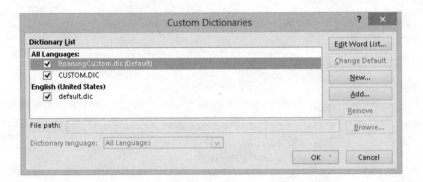

Click New to create a new dictionary file, or click Add to add another existing dictionary file to the list. (You can use multiple custom dictionaries.) A dictionary file is a plain-text file with each word on its own line. It should have a .dic file name extension, although that's not required. Previous Office versions used a file called Custom.dic, which is stored in %AppData%\Microsoft\UProof (C:\Users*username*\AppData\Roaming\Microsoft\UProof on a Windows system with default configuration), as part of your local profile. Office 365 adds a new default dictionary location called RoamingCustom.dic. Stored in the cloud, this custom dictionary roams with you and is available whenever you sign in to Office with your Microsoft account.

To assign a language to a dictionary, select the dictionary name and then make a selection in the Dictionary Language list. If you specify a language, Office uses the dictionary only when checking words that are tagged as being in that language.

To view or modify the words in a custom dictionary, select the dictionary name and then click Edit Word List. This leads to a dialog box similar to the one shown next.

To enter a new word, type it in the Word(s) box and click Add. To delete a word from the dictionary, select it and click Delete.

Using the thesaurus

If you're unable to come up with the perfect word, the thesaurus might help. To use the thesaurus in an Office program, select the word you want to look up, and then press Shift+F7. Alternatively, in the Proofing group on the Review tab, click Thesaurus. Office then opens the Thesaurus pane, shown in Figure 4-14.

Figure 4-14 To look up a different word, type it in the search box and then press Enter or click the search icon.

If the thesaurus offers a word that's better than your original, point to it, click the arrow next to it, and choose Insert. The word replaces your original typing. If the suggested word is close but not quite what you're looking for, click it; Office then looks up that word in the thesaurus. Perhaps the first suggestions were better; the Back and Forward buttons let you step through your lookup history, much like the comparable buttons in a web browser.

Setting language and regional options

As mentioned earlier in this chapter, each Office document has a language assigned to it, and Office uses that designation to determine which dictionaries to use for checking spelling and grammar, which reference books to use, and which language to use as the source when translating documents to another language. Language settings also affect sort order and regional options such as date format and page size. (These system-wide options are set in the Region And Language dialog box in Control Panel.)

To set the default language used by new documents you create and to set other options related to language, in the Language group on the Review tab, click Language, Language Preferences. (This option doesn't appear on the ribbon in Excel, but you can get to the same place by clicking File, Options, Language.)

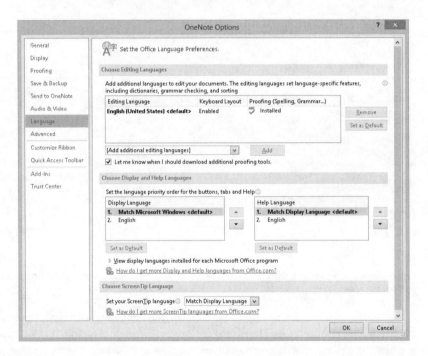

If you plan to work in a language that doesn't appear in the Editing Language list, select it from the drop-down list immediately below, and then click Add. If the keyboard layout and proofing dictionaries for the new language are not yet configured, links in those columns lead to more information.

Note that you can also specify the language for the user interface in Office, for Help text, and for ScreenTips. Not all languages are included in each Office edition, however.

To set the proofing language for selected text within a document, in the Language group on the Review tab, click Language, Set Proofing Language. In the dialog box that appears, select the language.

Translating text to another language

Office includes several tools for language translation. Bear in mind that this is strictly computer translation, and the results are unlikely to be as good as that done by a native-speaking human translator. However, it can be useful for rough translation. Office programs offer two translation tools: one that works in the Research task pane and a Mini Translator that pops up in a document window.

To use the first method on selected text, in the Language group on the Review tab, click Translate, Translate Selected Text. The Research task pane opens, where you can select a target language, as shown next. Click Insert to replace the selection, or scroll down for additional options.

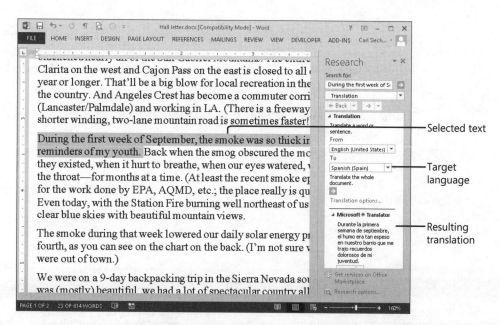

To set up the Mini Translator (not available in Excel), on the Review tab click Translate, Mini Translator. After you select a language, you simply point at a word or selected text, and the

Mini Translator appears in a Mini toolbar, as shown next. (Like the formatting Mini toolbar, it fades away unless you point at it.)

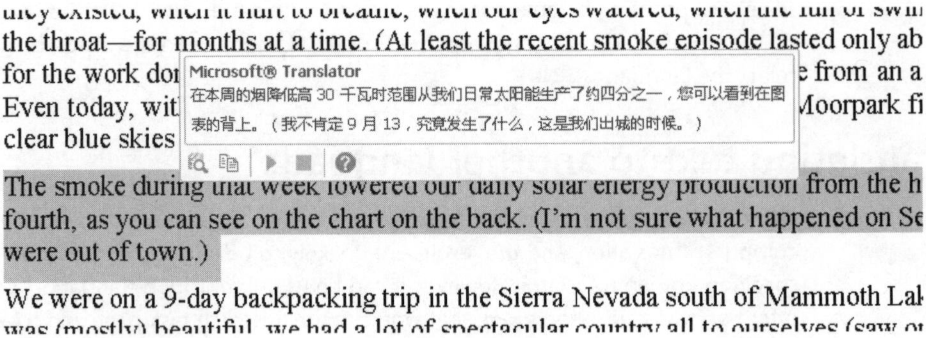

they existed, when it hurt to breathe, when our eyes watered, when the fun of swin the throat—for months at a time. (At least the recent smoke episode lasted only ab for the work do| e from an a Even today, with | Moorpark fi clear blue skies

> Microsoft® Translator
> 在本周的烟降低高 30 千瓦时范围从我们日常太阳能生产了约四分之一，您可以看到在图表的背上。（我不肯定 9 月 13，究竟发生了什么，这是我们出城的时候。）

The smoke during that week lowered our daily solar energy production from the h fourth, as you can see on the chart on the back. (I'm not sure what happened on Se were out of town.)

We were on a 9-day backpacking trip in the Sierra Nevada south of Mammoth Lak was (mostly) beautiful, we had a lot of spectacular country all to ourselves (saw on

CAUTION

Be aware that the Mini Translator works only when you have an active Internet connection, and it sends your text over the Internet in unencrypted format.

You can use the translated text in your document by clicking the Copy button, which places the translation on the Clipboard. Alternatively, click the Expand button to display the text in the Research task pane, where you can use the Insert button to replace the selected text with the translated version.

To stop using the Mini Translator, click Translate, Mini Translator again to turn it off.

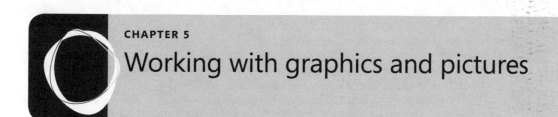

Working with graphics and pictures

E FFECTIVE communication of ideas often requires much more than verbal skills. With Office 2013, you can easily add pictures and other types of graphics that make your documents more visually appealing while at the same time supplanting the proverbial thousand words.

We begin our exploration of the picture-handling capabilities of Office, naturally, with a picture. Figure 5-1 shows the Insert tab on the ribbon in PowerPoint. The Insert tabs in Word, Excel, Outlook, and Publisher (and, to a lesser degree, OneNote) are quite similar, and this tab is the starting point in each program for adding graphics and pictures to a document.

Figure 5-1 The Insert tab for each Office program has a few program-specific options (such as Photo Album in this example from PowerPoint), but most options are found across Office programs.

In this chapter, we describe how to insert and modify each of the following types of graphical objects:

- **Picture** This option includes photographs, of course, but can also be used to insert a file saved in any of numerous picture file formats. (See "Inserting pictures into Office documents.")

- **Online Picture** This option comprises photographs, illustrations, and even audio and video clips from online sources, including clip art from Office.com, images you find via a web search, and images you've stored in an Internet-based service such as SkyDrive or Flickr. (See "Finding and using online pictures.")

- **Shapes**   This option provides line illustrations in a wide variety of shapes that you can further customize. (See "Adding shapes and text boxes.")

- **SmartArt**   SmartArt is a collection of templates for drawings, diagrams, flow charts, organizational charts, and so on. (See "Adding SmartArt to documents.")

- **Chart**   Office supports a large number of ways to display numeric data as an image for easier interpretation and analysis. (See "Displaying data graphically with charts.")

- **Screenshot**   This option captures any open window (even those that are covered by other windows) or part of your screen and inserts it in your document. (See "Capturing and inserting screenshots.")

- **Text Box**   As you would expect, a text box holds text, which gives you greater flexibility in placement and formatting vis-à-vis surrounding text. (See "Adding shapes and text boxes.")

- **WordArt**   WordArt provides a number of effects (such as skewing, stretching, rotating, shading, coloring, and distorting) that can be applied to text for use in logos, titles, and similar display purposes. (See "Applying text effects with WordArt.")

At the end of the chapter we describe another way to apply art, colors, and shapes to your documents: Office themes.

Working with drawing layers in Office documents

Before we dive into the specifics of inserting pictures, shapes, SmartArt, and other graphical elements, it helps to understand how Office manages those objects. In this section, we explain the concept of layers in Office documents, how to select graphical elements, and how to manipulate those graphics in ways that are common to all Office programs.

Although the finished product from Office is two-dimensional—whether it's printed on a sheet of paper or displayed on a flat-screen monitor—a graphics-laden document has a layer for each graphic, arranged in a virtual three-dimensional stack. It's as though you took a blank sheet of paper, wrote some text on it, and then started laying printed photographs and graphics clipped from a magazine atop the sheet. You'd soon have a stack of clippings, with some obscuring part or all of the ones behind them.

In Word and Outlook you can, in effect, peel the text off the page and lay it in front of the stack of graphics. PowerPoint can also place a slide's text in front of the stacked graphics, but the implementation is slightly different; in PowerPoint, slide text (with a transparent background) is itself stored in a placeholder (a type of graphics container), so placing the text in front of other graphics is simply a matter of bringing that layer to the front. Graphics in Excel always remain in front of text and numbers in cells, so you need to be sure that you move your graphics to a place where they don't cover important data.

Selecting graphics and pictures

To work with a graphic or picture after it is placed in a document—whether you want to move it, resize it, adjust its colors, or whatever—you must select it. The simplest way to select an object is to click it. A selected object is shown with a frame, as you can see in Figure 5-2.

Rotate handle
Sizing handles

Figure 5-2 A selected picture or graphic has a frame with handles.

Selecting text boxes and WordArt

When you click a text box or a WordArt object, the frame initially appears as a dashed line, as shown in Figure 5-3. With the frame in this state, you'll also notice the appearance of an insertion point or a text selection, for this is the way you edit the text in such objects. To work with the object itself rather than the text it contains, move the mouse pointer to the dashed line, where the pointer changes to a four-headed arrow, and click. The insertion point or text selection disappears, and the frame becomes a solid line. To return to text editing, click the text inside the frame. Alternatively, once an object is selected, you can toggle between text selection and object selection by pressing Enter and Esc. Table 5-1 shows other keyboard shortcuts for selecting objects.

Figure 5-3 To select a text object with a dashed frame, point to the frame and click.

TABLE 5-1 Keyboard shortcuts for selecting graphics and pictures

Action	Keyboard shortcut
Select an object when another object is selected	Tab or Shift+Tab
Select all objects	Ctrl+A
Open the Selection pane*	Alt+F10
Select the object when text in a WordArt or text box object is selected	Esc
Select text when a WordArt or text box object is selected	Enter

*Does not work in Outlook

Working with multiple graphics and pictures

Selecting objects becomes more complicated when your document contains several objects, especially if they are stacked one in front of another. When objects are stacked, clicking selects only the front-most one. If objects further back are not completely covered, you can click an uncovered part to select that object. Alternatively, after you select an object, you can press Tab to cycle the selection through the objects back to front (or Shift+Tab to cycle from front to back).

A complex document with many graphics and pictures becomes much easier to manage when you use the Selection pane (see Figure 5-4), which you can display in any of the following ways:

- On the Home tab, in the Editing group, click Select, Selection Pane. (In Excel, click Find & Select, Selection Pane.)

- If an object is already selected, under Picture Tools or Drawing Tools, click the Format tab. Then, in the Arrange group, click Selection Pane.

- Press Alt+F10.

The Selection pane lists all objects on the current page, worksheet, or slide. To select an object, simply click its name.

The default object names aren't particularly helpful in determining which object is which, so in a document with many objects that you manipulate often, you might want to take the time to give each object a more meaningful name. To do so, click the object name, click it a second time to enter edit mode, and then type the new name.

The Selection pane has another handy trick: the ability to hide objects. Click the icon to the right of an object's name to hide it or to make it visible again. (Note that objects in Word with Wrap Text set to In Line With Text can't be hidden.)

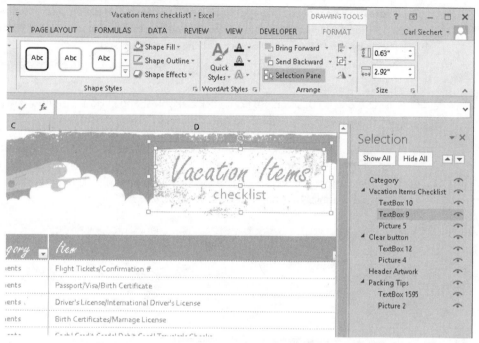

Figure 5-4 The Selection pane, shown on the right side of this graphics-heavy screen, lets you select individual objects—no matter how deeply they're buried.

To select multiple objects, hold Ctrl as you click each one. This works whether you click the objects directly or click their names in the Selection pane.

Positioning objects

To move a selected object (or multiple selected objects), move the mouse pointer over the object until the pointer becomes a four-headed arrow, and then drag. (For some types of objects, such as SmartArt, WordArt, or text boxes, you must point at the object's border frame. For other objects, you can point to any part of the object.)

Chapter 5

> **Note**
>
> Word and Outlook support a positioning style called In Line With Text, which is not available in Excel or PowerPoint. Inline objects move as part of the text flow, and therefore can't be moved by dragging or by using the Layout dialog box, described next. To position an object using these features, you must first select a different text wrapping style by right-clicking the object and choosing Wrap Text.

For more precise positioning, right-click the object and choose Size And Position (Word, PowerPoint, and Outlook) or Size And Properties (Excel). Then:

- In Word or Outlook, the Layout dialog box appears. Click the Position tab, where you'll find options for aligning the object with margins and other page landmarks as well as for specifying a precise location on a page. For details, see "Adding pictures and graphics" in Chapter 9, "Inside Word 2013."

- In Excel, the Format Picture (or Format Shape, depending on the type of object selected) pane appears. Click Properties to expand it. Although you can't enter dimensions to identify a precise location, options here allow you to specify whether and how an object's position and size change when you change the width and height of underlying cells.

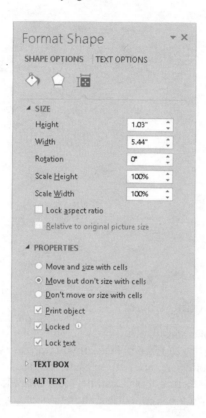

- In PowerPoint, the Format Picture or Format Shape pane appears. Click Position to expand it, whereupon you'll see options for specifying the position relative to the upper-left corner or center of the slide. For more information, see "Adding graphics, video, and audio" in Chapter 18, "Inside PowerPoint 2013."

Aligning and evenly distributing objects

In many cases, you won't want to fiddle with precise positioning of individual elements. Instead, you want to quickly align one or more objects, or you want to evenly space several objects on a page or slide. Office offers a quick path to each goal. To find that path, select the object (or objects); then, under Picture Tools, Drawing Tools, Chart Tools, or SmartArt Tools, click the Format tab. In the Arrange group, click Align to display an array of options, as shown in Figure 5-5.

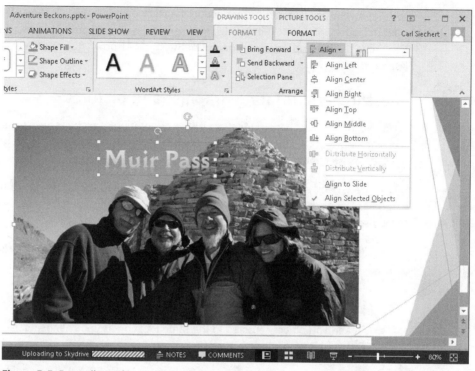

Figure 5-5 Regardless of how carelessly you place objects, you can whip them back into place by choosing an Align option (to align objects with the page or each other) or a Distribute option (to evenly space objects).

Changing the Z-order of stacked objects

As we explained earlier in this chapter, graphics and pictures are layered one in front of another in a virtual stack. You'll sometimes need to change the order so that one object doesn't improperly obscure another. For example, if you place a caption for a picture in a text box, you'll want the text box to be in front of the picture.

To move an object forward or back in the stack, select the object and, under Picture Tools, Drawing Tools, Chart Tools, or SmartArt Tools, click the Format tab. In the Arrange group, click either Bring Forward or Send Backward, which moves the object forward or backward one position in the stack. (Clicking the arrow next to these buttons exposes an additional command that moves the object all the way to the front or back of the stack.)

Alternatively, you can move items within the stack by using the Selection pane, shown earlier in Figure 5-4. Select the item to move, and then click an arrow button (next to Hide All) to move the item up (toward the front of the stack) or down (toward the back) in the list of shapes.

Resizing and rotating graphics and pictures

The techniques for changing the size or the orientation of pictures are similar to those for positioning objects. You can directly manipulate objects by clicking and dragging, or for more precise control, you can enter specific values in a dialog box or a pane.

To resize an object using the mouse, select the object and then drag one of the sizing handles (shown earlier in Figure 5-2). Your results might not match your expectations unless you use these techniques:

- To maintain the object's aspect ratio, use one of the corner sizing handles and hold down the Shift key as you drag. (For pictures, it's not necessary to hold Shift to maintain the aspect ratio. But it doesn't hurt, and that way you can use a consistent technique for all object types.)

- To keep an object centered in the same location as you change its size, hold down Ctrl as you drag.

- To maintain the aspect ratio and the center location, hold Ctrl and Shift as you drag.

To resize using the keyboard, select the object and then hold Shift as you press an arrow key. Hold Ctrl+Shift to enlarge or reduce in smaller increments.

You can achieve greater precision when you resize by entering dimensions in the Size group on the Format tab or in a dialog box. Right-click the object, and choose Size And Position (Word, PowerPoint, and Outlook) or Size And Properties (Excel). In the resulting dialog box or pane, you can specify the dimensions or enter a scaling factor, which calculates the size as a percentage of the object's original size.

You'll sometimes want to rotate graphics and pictures in a document. This might be required because your camera doesn't automatically rotate pictures when you shoot in portrait orientation. Or you might want to tilt an item slightly as an artistic effect.

To rotate a graphic or picture with the mouse, select it and then point to the rotate handle (shown earlier in Figure 5-2). Drag in either direction around the center of the object, and it rotates in that direction.

Drag to rotate

You'll find that the image "snaps" into position at each 90-degree mark when you rotate it using the mouse. If your intent is to rotate an image 90 degrees, an easier method is to use the Rotate tool, which is in the Arrange group on the Format tab (under Picture Tools or Drawing Tools).

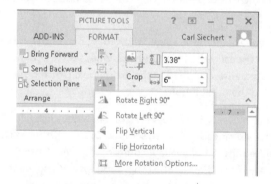

Rotate the selected object with the keyboard by holding the Alt key as you press the Left Arrow (for counterclockwise rotation) or Right Arrow key. Each keypress rotates the object 15 degrees. Press Ctrl+Alt with an arrow key to rotate 1 degree at a time.

The last command on the Rotate menu, More Rotation Options, opens the Layout dialog box (Word and Outlook) or Format Shape/Format Picture pane (Excel and PowerPoint), where you can specify a rotation angle with one-degree precision.

Office also supports three-dimensional rotation of graphics and pictures. For more information, see "Adding shapes and text boxes" and "Applying picture styles" later in this chapter.

INSIDE OUT Specify dimensions using your preferred unit of measure

By default, Office displays measurements using the units associated with your computer's Region settings, which turns out to be inches in the United States and millimeters in other countries. Nevertheless, in any Office dialog box, you can enter dimensions using any of the following units:

- Inches: in or "

- Centimeters: cm

- Millimeters: mm

- Points (a printer's measurement equal to 1/72 inch): pt

- Picas (a printer's measurement equal to 12 points, or 1/6 inch): pi

- Pixels (normally 1/96 inch; dots per inch [dpi] can be changed in Control Panel): px

To use one of these units, type the numeric value followed by one of the abbreviations in the list above. (If you don't specify the unit, Office assumes you're using the default unit.) As soon as you move to a different field in the dialog box, Office displays the dimension you entered using the default unit.

To change the default unit of measure in Word, Excel, or OneNote, click File, Options. In the Options dialog box, click Advanced, and then scroll to Display (Other in OneNote). Under that heading, you'll find the list of available units of measure. Note that your setting in one Office program doesn't affect the other programs. If you want to change the default setting for all programs (not just Office), visit Clock, Language, And Region in Control Panel.

Grouping objects

When you have several objects properly positioned in relation to each other, you'll want to group them. Doing so makes it easier to move or manipulate all the component objects as one, and it prevents inadvertently modifying part of the graphic or picture.

A simple example of the benefit of grouping is a logo that comprises two objects: a design saved as a picture and a slogan in a text box. After resizing and moving the objects individually until they're in proper position, select them both. Then, on the Format tab, click the Group button (see Figure 5-6), and then click Group.

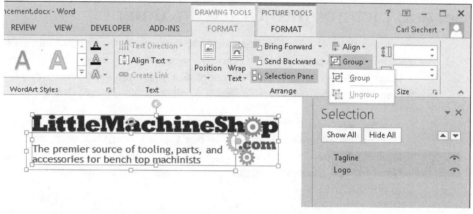

Figure 5-6 Choosing Group causes the selected objects to be combined into a single object, as shown in Figure 5-7.

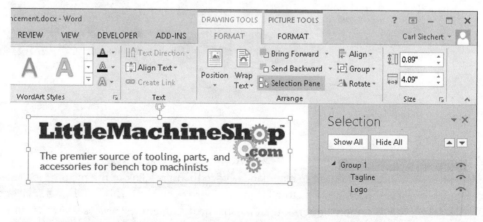

Figure 5-7 After grouping, the grouped objects share a single selection frame. Note that the Selection pane shows the objects within the group.

TROUBLESHOOTING

Grouped objects remain grouped after you choose Ungroup

After you choose the Ungroup command, it might appear that the objects remain grouped. For example, if you drag one of the formerly grouped objects, all objects move together. The problem is that Office leaves all objects selected after you choose Ungroup. The solution is simple: Click outside any of the grouped objects, which clears the selection. You can then select individual objects.

Inserting pictures into Office documents

In the context of Office, "picture" refers to much more than photographs. Regardless of composition, a picture is a file in any of many popular graphics formats, including JPEG (.jpg), Portable Network Graphics (.png), Graphics Interchange Format (.gif), Windows Bitmap (.bmp), Windows Metafile (.wmf), and Encapsulated PostScript (.eps).

To insert a picture, click the Insert tab, and in the Illustrations group (Images in PowerPoint), click Picture. The Insert Picture dialog box appears, which has all the same features as the familiar File Open dialog box. Navigate to the picture you want, select it, and click Insert. Note that you can select and insert multiple pictures simultaneously; hold Ctrl as you click to select each picture.

Also note the arrow next to the Insert button, which exposes two additional insert options.

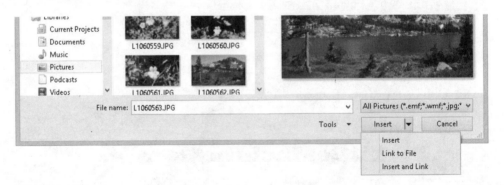

Choosing Link To File commands Office to insert a link to the picture file's location instead of embedding the picture file in the Office document. This results in a smaller document file size, but, more importantly, it means the document will always show the current version of the picture file. If you change the file in its original location, you'll see the updated version the next time you open the Office document. If the file is not available at the linked location (if, for example, it has been renamed or deleted, or if it's on a server drive that's not currently available), a red X appears instead of the picture.

Insert And Link embeds the picture file in the document *and* includes a link to the original file. When you open a document, if the linked file is available, Office displays it; if not, Office displays the embedded version.

That's all there is to it. After you insert a picture, you can select it, move it, resize it, and work with it in various ways, as described in the next section, "Making your pictures look great."

INSIDE OUT   Choose a better default wrapping style for pictures in Word

When you insert a picture or screenshot in Word, by default it is placed at the insertion point. A graphic positioned this way (which is called In Line With Text) acts like any other letter or symbol in the text stream: when you type to the left of the graphic, it shifts to the right until it no longer fits and then wraps to the next line. In-line graphics work best in layouts that have text above and below each picture (like most of the screen illustrations in this book, for example) but not beside them. Place each picture in its own paragraph to use this style.

You can be much more creative in your layouts by setting pictures so that text "wraps" around them. To change the wrapping style for a picture, right-click it and choose Wrap Text. For details, see "Adding pictures and graphics" in Chapter 9.

If you find yourself frequently changing the wrapping style, you should change the default. To do that, click File, Options. In the Word Options dialog box, click Advanced. Under Cut, Copy, And Paste, locate Insert/Paste Pictures As, and select an option.

Making your pictures look great

Programs in Office 2013 include picture editing tools that rival many stand-alone programs for editing digital images. Using just the tools in Word, Excel, PowerPoint, or Outlook, you can apply artistic touches such as blurs, paint strokes, and mosaic effects. A number of predefined picture styles include borders, reflections, 3-D effects, and perspective tilting. You can automatically outline the subject of a photo and remove the background. Other tools let you overlay text in creative ways. And then there are the more mundane tasks: making color corrections; adjusting brightness, contrast, and sharpness; and resizing photos. Unlike earlier Office versions, the cropping tool makes it easy to see what you're removing from the image.

A complete description of the picture-editing capabilities of Office could fill a chapter—or a book—so we don't explain every option in detail. Fortunately, with the start we provide here, you'll find that these features are easily discoverable. And the Live Preview capability provided by most of the picture-editing tools makes them intuitive to use as well.

For information about two other common tasks that apply to other types of graphics as well as pictures, see "Resizing and rotating graphics and pictures" earlier in this chapter.

Cropping pictures

You're an exceptional photographer if each picture you take is perfectly composed. For those pictures that aren't perfect, you'll want to crop to remove unnecessary background or to better fit the space in your document.

To crop a picture, select it, click the Format tab (under Picture tools), and in the Size group, click Crop. Cropping handles appear on your picture; drag a handle to adjust the cropping. Alternatively, you can drag the picture. Either way, note that the area to be cropped out remains visible but shaded. To crop equally from both sides of a picture, hold Ctrl as you drag one of the side cropping handles. To crop equally from all four sides, hold Ctrl and drag one of the corner handles. Press Esc or click outside the picture when you're done.

As shown in Figure 5-8, you can also crop to a particular aspect ratio (that is, the ratio of width to height). This is useful when you want an image to perfectly fill a screen or a particular size of photo paper or picture frame, for example. Click the arrow by the Crop button, and then click Aspect Ratio and select the ratio you want. To maintain the aspect ratio after you make a selection, drag the picture instead of dragging the cropping handles that appear.

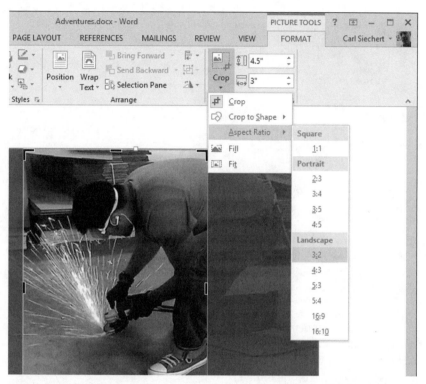

Figure 5-8 If cropping handles are already displayed when you click Crop, Aspect Ratio, Office applies the selected aspect ratio within the bounds of the cropping handles.

Note that when you drag a cropping handle, the aspect ratio is not maintained; you get free-form dragging just as if you used the normal Crop command. You'll sometimes find that getting the best results when cropping to a particular aspect ratio requires an iterative process of resizing and cropping. Those iterations might also include choosing the Fill or Fit command on the Crop menu. Both commands maintain (or restore, if necessary) the original picture's aspect ratio, but they crop the image to fit the current picture shape and size.

For more precise cropping control, right-click the picture and choose Format Picture. In the Format Picture pane, click the Picture icon, expand Crop, and then enter the dimensions.

Chapter 5

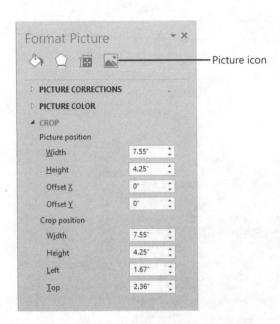

If you find rectangular cropping to be too dull, you might enjoy experimenting with the Crop To Shape command on the Crop menu. With it, you can get some truly strange (and sometimes wonderful) effects by using predefined shapes as crop outlines. (Figure 5-9 shows an example of the former.)

Figure 5-9 When you crop to a shape, Office resizes and distorts the shape to fill the picture frame.

Adjusting colors and applying artistic effects

Features in Office for correcting picture colors and applying special effects range from the essential to the bizarre. Yet they're generally easy to understand, and, best of all, with Live Preview you're able to see how a particular setting looks with *your* picture. You don't need to rely on a thumbnail of a sample picture or try to guess how numeric settings translate to visual images.

The tools for adjusting color are on the Format tab (under Picture Tools) in the Adjust group. Select a picture, click the Format tab, and then click Corrections to see a gallery of options for adjusting the picture's sharpness, brightness, and contrast. As shown in Figure 5-10, clicking Color displays a gallery for adjusting saturation and tone, as well as for applying a color tint to the picture. To see how a setting will look, simply hover the mouse pointer over it, and the setting is temporarily applied. When you find the one you like, click it.

Figure 5-10 The current settings have a bold outline in the gallery.

The third gallery in the Adjust group, Artistic Effects, works in an identical fashion. The effects include an assortment of filters and simulated techniques, such as pencil sketch, paint brush, looking through frosted glass, and so on. Most defy description, so the best way to learn about them is to open the gallery and point.

At the bottom of each gallery is a command that leads to additional settings in the Format Picture pane. You can view and edit numeric values that correspond to the gallery settings, and you can make precise adjustments to the settings. In addition, a Presets button in each section provides another gallery view. One difference here: to see the effect on your picture, you must click the thumbnail in the gallery; pointing to it does nothing.

Applying picture styles

The Picture Styles group on the Format tab contains tools for adding a border to your picture and for applying effects such as shadows, reflections, glows, and three-dimensional rotation. The Picture Styles group also includes a Quick Styles gallery, which contains pre-configured combinations of each of these settings.

To use the Quick Styles gallery, select one or more pictures, and then point to one of the visible thumbnails. If none of those suit your fancy, you can scroll down in the gallery or, better yet, click the More button, the arrow at the bottom of the scrollable window. Figure 5-11 shows an example. When you find a suitable option, click it to apply the settings.

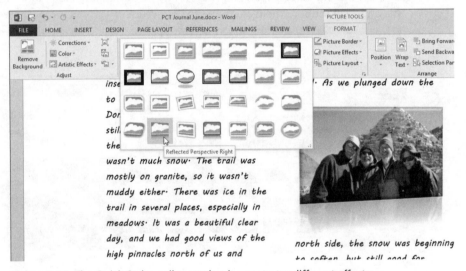

Figure 5-11 The Quick Styles gallery makes it easy to try different effects.

To make your own settings—or to adjust the ones made by a Quick Styles preset—click Picture Border (where you can select a color, line width, and line style) or Picture Effects (where you can choose shadows, reflections, glows, softened edges, bevels, and three-dimensional rotation from galleries). Each of these options can be viewed and fine-tuned in the Format Picture pane. Click the Options command at the bottom of a gallery to open the relevant section of Format Picture.

Another option in the Picture Styles group, the Picture Layout gallery, embeds your selected pictures into SmartArt objects. With this feature, you can make some professional-looking presentation materials with just a few clicks. For more information, see "Adding SmartArt to documents" later in this chapter.

Removing the picture background

Office includes a feature that automatically removes the background from a picture, leaving only the picture subject visible. To use this feature, it helps to have a picture with the subject in sharp focus, and with good contrast. Yet you can sometimes get surprisingly good results even with less-than-perfect pictures.

To remove the background from a picture, select the picture, click the Format tab, and in the Adjust group, click Remove Background. Office quickly makes its best guess at cropping and masking the background, which it identifies with a magenta overlay. As shown in Figure 5-12, this initial attempt isn't always perfect.

Figure 5-12 Initially, Office omitted these hikers' bodies and included part of the background structure.

If the initial results aren't quite right, click Mark Areas To Keep, and then click the additional areas to include (such as the hikers' bodies in Figure 5-12). Click Mark Areas To Remove and then click any unwanted areas that Office left in. If a single click merely deposits a mark but doesn't include or exclude the area of interest (as indicated by the colored mask), try dragging through the area. When you're done, click Keep Changes. In our example, we zoomed in, and then it took just a drag through the clothing and a few clicks in the background structure to produce this result.

INSIDE OUT   Adjust the cropping area

You'll find that with some photos, automatic background removal doesn't work well, and the initial results mistakenly include or exclude several areas. Before you start making manual corrections, the first thing you should do is adjust the cropping indicators to more closely match the final outline you want. When you change the cropping, Office modifies the background selection and, in our experience, often does a much better job with your assistance here.

Undoing picture edits

As you experiment with the picture formatting features in Office, not every shot is going to be a keeper. Mistakes that you recognize right away, of course, can always be undone in the usual manner: click Undo on the Quick Access Toolbar, or press Ctrl+Z. But you might decide much later to revert to the original photo settings.

Doing so is quite simple: Select the picture, click the Format tab, and in the Adjust group, click Reset Picture (to restore the background, remove borders and other picture styles, and restore the original colors) or Reset Picture & Size (to do all of the foregoing, plus remove any cropping and restore the picture's original size).

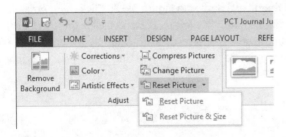

TROUBLESHOOTING

Changes to pictures can't be undone, or edits disappear

A setting buried deep in Office options can lead to some head-scratching moments if it's not set properly. The symptoms can be either of the following:

- After making various picture edits, as described in the preceding sections, you decide you don't like the changes and want to restore the original picture—but the Reset button is unavailable.

- Each time you open a document containing a picture inserted with the Link To File or Insert And Link command, all the artistic effects and other edits you've added are gone, and the original picture file appears.

These seemingly opposite symptoms can arise from the same root cause: the Discard Editing Data setting. To review the setting, click File, Options. In the Options dialog box, click Advanced, and scroll to Image Size And Quality. Unless reducing the file size of your Office document is paramount, clear Discard Editing Data.

Finding and using online pictures

In Office 2013, the Clip Art option that appeared in earlier Office versions has been replaced by Online Pictures, a term that encompasses not just an online catalog of line art, illustrations, photographs, audio clips, and video clips—as before—but also access to other pictures stored online. This includes your own images that you've stored on SkyDrive or other photo storage sites as well as images you find with a web search.

For more information about working with video, see "Adding graphics, video, and audio" in Chapter 18.

To find and insert pictures stored online, click the Insert tab, and click Online Pictures. The Insert Pictures dialog box appears, as shown in Figure 5-13.

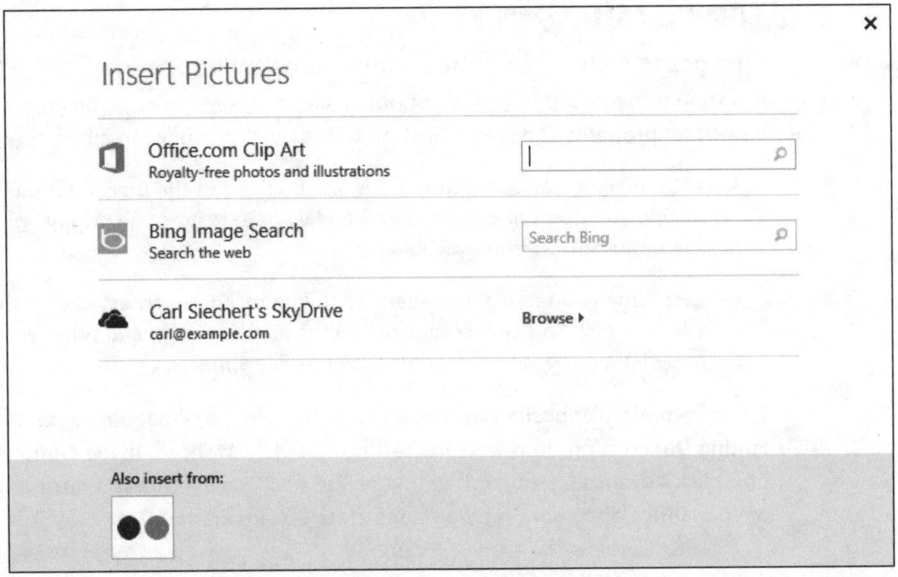

Figure 5-13 Additional sources you can link to your account (such as Flickr) appear at the bottom of the dialog box.

For the first two picture sources—Office.com Clip Art and Bing Image Search—you type a word or two that describes what you're looking for and then click the search icon or press Enter. As shown in Figure 5-14, web search results initially include only images licensed under Creative Commons. (After you click Show All Web Results, a warning about using copyrighted images appears. To find royalty-free images, search Office.com Clip Art.) Select one or more items from the results and then click Insert to place the selected pictures in your document.

With other sources of online pictures—namely, SkyDrive and Flickr accounts—click Browse or See More to explore your stored images. Select the ones you want and click Insert.

For information about using SkyDrive, Flickr, and similar services, see Chapter 7, "Connecting Office 2013 to SkyDrive and other online services."

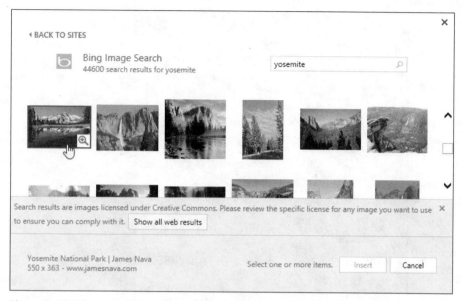

Figure 5-14 When you point to a picture, details about the image appear in the lower-left corner. Click the plus sign to get a larger view.

Adding shapes and text boxes

Office includes a variety of shapes that can be inserted as line illustrations. Shapes include arrows and other symbols to use in diagrams, various polygons, boxes for callouts and other text, and some that'll leave you wondering what possible use they could have. Although the unadorned shapes are not much to look at, Office includes a full range of effects, colors, shading, and other customizations that can add some pizzazz to your document.

The tools for inserting and customizing shapes also work on text boxes. A text box is, in fact, merely a rectangular shape that can contain text.

To insert a shape, click the Insert tab, and in the Illustrations group, click Shapes. A gallery of predefined shapes appears. (If you're inserting a text box, you can bypass the Shapes gallery by clicking Text Box, which is in the Text group on the Insert tab.)

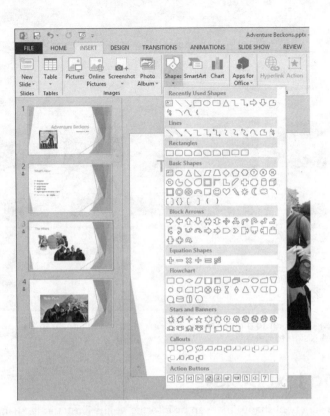

Click a shape, and then drag in the document to create a container for the shape. Don't worry if the size or position isn't quite right; you can easily change, move, resize, or rotate the shape by selecting it and dragging its handles. (For details, see "Positioning objects" and "Resizing and rotating graphics and pictures" earlier in this chapter.) To modify a shape, select the shape and look for shape handles, which appear as yellow squares.

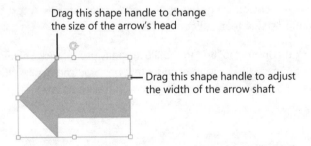

For more fine-grained control, right-click the shape and click Edit Points. Each point that defines the shape appears as a black square, which you can drag in any direction. To add a new point, hold down Ctrl and click anywhere on the shape's outline; Ctrl+click an existing point to remove it. When you click a point to select it, two additional handles appear; together, these three points define the point and the line segment on either side of it. You can drag the point or one of its handles to get different effects. To change the type of point, hold Shift (for a smooth point), Ctrl (straight point), or Alt (corner point) as you drag a handle.

The real fun begins when you apply shape styles. Select a shape, click the Format tab (under Drawing Tools), and click the More button in the Shape Styles group to see a gallery of predefined styles, as shown in Figure 5-15. Like the Picture Styles gallery, this one uses Live Preview; as you point to a thumbnail, its formatting appears in your document as well. Click a gallery item to apply the formatting.

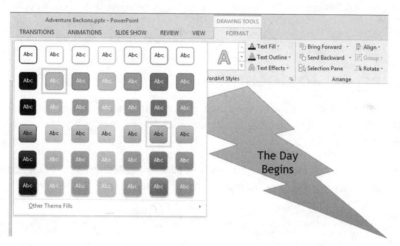

Figure 5-15 The Shape Styles gallery can apply pleasing combinations of colors and effects with a single click.

The Shape Styles gallery displays colors and styles that conform to the currently selected theme; changing the theme also changes the gallery contents. (For more information, see "Using Office themes" later in this chapter.) If none of the options in the Shape Styles gallery tickles you, use the tools on the right side of the Shape Styles group on the Format tab:

- **Shape Fill**   Options here let you fill the shape with a color (either solid or as a gradient), a picture from a file on your computer, or a texture (from a gallery that includes various fabrics, stones, wood grains, and other materials).

- **Shape Outline**   Select a color, line weight, and line style for the shape's outline.

- **Shape Effects**   Available effects are similar to the ones you can apply to pictures: shadows, reflections, glows, soft edges, bevels, and three-dimensional rotation, each of which is displayed in a Live Preview gallery.

Chapter 5

INSIDE OUT   Copy and move graphics and formatting

To copy or move a selected graphic or picture, you can use the Clipboard as you would with ordinary text. The usual keyboard shortcuts (Ctrl+X for Cut, Ctrl+C for Copy, and Ctrl+V for Paste), Home tab commands, and menu commands do the job.

But—just as you can with text—you can copy all the formatting for a graphic or picture, which is handy when you need to apply extensive (but consistent) styles and formats to many pictures. Use the Format Painter or use keyboard shortcuts: Ctrl+Shift+C to copy formatting, and Ctrl+Shift+V to paste formatting. For more information, see "Copying formatting" in Chapter 4, "Entering, editing, and formatting text."

Adding SmartArt to documents

SmartArt graphics provide an easy way to create graphical lists, process diagrams, organizational charts, and similar diagrams that meld shapes, text, and pictures into compelling visuals.

To insert SmartArt, click the Insert tab, and click SmartArt. A dialog box appears, in which you can select from an array of layouts, as shown in Figure 5-16. Select one and click OK.

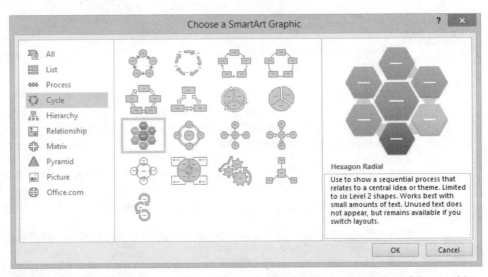

Figure 5-16 When you select a graphic, a larger visualization and a description of the graphic's use appear in the right pane.

The next step is to enter text into the SmartArt graphic. If the Text pane isn't displayed, select the graphic and click the arrow at the center of the left side of the frame. Within the Text pane, shown in Figure 5-17, use the keyboard shortcuts shown in Table 5-2. Alternatively, right-click an item in the Text pane, and choose from the menu. Tools in the Create Graphic group on the Design tab under SmartArt Tools provide a third (and sometimes best) method for organizing the text in a SmartArt graphic.

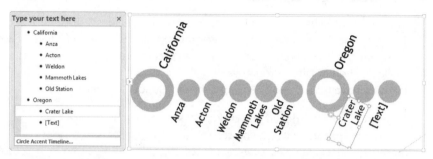

Figure 5-17 Although you can enter text directly into the graphic, it's usually easier with the aid of the Text pane.

TABLE 5-2 Keyboard shortcuts for text entry in SmartArt graphics

Action	Keyboard shortcut
Go to next entry	Down Arrow
Go to previous entry	Up Arrow
Create new entry	Enter
Delete entry	Delete (with some shapes, you must first delete any text in the entry)
Demote current entry	Tab
Promote current entry	Shift+Tab

The Design tab under SmartArt Tools includes galleries in which you can select a different SmartArt design (in the Layouts group), a different color scheme (in the SmartArt Styles group), or a different style (a predefined configuration of fill, outline, and effects settings for shapes and text in the SmartArt graphic).

You'll find more granular controls on the Format tab under SmartArt Tools. You can modify shapes individually or en masse (a SmartArt graphic is an assemblage of individual shapes)

by using the tools and techniques described earlier in this chapter for individual shapes. (See the preceding section, "Adding shapes and text boxes.") In addition, you can format text using all the options available for WordArt, as described in "Applying text effects with WordArt," later in this chapter.

Displaying data graphically with charts

Data charts have been a key feature of Excel since its earliest appearance back in 1985. The chart capabilities and features increased dramatically over the years, of course, but full-featured charting remained primarily an Excel feature, with lesser charting capabilities available in other Office programs. With Office 2013, however, the full range of charting features is available in Word, PowerPoint, and Outlook, as well as Excel.

To insert a chart in a document, click the Insert tab and then click Chart. The Insert Chart dialog box appears, in which you can select from an astonishing gallery of chart types. (Because charting remains a central part of Excel, there isn't a single Chart tool on the Insert tab. Instead, each chart type appears in its own gallery. You can, however, open Insert Chart by clicking the dialog box launcher in the Charts group on the Insert tab.)

Hover the mouse pointer over the sample chart for an enlarged view

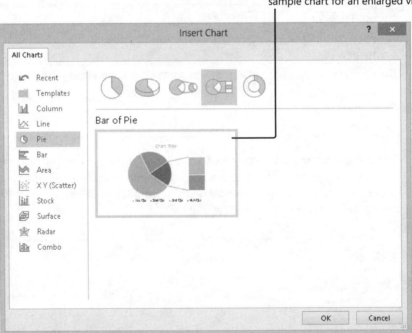

Select a chart type (you can change it later) and click OK. A worksheet then opens in an Excel-like window (see Figure 5-18); this is where you enter the data for your chart. You can then switch back and forth between entering data in the worksheet window and viewing and formatting the resulting chart in your document window. Contents of the Office Clipboard appear in the Clipboard pane for easy pasting into the worksheet. (If you're inserting a chart in Excel, the data and the chart appear in different parts of the same worksheet.) If you need to reopen the worksheet after closing it, select the chart, and on the Design tab, under Chart Tools, click Edit Data.

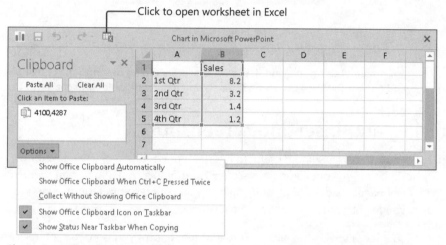

Figure 5-18 The worksheet initially contains sample data. Type in the worksheet or paste from the Clipboard. (If the Clipboard doesn't appear as shown here, return to the document window and click the Clipboard dialog box launcher on the Home tab to display the Clipboard pane. Then click in the worksheet window and double-click the Clipboard icon in the taskbar notification area.)

To change the appearance of your chart, select the chart and click the tabs under Chart Tools:

● Use the Design tab to change overall settings, such as chart type, data orientation, and styles.

● The Format tab is the place to manage shape styles, position, and size—settings we cover elsewhere in this chapter. (See "Adding shapes and text boxes," "Positioning objects," and "Resizing and rotating graphics and pictures.")

When you select a chart, a set of tools appears on its right side. With these tools, you can modify specific chart elements, such as titles, axes, and legends, and you can filter the data to exclude unwanted parts. This toolbar offers functionality comparable to the Layout tab under Chart Tools in Office 2010.

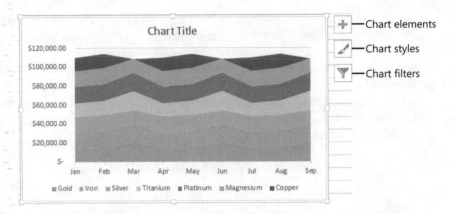

For details about displaying data with charts, including descriptions of features on the Design and Format tabs, see Chapter 13, "Analyzing data with tables and charts."

Capturing and inserting screenshots

You'll sometimes find it useful to insert a representation of a window (or part of a window) clipped from your computer's screen. For example, you might want to include part of a webpage in a document, or if you're documenting computer procedures for your office, you might want to show a program window.

To insert a screenshot, first be sure that the window you want to capture is not minimized to the taskbar. (It's okay if it's covered by other windows, including the Office window you're working in.) Then click the Insert tab, and in the Illustrations group, click Screenshot. Thumbnail images of each window appear, as shown in Figure 5-19.

Click a thumbnail to insert an image of the entire window. If you want to show only part of the screen, you can crop the window image after you insert it, or you can click Screen Clipping. When you click Screen Clipping, the Office window disappears from view, exposing the underlying screen—whatever it may contain. Use the mouse to drag across the area you want to capture, creating a rectangular clipping area. When you release the mouse button, Office immediately inserts an image of the area you outlined.

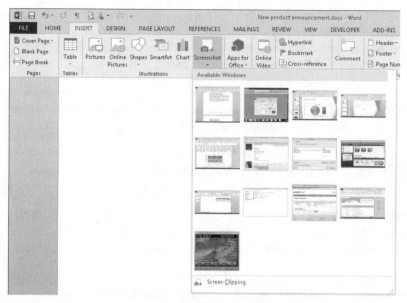

Figure 5-19 Available windows include all windows and dialog boxes that are not minimized, except for the Office window in which you're working.

> **Note**
>
> Although OneNote doesn't have the ability to capture and insert entire windows, you can grab screen clippings in OneNote. On the Insert tab, in the Images group, click Screen Clipping. For more information, see "Screen clippings" in Chapter 21, "Inside OneNote 2013."

INSIDE OUT Capture the Office window

Ironically, the screenshot feature in Office 2013 doesn't let you capture an image of the Office program itself. Workarounds abound, but the simplest is to press Alt+Print Screen (which copies the current window to the Clipboard) and then press Ctrl+V to paste the Clipboard content into your document. In Windows 8, press Windows logo key+Print Screen to capture the entire screen to a file in the Screenshots folder of your Pictures library. Insert the screenshot into your document, and then use the Office cropping tools to zero in on the portion you want to use.

Inserted screenshots are handled by Office programs exactly like pictures. When you select a screenshot, Picture Tools appears on the ribbon. The Format tab contains the same tools and features, and you can apply to a screenshot any of the changes described in "Making your pictures look great" earlier in this chapter.

Unlike pictures that you insert, however, screenshots don't exist elsewhere as an image file. In Word, OneNote, PowerPoint, and Outlook (but not Excel), it's easy to create such a file. Simply right-click the image and choose Save As Picture.

Applying text effects with WordArt

A fixture in Word for many years, WordArt has changed significantly (for the better) in recent editions. It's now easier to use, more flexible, and can create attractive text effects—instead of the funhouse mirror–style distortions that typified its output in earlier editions. Moreover, you can now use WordArt in Excel, PowerPoint, and Outlook as well as Word.

To convert existing text to WordArt, first select the text. Then (whether you have text selected or not) click the Insert tab, and in the Text group, click WordArt. A gallery of colorful styles appears. Click one, and you'll see your text (or placeholder text, if you didn't have any selected) in the new style. When the selection frame is a dashed line, you can select and enter text. (Use the Esc and Enter keys to switch between text entry and formatting modes.) You also specify a font, font size, and effects such as bold and italic while you're in text entry mode; use the usual text formatting tools on the Home tab or the Mini toolbar.

With your text in place, you can proceed to modify other aspects of its appearance. Select the WordArt object and then click the Format tab (under Drawing Tools). Here, in the WordArt Styles group, you can select a different predefined lettering style from the gallery. (If a Quick Styles button appears, click it to display the gallery.) The three tools to the right of the gallery offer additional customization options similar to those available for shapes:

- Click Text Fill to select coloring options for the letters. You can select a color (solid or gradient). Or go crazy: use a picture from a file or a texture cropped to the shape of the letters.

- Click Text Outline to specify the color, line weight, and style of the letter outlines.

- Click Text Effects (see Figure 5-20) to add shadows, reflections, and other effects. Each item on the Text Effects menu leads to a gallery submenu with Live Preview.

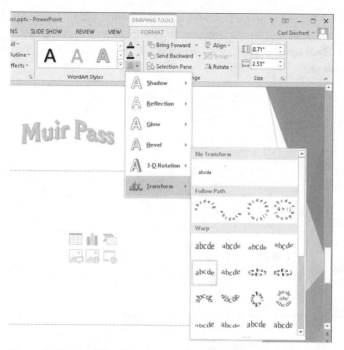

Figure 5-20 You'll find the funhouse-mirror effects in the Transform gallery.

All the settings and effects available on the Format tab, along with additional options, can be viewed and configured in the Format Shape pane. To open it, click the WordArt Styles dialog box launcher.

Using Office themes

The final section of this chapter deals not with individual graphic objects but with a feature that can change the overall appearance of your document with just a few clicks. That feature is document themes. A *theme* is a collection of formatting options that include a set of colors, a set of fonts (one for headings and one for body text), and a set of effects (such as line styles and fill effects).

A theme in PowerPoint also includes backgrounds. For more information about themes in PowerPoint, see "Applying themes" in Chapter 18.

Selecting a theme causes all these theme elements to be applied to a document. (You can override theme settings for any part of a document, and those parts won't be affected by theme changes.) Themes are consistent across all Office programs. You can, for example, apply a theme to a Word document and apply the same theme to an Excel worksheet and a PowerPoint presentation, giving them a consistent look and feel.

Chapter 5

To apply a theme to the current document, click the Design tab (in Word and PowerPoint), the Page Layout tab (Excel), or the Options tab (Outlook) and then click Themes, as shown in Figure 5-21. Point to a theme to see a live preview of your document, and click a theme to apply its settings.

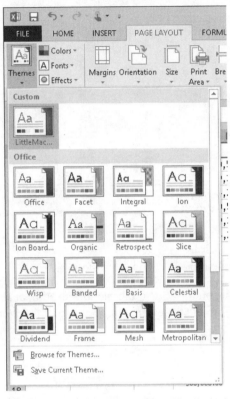

Figure 5-21 The Custom section appears only if you have saved one or more themes.

To see what components constitute a theme (and to change them to your liking), use the other buttons in the Themes group on the Design (or Page Layout or Options) tab.

- **Colors**   A theme includes a dozen (usually complementary) colors that are applied to different document elements. You can select one of the 20-odd built-in color collections, or you can click Customize Colors to make a custom collection.

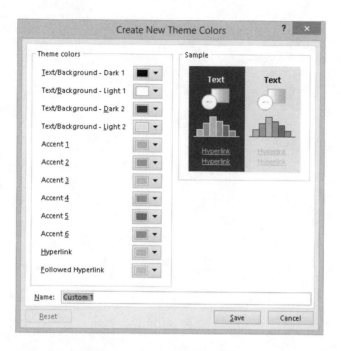

- **Fonts**   A theme comprises two fonts: one for headings and one for body text. Select a built-in pairing, or click Customize Fonts to mix your own. Office differentiates between headings and body text based on the paragraph style (Word), cell style (Excel), or placeholder type (PowerPoint).

- **Effects**   Select one of the built-in line and fill effects combinations. You can't create your own variation.

After you've made your selections and customizations in each of these three areas, you might want to save this combination as a new custom theme. To do that, click Themes, Save Current Theme. Each theme is stored in its own file, so it's easy to copy the theme file to other computers, thereby enabling consistent appearance throughout an organization. Theme files are stored by default in %AppData%\Microsoft\Templates\Document Themes (C:\Users*username*\AppData\Roaming\Microsoft\Templates\Document Themes on a computer with default settings), but you can store them in any folder.

If your custom theme doesn't appear in the Themes gallery after it's been copied to a computer, click Themes, Browse For Themes to locate it.

Chapter 5

PART 2

Office on the desktop and in the cloud

Managing Office files

I T's EASY to get lost in discussions of features, user interface elements, and design decisions in Office 2013 and lose the much larger point. No one uses the individual programs that are part of Office for the sheer joy of clicking items on a ribbon or typing bullet points. Those programs and their accompanying tools and techniques are merely a means to an end: a report, a slide deck, or an annual budget, for example, which in turn might be printed, posted, published, or shared in real time.

In this chapter, we examine the data files that you create and use with the four document-centric Office programs. The end product—a Word document, an Excel workbook, a PowerPoint presentation, or a Publisher publication—is contained in a single file that you can open, move between folders, attach to an email message, and so on. In this chapter, we explain which file formats each Office program supports, how to convert files to alternative formats, and how to make sure you don't lose the work contained in those files because of a power failure or (ahem) user error.

Three other Office programs described in this book—OneNote, Access, and Outlook—store discrete data items (pages in OneNote and email messages in Outlook, for example) in large files that act as *data stores*. You manage and manipulate individual items from within the program and generally don't need to concern yourself with document files (except when you export an item as a separate file). You'll find more details in the chapters devoted to those programs. But don't head back there just yet; you'll find plenty of information in this chapter that you can use to understand and better manage Office files.

> **Note**
>
> Throughout this chapter—indeed, throughout this book—you might be confused about our use of the term *document*. In its narrowest definition, it refers to a data file saved in the Microsoft Word Document (.docx) format. However, *document* can also refer generically to user-created files from any program—files that are stored by default in your Documents library or Documents folder. You'll find both definitions in use here.

Where (and how) Office stores files

When you use the default Office 2013 settings, opening Word, Excel, PowerPoint, or Publisher takes you to a Start screen like the one shown in Figure 6-1. Like most other items in Backstage view, the targets here are large, making them particularly easy to use on a touch screen device.

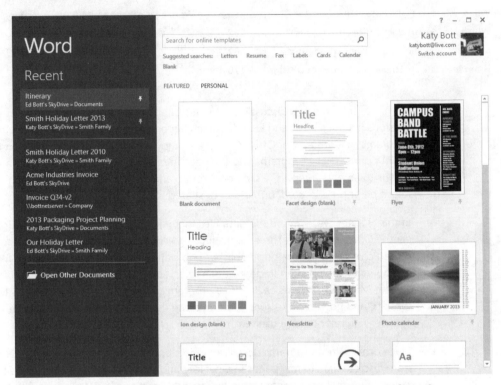

Figure 6-1 The only way to open this Start screen is to open a new instance of Word. PowerPoint, Excel, and Publisher have similar Start screens.

The column on the left shows a list of files you've opened recently, with two documents pinned to the top of the list in this example. The pane on the right offers a selection of templates, with Blank Document in a permanent position as the first item in the list. (You'll see Blank Workbook and Blank Presentation in Excel and PowerPoint, respectively. Publisher offers a choice of blank projects in varying sizes on its Start screen.)

INSIDE OUT
Bypass Backstage view completely for file management

If you're a traditionalist using Office 2013 on a device that doesn't have a touch screen, you might prefer to skip the layover in Backstage view and go directly to the familiar Open and Save As dialog boxes when you want to work with files. Your wish is our command.

You can go straight to the Open dialog box at any time by pressing Ctrl+F12. To open the Save As dialog box, press F12. The familiar Ctrl+O (Open) and Ctrl+S (Save) shortcuts go to Backstage view by default.

In Word, Excel, or PowerPoint, click the General tab in the Options dialog box and clear Show The Start Screen When This Application Starts. (In Publisher, this option is Show The New Template Gallery When Starting Publisher.) Next, go to the Save tab and select Don't Show The Backstage When Opening Or Saving Files. Click OK to save your changes.

You must make these changes separately using the Options dialog box in each program. There's no master switch.

When you move the mouse pointer over an unpinned item in the Recent list, a pushpin icon appears; click the icon to pin that file to the top of the list. You can also right-click any item in the list to see a more comprehensive menu of customization options like the one shown here.

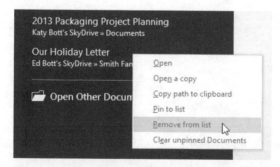

The Open A Copy option is worth calling out here. It's the preferred way to create a new document based on one you previously saved, without the risk of accidentally overwriting the original. The Remove From List option allows you to prune unneeded entries from the list. Click Clear Unpinned Documents/Workbooks/Presentations to remove all entries from the Recent list except those you've pinned. (This choice appears as Clear Unpinned Items in Publisher.)

> **Note**
>
> These same customization options for the Recent list are available when you click the Recent Documents/Workbooks/Presentations/Publications link that appears at the top of the pane when you click File, then Open. You can customize the templates pane, too, as we explain in "Using templates to streamline document creation" later in this chapter.

The individual pieces of the Start screen are available when you click File from Word, Excel, PowerPoint, or Publisher. Click New to see available templates; choose Open or Save As to display a list of available locations where you can browse for files or folders. Figure 6-2 shows the Save As pane in Backstage view.

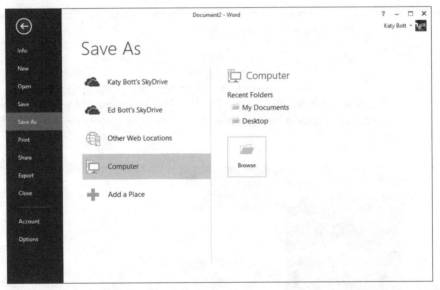

Figure 6-2 Click Browse from Backstage view to open the standard Windows dialog boxes for opening and saving files.

If the file you want to open isn't in the Recent list or you're saving a file for the first time, click a location and then click Browse. That action displays an Open or Save As dialog box similar to the ones you've seen in countless other Windows programs.

Note we said *similar*, not identical. The Office versions of these common dialog boxes include a few extra features that you won't find in their Windows-standard equivalents. Figure 6-3 shows the Save As dialog box from Word running in Windows 8.

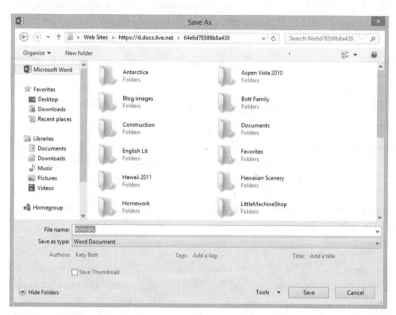

Figure 6-3 When you use the Office Save As dialog box, you can enter metadata and choose some options from the Tools menu.

The Open and Save As dialog boxes are, in effect, special-purpose instances of Windows' built-in file management tools—File Explorer in Windows 8, Windows Explorer in Windows 7. That means you can right-click a folder or file to display a menu of available actions, and you can use all the tricks you use in Windows to move, rename, delete, and otherwise manipulate files, without leaving Office.

The Back and Forward buttons, address bar, and search box are identical to those you'll find in File Explorer (Windows Explorer in Windows 7). The Up button is available if you're using Windows 8, but isn't there for Windows 7. The navigation pane is nearly the same; the only difference is that the name of the Office program appears at the top of the pane.

Entering text in the search box filters the window contents to include only documents in the current folder and its subfolders that contain that text. You can further narrow your search with the use of search filters, which we discuss in "Organizing and finding Office files" later in this chapter.

> **Note**
>
> In this chapter, we discuss opening and saving documents, regardless of where they're stored. For information about the special challenges of working with documents in the cloud, see Chapter 7, "Connecting Office 2013 to SkyDrive and other online services," and Chapter 8, "Using Office 2013 with an Office 365 subscription."

Custom options in the Save As dialog box

You see the Save As dialog box when you save a document for the first time or save an existing document with a new name or in a different file format. You can optionally choose to enter properties about the document and its authors, which are saved as *metadata* in the file; then enter a file name, choose a file type, and click Save.

For general information about Office file formats, see "Which file formats does Office 2013 support?" later in this chapter.

Other options available here vary depending on the file format you select. If you select the default file format in Word, Excel, PowerPoint, or Publisher, you see a selection of document properties below the Save As Type list: Authors, Tags, and Title are visible by default, but you can see additional properties if you widen the dialog box. You are free to edit or ignore the values stored in these fields. Select Save Thumbnail (Word and Excel only) to create a thumbnail image of the document to appear in File Explorer (and in the Open and Save As dialog boxes) in place of the standard document icon.

INSIDE OUT   Change the default entry in the Authors field

In a new document created using one of the default Office formats, the Authors field is initially populated with the name of the user who created the document. This name is set when you sign in to Office; you can change the name shown here (as well as the names or initials used in comments and tracked changes) by clicking File, Options, and then changing User Name and Initials on the General tab. If you want to use one name and set of initials regardless of which account you're using, select the option Always Use These Values Regardless Of Sign In To Office.

The Tools menu at the bottom of the Save As dialog box displays a menu of additional options, which vary depending on which program you're using.

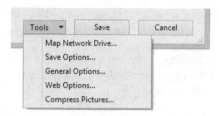

These three options are worth noting:

- **Save Options**   This command opens the Options dialog box and displays the Save tab. For the most part, the options here affect all documents. The Preserve Fidel-ity When Sharing This Document area at the bottom of the dialog box is the major exception, allowing you to embed fonts in Word and PowerPoint files.

- **General Options**   This command opens a dialog box in which you can set security-related options for encryption, password protection, and macro handling.

- **Web Options**   This command opens a dialog box in which you can set various com-patibility options for webpages you create in Office.

Custom options in the Open dialog box

The Open dialog box, like its counterpart Save As, is essentially a special-purpose Explorer window. Naturally, you can select any file from any folder and click Open to begin working with that file. But click the arrow to the right of the Open button and you'll see additional options, as shown here:

- **Open Read-Only**   When you open a document in read-only mode, Office doesn't prevent you from making changes. However, to save any changes, you must save the document with a new name, preserving the original unedited document.

- **Open As Copy**   This option creates a copy of the selected file, inserting the word Copy and a number before the file name, and then opens the copy. Use this option if you want to create a new version of an existing document without the risk of accidentally overwriting it.

- **Open In Browser**   This option is available only when you select a file saved in an HTML format. Click Open to edit the document in Word; use this option to view the saved document in your default web browser.

- **Open In Protected View**   Protected View is designed primarily for potentially risky files, such as documents you download from the Internet or a message attachment from a sender identified as potentially unsafe. In Protected View, you're prevented from editing or saving the document unless you explicitly enable these features after the document opens. For more information about Protected View, see "Working with (and around) Office security features" later in this chapter.

- **Open And Repair**   If your file doesn't open properly, try this option, which attempts to repair corrupted files or, if that's not possible, extract the valid data.

Which file formats does Office 2013 support?

If you never share Office 2013 files, you don't need to worry too much about file formats. Create a workbook in Excel 2013, for example, and you can save it in the default format (without even being aware what the default format is) and reopen it later without a hitch. Historically, however, one of the pain points for Office users has been exchanging documents with other users.

Office file formats have evolved over the decades as new document features are supported. When you share a document with people who don't have the same version of Office as you, the document might not look the same when they open it—or they might not be able to open it at all. Compatibility becomes even more problematic when you need to share documents with someone who doesn't have any version of Microsoft Office and uses a different suite of programs (or none at all).

The document-centric programs in Office 2013 store files by default in XML-based file formats, which we'll discuss in more detail shortly. In addition to these native formats, you can save and open files as templates, with or without support for macros. You can open and save files in the binary formats that were used with Office 97–2003, or in the OpenDocument format used by the free OpenOffice.org program. You can also export most documents created with Office programs to a variety of non-native formats, including HTML files destined for viewing in browsers.

When you save a document in a format other than the default Office format, you might see a warning similar to the one in Figure 6-4. This lets you know that not all features are supported by the selected file format and that you can expect some loss of fidelity when you open the document in its native program—or even when you reopen it in the Office 2013 program that you used to create it.

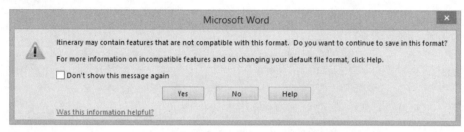

Figure 6-4 This generic compatibility warning may appear when you save a document using an alternative format.

Understanding the Office 2013 default formats: Office Open XML

By default, Word, Excel, and PowerPoint use documents stored in the Office Open XML (OOXML) format. This XML-based format, which was introduced with Office 2007, offers several advantages over the binary formats used in Office 2003 and earlier versions. Most notably:

- **Smaller files**   Each document file (.docx for Word, .xlsx for Excel, and .pptx for PowerPoint) is actually a container file in the ZIP archive format. The document parts—including the document text, embedded images, formatting commands, and so on—are saved as individual files within the container. Zip compression technology reduces the file size as much as 75 percent. Office automatically unzips the container when you open a document and rezips it when you're done.

  This not only means you need less disk space to store documents, but it facilitates sending documents as email attachments and reduces the time needed to move files to and from network or Internet locations.

- **More robust files**   Because the document file contains discrete files within a ZIP archive, you should be able to open and work with the document even if some component parts are missing or damaged. To open a damaged file, you might need to change its file name extension and use a third-party utility.

- **Better control over personal information**   With the older binary formats, some notoriously embarrassing incidents arose in which snoops were able to find personal information and earlier edits to a document. The Open XML formats support the use of the document inspector (see Figure 6-5), which identifies potential privacy problems (and other issues) and allows you to remove personally identifiable information such as author names, document revisions, file paths, and so on. For more information about the document inspector and privacy concerns, see "Inspecting and removing personal and confidential information" later in this chapter.

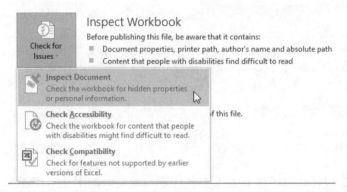

Figure 6-5 On the Info pane in Backstage view, a summary of potential privacy issues appears next to Check For Issues. Click the button and choose Inspect Document for details.

INSIDE OUT   Dig into an Open XML document

If you're curious about the structure and content of an Open XML document, it's easy to take a look inside. Start by changing the file name extension to .zip, and then open the file as a compressed folder in File Explorer. In the root of the compressed folder, you'll see a document named [Content_Types].xml. This file, which you can view in a web browser, identifies the parts of the document. The files that make up these parts are located within subfolders of the compressed folder.

"How to: Manipulate Office Open XML Formats Documents" provides an introductory tour of the structure and content of the files within a document file; you can find this article in the MSDN library at *w7io.com/10402*.

Setting a default file format

As we noted earlier, the default formats used for document-centric programs in Office 2007–2013 are based on Open XML. "Default," in this case, merely means that when you save a document for the first time, that format is preselected in the Save As dialog box. (When you open a document that was previously saved in a different format, Office uses the file's current format as the default choice when you resave it.)

You might want to select a different format as the default choice, particularly if you frequently share documents you create with people who are using programs other than Office

2007–2013. Changing the default format for Word, Excel, or PowerPoint is easy, but it's not particularly intuitive. Here's how:

1. In Backstage view, click Options.

2. In the Options dialog box, click Save.

3. Next to Save Files In This Format, select the format you want to use by default.

You can override your new default format at any time by choosing a different file type in the Save As dialog box.

> **Note**
>
> In some countries, the first time you run an Office 2010 or 2013 program, it asks you to choose between two default formats: Office Open XML or OpenDocument (ODF). (OpenDocument formats were developed for the OpenOffice.org office suite. Selecting ODF as your default format provides compatibility with other programs, but it doesn't support all features of Office.) Your choice in this dialog box sets the default for all Office programs that support OpenDocument formats.

INSIDE OUT   Using Office 2013 formats with earlier Office versions

Microsoft offers a free compatibility pack for earlier versions of Office that enables users of those versions to read, modify, and save Word, Excel, and PowerPoint documents in the Office Open XML format—the default format used by Office 2007–2013. If you regularly exchange documents with someone who uses Office 2003 or (shudder) an earlier, unsupported version, the compatibility pack provides a way to help them.

The Microsoft Office Compatibility Pack for Word, Excel, and PowerPoint File Formats works with any of these earlier Office versions:

- Microsoft Office 2000 with Service Pack 3

- Microsoft Office XP with Service Pack 3

- Microsoft Office 2003 with Service Pack 3

To download the Microsoft Office Compatibility Pack for Word, Excel, and PowerPoint File Formats, visit *w7io.com/10401*. For more details about installing, using, and troubleshooting the compatibility pack, see Microsoft Support article 924074 (*w7io.com/924074*).

Chapter 6

Checking for compatibility with an earlier Office version

Not surprisingly, newer versions of Office include features that were not part of earlier Office versions—features as varied as numbering formats in Word, sparklines (in-cell graphs) in Excel, and reflection shape effects in PowerPoint.

If you exchange documents with users who plan to open them using programs other than Office 2013, you'll want to know whether your documents will appear the same when those users open your files. Word, Excel, and PowerPoint include a compatibility checker feature that identifies items in your document that won't work properly with earlier Office versions. On the Info tab in Backstage view, click Check For Issues, and then click Check Compatibility. If the compatibility checker finds incompatible items in your document, it displays a dialog box that identifies each problem, similar to the one shown in Figure 6-6.

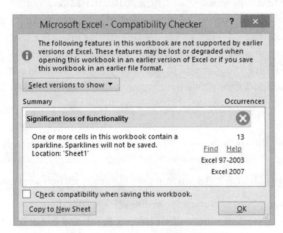

Figure 6-6 For each compatibility issue, the compatibility checker provides details about the issue and explains which Office versions are affected.

The compatibility checker runs automatically when you save a document in one of the downlevel formats such as Word 97–2003 Document (.doc), Excel 97–2003 Workbook (.xls), and PowerPoint 97–2003 Presentation (.ppt). When a dialog box like this appears, click Continue to proceed with the save operation (with full knowledge of the limitations and consequences) or click Cancel to return to the Save As dialog box without saving.

When you open a document in an Office 2013 program that was originally created using an earlier version, Office opens that document in Compatibility Mode. You can readily identify any such document by the [Compatibility Mode] label in the title bar and a similar label at the top of the Info pane in Backstage view, next to the Convert button.

To restore the full set of Office 2013 features to a document that has been opened in Compatibility Mode, open the Info pane and click Convert.

Exporting files and data to alternative formats

The native formats in Office 2013 are the preferred choice for documents you create, store, and manage. But there are at least three circumstances under which you might prefer an alternative format:

- **You want anyone to be able to view your document and have it look identical to what you've created.** The preferred universal format for this scenario is Adobe Portable Document Format (PDF). A PDF reader is included with Windows 8, and native or third-party readers are available for other versions of Windows, for Macs and PCs running Linux or UNIX, and on every modern mobile device. We'll discuss PDF options in more detail shortly.

INSIDE OUT   What is the XPS format good for?

The Open XML Paper Specification (OpenXPS) was originally developed by Microsoft as a PDF alternative, but it never achieved any traction. It has some theoretical advantages for sharing read-only documents (XPS can more closely match the appearance of your original Office document), but it is not as widely known or supported as PDF. An XPS viewer program is included with Windows Vista, Windows 7, and Windows 8. Users of Windows XP can get XPS-viewing capabilities by installing Internet Explorer 8 or a viewer such as the free one from Microsoft (*w7io.com/10403*). Other options for Windows as well as for other operating systems can be found at *w7io.com/10404*.

- **You plan to publish the output of an Office program on a website for viewing directly in a browser.** Word, Excel, and Publisher allow you to save their output in Web Page (HTML) format. (An alternative format allows you to save the output as a single file webpage, which can be opened in Internet Explorer.) These formats are available when you choose Save As from Backstage view. The resulting output consists of an HTML page, with a file name extension of .htm; additional elements, such as pictures and style sheets, are stored in separate files and saved in a subfolder with the same name as the .htm file. To make a PowerPoint presentation viewable in a web browser, use the Present Online option; for details, see "Delivering a live presentation online" in Chapter 20, "PowerPoint 2013 inside out."

- **You want to use part of a document you created using Office in another program or file.** For example, you might want to save individual PowerPoint slides as image files, or use a range of data from an Excel list in an Access database. Where they're useful, we discuss these export options in more detail in the chapters devoted to specific programs.

The most obvious advantage of saving a document in PDF format is that you can have confidence that your reader will see exactly what you created. Embedded fonts and images go a long way toward ensuring a high level of fidelity.

To save a Word document, Excel workbook, PowerPoint presentation, or Publisher project in PDF format, you can click Save As in Backstage view and select PDF from the Save As Type list. As an alternative, you can click Export in Backstage view and then click the Create PDF/XPS button.

Both options lead to essentially the same destination: a variant of the Save As dialog box, with a few PDF-specific options below the Save As Type box, as shown in Figure 6-7.

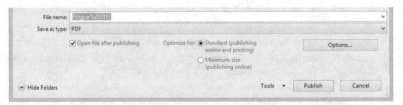

Figure 6-7 These options are specific to files you save in PDF format.

Choose a file name and a destination folder, but don't click Publish just yet. Instead, review the following options:

- **Open File After Publishing**   If this option is selected, the PDF or XPS document opens in the program registered for that document type (by default, this is the Reader program in Windows 8, although you can substitute a desktop program such as Adobe Reader).

- **Optimize For**   Choosing Standard produces high-resolution files suitable for use by a commercial printer, but the files can be quite large. Choosing Minimum Size produces files that are smaller and are usually good enough for viewing on a computer screen.

- **Options**   In the Options dialog box, you can specify which parts of a document, workbook, or presentation you want to include in the output. In Word, you can create bookmarks in the output file using document headings. The options you see here vary slightly depending on the program you're using, but they're generally similar to the Options dialog box for PowerPoint, shown in Figure 6-8.

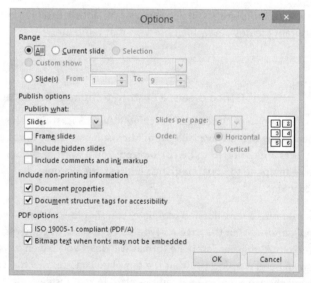

Figure 6-8 These additional settings are available for the current file if you select PDF as the file type and then click the Options button.

Using templates to streamline document creation

Do you create the same type of document over and over? Do you want to apply a consistent look and feel to all new documents? Do you regularly make the same changes to every new document?

If you answered yes to any of those questions, then this section is for you. Customizing the default file template that each Office program uses when you choose a blank document, workbook, presentation, or project allows you to replace the Office defaults with settings that mirror your preferences. Creating additional custom templates (or adapting third-party templates to your own preferences) allows you to eliminate much of the drudgery of creating new documents with common elements.

Templates are essentially special-purpose versions of the equivalent file format, with a different file name extension. Thus, the Word Document Template format uses .dotx instead of .docx, PowerPoint templates use .potx instead of .pptx, and so on. Templates can contain boilerplate text, pictures, placeholders, styles, and macros (if you choose a macro-compatible template format).

If you double-click a template file in File Explorer (Windows Explorer in Windows 7), the associated program creates a new file based on that template.

INSIDE OUT Let Office create a custom templates folder automatically

On a clean installation of Office 2013, clicking New in Backstage view takes you to a listing of templates that are available from Microsoft's website, *Office.com*. Many of those templates are designed to be customized; you'll want to change the generic text on an invoice template to your company's address, for example, and add a logo in place of the placeholder.

After you customize a downloaded template, you should click Save As and select one of the template formats in the Save As Type box. For most documents, the basic Word/Excel/PowerPoint/Publisher Template format will do. If you see an error message like the one shown here, warning you that the template includes macros, cancel the Save operation and choose a macro-enabled template format instead.

When you save your first custom template in any Office 2013 program, Office creates a new Custom Office Templates folder in your Documents folder (if it doesn't already exist) and uses that as the destination folder. Any additional templates you save in any Office program go in this folder.

After you have created your first custom template in Word or Excel, you'll see a new option at the top of the New pane, beneath the search box for those two programs. Click Featured to see the online templates, or click Personal to see only templates that you have saved in your Custom Office Templates folder. (In Publisher, you see Featured and Built-In as options; PowerPoint omits these navigational aids.)

Options such as these appear after you save your first custom template

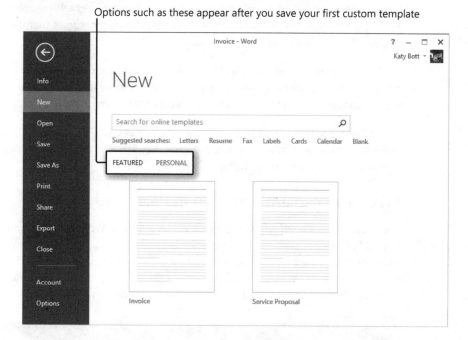

If you have many templates and you want to organize them, use subfolders of the template folder. Each subfolder appears as a folder icon in the New pane when you click Personal.

Working with (and around) Office security features

Office macros are a form of programming used for automation that allow a Word document, an Excel workbook, or another macro-enabled file to perform actions on its own, including interacting with the operating system.

Chapter 6

In the wild, woolly, and distant past, Word documents (and, to a lesser extent, documents from other Office programs that include a macro language) were sometimes used by malicious hackers to spread viruses and other malware. This came about largely because of the unfortunate combination of Word's powerful macro capabilities and its default settings, which allowed naïve users to open documents that automatically executed malicious macros. Other risks arose from the use of ActiveX controls (another type of program) embedded in documents.

Malware that exploits Office documents reached its peak in the late 1990s but is thankfully rare today. Although Office documents still support the use of macros and ActiveX controls (topics beyond the scope of this book), features in newer versions of Office greatly mitigate the risks associated with them. Office settings are secure by default, meaning that you must take positive steps to enable macros, ActiveX, or other technologies that have the potential of doing harm—as well as working to your benefit.

By default, Office prompts you and requests your permission whenever a document uses macros or ActiveX controls. In addition, Protected View—a feature-restricted, read-only mode—prevents documents of unknown provenance from doing any harm.

Office has other, less apparent, protections in place as well. For example, Data Execution Prevention disables add-ins that work in ways that can lead to a crash or might be a sign of a program trying to do some harm.

What you can and can't do in Protected View

The most visible sign of Office security is Protected View. When you open an Office file from an untrusted location—a website, for example, or as an attachment in an email message—that document opens in Protected View. In Protected View, most editing functions are disabled, as is the ability to print the file. Office displays several prominent indications to let you know that Protected View is in effect, as shown in Figure 6-9.

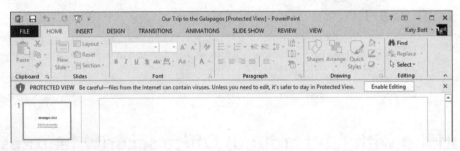

Figure 6-9 Office warns you that a file has been opened in Protected View with a label in the title bar, disabled tools on the ribbon, and, most prominently, a yellow message bar below the ribbon.

If you open the Info pane for that file, you'll see a similar prominent warning.

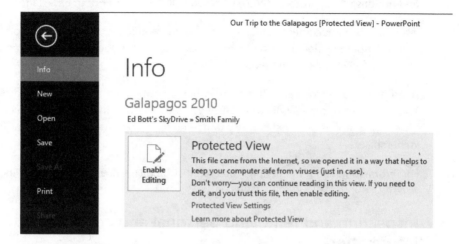

A document opens in Protected View for any of several reasons, including:

- The file originated from an Internet location. Because the Internet is the source of most viruses and other malware, Office invokes Protected View whenever you open a document directly from an Internet location or when you open a document that was downloaded from the Internet.

- The file was received as an email attachment and the sender has not been identified as safe.

- The file is stored in an unsafe location, such as the Temporary Internet Files folder.

- The file is blocked by File Block, a feature that causes documents from older versions of Office (by default, documents from Word 95 and earlier and from Excel 4 and earlier) to open in Protected View. The code used to open and save these outdated file types has security vulnerabilities.

- The file is corrupt. Office validates each file when it opens it; files that fail validation open in Protected View.

In Protected View, all the tools for viewing, searching, reviewing, and navigating within a document are available. However, you cannot edit, print, or save a document in Protected View.

If you trust the source of the document and are confident that it's safe, you can exit Protected View, thereby enabling the full panoply of Office tools and features. To exit Protected View when a yellow message bar appears, simply click Enable Editing in the message bar. Alternatively, click the File tab and click Enable Editing on the Info pane. (You will also find options to exit Protected View when you click Save or Print in Backstage view.)

If the untrusted document contains active content—macros or ActiveX controls—this content is disabled by default. A separate message bar warns you of the change and allows you to enable the macros or content.

A red message bar indicates that a binary file did not pass the Office file-validation tests. This type of error occurs only with Office 97–2003 formats and can indicate a corrupted file or one that has been deliberately tampered with in an attempt to exploit a security vulnerability.

For information about modifying Protected View and File Block settings, see "Fine-tuning security settings" later in this chapter.

Inspecting and removing personal and confidential information

The biggest threat to your privacy comes from your Office files themselves. Although the information that Office stores in a document is generally pretty innocuous—items such as your name, the amount of time spent editing a document, and so on—you might not want it revealed, perhaps for competitive reasons. In addition, documents can contain comments, annotations, content from earlier revisions, or hidden text that might cause embarrassment (or worse) if revealed.

Word, Excel, and PowerPoint include a feature that examines a document to find any personal information stored in the file and offer you the option to permanently remove it. You'll find this option on the Info tab in Backstage view. Click Check For Issues, Inspect Document. Figure 6-10 shows the Document Inspector dialog box for PowerPoint.

We strongly recommend that you use this feature anytime you share an Office file with anyone else or post it in an online location that might be accessible outside your circle of trusted associates.

For more information about options available when you click Check For Issues in a Word document, see "Checking a document" in Chapter 10, "Working with complex documents."

Figure 6-10 Clicking the Inspect button checks a presentation for potential privacy issues. Word and Excel have similar features.

INSIDE OUT   Protect documents from unwanted access or copying

Office also includes tools for protecting your documents from snooping and for ensuring that your document has not been altered. With Word, Excel, and PowerPoint, you can encrypt a document so that it can be opened only by someone who knows the password, and you can configure permissions (enforced by an Information Rights Management server) so that only people you authorize can view or edit a document. You can also apply a digital signature that people can use to verify who created the document and confirm that it hasn't been changed since the signature was applied.

For more information about these options, see "Protecting a document" in Chapter 10.

Fine-tuning security settings

As with so many activities in computing (and in life generally), there's a tradeoff between security and convenience. You could lock down your computer and Office so that they're perfectly safe—but you wouldn't be able to share usable documents or get anything done.

Chapter 6

On the other hand, you could throw caution to the wind; you wouldn't be slowed down by extra clicks to clear warning messages, so you could work quickly and efficiently—until the first malware strikes. The trick, of course, is to find the proper balance between security (annoyance and inefficiency) and convenience (danger).

We find that the default settings for Office straddle the line nicely, but if you want to make adjustments to the security settings, you need to visit the Trust Center. To get there, click File and then click Options. Click the Trust Center tab, and then click Trust Center Settings. (If a document is currently open in Protected View, you can get here more quickly by clicking File and then clicking Protected View Settings on the Info pane.)

Tabs in the Trust Center dialog box, shown in Figure 6-11, provide access to settings for managing various security risks.

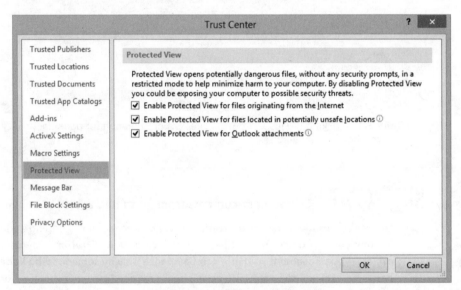

Figure 6-11 Clearing check boxes on this tab in the Trust Center reduces the number of warning messages you see—but at a possible cost in lowered security.

If you routinely open files created in older versions of Office, or if you share files with associates who have standardized on alternative file formats, take a look at the File Block Settings tab, shown in Figure 6-12. Each file type that does not have a check mark can be opened and saved normally. A check box in the Open column causes the file to open according to the setting at the bottom of the dialog box (in Protected View by default). A check box in the Save column prevents you from saving the file in its original format; you must save it as another supported file type. (For information about supported file types, see "Which file formats does Office 2013 support?" earlier in this chapter.)

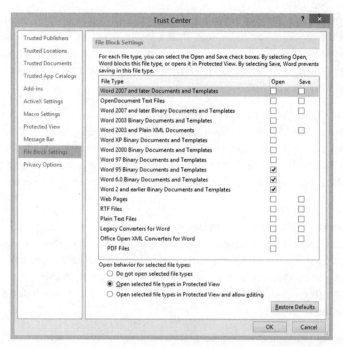

Figure 6-12 Use these options to warn or block the current Office user when opening or saving files in formats that might be unsafe or cause compatibility problems when shared.

Options you set in Trust Center apply to all Office programs.

If you're a security geek, the Trust Center is filled with interesting options that we don't have space to discuss here. We encourage you to explore its other options—but do so *carefully*. Playing "what if" with security settings can work out badly. Before you make a change, be sure you understand the security implications.

Organizing and finding Office files

The time-honored method for organizing documents in Windows is to save them in a hierarchical structure of folders. Then, to retrieve a document, you navigate through the folder structure until you find the one that contains the document you want. This system is useful, but it also imposes some arbitrary limitations. For example, do you create folders by project? By date? By type of document? You'll often encounter situations where it would be perfectly logical to save a document in any of several folders—so which do you choose? And will you remember the location when you go to retrieve the document later?

Chapter 6

The use of tags, categories, and other editable fields—as well as system-maintained properties such as the modification date—makes the folder structure and file location much less important. With the search capabilities built in to Windows 7 and 8, it's easy to search across multiple folders and drives to find a specific document based on its content, author, tags, title, and other properties.

As we noted at the beginning of this chapter, the Open and Save As dialog boxes use the same plumbing as File Explorer (in Windows 8) and Windows Explorer (in Windows 7). That means you can use the View button to switch between Details view (which includes Date Modified, File Type, File Size, and other fields), small icons, large icons, and so on. In the Open dialog box, you can use the Preview pane to view the file that's selected in the file pane.

And, of course, you can use the search box in the Open or Save As dialog box to filter the list of files to those that include the text or keyword you enter there. You can also use one or more properties as filters. When you click in the search box, commonly used filters appear in blue; click a filter name (for example, Authors), and then select from the list that appears. To use other filters in the search box, type the property name followed by a colon and then type the filter text.

In Details view, you can click the heading to the right of a column name to select from a drop-down list of items in that column. Use this option with the Type column to restrict the display of files to Microsoft Word Document, for example.

You can greatly improve the quality of search results by filling in document properties for files you want to retrieve later, especially when those files are part of a large data store that multiple people contribute to and access.

In addition to the content of a document, files in the Office Open XML document formats (as well as many other file formats) can contain other details about the document in the form of metadata. Metadata can include properties such as the name of the document author; the number of pages, paragraphs, lines, words, and characters in the document; the date and time it was last printed; and much more.

You can see a limited selection of these properties in fields in the Save As dialog box, as we discussed earlier in this chapter. To view the full set of properties of a file in Office, open Backstage view. Document properties are displayed in a list along the right side of the Info pane, as shown in Figure 6-13.

Properties ˅

Size	113KB
Pages	1
Words	2306
Total Editing Time	7 Minutes
Title	Add a title
Tags	Add a tag
Comments	Add comments

Related Dates

Last Modified	Today, 11:19 AM
Created	7/20/2012 11:13 AM
Last Printed	

Related People

Author	Add an author
Last Modified By	Ed Bott

Related Documents

Open File Location

Show All Properties

Figure 6-13 This abbreviated list of document properties appears on the Info pane. Click Show All Properties to see additional fields.

Some properties, such as the number of words and total editing time, are generated automatically by Office and can't be edited. The Title, Tags, and Comments fields can be edited at any time; simply click and type. You can display and edit a more comprehensive list by clicking Properties on the Info tab. Doing so offers two choices:

- **Show Document Panel**   This option displays a pane at the top of the document window that includes some of the most common editable properties.

- **Advanced Properties**   This option displays a multitabbed properties dialog box that provides access to more properties than you thought possible. And if that's not enough, you can create your own custom properties. (You can reach this same dialog box by clicking Document Properties, Advanced Properties in the upper-left corner of the document panel.)

Chapter 6

INSIDE OUT Use tags for pinpoint searches

Tags (which appear under Keywords on the document panel) are an extraordinarily effective way to make your searches more effective. For example, you can enter the name of projects (Project X) or clients (Acme Corp.) or document types (proposal) in the Tags field. Later, you can use those search terms to find matching documents regardless of the file name and document contents.

To enter multiple tags, separate them with semicolons. To search using tags, open File Explorer (Windows 8), Windows Explorer (Windows 7), or the Open or Save As dialog box in an Office program. Select a location to search, click in the search box, and type **tag:** (including the colon). Windows will show a list of tags associated with files in that location; pick one to narrow your search.

Backup and recovery options

Throughout this chapter, we focus on saving files as you work. It's wise to periodically save your work by pressing Ctrl+S, but unfortunately, we don't always remember to do that. To prevent accidental loss of your documents, Office 2013 includes AutoRecover and Autosave, options that can save your bacon (as well as your document) in situations when Office closes before you save the file. This can occur if you experience a power outage; if a program closes unexpectedly or hangs, requiring you to forcibly close it; or if you close the Office program without first saving your document.

When AutoRecover is enabled, it automatically saves a copy of your document as you work, at regular intervals that you define. (Note that this feature saves a copy of the current document; it does not overwrite your previously saved file.) The AutoRecover versions are discarded when you save your document and close the program. Autosave keeps the last AutoRecover version if you close the Office program without saving.

AutoRecover and Autosave settings are maintained separately for each of the four document-centric programs. Open Backstage view, click Options, and then click Save in the Options dialog box. Word, Excel, and PowerPoint offer options similar to those shown next. (Publisher allows you to set the AutoRecover interval only.)

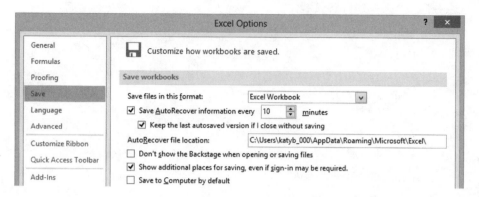

AutoRecover is enabled by default, and we don't recommend disabling it. To change the interval, use the Save AutoRecover Information Every *nn* Minutes control, choosing a value between 1 and 120 minutes. If you want to change the location where saved files are kept, enter a folder path in the AutoRecover File Location box (we recommend using the default location). Finally, make sure that Keep The Last Autosaved Version If I Close Without Saving is enabled; this option is available only when AutoRecover is enabled.

AutoRecover is especially useful if you discover that you accidentally overwrote a crucial portion of your document, or if you decide that you're not happy with your last few edits and you want to roll back to a previous version. Click File to open Backstage view. On the Info pane, saved versions appear alongside the Manage Versions button, as shown here.

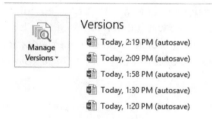

Click any version to open a read-only copy of the file. Note the message bar that appears at the top of the document window, informing you that this is not the last-saved or most recent version of the document. Click the Restore button to replace the last-saved version with the currently displayed version—the one you selected from the versions list.

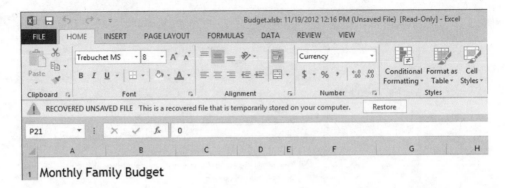

Monthly Family Budget

If you just want to recover a portion of the recovered previous version, select it from the restored document and copy it to the Clipboard or to a new file. Then close the recovered document without saving it.

> **Note**
>
> **If you're using Word (but not Excel or PowerPoint), you can compare the currently displayed document and the last-saved version by clicking Compare. This opens a new document that shows the differences between the versions. For more information about document comparison, see "Reviewing tracked changes" in Chapter 10.**

If you close Office without saving your document and you've enabled Autosave, Office saves your document for up to four days in a well-hidden folder in your local user profile: %LocalAppData%\Microsoft\Office\UnsavedFiles. You can open a document directly from that folder in File Explorer, or you can open it from within Office, using either of two methods:

- In Backstage view, click Open. At the bottom of the Open pane, click Recover Unsaved Documents (in Word), Recover Unsaved Workbooks (Excel), or Recover Unsaved Presentations (PowerPoint).

- On the Info pane in Backstage view, click Manage Versions, and then click Recover Unsaved Documents (in Word), Recover Unsaved Workbooks (Excel), or Recover Unsaved Presentations (PowerPoint).

Regardless of how you retrieve the document, Office displays a message informing you that it's an unsaved file and prompting you to use Save As to give it a file name and location.

Note that AutoRecover is not a substitute for a good backup routine. Saving files to SkyDrive and then synchronizing them with multiple PCs offers excellent protection from hard drive crashes and accidental deletion.

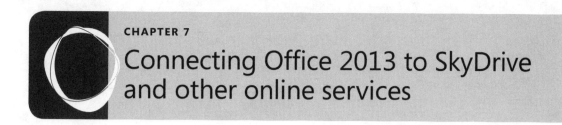

Connecting Office 2013 to SkyDrive and other online services

S OME OF the most interesting and useful new features in Office 2013 involve its deep connections to online services. By signing in using a Microsoft account, you gain access to a generous allotment of free online storage, and your Office settings roam with you as you move from one device to another. You can save a Word document on your desktop PC, for example, and then resume editing it on a tablet, with the Office Roaming Service telling Word exactly where you left off.

Saving documents in SkyDrive and synchronizing them with local copies gives you easy backup capability. It also allows you to work with documents from anywhere—in a web browser, on a mobile device, or on a PC using the full range of editing tools in the Office programs.

In this chapter, we take a closer look at what you can do when you sign in with an Office account, and we explain how to make the most of Office with SkyDrive and Office Web Apps. (If you have an Office 365 subscription, you get some additional capabilities, which we describe in Chapter 8, "Using Office 2013 with an Office 365 subscription.")

What happens when you sign in with an Office account?

If you're using the Office 2013 programs as part of an Office 365 subscription, signing in with your Office 365 user name and password is mandatory. With the stand-alone version of Office 2013, you can elect not to sign in. In that configuration, your settings and preferences won't roam, and you won't be able to open or save documents stored in SkyDrive using Office programs, but you'll still be able to create, edit, and save documents on local and network drives.

You can sign in to Office (or switch to a different account) from the Me control in the upper right corner of every Office 2013 program (except Lync) or from the Account pane in Backstage view.

When you choose to sign in to an Office account for the first time, you see the dialog box shown in Figure 7-1.

Figure 7-1 Sign in using a free Microsoft account to sync settings and access your personal SkyDrive. The Organizational Account option is for business Office 365 accounts.

If you use a free Microsoft account (formerly known as a Windows Live ID) with a retail copy of any edition of Office 2013, you can access the following services:

- 7 gigabytes (GB) of SkyDrive storage (you can increase this amount by 20 to 100 GB for an annual fee).

- Connections to Microsoft's free mail and calendar services hosted at Outlook.com (formerly Hotmail).

- Connections to other services that are associated with your Microsoft account, including Facebook, LinkedIn, Twitter, Flickr, and YouTube.

- Synchronization of Office settings using the Office Roaming Service.

INSIDE OUT   Disconnect Office from the Internet

Some people are suspicious of cloud-based services, fearing the loss of confidential data or unauthorized access by outsiders. We're confident that SkyDrive and the Office Roaming Service are reliable, secure, and private, and we're also confident that Microsoft will support these services for the long term. But if you're not so trusting, you can cut all ties between Office and the Internet.

The first step is to avoid signing in in the first place. Office programs exchange no information with the Internet in that configuration (unless you've opted in to the Customer Experience Improvement Program). To eliminate the possibility of any data being shared, open the Options dialog box in any Office program, click Trust Center Settings on the Trust Center tab, select Privacy Options, and clear the Allow Office To Connect To The Internet check box. This setting applies to all Office programs immediately.

Note

If you have an email address in the Hotmail.com, Live.com, or Outlook.com domain, that account is automatically a Microsoft account, with its own SkyDrive storage allotment and web-based email and calendar services. You are not required to use an email address in one of these Microsoft owned and operated domains, however. You're free to set up a Microsoft account using an email address on a domain you control or from a service such as Yahoo or Gmail.

The list of roaming settings that are synchronized automatically between devices is relatively short: it includes the contents of the Recent Documents list on the Open pane in Backstage view, as well as recently used templates on the New pane. The Office Personalization settings (background and theme) synchronize automatically, as does the list of connections to other services. Custom dictionaries are synchronized, and Office can remember the Resume Reading position in a Word document and the Last Viewed Slide setting in PowerPoint.

Customizations you make to individual programs, including changes to the ribbon and Quick Access Toolbar, are not synchronized.

When you're signed in, you can view details of your account and connected services on the Account pane in Backstage view (this option is called Office Account in Outlook). Figure 7-2 shows a typical account.

Account

User Information

Katy Bott
katybott@live.com

Change photo
About me
Sign out
Switch Account

Office Background:

No Background ▼

Office Theme:

Dark Gray ▼

Connected Services:

f Facebook   Manage
Katy Bott

☁ Katy Bott's SkyDrive
katybott@live.com

Add a service ▼

Figure 7-2 This block of information in Backstage view lets you view your Office account at a glance, change some details, and add connections to other services.

Note

When you sign in to Office on a new PC for the first time using a Microsoft account, you might need to reenter credentials for any additional storage services you've connected to your Office account. This is a security precaution, to prevent someone who compromises one set of credentials from being able to access all connected services. If you've added a second SkyDrive account or connected to Office 365 SharePoint, you'll see a yellow box like the one shown here, where you'll need to reenter the credentials for the secondary storage.

☁ Ed Bott's SkyDrive
To connect to Ed Bott's SkyDrive, you'll need your user name and password.

Connect   Remove service

Under the User Information heading, you can change your profile photo and view or edit the details in your Microsoft account profile. Links in this block also allow you to sign out (unless the address you signed in with is also used as a Windows 8 account on the same PC) or switch accounts.

The contents of the Add A Service menu vary, depending on the account type you used when signing in. If you're signed in with a Microsoft account, you have the options shown here.

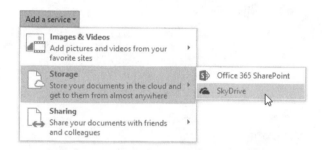

Any services you connect to here become available in the appropriate places within Office 2013 programs. For example, if you connect Flickr to your Office account (from the Images & Videos menu under Add A Service), it becomes a source of images when you choose Online Pictures from the Insert tab in Word, PowerPoint, Excel, and Publisher. Likewise, connecting your LinkedIn or Twitter account (from the Sharing menu) makes those options available on the Share pane for documents that are stored on SkyDrive.

Figure 7-3 shows the Share pane with three connected social networks available.

After you share a file using a social network, its link is added to the Share pane for that document, where you can right-click the item to stop sharing it or change its permissions, as shown in Figure 7-4.

Figure 7-3 Connecting social networks to your Office account allows you to post links to documents you've saved on SkyDrive.

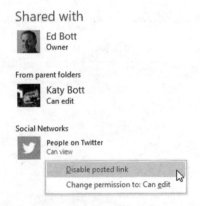

Figure 7-4 Documents you share on social networks get an entry in the Share pane, where you can change their sharing settings.

Saving, sharing, and syncing Office documents with SkyDrive

Microsoft launched its SkyDrive service in 2007 and added explicit connections to Office (including web-based Office apps) with the launch of Office 2010. Today, the service is available worldwide, offering 7 GB of online storage to anyone with a free Microsoft account, and its connections to Office 2013 are much more tightly integrated than in previous Office versions.

You can store any type of file on SkyDrive, but our focus in this chapter is on documents saved in one of the four Office 2013 formats that are explicitly supported with Office Web Apps in SkyDrive: Word document, Excel workbook, PowerPoint presentation, and OneNote notebook. (A fifth format, Excel survey, is also available for collecting input from webpages and tabulating it in worksheet form. We cover this option in more detail in "Using online forms to collect survey data" in Chapter 14, "Excel 2013 inside out.")

> **Note**
>
> One challenge we face in documenting a web-based service like SkyDrive is that the service can change at any time. By adding or changing bits on its web servers, Microsoft can make new features available, increase or decrease the amount of available storage, and change the user interface. We fully expect that the SkyDrive feature set and user interface will change over time, so in this section we've avoided detailed descriptions and step-by-step procedures in favor of more global instructions.

Your view of SkyDrive and its contents varies, depending on your starting point.

Using SkyDrive in a web browser

If you visit skydrive.com (which redirects to skydrive.live.com for now) in a browser window, you see a display like the one in Figure 7-5. Think of it as a simplified version of the venerable Windows Explorer (now File Explorer in Windows 8). Note that we've switched to Details view and made the properties pane visible.

In Windows 8 (and Windows RT), you can also access the contents of your SkyDrive folder from a built-in app.

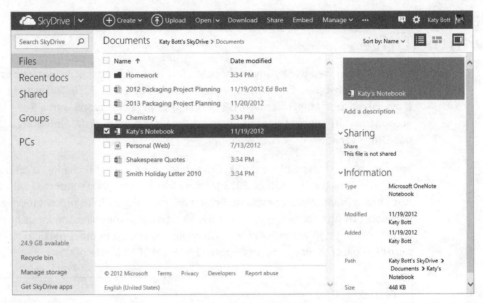

Figure 7-5 In a web browser, the contents of a SkyDrive folder resemble a simplified File Explorer window.

Using SkyDrive from an Office program

From Office Backstage view, you can connect directly to a SkyDrive folder. If you've signed in to Office using your Microsoft account, your SkyDrive folder appears as a destination in the Open and Save As panes in Backstage view.

Choose SkyDrive as a destination and then click Browse to display the contents of your SkyDrive folder, including any custom folders you've created, in a standard Windows dialog box. If you want to reopen a specific folder, select that location from the list of recently used folders before you click Browse.

Synchronizing SkyDrive files with Windows

Opening files directly from SkyDrive is fine if you're online, but what if you're temporarily disconnected from the Internet? You can't browse those folders without an Internet connection. The solution is to install the SkyDrive app for Windows, which sets up a synchronization process that runs in the background and keeps your local files in sync with the contents of the SkyDrive folder.

You'll find the Windows app (as well as apps for iOS and Android devices and Apple Macs) here: *https://apps.live.com/skydrive*.

Note that you can sync only one SkyDrive account with your PC. A Choose Folders tab in the Settings dialog box for the app lets you choose which folders are synchronized. If you have stored a large amount of data in SkyDrive, you can lessen the burden on your PC by telling the app not to synchronize folders you use for archive purposes, or those that contain files you don't need when offline.

You can open any file from the local folder or from its online location. Changes you save in either place are reflected during the next synchronization. If you're online, your changes are synced continuously.

INSIDE OUT   Use multiple SkyDrive accounts in Office

When you sign in to Office using a Microsoft account, the SkyDrive storage associated with that account is available in the Open and Save As dialog boxes. But you're not limited to a single SkyDrive account. If you've set up a second (or third or fourth...) Microsoft account, you have a separate SkyDrive storage allocation for each one, and you can access the SkyDrive folders for that secondary account by clicking File, Account and using the Add A Service link at the bottom of your account settings in Backstage view. Adding multiple SkyDrive locations gives you a way to increase available online storage without paying extra. It also allows you to share files with other people without mixing them into your primary SkyDrive account.

Using Office Web Apps

Before SkyDrive came into existence, you could share an Office document with friends or colleagues, but they needed their own copy of Office (or a compatible program) to edit the contents of the file, and even viewing a document required installing software.

Office Web Apps, a key feature in SkyDrive that made its debut with Office 2010, makes that extra layer of software unnecessary. You can view and edit Word documents, Excel workbooks, PowerPoint presentations, and OneNote notebooks directly in a browser window, with no additional software required. Using SkyDrive's built-in sharing features, you can grant access to those documents to anyone you choose, and they in turn can view those documents (and edit them, if you allow them to) in their browser window using Office Web Apps.

Most remarkably, Office Web Apps work with virtually all modern browsers and operating systems, even those not made by Microsoft. Internet Explorer doesn't offer any significant advantages; you can use Office Web Apps with Firefox, Chrome, or Safari on Windows, OS X, and Linux.

Microsoft describes Office Web Apps collectively as "online companions" to the corresponding programs that are part of the Office family, and that's an accurate description. Even though you can accomplish some impressive tasks with Office Web Apps, they have nowhere near the power or flexibility of the full programs.

Figure 7-6 shows a Word document stored on SkyDrive and viewed in a browser using Microsoft Word Web App. The font formatting, graphics, and layout are indistinguishable from the same document opened in the full Word 2013 program.

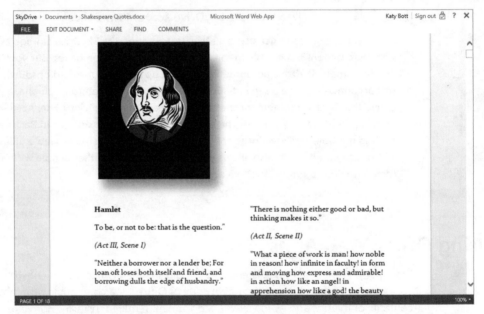

Figure 7-6 This document viewed in Word Web App displays the same graphics, formatting, and layout as in the Word desktop program.

In this "viewer" mode using Word Web App, the page's appearance is virtually identical to the document as it was created in the full-strength Word program. The display fidelity is very high: you can see page borders, columns, and accurate font formatting. Even complex layout elements like the black matte border and shadow around the accompanying graphic appear where the document author placed them. Anyone who uses a browser to open this document can read it with full fidelity. The other Office Web Apps offer similar fidelity in rendering worksheets, presentations, and OneNote pages.

For more on how to lay out graphics in Office documents, see Chapter 5, "Working with graphics and pictures."

Although the document looks identical in both places, the web app itself has some significant differences from the corresponding full program. For starters, notice the breadcrumb
bar at the top of the document, which shows you that the document is stored in a SkyDrive
folder. The simplified status bar at the bottom shows you the number of pages in the document and allows you to zoom in or out.

This default view allows you to read the fully formatted document. To make changes, click
Edit Document and choose the Edit In Word Web App option. Doing so exposes a ribbon
with a limited selection of editing options. Right-click shortcut menus are also available
within the document, as shown here.

Each Office Web App offers a subset of the features available in the corresponding full program. In theory, any of the features and formatting in a document that are not supported
in a web app are preserved when you edit and save a document using the less capable
browser-based version. In practice, you might find that seemingly minor changes made
using the Word or PowerPoint Web App can affect formatting in unexpected ways.

Making changes using an Office Web App works fine with simple documents. For more
complex documents, or to use features not available in the web app, click Edit In *Program
Name* (where *Program Name* is Word, Excel, or PowerPoint. (The equivalent option in
OneNote Web App is Open In OneNote.)

What if you make an editing mistake and save a document after inadvertently deleting an
important section or mangling formatting? The three document-centric Office Web Apps
(Word, Excel, and PowerPoint) include a handy feature that allows you to roll back any
changes, regardless of who made them. Click File to open the greatly simplified web-based
Backstage view, click Info, and then click Previous Versions. That action shifts the open document to the right and shows a list of previously saved versions to its left, with the date and
time the document was saved as well as the name of the user who saved it.

Click any of those previous versions to display the saved document and scroll through it.
Options below the date and time stamp allow you to restore the document (overwriting

the current version) or download a copy. Figure 7-7 shows this feature in action in Excel Web App.

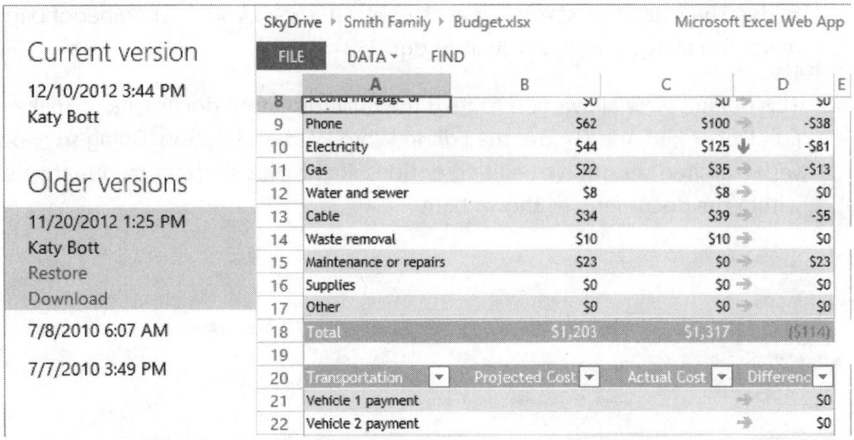

Figure 7-7 Restore a previous version of a file using this simplified Info pane in Backstage view.

To stop editing a file and return to read-only view in an Office Web App, click the View tab and click Reading View.

You can adjust permissions to grant other people access to a shared SkyDrive folder. When you do that, other people can create, open, and edit files directly in that folder, depending on the permissions you've assigned.

But you can also share an individual file via email, on a social network, or by creating a link. The Share option is available in both Editing View and Reading View (the exact location varies depending on which Office Web App you're using). The interface is similar to the desktop options available on the Share pane in Backstage view when using an Office desktop program.

Editing a shared document in real time

When you share a document stored on SkyDrive or in a SharePoint or SkyDrive Pro folder, you and your collaborators have the option to work on that document at the same time, with your separate changes merging into the shared copy with little or no effort on your part.

This magic requires, of course, that you grant Can Edit permissions to the other member (or members) of your team. The program you're using also has to support simultaneous editing. The rules vary for different Office programs:

- Word documents, PowerPoint presentations, and OneNote notebooks can be edited simultaneously by different parties using the respective Office Web App, the desktop app, or both.

- Excel workbooks can be edited simultaneously only if all parties are using the Excel Web App. Attempting to open the shared workbook in the Excel desktop app while it is being edited by another person results in an error. Likewise, you'll see an error message if you try to open the workbook when someone already has it open in the Excel desktop app.

When two or more people are editing the same document simultaneously, Word and PowerPoint provide cues in the status bar. Click the Authors indicator, for example, to pop up a list showing who's working on the current document. In the case of Word, you'll also see an indication that updates are available, but those updates won't appear in the document automatically.

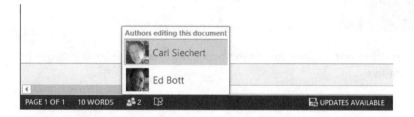

In the PowerPoint and Excel Web Apps, any changes you make to an open presentation or workbook are saved automatically; don't bother looking for a Save command, because it's not there. Likewise, any changes other people make to a shared document also appear in your editing window with no action required on your part.

In the Word Web App, you must explicitly save changes using the Save command on the File menu or the Ctrl+S shortcut. The Word Web App does not automatically save changes, and if you exit without saving (or if your browser crashes in midsession), you will lose all your work. (This is true even if you're working solo.)

In the desktop versions of PowerPoint and Word, you must save your changes to a shared file before anyone else editing that file will be able to see your updates. Shortly after you make those changes, your online collaborators will see an Updates Available message in the status bar. A similar, prominent notification is available in the Info pane in Backstage view.

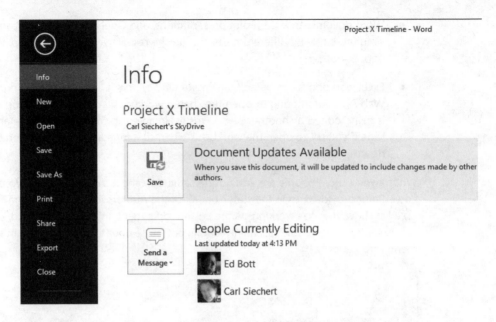

Press Ctrl+S or click Save to refresh the document with the latest changes from other coauthors.

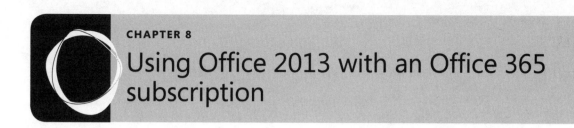

CHAPTER 8

Using Office 2013 with an Office 365 subscription

W HEN YOU subscribe to Office 365, you get a license to use Office 2013 on multiple devices as part of the package. The programs in the Office suite—Word, Excel, and so on—all look and act the same as their stand-alone counterparts, but there are some extra benefits included with your subscription.

In this chapter, we explain how to get the most from the web-based dashboard where you manage an Office 365 subscription. We also explain how to use a feature called Office on Demand, which lets you run full-featured programs on a Windows PC without having to use one of your allowed Office installations. And finally, we discuss how SkyDrive Pro in Office 365 differs from the free SkyDrive service.

How Office 365 and Office 2013 work together

Office 365 subscriptions are available in a broad range of plans at many different price points, but for our purposes it's sufficient to divide them into two groups: consumer and business. (You'll find a detailed list of plans in "Choosing an Office edition," in Chapter 2, "Installing and updating Office 2013.")

If you've already set up an Office 365 account, you can access it on the web by visiting *Office.com*, where you'll be prompted to enter your credentials: a Microsoft account if you are using Office 365 Home Premium, an organizational account if you are using a business, education, or government plan.

Sign in to Office.com
Start working in the cloud

Microsoft account
Sign in with the account you use for
SkyDrive, Xbox LIVE, Outlook.com, or other
Microsoft services.

Organizational account
Sign in with the account provided by your
work or school to use with Office 365 or
other Microsoft services.

The most common consumer plan is Office 365 Home Premium, which allows you to use the latest version of Office in a single household on up to five PCs or Macs. (Office 365 University offers nearly identical features, except that it is limited to two devices.) To perform management tasks, you sign in using your Microsoft account. Other members of your household can use the copies of Office you install, but they have no Office 365 subscription benefits.

Office 365 business plans start with Small Business Premium (25 users maximum) and work their way up to enterprise offerings that can include thousands of users. All of these accounts come with Exchange Online, SharePoint Online, and Lync Online and a default domain (*contoso.onmicrosoft.com*, for example), which you can customize to use your own domain (*contoso.com*).

As an administrator of a business Office 365 plan, you sign in at *Office.com* using your organizational account (edbott@contoso.com, for example) and then create individual user accounts from a comprehensive management dashboard.

After an administrator creates an Office 365 account for you, you sign in using your organization credentials (katy@contoso.com, for example) to gain access to your personal dashboard. There, you can manage Office 365 installations on your own devices, read and respond to email using Outlook Web Access, open and save files from your organization's SharePoint site, and customize settings for your own profile.

Managing your Office 365 account

In this section, we assume that you've already set up your Office 365 account and that you will sign in using the credentials assigned to your subscription: a Microsoft account for Office 365 Home Premium, organizational credentials for a business Office 365 account.

Working with Office 365 Home Premium

When you sign in at *Office.com* using the Microsoft account attached to your Office 365 subscription, your starting point is the My Office page, shown in Figure 8-1. (You can return to this page anytime by clicking My Office in the navigation bar at the top of the page.)

You don't need an Office 365 subscription to sign in at *Office.com*. In fact, the only visible difference on the My Office page is in the row of program icons just below the Recent Documents list. Without an Office 365 subscription, you see four icons, under the heading Create New, each of which creates a new file in your SkyDrive account and opens it using the associated Office Web App. With an Office 365 account, you see five icons under the Office On Demand heading. We discuss their function later in this chapter.

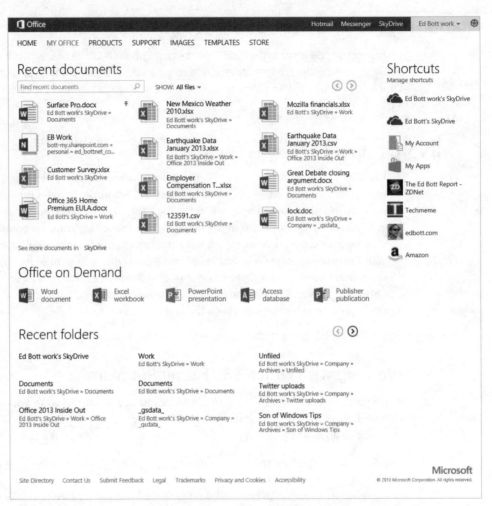

Figure 8-1 After you sign in with a Microsoft account, the My Office page shows a list of recently accessed SkyDrive files and folders, plus a customizable list of shortcuts.

To reach the Office 365 Home Premium account management dashboard, click My Account on the Shortcuts list, or click your name in the upper-right corner of the Office bar and then click My Account on the menu. Either way, you end up at a page like the one shown in Figure 8-2.

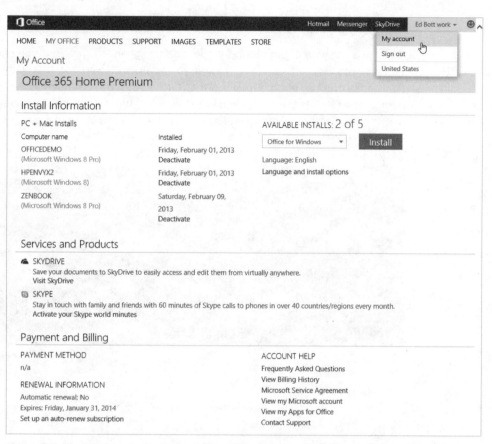

Figure 8-2 The My Account page for Office 365 Home Premium allows you to manage your Office installs, access related services and products, and set up or change payment methods.

The most important section of this page is at the top, where you can see at a glance which PCs or Macs you've assigned Office licenses to.

To install Office on a new device, sign in at *Office.com* on that device by using the Microsoft account associated with your subscription. Click Install to launch the Click-to-Run installer and begin setting up a 32-bit copy of Office 2013; if you want to customize the installation using a different language or a 64-bit copy of Office, click Language And Install Options.

To remove a PC or Mac from the list of authorized devices, click Deactivate next to its name. You don't have to sign in on the device to remove it from the list. Deactivating an installation does not uninstall the Office programs from the device.

For a more detailed discussion of how to install Office on a new device, see "Setting up Office," in Chapter 2.

Working with Office 365 business plans

When you use your organizational credentials to sign in at *Office.com*, you end up at a portal that looks very different from the one you access with a Microsoft account. When you first sign in using an account that is not an Office 365 administrator, you see a Get Started page that resembles the one shown in Figure 8-3. It has a large Install button for the Office desktop programs and links to equivalent Windows 8 apps. At the time we wrote this, the latter list consisted only of OneNote and Lync.

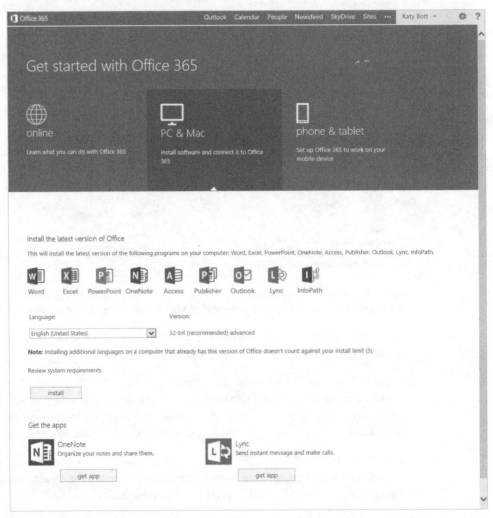

Figure 8-3 This Get Started page includes training links and options to install the latest version of Office and set up mobile devices.

The Office 365 navigation bar for a business account is decidedly different from the Home Premium version. Instead of the free Hotmail, Messenger, and SkyDrive links, you get direct access to your organizational Exchange account from the Outlook, Calendar, and People links. Click your name in the upper-right corner to set your instant messenger status and change your account information or sign out.

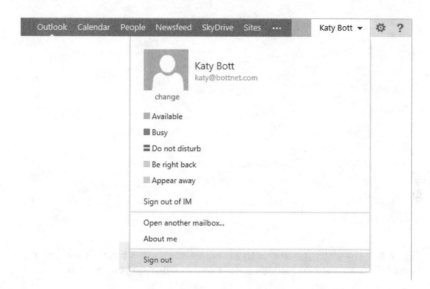

The Office 365 account management dashboard for a user is clean and simple. Click the gear icon to the right of your user name in the navigation bar and then click Office 365 Settings. From this abbreviated list, shown in Figure 8-4, you can change the information that other members of your company see on your About Me page, manage software installations, and change your password and language.

If you're an administrator of a business account, the Office 365 navigation bar includes an Admin link, which leads to a dashboard where you can manage user accounts and groups, assign licenses, attach one or more custom domains to your Office 365 account, and track service status.

Figure 8-4 The settings available to a user in an Office 365 business account are relatively limited. Click Software to manage installations of Office on your devices.

Figure 8-5 shows the management dashboard for an Office 365 Small Business Premium account. The Admin Center for an enterprise account is considerably more complex.

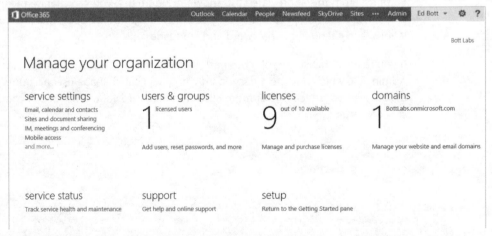

Figure 8-5 If you're an administrator of an Office 365 Small Business Premium account, clicking the Admin link (just to the left of the user name) opens this management dashboard.

Using Office on Demand

On any device you use regularly, you can and should assign one of your allowed Office 2013 installations. Installing the Office software locally allows you to quickly use any Office program, including Outlook, in a matter of seconds.

But what do you do if you're sitting at a computer you don't normally use, and Office isn't already installed?

For documents that are stored on SkyDrive, you can handle most editing tasks directly in the corresponding Office Web App. Sometimes, though, you need the full strength of the desktop Office program to accomplish a specific goal, such as reviewing comments and group edits in a Word document.

The relatively quick solution is to use Office on Demand, a feature of all Office 365 sub-scriptions that allows you to stream and install a temporary copy of the program you want to use. Office on Demand works with Word, Excel, PowerPoint, Publisher, and Access (the OneNote and Outlook desktop programs must be installed locally to run) on PCs running Windows 7 or Windows 8. (OS X is not supported.)

To start an Office on Demand session, open a SkyDrive file using its Office Web App, and then click Edit In *Program Name*. You can also create a new file using an Office on Demand program. Using Office 365 Home Premium, go to *Office.com*, sign in with the Microsoft account associated with your subscription, and click My Office. Below your list of recently opened files you'll see this set of options:

Office on Demand

 Word document   Excel workbook   PowerPoint presentation   Access database   Publisher publication

In business-focused Office 365 plans, the equivalent options are in a slightly different loca-tion. Click Use Office On Demand (at the bottom of the navigation pane on the left of the SkyDrive Pro page), which takes you to the page shown in Figure 8-6.

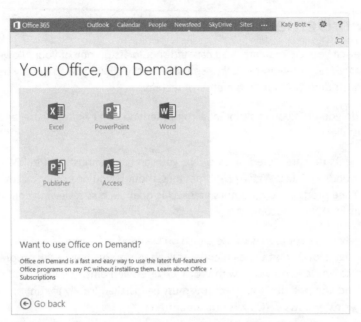

Figure 8-6 The entry points for Office on Demand in a business Office 365 account are slightly different from those in Home Premium, but the result is the same.

Click the icon for the program you want to begin using. If this is the first time you've used Office on Demand, you'll prompted to install the Microsoft Office on Demand Browser Add-ons. The exact procedure is slightly different, depending on which browser you're using.

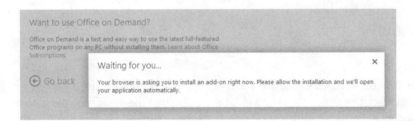

The browser add-on authenticates you and hands things off to the Microsoft Office Click-to-Run program, which begins the streaming process. Within a few minutes (the exact time depends on the speed of your Internet connection), you're running that program. You're signed in using your Office account, you can access all your files and services (in the cloud and locally), and you can create, open, edit, and save any document whose format is supported by that program.

The experience is exactly like using a locally installed version of the program. All its features are available, and you can work with files in the cloud, on a local PC, or on a portable storage device.

The Office program streams features on demand, giving you the chance to begin using the program immediately. If you try to use an advanced feature, you might experience an additional delay as the features you requested move to the front of the streaming queue. Look for a warning like this one in the lower-right corner of the desktop.

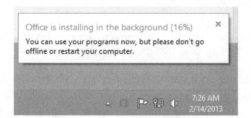

It's all done through the magic of Microsoft Office Click-to-Run, as you'll discover if you poke around in Task Manager and see that Roamingoffice.exe (that's the formal, command-line name for Click-to-Run) is running. (For more details on how Click-to-Run works, see "Using the Click-to-Run Office installer" in Chapter 2.)

When you close the Office on Demand program you were using, it (mostly) disappears. Click-to-Run doesn't leave any shortcuts or signs that it was installed, and it erases all of your temporary data files. It does save a cached copy of the files you downloaded (they're stored in an Office 15 folder in the user profile you were signed in with); having those cached files on hand means your Office on Demand session can start much more quickly next time.

Working with SkyDrive Pro

For free Office accounts as well as Office 365 Home Premium, SkyDrive is the default cloud storage location. With a business-class Office 365 account, you can still use SkyDrive, but you also have access to private cloud storage managed by your company. And a local utility, SkyDrive Pro 2013, allows you to sync the contents of that online storage with a local PC so you have access to important work files even when you're offline.

When you sign in with an organizational account that includes SharePoint Online, the SkyDrive link in the navigation bar takes you to a page that looks like the one in Figure 8-7.

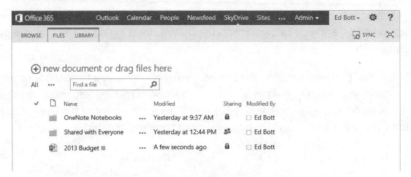

Figure 8-7 Click Sync (in the upper-right corner of this page) to use the SkyDrive Pro Windows utility to sync your online documents with local storage.

In the upper-right corner of that window is a small Sync button. Click it to immediately begin setting up SkyDrive Pro so that it synchronizes the contents of your online documents to your local user profile. With that task done, you can open, edit, and create documents directly in that folder, without having to go online. All your changes will be synced automatically.

You can also sync other SharePoint libraries on team sites to your computer using SkyDrive Pro. To add a location, start by right-clicking the SkyDrive Pro icon in the notification area of the taskbar to display the menu shown here:

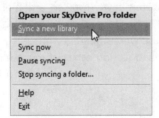

Copy the URL of the SharePoint site you want to sync and paste it into the SkyDrive Pro dialog box. Your files will begin synchronizing automatically.

The synchronization utility adds SkyDrive Pro and SharePoint shortcuts to the Favorites section of File Explorer (Windows Explorer in Windows 7), where you can view, open, and manage the synced files. It also adds a SkyDrive Pro item to the right-click menu in File Explorer, allowing you to open a synced file in your default web browser, copy a link to the file (useful for pasting into an email message), or share a file with another member of your team.

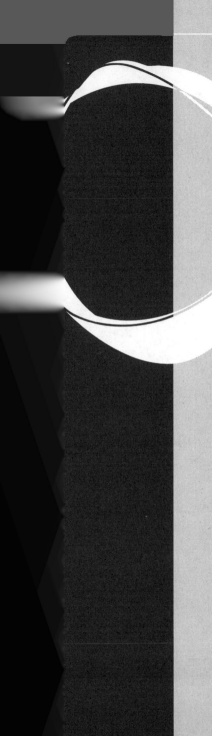

PART 3
Word

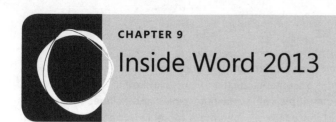

CHAPTER 9

Inside Word 2013

S HOULD the paperless office ever become a reality, computer users' reliance on Word won't diminish, because it's also ideal for creating online documents, including blog posts and documents distributed in PDF, XPS, and other electronic formats. In the early days of personal computers, a "word processor" processed only words and text. A modern word-processing program like Word 2013 melds text and graphics in ways that used to be possible only with high-end desktop-publishing programs.

In this chapter, our focus is on how you build and format documents—regardless of the final output medium. We cover the basics of creating a document, searching and navigating in a document, adding commonly used elements such as pictures and lists, and formatting to improve a document's appearance and readability.

In the two chapters that follow, we cover more complex formatting tasks, explain Word's features for reviewing and sharing documents, and wrap up our Word coverage with a compendium of advanced topics.

What's in a Word document?

A "document" in Word can be any in a wide range of items, including letters and other types of correspondence, brochures, reports, books, forms, certificates, and other items that typically end up being printed on paper. In addition, Word is a capable tool for producing documents that usually appear only on-screen, such as blog posts and webpages. There's not much in common among these disparate document types, although most contain primarily text, perhaps embellished with some pictures or other graphics.

With its printer-centric roots, a Word document consists of one or more pages. Page sizes are normally based on paper sizes used in desktop printers, although you can define a page as any size up to 22 inches (558.7 mm) square.

Figure 9-1 shows a data sheet for a new product. In the figure, you can see some features that can be incorporated into Word documents, such as pictures and other graphics, text wrapped around irregular shapes, multiple-column layouts, tables, and bulleted lists. We explain how to implement each of these features (and many more) in this and the following two chapters.

Navigation pane   Ruler

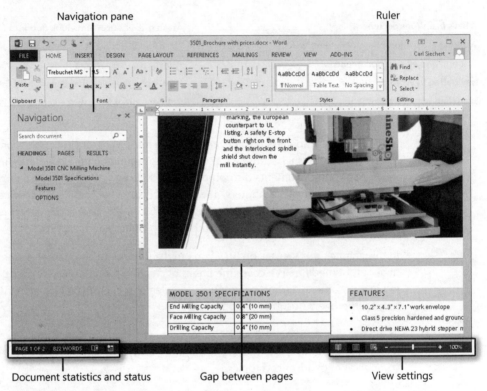

Document statistics and status   Gap between pages   View settings

Figure 9-1 In Print Layout view, the document's on-screen appearance closely matches its printed output.

The Word window shown in Figure 9-1 shows a couple of optional (but very useful) components. The Navigation pane is handy not only for navigating within a document (for more information, see "Navigating within a document" later in this chapter), but also for organizing documents (see "Using outlines to plan, organize, and edit documents" in Chapter 10, "Working with complex documents"). The Navigation pane is also the primary search interface in Word (see "Searching within a document" later in this chapter). The other non-standard element shown in the figure is the ruler along the top and left edges of the document workspace. The ruler allows you to see and adjust margin, indent, and tab settings (see "Setting page layout options," "Formatting paragraphs," and "Using tabs" later in this chapter).

To display or hide these items, visit the View tab, shown in Figure 9-2.

Figure 9-2 Options for displaying rulers and the Navigation pane are in the Show group on the View tab.

INSIDE OUT   Work with documents in Compatibility Mode

To maintain compatibility with earlier versions of Word, Word uses Compatibility Mode. If you and the people with whom you exchange documents work exclusively in Office 2013 (and you use default settings for saving documents), your documents are stored in Office Open XML format, which has a .docx file name extension. Compatibility Mode never enters the picture.

If you exchange documents with users of earlier Word versions (or you open documents that you created in an earlier version), you might see "[Compatibility Mode]" in the title bar of the Word window. This indicator appears in documents saved in the binary format (.doc extension) used by Word 2003 and earlier versions. Similarly, it occurs with .docx files saved in Word 2007 and Word 2010, which don't support all the features of Word 2013. (In fact, Word has a separate Compatibility Mode for each of these three versions. To see which is in use, click File, and on the Info tab click Check For Issues, Check For Compatibility. In the dialog box that appears, click Select Versions To Show; a check mark appears by the current Compatibility Mode.)

You enter Compatibility Mode automatically whenever you open a document that you saved with compatibility features maintained, or when you open a document created in an earlier Word version. In Compatibility Mode, you're likely to notice some changes other than the title bar notice:

- Some features are unavailable. (For example, in the Font group on the Home tab, Text Effects is unavailable. And in the Illustrations group on the Insert tab, Screenshot is unavailable.)

- Other features are noticeably different in their implementation. (For example, if you select a picture and then click the Format tab under Picture Tools, the Adjust group contains different options than you see when a file is not in Compatibility Mode, and the Picture Styles group is replaced with less-capable Shadow Effects and Border groups.)

- You might see some artifacts that Compatibility Mode doesn't fully address, such as minor layout changes.

Disabling these features in Compatibility Mode ensures that you won't incorporate elements in your document that can't be properly rendered when the document is opened in an earlier Word version. If you don't plan to use a document in the old Word version again, it's easy to upgrade the current document to pure Word 2013 format. Click File, and on the Info tab, click Convert.

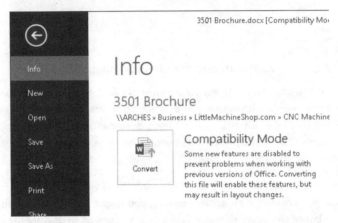

If, on the other hand, you need to share a document with someone using an older version, be sure to use a compatible format. When you save a document while in Compatibility Mode, it maintains its original format. To convert a Word 2013 document (such as a new one you create), when you save the document, do this: Click File, Save As, select a folder, and then select Word 97–2003 Document in the Save As Type box. (Unfortunately, you can't save in the Word 2007 or Word 2010 format. If you need to exchange documents with a user of those versions and you don't want to use the older Word 97–2003 Document format, you have two less-than-desirable options: You can save in Word 2013 format, but any Word 2013–unique features are lost if the other user resaves the file. Or you can ask the other user to create and save a document—even a blank document; your subsequent edits are then restricted to features supported by the other user's version.)

A number of advanced settings can be made to ensure compatibility with particular Word versions. To work with these settings, click File, Options. In the Options dialog box, click Advanced, and then scroll all the way to the bottom. In the drop-down lists, select which documents you want to affect and which version of Word you want to ensure compatibility with. Each version has its own collection of predefined compatibility settings; you can review or modify the individual settings. Note that these options are available only in Compatibility Mode; no options appear for documents saved in the native Word 2013 format.

Supported file formats in Word 2013

In this book, we assume that you are using the standard Word Document (.docx) format. Word can also open, edit, and save files in several other formats, albeit with some limitations. Not all Word features are available when using other file formats, and you might notice minor (or even major) layout changes when you view a document in Word versus the document's native program.

Word 2013 can open and save documents in any of these formats:

- **Word Document (.docx) and Word Macro-Enabled Document (.docm)**   These XML-based formats provide full functionality in Word 2007 and later. The first type, the default in Word 2013, cannot contain VBA macro code; the latter can.

- **Word Template (.dotx) and Word Macro-Enabled Template (.dotm)**   Word Template is the default format for templates in Word 2007 and later; Word Macro-Enabled Template adds VBA macro capability.

- **Word 97–2003 Document (.doc) and Word 97–2003 Template (.dot)**   These are the native formats used by versions of Word prior to Word 2007.

- **PDF (.pdf)**   This format lets you create documents that can be viewed on nearly any computer or mobile device. The ability to open and edit PDF files is new with Word 2013. For details about working with PDF files, see "Exporting files and data to alternative formats" in Chapter 6, "Managing Office files."

- **Single File Web Page (.mht or .mhtl)**   This format stores all components of a webpage in a single file for easy portability, and can be viewed in most web browsers.

- **Web Page and Web Page, Filtered (.htm or .html)**   An HTML file contains only text and commands; other webpage elements, such as pictures and style sheets, are stored in separate files, which Word saves in a subfolder with the same name as the HTML file. The filtered format removes all Office-specific tags for compatibility with a wider range of web browsers.

- **Rich Text Format (.rtf)**   This format is widely supported by word-processing programs, including the WordPad program included with all versions of Windows except Windows RT.

- **Plain Text (.txt)**   This lowest-common-denominator format contains only unformatted text.

- **Word XML Document, Word 2003 XML Document, and Strict Open XML Document (.xml)**   These formats are compatible with the XML schema used by various programs.

- **OpenDocument Text (.odt)** This XML-based format was originally developed for the OpenOffice.org office suite.

- **Works 6–9 Document (.wps)** This is the format used by Microsoft Works for word-processing documents.

Word 2013 can open (but not save) documents in these formats:

- **WordPerfect 5.x (.doc) and WordPerfect 6.x (.wpd or .doc)** These formats let you read documents created in WordPerfect. To make changes, you must save in a different format.

Word 2013 can save (but not open) documents in this format:

- **XPS Document (.xps)** This format provides an alternative to PDF. A viewer for XPS documents is built in to Windows 8, Windows 7, and Windows Vista; viewers for some other platforms are available.

Working in an appropriate document view

By default, documents in Word are displayed in Print Layout view, which closely approximates the appearance of ink on paper. Within the document area of the Word window, you see a white background (or other color if you change the page color) scaled to represent a single sheet of paper. In Print Layout view, document content is laid out just the way the document will print, faithfully rendering margins, line breaks, page breaks, and graphics positioning. For most purposes, Print Layout view is best, and it's therefore a good default.

INSIDE OUT Set the page color

You can set the background color for your pages by clicking the Design tab and then, in the Page Background group, clicking Page Color and selecting a color. The color you select doesn't print, but choosing a color in this way is useful in two situations:

- You're going to print on colored paper. (Your on-screen document looks more like the finished product.)

- You're creating a document for on-screen use, whether as a Word document or another file format, such as PDF, XPS, or HTML. When you save in any of these formats, the background color is preserved as part of the document.

Print Layout view is one of five available document views. The others are covered in the following sections.

Read Mode

Read Mode (known as Full Screen Reading view in previous editions of Office) can optionally fill the screen and omit the usual window trappings (borders, scroll bars, and so on) except for a single narrow toolbar at the top, as shown in Figure 9-3. This offers a fully immersive reading experience similar to that of a dedicated e-book reader.

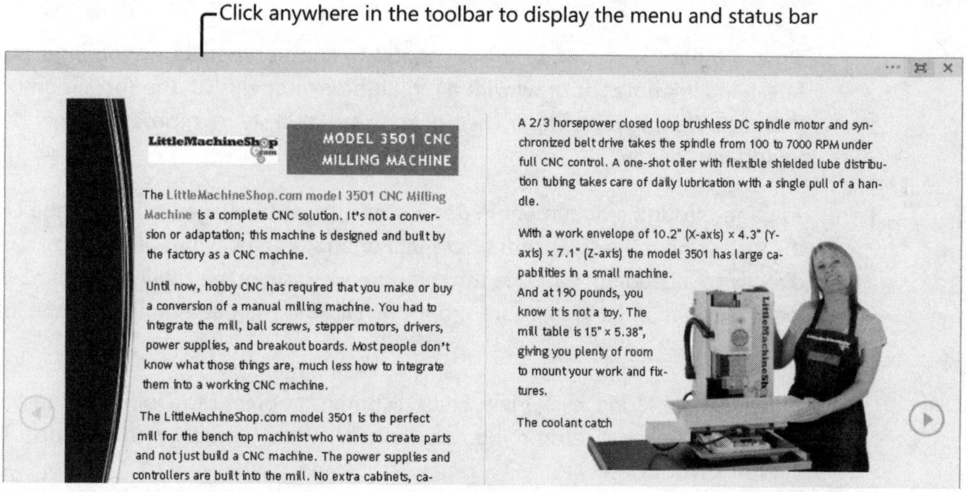

Click anywhere in the toolbar to display the menu and status bar

Figure 9-3 Read Mode provides a convenient way to read and review documents.

As its name suggests, Read Mode is designed for reading documents, not editing them. Like an e-book reader, Read Mode reformats text to properly fit the screen pages at a legible size. You can adjust the text size with the zoom slider in the status bar. The View menu offers a few more layout options, such as column width, whether to display the Navigation pane, and so on.

As with any good e-book reader, you can highlight passages, insert comments similar to sticky notes, look up a highlighted word or phrase in a dictionary or other online research tool, or translate text. Commands for some of these options are on the Tools menu, but you get more choices by right-clicking in the document.

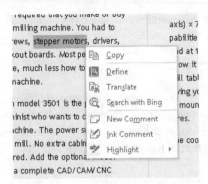

On a computer with pen or touch capability, another markup option—the ability to write free-hand ink notes or draw with a highlighter—appears on the Tools menu only when you first click View, Layout, Paper Layout. You can use a stylus, mouse, or other pointing device to add your scrawl.

To page through a document in Read Mode, press the Page Down or Page Up key, or click the arrows near the sides of the screen. For additional navigation options, such as jumping directly to a heading, page, or other landmark, display the Navigation pane by choosing View, Navigation Pane or, more simply, by clicking the page number at the left end of the status bar.

To leave Read Mode, click View, Edit Document or press Esc. Doing so doesn't close Word altogether; rather, it returns you to a "normal" Word window with your document displayed in Print Layout view.

> **Note**
>
> By default, email attachments open in Read Mode. If you find this behavior annoying, you can change it: Click File, Options. On the General tab, under Start Up Options, clear Open E-Mail Attachments And Other Uneditable Files In Reading View.

Web Layout view

Web Layout view shows how your document would appear as a webpage. Text wrapping is determined by window width rather than page (paper) width. There are no margins around the edge of the page (because there is no "page"), and there are no headers or footers. Text wrapping and positioning of pictures and graphics observe the limited capabilities of the HTML language and rendering by web browsers. Although this view is useful mainly for working with documents to be viewed online, because of the way it wraps text to fit the window it's occasionally handier than Print Layout view for the phase in document preparation where you're more interested in what the words say than how they're laid out on the page. Unlike Draft view, pictures and graphics are displayed.

Outline view

Outline view displays your document's headings as a hierarchical outline and shows tools specifically for working in this view on the Outlining tab. For more information, see "Using outlines to plan, organize, and edit documents" in Chapter 10.

Draft view

Draft view shows only the text in the body of your document. Headers, footers, pictures, and other graphics are not displayed. In years past, when computers were much less powerful than those available now, Draft view was commonly used instead of Print Layout view, which could be dreadfully slow. With modern computers, there's seldom reason to invoke Draft view unless your goal is to focus exclusively on text content.

INSIDE OUT   Show more in Print Layout view

By design, Print Layout view shows an accurate representation of each page, including its margins and any headers or footers. This information can occupy a lot of vertical space, leaving less room on the screen for the document content you're working on. You can hide this space by pointing to the gap between pages and double-clicking when the mouse pointer appears, as shown here.

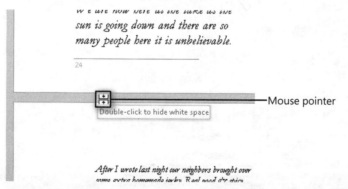

To again display the header and footer area, double-click the (now thinner) page separator.

Switching views and zooming

To switch between views, click an option in the Views group on the View tab, shown in Figure 9-2. Easier yet, click one of the buttons in the lower-right corner of the Word window, each of which corresponds to a document view. (See Figure 9-1.) If you prefer keyboard shortcuts, use the ones in Table 9-1.

TABLE 9-1 Keyboard shortcuts for selecting a document view

Action	Keyboard shortcut
Switch to Print Layout view	Ctrl+Alt+P
Switch to Outline view	Ctrl+Alt+O
Switch to Draft view	Ctrl+Alt+N

Another factor in choosing a view that works best for you is zoom level, or magnification. Your ideal zoom percentage might vary depending on your screen size and resolution, your visual acuity, your manual dexterity (for precise touching or mouse positioning), the fonts you choose, and the type of work you're doing (for example, you might need to zoom way in while editing a picture, and then zoom back out to work on text).

You adjust the zoom percentage using the slider in the lower-right corner of the Word window, next to the document view buttons. For more precise control, click the View tab and then click Zoom to display the dialog box shown in Figure 9-4.

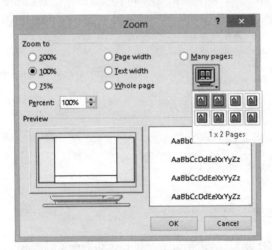

Figure 9-4 The Many Pages option adjusts the zoom level to precisely fit the selected number of pages in the window.

The Zoom group on the View tab (shown earlier in Figure 9-2) also provides options for quickly returning to 100 percent scaling or to certain preset zoom levels that scale to fit one or two pages in the window or fit the page width to the window width. With these presets (other than 100 percent), the zoom level automatically adjusts when you change the window size. Note that these presets generally have no effect except in Print Layout view.

Creating and editing documents

In this section, we take a look at some document editing techniques that are used only in Word. The nature of text-centric documents produces some unique requirements, and in this section we discuss the solutions provided by Word 2013.

The process of starting a new document is essentially the same in all Office programs. For details, see "Using templates to streamline document creation" in Chapter 6, "Managing Office files." Likewise, the methods for opening existing documents and saving documents are the same in Word as they are in other Office programs. For details, see "Where (and how) Office stores files" in Chapter 6. For information about basic editing techniques that apply to all Office programs, see Chapter 4, "Entering, editing, and formatting text."

Using tabs

Tabs are fixed locations that you can use to align lines of text. To insert a tab, press the Tab key; the insertion point advances to the next tab stop. You can set the positions of tabs and set other options, such as alignment type, by using the ruler or the Tabs dialog box.

To set tabs using the ruler, follow these steps:

1. If the ruler is not visible, select Ruler in the Show group on the View tab.

2. Click the box at the left end of the ruler until it displays the tab alignment type you want.

    Left-aligned tab   Text starts at the tab position.

    Center-aligned tab   Text is centered on the tab position. (Text automatically re-centers as you type.)

    Right-aligned tab   Text ends at the tab position. (Characters shift to the left as you type.)

    Decimal-aligned tab   Numbers with a decimal point align the decimal point at the tab stop. (Numbers or text without a decimal point or period are right-aligned.)

    Bar   This is not a tab stop; rather, it inserts a vertical line at the tab position as a column divider.

3. Click the ruler where you want to set the tab stop. If you don't click precisely where you want the tab stop, you can drag the tab-stop marker along the ruler.

The Tabs dialog box lacks the ability to show your tab stops in position, but it offers one feature not available via the ruler: the ability to specify leader characters. (In the typesetting world, a leader is a repeated character to the left of a tab stop—often a row of periods.) To use the Tabs dialog box to set one or more tab stops:

1. On the Home tab, click the Paragraph dialog box launcher (the arrow in the lower-right corner of the Paragraph group). Then, in the Paragraph dialog box, click Tabs.

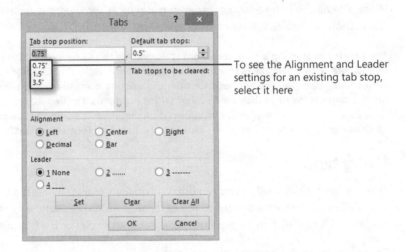

To see the Alignment and Leader settings for an existing tab stop, select it here

2. In the Tab Stop Position box, enter the position, as measured from the left margin.

3. Under Alignment, select one of the five alignment types.

4. Under Leader, select periods, hyphens, underlines, or no leader character. The leader character fills the gap between the tab stop and any text to its left.

5. Click Set.

6. To set additional tab stops, repeat steps 2 through 5. Click OK when you're done.

By default, left-aligned tabs are set every one-half inch. However, if you set any tab stops yourself, all default stops to the left of your tabs are ignored.

Tab stops are included in a paragraph style. This means that each time you press Enter (to start a new paragraph) at the end of a paragraph with tab stops set, the following paragraph will have the same tab-stop settings. More importantly, it means you can store tab stops as part of a paragraph style in a template.

To remove a tab stop using the ruler, simply drag the marker off the ruler. Using the Tabs dialog box, you can remove a tab stop by selecting it and clicking Clear.

INSIDE OUT   Don't use tabs for the wrong reasons

It's easy to spot a document created by someone who's not proficient in using Word. Press Ctrl+* or click Show/Hide ¶ (in the Paragraph group on the Home tab) to display formatting characters, and if the page is littered with right arrows (→)—the symbol for tab characters—it has been created in a way that makes editing difficult and inefficient.

Tabs provide the best way to align text from a single line with text in other lines. Word has better tools for other types of tabular text. Where each clump of text might consist of more than one line, don't fall for the amateur mistake of trying to use tabs and line breaks; instead use a table. (For details, see "Creating a table" in Chapter 10.) And if you want to set up snaking columns of text (as in a newspaper, where when the text reaches the bottom of the first column it continues in the next column), using tabs would be a nightmare; instead, use columns. (For details, see "Formatting columns and sections" in Chapter 10.)

Tabs are also a poor solution for indenting text from the left margin and for indenting the first line of a paragraph. Both of these tasks are better accomplished with paragraph formatting; see "Formatting paragraphs" later in this chapter.

Chapter 9

Inserting special characters

Office 2013 offers several tools for inserting symbols that don't correspond to a key on your keyboard, such as math symbols, arrows, and letters used in foreign languages. Tools that work in all Office programs include the Symbol option on the Insert menu, Auto-Correct, and entering character codes. For details about these tools, see "Entering symbols and other special characters" in Chapter 4.

Word adds a few additional methods to the mix:

- In the Symbol dialog box (to open it, on the Insert tab, click Symbol, More Symbols), the Special Characters tab offers easy access to characters often used in documents, such as dashes and trademark symbols. (By visiting that tab, you can quickly learn the keyboard shortcuts for characters you use often.)

- Additional AutoCorrect options enable automation beyond the ability to replace one character string with another. To view and modify AutoCorrect options, click File, Options, click the Proofing tab, and click AutoCorrect Options. In addition to the options on the AutoCorrect tab, be sure to review the options on the AutoFormat As You Type tab, shown next. Options here automate the entry of characters such as fractions and dashes; other options automate the formatting of lists, paragraphs, and other elements.

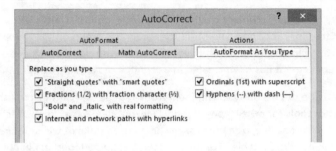

Changing case

Not everyone has the foresight to correctly capitalize text while typing. Fortunately, Word offers two methods for the common task of switching between uppercase (capital) and lowercase letters in existing text. With both methods, you begin by selecting the text in which you want to correct the capitalization.

The first method is to click Change Case, which you'll find in the Font group on the Home tab. A menu of capitalization styles appears.

The other method is to press Shift+F3, which cycles through lowercase, uppercase, and either sentence casing (if the selection ends with a period) or capitalizing each word.

Changing case using these methods actually changes the characters, just as if you pressed (or didn't press) the Shift key. You can also change case with a character format, which changes the appearance of each letter but not the underlying text. For details, see "Formatting text" later in this chapter.

Controlling line breaks and hyphenation

As you type text, word-processing programs ordinarily move to the next line when you reach the right margin, breaking the line at the last space before the word that would go beyond the margin. Sometimes you'll want to force a new line in specific places; in other cases you might want to prevent a line from breaking, such as between words in a proper name or in the middle of a phone number. Table 9-2 shows the keys for controlling breaks.

Inserting a nonbreaking space or hyphen ensures that the line won't end at that character; instead, the word preceding the nonbreaking character moves down to the next line. An optional hyphen is normally invisible, but if it falls near the end of a line, Word inserts a hyphen and a line break at that point.

TABLE 9-2 Break characters

To insert	Press
Line break	Shift+Enter
Page break	Ctrl+Enter
Column break	Ctrl+Shift+Enter
Nonbreaking space	Ctrl+Shift+Spacebar
Nonbreaking hyphen	Ctrl+Shift+Hyphen
Optional hyphen	Ctrl+Hyphen

Word has two other characters for managing line breaks: a no-width optional break and a no-width non break. These work like spaces and nonbreaking spaces, respectively, except that they don't occupy any space. By default, no shortcut key exists for these characters. To enter them, go to the Special Characters tab in the Symbol dialog box. (If you use them often, select one in that dialog box and click Shortcut Key to assign your own shortcut key.)

You manage hyphenation by clicking Hyphenation (in the Page Setup group) on the Page Layout tab. Hyphenation is turned off by default. If you choose Automatic, Word hyphenates your entire document without further intervention. If you choose Manual, Word asks about each word it proposes to hyphenate. You can accept Word's suggestion (indicated by a flashing cursor) by clicking Yes; move the insertion point to your preferred break and click Yes; or click No to prevent hyphenating the word.

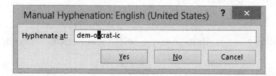

Inserting the date, time, and document properties

You'll often want to include the current date in a document, such as when you're typing a letter. The simplest way to do this is to let AutoText take over. Begin typing the date (spelled out or in m/d/y format), and after you type the fourth character, a pop-up tip offers to complete the date if you would be so kind as to press Enter. Fair enough.

If you want additional formatting options, or if you want to enter the date in a way that can be updated to the current date when you use the document at another time, click Insert, Date & Time (in the Text group). Doing so displays a dialog box showing the current date and time formatted in various ways.

If you've been diligent about maintaining document properties (details such as the document title and author), you might find it useful to include some of these properties in your document text. To do so, on the Insert tab click Quick Parts, Document Property, and then click the name of the property to include. If you select a property that hasn't yet been defined in this document, Word enters a placeholder where you can type the property value. There's a real advantage to entering properties using the Quick Parts feature instead of typing the property value as ordinary text in your document: if you later change the property value, all occurrences of it in your document update automatically.

For more information about document properties, see "Organizing and finding Office files" in Chapter 6.

Navigating in Word documents

Naturally, the same techniques for browsing through a document in virtually any Windows-based program—scroll bars, Page Up and Page Down keys, and so on—work in Word 2013. But finding your way around a long document in these ways can be tedious, to say the least. Fortunately, Word includes a host of its own navigation features that make it easier to go directly to a particular location in a document.

Navigating within a document

A key component of the navigation toolkit in Word 2013 is the Navigation pane, shown earlier in Figure 9-1. To display the Navigation pane, select its check box on the View tab, or press Ctrl+F.

The Navigation pane has three tabs near its top:

- The Headings tab shows each of the headings in your document, and you can jump directly to any heading by clicking it in the Navigation pane. (For information about what defines a heading, see "Formatting paragraphs" later in this chapter.)

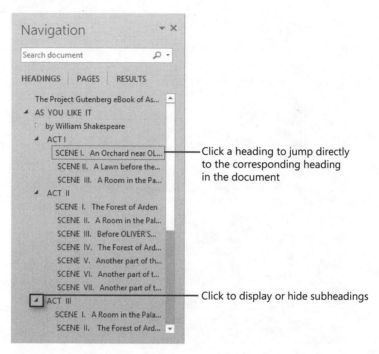

Click a heading to jump directly to the corresponding heading in the document

Click to display or hide subheadings

You can expand or contract this outline view so that it shows the headings you want without you having to scroll a long way to find a particular heading: Click the triangle at the left edge of a parent heading to expand or contract its subheadings. To expand or contract the entire outline to a particular heading level, right-click any heading and then click Show Heading Levels.

The headings tab is not just for navigation, however. With it, you can add, remove, promote, and demote headings, and you can reorganize your document by dragging headings in the Navigation pane. For details, see "Using outlines to plan, organize, and edit documents" in Chapter 10.

- The Pages tab shows a thumbnail image of each page in your document. You can skip immediately to a document page by clicking its thumbnail.

Chapter 9

- The Results tab shows search results. For details about using the Navigation pane for searching, see "Searching within a document" later in this chapter.

In addition to browsing by heading and by page, a less apparent feature of the Navigation pane lets you browse by other elements in a document, including graphics, tables, and reviewer comments. Click the magnifier icon next to Search Document to display a list of browse targets.

Click Tables, for example, and on the left tab each heading under which a table resides is highlighted. On the Pages tab, only pages that contain a table appear as thumbnails. And in the document itself, every table is highlighted. You can move to the next or previous table by clicking the arrow buttons to the right of the tabs. To return to the normal Navigation pane views, click the X that replaced the magnifier you clicked earlier.

Word offers another way to navigate by object with its Go To command, which opens the Find And Replace dialog box to the Go To tab. You can display this dialog box, shown in Figure 9-5, in any of the following ways:

- In the Navigation pane, click the magnifier icon next to Search Documents and then click Go To on the menu that appears.

- On the Home tab, click the arrow next to Find (in the Editing group) and click Go To.

- Press Ctrl+G or F5.

Figure 9-5 Go To offers some navigation capabilities not available in the Navigation pane.

Unlike the Navigation pane, Go To is designed for going directly to a specific occurrence of an object as well as browsing from one to the next. For this reason, Go To has a couple of additional navigation tricks. For some types of objects (such as pages, sections, and lines), you can enter a number to go directly to a numbered item (for example, select Graphic and type **4** to go to the fourth picture or graphic, counting from the beginning of the document). If you precede the number with a plus or minus sign, you jump forward or back the specified number of objects; for example, select Line and type **+10** to advance ten lines. For other object types (such as bookmarks), Go To provides a list of valid destinations to which you can go.

You'll sometimes want to move around in a document while you're typing or editing text—when it might not be convenient to take your hands off the keyboard. Rest assured that Word has plenty of keyboard shortcuts for navigating around a document. Some of them are common to all Office programs, and you'll find them listed in Table 4-1 in Chapter 4. Table 9-3 supplements the list with shortcuts that are unique to Word.

Chapter 9

INSIDE OUT Jump to your last edit location when you open a document

When you open a document, you can pick up where you left off the last time you worked on the document. Word displays a "Welcome back!" message, which you can click to go to the location of the last edit when the document was closed. If that message disappears before you act, press Shift+F5 to jump to the location.

TABLE 9-3 Keyboard shortcuts for navigating in Word

Action	Keyboard shortcut
Open the Navigation pane	Ctrl+F
Go to a page, section, bookmark, graphic, or other location	Ctrl+G or F5
Go to the next location of the same type	Ctrl+Page Down
Go to the previous location of the same type	Ctrl+Page Up
Cycle through the locations of your last four edits	Ctrl+Alt+Z or Shift+F5
Go to top of current screen	Ctrl+Alt+Page Up
Go to bottom of current screen	Ctrl+Alt+Page Down

Working with multiple document windows

It's not just hard-driving multitaskers who sometimes need to have several document windows open simultaneously. For example, while you're working on a new document, you might want to have one or more reference documents open, or you might want to have an earlier, similar document open so that you can copy text and pictures from it.

Each document you open—whether you open it from File Explorer, a pinned icon, or the File menu in Word—appears in its own window. The standard Windows tools for arranging windows (easiest: right-click the taskbar and choose an arrangement) and for switching between windows (press Alt+Tab or click the taskbar button) apply to Word windows, of course. However, when you use these tools, you typically end up resizing or switching among all your open windows, including those for your web browser, email program, games, and so on. Word has a few tricks for working exclusively with open Word windows without disturbing any of your other windows.

You'll find the window-management commands in the Window group on the View tab, shown earlier in Figure 9-2. These commands act as follows:

- **New Window** Opens a new window that also contains the current document. To differentiate the windows, the caption (title bar) for each window shows a colon and a number after the file name.

- **Arrange All**   Places all open Word windows on the primary monitor, splitting the space equally among them so all are visible.

- **Split**   Splits the current window into two panes; see the following tip for details.

- **View Side By Side**   If two Word windows are open, this displays them side by side, each filling half the screen, so that you can easily compare the documents. (If more than two Word windows are open, Word asks which one you want to display next to the current window.)

- **Synchronous Scrolling**   When this option is selected, scrolling in either side-by-side window scrolls both windows together. (Again, this feature is most useful for comparing versions of a document.) This option is available only when View Side By Side is selected.

- **Reset Window Position**   Restores the position of side-by-side windows so that each occupies half the screen. This option is available only when View Side By Side is selected, and it has an effect only if one or both windows have been resized.

- **Switch Windows**   Displays a menu of all open Word windows, allowing you to quickly switch to another.

INSIDE OUT   Use a split-screen view of a document

When you're editing a document, it's often useful to look at two different parts of a document simultaneously. You might want to refer to a picture or table in one part of your document while you enter a textual description in another part, for example. You can click New Window (in the Window group on the View tab) to open the same document in a second window, but sometimes it's more convenient to split a single document window into two panes. To split a window horizontally, click Split (in the Window group on the View tab) or press Ctrl+Alt+S. You can drag the divider up or down to adjust the pane sizes.

You can then work in either part of the window. The panes scroll independently, and you can set each one to a different zoom level or document view. To switch to the other pane, click in it or press F6. (You might need to press F6 several times. Once you figure out the sequence, you can alternate between F6 and Shift+F6 to switch directly between the two panes.)

To remove the split, click Remove Split (in the Window group on the View tab), double-click the pane divider, drag the pane divider to the top or bottom of the pane, or press Ctrl+Alt+S.

Chapter 9

Microsoft hasn't forgotten lovers of keyboard shortcuts when it comes to managing windows. Table 9-4 shows the ones that are unique to Word.

TABLE 9-4 Keyboard shortcuts for working with windows

Action	Keyboard shortcut
Move to the next or previous Word window	Ctrl+F6 or Ctrl+Shift+F6
Move to the next or previous pane (applies to panes in a split document, task panes, the ribbon, and status bar tools)	F6 or Shift+F6
Maximize or restore the current window	Ctrl+F10
Split the current window or remove the split	Ctrl+Alt+S

Searching within a document

Our discussion of the Navigation pane in the preceding sections touches on various items you can look for to quickly reach various locations in a document. But we haven't yet explored the topic of searching for text, which can also serve as a sort of navigational aid.

The easiest way to search for a particular text string is to type the text in the Search Document box at the top of the Navigation pane. (Press Ctrl+F to go directly there, regardless of whether the Navigation pane is already displayed.) As you enter your search text, Word immediately searches the document and displays its results, as shown in Figure 9-6. When you press Enter, Word selects the first occurrence of your search text.

To go to a particular search result, simply click the item in the Navigation pane. Note that the other tabs work as they do with object searches, described earlier in this chapter. On the Headings tab, each heading above each occurrence of the search text is highlighted, so you can see at a glance which parts of the document contain the text. The Pages tab is filtered so that it shows thumbnail images only of pages that include the search text.

As an alternative to clicking a search result, you can click the up or down arrow to the right of the tabs to go to the previous or next occurrence of the search text.

Searching for nonstandard characters

Searches in Word are not limited to letters, numbers, and other symbols. You'll often want to search for line-ending codes, perhaps to eliminate repeated line breaks or to find an occurrence of text that is at the end of a paragraph, for example. Table 9-5 lists the special characters and other items you can search for and the character string you enter to find them.

Enter your search text here

Word displays each occurrence in context on the Results tab...

...and highlights all occurrences in the document

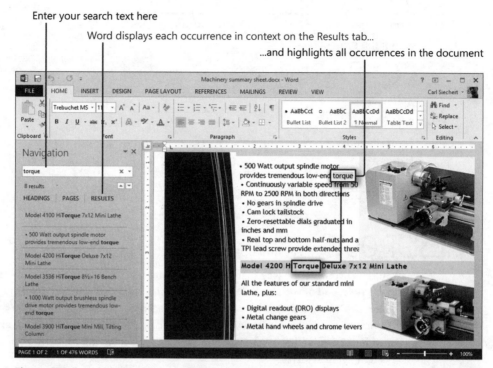

Figure 9-6 Search results in the Navigation pane are refined as you type each character in the search box.

TABLE 9-5 Search strings to find special characters

Item to find	Search string
Manual line break	^l (lowercase letter L)
Paragraph break	^p
Column break	^n
Manual page break	^m
Section break	^b
Tab character	^t
White space (space or tab)	^w
Nonbreaking space	^s
Nonbreaking hyphen	^~
Optional hyphen	^-
En dash (–)	^=
Em dash (—)	^+
Caret (^)	^^
Section symbol (§)	^%

Chapter 9

Item to find	Search string
Paragraph symbol (¶)	^v
Any character	^?
Any letter	^$
Any digit	^#
Endnote mark	^e
Footnote mark	^f
Field	^f
Graphic	^g

INSIDE OUT   Set find options

You can customize the way that Navigation pane searches work by clicking the arrow at the right end of the Search Document box and choosing Options. The Find Options dialog box enables the use of wildcards (? for a single character, * for one or more characters) and lets you narrow (Match Case or Find Whole Words Only, for example) or widen (Sounds Like, Ignore Punctuation Characters, or Find All Word Forms, for example) your search.

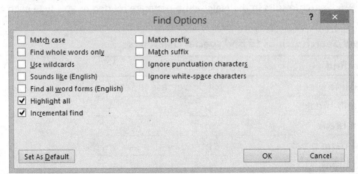

Sounds Like looks for your search word and its homonyms (words that sound the same but are spelled differently, such as *bread* and *bred*). It's great (grate?) for finding commonly confused words such as *there* and *their*.

Find All Word Forms uses a lexicon of related terms to include in search results. For example, with this option selected, a search for "buy" will find all occurrences of *buy*, *buying*, and *bought*.

Note that with some of these options selected, Word doesn't begin searching until you press Enter after entering your search text.

Including formatting in your search criteria

You might've noticed the Advanced Find command, either on the menu in the Navigation pane or on the Find menu in the Editing group on the Home tab. Selecting this command opens the Find And Replace dialog box and displays the Find tab. Longtime Word users will recognize this as the Find interface from earlier (pre–Navigation pane) versions of Word, but it continues to offer one capability that's not available in the Navigation pane: search for formatting.

You might want to use this feature to find an instance of a word in a heading or in bold-face text, for example. To do that, on the Find tab in the Find And Replace dialog box, click More to expose additional options. Enter the text you want to find in the Find What box, and then click Format to specify the formatting you're looking for.

INSIDE OUT   Search for highlighted text

Highlighting text can be useful for students and others who want to mark important passages and for content authors who want to mark a section for later review. Because highlighting isn't treated like other character formats, you might conclude that the only way to return to the highlighted sections is to visually scan your pages. Fortunately, that's not the case.

To go to the next highlighted section, click Advanced Find. Don't enter any text in the Find What box; just click Format (if the Format button doesn't appear, first click More), click Highlight, and then click Find Next.

Repeating a search

If you use Advanced Find, you can leave the Find And Replace dialog box open even as you work in your document. You can go to the first search result, make some edits, and then click Find Next in the still-open Find And Replace dialog box to go to the next search result. (Note, however, that you might encounter some limitations while the dialog box is open. For example, you can't move text by dragging and dropping.)

Similarly, the Navigation pane can stay open while you switch back and forth between document and task pane, making it easy to go to the next result. Although the search results and highlights in the Navigation pane disappear when you edit in the document, they reappear when you click either of the arrows (the Previous Search Result or Next Search Result button) to the right of the tabs.

If you do close the Find And Replace dialog box or the Navigation pane, however, you can still go to the next result from your previous search: Simply press Ctrl+Alt+Y.

Searching and replacing

A common editing task is to replace all occurrences of a certain word or phrase with another. To do that, press Ctrl+H to open the Find And Replace dialog box to the Replace tab, as shown in Figure 9-7.

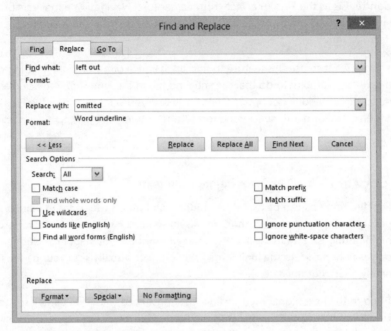

Figure 9-7 For a straight replacement of one bit of text with another, you can hide the clutter of this busy dialog box by clicking Less.

Clicking More displays additional options that let you refine your search, search for text formatted in a certain way, and apply formatting to the replacement text. If the insertion point is in the Find What box when you click Format, Word searches for text that has the formatting you specify. If it's in Replace With, Word applies the formatting when it replaces text.

Making your documents look good

An important part of "processing" words is formatting them to be legible and visually compelling. As with so many other tasks in Office, formatting can be done in several ways. In the next few pages, we describe how to apply formats directly to characters, paragraphs, and pages.

Direct formatting is the most obvious and most intuitive way to apply formatting, but as you'll see in "Giving your documents a consistent appearance" later in this chapter, the use of styles, themes, and templates offers more powerful ways to format a document. None-theless, the principles of direct formatting apply to those methods as well.

To apply formatting, you select the text you want to format and then apply the format.

> ### Note
>
> You can also apply formats without selecting text. Place the insertion point in a word, and any character formats you choose are applied to the entire word. Any paragraph formats you choose apply to the entire paragraph.

INSIDE OUT   Use Word tricks for selecting text

All the usual techniques you know for selecting text in other Windows-based programs (for an overview, see "Entering, selecting, and deleting text" in Chapter 4) work equally well in Word. Because manipulating text is one of its core functions, Word offers additional features for quickly and easily selecting text.

Touch typists and others who prefer keyboard shortcuts have an alternative to holding the Shift key as they use arrow keys to extend the selection. Press (and release) F8. Then use the arrow keys or other methods to extend the selection. Press Esc to cancel the F8 extend mode.

F8 is also handy for quick selections: Press it a second time to select a word, a third time to select a sentence, a fourth time to select a paragraph, and a fifth time to select the entire document. Press Shift+F8 to reduce the size of the selection.

Have you ever tried to make a vertical selection? Doing so is useful, for example, in tabular text, where you want to select text in one column to format it. The trick for doing that is to hold Alt or Ctrl+Alt as you drag, or press Ctrl+Shift+F8 and then use arrow keys to extend the selection.

Other tricks for mouse users: Double-click to select a word, triple-click to select a paragraph. Click in the left margin to select a line, or double-click in the left margin to select a paragraph.

To make multiple selections (which allows you to apply formatting to many different parts of a document simultaneously), hold the Ctrl key as you click and drag to make each selection. If you accidentally select something you didn't want to select, keep holding Ctrl and click the wrong selection again; that selection is cleared, while the rest of your selections remain.

Formatting text

In Chapter 4, we showed how to format text by selecting the text and then choosing options on the Home tab or the Mini toolbar (or using keyboard shortcuts) to apply a font, point size, and basic formats such as bold and italic. For details, see "Applying character formatting" in Chapter 4.

Word supports several additional character formats that you can apply to text. Although some can be controlled from the Home tab, others require a visit to the Font dialog box, which you can launch by clicking the arrow in the lower-right corner of the Font group on the Home tab or by pressing Ctrl+Shift+F. (Many of these formats can also be applied with shortcut keys, as shown in Table 9-6.)

TABLE 9-6 Keyboard shortcuts for formatting characters

Action	Keyboard shortcut
Open the Font dialog box	Ctrl+Shift+F
Change to Symbol font	Ctrl+Shift+Q
Increase font size	Ctrl+Shift+>
Decrease font size	Ctrl+Shift+<
Increase font size by 1 point	Ctrl+]
Decrease font size by 1 point	Ctrl+[
Turn bold on/off	Ctrl+B
Turn italics on/off	Ctrl+I
Turn underlining on/off	Ctrl+U
Turn word underlining (not spaces) on/off	Ctrl+Shift+W
Turn double-underlining on/off	Ctrl+Shift+D
Turn superscript on/off	Ctrl+Shift+Plus
Turn subscript on/off	Ctrl+=
Turn small caps format on/off	Ctrl+Shift+K
Turn all caps format on/off	Ctrl+Shift+A
Turn hidden text on/off	Ctrl+Shift+H
Clear all manual character formatting	Ctrl+Spacebar

INSIDE OUT   Deal with fonts that aren't installed on your computer

A document that was created on a different computer might use fonts that are not installed on your computer. If you open such a document, Word does its best to find a similar font on your system to use for display and printing.

And if you're not happy with Word's best? Specify your own substitute fonts. Click File, Options. On the Advanced tab, under Show Document Content, click Font Substitution. In the dialog box that appears, Word lists all the fonts that are used but not installed. To specify a different font, select a missing font and then choose from the Substituted Font list.

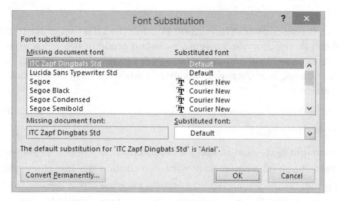

If you subsequently open the document on a computer where the original font is installed, Word uses that font. To change all occurrences in the document so that the substitute fonts are always used, click Convert Permanently.

Chapter 9

Most options in the Font dialog box need no further explanation, but some people are unfamiliar with the following:

- **Small Caps**   In this format, capital letters appear as they always do, but lowercase letters appear as smaller versions of the capitals—LIKE THIS.

- **All Caps**   As you would expect, in this format all letters appear as capital letters. The important thing to note is that the character codes do not change; Word merely changes the way lowercase letters are displayed. This difference means that if you turn off the All Caps format (or change to a style that doesn't have All Caps turned on), all the text reverts to its previous capitalization. Conversely, if you actually change case (by using the Change Case option in the Font group on the Home tab, or by using the Shift+F3 shortcut), the original capitalization is lost.

- **Hidden**   Text with this format disappears altogether except when you select Show/Hide ¶ (in the Paragraph group on the Home tab) or press Ctrl+*. Hidden text is handy for notes to yourself that you don't want to include in printed documents. (By default, hidden text doesn't print, even when it's displayed on the screen. To change this setting, click File, Options. On the Display tab, under Printing Options, select Print Hidden Text.)

CAUTION!

Don't rely on hidden text to retain your deepest, darkest secrets. Anybody who has access to your document file can display the hidden text.

In this chapter, we describe text formatting through the selection of fonts and basic attributes. Word can do much more, however, including gradient fills, reflections, and other effects. For details, see "Applying text effects with WordArt" in Chapter 5, "Working with graphics and pictures," and "Applying advanced text-formatting capabilities" in Chapter 11, "Word 2013 inside out."

Highlighting text

You can highlight text—that is, apply a background color much as you would with a highlighter felt pen on a paper document—by clicking the Text Highlight Color tool in the Font group on the Home tab. (Optionally, click the arrow next to the tool to select a different pen color.) The mouse pointer changes to a highlighter pen, and you can then highlight various passages by dragging over them. Click the tool again or press Esc to turn off the highlighter pen. (Alternatively, you can highlight text by selecting it and then clicking the Text Highlight Color tool on the Home tab or on the Mini toolbar.)

Although you apply highlighting in the same fashion as character formats (such as bold or a point size), it is not a character format. Highlighting can't be included in a character or paragraph style, and it is not removed when you click Clear All Formatting (in the Font group on the Home tab) or press Ctrl+Spacebar. To remove highlighting, click the arrow by the Text Highlight Color tool and then click No Color.

You can choose to hide highlighting on-screen and in printed documents without removing it. (Click File, Options. On the Display tab, under Page Display Options, clear Show Highlighter Marks.)

Although you can't include highlighting in a style, you can use the Shading tool (in the Paragraph group on the Home tab) to achieve a similar effect. Shading can be included in character and paragraph styles.

Formatting paragraphs

Options for managing paragraph formatting appear on the Home tab and on the Page Layout tab (in the Paragraph group on both tabs).

The basics of paragraph formatting are the same in Word as in other Office programs; for more information, see "Applying paragraph formatting" in Chapter 4.

On either tab, clicking the arrow in the lower-right corner opens the Paragraph dialog box, shown in Figure 9-8. Here you can precisely set indents from the margins and line spacing.

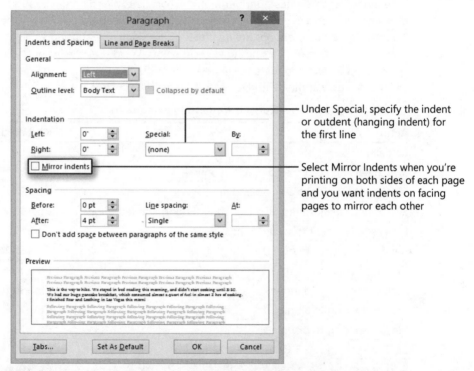

Under Special, specify the indent or outdent (hanging indent) for the first line

Select Mirror Indents when you're printing on both sides of each page and you want indents on facing pages to mirror each other

Chapter 9

Figure 9-8 Under Spacing, you specify the space between lines in a paragraph and the amount of space above and below each paragraph. Create heading styles with an Outline Level setting.

As an alternative to the ribbon tools and the Paragraph dialog box, you can set indents by using the ruler, shown in Figure 9-9. Simply drag the indent markers to relocate them. To move the left indent and first indent simultaneously, drag the box below the left indent marker. Note that indents can extend into the page margins (notice the right indent in the figure); because indents are measured from the margin, the numeric values under Indentation in the Paragraph dialog box are negative in this case.

Figure 9-9 The colored background in the ruler indicates the page margins.

Standard line spacing settings (single, double, and so on) are readily made with the Line And Paragraph Spacing tool on the Home tab or by using keyboard shortcuts (see Table 9-7). Additional options are available only in the Paragraph dialog box. The Single option accommodates the largest font or graphic in each line, plus a bit of extra space. (If you have different point sizes in each line, the spacing within a paragraph will vary.) The 1.5 Lines, Double, and Multiple options are multiples of the Single line spacing value. With the At Least option, you specify a spacing value in points; Word uses the lesser of this value or the size needed to accommodate the largest font or graphic in a line. The Exactly option spaces all lines precisely at the height you specify, regardless of their content.

TABLE 9-7 Keyboard shortcuts for formatting paragraphs

Action	Keyboard shortcut
Left align	Ctrl+L
Switch between centered and left-aligned	Ctrl+E
Switch between right-aligned and left-aligned	Ctrl+R
Switch between justified (aligned left and right) and left-aligned	Ctrl+J
Increase left indent to next 0.5 inch	Ctrl+M
Reduce left indent to next 0.5 inch	Ctrl+Shift+M
Create a hanging indent	Ctrl+T
Reduce the hanging indent	Ctrl+Shift+T
Set line spacing to Single	Ctrl+1
Set line spacing to Double	Ctrl+2
Set line spacing to 1.5 Lines	Ctrl+5
Add or remove space before (12 pt)	Ctrl+0
Clear all manual paragraph formatting	Ctrl+Q

You also specify the space before (above) and after (below) each paragraph in the Paragraph dialog box. Note that the space after one paragraph is not added to the space before the following paragraph; instead, Word always uses the larger of the two values. The Paragraph dialog box also includes an option to suppress the space before and after paragraphs of the same style. This is useful, for example, with a bulleted list. You might want space before and after the list to set it off from other text, but not have space between each bullet item.

TROUBLESHOOTING

Text or graphics get clipped

If you set line spacing to Exactly, you might find that tops and bottoms of some letters don't appear. The problem could be that you're using text that's too big to fit in the allotted space; increase the line spacing or reduce the point size of the text.

If your in-line graphics are being clipped, you have two alternatives: use a line spacing option other than Exactly, or change the graphic's text-wrapping style. (For details, see "Adding pictures and graphics" later in this chapter.)

Paragraph formatting is associated with the paragraph mark at the end of each paragraph. (The paragraph mark is normally hidden, but you can display it and other formatting marks by pressing Ctrl+*.) You can demonstrate this by selecting and copying a paragraph mark and then pasting it elsewhere; the paragraph that ends with the newly pasted mark uses the same paragraph styling as the paragraph from which it was copied.

Setting page layout options

Options on the Page Layout tab determine the page size, orientation, and margins for a document—settings you can also make via the Page Setup dialog box.

To quickly adjust the page margins, use the ruler. As shown earlier in Figure 9-9, the "live" area within the margins is indicated by a white background in the ruler. To move a margin, drag the edge of the colored area.

On the Design tab, options in the Page Background group provide access to some interesting, but seldom used, page layout features. You can select or create a "watermark"—some text or a picture that prints as a background on each sheet. Watermarks are often used to identify proprietary information (with a message like "CONFIDENTIAL" or "DO NOT COPY"), but the feature makes it easy to use a picture (which can be optionally washed out so it doesn't interfere with text) as a background. Clicking Page Borders opens the Borders And Shading dialog box, wherein you can define a rectangular frame to surround each page.

For information about multicolumn and other complex layouts, see "Formatting columns and sections" in Chapter 10.

Adding headers, footers, and page numbers

A header or footer is a block of text at the top or bottom of each page. Some headers and footers are constant throughout a document—perhaps showing your company name or a document's date. Headers and footers can also incorporate variable text; this can be as simple as a page number, or it can vary depending on the page content. (For example, notice the headers in this book. The ones on left-hand pages include a page number, the chapter number, and the chapter title; headers on right-hand pages include heading text, which changes throughout the chapter.)

You'll want to decide whether to use different headers and footers on left and right pages (something to consider only if your document will be printed on both sides of the paper), and whether you want to use a different header and footer (or none at all) on the first page of the document. You can make those settings on the Layout tab of the Page Setup dialog box, but it's simpler to just go directly to the Insert tab and click Header or Footer. Either way, a gallery appears, from which you can select a predefined or a blank header or footer.

After you make your selection, you're working in the header and footer area of the document. Many of the predefined headers and footers have content controls, which are defined areas where you can type. Many content controls are linked to document properties. For example, many headers and footers use the Title property to incorporate the document title into the document. If you've already defined the title, it appears in place when you insert a header or footer that uses it. If you haven't yet defined the title, placeholder text appears, as shown in Figure 9-10.

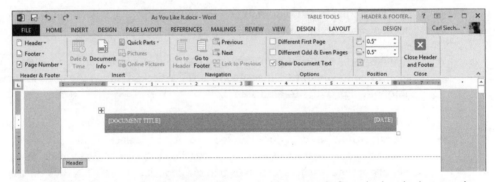

Figure 9-10 Typing over the document title placeholder not only fixes the header but sets the Title property. Headers update automatically if you change the value of the Title property.

INSIDE OUT   Prevent content controls from updating

To convert the text in a content control to static text—regardless of whether it comes from a property setting or you typed it—right-click it and then click Remove Content Control.

To work in the header and footer area, double-click it. To switch back to the body of your document, double-click it or click Close Header And Footer on the Design tab under Header & Footer Tools (see Figure 9-10). While working in the header and footer area, use tools in the Navigation group to jump back and forth between header and footer and to jump to the previous or next footer in a document with multiple sections. Each section has its own header and footer. If you want to use the same one in successive sections, go to the section *after* the one whose header and footer you want to continue; then click Link To Previous. (For more information about sections, see "Formatting columns and sections" in Chapter 10.)

Editing in the header and footer area is the same as editing in the document body: click and type.

Also on the Design tab, you can select a different header or footer; insert the date, the time, a picture, or other items; specify whether to use different headers on the first, odd, and even pages; and specify the distance between the header or footer and the edge of the page.

Giving your documents a consistent appearance

In the preceding pages, we explain how to apply formatting directly. Although this technique is useful for short documents, if you try to directly format a longer document you'll discover the shortcomings of this method. First, it's tedious; you need to make a lot of individual settings separately. Second, it's difficult to maintain consistency throughout a document. And third, it's difficult to modify your document if you decide to implement a different design.

Word has three related features that overcome the weaknesses of direct formatting:

- **Themes**   An Office *theme* is a set of theme colors, theme fonts, and theme effects. Switching to a different theme changes all those components at once—as long as the document uses styles that rely on theme fonts and colors. For information about selecting and modifying themes, see "Using Office themes" in Chapter 5.

- **Styles**   A *style* is a collection of formatting settings that can be applied to characters, paragraphs, lists, or tables. A character style, for example, might specify a font, size, font style, and color. A paragraph style typically includes character formatting information (font, size, and so on) as well as formats that apply strictly to paragraphs, such as line spacing, indents, borders, and tab-stop settings. You can apply a style—and all the formatting steps it includes—with a simple selection in the Styles gallery.

  Word 2013 includes a number of predefined styles—indeed, several sets of predefined styles—that you can use right away, or you can define your own styles.

- **Templates** A *template* is a file in which you can store styles. Each document you create is based on a template. Word uses the template called Normal.dotm by default, but you can select a different template (one that's included with Word, one you download, or one you create yourself) when you create a new document. When you create a new document, Word copies all the styles (along with AutoText entries and any text, pictures, or other document elements included in the template) into the new document.

Understanding how themes, styles, and templates work together is an essential part of Word mastery. It might seem daunting because Word offers numerous choices—several predefined themes, countless styles (and style sets, which are collections of styles), and an online library of sample templates—and on first appearance you might think these all work independently. That's not the case.

A template brings its own collection of styles, so once you apply styles to a document, if you select a different style set (or change templates), your document instantly changes to reflect the formatting for the like-named styles in the new style set or template. And if the styles are defined to use theme fonts and theme colors, when you change themes, you get the fonts and colors from the new theme. You can make these changes in any order, and through the use of galleries and Live Preview, you can easily see how each change in styles affects the document.

As an example, Figure 9-11 shows a document that was created using a template downloaded from Office.com. The screen on the right shows the same document, with the Fancy style set and Facet theme applied.

Using these formatting techniques instead of direct formatting is a trait of advanced Word users—yet once you understand the concepts, you'll find that using styles, themes, and templates is actually much easier than direct formatting. Using styles and themes allows you to provide consistency throughout a document, and by saving and using templates, you can employ a consistent appearance from one document to another and throughout your organization.

Applying styles

The simplest way to apply a style is to make a selection in the Styles gallery on the Home tab, as shown in Figure 9-12. As you point to different options in the gallery, Live Preview shows how each option looks in your document.

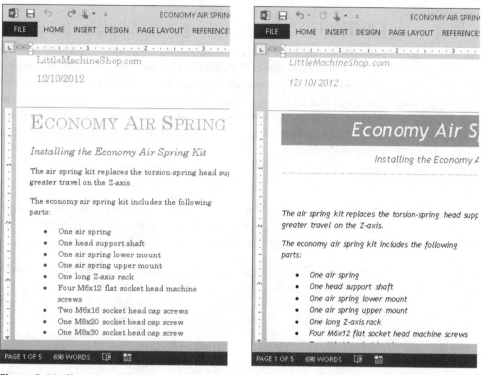

Figure 9-11 Changing the style set added paragraph borders and backgrounds; changing the theme applied different fonts and colors.

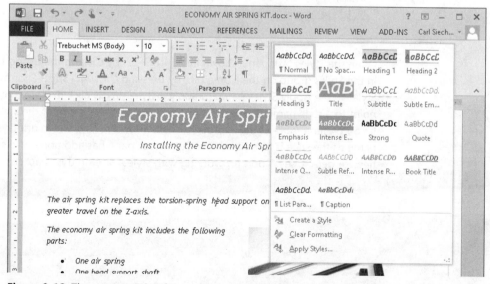

Figure 9-12 The current style of the selection is highlighted in the gallery.

Chapter 9

CAUTION!

As noted earlier, if you apply a paragraph style when no text is selected, Word applies the style to the paragraph that contains the insertion point. Likewise, if all or parts of more than one paragraph are selected, Word applies the paragraph style to each paragraph that is fully or partially selected. However, if less than one full paragraph is selected, Word applies only the character formats from the paragraph style and does not apply any paragraph formats. For more information, see "Understanding linked styles" in Chapter 11.

Handy as it is, the Styles gallery has some drawbacks. It doesn't show all available styles in a template, and it can be a bit cumbersome to use. Fortunately, as with so many operations in Office, alternative methods abound. You can apply styles with any of these techniques:

- Press Ctrl+Shift+S to open or switch to the Apply Styles task pane, which normally appears as a floating window. Begin typing the name of the style you want, and when the full name appears, press Enter to apply the style. The task pane remains open, so you can switch to it at any time by clicking it or pressing Ctrl+Shift+S.

- Open the Styles task pane, shown in Figure 9-13, by clicking the dialog box launcher in the Styles group on the Home tab; by pressing Ctrl+Alt+Shift+S; or by clicking Styles in the Apply Styles pane. To apply a style, simply click it. Note that when you point to a style name, a ScreenTip shows a textual description of the style's attributes. If you prefer a more visual approach, select Show Preview, which displays each style name as the style is formatted. The Styles task pane has additional tricks and capabilities; for details, see "Tools for working with styles" later in this chapter.

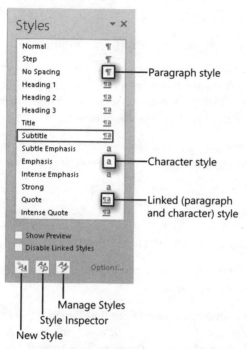

Figure 9-13 The Styles pane includes a symbol that identifies each style's type.

- Use a keyboard shortcut to apply a style to the current selection. Table 9-8 shows predefined shortcuts for applying styles, and you can define your own shortcuts for applying other styles. To do that, open the Modify Style dialog box (for details, see "Creating a new style" later in this chapter) and click Format, Shortcut Key.

TABLE 9-8 Keyboard shortcuts for applying styles

Action	Keyboard shortcut
Open the Apply Styles task pane	Ctrl+Shift+S
Open the Styles task pane	Ctrl+Alt+Shift+S
Apply the Normal paragraph style	Ctrl+Shift+N
Apply the Heading 1 style	Ctrl+Alt+1
Apply the Heading 2 style	Ctrl+Alt+2
Apply the Heading 3 style	Ctrl+Alt+3
Apply the List Bullet style	Ctrl+Shift+L

INSIDE OUT   Show style names in Draft and Outline views

If you use Draft view or Outline view to work in your document, it's sometimes diffi-cult to see which styles are in use. To overcome this difficulty, click File, Options. In the Word Options dialog box, click the Advanced tab and scroll down to Display. Next to Style Area Pane Width In Draft And Outline Views, enter 1".

Now you'll see a pane along the left side of your document that shows the style for each paragraph. To adjust the width of this pane, simply drag the line that separates it from the document content.

Making global changes to your document

Having applied styles to the paragraphs and text in your document, you can now experi-ence the magic of themes and style sets.

You can select a different theme by choosing from the Themes gallery on the Design tab. As you point to each theme, Live Preview shows its effect on your document. To remove theme settings and revert to settings in the template, click Themes again and then click Reset To Theme From *TemplateName* Template.

To select a new style set, in the Document Formatting group on the Design tab, click the arrow in the lower-right corner of the Style Sets gallery. A menu of predefined style sets appears, and again Live Preview shows the result. Commands at the bottom of the Style Sets gallery restore the style set from the template or from the current document. (Although a new document gets its styles from a template, you can subsequently modify those styles and keep the changes only in the document, without updating the template.)

You can also make global changes by modifying your existing styles or by applying a differ-ent style to certain paragraphs. When you modify a style, all instances of that style in your document are updated to use the new attributes. For more information, see "Creating a new style" later in this chapter.

INSIDE OUT   Prevent formatting changes

If your intent is to enforce a uniform look throughout your organization's documents, having the freedom to select different themes and style sets works against this goal. To limit formatting changes in a document, click Restrict Editing in the Protect group on the Review tab. In the Restrict Editing pane, click Settings (under Formatting Restrictions). In the Formatting Restrictions dialog box, shown next, select the styles you want to allow, and select options to prevent changing style sets and themes. Click OK. Back in the Restrict Editing pane, click Yes, Start Enforcing Protection.

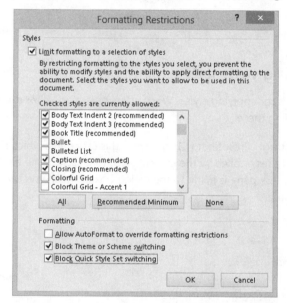

Restrictions you impose this way protect only the current document. Through the Manage Styles dialog box, you can impose additional restrictions, and you can apply these restrictions to the current document or to the current template, which then enforces the restrictions on any new documents created from the template. For more information about Manage Styles, see the following section, "Tools for working with styles."

INSIDE OUT Change all occurrences of one style to another

You might have a need to change all instances of a style to another. This is often the case when you import text from a document that uses different styles, for example. You can use search and replace to find and replace each one, but there's a simpler way to select all occurrences of a style. In the Styles gallery, right-click the style of interest and then click Select All *nn* Instance(s). (Alternatively, in the Styles task pane, click the arrow to the right of a style name to find this command.) With all instances selected, you can then apply another style, apply direct formatting, or even delete all paragraphs formatted with that style.

Tools for working with styles

In addition to the tools for applying styles, Word offers several tools for examining formatting and styles, including these:

● **Reveal Formatting**   Press Shift+F1 to display this task pane, which shows all the formatting attributes applied to the current selection. Each of the blue underlined headings in this task pane is a link to the dialog box in which you can change that particular attribute.

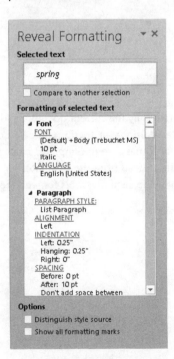

Under Selected Text, select Compare To Another Selection to open a second sample text box. Select some other text, and Reveal Formatting lists the formatting differences between the two selections.

● **Style Inspector**   In the Styles task pane (see Figure 9-13), click Style Inspector (the second button at the bottom of the pane) to open the task pane shown next. In its first and third boxes, the Style Inspector shows which styles have been applied at the paragraph and character level. The second and fourth boxes identify any direct formatting that has been applied. A button next to each of these boxes clears that formatting from the selection.

● **Manage Styles**   The Manage Styles dialog box, which you open by clicking the third button at the bottom of the Styles task pane (see Figure 9-13), is the place to make a variety of style-related settings, including these:

○ On the Set Defaults tab, specify the format for text and paragraphs that don't have any style applied, for which Word uses the built-in Normal style. (A common gripe about earlier versions of Word was the difficulty of changing the default style of 10-point Times New Roman. Although Manage Styles is deeply buried, once you find it you'll see that changing the default formatting is easy.)

○ The Edit tab includes a complete list of styles from the current document; select any one and click Modify to make changes to the style.

○ To limit the formatting changes that users can make, visit the Restrict tab.

○ On the Recommend tab, you can identify certain styles as "recommended" and specify the order in which they appear in the Styles or Apply Styles pane. (To show recommended styles or other styles, click Options in the Styles pane, shown earlier in Figure 9-13.)

○ To copy styles from one document or template to another, click Import/Export to open the Organizer dialog box.

Chapter 9

> **Note**
>
> To add a style to the Styles gallery, open the Styles pane, click the arrow to the right of the style name, and click Add To Style Gallery. To remove a style from the gallery (but not delete the style from the document), right-click the gallery entry and then click Remove From Style Gallery.

Creating a new style

When the template you're using doesn't have a style you need, create a new one. You can do this in either of two ways:

- Use any combination of styles, themes, and direct formatting to create an example of the style you want. Then right-click it, point to Styles, and click Create A Style. Word displays a dialog box in which you can give the new style a name, which appears in the Styles gallery, the Styles pane, and the Apply Styles pane. By default, the new style is stored in your document, but it is not added to the template from which the document was created. To add it to the template, you need to modify the style, which you can do by clicking Modify in the Create New Style From Formatting dialog box.

- Create a new style "from scratch." In the Styles pane (shown earlier in Figure 9-13), click New Style (the first button at the bottom of the pane). A dialog box similar to the one shown in Figure 9-14 appears.

Some items in this dialog box require a bit of explanation:

- **Style Type**   Your choice here determines which options are available elsewhere in the dialog box, so it should be your first stop after you give the style a name. For more information about the Linked style type, see "Understanding linked styles" in Chapter 11.

- **Style Based On**   If you want to make a style that's similar to another one, you can save time by selecting that style here. You won't need to repeat its settings, and you ensure that the two styles stay in sync. That is, if you make changes to the base style, those changes appear in the new style automatically. If you want to be sure that the new style does *not* change when you update another style, select No Style here.

- **Style For Following Paragraph**   This feature adds a bit of automation to your document when you enter text by setting the style for the next paragraph when you press Enter in a paragraph that uses this style. It's typically used for heading styles, so that the paragraph following a heading is automatically formatted as body text.

- **Font** Select one of the first two entries, which include the word *Body* or *Headings*, if you want changes to the font theme to affect this style. Note that if you click Format, Font to select font details, the two theme options are identified as +Body and +Headings.

- **Font Color** To enable theme colors to affect this style (and other style colors you can set, such as the colors for underlines, borders, and shading), in the Font Color box select an option under Theme Colors. To prevent theme influence, select an option under Standard Colors.

- **Automatically Update** If you select this check box, whenever you apply direct formatting to a paragraph that uses this style, Word automatically updates the style (and thereby updates all paragraphs in the document that use the style). We don't recommend this option, as too often it makes changes you don't expect.

    If you don't select Automatically Update, you can update a style to match the currently selected text by right-clicking the style in the Styles gallery and then clicking Update *StyleName* To Match Selection.

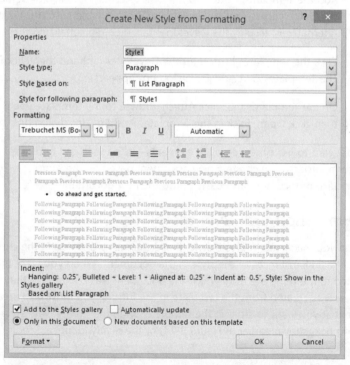

Figure 9-14 Basic character and paragraph formatting options are in this dialog box. Click Format for additional options.

If you prefer to use a dialog box similar to the one shown in Figure 9-14 to make changes to a style, you can do so by right-clicking a style in the Styles gallery (or clicking the arrow to the right of a style name in the Styles task pane) and choosing Modify.

Applying a template to an existing document

When you create a document based on a template, the new document begins as a copy of the template, incorporating all its text, graphics, macros, and AutoCorrect entries—as well as its styles.

For details about selecting a template when you create a new document, see "Using templates to streamline document creation" in Chapter 6.

You can apply a template to an existing document if, for example, you want to use the styles from the template. Note, however, that when you apply a template this way, you don't get its text, graphics, and page layout. But if your goal is to pick up styles, follow these steps:

1. Add the Templates button to the Quick Access Toolbar. (For details, see "Customizing the Quick Access Toolbar" in Chapter 3, "Using and customizing the Office interface.") Alternatively, display the Developer tab. (See "Personalizing the ribbon" in Chapter 3.)

2. Click the Templates button (or the Developer tab) and then click Document Template. The Templates And Add-Ins dialog box appears.

3. On the Templates tab, click Attach. Browse to the template you want to apply, and then click Open. Back in the Templates And Add-Ins dialog box, click OK.

If you want to use other template elements—its page layout and graphics, for example—a better approach is to create a new document based on the template. Copy all the text from your current document and paste it into the new document.

Saving and modifying templates

When you make changes to a style, those changes are stored in the current document and affect all instances of the style in the document. When you want those changes to be copied to the template from which the document was created (so that the changes affect documents created from the template in the future), you must take an extra step. For each style that you want to store in the template, open the Create New Style From Formatting dialog box (shown earlier in Figure 9-14) or the nearly identical Modify Style dialog box. Be sure that New Documents Based On This Template is selected, and then click OK. When you close the document, Word asks if you want to save any unsaved changes, and also asks if you want to save changes to the template. Click Save.

To incorporate the currently selected style set and theme selection into the template, on the Design tab, click Set As Default. Doing so includes these styles and settings in the template and also uses them as the defaults when you create a new document based on the template.

INSIDE OUT   Make changes to the Normal style

You can quickly change the font and paragraph style for the Normal style—the template style used for paragraphs to which no other style has been applied—without digging down to the Modify Style dialog box. Simply open the Font dialog box or Paragraph dialog box (easiest way: click the dialog box launcher in the Font or Paragraph group on the Home tab), make your changes, and click Set As Default.

Adding pictures and graphics

In many cases, a Word document consists of much more than just words. Pictures, line drawings, charts, screenshots, and other types of graphics can visually enhance nearly any document. SmartArt graphics combine text and graphics to produce compelling charts and presentations.

The techniques for creating, inserting, resizing, rotating, and formatting each of these graphical object types are the same in Word as they are in other Office programs. We describe these object types and the techniques for using them in Chapter 5.

Although the object types are consistent throughout Office, Word offers unique ways to position such graphics within a document. Word uses one of two basic methods to position a graphic:

- **In Line With Text**   In-line graphics are treated as part of the document's text stream. They maintain their position between the characters or paragraphs where they are inserted, and they move to the right or down with each character or line you insert before them.

- **With Text Wrapping**   Word offers several text-wrapping variants, which we explore next. In each of these variants, a graphic's horizontal and vertical position is specified relative to the page, margins, or other landmark. The graphic moves automatically only if the landmark to which it's tied moves.

TROUBLESHOOTING

A graphic is cropped to just one line high

You might find that after you insert a picture or other graphic, it's severely cropped, so that only the bottom of the picture appears. This happens when an in-line graphic is placed in a paragraph that has fixed line spacing. You can fix the problem—and show the entire picture—in either of two ways:

- Change the text wrapping to an option other than In Line With Text.

- Change the line spacing for the paragraph to a setting other than Exactly.

For the simplest placement options, select a graphic and, on the Page Layout tab, click Position. A gallery appears, and Live Preview shows the effect of each gallery option as you hover the mouse pointer over it. Options in the Position gallery let you place a graphic at any margin or centered between the margins.

To more precisely control the positioning of a picture or graphic in Word, you use the Wrap Text option. You can get to Wrap Text by selecting the object and then clicking the Page Layout tab; Wrap Text is in the Arrange group. (You'll also find Wrap Text in the Arrange group on the Format tab under Picture Tools or Drawing Tools.) Alternatively, select an object and click the Layout Options icon to display a menu of text wrapping options, as shown in Figure 9-15.

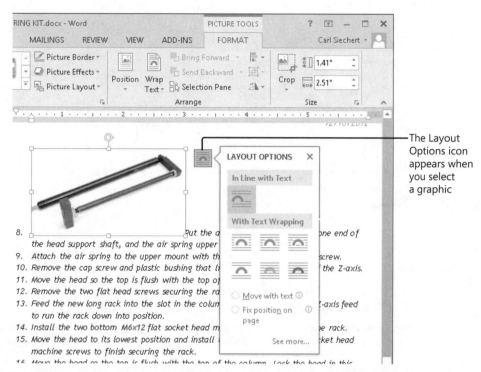

The Layout Options icon appears when you select a graphic

Figure 9-15 Clicking Wrap Text on the Format tab or Page Layout tab offers options like those that appear when you click the Layout Options icon. The difference is that Wrap Text displays a Live Preview as you hover over each option.

Clicking See More (or clicking More Layout Options on the Wrap Text menu) opens the Layout dialog box, shown in Figure 9-16, in which you can specify additional wrapping parameters, such as whether text wraps on both sides of the graphic or only one side, and the distance between the wrapped text and the graphic.

Graphics that use text wrapping can also be dragged into position. As you drag a graphic close to a margin, the center of a column or page, the top of a paragraph, and certain other objects, an alignment guide appears. This green line, a feature new to Word 2013, makes it easy to snap pictures and other graphics into alignment.

You'll sometimes want to wrap text around an irregular shape, such as the picture shown in Figure 9-17. You do this with the Edit Wrap Points command on the Wrap Text menu. Hold down Ctrl and click on the red outline to create a wrap point, which you can then drag into position. To remove a wrap point, Ctrl+click it again.

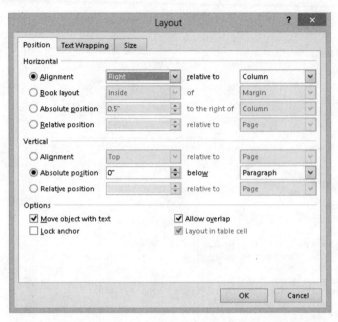

Figure 9-16 The Position tab allows you to place the graphic at an absolute position or relative to various document landmarks, such as a margin, the edge of the page, or a paragraph.

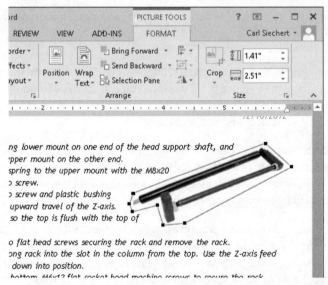

Figure 9-17 Wrap points let you determine how text wraps around a graphic, regardless of the graphic's actual shape.

Working with bulleted and numbered lists

A common element in Word documents is a list. Bulleted lists are typically used when the order of the items is unimportant, whereas numbered lists are often used for procedural steps or in legal documents where each section can be identified by its number.

For simple bulleted and numbered lists, Word formats the paragraphs automatically as you type. Begin a paragraph with an asterisk followed by a space, for example, and Word removes the asterisk and applies an appropriate style that includes a bullet character and is indented properly. A similar conversion occurs when you begin a paragraph by typing the number 1 followed by a period and tab. The AutoFormat process continues when you press Enter twice after the last list item: Word removes the extra paragraph and reverts to the Normal paragraph style for subsequent paragraphs.

To apply standard list formats to existing paragraphs, select the paragraphs and then select the Bullets tool or Numbering tool in the Paragraph group on the Home tab. Click the arrows on the right side of these tools to expose additional options, such as different bullet characters or different numbering styles, as shown in Figure 9-18.

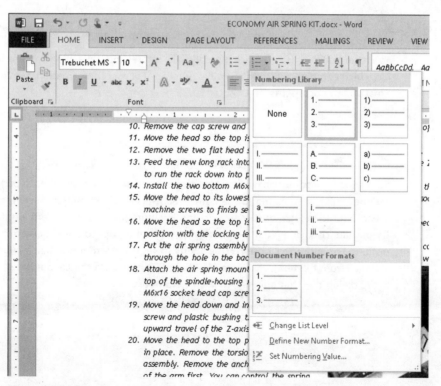

Figure 9-18 If you don't like any of the numbering styles in the library, click Define New Number Format.

Numbered lists are renumbered automatically as you add and remove paragraphs. Ordinarily, numbering restarts at 1 following an unnumbered paragraph. If you want to continue numbering from the previous list, right-click the incorrect number 1 paragraph and choose Continue Numbering. Conversely, you can begin numbering anew at any point by right-clicking and choosing Restart At 1.

To create a list within a list, press Tab at the beginning of a list paragraph. Word further indents the paragraph and applies a different bullet character or numbering style. (For example, if your top-level list is numbered 1, 2, 3, and so on, Word numbers the next level as a, b, c.... If you don't like this standard convention, click the Bullets or Numbering tool and select a different style.) Word restarts numbering for a lower-level list after each higher-level list.

For additional options for multilevel numbered lists, click Multilevel List, the tool to the right of Numbering in the Paragraph group on the Home tab. Here you can make settings that aren't available in the standard Define New Number Format dialog box, and you can make settings for each level (up to nine levels deep) without leaving the dialog box.

INSIDE OUT   Use SmartArt to create compelling lists

To create bulleted lists that are more visually interesting, take a look at SmartArt graphics, which combine lists with chartlike graphics. For more information, see "Adding SmartArt to documents" in Chapter 5.

One other type of numbering: line numbers

Some documents must have line numbers printed in the margin of each page. This feature, which is unrelated to the numbered lists described on the preceding pages, is widely used in legal documents. To add line numbers to a document, on the Page Layout tab, click Line Numbers (in the Page Setup group) to see a menu of numbering options. For additional options (the ability to set the starting number, increment, and distance from the text), click Line Numbering Options. On the Layout tab of the Page Setup dialog box that appears, click Line Numbers.

Checking grammar and spelling

Office 2013 has a spelling checker that, for the most part, works the same in all Office programs. For details about its use, see "Checking spelling" in Chapter 4. As we noted in that
section, however, Word also incorporates tools for checking grammar and style into the
spelling checker.

Grammatical errors that Word detects are marked in your document with a squiggly blue
underline. As with spelling errors (which are marked with a squiggly red underline), you
can right-click the offending phrase or sentence to see a list of proposed corrections from
which you can choose, along with links to more information about the error. Results of the
grammar review also appear when you check spelling throughout a document by clicking
Spelling & Grammar on the Review tab (or by pressing this option's shortcut key, F7).

Correct grammar is somewhat subjective, and you might want to limit the items that Word
flags for review or customize the rules to your personal style guidelines. For example, while
there is consensus on proper subject/verb agreement, grammar nitpickers still debate the
serial comma. To change how the grammar review works, click File, Options. On the Proofing tab, scroll down to When Correcting Spelling And Grammar In Word. First, decide
whether you want Word to check for stylistic faux pas (such as passive sentences) in addition to grammar; next to Writing Style, select Grammar Only or Grammar & Style. Then
click Settings to examine the available grammar options.

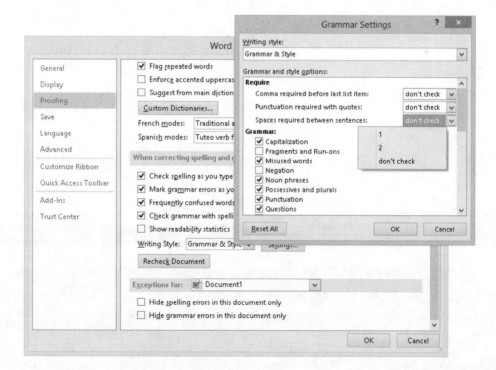

Chapter 9

The options you set here apply to all documents you open in Word.

After you close Grammar Settings, you can click Check Document (or Recheck Document, if you've already performed a spelling and grammar review) to proof your document using your new settings.

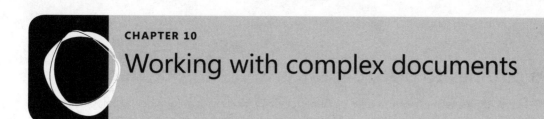

WORD is a workhorse that excels at producing documents with complex layouts, such as newsletters, brochures, and other multicolumn designs. Word also has the features to manage extremely long documents, such as reports, scripts, and books. (You shouldn't be surprised to learn that we prepared the manuscript for this book using Word 2013.)

In this chapter, we focus on tasks that are usually associated with complex or long documents, including outlining, inserting cross-references, and creating tables of contents and indexes. We also explain how to use sections both to break up long documents and to create complex layouts. And we show how to create and format tables, which can be useful in documents of any complexity or length.

Whether you're writing a sales proposal or the great American novel, you probably don't work alone. Coworkers, managers, editors, proofreaders, and others are likely to have suggestions for improving your document. Your cohorts can make their suggestions directly in your Word document, and you can then review them and decide whether to accept or reject them. In this chapter we describe comments and tracked changes, two features for providing document feedback.

We conclude with a discussion of methods for sharing a document with others. You want to be certain that a document doesn't include information that it shouldn't, and you might want to prevent others from making changes to the document.

Using outlines to plan, organize, and edit documents

Writing a well-organized long document usually starts with an outline of topics, headings, and notes. With Outline view, Word provides a work environment that is ideal for planning a document before you begin writing and is also useful for reviewing and organizing your document as writing progresses. In Outline view, you can hide some or all of the body text, allowing you to concentrate solely on the headings.

For details about switching views, see "Working in an appropriate document view" in Chapter 9, "Inside Word 2013."

In Outline view, paragraphs that have a heading style appear in outline form, with each successive heading level indented a bit more from the left margin, as shown in Figure 10-1. When you work in Outline view, only the document's text appears; graphics are hidden. Although text formatting remains intact, paragraph spacing and indents follow outline style. (If you want to suppress text formatting so that it's easier to focus on the outline's content, clear Show Text Formatting on the Outlining tab.)

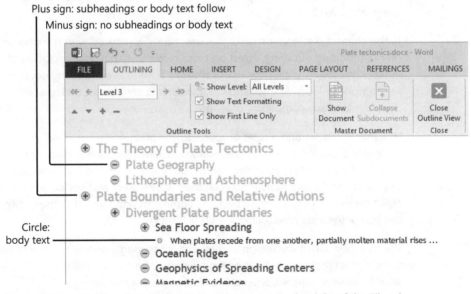

Figure 10-1 In Outline view, the Outlining tab appears to the right of the File tab.

The outline feature uses heading styles to determine outline levels. In the style sets that are included with Word 2013, these heading styles are called Heading 1, Heading 2, Heading 3, and so on. (Any paragraph or paragraph style can be modified so that it appears in the outline hierarchy. You do that in the Paragraph dialog box, where you'll find Outline Level under General on the Indents And Spacing tab.) For more information about paragraph styles, see "Formatting paragraphs" in Chapter 9.

Tools on the Outlining tab make it easy to promote, demote, and view different outline levels:

- The Outline Level box (shown as Level 3 in Figure 10-1) sets the heading level for the current selection.

- The left and right arrows on either side of the Outline Level box promote or demote the selection by one level. For example, if the current selection is formatted as Heading 2, clicking the right arrow demotes it to Heading 3.

- The double left arrow promotes the selection to a top-level heading, Heading 1.

- The double right arrow demotes the selection to body text, applying the Normal style.

- The Move Up and Move Down arrows move the selection within the outline. (This tool moves up or down one entry with each click. To move a selection a greater distance, you'll find it easier to drag an outline marker—the circle at the left end of each heading or paragraph. Doing so moves all subheadings and body text as well as the selected heading.)

- The Expand (plus sign) tool expands the selection to show its subheadings or body text.

- The Collapse (minus sign) tool hides subheadings or body text below the selected heading.

- Show Level collapses and/or expands all headings to show the level you select and all higher-level headings.

When you're typing in Outline view, you can use the usual keyboard shortcuts for applying styles (including Ctrl+Alt+1 for Heading 1 and Ctrl+Shift+N for Normal), but you might find it easier to use Tab and Shift+Tab to set heading levels. Indeed, most of the work you do through the Outlining tab can be performed with keyboard shortcuts, which are listed in Table 10-1.

Chapter 10

TABLE 10-1 Keyboard shortcuts for working with outlines

Action	Keyboard shortcut
Switch to Outline view	Ctrl+Alt+O
Show Level 1 headings only	Alt+Shift+1
Show headings to Level 2	Alt+Shift+2
Show headings to Level 3	Alt+Shift+3
Show headings to Level 4	Alt+Shift+4
Show headings to Level 5	Alt+Shift+5
Show headings to Level 6	Alt+Shift+6
Show headings to Level 7	Alt+Shift+7
Show headings to Level 8	Alt+Shift+8
Show headings to Level 9	Alt+Shift+9
Promote by one level	Shift+Tab or Alt+Shift+Left Arrow
Demote by one level	Tab or Alt+Shift+Right Arrow
Expand a collapsed outline	Alt+Shift+Plus Sign
Collapse an expanded outline	Alt+Shift+Minus Sign
Move up	Alt+Shift+Up Arrow
Move down	Alt+Shift+Down Arrow

Navigating in long documents

Outline view also provides a method for jumping directly to a particular part of a document. When you exit Outline view and return to Print Layout view, you'll find that the insertion point or selection remains in the same heading and that the heading is near the top of the screen.

While that's convenient if you happen to be working in Outline view, there's no reason to switch to Outline view to jump to a heading. A much better tool for that purpose is the Navigation pane. (For details, see "Navigating within a document" in Chapter 9.)

Notice that the Navigation pane has many of the capabilities of Outline view. It shows a hierarchically organized outline of your document headings. You can selectively expand and collapse the hierarchy by clicking the triangle next to a heading name. And, just as you can in Outline view, you can drag headings up or down within the Navigation pane to reorganize your document; all subheadings and body text move with the heading you move.

Other outlining features are exposed when you right-click a heading in the Navigation pane, as shown here.

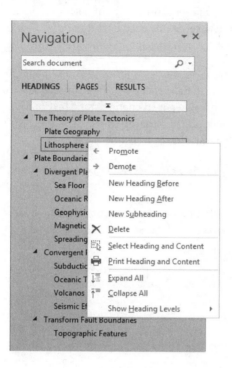

Chapter 10

INSIDE OUT Collapse headings in Print Layout view and Read Mode

When you point to or tap a heading in a document, a small triangle appears at its left end. Click that triangle to collapse the text below the heading, including all subheadings. This feature, which is new in Word 2013, allows you to hide the text below a heading, similar to Outline view, allowing the reader to focus on the remaining text. When you collapse a heading this way, the collapsed text is also hidden when you print the document. Click the triangle again to expand the text and subheadings.

Normally, after you close and reopen a document with headings collapsed in this way, all headings are expanded. If you want headings to remain collapsed each time you open the document, place the insertion point in a heading. Then open the Paragraph dialog box (on the Home tab, click the dialog box launcher in the lower-right corner of the Paragraph group) and select Collapsed By Default.

Formatting columns and sections

Word uses *sections* to enable the independent formatting of parts of a document that have a different page layout. A section break separates each part that has different page margins, different orientation, a different column layout, or even different headers and footers.

Within a section, you can have different headers and footers for odd pages, even pages, and the first page of a section. And those headers can include variable text, such as the text of the most recent heading. But if you want to change static text or the layout of the header or footer—or if you want a first-page header to appear, say, on the first page of a new chapter in your document—you must insert a section break.

For more information about headers and footers, see "Adding headers, footers, and page numbers" in Chapter 9.

To insert a section break, place the insertion point where you want the break to go, click the Page Layout tab, and click Breaks (in the Page Setup group), as shown in Figure 10-2.

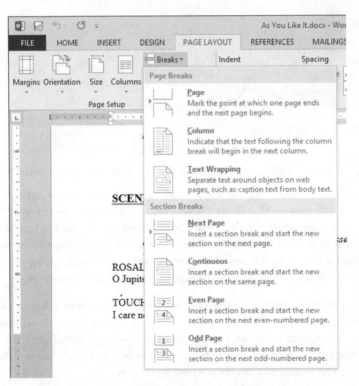

Figure 10-2 Any of the last four options on the Breaks menu inserts a section break.

You can choose a continuous break (one that begins the new section immediately below the break without beginning a new page) or a break that starts the new section on a new page. If you want to start on a new page, you must choose whether you want to begin on the next page (regardless of whether it's odd or even), the next even page, or the next odd page. The last two options, which are often used in book layouts (for example, in this book each chapter begins on an odd-numbered page), insert an extra blank page if necessary.

With section breaks in place, page layout changes you make with options in the Page Setup group on the Page Layout tab apply by default to the current section only (the one that contains the insertion point or selection). To change the margins, orientation, paper size, or column layout for more than one section, select all or parts of the sections you want to format before you apply the format. Alternatively, click the dialog box launcher in the Page Setup group. At the bottom of each tab in the Page Setup dialog box, you'll see options similar to the ones shown here that let you specify the scope of your formatting change. You'll find options like these on the Page Border tab of the Borders And Shading dialog box as well.

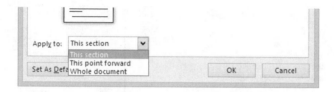

When you insert a section break, thereby creating a new section, both sections inherit the page layout settings of the section you split. Much as paragraph formatting is associated with the paragraph mark at the paragraph's end, section formatting is associated with the section mark at the end of a section. Understanding that little factoid makes it easier to anticipate what happens if you delete a section mark—the new, combined section uses the settings of what was its second section.

INSIDE OUT   Copy section formatting

Understand too that you can copy a section mark; when you paste it elsewhere, the section that it completes has the same page layout settings as the section from which it was copied.

Creating a multicolumn layout

Word can format text in columns, which flow text in such a way that when the bottom of a column is reached, the text continues at the top of the next column, similar to the way newspapers (remember those?) look. Aside from its visual appeal, a multicolumn layout has an important practical benefit: shorter line lengths are easier to read, particularly in smaller point sizes.

To format your document so that it has more than one column, click the Page Layout tab, click Columns (in the Page Setup group), and select a number of columns.

It's a rare document that is formatted using a multicolumn layout throughout, however. A more common scenario is to have a heading or picture that spans the full page width, with multiple columns below. Figure 10-3 shows an example.

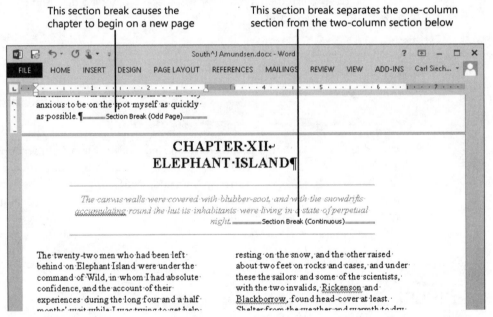

Figure 10-3 It's easier to work with sections and columns when formatting symbols are displayed.

To set up a document like this, follow these steps:

1. If formatting symbols are not displayed, press Ctrl+* or click Show/Hide ¶ on the Home tab.

2. Place the insertion point where you want the multicolumn layout to begin, and then click Page Layout, Breaks, Continuous to insert a section break.

3. Place the insertion point where you want the multicolumn layout to end, and then insert another section break.

4. Click somewhere between the two section marks, and then click Page Layout, Columns. If the basic options on the Columns menu don't suit you, click More Columns to display the Columns dialog box.

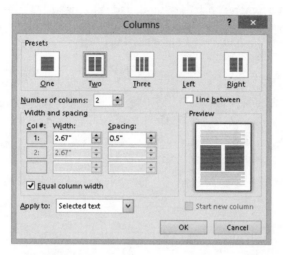

Here you can format as many columns as will fit on the page (the minimum column width is 0.5 inch), and you can set the amount of space between each one. By clearing Equal Column Width, you can set the column width and the spacing independently for each column.

In a multicolumn layout, you can insert a manual column break by choosing Column on the Breaks menu (shown earlier in Figure 10-2) or by using its keyboard shortcut, Ctrl+Shift+Enter.

INSIDE OUT   Balance columns on the last page

Ordinarily, on the last page of a multicolumn layout (or the last page of a multicolumn section followed by a section break that starts a new page), text tends to end up on the left side of the page. That's because Word flows text in the usual way: it doesn't begin a new column until the current column is filled all the way to the bottom.

Your document will look more professional if the last page flows text in all columns to an equal depth. Forcing that to happen is easy: insert a continuous section break at the end of the multicolumn text. (If you already have a new-page section break, as shown in Figure 10-3, this means you'll end up with two consecutive section breaks.)

Working with tables

Tables, of course, are ideal for tabular data—text or numbers in a gridlike layout of rows and columns, such as the list of keyboard shortcuts shown earlier in Table 10-1. But resourceful Word users find many other uses for tables. For example, when you want to have headings in the left column that align with text in the right column, use a table. Such a layout is used in documents such as resumes and in forms such as the fax cover sheet created by the Professional design template. Figure 10-4 shows this template, which is available from Office.com. (To find it, click File, New, Fax.)

Figure 10-4 This template uses a table to align text. The gridlines in the table do not print.

Creating a table

Word provides several ways to add a table to your document:

- **Insert Table**   Using either a quick-entry gallery or a dialog box, you can insert an empty grid into your document.

- **Draw Table**   You can use a mouse or a stylus to sketch out a table layout, which Word converts to carefully aligned columns and rows.

- **Convert Text To Table**   If you have existing document text with some sort of separator between column data (a paragraph mark or a tab, space, or other character), Word can create a table and place the text in table cells.

- **Quick Tables**   Word includes a gallery of predesigned tables that you can insert. You can add your own tables to the gallery.

Using the Insert Table command

To add a table to a document, place the insertion point where you want the table to go, and then on the Insert tab, click Table. Now you're faced with a choice. If your table won't exceed 10 columns in width or 8 rows, point to the grid that appears, as shown here.

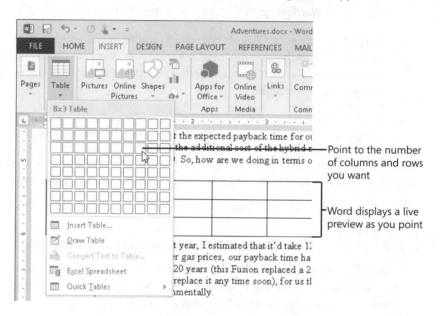

Point to the number of columns and rows you want

Word displays a live preview as you point

You can always add more columns or rows later (see "Adding and removing rows and columns" later in this chapter), but if you want to start out with more (up to 63 columns and 32,767 rows) or want to set other table options, click Insert Table on the menu to open the dialog box shown next.

Chapter 10

Under AutoFit Behavior, you have three options for controlling column width:

- **Fixed Column Width** Sets each column to the width you specify. If you leave it set to Auto, Word evenly divides the space between the left and right page margins by the number of columns. If you subsequently add or remove columns and the width is set to Auto, Word readjusts the column widths to fit the space.

- **AutoFit To Contents** Adjusts the column widths as you enter information to get the best fit for each column—"best" meaning that Word adjusts each column to accommodate each row's contents in the fewest number of lines without going beyond the page margins.

- **AutoFit To Window** Evenly divides the space between margins by the number of columns—just like choosing the first option with the width set to Auto.

You can select an AutoFit option any time after you insert a table by clicking in the table and then clicking AutoFit in the Cell Size group on the Layout tab under Table Tools.

INSIDE OUT Change the default number of columns and rows

If you often create tables with the same number of columns or rows, you can change the default values in the Insert Table dialog box. Specify the values, and then select Remember Dimensions For New Tables before you click OK.

Drawing a table

This method is the best one for drawing complex tables, such as tables with a cell that spans several columns or rows, or tables that have a different number of cells in each row. To draw a table, on the Insert tab click Table, Draw Table. The mouse pointer becomes a pencil. Drag diagonally to draw a rectangle that defines the outer boundaries of the table. Then draw horizontal and vertical lines within that rectangle to create rows, columns, and cells. You can also draw diagonal lines within a cell, as shown here.

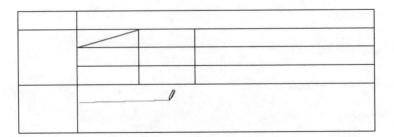

To exit drawing mode, click anywhere (in a table cell or outside the table) and begin typing, or simply press Esc. To resume drawing, click in the table, click the Layout tab under Table Tools, and click Draw Table in the Draw group.

To erase a line, click Eraser (on the Layout tab under Table Tools), and then click the line you want to erase.

Using tools in the Borders group on the Design tab, you can specify the style, weight, and color of lines you draw. You can make your selections before you draw or, to change an existing line, make your selections, click the Border Painter tool (new in Word 2013), and then click the line.

Converting text to a table

Word can take text that's in a standard data format and place it in a table. Begin by entering the data, inserting a separator character after each data item (that is, each item you want to go into a table cell), and pressing Enter each time you want to start a new table row. You can use any character as a separator, but commas, spaces, or tabs are the most commonly used. The only limitation is that the separator character can't be part of the data you want to include in the table.

With your data in place, select the text, and then click Insert, Table, Convert Text To Table. In the dialog box that appears (shown in Figure 10-5), Word shows its best guess at which separator character is in use and how many columns and rows will appear in the table. You can, of course, override those guesses.

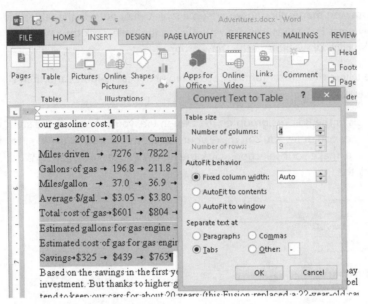

Figure 10-5 Because formatting characters are displayed here, you can see that we used tabs as the separator character.

TROUBLESHOOTING

Comma-separated values files don't convert properly when imported into a Word table

A widely used data interchange format is a comma-separated values file, or CSV file. A CSV file is a plain-text file that uses a comma to separate each item in a row of data and a paragraph mark at the end of each row. So far, perfect for conversion.

Problems arise when a data item that's intended to go in a single cell contains a comma. Programs that create CSV files deal with this situation by enclosing the item in quotation marks. Unfortunately, Word doesn't recognize this convention, so it ends up splitting data at every comma (and erroneously preserving the quotation marks, to boot).

You can work around this problem in either of two ways. If possible, use a different separator character in your data file; many programs can produce a tab-separated values file as an alternative to CSV. If that's not possible, open the file in Excel, which properly handles quotation marks. You can then use Excel to save the file as a tab-delimited file, or simply copy the data from Excel and paste it into your Word document.

Using Quick Tables

Word includes a gallery of tables that are already formatted and even filled with data. These include several calendar layouts as well as various data tables. Although the data is unlikely to be useful to you, Quick Tables provide handy templates that take care of the layout and formatting tasks, leaving you only the job of filling in the data. To view the gallery and insert a Quick Table, on the Insert tab click Table, Quick Tables.

INSIDE OUT   Add your own tables to the Quick Tables gallery

After you lay out and format a table to perfection, you might want to reuse it (albeit with different data) elsewhere. To add it to the Quick Tables gallery, select the table and then click Insert, Table, Quick Tables. At the bottom of the gallery, click Save Selection To Quick Tables Gallery. In the dialog box that appears, you can give this new building block a name and modify other details—or you can simply click OK.

Working with table data

You enter and edit data within a table in much the same way as you do elsewhere in a document. A table cell can contain any amount of text. It can also include pictures and graphics; you can even insert another table within a table cell.

Just as it does in normal text, pressing Enter in a table cell inserts a paragraph mark. To move to another cell, press Tab or Shift+Tab. Pressing Tab moves to the next cell to the right or, at the end of a row, to the first cell in the next row. Shift+Tab moves in the opposite direction. If you press Tab in the table's last cell (the one in the lower-right corner), Word appends a new row that's formatted the same as the current last row. Table 10-2 shows other keyboard shortcuts you can use for moving within a table.

TABLE 10-2 Keyboard shortcuts for moving in tables

Action	Keyboard shortcut
To next or previous cell	Tab or Shift+Tab
To first or last cell in a row	Alt+Home or Alt+End
To first or last cell in a column	Alt+Page Up or Alt+Page Down
To previous or next row	Up Arrow or Down Arrow
Move current row up or down by one row	Alt+Shift+Up Arrow or Alt+Shift+Down Arrow

Chapter 10

> **Note**
>
> To insert a tab character in a table cell, press Ctrl+Tab.

Selecting table data

To select text within a cell, you use the usual Office and Word techniques. (See "Entering, selecting, and deleting text" in Chapter 4, as well as "Entering, editing, and formatting text" and "Making your documents look good" in Chapter 9, "Inside Word 2013.")

To select one or more table cells, you can use tools on the Layout tab under Table Tools. Click Select in the Table group, and then you can choose to select the current cell, column, or row—or the entire table. To select the entire table, you can also use the Alt+Shift+5 keyboard shortcut. (You must use the 5 on the numeric keypad.)

You can also use the mouse to select a cell (click in the cell's left margin), a row (click to the left of a row), or a column (click at the top of a column). You'll know you're in the right place when the mouse pointer changes to an arrow (a small black arrow to select a cell or column, or a white arrow for a row). Drag to extend the selection to include multiple cells, rows, or columns. To select the entire table, point to the upper-left corner of the table and click when the mouse pointer appears as a four-headed arrow.

Sorting table data

You can sort rows of data according to the content of the cells in a column. You can, in fact, perform a multilevel sort on up to three columns. For example, if you have a directory of names and addresses, you might want to organize the list alphabetically by name within each town. To do that, you sort on postal code, then by last name, and then by first name.

To sort data in a table, click in the table. (Be sure the insertion point is in the table and that nothing is selected.) Then click the Layout tab (under Table Tools) and click Sort in the Data group. The Sort dialog box appears, as shown in Figure 10-6.

If the first row of your table contains descriptive titles instead of data, select Header Row. Then choose the column (or columns) by which you want to sort. Indicate the type of data in each column (text, numbers, or dates) and the sort order to use.

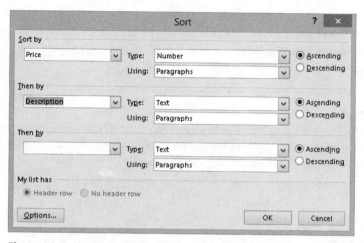

Figure 10-6 The settings shown here sort all items by price, from lowest to highest, and within each price group alphabetize items by description.

Using formulas in tables

Within a Word table cell you can use a small subset of Excel functions for performing numeric calculations. Word identifies cells in a table in the same way that Excel does: a letter/number combination that specifies the column and row, beginning with cell A1 in the upper-left corner of the table.

To enter a formula at the insertion point, on the Layout tab (under Table Tools), click Formula in the Data group. The Formula dialog box appears, as shown in Figure 10-7.

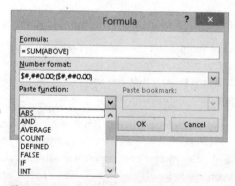

Figure 10-7 Click Paste Function to see the full list of available functions.

Just as you do when entering a formula in Excel, begin your entry in the Formula box with an equal sign. You can then use cell and range references, constants, mathematical operators, and functions from the Paste Function list to complete the formula. For more information, see "Using formulas and functions" in Chapter 12, "Inside Excel 2013."

Chapter 10

Word has four range names that you won't find in Excel: ABOVE, BELOW, LEFT, and RIGHT. With these ranges, you can create a formula that includes all the cells in the direction you specify. For example, to display the total of the values in a column, in a row at the bottom of the column you would insert the formula =SUM(ABOVE).

> **Note**
>
> Unlike formulas in Excel, formulas in a Word table don't recalculate automatically when you change data in the table. To update the formula results, include all formulas in the selection and press F9, the keyboard shortcut for updating fields.

INSIDE OUT Enter formulas without the Formula dialog box

It requires several clicks to get to the Formula dialog box, so you might prefer an easier way to enter a formula, which is actually a Word field. Press Ctrl+F9 to insert a new field, and then type the formula (being sure to include the equal sign) between the braces that identify the field. With the field included in the selection, press Alt+F9 to display the field result. For more information about fields, see "Using fields to automate documents" in Chapter 11, "Word 2013 inside out."

INSIDE OUT Use an Excel table for more demanding calculations

As noted, the formula capabilities of Word don't compare favorably with those of Excel. If you need text functions, date calculations, or more advanced mathematical calculations, you need to use Excel. That doesn't mean that you can't include the data and the resulting calculations in your Word document, however.

You insert an Excel worksheet into your document in much the same way you insert a table: on the Insert tab, click Table, Excel Spreadsheet. While you work in the Excel spreadsheet, you have the full capabilities of that program. In fact, the ribbon changes to show the same tabs and tools you see in Excel.

To include more or fewer Excel columns and rows in your Word document, drag the borders of the Excel object. When you click outside the worksheet, the Excel interface (such as row and column headings) disappears, and the Word ribbon returns. Double-click in the worksheet to resume editing in Excel.

Formatting a table

The table you get when you use the Insert Table or Convert Text To Table command is not much to look at: a simple grid of thin black lines, with text aligned at the top and left of each cell. With a few simple commands on the Design and Layout tabs under Table Tools (see Figure 10-8), you can quickly spruce up the table's appearance.

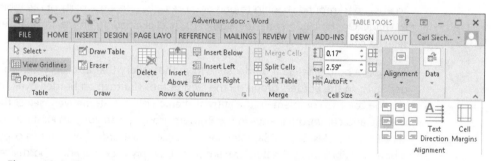

Figure 10-8 These tabs appear under Table Tools whenever the insertion point or selection is in a table.

Aligning text

When a cell is wider or taller than its contents, where should the text go within that space? You'll probably want ordinary text to be left and top aligned, but you might want to set column headings so that they're centered and bottom aligned. You might want a column of numbers to be right aligned.

To get any of these permutations (or others), select the cells you want to align. Then, in the Alignment group on the Layout tab (see Figure 10-8), select one of the nine options (every combination of left, center, and right; and top, middle, and bottom).

Note that you can use paragraph formatting and styles within a table cell, which allows you to set other alignment options, such as paragraph indents, hanging indents, bullet lists, and so on.

Chapter 10

Rotating text

To rotate text in the selected cells 90 degrees in either direction, click Text Direction (in the Alignment group on the Layout tab).

Rotating text to a nonperpendicular angle is not so easy. You can select the text to rotate (but not the entire cell), convert it to WordArt (click Insert, WordArt), and then rotate the WordArt object. (For details, see "Applying text effects with WordArt" and "Resizing and rotating graphics and pictures," both in Chapter 5, "Working with graphics and pictures.") Alternatively, insert an Excel worksheet in your document, and use Excel to rotate the text in selected cells to any angle.

Adding borders and shading

To apply background shading to one or more cells, select the parts of the table you want to shade. On the Design tab (see Figure 10-8), click Shading (in the Table Styles group) and select a color.

To apply a border, select a border style from the gallery that appears when you click Border Styles in the Borders group on the Design tab. The themed border styles in the gallery change color to complement the current theme colors. (Alternatively, select the line type, weight, and color from menus in the Borders group. Or, to copy an existing border style, click Border Styles, Border Sampler and then click the border you want to copy.) Selecting a border style enables the Border Painter tool; simply click individual border segments in the table to apply the selected style. As an alternative to the Border Painter tool, click the arrow below Borders to display a menu of locations to which you can apply the border. Your menu choice becomes the default, so you can apply the same border (for example, a border around the outside of the selection) to another selection simply by clicking Borders without opening its menu.

Applying styles

The quickest way to dress up your table is to use a style. On the Design tab (see Figure 10-8), click the More button by the Table Styles gallery to see more than 100 colorful table styles from which you can choose.

Check boxes in the Table Style Options group on the Design tab determine which parts of a style are applied:

- Select Header Row if the first row of your table has column titles. Similarly, select First Column if the first column contains row titles.

- Select Total Row if you want a specially formatted row at the bottom of the table—one that is typically used for numeric totals or summary data. Last Column serves a similar purpose for the rightmost column.

- Select Banded Rows or Banded Columns if you want to use bands of alternating colors to make your table easier to read.

To customize the table style currently in use, open the Table Styles gallery and click Modify Table Style. In the Modify Style dialog box, shown next, you can change any component of the style—fonts, borders, shading, alignment, banding, and so on—for the entire table or independently for each part of the style (such as the header row or last column).

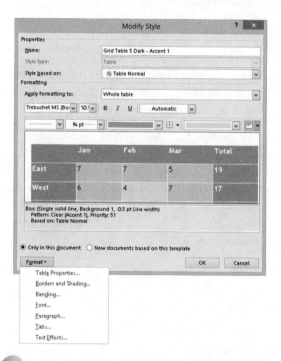

For more information about customizing styles, see "Creating a new style" in Chapter 9.

Changing the table layout

Not surprisingly, you'll find tools for modifying a table's layout—the number of rows and columns—on the Layout tab under Table Tools. See Figure 10-8.

Adjusting column widths and row heights

Using options in the Cell Size group on the Layout tab, you can set the height of the selected rows and the width of the selected columns. You might find it easier to adjust the size directly. Position the mouse pointer on a table gridline, where it becomes a two-headed arrow around a separation line. At that point, you can drag to resize the row or column.

Chapter 10

INSIDE OUT   Resize a single column

When you drag the border between columns to the left, the column on the left side of the border gets narrower and the column on the right gets wider; the opposite happens when you drag to the right. To resize only the column on the left without affecting the column on the right, hold Shift as you drag.

Setting column widths using these methods specifies a precise dimension for each column. To set widths automatically, choose one of the AutoFit options (for details, see "Using the Insert Table command" earlier in this chapter). Another option is to click Distribute Columns, which divides the space evenly among the selected columns.

For additional control over column widths, click the arrow in the lower-right corner of the Cell Size group to open the Table Properties dialog box, shown in Figure 10-9. On the Column tab, you can specify the width for each column as an absolute dimension or a percentage of the total. On the Row tab, you can set the row height to an exact dimension, or you can select At Least, which allows the row to grow to accommodate its content.

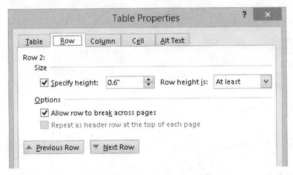

Figure 10-9 You can cycle through your entire table by clicking Previous Row and Next Row (or comparable buttons on the Column tab).

INSIDE OUT   Resize columns and rows using the ruler

Another way to adjust widths and heights is by dragging the column and row separators on the ruler. But here's a neat trick: Hold down Alt as you drag, and Word shows precise measurements of each column or row in the ruler.

Adding and removing rows and columns

Tools for adding or removing rows or columns are in the Rows & Columns group on the Layout tab. You'll find similar options on the menu that appears when you right-click in a table. To insert a single row or column with one click, point to the left edge of a row divider or top edge of a column divider; an add icon appears, as shown next.

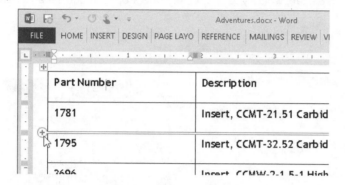

If you click Delete, Delete Cells, a dialog box appears, as shown here. You must tell Word whether to move the remaining cells in the row to the left, or to move the remaining cells in the column up.

Merging and splitting table cells

In its Merge group, the Layout tab includes a tool for merging selected cells into a single cell and another tool for splitting selected cells into the number of columns and rows that you specify.

When you merge two or more cells into one, the content of all the original cells is preserved in the new, single cell. Text that was once separated into individual cells is now placed in separate paragraphs in a single cell.

As an alternative to the Merge Cells and Split Cells tools, you can perform these tasks with the Eraser and Draw Table tools. Click Eraser and then click the border between two cells to merge them. Click Draw Table and draw a line in a cell to split it in two.

Positioning a table

In much the same way that a picture or other graphic can be positioned in the normal flow of text (in line) or placed on the page so that text wraps around it, you can specify text wrapping options for a table. To control a table's position on the page, on the Layout tab click Properties in the Table group. In the Table Properties dialog box, shown in Figure 10-10, click the Table tab, where you can set alignment options and set an indent from the left margin.

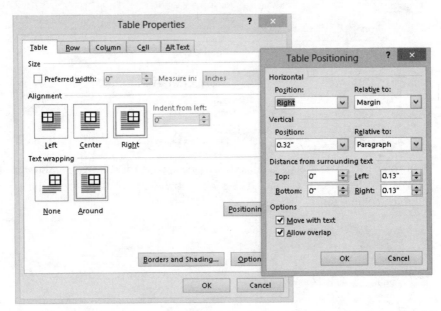

Figure 10-10 To flow text around the table, under Text Wrapping click Around, and then click Positioning to specify placement options.

As an alternative to the dialog box routine, point to the upper-left corner of the table. When the mouse pointer turns into a four-headed arrow, drag the table to the position you want. To adjust text wrapping options, you'll need to visit the Table Positioning dialog box.

Working with tables that span a page break

Two issues come into play when a table goes beyond the end of a page:

- Should rows be allowed to break across pages, or should the contents of each row be kept intact?

- Do you want to repeat one or more rows as column titles at the top of each page?

You'll find settings for both options on the Row tab of the Table Properties dialog box, shown earlier in Figure 10-9.

INSIDE OUT   Insert a paragraph at the top of a page

In a document that begins with a table, if you press Ctrl+Home to go to the beginning of the document and then begin typing, your text goes into the first cell, not in a new paragraph. Solving this problem requires creative use of Split Table, a tool in the Merge group on the Layout tab. As you might guess, that tool splits a table into two tables, with an empty paragraph separating them.

To insert an empty paragraph before the table, place the insertion point in the table's first row, and then click Split Table. Alternatively, you can use the keyboard shortcut for Split Table, Ctrl+Shift+Enter.

Deleting a table

If you select one or more cells in a table—or even the entire table—and press the Delete key, Word deletes the contents of the selected cells, but leaves the table grid intact. Depending on what you're trying to do, you might consider this to be a feature; after all, it makes it easy to clear the contents of a table or form so that you can reuse it.

If you're intent on removing the table as well as its contents, you have three options:

- On the Layout tab under Table Tools, click Delete (in the Rows & Columns group), Delete Table.

- Select all cells in the table and then cut the selection to the Clipboard. (Note that doing so replaces the current Clipboard content.)

- Extend the selection so that it includes the table and at least one character outside the table, and then press Delete.

Inserting references to other parts of a document

Cross-references are a common part of many document types, including legal documents (which often refer to other sections by paragraph number) and reference books (which sometimes include page number references to other sections of the book).

Cross-references update automatically when the document content changes. For example, if edits to your document change the page number on which a referenced heading falls, a reference like "see 'Summing It All Up' on page 47" gets the correct page number. And if you change the text of the heading, all references to it update as well. Similarly, if you use captions to number and identify figures or tables, the numbers update automatically when you add, remove, or reorder the numbered items.

Defining reference targets

You can insert references to a variety of document elements, as listed next. Notes in the following list explain how to ensure that Word recognizes each reference target as such.

- **Numbered Item** To use a numbered item as a target, apply a numbered list style. (For details, see "Working with bulleted and numbered lists" in Chapter 9.)

- **Heading** To refer to a heading, you must apply a heading style to the heading paragraph. (For details, see "Applying styles" in Chapter 9.)

- **Bookmark** A bookmark can serve as a browse target as well as a cross-reference target, making it useful for returning to a specific document location. To insert a bookmark, first place the insertion point where you want to place a bookmark, or select the text you want to use as a bookmark. Then click the Insert tab and click Bookmark (in the Links group). In the Bookmark dialog box, type a name for your bookmark; the name can contain letters, numbers, and underscore characters, but it can't contain spaces or other punctuation.

> ## Working with bookmarks
>
> To jump to a bookmark you've defined, press Ctrl+G to open the Go To tab in the Find And Replace dialog box, select Bookmark, select the bookmark name, and then click Go To.
>
> You can make your bookmarks visible. Click File, Options to open the Word Options dialog box. Click Advanced, and then, under Show Document Content, select Show Bookmarks. A bookmark set to a single point appears as an I-beam; bookmarked text appears between colored square brackets. The bookmark indicators are not included when you print a document.

- **Footnote** A footnote consists of a footnote reference (a superscript number or symbol in the document text) and a note at the bottom of a page; footnotes are typically used to include explanatory notes or bibliographic citations. To use a footnote as a cross-reference target, you must create it using the Insert Footnote tool, which you can find in the Footnotes group on the References tab.

- **Endnote** Endnotes are similar in form and function to footnotes, except the notes appear at the end of the document. To use an endnote as a cross-reference target, create it with the Insert Endnote tool, also in the Footnotes group on the References tab.

- **Equation**   To refer to a numbered equation, add a caption that includes a {SEQ Equation} field code, as explained in the following section.

- **Figure**   To refer to a numbered figure, add a caption that includes a {SEQ Figure} field code, as explained in the following section.

- **Table**   To refer to a numbered table, add a caption that includes a {SEQ Table} field code, as explained in the following section.

Creating captions for equations, figures, and tables

In this book, figures and tables are identified by a sequential number and caption. This common arrangement is easy to create in Word. To create a caption, follow these steps:

1. Select the item for which you want a caption—an equation created with Insert Equation, a picture or graphic, or a table. (In fact, you can apply a caption to *anything* in a document; there's nothing magical about equations, figures, and tables. It's just that Word has predefined caption handling for these common document elements.)

2. On the References tab, click Insert Caption (in the Captions group). The Caption dialog box appears.

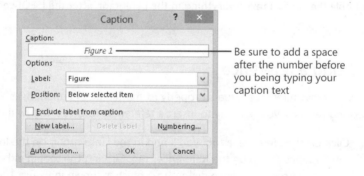

Be sure to add a space after the number before you being typing your caption text

3. Under Options, select the label and position you want to use. If you're not satisfied with the label options, click New Label and define your own.

4. In the Caption box, append your caption text to the label and number that appears.

INSIDE OUT Use field codes to insert captions

The Insert Caption tool provides a convenient way to insert a caption, but you might find it easier to type captions directly into your document. The cross-reference feature in Word (described in the next section) relies on the presence of a field code to identify equations, figures, and tables. Specifically, any paragraph that includes a {SEQ Figure} field code is assumed to be a figure caption, which can serve as a cross-reference target. Equations and tables are identified by {SEQ Equation} and {SEQ Table} codes, respectively.

To insert a field code at the insertion point, press Ctrl+F9. Then type the field code text between the braces that appear. Before you finish your document, you need to press Alt+F9 to display the field code results instead of the field codes, and you'll need to press F9 to update the fields. Although these extra steps might seem burdensome, typists who don't like to interrupt their typing by reaching for the mouse might find this method to be easier in the long run, especially if tasked with inserting many captions. For more information about working with field codes, see "Using fields to automate documents" in Chapter 11.

As you'll see in the next section, a reference to one of these items can include the entire caption (the entire paragraph that contains the {SEQ} field code), only the label and number (everything in the paragraph before the {SEQ} code and the field code result), or only the caption text (everything in the paragraph after the {SEQ} code).

Inserting a reference

With your cross-reference targets properly formatted and captioned, as described in the preceding sections, you're ready to insert a reference. To do so, follow these steps:

1. Click Cross-Reference, a tool you'll find in the Links group on the Insert tab *and* in the Captions group on the References tab. Clicking the tool in either ribbon location opens the Cross-Reference dialog box, which is shown in Figure 10-11.

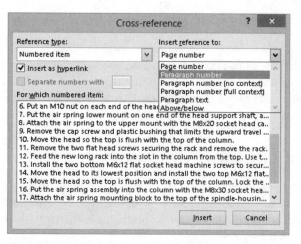

Figure 10-11 The bottom of the dialog box is populated with a list of the document's headings, bookmarks, figures, or other reference targets, based on your selection under Reference Type.

2. Select a Reference Type (Numbered Item, Heading, Bookmark, Footnote, Endnote, Equation, Figure, or Table). When you make a selection here, Word displays the available cross-reference targets in the main part of the dialog box and includes appropriate options under Insert Reference To.

3. Select a cross-reference target.

4. Select an option under Insert Reference To.

   Some reference types include references to two types of numbers: No Context and Full Context. This distinction applies to multilevel lists. Full Context includes the complete path to the referenced item, such as 2.a.ii or 507(a)(4), whereas No Context includes only the number of the nested item—using the preceding examples, ii or (4).

   The Above/Below option inserts only the word *above* or *below* depending on the position of the target relative to the inserted reference. In many cases the reference and its target are separated by several pages, making "above" and "below" less helpful to a reader. A more elegant solution is to select Page Number under Insert Reference To and also select Include Above/Below (not visible in Figure 10-11). This way, Word inserts "above" or "below," as appropriate, if the reference and target are on the same page; if they're on different pages, Word instead inserts "on page *xx*," where *xx* is the page number.

5. If you want the cross-reference to be a hyperlink to the target, select Insert As Hyperlink. When you create a cross-reference this way, clicking the cross-reference jumps to the target. This works in Word and, if you save the document as a webpage,

Chapter 10

in a web browser. (For other ways to insert hyperlinks, see "Entering hyperlinks" in Chapter 4.)

6. Click Insert. The dialog box remains open, allowing you to move the insertion point in the document and insert another cross-reference without repeating the first several steps of this procedure. Click Close when you're through inserting cross-references.

Creating tables of contents and indexes

A common feature of long documents is a table of contents, which typically lists all the headings in the document in the order in which they appear, along with the page number each appears on. Bookending many long documents is an index, which lists topics in alphabetical order, with page numbers.

Inserting a table of contents

To insert a table of contents in a document, place the insertion point where you want it to go. Then click the References tab and click Table Of Contents. The small gallery that appears has, by default, two viable options (Automatic Table 1 and Automatic Table 2) and one (Manual Table) that's more trouble than it's worth. Automatic Table 1 and Automatic Table 2 are identical except for the title ("Contents" versus "Table of Contents"), which is ordinary text that you can easily edit to your liking. Select one of these options, and Word inserts a table similar to the one shown in Figure 10-12. The built-in automatic options include heading levels 1 through 3 in the table of contents.

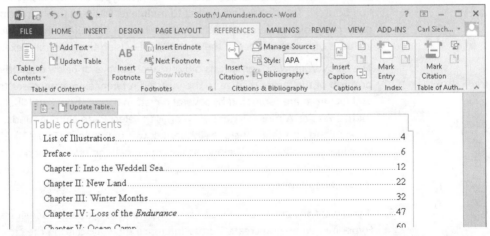

Figure 10-12 When you click inside the table of contents, a frame appears around the table, and a small toolbar appears at the top.

The table of contents doesn't update automatically as you make changes to your document. To make it reflect the current document content, click Update Table (in the toolbar shown in Figure 10-12 or in the Table Of Contents group on the References tab). You're then given a choice of updating page numbers only (this option is faster, but it doesn't take into account headings that have been added, removed, moved, or edited) or rebuilding the table from scratch.

If this predefined table of contents doesn't suit your fancy, define your own parameters. Below the Table Of Contents gallery, click Custom Table Of Contents, which opens the Table Of Contents dialog box, shown in Figure 10-13.

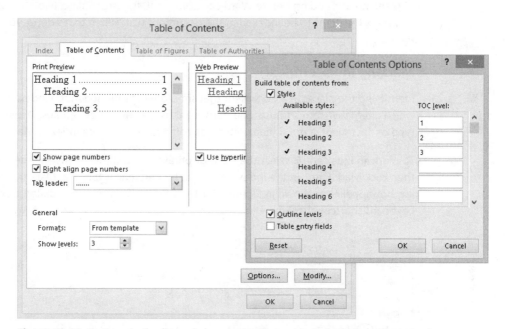

Figure 10-13 Options in the Formats box under General include designs that complement certain style sets.

Here you can specify how many heading levels to include, among other options. To include paragraphs that use styles other than the built-in Heading 1, Heading 2, and so on, click Options. In the Table Of Contents Options dialog box, you can specify each style you want to include and which contents level to assign it.

As shown in Figure 10-13, Word builds a table of contents using up to three different input types: styles (that is, each paragraph that has a particular style applied), outline levels (paragraphs that have an outline level assigned that's within the Show Levels range in the Table Of Contents dialog box), and table entry fields.

These last two options provide alternative ways to include in the table of contents items that wouldn't otherwise be included. To include a paragraph, you can click Add Text (in the Table Of Contents group on the References tab) and select a level; doing so sets an outline level for that paragraph without affecting the underlying style. Alternatively, you can use {TC} field codes to mark table of contents entries, although this method is more complex.

Preparing and inserting an index

Unlike a table of contents, which practically creates itself as long as you have consistently applied styles in your document, creating an index—especially a good index—requires a lot of planning and coding before Word can compile it. It's essentially a two-step process: First you mark the items to be indexed in the document text. When that's done, you generate the index.

Marking index entries

Identifying the places in a document that should be mentioned in the index, figuring out which alternative terms to use, and marking those terms can be tedious. Depending on the type of document, a good index often has half a dozen or more index entries on each page.

To mark an index entry, select the word or phrase you want to use as an index term, and then click Mark Entry, in the Index group on the References tab. The Mark Index Entry dialog box appears, as shown in Figure 10-14. (You can also display this dialog box by using its keyboard shortcut, Alt+Shift+X.)

Figure 10-14 Clicking Mark All marks all occurrences of the selected word or phrase in the document.

When you click Mark or Mark All to mark an index entry, Word inserts an {XE} field code. Because this field code is normally hidden, Word turns on the display of hidden text, allowing you to see and edit the field codes directly. Click Show/Hide ¶ (in the Paragraph group on the Home tab) or press Ctrl+* after you've seen enough.

INSIDE OUT   Create multilevel indexes

You might notice in the {XE} field codes that Word inserts that the main entry is separated from the subentry by a colon. For example, the code generated by the text shown in Figure 10-14 looks like this: { XE "tern:white-rumped" }

You can use colons to create multilevel indexes—up to seven levels deep, in fact. You can enter text for additional levels in the field code, of course. But you can also enter it in the Mark Index Entry dialog box, even though it has spaces only for the first two levels. The trick is simple: In either the Main Entry or Subentry box, insert the text for each level, using a colon to separate them. For example, you could type **tern:white-rumped:habitat and range** to add a third level.

Generating the index

After the hard work of marking entries is out of the way, the remaining task is easy. Place the insertion point where you want the index to go, and then on the References tab, click Insert Index (in the Index group). A dialog box like the one shown in Figure 10-15 appears.

Your options in the Index dialog box are few. You can choose between Indented (each index entry starts on a new line, indented appropriately to indicate the level) or Run-In (subentries run together in paragraph style) types, and you can specify the number of columns in the page layout.

The alluring AutoMark button deserves some explanation. This feature uses a separate document (called an AutoMark file or, more generically, a concordance file) that contains the terms you want to mark in the document. The AutoMark file is a Word document that contains a two-column table. The left column contains each term you want to search for in the document ("Adelie," for example) and the right column contains the index entry you want to make at each occurrence of the search term (such as "penguin:Adelie"). Invoking AutoMark searches the current document for all occurrences of the terms and inserts the corresponding index entries. While this concept sounds tempting, in practice it generally doesn't produce a useful index.

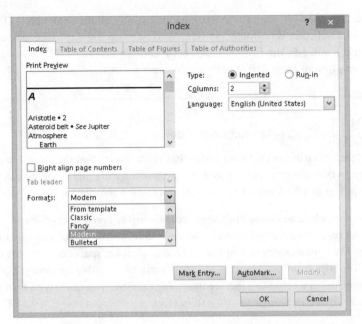

Figure 10-15 You can pick up styles and layout from the current template or use one of the built-in style sets. A sample index in the Print Preview box shows you what to expect.

If you make edits to your document after inserting an index, you need to update the index. To do that, click in the index and then click Update Index (in the Index group on the References tab). Easier yet, click in the index and press F9, the keyboard shortcut to update fields; the index itself is created by an {INDEX} field.

Using review comments in a document

A comment added to a document provides a way to offer an explanatory note or a suggestion, or to pose a question to the author. A time-honored way to add comments to a document author is to write notes in the margin. Word includes a feature that emulates this method: by default, a comment appears in the document's right margin.

In its 2013 iteration, Word adds several enhancements to the comments feature: a new look with pictures, full names, and a time stamp; an uncluttered view; a cleaner way to respond to comments; and a way to mark comments as done.

INSIDE OUT   Make changes directly in the document

Comments are great for making suggestions, asking questions, or explaining an edit. But when you want to make corrections to a document, don't use comments; transcribing those comments into the document creates more work later. Instead, turn on change tracking and make changes directly in the document. For details, see "Tracking and highlighting changes made to a document" later in this chapter.

Inserting a comment

To insert a comment, begin by selecting the text you want to highlight or place the insertion point at the item you're commenting on. Then click the Review tab and click New Comment; alternatively, press the command's keyboard shortcut, Ctrl+Alt+M. As shown in Figure 10-16, a panel appears in the right margin. Type your comment in the panel.

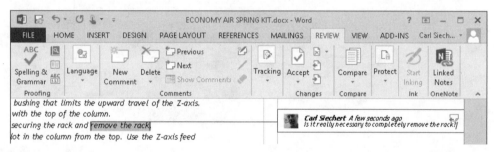

Figure 10-16 Word inserts the commenter's name and a time stamp at the beginning of the comment.

If your computer supports pen input, you can write your comments if you prefer. Select the document text to highlight, and then click Ink Comment (in the Comments group on the Review tab). As with typed comments, Word inserts the commenter's name and a time stamp, but the panel displays ruled lines in the writing area. Word expands the handwriting input area if needed. When you're finished writing, Word removes the lines and unused space. Although this method is sometimes more convenient, particularly if you're editing while using a stylus-equipped tablet, it has a drawback: Word doesn't attempt to recognize handwriting, which means that handwritten text won't be included in search results. If you expect to search your document for text contained in comments, you're better off using an input method that converts handwriting to text, such as the Touch Keyboard in Windows 8 or its predecessor, Tablet PC Input Panel in Windows 7.

Reviewing comments

When a document contains one or more comments, by default the location of each comment is indicated by a colored highlight in the document (a different color for each reviewer) and a balloon in the right margin, as shown in Figure 10-17. If you prefer to view the comments in the document (as shown in Figure 10-16), click Show Comments (in the Comments group on the Review tab). Note that this command is available only when Simple Markup is selected in the Tracking group. (For more information, see "Changing view options" later in this chapter.)

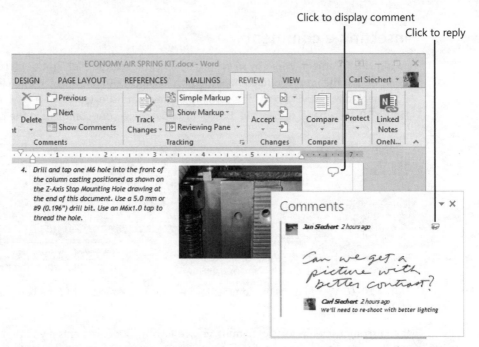

Click to display comment

Click to reply

Figure 10-17 Click a balloon icon to open the comment in a window. This example shows an ink comment with a reply.

As shown in Figure 10-17, three tools in the Comments group on the Review tab become available when a document contains one or more comments: Delete, Previous, and Next. Instead of tediously paging through a document in search of comments, you can skip instantly to the next or previous comment by clicking one of these buttons.

You can also browse by comment using either of these navigation tools:

- **Navigation pane** Click the arrow at the right side of the search box, click Comments, and then choose the name of the reviewer whose comments you want to see or choose All Reviewers. Then click the arrow buttons to the right of the tabs to jump to the next or previous search result.

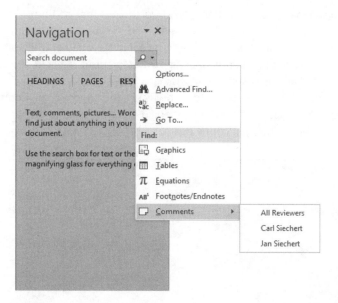

- **Go To command**   Press Ctrl+G and select Comment under Go To What. You can jump to the previous or next comment by a particular reviewer, or you can enter a number to jump directly to a specific comment.

For more information about these browse methods, see "Navigating within a document" in Chapter 9.

Comments also appear in the Revisions pane, which you display by clicking Reviewing Pane, a button in the Tracking group on the Review tab. For details about working in the Revisions pane, see "Reviewing tracked changes" later in this chapter.

Once you get to a comment of interest, you have some options that are new with Word 2013:

- You can reply to a comment by clicking the icon in its upper-right corner (see Figure 10-17). You enter a reply in the same way you enter a new comment; the key difference is that the reply appears indented below the original comment, forming a discussion thread. Comment replies are preserved if you open the document in an earlier Word version, but they appear as separate, unindented comments.

- You can contact the commenter immediately. Point to the commenter's picture, and a window appears with buttons that let you reach the commenter by instant message, phone, video, or email if your communications programs are properly configured.

Click the arrow at the right end of the window to open a contact card that includes additional details about the commenter and links for making contact.

- You can mark a comment as "done." Documents that go through several review cycles can become cluttered with comments, and this feature lets you signal that you've taken care of the comment without deleting it altogether. The comment remains part of the document, but when Show Comments is selected, the comment text is truncated and appears dimmed, making it less intrusive, as shown in Figure 10-18. To mark a comment complete, right-click it and choose Mark Comment Done. If you need to see the full comment again, simply click it. To unmark it, right-click and choose Mark Comment Done again.

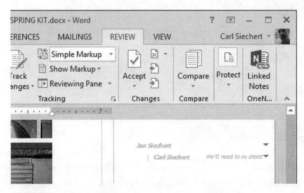

Figure 10-18 The comments shown earlier in Figure 10-17 appear truncated and dimmed when marked as done.

Printing comments

When you print a document that contains comments (or other changes, as described in the following sections), by default Word includes the comments when you print. It does this by reducing the size of each page to create a markup area on the right side large enough for the comment balloons, as shown in Figure 10-19.

To print your document without comments, under Settings click Print All Pages. Then click Print Markup to remove the check mark.

You can also choose to print only the comments and tracked changes without printing the entire document. To do that, click Print All Pages and then click List Of Markup.

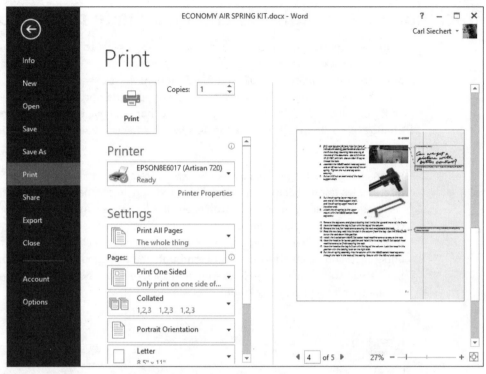

Figure 10-19 As shown in the preview image, Word prints comment balloons and other markup along the right side of each page.

If you're not satisfied with the width of the comment area on the right side of each page, return to the Review tab and click the dialog box launcher in the lower-right corner of the Tracking group. In the Track Changes Options dialog box, click Advanced Options. Near the bottom of the Advanced Track Changes Options dialog box, under Balloons, you'll find options for adjusting the page layout and comment appearance.

Tracking and highlighting changes made to a document

Comments replace the functionality of sticky notes applied to document printouts. Like applying a sticky note, adding a comment to a document file can provide some useful guidance, but it doesn't actually get the document any closer to completion. To do that, contributors must make their edits and corrections in the document. However, if a reviewer edits your document, you can't easily tell what changes have been made—unless Track Changes is on. To turn it on, click the Review tab and click Track Changes in the Tracking group.

When change tracking is on, you end up with a "redlined" document, so named because it resembles traditional markup done with a red pen. In a departure from earlier Word versions, however, by default you won't see all the changes. As shown in Figure 10-20, a colored line in the left margin identifies the location of each edit. Click the line (or choose All Markup in the Tracking group) to show exactly what has changed: added text appears underlined and deleted text has a strikethrough line through it. These additions and deletions are in color so they're easy to spot, and each reviewer's comments are in a different color, making them easy to differentiate. See Figure 10-21.

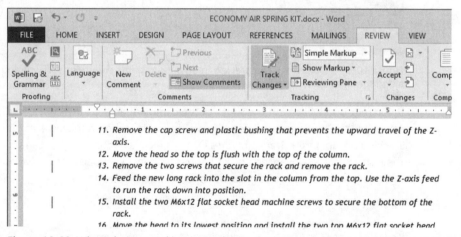

Figure 10-20 When change tracking is on, the Track Changes button is highlighted. A line in the left margin identifies each line with a change. Click the line to show changes.

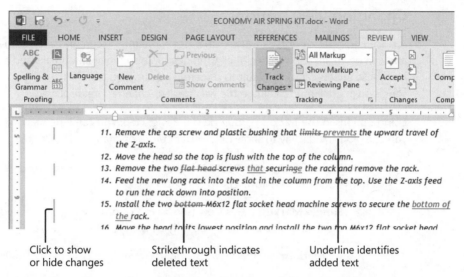

Click to show
or hide changes

Strikethrough indicates
deleted text

Underline identifies
added text

Figure 10-21 Choose All Markup or click the change indicator to show redlined changes.

INSIDE OUT   Use traditional markup

Some reviewers prefer going old school by using a red pen on printed output. In Word, you can mark up a document this way without even printing it! On a computer with pen or touch support, the Review tab includes a Start Inking tool in the Ink group. Click or tap this tool, and Word displays the Pens tab under Ink Tools, where you can select a pen style and color. You then use the pen or your finger to draw directly on the document. (For a list of standard proofreaders' marks, go to *w7io.com/10901*.)

This method provides a handy way to mark up a document when using a keyboard isn't convenient, but it has some disadvantages. First, Word makes no attempt to interpret your scrawl, so it's up to someone else to actually make changes to the document text. And when that happens, another disadvantage becomes apparent: Deleting all the ink marks is a tedious task. Therefore, if you want to employ this method, we recommend that you first turn on change tracking. That way, the ink marks are preserved as a change. Turn off change tracking after you complete the ink markup and before you make changes in the document. After you make the text corrections, you can hide all ink marks by changing the view to Original, or remove them all by rejecting all changes in the document. (These two tasks are described in the following sections.)

Changing view options

A document that has lots of tracked changes sometimes resembles a graffiti-covered wall and can be challenging to decipher. Changes can also move line breaks and page breaks, and these effects can be difficult to discern when tracked changes are shown. For these reasons, you might want to change the way tracked changes are displayed.

Using options in the Tracking group on the Review tab, you can hide markup altogether, or you can filter the display to show only certain types of changes. Here's how:

- Click Display For Review (the button that shows Simple Markup by default), and choose one of the following:

  ○ **Simple Markup** This view (shown in Figure 10-20) shows the edited document, but edits are indicated only by a line in the margin.

  ○ **All Markup** In this view (shown in Figure 10-21), edits are shown as redlines.

  ○ **No Markup** Like Simple Markup, this view shows the final, edited document; the difference is that no indications of tracked changes appear.

  ○ **Original** This view shows the original document without changes.

  Note that you can make changes in any view and Word continues to track changes, even when you choose a view that doesn't display the markup. However, if you're using Original view and you make a change in the document, Word immediately switches to showing markup.

- To selectively show markup, click Show Markup. On the menu that appears, shown next, you can select which types of markup you want to display and you can select which reviewers' markup to display. The Balloons submenu includes an option—Show Revisions In Balloons—that moves deleted text to a balloon in the markup area in the right margin instead of using strikethrough text; this option shows final line and page breaks more accurately.

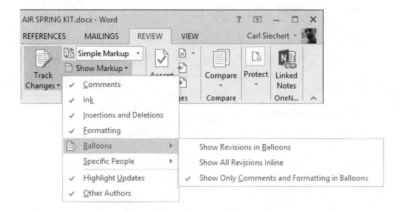

Reviewing tracked changes

After one or more reviewers have added their two cents to your writing masterpiece, you'll want to review the changes before committing them. To do that, you use tools in the Changes group on the Review tab.

From the beginning of the document, click Next (or Accept) to jump to the first change or comment. If you agree with the change, click Accept, which removes the markup from the change and advances to the next change. If you don't want to accept the reviewer's change, click Reject, which undoes the change and advances to the next one. Can't decide? Click Next to jump to the next change while leaving the markup in place.

You needn't examine every single change. Click the arrow on the Accept button or the Reject button to display a menu of additional options, most notably the option to accept (or reject) all changes in the document without further review.

Another way to review changes and navigate among them is with the Revisions pane, which you display by clicking the Reviewing Pane button in the Tracking group on the Review tab. As shown in Figure 10-22, the Revisions pane shows the reviewer's name and, if you choose the horizontal display, the time of each change. An advantage of the Revisions pane is that you can search within it to quickly find specific text. You can click revision text to jump directly to that change or comment in the document. You can also edit and format text directly in the Revisions pane. Clicking the Accept, Reject, Previous, or Next button on the Review tab has the same effect whether you're working in the document or the Revisions pane.

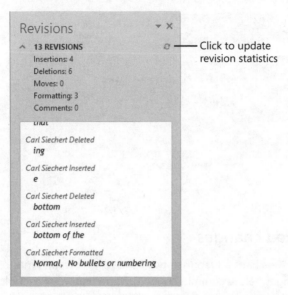

Figure 10-22 The Revisions pane also includes some interesting statistics at the top.

You'll sometimes want to distribute a document to more than one person for review. After the review copies come back, you're stuck with the unenviable job of merging comments and changes from multiple documents into one. And what if not all the reviewers remember to turn on change tracking? The Combine and Compare tools in the Compare group on the Review tab provide relief for these reviewing headaches.

Both tools use two documents as their input. Compare is designed for comparing a revised document with the original, whereas Combine is intended to merge changes from two different revised documents into one, leaving the tracked changes intact. In practice, the difference between the two tools is slight.

You select the documents to combine or compare in a dialog box similar to the one shown next. You fine-tune the comparison operation by clicking More, which exposes the options shown in the bottom part of this dialog box.

After you click OK, your documents appear in a multipaned window, as shown in Figure 10-23. The usual collection of Review tab tools for browsing, accepting, and rejecting changes and comments apply here as well.

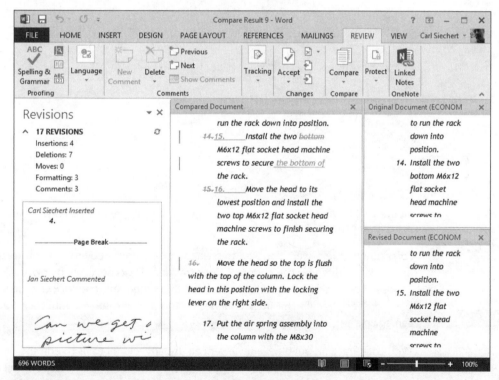

Figure 10-23 The document panes scroll synchronously, making it easy to compare the documents.

Setting options for tracking changes

The default behavior of underlining text additions, striking out deletions, and so on works well for most people—but you're not stuck with it. You can select different ways of marking (bold text for additions, for example), specify which color to use for edits you make, and select which types of changes you want to track. (For example, you might choose not to mark changes to formatting.) You make all these choices in the Advanced Track Changes Options dialog box, which is shown in Figure 10-24. To open this dialog box, on the Review tab, click the dialog box launcher in the lower-right corner of the Tracking group and then, in the Track Changes Options dialog box, click Advanced Options.

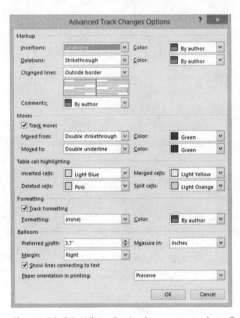

Figure 10-24 When By Author appears in a Color box, Word uses a different color for each reviewer's changes.

To ensure that reviewers don't try to sneak some changes in by turning off Track Changes and making edits, you can choose to lock tracking. Click the arrow below Track Changes, choose Lock Tracking, and enter a password that's required to unlock change tracking. (The password is optional.) The Track Changes button is then disabled until Lock Tracking is chosen again.

With Lock Tracking enabled, a reviewer can use any and all tools to edit the document, but all edits are marked as tracked changes, and the reviewer cannot accept or reject changes.

INSIDE OUT   Allow comments only

Sometimes you want reviewers to make comments, but don't want them making other changes to a document. To enable this restriction, follow these steps:

1. Click the Review tab and then click Restrict Editing in the Protect group. This opens the Restrict Editing pane.

2. Select the check box under Editing Restrictions. Then select Comments. (Choosing Tracked Changes, which also allows comment entry, is the same as choosing Lock Tracking, described above.)

3. Click Yes, Start Enforcing Protection.

4. In the Start Enforcing Protection dialog box, enter a password if you want to make it a little harder for a reviewer to remove the protection. For working with trusted associates, leave the password boxes blank. Then click OK.

When you allow only comment editing, reviewers are rebuffed with an error message if they try to make any edits other than inserting a comment or deleting one of their own comments.

Chapter 10

Preparing a document for distribution

Before you share an electronic document with the world, you should review the file to be sure it doesn't contain information that you don't want others to see. You might also want to check for improvements you can make that render the document more accessible to people with disabilities. If you're planning to share with users of earlier versions of Word, you'll want to be sure that they can open the file. (For details, see "Checking for compatibility with an earlier Office version" in Chapter 6, "Managing Office files.")

You might also want to protect your document from unwanted changes, and you might want to prevent unauthorized users from opening the document. You can also apply a digital signature to a document, which provides assurance to recipients of the document that it came from you and that it hasn't been altered.

You'll find tools for each of these tasks by clicking the File tab to display the Info pane in Backstage view, as shown in Figure 10-25.

Figure 10-25 Explanatory text under Protect Document and Inspect Document highlights potential issues with the current document.

Checking a document

Several notorious incidents have occurred in which a publicly released Word document disclosed embarrassing information. It doesn't take an Office whiz to discover the name of the document creator and, in fact, it's pretty easy to snoop in a file to find hidden text or even text that has been deleted during editing—especially with documents in the Word 97–2003 Document (.doc) format.

To prevent information in your document from becoming tabloid fodder, in the Info pane in Backstage view click Check For Issues, Inspect Document. Doing so opens the Document Inspector dialog box, in which you select the types of personal information you want to expunge. (For more information about each of these categories, see *w7io.com/10902*.) Make your selections and click Inspect, whereupon you'll see the inspection results, as shown in Figure 10-26.

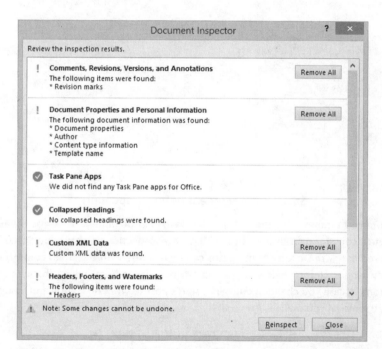

Figure 10-26 Click Remove All for each category to sanitize your document file.

Making a document accessible to the widest group of readers isn't just political correctness; it's smart business. Furthermore, it's required for some business and government documents. Most issues identified make it easier for visually impaired users to read a document. For example, adding alt text to each picture (which text-to-speech software can read aloud) can improve your document's accessibility. If your document contains potential accessibility issues, a notice to that effect appears on the Info tab under Inspect Document. To learn more, click Check For Issues, Check Accessibility. An Accessibility Checker pane then appears next to your document. As you expand and click each item under Errors, Warnings, and Tips, the offending item is selected and explanatory text appears at the bottom of the Accessibility Checker pane.

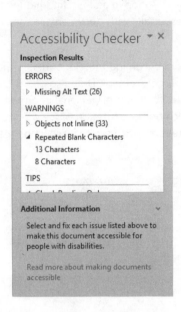

INSIDE OUT   Save your document before inspecting

Before you summon Document Inspector, save your document. Then use Save As to create a copy for distribution, and perform the inspection on that copy. Some items you remove with Document Inspector can be restored with the Undo command, but many cannot. Unfortunately, there's no obvious way to know which changes can be undone in case you change your mind, so it's best to work on a copy and assume that every removal you make is irreversible.

Protecting a document

The Protect Document button in the Info pane in Backstage view, shown in Figure 10-27, offers links to several tools you can use to prevent unauthorized changes to your document and to assure document recipients that the document is indeed yours.

Figure 10-27 Commands under Protect Document limit access to a document.

Options under Protect Document perform the following tasks:

- **Mark As Final**   Choosing this command sets a flag in the file so that it opens in read-only mode. You can't type in the document or edit it in other ways, and most buttons on the ribbon are disabled. This provides adequate protection from inadvertent changes, but it doesn't defend against malicious changes. Anyone can remove the final status by revisiting the Info tab and clicking Mark As Final again or, more simply, clicking Edit Anyway in the message bar that appears, as shown here.

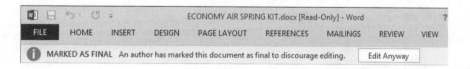

- **Encrypt With Password** When you choose this command, Word asks you to provide a password, which it then uses as a key for encrypting the document. Thereafter, Word asks for the password each time someone tries to open the document. Be sure you save the password in a safe place because there's no practical way to recover it.

- **Restrict Editing** This command displays the Restrict Editing task pane, which you can use to limit formatting changes and edits. For more information, see "Making global changes to your document" in Chapter 9 and "Setting options for tracking changes" earlier in this chapter.

- **Restrict Access** This command uses Information Rights Management (IRM) to keep track of which people are allowed to view or edit a document. Your network must have an IRM server to use this feature.

- **Add A Digital Signature** A digital signature is a code embedded in the document file that ensures that the document came from you (or someone who has access to the private key for your digital ID) and that the document hasn't been altered. In addition, it provides a tamper-proof time stamp for the document. Choose this command to learn about options for obtaining a digital ID if you don't have one already.

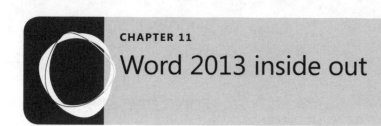

I N THE first two chapters of this section about Word, we cover the basic tasks that nearly anyone who uses Word—whether casual user or full-time writer—needs to master to be proficient. We follow a steady progression from simple tasks to complex documents. In this chapter, we dig deeper. The format is a bit more freewheeling, as we cover a range of advanced, but largely unrelated, topics. These are the ones that'll make you go "Wow!"

We look at some advanced text-formatting capabilities that traditionally have been the realm of desktop publishing and high-end typesetting programs. We show how to use Word to manage your blog. Another topic we tackle in this chapter is mail merge, a task that has confounded word-processing users for a long time; we try to bring some clarity to the subject. We also look at building blocks and fields, features that help you to add content to your document and keep it fresh.

Finally, we describe some of our favorite Word tweaks and tips.

Applying advanced text-formatting capabilities

Earlier in this book, we described how to format text in any Office program (see "Applying text formatting" in Chapter 4, "Entering, editing, and formatting text") and showed additional formatting options and techniques that are unique to Word (see "Formatting text" in Chapter 9, "Inside Word 2013"). But we're not done with this subject yet. Word 2013 includes still more options for dressing up the text in your documents. You probably won't use these effects every day, but when you do have occasion to use them, the results can be spectacular.

Applying shadows, reflections, and other text effects

Word has several types of effects that can be applied to document text:

- **Outline** effects add a border around each text character in a color, weight, and line style that you select.

- **Fill** effects, including gradients, control the color of characters.

- **Shadow** effects create a three-dimensional look by making the text appear as if it is floating in front of the screen or paper.

- **Reflection** effects also provide the appearance of depth by showing a mirror image of the text, as if it's on a reflective surface.

- **Glow** effects add a radiant appearance to each character.

You can combine these effects to create some wonderful results. But don't overdo it; you can also end up with something hideous.

To apply any of these effects except fill color, find the Font group on the Home tab and click Text Effects And Typography. A gallery of effects appears, as shown in Figure 11-1. To specify a fill color or to apply a gradient effect to text, click the arrow next to the Font Color button, which is also in the Font group on the Home tab. (If you click the Font Color button, it applies the last color you used or, if you haven't yet used the tool, red.)

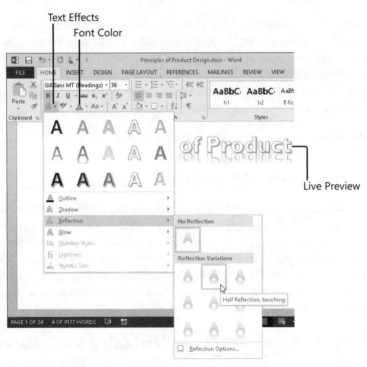

Figure 11-1 As you point to each effect in the gallery, Live Preview shows how it will look.

As an alternative to choosing from the gallery, you can use the Format Text Effects pane, which offers more precise control and options not available in the gallery presets. Additional options include gradient fills, gradient lines, shadow colors, and three-dimensional bevel effects. To summon Format Text Effects, which is shown in Figure 11-2, choose the Options command at the bottom of the Shadow, Reflection, or Glow gallery. Or in the Font dialog box, click Text Effects.

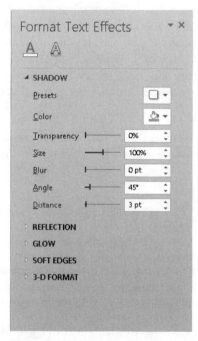

Figure 11-2 For each effect, you might find it easiest to start with a preset and then tweak the settings.

These effects are similar to those available for WordArt; indeed, you can apply any of these effects to text within a WordArt object. However, there are some good reasons to apply text effects to normal document text instead of using WordArt. For example, you don't need to mess with positioning and text wrapping because formatted document text flows with other text. On the other hand, WordArt objects can be inserted in Word, Excel, PowerPoint, and Outlook documents, whereas the text effect techniques described in this section are available only in Word. If you want to reuse your fancy formatted text in another program, use WordArt so you can paste it in the other program. For more information about Word-Art, see "Applying text effects with WordArt" in Chapter 5, "Working with graphics and pictures."

Chapter 11

Text effects can be included in paragraph, character, list, and table styles. For information about working with styles, see "Giving your documents a consistent appearance" in Chapter 9.

Using ligatures and other fine typography effects

Traditional typesetting uses several subtle techniques that make typeset documents look better than anything produced by a word-processing program. These techniques have been used throughout the history of typesetting—in hand-set type, hot metal, photo-typesetting, and (more recently) desktop publishing programs. When these techniques are used, graphic designers and typographers can spot the difference at a glance, whereas others might recognize that the text looks better and "more professional," but they can't tell you why. With Word, many of these features are available in word-processing documents, including:

- **Ligatures** A *ligature* is two or three letters that are combined into a single character because the shapes of the letters are more aesthetically pleasing when combined this way.

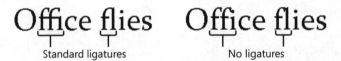

Standard ligatures   No ligatures

Whether a particular font has ligatures in a particular category (as defined by the OpenType specification) is up to the font's designer, and that decision determines which ligatures are used when any of these options is selected in Word:

- ○ **Standard Only** Standard ligatures vary by language. In English, common ligatures combine an *f*, *l*, or *i* when it follows an *f*, but other combinations exist in some fonts.

- ○ **Standard And Contextual** In addition to standard ligatures, this setting includes character combinations that the font designer thinks are appropriate for a particular font, perhaps due to the unusual shapes of some letters.

- ○ **Historical And Discretionary** Historical ligatures are ones that were once standard (*ct* and *st* combinations, for example, often have a small swash tying the letters together).

- **Number Forms** *Old-style* numbers have varying heights and are often used when numbers appear within text because the numbers align well with mixed-case text. Modern numbers (called *Lining* in Word) align on the baseline and are of uniform height; these are best for numerical data. Each font has a default setting based on the font's typical usage. For example, the default for Candara, Constantia, and Corbel is old-style, whereas Cambria, Calibri, and Consolas use lining as the default number form.

1,234,567,890   1,234,567,890 ___ Baseline

Old-style numbers   Lining numbers

- **Number Spacing**   *Proportional* numbers have varying widths; because that generally looks better, proportionally spaced numbers are usually used for numbers within text. *Tabular* numbers all have the same width (more accurately, they all occupy the same space, as the numbers themselves look the same), which is useful for tables of numerical data because the digits align vertically. As with number forms, each font has a default setting. For example, Candara, Constantia, and Corbel default to proportional spacing, whereas Cambria, Calibri, and Consolas use tabular spacing by default.

1,112,112,112   1,112,112,112
1,234,567,890   1,234,567,890

Proportional spacing   Tabular spacing

- **Stylistic Sets**   Some fonts include letter combinations with swashes and other flairs that can be used for decorative text in titles and on certificates, for example. Fonts that include stylistic sets often include more than one, with each one identified by an arbitrary number.

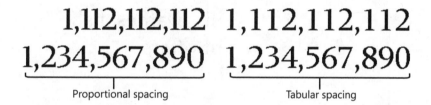

1 Am, Therefore 1 Think —— Gabriola stylistic set 1

1 Am, Therefore 1 Think —— Gabriola stylistic set 2

1 Am, Therefore 1 Think —— Gabriola stylistic set 3

Stylistic sets are best reserved for occasional decorative text, such as a title or heading. Getting just the right look often requires much experimentation. You'll sometimes want to apply stylistic sets on a letter-by-letter basis.

Chapter 11

These typographical effects are available only with OpenType fonts and, more specifically, only certain OpenType fonts. You're likely to find these features in the newer fonts included with Windows and with Office, including Calibri, Cambria, Candara, Constantia, Corbel, and Gabriola.

You apply any of these typographic effects in much the same way as you apply other text formats: you select the text, and then click Text Effects And Typography (in the Font group on the Home tab). The menu that appears, shown next, has submenus for Number Styles, Ligatures, and Stylistic Sets. If the selected font doesn't support one of these features, the corresponding command is unavailable. Point to an option to see a live preview.

Alternatively, click the arrow in the lower-right corner of the Font group on the Home tab or press Ctrl+Shift+F to open the Font dialog box, and then click the Advanced tab, which is shown in Figure 11-3. Make your selections under OpenType Features. Although this method also provides a preview (in the dialog box, not in the document), all options are available for all fonts—even though in most cases your selection has no effect.

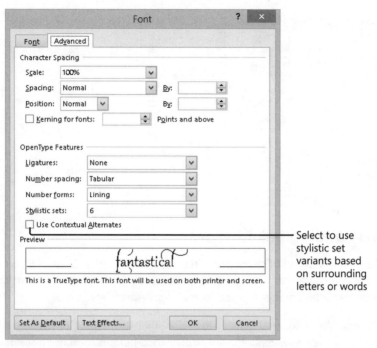

Select to use
stylistic set
variants based
on surrounding
letters or words

Figure 11-3 In lieu of Live Preview showing changes in your document, the Preview box shows the font name or the selected text using the current font settings.

OpenType typographic effects can be included in styles. For information about working with styles, see "Giving your documents a consistent appearance" in Chapter 9.

Beginning a paragraph with a drop cap

Another typographic nicety that graphic designers are fond of is a *drop cap*, which is where the first letter or first word of a paragraph is larger than the rest of the text. You can see an example on the first page of each chapter in this book. Creating a drop cap requires not just formatting the letter in a larger font, but also aligning the top of the drop cap with the top of the other paragraph text. (If you simply format the first letter in a larger size, it doesn't "drop.")

Word makes this task easy. Click anywhere in the paragraph (if you want to drop the entire first word, you must select it), click the Insert tab, and in the Text group click Drop Cap. Select a drop cap option, or click Drop Cap Options to specify a font (by default, Word uses the paragraph font) or adjust the size or position using the dialog box shown next.

Chapter 11

Understanding linked styles

In our earlier discussion of styles (see "Creating a new style" in Chapter 9), we covered character styles and paragraph styles, which are methods for reusing and consistently applying character formatting and paragraph formatting, respectively.

As you work with styles, you're likely to see another style type: Linked (Paragraph And Character). As the name implies, a linked style incorporates formatting settings for paragraphs (line spacing and indents, for example) *and* for characters (such as font and point size). Confusingly, however, paragraph styles can also incorporate character formats. So what's the point of linked styles?

Linked styles were introduced in Word 2002 (part of Office XP) to enable the use of run-in headings. (A *run-in heading* is one that, instead of being on a line by itself, is immediately followed by paragraph text.) A linked style can be applied to a full paragraph—just like a paragraph style—or it can be applied to a selection of text within a paragraph, much like a character style. Either way, Word recognizes the style's heading level for use in outlines, the Navigation pane, and tables of contents.

In Word 2002 and Word 2003, the default style type for a new style was linked, so when you use templates developed in earlier versions of Word, you're likely to see this type. (In Word 2013, as in Word 2007 and Word 2010, new styles are paragraph styles by default.)

Linked styles serve a useful purpose, but they can sometimes cause confusion or annoyance because if text is selected when you apply a linked style, the style is applied only to the selection instead of the entire paragraph. You can avoid the problem in two ways:

- When you create a new style, if you don't plan to use it as a run-in heading, set the style type to Paragraph.

- To work with an existing template that contains linked styles, open the Styles pane (click the arrow in the lower-right corner of the Styles group on the Home tab or press Ctrl+Alt+Shift+S), and then select Disable Linked Styles. This setting doesn't actually disable the styles; it merely changes their behavior to work like paragraph styles.

Using Word to create and edit blog posts

If you maintain a blog, you've probably tried using the web-based interface provided by the blogging service for creating, editing, and posting entries. Many of these interfaces are awful. For users of some popular blogging services, Word 2013 offers a better solution.

With Word, you can create a new post from scratch, or you can publish an existing document to a blog. Word works with most popular blogging platforms, including SharePoint, WordPress, and Blogger. You create your post using Word's familiar tools, and then with a single click Word publishes it to your blog.

To create a new post, click File, New, and then double-click Blog Post. To publish an existing document, open it, and then click File, Share. Under Share, click Post To Blog, and then click the Post To Blog button.

Either way, a new window opens, as shown in Figure 11-4. (The main difference between the two methods is that one includes the content of the currently open document, whereas the other starts with a blank page.) You'll notice some differences from an ordinary document window: a Blog Post tab replaces the Home tab, and most other tabs are missing. (That's because blogs don't support the full range of Word capabilities, so Word doesn't expose the unavailable options.) And a content control at the top of the document commands you to Enter Post Title Here.

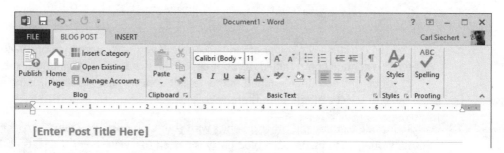

Figure 11-4 The Blog Post tab incorporates features from the standard Home and Review tabs in addition to the blog-specific features in the Blog group.

Chapter 11

Managing blog accounts

If this is your first time using the blogging feature, Word asks you to register your blog account, as shown in Figure 11-5. Click Register Now to configure Word to work with an existing blog or to set up a new blog. The few steps to register a blog account vary depending on the service, but the on-screen descriptions are reasonably clear and include links to webpages with more details about completing the process. In any case, it takes only a minute or two—but you can postpone the operation if you want to by clicking Register Later. If you take that option, you can create, edit, and save blog entries, but you can't post them until you register your account, which you can do at any time.

Figure 11-5 If you choose Register Later, you can initiate the process by clicking Manage Accounts in the Blog group on the Blog Post tab—or simply wait until Word prompts you when you attempt to post an entry.

To view or modify your blog account settings, or to register another blog, click Manage Accounts in the Blog group on the Blog Post tab.

You can register any number of blog accounts. If you have more than one account registered, a content control titled Account appears in the document window just below the post title. The account identified as the default appears here initially; click the account name to select a different registered account.

To include pictures and other graphics with your blog posts, you need to specify a server for storing pictures. (When a blog entry is posted to a web server, the text—in HTML format—is stored separately from pictures or other images in the post.) During the registration process (or later, by selecting an account in Blog Accounts and clicking Change), click Picture Options. In the Picture Options dialog box, select SharePoint Blog or My Blog Provider, if available. These options store pictures in a designated pictures library associated with your blog account.

TROUBLESHOOTING

Word doesn't recognize your blogging service's picture provider

Unfortunately, Word doesn't recognize the picture-hosting capabilities of some blogging services and instead leaves you with only two choices: None—Don't Upload Pictures (this option is fine if your blog contains only text) and My Own Server.

Don't be dissuaded by the phrase "my own." Although you can use your own web server to host pictures, this is also the option to choose if you plan to use a third-party image provider. Such services are widely available, often at little or no cost to you. Flickr, Photobucket, and Shutterfly are popular services you can use, and a web search for "image hosting service" turns up scores more. To use one of them, select My Own Server in the Picture Options dialog box, and then in the Upload URL box, enter the FTP or HTTP address that the hosting service provides for uploading your pictures. In the Source URL box, enter the HTTP address for viewing your picture collection; Word includes this information in the <img> tag in the blog post.

Unfortunately, you can get into the deep weeds pretty quickly with image providers, which often make it difficult to find the appropriate URLs to use for uploading and viewing. If you run into trouble, we recommend trying Windows Live Writer (a component of the free Windows Essentials collection, which you can download from Microsoft) or—if you're just starting a new blog—switching to a better-supported blogging service, such as WordPress.com.

Working with blog posts

You create and edit your blog post as you do any other document, albeit with a limited set of tools. The Blog group on the Blog Post tab includes a handful of tools that aren't seen elsewhere in Word:

- **Publish**   When you finish your post, click Publish to upload it to your blog account. Click the arrow below the Publish button to expose a second option: Publish As Draft. This option uploads the post but saves it as a draft instead of publishing it to the publicly available blog. This allows you to review the post and edit it—either in Word or using your blogging service's editing tools—before making it public.

- **Home Page**   Click this button to open your blog's home page in your web browser.

- **Insert Category**   Click this to display a content control below the post title. This content control lets you select a category from a list or type a new one; categorizing your posts makes it easier for visitors to your blog to find posts about a particular topic.

- **Open Existing**   Click this button to open a list of posts that have been published on your blog. You can then select a post, download it, edit it, and republish it.

- **Manage Accounts**   Click to open Blog Accounts, a dialog box in which you can add, modify, or remove blog accounts, as described in the previous section.

INSIDE OUT   Add the Blog Post template to your Jump List

You can pin the Blog Post template to the Jump List for Word, which allows you to start a new blog post directly from your desktop, without even starting Word first.

To set this up, you must have a Word icon pinned to your taskbar. Right-click the Word icon on the taskbar. If you've recently created a blog post, as described in the preceding sections, a template named Blog Post should appear under Recent. As shown next, click Pin To This List next to Blog Post, which ensures that it stays on the list permanently.

Thereafter, when you open the Jump List, you can simply click Blog Post to open a new blog post window in Word.

When you publish a blog post, it's stored on a web server, but you might also want to save a local copy so that you can work with it when you don't have Internet access. Simply save the file as you would any other document (press Ctrl+S or click File, Save); by default, Word uses its standard .docx file format. Note, however, that after you publish a post to your blog, some formatting is lost, even in your locally saved copy.

INSIDE OUT   Editing your blog's HTML code

Many blog editors—including stand-alone programs and your blogging service's online editing tools—let you switch between a "preview" view (comparable to Print Layout view in Word) and HTML code view. Not Word.

If you need to examine and edit the HTML code, create your post in Word and publish it as a draft. Then use your blogging service's editor to open the draft, where you can tweak away.

Inserting video

In previous versions of Office, you can embed video clips in a PowerPoint presentation. (That ability continues with PowerPoint 2013; for more information, see "Working with video" in Chapter 18, "Inside PowerPoint 2013.") Now a new feature in Office 2013 enables video in Word documents. Naturally, this capability makes more sense when you're preparing a document to be viewed on a computer rather than printed.

You insert a video clip in a document in much the same way you insert other objects: place the insertion point where you want the video and then click Online Video (in the Media group on the Insert tab). The Insert Video dialog box appears, as shown in Figure 11-6.

The Bing Video Search option works much like the comparable Online Pictures search: you enter a search term and press Enter (or click the search icon), and thumbnail images of search results appear in a window. Point to a thumbnail to see more information about the video and to display a View Larger icon. Click that icon to play the video in a small preview window. After you make your selection, click Insert. The YouTube option works in an identical fashion.

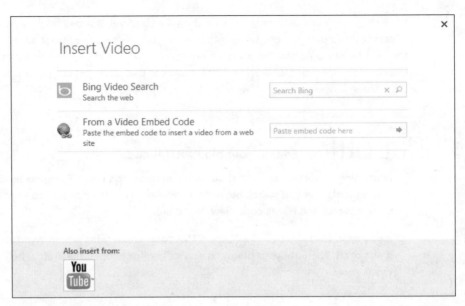

Figure 11-6 Clicking an available option at the bottom of the screen adds it to the list of online video sources.

For videos on sites that aren't directly supported by Word (or that you can't find with a Bing Video Search), use the From A Video Embed Code option. Note that you don't enter the URL of a video here; you must enter HTML code for embedding the video. Most sites provide an embed code as one of their sharing options. For example, with Vimeo or You-Tube, go to the webpage for a video, click Share, and then copy the HTML code in the Embed box.

INSIDE OUT   Using SkyDrive videos

PowerPoint has an option in the Insert Video dialog box for inserting a video from your SkyDrive; this option doesn't appear in Word. Nonetheless, it's easy to insert a video stored on SkyDrive to a Word document. Use the SkyDrive web client (not the Windows 8 app) to find your video, right-click it, and choose Embed. Copy the HTML code and paste it into the From A Video Embed Code box.

The image of a video inserted in a Word document can be manipulated in the same ways as other types of graphics: crop it, resize it, apply effects, and so on. None of these changes affect the way the video plays, however. When you play an embedded video (by clicking the Play button on the video image), the video opens in a player window before a darkened Word window. To stop play and return to the document, click outside the player window.

Combining documents and data with mail merge

Mail merge is the process of marrying a document (such as a letter) with data (such as a list of addresses). Although it's typically used for generating form letters and bulk mailings, you can apply mail merge techniques to just about any kind of document and any kind of data. Your data, for example, might include the name of a product a customer has purchased, or the registration number for a seminar attendee, or test scores, or ... well, you get the idea.

With mail merge features in Word, you can sprinkle data fields throughout a document, you can sort and filter the data, and you can perform conditional merges in which the output depends on information in the data. You're not limited to a single data record per document either; you can use mail merge to create a page of labels (each addressed to a different person) or to print a roster, directory, or catalog (which allows you to format it in far more interesting ways than you could, say, with Excel or Access).

INSIDE OUT   Print a single envelope or label

Merging data from a list is a powerful way to print many envelopes or labels, each addressed to a different person. But often you need just a single envelope or label, which is somewhat difficult to create when starting from a standard blank document. Word has you covered.

Simply click the Mailings tab, and in the Create group click Envelopes or Labels. The dialog box that appears, shown in Figure 11-7, is the same either way; the only difference is which tab is displayed initially.

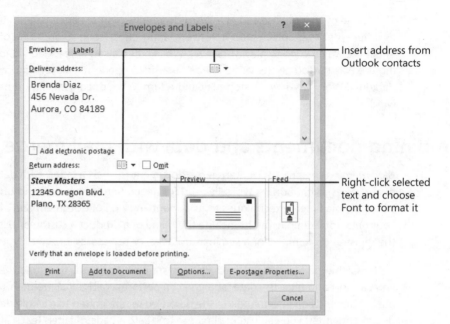

Insert address from
Outlook contacts

Right-click selected
text and choose
Font to format it

Figure 11-7 On either tab, click Options to select a paper size and type and to set printer options.

Type the addresses (or other information) directly in the dialog box or click the button to select an address from your Outlook contacts. (Bonus tip: If you select text in your document before you click Envelopes or Labels, your selected text appears in the Delivery Address text box.) If you have an account with Stamps.com or another supported electronic postage vendor, you can print a postage "stamp" on your envelope or label.

To complete the task, click Print to send the job to your printer. Alternatively, click Add To Document (Envelopes tab) or New Document (Labels tab) to open the envelope or label in an ordinary Word document window, allowing you to modify it (add a logo, perhaps) or save it for reuse.

Using the mail merge wizard

Word includes a wizard that leads you through the process of selecting data, preparing a document, previewing the merge results, and sending the results to the printer or to a file. To start the wizard, click the Mailings tab, and in the Start Mail Merge group, click Start Mail Merge, Step-By-Step Mail Merge Wizard. This opens the Mail Merge pane, as shown in Figure 11-8.

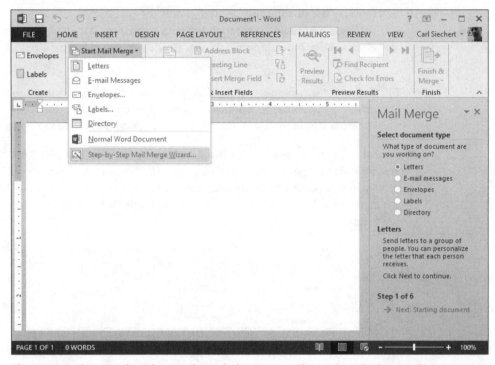

Figure 11-8 The wizard guides you through the process. Choose Step-By-Step Mail Merge Wizard at any time to display the Mail Merge pane.

The wizard takes you through the following steps:

1. **Select a document type.**   You begin by selecting a document type—letter, email message, envelope, label, or directory. Your choice here affects the layout (the last two choices print multiple records on a single sheet, for example) and the wording that appears in the following steps.

2. **Select a starting document.**   You can use the current document, open a previously saved document, or create a new document based on a template you choose.

3. **Select data records.**   You can draw data from an existing file or database, from your Outlook contacts, or from a list you type in Word. For more information, see the next section, "Working with data files."

4. **Lay out the document.**   In this step, you insert merge fields that link to data in your list. Throughout the process, you can work in the document window to type other information (such as common text that appears in all merged documents), format text, and so on. For more information, see "Inserting data fields in a document" later in this chapter.

5. **Preview the document.** Word replaces the field names with actual data from your database. You can page through the data records to verify that the merge works as expected. For more information, see "Previewing the merged output" later in this chapter.

6. **Complete the merge.** In the final step, you merge the data into the document. You can send the output to a printer, to a new document, or as individual email messages. For more information, see "Completing the merge" later in this chapter.

For most users, the wizard is a worthwhile assistant. It ensures that you don't overlook any steps, yet it doesn't get in the way of speed or efficiency, as some wizards do. Nonetheless, as you gain experience you might prefer to use the ribbon tools; you can switch back and forth at any time. Figure 11-9 shows which tools on the Mailings tab correspond to each wizard step.

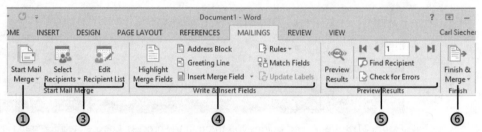

Figure 11-9 Numbers correspond to step numbers in the wizard. (Step 2 is comparable to choosing New or Open from Backstage view.)

Working with data files

In the wizard's third step, you connect the document to a data source.

For the simplest data requirements, type the list in Word. In the wizard, click Type A New List. Alternatively, on the Mailings tab, click Select Recipients, Type A New List. A dialog box appears in which you can enter your data, as shown in Figure 11-10. After you enter your data and click OK, Word prompts you to save the data as a file, which it saves as an Access database.

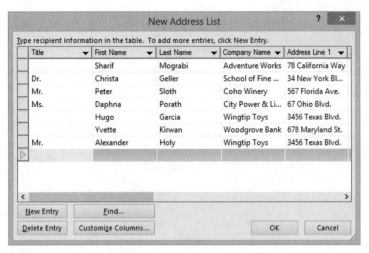

Figure 11-10 Click Customize Columns to add, remove, rename, or reorder columns to better suit your needs.

If the data you need already exists in your Outlook contacts or in a file, select one of those options instead. You can use as a data source any of numerous file types, including an Excel worksheet, a Word document (with data in a table), an Access database, an HTML file (with data in a table), or plain text files in comma-separated values (.csv) or delimited formats. You can also use information in a database that you access with an Open Database Connectivity (ODBC) connector.

> **Note**
>
> Be sure that your data file includes a header record—one that identifies the data field names. If it doesn't, Word uses the data in the first record as a header, which means you get undesirable field names and you lose access to the data in the first record.

After you connect to a data source, you can work with the list data by clicking Edit Recipient List (in the wizard or on the ribbon). The Mail Merge Recipients dialog box appears, as shown in Figure 11-11. Here you can select which records you want to include (select the check box by the ones you want), sort the list (tip: click a column heading to sort instead of clicking Sort), filter the list based on criteria you specify, and make other changes.

Chapter 11

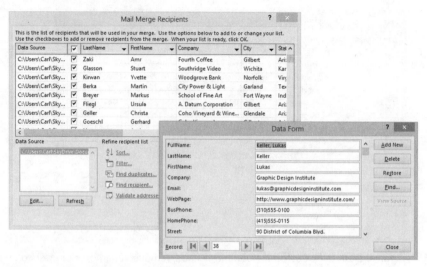

Figure 11-11 To edit a record, select the item in the Data Source box and then click Edit. Any changes you make are stored in the data source.

Inserting data fields in a document

Presumably, in step 2 of the wizard you created the parts of the document that should print with all merged records, such as your logo and company information, the text of the letter, and similar items. This information can find its way into your document from a template, from an existing document, or from edits you make during this session.

With the basics in place, you can then insert data fields—placeholders for data—into appropriate places in your document. Position the insertion point in the document where you want merge data to appear, and then insert fields. You can do this from step 4 of the wizard or by using tools in the Write & Insert Fields group on the Mailings tab.

To insert an individual data field, click More Items (in the wizard) or Insert Merge Field (on the ribbon), and then click the name of the field you want to insert. In the dialog box that appears (see Figure 11-12), you can choose to insert Database Fields (the field list shows the names of the fields in your database) or Address Fields (standard field names used in addressing applications).

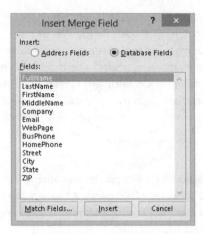

Figure 11-12 To correlate the field names in your database with those in the address fields, click Match Fields.

Note that you can put merge fields anywhere in your document, and you can repeat fields without limitation. For example, you might include in the body of a letter something like "Thanks for purchasing a «ProductName». You might be interested to know that we have a special deal for «ProductName» owners."

Inserting individual fields can be tedious, so Word includes a couple of "super" fields that you can insert: Address Block and Greeting Line. Click one of these, and a dialog box appears in which you can customize the field output. For example, in the Insert Greeting Line dialog box, shown in Figure 11-13, you can select a default greeting or create your own.

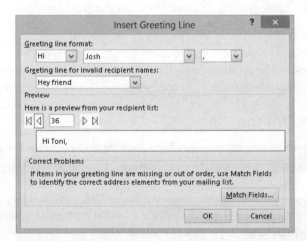

Figure 11-13 The predefined greetings are a bit more traditional than the ones we've typed.

The Address Block and Greeting Line fields have some intelligence built in. For example, if you select Mr. Randall as the greeting line format, each merged record uses the Title field followed by the Last Name field. But what if a record has no entry in the Title field? Word inserts First Name followed by Last Name. And what if a record has no name at all? Word inserts the text in the Greeting Line For Invalid Recipient Names box. The Address Block field performs similar tricks: it omits blank lines (for example, when a recipient record doesn't have a company name or a second address line) and properly formats addresses.

> **Note**
>
> Although merge field names appear between guillemets (for example, «First_Name»), you can't simply type the symbols and the merge field name. Although you can type your entry using a {MERGEFIELD} field code, the easiest and most reliable way to insert merge fields is with tools on the Mailings tab.

Previewing the merged output

In step 5 of the wizard, you can check your work. (As an alternative to using the wizard, click Preview Results on the Mailings tab.) The merge field placeholders are replaced by actual data, and you can click the Next Record and Previous Record buttons to page through the results.

Be on the lookout not just for misplaced fields, but also for missing data and for data that overflows the allotted space. (Perhaps it exceeds the boundaries of a label or adds an extra page to a letter.) When you see errors like this, you can choose to exclude the offending recipient, edit the data, or modify the document or its formatting so that each merged item prints properly.

One option appears in the Preview Results group on the Mailings tab that's not available in the wizard pane: Check For Errors. This review checks spelling and grammar, among other things, and (depending on which option you choose) can also complete the merge.

Completing the merge

The sixth and final step is to actually perform the merge. Whether you use the wizard or the Finish & Merge tool on the Mailings tab, you can send the merge results to a printer (choose Print Documents) or to a new document (choose Edit Individual Documents). With the latter option, you end up with all the completed documents (letters or whatever) in one humongous document, which opens in a new window. In that document, you can edit individual documents (perhaps to add a personal note) before you print.

Whether you print or merge to a new document, Word first asks which records you want to include. If you want to print a range of records, you need to know the numbers of the first and last records to include; you can determine that information by using tools in the Preview Results group on the Mailings tab.

A third output destination is available by clicking Finish & Merge on the Mailings tab: email. You need to have an email address in each record. In an effort to reduce spam, many Internet service providers limit the number of messages you can send in a given period of time. Therefore, this option is practical only for small distribution lists. (And, of course, you should send email only to those people who want to receive messages from you. Otherwise, you join the ranks of reviled spammers.)

Using building blocks

In Word, a *building block* is a stored chunk of content that can be used to quickly enter text and graphics in a document. Word organizes building blocks into galleries of blocks for similar purposes—headers, footers, equations, tables, cover pages, and so on. Dozens of building blocks of various types are included with Word; you can use these as is, modify them, or create your own building blocks. You can download additional building blocks from Office.com.

You insert building blocks into a document by using tools and galleries on the Insert tab and Design tab. We discuss some of these galleries elsewhere in this book. (See "Adding headers, footers, and page numbers" and "Setting page layout options" in Chapter 9; "Using Quick Tables" and "Creating tables of contents and indexes" in Chapter 10; and "Entering mathematical equations" in Chapter 4—as well as the following section, "Using AutoText.")

To view all the available building blocks, click the Insert tab, and in the Text group click Quick Parts, Building Blocks Organizer. The Building Blocks Organizer dialog box, shown in Figure 11-14, lists all building blocks, initially sorted by gallery. (Click a column heading to sort by another field.)

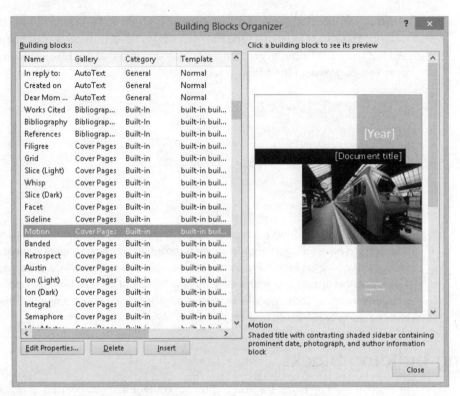

Figure 11-14 Select a building block to see its preview and description.

You can insert a building block directly from Building Blocks Organizer by selecting it and clicking Insert.

Using AutoText

One of the most useful types of building block is called AutoText. AutoText can contain any amount of document content, including formatting. It's typically used for boilerplate text, such as an "about this company" block that must go at the end of each press release, an oft-used disclaimer, or a title block including your logo and address.

To create an AutoText entry, select the content you want to reuse, and then press Alt+F3. (If you can't remember the keyboard shortcut, you can take the lengthier path: Click the Insert tab, and in the Text group click Quick Parts, AutoText, Save Selection To AutoText Gallery.) A dialog box appears, as shown in Figure 11-15. Enter a memorable name, which is how you identify the entry when you want to reuse it.

Figure 11-15 AutoText provides an easy way to enter frequently used text and graphics.

To insert your AutoText entry in a document, you can click Quick Parts, AutoText and then click the entry's thumbnail shown in the gallery. But there's a much easier way: Type the name you assigned to the AutoText entry, and then press F3. You don't need to type the entire name; you just need to type enough to uniquely identify it. For example, to enter an entry called Terms of Sale when you have no other AutoText entries that begin with the let-ter *T*, you could simply type **t** and then press F3. If you also have an entry called Trademark List, you'd need to type (at least) **te** before you press F3.

AutoCorrect provides an alternative way to enter blocks of text. For details, see "Entering boilerplate and other oft-used text" in Chapter 4.

Creating other types of building blocks

The process of creating other types of building blocks is nearly identical to the one just described for AutoText entries. For example, if you want to save a new header in the Header gallery, create and format the header just the way you want it, and then select it. Then, do one of the following to open the Create New Building Block dialog box:

- Click the gallery where you want to add the new entry. For example, to save a new header, click Insert, Header, Save Selection To Header Gallery.

- Click Insert, Quick Parts, Save Selection To Quick Parts Gallery. (Quick Parts is an all-purpose gallery that you might prefer to use simply to differentiate your stored building blocks from the Microsoft-furnished blocks.)

- Press Alt+F3.

Each of these actions opens the Create New Building Block dialog box; the only difference is the selection in the Gallery box, which you can change. Your choice here determines which gallery your building block appears in. Other than maintaining a sense of order, there's no reason you couldn't, for example, put a footer in the Cover Pages gallery. Other fields in Create New Building Block deserve a bit of explanation:

- **Category** You can create categories within each gallery. Items in a gallery are grouped by their category.

- **Description** Use this field to enter explanatory text, which appears in a ScreenTip when you hover the mouse pointer over a gallery item and when you view the item in Building Blocks Organizer.

- **Save In** Specify where you want to save the building block:

  - Select Normal to save the building block in the Normal.dotm global template, which makes it available in all documents.

  - Select the name of the current template to store it in that template, which makes it available in all new documents you create based on the template.

  - Select Building Blocks to save it in Building Blocks.dotx, a template file that's stored in a subfolder of %AppData%\Microsoft\Document Building Blocks. Building blocks you store here are available for all documents you create, but this template isn't easy to share with others.

- **Options** Specify whether the building block should be placed in a paragraph by itself, on a page by itself, or simply positioned at the insertion point without adding a paragraph or page break when you insert it.

Using fields to automate documents

A *field* is a specialized placeholder for document content. (Word fields are not the same as data merge fields, as discussed earlier in this chapter. In fact, data merge fields are a type of Word field.) Fields can update dynamically, and they can be used for a wide variety of purposes. They can show variable data, such as the name of the document author, the number of pages in a document, or the date the document was last printed. They can be used to generate number sequences or even to perform numeric calculations. You can use fields to include certain text based on conditions you specify. You can use fields to create buttons that run macros or perform other actions, and you can use fields to enable an interactive document (one that asks a question and then enters the answer into the document).

And we're just scratching the surface. There's much more you can do with fields, but detailing it all is beyond the scope of this book. What we can do, however, is show you how to work with fields in general. Armed with that knowledge, you should be able to start using fields in your documents.

You've probably already used fields, possibly without knowing it. Many features of Word that we discuss elsewhere in this book (for example, tables of contents, indexes, date and time, and document properties) are implemented with fields, but Word provides an interface that shields you from having to work directly with fields in these cases. Knowing how to work with fields empowers you to tweak those fields in ways that can't be done through the normal user interface.

Working with field codes

A field can be represented in either of two ways: a field code (the programming language, if you will) or the field result (the output of the field code as normally displayed or printed in a document). For example, this field code:

`{Author}`

might yield this field result:

`Lori Kane`

To switch views between field codes and field results, press Alt+F9. Table 11-1 shows more keyboard shortcuts for working with fields.

A field code looks like ordinary text between curly braces—but there's nothing ordinary about the braces. You must insert them using Ctrl+F9 or with the Field dialog box. The text within those magic braces includes the field name and, in some cases, properties and switches. For example, the field code { SEQ OrderNum \n \#"##0" * MERGEFORMAT } includes the field name (SEQ), a property (OrderNum), and switches (the rest).

TABLE 11-1 Keyboard shortcuts for fields

Action	Keyboard shortcut
Insert an empty field	Ctrl+F9
Switch views between field codes and field results (all fields)	Alt+F9
Switch views between field codes and field results (selected fields)	Shift+F9
Update selected fields	F9
Go to next or previous field	F11 or Shift+F11
Lock a field to prevent updates	Ctrl+F11
Unlock a field	Ctrl+Shift+F11

Inserting a field

Before you step up to the big leagues and start entering field codes directly, use the Field dialog box to insert a field. It lists all the available fields, includes a brief description about each one, shows the proper syntax, and provides a method for inserting valid switches. To get there, click the Insert tab, and in the Text group click Quick Parts, Field. Figure 11-16 shows the Field dialog box that appears.

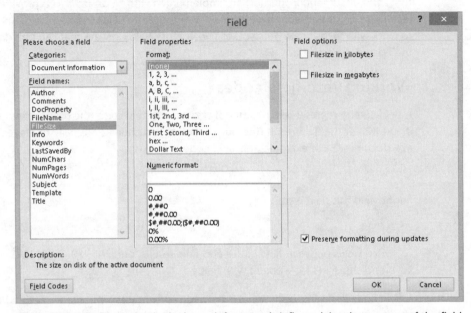

Figure 11-16 A description in the lower left corner briefly explains the purpose of the field selected in the Field Names box.

To narrow your choices a bit, select a category. Then select each field name and view its description to get an idea of what the field is used for. Make selections under Field Properties and Field Options, and then click Field Codes or the Options button (which appears after you click Field Codes) for assistance in entering other parameters.

There's much to learn about fields, and perhaps we've piqued your interest. If so, you can find additional details about using fields at *w7io.com/11001*, and a detailed reference at *w7io.com/31101*.

Our favorite Word tweaks and tips

We conclude our coverage of Word 2013 with descriptions of some seemingly esoteric customizations, tasks, and features. As it turns out, however, we use them often and it makes our use of Word a tad easier and more enjoyable. Perhaps you'll benefit from their use too. And while some authors wouldn't admit this, we finish off this section with a bit of filler text—but we think you'll like it!

Applying styles from the Quick Access Toolbar

On the Home tab, right-click an item in the Styles gallery and choose Add Gallery To Quick Access Toolbar. You can now apply gallery styles without displaying the Home tab; simply click the newly added icon on the Quick Access Toolbar to display the gallery. Note also that when you open the gallery on the Quick Access Toolbar, the dominant style of the current selection is highlighted, making this a handy way to see which styles are currently applied as well as a tool for applying a different style.

INSIDE OUT   Add any toolbar group to the Quick Access Toolbar

On the ribbon, a toolbar group is the collection of options between two vertical divider lines. You can add any toolbar group to the Quick Access Toolbar as a gallery-style menu. Right-click the group name and choose Add To Quick Access Toolbar. When you click the new icon on the Quick Access Toolbar, all the tools in the group appear below it.

Customizing the Quick Access Toolbar and the status bar

Some of our other favorite additions to the Quick Access Toolbar include the following:

- **Switch Windows**   If you frequently have more than one document window open, this tool makes switching between them quick and easy.

- **Open**   This tool is equivalent to clicking File, Open, saving you one click every time you want to reopen a recent file.

- **New...**   Similarly, this tool saves one click each time you create a new document by jumping directly to the New pane in Backstage view. (Note that the New... command is different from the New command, which opens a new document using the default template.)

- **Navigation Pane**   This tool lets you easily display or hide the Navigation pane.

- **Quick Print**   This tool immediately sends a document to the printer using default settings, thereby reducing three clicks (File, Print, Print) to one.

- **Show All**   When your document isn't laying out the way you expect it to, it's easier to figure out what's going on when you can see paragraph marks, new line characters, tabs, and other nonprinting characters.

Chapter 11

- **Insert A Comment** When collaborating on documents, we often use comments, and this tool saves a trip to the Review tab.

- **AutoCorrect Options** If you often add AutoCorrect entries, this tool saves you the drudgery of clicking File, Options, Proofing, AutoCorrect Options.

- **Building Blocks Organizer** This tool provides an alternative way to insert any type of building block, including AutoText entries.

For details, see "Customizing the Quick Access Toolbar" in Chapter 3, "Using and customizing the Office interface."

Because we often use change tracking, we also like to add an item to the status bar. Right-click the status bar and choose Track Changes. You can then click this status item to turn change tracking on or off.

Installing and using apps for Word

Like the other main applications in Office, Word 2013 is an extensible platform that allows the use of apps to supplement Word's capabilities in a variety of ways. Numerous research tools are available, including dictionaries (which not only expand the spelling-check capabilities of Word, but also provide definitions), thesauruses, encyclopedias, web search engines, and more. Other apps include templates, forms, calculators—and on and on.

We currently use only a few add-ins—a dictionary, a library of legal forms, and a "word cloud" generator—but we encourage you to see what's available and to find the ones that'll make you more productive.

To explore the options, on the Insert tab click Apps For Office, See All. On the My Apps tab, click the link to the Office Store. If you're looking for a particular type of app (for example, a dictionary), you can instead click Featured Apps and then enter a term in the search box.

Reading document text aloud

It's often useful to have a document read aloud. When you're proofreading text that you've retyped, you can read the original while Word speaks what you typed. And sometimes having something you've written spoken out loud exposes errors that you might miss by staring at the words on the screen or on paper.

Word has a well-hidden Speak command that can assist in these situations. Some very good text-to-speech implementations are available for modern computers; this isn't one of them. The spoken text is unmistakably computer-generated, yet it can be good enough for some purposes.

If you want to try it, you need to dig a bit. Right-click the ribbon and choose Customize The Ribbon. Under Choose Commands From, select Commands Not In The Ribbon. Scroll down to find the Speak command, and add it to the ribbon. (If you don't already have a custom group on the ribbon, you need to create one.) The Review tab is an appropriate location.

For details about adding a command to the ribbon, see "Personalizing the ribbon" in Chapter 3.

With the Speak command now ensconced on the ribbon, select some text and click Speak to hear a voice reminiscent of early science fiction movies.

Creating a cover page

A well-designed cover for a report or booklet can build brand awareness, entice readers, and even "cover" up some less-than-stellar content that follows. Recent versions of Word have included a gallery of cover pages, but this feature is not well known.

To view the gallery and insert a cover page, click Cover Page, in the Pages group on the Insert tab. The built-in cover pages rely on the current template, theme, and style set for colors, fonts, and other formatting, so they'll complement the rest of your document. They have content controls that pick up (and let you modify) document information, such as the name of the author, title of the document, and so on.

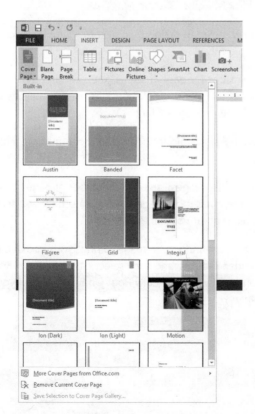

Chapter 11

In addition to the gallery of built-in cover pages, more are available at Office.com. You can also create your own cover page, select it, and add it to the gallery, using the command at the bottom of the Cover Page menu.

Printing booklets

Printing a multipage document in booklet form is a difficult task if you do it manually. You need to calculate page sizes and margins, and worst of all, you have to reorder the pages so that they come out in the proper order when the sheets are folded and collated. Fortunately, Word can do all the hard work for you.

> **Note**
>
> You'll have the most success setting up booklet printing if you follow these steps *before* you enter and format the document content.

To set up a document to print as a booklet, follow these steps:

1. On the Page Layout tab, click Margins, Custom Margins.

2. On the Margins tab of the Page Setup dialog box, next to Multiple Pages, select Book Fold.

3. Under Margins, enter dimensions for page margins. Keep in mind that the page size is now one-half of the paper size. (For example, if you're using letter size paper, the new effective page size is 5½ inches by 8½ inches.)

4. If you want to allow additional space along the fold to accommodate a binding, increase the Gutter value.

5. Next to Sheets Per Booklet (under Pages), select the number of pages you want in each booklet. If your document has more pages than the number you select, the document prints as multiple separate booklets.

After you create the document content and you're ready to print your booklet, choose File, Print. Click the second button under Settings, and then select either Print On Both Sides (if your printer can duplex automatically) or Manually Print On Both Sides (if your printer prints on only one side of the sheet).

Generating "greek" text

When you work on a design-oriented project in Word, you'll sometimes want to get an idea of how the document will look even before the copy for the document has been written. Graphic designers have long used filler text to show off design concepts without worrying that the client will get bogged down in the content. The technique is sometimes called "greeking"—which is somewhat ironic because the text most commonly used for greeking is in Latin.

That text begins "Lorem ipsum," and it's widely used because it approximates standard English text in word length and letter selection, yet it can't be mistaken for English. To enter that filler text in a document, start a new paragraph, type **=lorem()**, and press Enter. Word replaces this with five paragraphs of filler text.

If you want more or less filler text, insert two parameters within the parentheses: the number of paragraphs and the number of sentences in each paragraph. For example, typing **=lorem(2,4)** generates this text:

Lorem ipsum dolor sit amet, consectetuer adipiscing elit. Maecenas porttitor congue massa. Fusce posuere, magna sed pulvinar ultricies, purus lectus malesuada libero, sit amet commodo magna eros quis urna. Nunc viverra imperdiet enim.

Fusce est. Vivamus a tellus. Pellentesque habitant morbi tristique senectus et netus et malesuada fames ac turpis egestas. Proin pharetra nonummy pede.

Use just a single parenthetical parameter, and Word interprets that as the number of paragraphs you want, with each containing three sentences.

If you'd rather have something that looks more like English, use =rand() or =rand.old() in the same way.

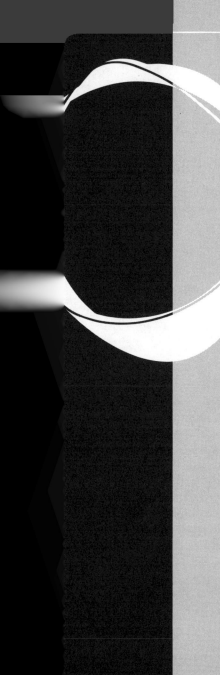

PART 4

Excel

ERHAPS because of its long association with accountants, Excel has a reputation as staid, even dull. It's the software equivalent of a gray flannel suit. We think that characterization is unfair. Yes, it's true that you can use Excel to count beans and widgets and calculate profits and losses with incredible precision. But you can also use this all-purpose tool for tasks that are completely unrelated to numbers. In the three chapters that begin here, we cover as many of those possibilities as we can.

We start with the nuts and bolts of Excel: what's in a workbook and how to navigate through the multiple dimensions of cells, rows, columns, and worksheets. Most of these elements will be familiar if you've used previous versions of Excel.

When you look past the grid-style layout, you can think of Excel as a powerful engine for performing calculations using numbers, dates, and text. The key to making these calculations work for you is understanding how to create formulas using arithmetic, logical, and comparison operators. Most valuable of all is a long list of functions that perform scientific, engineering, and statistical calculations that would take hours to work out manually. We cover Excel's extensive library of built-in functions in this chapter.

Also in this chapter, we explain how to enter data quickly and accurately and dive into the details of how Excel transforms what you type or paste into what you see on the screen with a look at number formatting. In the same spirit, we explain how to move, modify, and transform cells and ranges so the results are as you expect.

What's in an Excel workbook?

The sheer breadth of things you can create using Excel is staggering. Starting from a blank sheet, you can enter simple lists, take inventory of a collection, or prepare a consolidated financial report for a business of any size. With the right formatting, you can produce reports that look like they come from a desktop publishing shop, generate easy-to-read forms, and even construct calendars for use online or on paper. All of these uses start with a workbook, which is the default document format for Excel.

In this section, we assume that you are using the standard Microsoft Excel Worksheet (.xlsx) format. For a description of other available formats, see the sidebar "Supported file formats in Excel 2013," immediately following this section.

A workbook consists of one or more worksheets, each of which is made up of a maximum of 16,384 columns and 1,048,576 rows (although it's highly unlikely you'll ever create a worksheet big enough to need all of those theoretically available 17 billion-something cells). At the intersection of each row and column is a cell, which is identified by combining the letter from its column heading and the number from its row heading. Cell A1 is in the upper-left corner of every worksheet; C11 is the active cell if you move two columns over and 10 rows down; XFD1048576 is in the lower-right corner of the sheet. Click in any cell to begin entering text, a number, or a formula that performs a calculation using a worksheet function, with or without references to the contents of other cells. (We discuss formulas in much greater detail later in this chapter.)

Figure 12-1 shows a packing slip created in Excel. An employee who pulls up this template can fill in values in a few cells (or draw them directly from a database with a little programming help) and print out the resulting sheet to include with a shipment. The bold black lines identify the current cell, whose address, F3, appears in the Name box. The formula bar indicates that the cell contains a formula that returns the value of today's date. The formula result (December 23, 2012, in this example) appears in the worksheet.

Excel also allows you to create specialized data structures on a worksheet. You can define a range of cells as a table, for example, which lets you sort, filter, and format data arranged as a list. You can use PivotTables and PivotCharts to slice, filter, and summarize large sets of data. And you can create a chart from data on a worksheet to analyze trends and relationships visually.

For a full discussion of charts and tables, see Chapter 13, "Analyzing data with tables and charts." For a full discussion of PivotTables, see Chapter 14, "Excel 2013 inside out."

Although you can put together a workbook using a single worksheet, using multiple worksheets offers some notable advantages, especially in terms of organizing complex collections of data. Examples include:

- For a consolidated budget or financial report, you might keep the figures for each department on a separate worksheet. Each department fills in its own numbers using a standard template, and you "roll up" the results into a summary worksheet that uses the same structure to calculate a grand total for each row and column.

- For a workbook that contains details about a loan, you might keep the summary of interest rates, principal amounts, and payments on one worksheet and display a full amortization table on its own sheet, where you can view and print it separately.

As we discuss elsewhere in this book, you can display charts on their own worksheet, away from potentially distracting source data, and you can reduce complex data sets to easy-to-read summaries by adding a PivotTable on a separate sheet. You can also use multiple extra worksheets to perform back-of-the-envelope calculations without disturbing a carefully constructed and formatted main worksheet.

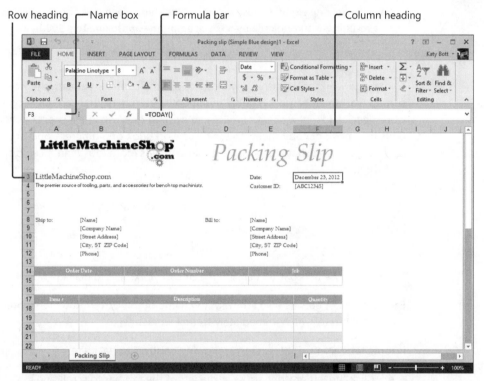

Figure 12-1 The contents of the current cell appear in the formula bar. The cell address, defined by intersecting column and row headings, is called out in the Name box.

INSIDE OUT Change the default number of worksheets

By default, each blank workbook you create contains a single blank worksheet. This is a change from previous versions, which insisted on giving you three worksheets with a new workbook. To modify this default for all new Excel workbooks you create, click File, and then click Options in Backstage view. On the General tab of the Excel Options dialog box, under the When Creating New Workbooks heading, adjust the Include This Many Sheets setting. The minimum is 1; the maximum is 255, although we can't imagine why anyone would choose a number that high. Each new sheet increases the size of the resulting workbook file by a trivial amount—approximately 500 bytes per sheet.

To manage worksheets within a workbook, use the controls beneath the worksheet. The current worksheet name is highlighted in bold. From here, you can select one or more worksheets, add a new sheet or delete an existing one, rename a sheet or change the color of its tab, move or copy sheets to the same workbook or a different one, and hide a worksheet. Figure 12-2 shows a worksheet that contains more tabs than it can display in the current window.

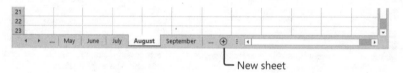

New sheet

Figure 12-2 Use the controls beneath the current worksheet to manage worksheet tabs.

Each worksheet gets its own tab, with the name of the current tab highlighted in bold. Click any visible tab to switch immediately to that worksheet.

If some tabs aren't visible, use the following controls to navigate:

- Click the left or right arrow at the left of the tab bar to scroll one tab at a time in either direction without leaving the current worksheet.

- Press Ctrl and click the left or right arrow to scroll to the first or last tab, respectively, in the current workbook.

- Click the ellipsis (...) on either side of the visible tabs to show the first hidden tab on that side and switch to that worksheet immediately. Continue clicking to scroll in that direction, displaying the contents of each worksheet as you go.

To create a new worksheet, click the large New Sheet button at the right of the worksheet tabs section, or use the keyboard shortcut Shift+F11. Newly created worksheets appear to the right of the selected worksheet tab in the current workbook and get a generic name with a number that is one higher than the most recently used number—Sheet2, Sheet3, and so on. To create a new sheet from a saved template, right-click the tab to the left of where you want the new sheet to appear, and then click Insert on the shortcut menu.

To rename a worksheet, double-click its name on the sheet tab and begin typing. A sheet name can have a maximum of 31 characters and can include spaces, parentheses, and most punctuation marks, with the exception of the following prohibited characters: [ ] / \ ? * : (brackets, slash and backslash, question mark, asterisk, and colon).

CAUTION !

> Just because you can create a 31-character sheet name doesn't mean you should. The names of worksheets are used in formulas when a referenced cell location is on a sheet other than the one containing the formula. Short, simple, descriptive names work best for this purpose; long, complex sheet names make it difficult to understand the design of a workbook or to debug a formula.

To color-code a worksheet tab (or a group of tabs selected using the standard Ctrl+click method), right-click the selected tab and click Tab Color. You can choose any standard color or a color from the current theme. Colored tabs are best used sparingly to help visually identify a group of related tabs or to make it easier to spot summary sheets.

To move a worksheet within a workbook, drag the sheet tab left or right. When the black triangular marker is over the location where you want the sheet to appear, release the mouse button. To move a sheet to a different workbook, make sure the destination work-book is open; then right-click the tab you want to move, and click Move Or Copy. In the Move Or Copy dialog box, select the name of the destination workbook from the To Book list and the tab location from the Before Sheet list, and then click OK.

To copy a worksheet to the same workbook, hold down the Ctrl key and drag the sheet tab left or right. The contents of the copied sheet are identical to the original, and the name is the same except for a numeric suffix. To copy a sheet to another open workbook, follow the same steps as for moving the sheet, but select Create A Copy in the Move Or Copy dialog box before clicking OK.

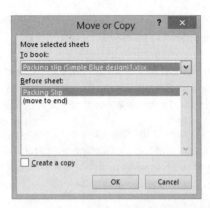

To hide a worksheet, right-click its tab and select Hide from the shortcut menu. The contents of that sheet are still available for formulas, but they are unavailable for casual inspection. This isn't a security feature—its primary purpose is to remove potentially distracting elements that are necessary for workbook calculations but shouldn't be changed. To see a list of hidden sheets so you can make one or more visible, right-click any sheet tab and click Unhide.

Supported file formats in Excel 2013

In this book, we assume that you are using the standard Microsoft Excel Worksheet (.xlsx) format. Excel can also open, edit, and save files in several other formats, with some limitations. Not all features are available when using other file formats, and you might notice minor (or even major) layout changes when you switch between formats.

Excel 2013 can open and save documents in any of these formats:

- **Excel Spreadsheet (.xlsx) and Excel Macro-Enabled Spreadsheet (.xlsm)** These formats use the Transitional Open XML format and provide full functionality in Excel 2007 and later. The first type, the default in Excel 2013, cannot contain VBA macro code; the latter can. In the Save As dialog box, these formats are called Workbook and Macro-Enabled Workbook, respectively.

- **Strict Open XML Spreadsheet (.xlsx)** This file type, which is fully supported in Excel 2013, uses a variation of the Open XML format that does not rely on Microsoft data formats. This format can be opened (but not saved) in Excel 2010; it is incompatible with Excel 2007 and earlier versions.

- **Excel Binary Workbook (.xlsb)** This format provides extremely fast performance for opening and saving data files. File sizes are larger than comparable .xlsx files, and this format is less secure.

- **Excel Template (.xltx) and Excel Macro-Enabled Template (.xltm)**   Excel Template is the default format for templates in Excel 2007 and later; the Excel Macro-Enabled Template format can contain VBA code. When you save a workbook created from a macro-enabled template that includes macro code, Excel prompts you to save the workbook as macro-enabled.

- **Excel 97–2003 Worksheet (.xls) and Excel 97-2003 Template (.xlt)**   These are the native formats used by versions of Excel prior to Excel 2007.

- **Microsoft Excel 5.0/95 Workbook (.xls)**   This format was widely used in the mid-1990s.

- **Web Page (.htm or .html) and Single File Web Page (.mht or .mhtl)**   An HTML file contains only text and commands; other webpage elements, such as pictures and style sheets, are stored in separate files, which Excel saves in a subfolder with the same name as the HTML file. The Single File Web Page format saves all components in a single portable file that can be viewed in a web browser. You can save an entire workbook or a single worksheet using these formats.

- **Text (Tab Delimited), Unicode Text, Text (Macintosh), and Text (MS-DOS) (.txt)**   Each of these formats creates a plain-text file in which each cell in a row is separated by a tab character. The difference among the four variants is the character encoding.

- **CSV (Comma Delimited), CSV (Macintosh), CSV (MS-DOS) (.csv)**   These formats are similar to the preceding format, except that a comma separates each cell value.

- **Formatted Text (Space Delimited) (.prn)**   This plain-text file uses spaces to align columns of data.

- **DIF (Data Interchange Format) (.dif)**   This is a text file format that dates back to the 1980s; it's designed for moving data between different spreadsheet programs.

- **SYLK (Symbolic Link) (.slk)**   This is another format for exchanging data between different spreadsheet programs.

- **XML Data (.xml)**   This format can be used in custom data interchange applications.

- **XML Spreadsheet 2003 (.xml)**   This format uses XML tags that correspond to an XML schema, making it useful for some custom data interchange applications.

- **Excel Add-In (.xlam)**   This format is used for supplemental programs that run code. It supports the use of VBA projects and Excel 4.0 macro sheets.

Chapter 12

- **Excel 97-2003 Add-In (.xla)**   This is the add-in format used by earlier versions of Excel.

- **OpenDocument Spreadsheet (.ods)**   This XML-based format was originally developed for the OpenOffice.org office suite.

Excel 2013 can open (but not save) documents in these formats:

- **Excel 4.0 Workbook (.xlw)**   This format dates to the early 1990s.

- **Excel 4.0 Macro (.xlm, .xla)**   This import-only format lets you open macro sheets created with ancient Excel versions and convert them to VBA.

- **Access Database (.mdb, .mde, .accdb, .accde)**   Selecting one of these formats allows you to import data from an Access database.

- **Query File (.iqy, .dqy, .oqy, .rqy)**   These import-only formats allow you to use data from a SQL Server database.

- **dBase File (.dbf)**   Select a file saved in this format to import data from a dBase database.

Excel 2013 can save (but not open) documents in these formats:

- **PDF (.pdf)**   This export-only format lets you create documents that can be viewed on nearly any computer. For details about working with PDF files, see "Exporting files and data to alternative formats" in Chapter 6, "Managing Office files."

- **XPS Document (.xps)**   This format provides an alternative to PDF. A viewer for XPS documents is built in to Windows 8, Windows 7, and Windows Vista; viewers for some other platforms are available.

Navigating in worksheets and workbooks

You can plod your way through any worksheet by clicking and typing in individual cells, but worksheets and formulas become much more powerful when you work with multiple cells simultaneously. In Excel's parlance, any selection of two or more cells is a *range*. You can use a range as the argument in a formula and to define data series and labels in charts. You can also enter, edit, and format data in multiple cells simultaneously by selecting a range first. In a budget worksheet, for example, you can select the range containing totals and apply the Currency format to all the cells in that range with a single action.

If you click in any cell and drag in any direction, your selection of adjacent cells is called a *contiguous range*. As you expand your selection, the Name box provides feedback about the size of the range. In this example, the current range consists of four rows and three columns:

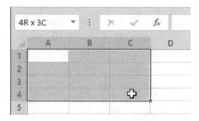

A reference to a contiguous range consists of two cell addresses separated by a colon. The two addresses identify the upper-left and lower-right corners of the range, respectively. In the previous example, the range address is A1:C4. You can also define a *noncontiguous range* by holding down the Ctrl key as you select any combination of individual cells and ranges on a single worksheet. You can apply cell formatting to a contiguous or noncontiguous range, and you can use either type of range as the argument in a formula.

One related navigational concept is worth noting here as well. Excel defines the current *region* as the area around the active cell that is separated from the rest of the worksheet by blank rows and blank columns. If you define a table, for example, Excel expands the default selection to include the current region.

INSIDE OUT   Select rows, columns, and entire sheets

To select an entire row or column, click the row heading or column heading, respectively. To select multiple columns or rows, drag the selection across multiple headings (or hold down the Ctrl key as you select additional rows or columns). To select all cells in a worksheet (so that you can apply global formatting, for example), click the unlabeled Select All button in the upper-left corner of the sheet, just below the Name box. To reference a range that includes all the cells in a given row or column, use the row number or column letter by itself. Thus, a reference to 5:5 means all cells in row 5, and AC:AE refers to all cells in columns AC, AD, and AE.

Chapter 12

Using cell addresses and range names

The Name box, just to the left of the formula bar (above the current worksheet contents), shows the address of the active cell. This is true even if the current selection consists of a range.

You can jump to any cell by entering its address in the Name box and pressing Enter. If you enter the address of a contiguous range in the Name box (H8:J10, for example), pressing Enter selects that range and makes the cell in the upper-left corner of that range active and ready to accept input.

The Name box has a much more practical use, however. Excel allows you to assign names to any cell or range or to a formula or constant. If your worksheet includes a table listing sales-tax rates by state, you can define each rate using a descriptive name: CASalesTaxRate, AZSalesTaxRate, and so on. You can then use those names in place of the corresponding cell or range address in formulas. On an invoice worksheet, for example, you can define Items_Total as the name for the cell that sums up the price of all items in the order and then use a formula like this one to calculate the sales tax for California residents:

```
=Items_Total*CASalesTaxRate
```

That's easier to understand than =D14*E76, isn't it? The advantage of using a range name is especially apparent when you have to review and revise a worksheet that someone else created (or even one that you created months or years earlier). Think of range names as a part of the documentation of the logic and structure of a worksheet and workbook.

Excel creates some names automatically—when you define a table or a print range, for example—but you can also define names manually. The simplest way to define a name is to select a cell or range, click in the Name box, type a name, and press Enter. For more control over the naming process, click the Formulas tab, and then click Define Name in the Defined Names group. That opens the New Name dialog box, shown in Figure 12-3.

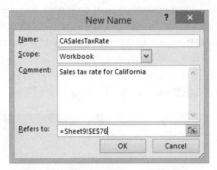

Figure 12-3 Using the Define Name command allows you to add comments to the name you assign to a cell or range.

By default, all names you create use absolute cell references. For an explanation of this type of reference, see "Using formulas and functions," later in this chapter.

The rules for a cell or range name are strict: Names are not case-sensitive. The first character must be a letter, an underscore, or a backslash, and remaining characters (up to a total of 255) can be letters, numbers, periods, and underscore characters. Spaces, punctuation, and other special characters are prohibited. You cannot use any name that could be confused for a cell reference, and you cannot use the single letters C or R (capitals or lowercase), which could be misinterpreted as "column" or "row."

To pick from a list of all named cells and ranges in the current workbook, even those on different worksheets, click the drop-down arrow to the right of the Name box.

Using keyboard shortcuts

For the productivity-obsessed, mouse pointers and scroll bars are like roadblocks and speed bumps. Keyboard shortcuts are almost always faster, and they sometimes offer unique navigation and tricks that aren't available any other way. Excel shares a few keyboard shortcuts with its fellow Office programs, including F2 to make the contents of the current selection available for editing and F4 to repeat the previous action. Ctrl+X, Ctrl+C, and Ctrl+V work for Cut, Copy, and Paste; Ctrl+Alt+V for Paste Special; and Ctrl+Z and Ctrl+Y for Undo and Redo. For formatting, you can count on the old standbys Ctrl+B, Ctrl+I, and Ctrl+U to apply bold, italic, and underline formatting, respectively, to the current selection.

In Table 12-1, we list some useful and unjustly obscure shortcuts available only in Excel.

TABLE 12-1 Keyboard shortcuts used only in Excel

Action	Keyboard shortcut
Move to beginning of current row	Home
Move to upper-left corner of current sheet	Ctrl+Home
Move up one window	Page Up
Move down one window	Page Down
Move to previous worksheet	Ctrl+Page Up
Move to next worksheet	Ctrl+Page Down
Expand/collapse the formula bar	Ctrl+Shift+U
Select the current region	Ctrl+*
Select all cells containing comments	Ctrl+Shift+O
Display the Insert dialog box	Ctrl+Plus Sign (+)
Display the Delete dialog box	Ctrl+Minus Sign (–)
Hide selected rows	Ctrl+9
Hide selected columns	Ctrl+0

Chapter 12

A few useful keyboard shortcuts require more explanation than we can pack into a table.

In other Office programs, Ctrl+A is the shortcut for Select All. In Excel, however, this keyboard shortcut has at least three separate actions. If the current worksheet contains data, pressing Ctrl+A selects the current region. Press Ctrl+A again to select the entire worksheet. If you select a cell and type an equal sign followed by a function name, pressing Ctrl+A opens the Function Arguments dialog box.

Moving around within a selected range can be tedious, especially when the selection encompasses a long list with boundaries that extend well beyond the edges of the current window. In that case, press Ctrl+Period to move the active cell clockwise through the four corners of the selected range, without affecting the selection.

And then there's the End key, which enables a baffling set of navigation shortcuts collectively known as *End Mode*. When you press the End key in Excel, you might miss the small, subtle change along the left side of the status bar, where the words *End Mode* become visible. When this indicator is visible, typical navigation keys temporarily change their behavior in unusual ways.

- Press End and then press any arrow key to move the selection within the current row or column, in the direction of the arrow, to the next cell that contains data, skipping over any blank cells in between. You can accomplish the same movement using the Ctrl+arrow key shortcuts.

- Press End and then Home to move to the bottom-right corner of the portion of the worksheet that contains data—in other words, the cell that is at the intersection of the farthest data-containing row and column in the sheet. So, for example, if the outer reaches of the data in your worksheet (the row farthest from the top and the column farthest from the left) are in cell A277 and Z1, respectively, this shortcut takes you immediately to Z277. The keyboard shortcut Ctrl+End leads to the same destination.

- Press End and then Enter to move to the last cell in the current row, skipping over any blank cells. This End Mode trick has no corresponding Ctrl-key shortcut.

End Mode is enabled only until you press another key. If the next key you press is something other than one of the navigation keys in the previous list, such as a letter or number or function key, Excel turns End Mode off and processes that key press normally. If you accidentally enable End Mode, you can turn it off by pressing End again.

Entering and filling in data and series

For basic data entry tasks, Excel works about as you would expect. Click to select a cell, type something, and press Enter; or use the Clipboard to paste data copied from elsewhere. In this section, we explore a few techniques that are unique (and useful) in Excel.

When designing a worksheet, you might want to enter a constant value (such as 0) or an identical formula in a range of cells. Instead of filling each cell manually, speed things up by selecting the entire range (contiguous or noncontiguous) first. Type the text, value, or formula you want to include in each cell, and then press Ctrl+Enter. When you use this technique to enter a formula into multiple cells, the resulting entry uses relative cell references. If you want one or more references in the formula to use absolute or mixed references, adjust the formula before you press Ctrl+Enter.

For an explanation of the difference between absolute, relative, and mixed references, see "Using formulas and functions," later in this chapter.

To enter today's date into the active cell, press Ctrl+; (semicolon); to enter the current time, press Ctrl+: (colon).

A handful of keyboard shortcuts and mouse tricks allow you to copy data or formulas or fill a series through a range. Filling a range is a very powerful way to quickly build a worksheet, and you can take your pick of menus, keyboard shortcuts, and mouse gestures to accomplish the task.

Consider this scenario. You have a worksheet in which you have set aside column D for the results of this month's sales, which you plan to update daily. You've entered a formula in cell F2 to track performance against goal and formatted the cell so it uses the Percentage format. You now want to copy that value and formatting to column F for each of the remaining rows. Here's what this section of the worksheet looks like when we select the range we want to fill.

⊿	A	B	C	D	E	F
1	EmpID	LastName	FirstName	Sales	Goal	% of Goal
2	1	Bott	Ed	525	400	131%
3	2	Siechert	Carl	450	400	
4	3	Czernek	Pawel	375	400	
5	4	Cupala	Shiraz	700	400	

To copy the contents and formatting from the top cell in this range to all other cells, press Ctrl+D. If you prefer a ribbon-driven approach, click Fill (in the Editing group on the Home tab) and then click Down. If the top cell contains a formula, that formula is copied (with relative references) to the cells in the range below it. If the cell contains text or a number, that entry is copied exactly. If the selection contains more than one column, the contents of the first cell in each column of the range is copied to the cells beneath.

> ### CAUTION
>
> Using any of the Fill options completely replaces the contents of the destination cells. If those cells contain valuable data, you lose that data. To avoid this problem, use Ctrl+click to select the cells whose contents you want to replace and then use the Ctrl+Enter shortcut we discuss earlier in this section to enter the text, constant, or formula into only those selected cells.

A similar technique exists to fill a selection within a row. Enter the value, text, or formula in the first cell, and select the range to the right where you want to fill. Press Ctrl+R, or click Fill (in the Editing group on the Home tab) and then click Right. The Fill menu on the Home tab contains Up and Left options as well; there are no corresponding keyboard shortcuts for those operations.

Even more powerful is the ability to extend a series of numbers, dates, or values.

To fill in a series of numbers, enter the first value in the series and then select that cell and the remainder of the range where you want the series to continue. We want to begin a series with the year 1960, so we entered it in cell A2 and selected the balance of the range. Click Fill (in the Editing group on the Home tab) and then click Series to display the dialog box shown in Figure 12-4.

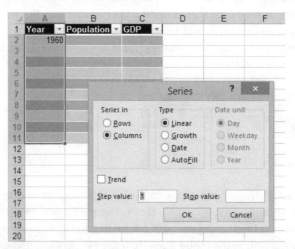

Figure 12-4 Click OK to fill in the values 1960 through 1969 in the selected range. Change the step value to 5 to fill in succeeding values with 1965, 1970, 1975, and so on.

Using the default step value of 1, Excel fills in 1961, 1962, and so on, all the way to 1969 in our selection of 10 cells. If we change that value to 5, each step in the series shifts accordingly, to 1965, 1970, and so on.

Ironically, the Date Unit section of this dialog box is unavailable in the previous figure even though we entered what looks like a date. Why? Because Excel didn't store our entry in date format. To make the Date Unit options available, we could change the entry in cell A2 to 1/1/1960; if we format that value using the mmm-yyyy format and choose a date unit of Month and a step value of 6, the series will progress through Jul-1960, Jan-1961, Jul-1961, and so on.

All the previous copies and fills can be accomplished just as easily by dragging the fill handle in the lower-right corner of a cell or range. Using the fill handle allows you to extend a surprising variety of series, some of which are not available from the Series option on the Fill menu. Besides numeric series, you can extend units of time, including hours of the day (9:00 AM, 10:00 AM, …) and days of the week or months of the year, abbreviated (Mon, Tues, … and Jan, Feb, …) or fully spelled out. As you can see in the following example, the fill handle looks like a thin black cross; as you drag, the border shows you which cells you've selected and a ScreenTip shows what will appear in the cell.

Drag the selection back up (or to the left, if you're working row-wise) to make the AutoFill range smaller. If you continue dragging down past Sunday, the series repeats. Months work the same way.

Excel knows that business runs on quarterly results. If you enter Q1 in a cell and then drag the fill handle down or to the right, Excel smartly assumes you want to continue with Q2, Q3, and Q4 and then start over with Q1. (You can get a similar result if you begin with 1st quarter or Quarter 1.) Excel continues repeating the series in this fashion until you release the mouse button.

If you start with a single cell containing a number and drag the fill handle down, Excel copies the contents of the initial cell into the remainder of the range (1, 1, 1, 1). Hold down Ctrl as you drag the fill handle to change to a series (1, 2, 3, 4). A small plus sign appears alongside the fill handle when it switches to series mode.

You can also fill a series containing text and a number. If you enter District 1 and drag the fill handle down, the series continues with District 2, District 3, and so on.

As with so many things in Office, you can also use the right mouse button to good advantage with the fill handle. When you release the mouse button after dragging, Excel displays a shortcut menu showing many of the options from the Series dialog box.

If you've already filled a range, use the AutoFill menu shown here to switch from Copy Cells to Fill Series or vice versa. You can also copy formatting only or choose Fill Without Formatting to add only the values in your series.

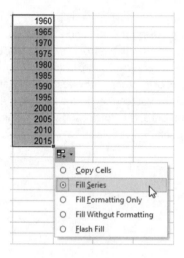

INSIDE OUT Give Excel some extra clues about your series

For most series, Excel uses the default step value of 1 when you extend the series using the fill handle or the Series dialog box. If you want to use a different series, enter values in two or more cells—enough to make it clear what the series is—and then select both cells and drag the fill handle down (to fill a column) or to the right (to fill a row). If you start with Jan 2014 and Apr 2014, for example, Excel assumes (probably correctly) that you want to continue with July 2014, Oct 2014, and Jan 2015. It formats the values as dates for you as well. And you don't have to mess with any dialog boxes to make it so.

The last entry on the AutoFill menu is a new option in Excel 2013 called Flash Fill. (You'll find it in the Editing group on the Home tab as well). This option allows you to perform some fills that would normally require you to use formulas. Flash Fill works by examining the contents of columns to the left of those in the column you want to fill. Enter two or three examples of the output you want to see, and Flash Fill tries to figure out what you're trying to do.

Figure 12-5, for example, shows a column of dates, formatted so that they show short months. We want to fill the column to its right with the value for just the month, as in the two examples we've entered manually.

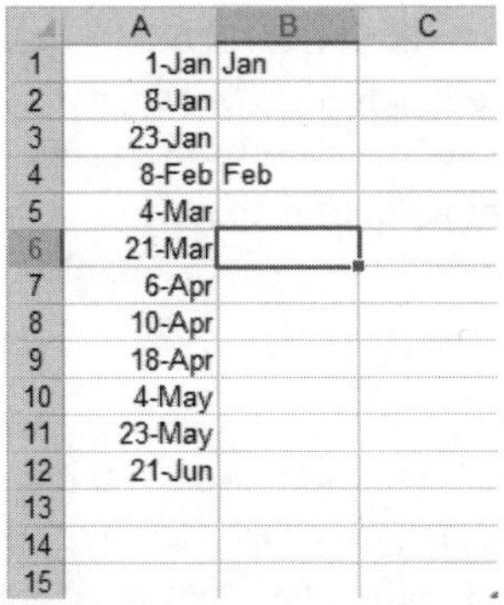

	A	B	C
1	1-Jan	Jan	
2	8-Jan		
3	23-Jan		
4	8-Feb	Feb	
5	4-Mar		
6	21-Mar		
7	6-Apr		
8	10-Apr		
9	18-Apr		
10	4-May		
11	23-May		
12	21-Jun		
13			
14			
15			

Figure 12-5 To use Flash Fill, enter a couple of examples of the results you want, as in column B here.

Leave the active cell in the same column as the two example entries and then press Ctrl+E (or use the Flash Fill option on the Fill menu on the Home tab). Excel guesses what you wanted to do and fills in the result in the column you selected (or tells you with an error message that you've stumped its algorithm). Figure 12-6 shows the result.

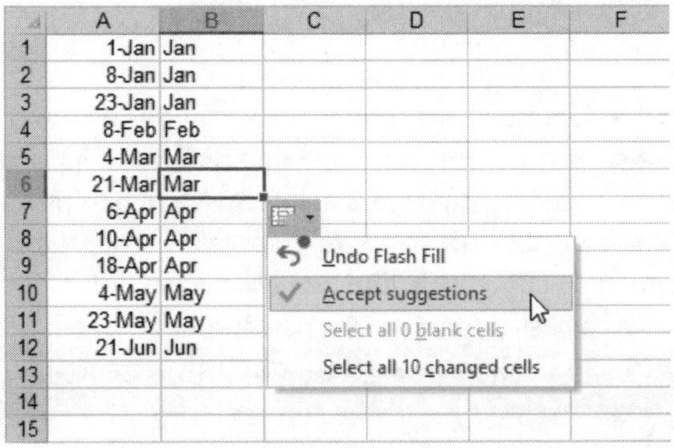

	A	B	C	D	E	F
1	1-Jan	Jan				
2	8-Jan	Jan				
3	23-Jan	Jan				
4	8-Feb	Feb				
5	4-Mar	Mar				
6	21-Mar	Mar				
7	6-Apr	Apr				
8	10-Apr	Apr				
9	18-Apr	Apr				
10	4-May	May				
11	23-May	May				
12	21-Jun	Jun				
13						
14						
15						

Figure 12-6 Flash Fill correctly deduced that we wanted to fill column B with the short form of the month from the previous column.

Click the icon in the lower-right corner of the active cell to open the Flash Fill Options menu, where you can undo the operation or accept it and make the menu indicator go away. You can also select all blank cells, perhaps to use Ctrl+Enter to insert a default value into those cells or all changed cells.

For more details on how to use and fine-tune Clipboard options, see "Using the Clipboard with Office programs" in Chapter 4, "Entering, editing, and formatting text."

Using formulas and functions

If the following section brings up unpleasant memories of high-school algebra assignments and nightmares about trigonometry, we apologize in advance. But we can't talk about Excel without discussing—at great length—its amazing ability to perform calculations. This section is all about formulas, which are equations that Excel uses to perform mathematical and statistical calculations, manipulate text, test logical conditions, look up information in databases, and much more. We promise: there won't be a test.

A formula is a self-contained set of instructions for Excel to follow, using a well-defined syntax. Excel evaluates the formula when you press Enter and displays the formula's result in the cell. (Unless the formula contains an error, that is, in which case you get an error message and help on fixing the error.) The formula itself remains visible in the formula bar when you select the cell.

To begin entering a formula, click in any cell and type an equal sign, followed by any valid combination of the following four elements:

- **Constants** are numbers or text values that you enter directly and that remain the same regardless of any ensuing calculations.

- **References** are cell or range addresses that incorporate the contents of the referenced location into the current formula.

- **Functions** are predefined formulas that perform calculations by using specific values, called *arguments*. The syntax of a particular function defines which arguments are required and which are optional. Arguments are enclosed in parentheses after the function name and can consist of constants, references, or other functions. Multiple arguments are separated by commas. A function used as an argument in another function is referred to as a *nested function*. A small number of functions use no arguments. NOW(), TODAY(), and PI(), for example, return the current time, today's date, and the value of pi, respectively.

- **Operators** define the types of calculations performed in a formula: arithmetic, comparisons, text concatenation, and reference. Excel has strict rules on the order in which calculations are performed; you can control the order of calculation by using parentheses.

We define each of these categories in more detail, with examples, in the following section.

Creating and editing formulas

The number of things you can do with Excel formulas and functions is literally limitless, especially when you learn to combine functions. We don't, alas, have limitless pages in this section, so we'll be sure we cover the fundamentals of how to add a formula to your worksheet and how to use built-in tools to find the correct syntax for any function and enter its arguments correctly. After we cover that ground, we'll dive into the built-in functions by category, providing examples that we think you're likely to find useful.

Although the examples we show in this section use capital letters, you don't need to wear out the Shift key when you use Excel. You can enter functions, references, and other parts of a formula in lowercase; Excel takes care of converting those elements to the proper case when you enter the formula.

The simplest formulas of all are those that use only constants and simple math operators without references to other cells or functions. The following formula, for example, is perfectly valid:

=2+2

If you're working in Excel, you can use any available cell as a quick-and-dirty calculator—presumably to figure something slightly more complex than 2+2. Just start with an equal sign and use any of the supported arithmetic operators as listed in Table 12-2.

TABLE 12-2 Arithmetic operators supported in Excel formulas

Operator	Usage
+ (plus sign)	Addition (=14+7, =C4+C5). If one of the values is negative, the result is the same as subtraction.
– (minus sign)	Subtraction (=17–3, =D1–D2) or negation (=–6, =–A7).
* (asterisk)	Multiplication (=3*10, =B5*B6).
/ (forward slash)	Division (=24/8, =B5/C5). The elements on either side of the operator are the dividend and the divisor, respectively. If the divisor evaluates to zero, you get a #DIV/0! error.
% (percent sign)	Percent (=10%, =F14%). The result is the same as dividing the number by 100; typically used with multiplication, as in =10%*42, which results in 4.2
^ (caret)	Exponentiation (=3^2, =C4^D8). Multiplies the number to the left of the operator by itself the number of times specified by the number to the right of the operator

When you use any of the arithmetic operators, the constants, references, functions, or formulas on both sides of the operator must result in values. If your formula is =C4+C5 or =D1*C5 and C5 is a text string, your result is the same: a #VALUE! error.

INSIDE OUT   Keyboard shortcuts for formulas

For touch typists who think moving one's hands away from the keyboard is a surrender to the forces of chaos and anarchy, we offer these productivity-salvaging keyboard shortcuts:

Ctrl+`   (The character shown is an accent grave, typically found beneath the tilde at the left of the number row on a standard PC keyboard.) This shortcut alternates between displaying cell values and displaying formulas in the worksheet and offers a useful way to see a worksheet's logic at a glance.

Ctrl+'   (The character shown is an apostrophe, typically found to the left of the Enter key on a standard PC keyboard.) Use this shortcut to copy a formula from the cell above into the active cell.

Ctrl+A   Enter an equal sign, followed by any function name, and then press this keyboard shortcut to open the Function Arguments dialog box

Ctrl+Shift+A   Enter an equal sign, followed by any function name, and then press this keyboard shortcut to insert the argument names and parentheses.

The most common of all formula tools is AutoSum—it's so useful in so many places that it gets its own button on both the Home tab and the Formulas tab in Excel *and* its own keyboard shortcut, Alt+= (equal sign). If you select a cell (empty or not) and click the AutoSum button, Excel inserts the =SUM formula. If Excel detects numbers in the column above or the row to the left of the active cell (even if some blank cells separate the range from the SUM function), it fills in that range as the argument. You can accept the default argument or adjust it as needed.

Click the AutoSum arrow to choose from a menu of other functions—Average, Count Numbers, Max, and Min—to automatically fill in those functions.

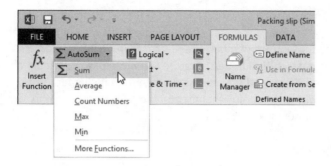

INSIDE OUT   Use names in place of formulas

Although names are most commonly used as cell or range references (as we described earlier in this chapter in "Using cell addresses and range names"), you can also assign a name to a formula. The named formula can refer to cells in the current worksheet or workbook, or it can stand on its own. To assign a name to a formula, click the Formulas tab and click Define Name. In the New Name dialog box, enter a name, and then type the formula itself in the Refers To box. For example, you could create the name End_Of_ Next_Month and apply it to the formula =EOMONTH(TODAY(),1). That formula checks today's date and then returns the last day of the next month. To use the name as part of a formula, click the Formulas tab, click Use In Formula, and select End_Of_Next_Month from the list of available names.

Making comparisons

Comparison operators allow you to compare two values and return a logical result of TRUE or FALSE. This type of comparison is usually combined with a logical function such as IF, which allows you to perform one calculation or return a specific value if the result of the logical test is TRUE and do something different if the result is FALSE. Table 12-3 lists all comparison operators that Excel supports.

TABLE 12-3 Comparison operators supported in Excel formulas

Operator	Usage
=	Equal to (A1=B1, C3=0)
>	Greater than (A1>B1, C3>0)
<	Less than (A1<B1)
>=	Greater than or equal to (A1>=B1)
<=	Less than or equal to (A1<=B1)
<>	Not equal to (A1<>B1)

Comparisons of similar data types work as you would expect. For values—including constants as well as references and formulas that evaluate to values—higher numbers are greater than lower and positive numbers are greater than negative numbers. Dates can be compared to other dates or to numbers. (For the technical reasons, see the discussion of date serial numbers in "Date and time functions," later in this chapter.) Text comparisons use alphabetical order, with letters before numbers and case ignored. (In other words, "District" and "district" are considered equal.)

Concatenating text

You can combine two or more text values to produce a single text value. What makes this magic possible is the concatenation operator—an ampersand (&). A very common use of this operator is in address lists where first and last names are in separate columns. To combine the names into a single cell, use a formula like the one shown here:

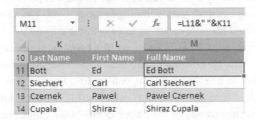

This sample uses two concatenation operators and illustrates that you can insert literal text (like the space between the two names) as long as you enclose it in quotation marks. So, if you have a list of opening and closing dates for a school, with one such date in cell E2, you could convert it to a more readable text value by using the following formula:

="Closing day: "&TEXT(E2,"mmmm dd, yyyy")

The formula grabs the date from the referenced cell, reformats it, and appends the introductory text. Compare the contents of the formula bar to the formula's result, as displayed in bold here:

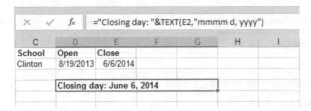

This example also illustrates a requirement for any concatenation operation: to concatenate other data types, such as dates and numbers, you must first convert those values to text. That's why we used the TEXT function in this formula.

For a more detailed discussion of functions used to convert and manipulate text, see "Text functions," later in this chapter.

Relative, absolute, and mixed references

Any formula can contain references to cells. Excel uses the value stored in the referenced cell to perform any calculations, just as though that value had been entered directly in the formula itself. You can combine ranges of cells for calculations by using three reference operators.

The most common is the range operator, which is a colon between two cell addresses. It includes the two referenced cells and all cells in between them. In the formula =SUM(C1:C10), the calculation adds up all values in all cells in the range C1 to C10.

You can also use a comma as an operator to refer to a discontiguous range. In the formula =SUM(C1,C3,C5-C10), Excel adds all values in cells C1, C3, and C5 through C10.

The most obscure reference operator of all is the rarely seen intersection operator, represented by a space. It returns the values from all cells that are common to the ranges on either side of the space. Thus =SUM(C1:C6 C5:C10) adds the contents of cells C5 and C6, which are the only ones that both ranges have in common.

Unless you specifically choose otherwise, every reference you enter in a worksheet is stored as a relative reference. When you move or copy a relative reference from one cell to another in a worksheet, the reference in the destination cell adjusts to reflect the same relative location. In Figure 12-7, we copied formulas from cell D7 to the corresponding cell in each data-containing row below it. We used the Ctrl+` (accent grave) shortcut to show the formula itself rather than the formula's results, demonstrating how the row number in each reference changes to reflect the correct relative location.

	A	B	C	D
1	Monthly Family Budget			
6	Housing	Projected Cost	Actual Cost	Difference
7	Mortgage or rent	1000	1000	=B7-C7
8	Second mortgage or rent	0	0	=B8-C8
9	Phone	62	100	=B9-C9
10	Electricity	44	125	=B10-C10
11	Gas	22	35	=B11-C11

Figure 12-7 When we copied the formula from the top of the Difference column to the cells beneath it, Excel adjusted the references so that they work properly with the data in each row.

In some cases, you want a reference in a formula to point to a specific cell even when you copy the formula to a new location. Say you set aside cell A1 as the input cell where you'll enter an assumption, such as the annual inflation rate, for use throughout your worksheet.

By trying different values in this cell, you can do what-if exercises with the remainder of the sheet.

To calculate the increase for the value shown in cell D4, you use the formula =D4*(1+A1). So far so good. When you copy the formula for use with D5, D6, and so on, the first reference changes just as you want. But so, unfortunately, does the second reference, so you end up with =D5*(1+A2). Because your assumption is entered only in A1, your formula returns an incorrect (or at least unexpected) result in each of the other cells.

The solution is to use an *absolute cell reference,* which is indicated by adding a dollar sign before the column letter and row number in the reference: =D4*(1+$A$1). When you copy this formula, Excel adjusts the first, relative reference but leaves the absolute reference alone. You can type the dollar signs for an absolute reference directly or click to position the insertion point in the cell reference you want to adjust and then press F4. (To make a range reference absolute, select the entire reference, including the range operator, before pressing F4.)

As we noted earlier in this chapter, named cells and ranges are always treated as absolute references. So, if you select cell A1 and define its name as Inflation_Rate, you can use that name in your formula and copy the formula to other rows and columns without making any adjustments.

Sometimes, a halfway approach is called for, in which either the row or the column reference remains fixed while the other half of the reference address changes. This construction is called a *mixed range,* with a dollar sign in front of either the row or column portion of the reference to indicate that that value should not change. Imagine a budget spreadsheet where you have category names in column C identifying each row, with month names over each column containing projected spending by that department for the month. In column D, you want to enter a fixed amount that represents the annual increase or decrease for that category, and you want to multiply the previous year's spending in that category by the same amount. As you copy the formula across each row, you want it to refer to the value in column D in that row. When you copy the formulas to the rows below, you want the row reference and not the column reference to change. Here's how a mixed reference solves that problem:

		f_x	=E15*(1+$D4)	
C	D	E	F	
Category	Annual adjustment	Jan	Feb	
Wages	5.60%	11,146	8,917	
Benefits	5.20%	2,931	2,655	
Payroll taxes	1.50%	1,068	855	
Insurace	8.90%	896	735	

The mixed reference $D4 tells Excel that no matter where you copy the formula, it should always point to the value in column D *for the current row*. To create a mixed range, type it manually or select the reference and then press F4 multiple times to cycle through each available option.

Controlling the order of calculation in a formula

The order in which Excel performs operations in formulas makes a difference. It's common for formulas to contain multiple operators. Unless you specify a custom order by using parentheses, Excel performs calculations in the following order:

- % (percent)

- ^ (exponentiation)

- * and / (multiplication and division)

- + and – (addition and subtraction)

- & (concatenation)

- =, < and >, <= and >=, and <> (comparison)

When the same operator is used multiple times in a formula, the calculations are performed in order from left to right.

When you use functions as arguments within functions, use multiple sets of parentheses to keep things separate. You can nest functions to as many as 64 levels within a formula.

Adding functions to a formula

Excel savants who've memorized the syntax of the functions they use regularly can enter a formula as fast as they can type. Start with an equal sign, spell each function name correctly, use arguments of the correct type, separate arguments with commas, and make sure every opening parenthesis is matched with a closing parenthesis. As long as you get all those details right, you'll have no problems.

If you've memorized the syntax for a particular function and the formula is simple enough, manual entry really can be the fastest option. But if you need a little assistance with one or more functions or your typing is less than perfect, Excel has lots of help to offer.

When you're not sure of the name of the function you want to use, click the Insert Function button to the left of the formula bar. That opens the Insert Function dialog box shown in Figure 12-8, where you can enter a search term and click Go or choose a category to filter the list of available functions.

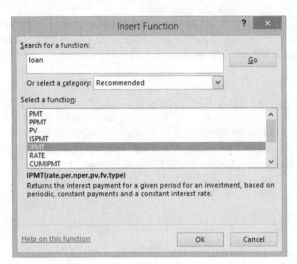

Figure 12-8 Use a search term to filter the list of functions, and then scroll through the Select A Function list to see descriptions and syntax.

After you select a function and click OK, Excel opens the Function Arguments dialog box shown in Figure 12-9, which includes fill-in-the-blank boxes for each argument.

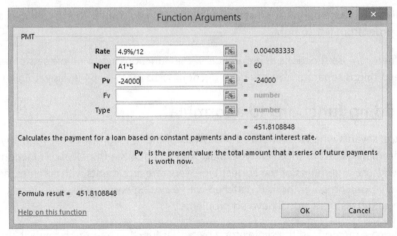

Figure 12-9 The value to the right of each input box shows the actual value that will be used by the formula based on your input. Below that column is the overall result of the formula.

The Function Arguments dialog box contains a wealth of useful information. A bold name means an argument is required. When you click in an input box, the descriptive text changes to help you understand what that argument is for. As you enter arguments, you can see Excel evaluate the results of each one on the right of the input box. The display below the input boxes shows the overall formula result based on all arguments entered so far.

TROUBLESHOOTING

An entry in the Function Arguments box shows as "Invalid"

When you fill in the blanks in the Function Arguments dialog box, you have the option to type a formula containing any combination of constants, operators, cell or range references, or names. If you enter a formula and Excel displays Invalid in bold red letters to its right, check that you got all those elements correct. If the formula is otherwise accurate, you probably added an equal sign at the beginning of the formula. The equal sign is used only at the beginning of a cell, not for formulas used as arguments in a function. Delete the equal sign, and the error should be replaced by a value.

The small button to the right of each input box collapses the dialog box temporarily so you can select a cell or range to insert in that box. After you select an address, click the button to expand the dialog box again.

Even when you type a formula directly in the formula bar (or in the cell itself), you get some help. After you enter an equal sign and begin typing a letter or two, Excel displays a list of all available functions that begin with that combination. As you type, the list narrows further. You can use the down arrow at any time to move through the list, select a function, and then press Tab to add it to the formula bar. When you do, the display beneath the formula bar changes to show arguments for the selected function. In some cases (as in the CONVERT function), one or more arguments might consist of a list of specific options, which are also available from a drop-down list. In this case as well, you can scroll through the list and then press Tab to enter a specific value from that list as an argument. (To see this feature in action, look at the example under "Engineering functions" later in this chapter.)

Mastering Excel's built-in functions

As we noted in the previous section, Excel divides its hundreds of built-in functions into categories that you can see and explore using the Insert Function dialog box or the Function Library group on the Formulas tab, as shown here in its fully expanded widescreen splendor.

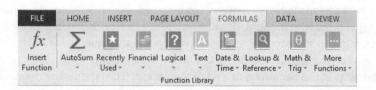

The arrow beneath each name leads to a complete list of functions available for that category. We looked at AutoSum functions earlier in this chapter. In this section, we look at some of the most useful options in each of the named categories. Even if you're an Excel veteran, it's worth exploring each category: Excel 2013 includes new functions, with the most significant changes coming in the Statistical functions group.

Financial functions

If you work in the accounting department at your business, or if you're involved in the banking or securities industry—or even if you just want to track stocks, bonds, and other financial instruments in your personal portfolio—then the functions in the Financial group will be useful to you.

These functions allow you to take details from a particular transaction or instrument and calculate accrued interest, yields, depreciation, internal rates of return, net present value, and future value for that item. In addition to all-purpose financial functions that can be used with any loan or investment, Excel includes functions that apply to specific classes of securities, such as treasury bills. (See the three functions that begin with TBILL for details.)

One set of financial functions that even nonprofessionals can use is the group of functions associated with loans and interest-bearing accounts of all types. For a mortgage, a consumer loan (such as an automobile loan), or a credit card, for example, you can calculate the monthly payment for a given rate of interest over a specific period of time. Or you can do the calculation from another perspective, figuring the actual interest rate you'll pay given a fixed payment amount over a fixed period. The online help can be confusing because it refers to "an investment," even though that description applies to the lender and not the borrower.

The five functions in this family mix and match the same group of arguments. Here, for example, is the syntax of the PMT function:

PMT(rate,nper,pv,fv,type)

You can use this function to calculate your monthly payment for a car loan or home mortgage. The first three arguments are required. If the interest rate (rate) is expressed in annual terms, you must divide by 12 to calculate a monthly payment. Likewise, you need to express the number of periods (nper) in months—so a 30-year loan is 360 months. Finally, the present value (pv) is the loan amount. Because you're the borrower, it needs to be expressed as a negative number. You can omit the two final arguments: future value (fv) is the amount you'll owe when the loan is paid off, or 0. And the type argument calculates whether you make payments at the beginning or end of the period. (The latter is the default if the argument is omitted.)

Here is the complete formula for a five-year loan of $24,000 at a stated interest rate of 4.9 percent:

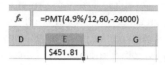

And here are two variations on that basic formula, using different functions to solve for a different variable:

- **NPER(rate,pmt,pv,fv,type)**　　Use this formula to calculate how many payments you need to make to fully pay off a credit card balance at a given payment. You can enter the minimum required payment for the pmt argument and then increase the amount to see how quickly extra payments accelerate the payoff. You can perform this what-if analysis in the Function Arguments dialog box, or you can set up input cells for each variable you want to play with and use references to those cells in the formula.

- **RATE(nper,pmt,pv,fv,type)**　　If a loan requires an up-front payment of fees or points, add that amount to the principal amount and plug that into the pv argument. The result tells you how much those fees add to the effective interest rate compared to the stated rate for the loan.

To calculate how much of a specific payment is interest and how much is principal, use the IPMT and PPMT functions, respectively. The syntax for the IPMT function is IPMT(rate,per,nper,pv,fv,type). Enter the payment number (per) to calculate the portion of that payment that is interest. Use the same syntax with the PPMT function (or subtract the result of the IPMT calculation from the result of the PMT calculation) to figure the principal.

Date and time functions

We can think of dozens of reasons to make date calculations in Excel worksheets. You might want to determine someone's age by comparing the value in the Birth Date column to today's date. Or perhaps you want to look over a list of invoices and compare invoice date to payment date to determine how long your customers typically take to pay their bills.

To master date calculations, you first have to understand how Excel stores date values. When you enter a date in a recognized format, Excel converts that date to a serial value— a number equal to the number of days that have elapsed beginning with January 1, 1900, which has a serial value of 1. Thus, September 29, 2013, is stored as 41546 and September 29, 2014, is 41911. Not surprisingly, subtracting those two dates, which are exactly one year apart, produces a result of 365.

TROUBLESHOOTING

Dates in an Excel worksheet are off by four years

As we noted earlier in this section, Excel 2013 (like all previous versions of Excel developed for Windows) uses a date system based on serial numbers where the start date is January 1, 1900. On a Macintosh, however, date serial numbers begin with January 1, 1904. If you create a worksheet in Excel for Windows and open it in the Mac version of Excel—or vice versa—your dates will look normal because both programs recognize and adjust for the different date formats. However, if you paste a date value from a worksheet created in Excel on a Mac into a new worksheet created in Excel on a Windows PC, your results will be off by approximately four years. The moral? Be very careful when pasting dates between worksheets if you even suspect that your data might have been created originally on a Mac.

INSIDE OUT   What's the serial number for a given date?

Under most circumstances, Excel handles the work of converting dates to serial values automatically. If you enter 9/29/2014 in a cell, Excel displays it using the default date format in the cell itself and in the formula bar. If you need to know the serial number, you can determine it easily. Select the cell, press Ctrl+1 to open the Format Cells dialog box, and click General. The Sample box shows the serial value. Click OK to change the cell format or click Cancel to return to the worksheet without changing it.

Time values also have a serial number associated with them, measured on a scale that runs from midnight (00:00:00 in hours, minutes, and seconds), to 11:59:59 PM (or 23:59:59, using the 24-hour format). Because the value of a single day is 1, the associated serial values for times run from 0 to 0.999988426, respectively. When you combine date and time into a single serial value, you get a single value that you can use to perform calculations of date and time. The serial value for 11:45 AM on September 29, 2014, is 41911.489583333. If you enter a time without including a date, Excel uses a date serial value of 0. If you then format the cell to show a date (or a combination of date and time), you'll see it listed, nonsensically, as January 0, 1900.

The SECOND, MINUTE, HOUR, DAY, MONTH, and YEAR functions allow you to break out the component parts of a date or time stored as a serial number. Each function takes a single argument and returns the respective parts as a number. Thus, if cell C3 contains the date 29-Sep-2014, the formula =MONTH(C3) returns 9 and DAY(C3) returns 29. To calculate the day of the week, use =WEEKDAY(serial_number,[return_type]), which returns a numeric value indicating the day of the week. If you leave the second argument blank, the result is between 1 and 7, where 1 equals Sunday. If you prefer an alternative numbering system, click the return_type argument and use any of the options shown here:

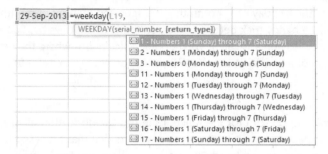

Two date functions are useful in nearly any worksheet. Neither one uses any arguments:

- **TODAY()** returns today's date

- **NOW()** returns the current date and time

You can perform date arithmetic by nesting these functions in formulas containing references to other cells containing dates. If cell E17 contains the date when you prepared and sent an invoice that has not yet been paid, you can calculate the number of days since that invoice was sent by using this formula:

=TODAY()–E17

TROUBLESHOOTING

Performing date arithmetic returns a date instead of a number

One quirk of date arithmetic in worksheets is that Excel tries, helpfully, to apply date formats when you use a date function in a formula. If you enter the formula =TODAY()–E17, where E17 is a date 76 days earlier, the result is displayed as April 10, 1900. That's the equivalent date for the serial number 76. The fix? Press Ctrl+Shift+~ (tilde) to apply the General format to the cell.

What if you're using a worksheet that has one or more columns of data containing dates or times formatted as text? If you're unwilling or unable to reformat those cells, use the DATEVALUE or TIMEVALUE functions to do the conversion. If the value is recognizable as a date or time, the respective functions should work properly.

The two new functions in this category for Excel 2013 are HOUR, which returns the hour of an argument that resolves to a time, and DAYS (not to be confused with DAY, which still exists), which calculates the number of days between two dates.

The list of functions under the Date & Time category heading includes a slew of esoteric entries. For example, the DAYS360 function (with European and U.S. options) is used for accounting systems that use a year made up of 12 30-day months. The EOMONTH function helps you calculate the last day of a month that is a specified number of months before or after a target date—a handy trick because Excel can't rely on "30 days has September, April, June, and November" as humans can. If you're doing calculations where the result must be a working day and not a weekend, use the WORKDAY (or WORKDAY.INTL) function.

Text functions

We confess to having a soft spot for the functions in this category. After all, we're writers and information managers, not accountants, so any tricks that make it easier to manipulate lists and blocks of text are always handy. In fact, we regularly use the functions we discuss in this section, singly or in combination, to split the output from database programs into different fields for use in Excel or Word tables.

The most common way to use the functions in this group is to paste a list from another source into one or more columns in Excel, and then use formulas in adjacent columns to manipulate that text. In this section, we focus strictly on the functions that are most useful for cleaning up and converting text.

The simplest functions are useful for removing unwanted characters from text: CLEAN and TRIM take a single argument (text) and remove nonprintable characters and spaces, respectively, from the string in the referenced location.

If your imported text uses inconsistent or inappropriate case formatting, you can use one of three functions to change it. UPPER, LOWER, and PROPER also use a single text argument. The effect is to change the referenced text to all capitals, all lowercase, or caps for the first letter in each word, respectively. The example shown here illustrates the PROPER function in action, transforming a column of text in all capital letters to easier-to-read initial caps.

f_x	=PROPER(D1)

D	E
ROMEO AND JULIET	Romeo And Juliet
CORIOLANUS	Coriolanus
TITUS ANDRONICUS	Titus Andronicus
TIMON OF ATHENS	Timon Of Athens
JULIUS CAESAR	Julius Caesar
MACBETH	Macbeth
HAMLET	Hamlet
TROILUS AND CRESSIDA	Troilus And Cressida
KING LEAR	King Lear
OTHELLO	Othello
ANTONY AND CLEOPATRA	Antony And Cleopatra
CYMBELINE	Cymbeline

That example also illustrates one of the problems with the PROPER function. It blindly capitalizes every word in the source text, even when those words are articles and conjunctions that shouldn't be capitalized in a title. It also automatically capitalizes the first letter after an apostrophe. That can lead to some inconsistent (and unwanted) results with possessives: FINNEGAN'S WAKE becomes Finnegan'S Wake, for example.

Another group of functions allows you to convert a value to text. This is a necessary step if you have a cell that contains a number and you want to concatenate that number with some text. Here are three useful functions in this group:

- **DOLLAR(number,decimals)**   This function converts a number to text using the $ (dollar) currency format. The second argument is optional; by default, Excel formats the number using two decimal places. If cell B5 contains the value 24.5, the formula =DOLLAR(B5) returns the text string $24.50.

- **FIXED(number,decimals,no_commas)**   Use this function to display a number as text, rounded to a fixed number of decimals. Only the first argument (number) is required. If you omit the decimals argument, Excel displays the result using the default of two decimal places.

- **TEXT(value,format_text)**   When you want to display a number as text using a custom format (perhaps so you can combine it with other text or symbols), use this function. The help text for this function is misleading. You can apply any number format using the same syntax as entries in the Custom category in the Format Cells dialog box. The format string must be enclosed in quotation marks. Thus, if cell B5 contains 24.44, the formula =TEXT(B5,"#,##0_);[Red](#,##0)") returns the text string 24.

If some cells in a column contain text and others contain numbers, you might want to use the T(value) function, which checks the contents of the referenced cell. If the cell contains text, the result of the function is that text; if the cell contains a value, the T function returns an empty text string.

Finally, you can use the VALUE(text) function to convert text to a number. If the text argument can't be evaluated as a number (for example, if it contains even a single letter), the function returns a #VALUE! error.

Logical functions

The functions in this group are some of the most powerful and useful in Excel. The IF function, for example, allows you to test for a specific condition and then return a result based on the answer to that test. Its syntax is IF(logical_test,value_if_true,value_if_false). In the following example, the formula in cell D2 uses a logical test of whether the invoice due date in B2 is less than today's date. If the result is true, it returns the text "Overdue," and if the result is false, it returns "Pending."

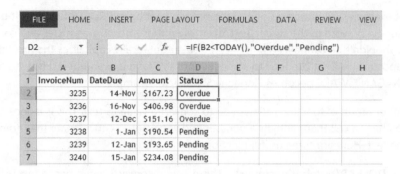

You can combine two or more logical tests, often in conjunction with IF. The AND function returns TRUE if all its arguments are true, and the OR function returns TRUE if any of its arguments are true.

Excel 2013 adds two new functions in this group: IFNA, which returns a custom value if a formula returns #N/A, and XOR, which returns the logical "exclusive OR" of all arguments.

Use the IFERROR function to avoid the possibility that a formula will return an error. Its syntax is IFERROR(value,value_if_error). If you're performing division operations and some cells in the column used for the divisor equal 0, you risk seeing #DIV/0! errors in those cells. To eliminate that possibility, use a formula like this one: =IFERROR(B2/C2,0), which returns 0 in place of any error.

To reverse the logic of any argument, use the NOT function.

Lookup and reference functions

The functions in this group allow you to identify cell addresses, row and column numbers, and other details about a cell or range. You can also use HLOOKUP and VLOOKUP to extract values from one row or column in a table based on a value from another corresponding row or column. A new function in this category is FORMULATEXT, which returns the text of a formula from another cell and is ideal for documenting the logic of a worksheet.

Statistical functions

For students of statistics, the functions in this group are invaluable. If you need to calculate confidence intervals, Poisson distributions, standard deviations, or even the "one-tailed probability of the chi-squared distribution," you've come to the right place.

INSIDE OUT   Watch out for deprecated functions

If you have experience with a previous version of Excel, you should pay close attention to the list of functions available in this group, which have changed significantly in Excel 2013. Some 38 statistical functions have been replaced with new functions, with the old versions deprecated and included only for backward compatibility. Microsoft warns that some of these functions might be dropped completely from a future Excel version.

For example, the CONFIDENCE function has been replaced with new functions CONFIDENCE.NORM and CONFIDENCE.T, and the old FDIST, FINV, and FTEST functions are replaced with five new functions, including F.DIST and F.TEST. For a full list of the changes, search the online help file for an article titled "Excel functions (by category)" and read the "Compatibility functions" section.

For those of us who aren't math majors, a few functions in this group are still handy for everyday use.

To calculate the arithmetic mean of a set of numbers, use the AVERAGE function. Although you can enter arguments individually, you're most likely to specify part of a row or column as the range to use for this calculation. The AVERAGEIF and AVERAGEIFS functions return the arithmetic mean of all cells that meet criteria you define.

The arithmetic mean is what most nonmathematicians think of when they hear the term *average*. For a slightly different calculation, use the MEDIAN function, which finds the number that is in the middle of a set of numbers.

To find the lowest or highest value in a set or a range, use the MIN or MAX function, respectively. Use the COUNT function to calculate how many numbers are in the referenced range or list of arguments. Four additional functions that begin with COUNT allow you to calculate the number of values (COUNTA), the number of blank cells (COUNTBLANK), or the number of cells that meet a single criterion (COUNTIF) or multiple criteria (COUNTIFS).

Math and trigonometry functions

We promised we wouldn't bring up unpleasant memories of math homework, and we'll be true to our word here. If you're a math student or an honest-to-goodness rocket scientist, you'll want to study the entire list of functions in this category. You'll find the usual suspects from trigonometry and math here: sine and cosine and tangent (SIN, COS, TAN), arcsine and arc cosine and arctangent (ASIN, ACOS, and ATAN), and even hyperbolic tangent (TANH) and inverse hyperbolic cosine (ACOSH).

Chapter 12

If you're a civilian (mathematically speaking), you'll benefit most from a group of math-oriented functions that all involve rounding numbers.

The ROUND function rounds a number to a specified number of digits. If you have a column full of calculated results and you don't mind permanently converting them to a result that is less accurate than the original, use this function. Its syntax is ROUND(number, num_digits). Two additional functions in the same family allow you to round numbers in a specific direction: ROUNDDOWN and ROUNDUP use the same syntax and round the value specified in the number argument down (toward zero) or up (away from zero).

If the details after the decimal point don't matter, use one of the following functions to round a number to an integer. INT rounds a number down to the nearest integer, EVEN rounds a number up to the nearest even integer, and ODD rounds a number up to the nearest odd integer. All three functions take a single number argument.

And we would be remiss if we left out one of our favorite math functions, which hasn't had much use in the past couple millennia but could be poised for a comeback. If you've been baffled by the intricacies of Roman numerals ("When was that movie copyrighted?"), let Excel help you out. The ROMAN function accepts any Arabic numeral as an argument and converts it to Roman numerals. So, =ROMAN(2014) correctly returns the result MMXIV, formatted as text. A second, optional argument lets you choose simpler, more concise formats (MXMIX for 1999 instead of the traditional MCMXCIX, for example), but we prefer the classic display.

Engineering functions

More than 50 functions are available in this category, and virtually all of them are useful only to professional engineers and engineering students. The single noteworthy exception is the CONVERT function, which allows you to create formulas for translating measurements between different systems. The function's syntax is CONVERT(number,from_unit,to_unit). The second two arguments, which must be enclosed in quotation marks, allow you to specify the type of conversion. To translate gallons to liters, for example, enter a value representing the number of gallons in cell A1, and then enter the following formula in cell B1:

=CONVERT(A1,"gal","l")

When you use the formula helper to enter the arguments for this function, the full list appears for the from_unit argument, with nearly 50 choices available, covering mass, distance, weight, temperature, and other measurement systems. You can convert meters to feet, angstroms to inches, light-years to parsecs, or Atomic mass units to grams, if you're so inclined. After you choose an option for the from_unit argument ("Light-year" in this example), the options for the to_unit argument are filtered to include only those that are appropriate for the measurement system from which you're converting, as shown next.

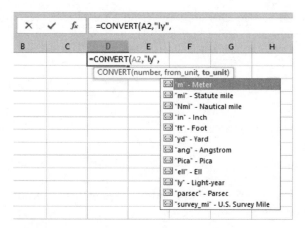

Information functions

Most of the functions in this group are of interest to advanced worksheet developers. The CELL function, for example, returns information about a cell—its contents, address, and formatting and the workbook in which it's located. The INFO function allows you to determine information about the environment of the system on which the current worksheet is being viewed, including the Windows version and which version of Excel is in use—extremely useful if you anticipate that someone might view your worksheet in an earlier Excel version that doesn't support specific features.

A long list of functions in this category are logical tests that begin with IS—ISERROR and ISBLANK, for example. Use them to add logic to a formula to suppress error messages, fill blanks with default values, and otherwise prevent you or anyone using a worksheet you design from running into unexpected conditions.

A particularly useful function in this group allows you to return a "Not Applicable" error message. You can use the NA function (which takes no arguments) as an argument with an IF function to add a neat #N/A value instead of an error message when a formula returns a particular result. Or use the ISNA function to identify cells where Excel returns that value automatically.

Formatting cells and ranges

When you enter values, text, or formulas in a cell, Excel applies default formatting to the contents of those cells based on its best guess as to the data type. You can adjust this formatting by using the commands in the Number group on the Home tab, as shown next. A far more extensive set of options is available in the Format Cells dialog box, which opens when you click the dialog box launcher in the lower-right corner of the Number group (or right-click any cell or range and choose Format Cells).

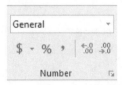

The commands in this group allow you to pick from a list of predefined number formats, apply a custom currency style, display a value in Percentage format, show or hide thousands separators (a comma for systems using U.S. regional settings), and increase or decrease the number of visible decimal places.

INSIDE OUT   Create custom formats with cell styles

The Number group on the Home tab mixes commands for predefined number formats and cell styles, which can be used to apply number formats. It also provides access to the Format Cells dialog box, where you can customize formats manually. The three buttons below the Number Format list apply the Currency, Percent, and Comma styles, respectively. (Confusingly, the Currency style actually uses the Accounting number format. Go figure.) You can see these styles in their normal location by expanding the Cell Styles list (from the Styles group on the Home tab) and then looking in the Number Format area.

Normally, clicking the Percent button in the Number group applies the Percentage format with no decimal places. If you want to replace that default result with one that applies the Percentage format with one decimal place, right-click the Percent style in the Cell Styles list and click Modify. Click the Format button and adjust the value in the Decimal Places box. Save your changes, and the result is complete. You can use this same technique to create additional styles, which you can add to the Quick Access Toolbar or access from the Cell Styles list. Note that this change applies only to the current workbook unless you save these changes to the default workbook template.

If none of the predefined formats work for you, try rolling your own. We explain how to do this in "Creating custom cell formats" in Chapter 14, "Excel 2013 inside out."

It's important to understand that most of the formatting options affect only the display of the data stored in that cell. You can change the number of decimal places and add a currency symbol to a number format, but the underlying data remains unchanged. Likewise, changing the date format for a cell does not change the date serial number displayed in that cell.

If you enter a number or text, Excel applies the General number format. In most cases, this means you see exactly what you typed. If a number you type is too wide to fit in the current cell and the width of the current column has not been manually set, Excel expands the column width to try to accommodate your entry. If you enter a formula, the General format displays up to 11 digits, including the decimal point, rounding the displayed result if necessary to show fewer decimal places than are actually stored for the value.

If you enter a value or a formula whose result won't fit in the defined cell width or that contains more than 12 digits to the left of the decimal point, Excel displays it using scientific notation.

You can override the formatting for any cell by using the drop-down list of available formats in the Number group on the Home tab. Conveniently, this list matches up neatly to the choices in the Number category of the Format Cells dialog box. In some cases, Excel overrides the General number format automatically, based on what you type or paste into a cell. You can manually apply a format at any time.

You can also use any of the keyboard shortcuts shown in Table 12-4 to quickly apply number formatting to the current selection. It's worth noting that all the shortcuts are applied using the Ctrl+Shift keys and the first seven keys in the number row of the standard U.S. keyboard layout.

TABLE 12-4 Keyboard shortcuts for common number formats

Shortcut	Action
Ctrl+Shift+~ (tilde)	Applies the General number format
Ctrl+Shift+!	Applies the Number format with two decimal places, a 1000 separator, and a minus sign (–) for negative values
Ctrl+Shift+@	Applies the Time format with the hour and minute, followed by AM or PM (11:30 AM)
Ctrl+Shift+#	Applies the Date format with the day, month (abbreviated), and year (31-Jan-11)
Ctrl+Shift+$	Applies the Currency format with the default currency symbol, two decimal places, and negative values in parentheses
Ctrl+Shift+%	Applies the Percentage format with no decimal places
Ctrl+Shift+^	Applies the Scientific number format with two decimal places

Chapter 12

The most useful Excel keyboard shortcut of all, in our opinion, is Ctrl+1. Pressing that combination opens the Format Cells dialog box and selects the Number tab. The options on this tab allow you to select, customize, or create formats in a variety of categories. In the remainder of this section, we look in detail at each of the available formatting options in the Format Cells dialog box.

Number formats

If you enter a number and use a comma to set off thousands, Excel applies the Number format using the default thousands separator for the region and language as defined in Windows. If the number you enter contains more than two decimal places, Excel stores the exact number you entered but rounds it for display purposes to no more than two decimal places.

Use the Increase Decimal and Decrease Decimal buttons (in the Number group on the Home tab) to add or subtract one decimal place at a time from the selection.

To manually set options for the Number format, make a selection and then open the Format Cells dialog box. Figure 12-10 shows which settings are available.

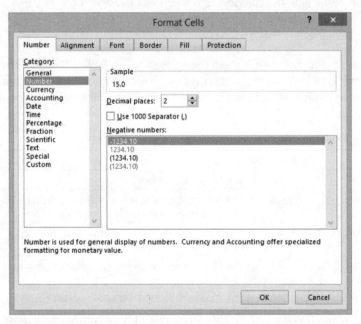

Figure 12-10 In addition to setting the number of decimal places and showing or hiding the 1000 separator, you can choose how negative values are displayed.

Currency and Accounting formats

Both the Currency and Accounting formats are designed for use with values that represent money. The difference? Currency formats allow you to choose an alternate format for negative numbers (a minus sign, parentheses, or red font formatting). Accounting formats line up decimals and move currency symbols to the left edge of the cell for a neater display in reports. The alignment used in Accounting formats can be hard to read in wide columns that contain small numbers; for readability's sake, choose a Currency format for those situations.

If you enter a number preceded by a dollar sign, Excel applies the Currency format, using the default currency symbol with up to two decimal places, regardless of how many decimal places you enter. Confusingly, when you click the command represented by a dollar sign in the Number group on the Home tab, Excel actually applies the Currency cell style (the Accounting format, with two decimal places). A drop-down list on this command allows you to pick an alternate currency symbol—Euro, pound, and so on.

INSIDE OUT   How to enter alternate currency symbols

Most PC keyboards sold in the United States allow you to enter only a single currency symbol—the dollar sign—directly. To enter a currency symbol that isn't represented on your keyboard, you need to jump through a hoop or two. The simplest option is to click the Insert tab and click Symbol. In the Symbol dialog box, select the Currency Symbols subset, choose a symbol, and then click Insert. If you regularly use one or two alternate symbols and you have a full-size keyboard with a numeric keypad, memorize the ASCII codes for those symbols so you can enter them as needed. To enter the Euro symbol (€), use the numbers on the numeric keypad (not those on the number row at the top of the keyboard) and enter Alt+0128. The British pound symbol (£) is Alt+0163. The currency symbol used in many Asian countries (¥), including Japan and the People's Republic of China, is Alt+0165. In Excel, you can use the Number tab of the Format Cells dialog box to choose from a list of hundreds of currency symbols when you choose either the Currency or Accounting format.

Date and Time formats

When the text or number you enter in a cell matches any of the built-in Windows date formats, Excel converts that entry to a serial number and formats the cell using the closest matching Date format. If the date you enter includes only the month and date, Excel adds the current year.

To choose a custom format, click the Date category in the Format Cells dialog box and choose one of the options in the Type list.

The formats at the top of the list, preceded by an asterisk, represent the Short Date and Long Date options as defined in the Region And Language section of Windows Control Panel. You can apply these two formats most quickly by using the Short Date and Long Date choices on the Number Formats list (in the Number group on the Home Tab). If you choose a different format, look at the Sample box above the Type list to see how the current cell contents will be displayed using that format.

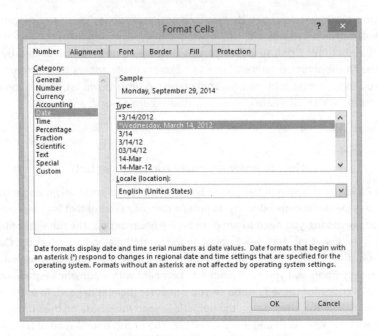

When you enter a set of numbers that contain a colon (:) and that can be interpreted as a time, Excel converts your entry to a serial number and applies the default Time format if possible. If the number is followed by a space and A, P, AM, or PM (in caps or lowercase), Excel adds AM or PM to the display format. Click the Time category in the Format Cells dialog box to see a list of alternative formats.

Percentage formats

When you enter a number that begins or ends with a percent sign, Excel applies the Percentage format, using up to two decimal places. The value you enter in this fashion is divided by 100 for storage. If you enter 5%, Excel stores it as 0.05. When you apply the Percentage format to a number that you previously entered using the General or Number format, Excel multiplies it by 100 for display purposes and adds a percent sign.

Fraction formats

In sharp contrast to the decimal options available elsewhere, the options in the Fraction category display values using old-style display formats like ½ and ¼. If the number is between 0 and 1, the fraction appears by itself. Excel also supports compound fractions, which include a whole number and a fraction, such as 8½.

To apply a Fraction format automatically when entering data, enter the whole number followed by a space and the fraction. If the number is less than 1, start with 0 and a space, like this: 0 7/16. (If you leave out the zero and space, Excel assumes you mean the date July 16 and will helpfully convert your entry to a date serial number and format.) The value is stored as a decimal, 0.4375 in this example.

For more control over the display of fractions, use the Fraction category in the Format Cells dialog box. The two most useful options are at the bottom of the list, where you can choose to format a cell or range so its contents show as tenths (3/10) or hundredths (30/100).

Scientific formats

Scientific (or exponential) format displays large numbers in a shorthand form—a value, followed by the letter E, a plus or minus sign, and another number. To convert that format to its decimal equivalent, move the decimal point by the number of places that appears after the E—if the value begins with a plus sign, move the decimal point to the right, adding zeros if necessary; if there's a minus sign, move the decimal point to the left, again adding zeros as needed. Here are some examples:

- 6.42E+06 is 6,420,000.

- 7.22E-05 is .0000722.

You can enter a number and apply the Scientific format with two decimal places as part of a single action. Just insert the letter E at the appropriate place.

INSIDE OUT   Show numbers with greater precision

Numbers expressed using the default settings for the Scientific format are rounded for display purposes to a maximum of six significant digits, regardless of the cell's width. To display numbers using more digits of precision, open the Format Cells dialog box, click Scientific in the Category list, and increase the number of decimal places (this value must be between 0 and 30).

Text formats

When is a number not a number? When you specifically want it to be treated as text. That happens with part numbers and product identifiers, for example, which can contain leading zeros and aren't typically used in calculations. If you enter a number in a cell, Excel drops the leading zero and aligns it to the right. To display the cell contents exactly as entered (including leading zeros), you must use the Text format, which is available at the bottom of the Number Format list in the Number group on the Home tab. This category in the Format Cells dialog box has no additional options.

You can apply the Text format automatically by entering an apostrophe before typing the number. The apostrophe is stored with the cell entry but is not displayed. Excel formats the number as text. A green triangular marker appears in the upper-left corner of the cell, indicating that Excel considers this an error. Select the cell to display a faint box with a yellow exclamation point, and then click that box to display a menu that includes an option to convert the entry back to a number or ignore the "error."

Special formats

The four entries in this category of the Format Cells dialog box are useful mostly for address and contact lists created in the United States. They allow you to quickly enter ZIP Codes, phone numbers, and Social Security numbers in any format and without punctuation. Excel handles the work of adding hyphens and splitting the entered values into groups of the correct length.

Even if you never use any of these formats, they're worth studying as examples of how to build your own cell formats for automatic formatting, a topic we cover in full in "Creating custom cell formats" in Chapter 14.

Finding, editing, moving, and copying data

Much of the work of building a workbook involves moving data between cells, ranges, and worksheets. For everyday cutting, copying, and pasting, the Clipboard is more than sufficient, especially when you discover some of the lesser-known options on the Paste Special menu and in the Find And Replace dialog box.

For an overview of common cut, copy, and paste techniques, see "Using the Clipboard with Office programs" in Chapter 4. For a discussion of common search and replace tools, see "Finding and replacing text and formatting," also in Chapter 4.

Knowing a few keyboard shortcuts can save you some time. Ctrl+F (or Shift+F5) opens the Find And Replace dialog box with the Find tab selected. Ctrl+H displays the same dialog box with the Replace tab selected instead. You can close the Find And Replace dialog box and then repeat the last Find by pressing Shift+F4. That obscure shortcut is worth memorizing if you regularly search through long tables where the search results might return hundreds of rows.

INSIDE OUT   Quickly copy the cell above

To copy the contents of the cell above the active cell, press Ctrl+' (apostrophe). If the cell from which you're copying contains a formula, this shortcut copies that formula exactly as it's entered—cell references in the formula are copied exactly as they appear in the original and are not converted to relative references. To copy the value from the cell above, press Ctrl+Shift+" (quotation marks). If the cell above contains a formula, the copy in the active cell consists of the text or value that is the result of that formula.

To learn about an expert tool that lets you find and select in ways that aren't possible with the Find And Replace dialog box, see "Navigating with the Go To dialog box" in Chapter 14.

Using the Clipboard to transform data

You can use the Paste Special dialog box in Excel, shown next, to perform some interesting and useful on-the-fly transformations. Under the Paste heading, for example, you'll find a Values And Number Formats option that allows you to paste the results of a range full of formulas into a new location.

The choices under the Operation category offer some interesting ways to perform mathematical operations on a cell or range using the contents of the Clipboard. Let's say you have a worksheet containing a year's worth of daily temperature data. You discover that for a two-week period in June, the thermometer was off, giving results 3 degrees lower than they should have been.

The fix? In a blank cell, enter the number you want to use as a constant—in this case, 3. Select that cell and press Ctrl+C to copy its contents to the Clipboard. Now select the cells in the 14 rows containing the incorrect temperature data, click the arrow under Paste, and click Paste Special. Click Add and then click OK. The content on the Clipboard (3) is added to the contents of all cells in the current selection.

You can use this same technique to apply an across-the-board 5 percent price hike to a list of prices. Enter 1.05 in a blank cell and copy it to the Clipboard. Then select all the prices to be adjusted and use the Multiply option in the Paste Special dialog box.

The last check box, Transpose, is our favorite. Want to convert all your rows to columns or vice versa? Select a range and use this option, with or without any of the choices above it.

Pasting text and formats into multiple worksheets

Entering data into multiple worksheets simultaneously is a useful trick when you're building a complex workbook. If you have many individual worksheets that share a common structure, you can enter text and format those common ranges without a lot of repetitive work.

You can select multiple worksheets one at a time by Ctrl+clicking each sheet tab, or use Shift+click to select a contiguous group of tabs.

If more than one sheet is selected, the bracketed text [Group] appears after the file name in the title bar. Any text you enter in the current cell appears in all matching cells on grouped worksheets. Any formatting you apply to the active sheet, including column widths and cell formats, is also applied to the same location in each grouped worksheet. Obviously, you wouldn't use this technique to enter data, but it's ideal for copying row labels and column headings.

The Paste and Paste Special commands work in ways that aren't immediately obvious in grouped worksheets—and you don't automatically get the same results as when you enter text directly in a group. When you copy a range in one location and then paste that range into a group, the Clipboard contents duplicate the contents of the range you originally selected. This means that if you copy some numbers from a range in Sheet1 where the corresponding cells in Sheet2 or Sheet3 are blank, pasting that range into a new selection will delete the values in the corresponding cells in Sheet2 and Sheet3 of the destination group. To perform Paste operations that copy the contents of a range on a single sheet to a group of sheets, you need to take one extra step. Copy the Clipboard contents to the current sheet, and then select the cell or range you just copied. Now click Fill (in the Editing group on the Home tab), and then click Across Worksheets. Although you don't have all the Paste Special options, the Fill Across Worksheets dialog box, shown here, gives you the choice of pasting contents, formats, or both.

To stop working with a group of worksheets and return to the normal one-sheet-at-a-time mode, right-click any of the grouped tabs (shown in bold) and click Ungroup Sheets.

Customizing the worksheet view

During the design and construction stages of any workbook, you probably want ready access to all of Excel's tools. But after construction is complete and you no longer need those tools, it's sometimes useful to hide them so you can focus on the contents of your worksheet, including any charts and tables. On the View tab, in the Show group, you'll find check boxes that allow you to temporarily remove any (or all) of four prominent features from the Excel interface:

The Ruler check box is available only in specialized views, as we explain in the Trouble-shooting note later in this section.

Clear the Gridlines option to remove the lines that define the edges of rows and columns and thus separate cells from each other. Clear the Headings check box to remove the labels above columns and to the left of rows. These two settings are saved on a per-worksheet basis.

Clear the Formula Bar check box to hide the formula bar, the Insert Function button, and the Name box. This setting is saved with the current workbook and affects all worksheets.

You'll find a few extra settings in the Excel Options dialog box. Click File, click Options, and then click the Advanced tab. Scroll down to the Display section, where you'll find the two groups shown next.

If you're obsessed with the idea of a clutter-free screen, you can clear the first three check boxes in the top group to hide the scroll bars and sheet tabs for the current worksheet. If you also double-click the current tab to hide the ribbon and leave only the tab names, you can create a view that will satisfy even the most diehard minimalist.

TROUBLESHOOTING

Excel won't allow you to remove the ruler

For most worksheet views, the Ruler check box (in the Show group on the View tab) is selected, and the option to remove the check mark is dimmed and unavailable. What's the problem? Check your view. The ruler isn't needed in Normal view, and thus it's not available to hide. It's only visible in Page Layout and Page Break Preview modes, where it's shown by default. Switch to either of those views to clear the Ruler check box.

The commands in the Zoom group on the View tab allow you to change the on-screen size of the worksheet contents. Click Zoom to open a dialog box where you can choose from five predefined magnification levels or enter a custom value. At zoom levels of 39 percent or less, gridlines are automatically hidden.

INSIDE OUT   Choose the right Zoom tools for maximum flexibility

Although you can open the Zoom dialog box and pick a magnification level, we recommend using the Zoom slider, on the status bar in the lower-right corner of the program window, instead. Drag the slider left or right to make the window magnification smaller or larger. Above 100%, the view increases in 6 percent increments, with much finer adjustments below 100%. Each click of the plus or minus button on either side of the slider increases the window magnification to the next multiple of 10 and then increases in 10 percent increments. To zoom up and down in 15 percent increments, hold down the Ctrl key as you roll the mouse wheel.

For any worksheet, the zoom scale ranges from a low of 10 percent (a bird's-eye view) to a high of 400 percent (an extreme close-up). By contrast, the Zoom dialog box offers only a single larger-than-normal setting (200%) and three evenly spaced smaller levels (25, 50, and 75 percent). Double-click the current Zoom percentage (to the right of the slider) to open the Zoom dialog box. The fastest way to return to normal magnification at any time is to click the 100% command in the Show group on the View tab.

The Zoom To Selection option lets you change the worksheet's magnification so that it shows the entire contents of the current selection, increasing or decreasing the width and height of the worksheet window as needed. This setting is saved as a custom magnification level; it applies to the current worksheet only and is not dynamic. If you change the size of the worksheet window or hide user interface elements, the magnification level remains the same percentage; after you make this type of change, you can resize the window's contents manually by clicking the Zoom To Selection command again.

Hiding rows and columns

Some worksheet data is required for calculations but isn't necessary for display purposes and might even be distracting in its raw form. For those occasions, you can hide one or more rows or columns. Click any cell within the row or column you want to hide (or click the heading to select the entire row or column). Then, in the Cells group on the Home tab, click Format, click Hide & Unhide, and then click Hide Rows or Hide Columns. As an alternative, you can right-click any heading and click Hide. You can also hide a column by dragging the right edge of the column heading to the left until its width is 0; to hide a row, drag the bottom edge of the row heading up until it disappears.

To make a hidden column or row visible, select cells on either side of the hidden column or above and below the hidden row, click Format on the Home tab, click Hide & Unhide, and then click Unhide Columns or Unhide Rows, as needed. If you want to unhide a single row or column without disturbing its hidden neighbors, click in the Name box, enter a cell address located in the hidden row or column, press Enter, and then use the Unhide Rows or Unhide Columns option from the Hide & Unhide menu. This technique is especially useful when the first row or column is hidden: type A1 in the Name box to jump to that location and unhide it.

Arranging worksheet windows

When you're creating a new worksheet, there's a good chance that you'll want to reuse data from another worksheet, in the same workbook or in a different workbook file. The tedious way is to click back and forth between the two maximized windows, copying, switching windows, pasting, and repeating those steps until everything's just right. The faster way—assuming your PC display is big enough—is to arrange the windows next to each other. You can then navigate through each one independently, comparing similar sections and editing or copying data to your heart's content.

In this version, Excel finally joins its Office-mates and assigns each workbook to its own window. It's no longer possible to display individual workbook files side by side in a single program window. Instead, each window gets its own ribbon, Quick Access Toolbar, status bar, and other common interface elements.

All the window-management controls you need are located on the View tab, in the Window group, as shown here:

If you have two or more workbooks open already and you want to rearrange them for simultaneous viewing, click Arrange All. That opens the dialog box shown here, which gives you four options (plus a check box that we'll discuss shortly):

The Tiled option arranges workbooks most efficiently, with the currently selected workbook on the left and additional workbooks stacked up in a checkerboard pattern. If you have three (or more) open workbooks to arrange, this is your best choice. The Horizontal and Vertical options arrange all open workbooks from top to bottom or side by side, respectively. Confusingly, the default action for the View Side By Side button in the Window group arranges two worksheet windows one over the other, rather than side by side. You can override this behavior by choosing the Vertical option in the Arrange Windows dialog box before you click View Side By Side. If you have three or more workbooks open, you're prompted to choose which one you want to compare with the current workbook.

If you've clicked View Side By Side, you can click Synchronous Scrolling and use your mouse wheel or either scroll bar to scroll both worksheets simultaneously. This option is especially useful when you're comparing two similar worksheets—last year's budget versus this year's, for example.

What if you want to see two tabs from the same worksheet side by side? Click New Window on the View tab to open a second view of the current workbook and worksheet; Excel appends a colon and a number to the title bar in each window. (Although you can scroll independently, each window represents the same file. Any changes you make in either window are reflected immediately in the other window.) If you use the Arrange All button, each instance is treated like any other open workbook. To ignore all other workbooks and just arrange multiple copies of the current window, click Arrange All, select Windows Of Active Workbook, and then click OK.

INSIDE OUT   Find worksheet tabs without scrolling

If you create a workbook with a large number of worksheets, you have to scroll one tab at a time to see each sheet name. This technique is especially tedious if you used the Tiled or Vertical option to arrange windows and thereby cut your worksheet to half (or less) of its normal width. The secret solution? Right-click either of the scroll buttons to the left of the sheet tabs to open the Activate dialog box, which contains the names of all worksheets in the current workbook. Double-click any name to jump straight to that worksheet.

Splitting, freezing, and locking panes

You don't need to open a second window to compare two different parts of the same worksheet. Instead, you can split the screen—vertically, horizontally, or both. Each split screen region scrolls independently, allowing you to compare the contents of widely separated columns or rows—you can see a block of data in rows 2 through 5 alongside the contents of rows 202 through 205, for example.

Compared to previous versions, Excel 2013 greatly simplifies the process of splitting a worksheet. You can add a horizontal split, a vertical split, or both. The split appears as a gray bar, with scroll bars on either side of the split allowing you to scroll through the split sections independently.

To split the current worksheet, select a cell and then click Split, in the Window group on the View tab. The split bars appear above and to the left of the location you selected. If you choose a cell in the first visible column in the current worksheet (even if there are other columns to its left), you get only a horizontal split bar above the selected cell. Likewise, choosing a cell in the top visible row produces only a vertical split. If you choose the top left cell in the current view, Excel splits the worksheet into four equal-sized panes.

Once the split bar is in place, you can scroll each pane independently and edit cell contents or adjust formatting in either location. Click and drag the split bar to change its location. Double-click either split bar to remove it. Click the Split button again to return to a normal, single-pane worksheet window.

In some worksheet designs, you might want to lock specific rows or columns into position so that they are always visible as you scroll through the data in the worksheet. This configuration is especially useful when your data range is taller or wider than the visible portion of the screen and you want to keep labels visible as you move through the worksheet.

In the following example, we used a conventional budget worksheet, with category names in column A, with an Annual Total column summarizing values for each month. For this view, we froze columns A and B into position and also froze the top row of column labels. As we scroll to the right and down, the intervening rows and columns disappear temporarily (see how the row headings jump from 1 to 16 and the column headings go from B to G?), but the row and column labels remain visible so we don't lose our place.

	A	B	G	H	I
D26		fx			
1	Category	Annual Total	May	Jun	Jul
16	Health Insurance	$10,283.00	$856.92	$856.92	$856.92
17	Licensing	$480.00	$0.00	$0.00	$0.00
18	Fuel	$2,880.00	$240.00	$240.00	$240.00
19	Maintenance	$1,080.00	$90.00	$90.00	$90.00
20	Home Insurance	$500.00	$0.00	$125.00	$0.00
21	Life Insurance	$2,000.00	$0.00	$0.00	$0.00

Freezing panes properly takes a little bit of practice and a trip to the Freeze Panes menu on the View tab. If your labels are in the top row or first column only, the procedure is simple: click Freeze Panes and then click either Freeze Top Row or Freeze First Column. The new configuration takes effect immediately regardless of which cell is currently selected.

To freeze multiple rows and/or columns, you must first select the cell that is immediately below and to the right of the rows and columns you want to freeze. Pick a cell in the first row if you want to freeze only columns, or pick a cell in the first column if you want to freeze only rows. To freeze columns A and B and row 1 as we did earlier, click to select cell C2 and then click Freeze Panes. To freeze column A and rows 1 and 2, select cell B3 first.

To restore normal worksheet scrolling, click the Freeze Panes menu again and choose the first option, Unfreeze Panes.

Analyzing data with tables and charts

EXCEL is no one-trick pony. Yes, the program works wonders with number-crunching tasks, but its rows and columns are also tailor-made for managing data that goes beyond basic bean counting. With minimal effort, you can keep address lists and membership rosters, track temperatures and rainfall, monitor stock prices, and record your performance in whatever sport or hobby you happen to fancy.

In this chapter, we look at the many options you have for entering, storing, sorting, filtering, cross-tabulating, and summarizing that data.

We also explain how to highlight trends and patterns in a sea of gray data to make it more interesting. You can use conditional formatting to add colors and custom text treatments, and you can make at-a-glance analysis easier by inserting tiny trend lines and markers called *sparklines*.

When that's not enough to tell a story, you can turn a collection of data into an elegant, information-based graphic and let *it* do the talking. In this chapter, we look at Excel's extraordinarily versatile charting engine and explain how to communicate a situation or a series of events in a single visual impression, with only a few well-chosen words required.

Building a visually compelling, information-rich chart from a series of numbers and dates is part science, part art. The science involves recognizing which series of data on a worksheet represent the patterns you're trying to describe. The art is in arranging and fine-tuning the colors, shading, shapes, labels, and other pieces of your chart so that they tell the story most effectively.

Sorting out your data analysis options

The single most important new feature of Excel 2013 is the Quick Analysis tool, which puts formatting, charting, tables, and other options in an easy-to-access place. You can still create charts, insert tables, and add totals manually, but this tool dramatically simplifies the process.

To get started, select a range (at least two cells containing data) and click the Quick Analysis tool that appears in the lower-right corner of the selection. (You can also press Ctrl+Q, or right-click and click Quick Analysis on the shortcut menu. If you choose the latter option, you can select a single cell and Excel will expand the selection to include the current region.)

Figure 13-1 shows the Quick Analysis tool in action. Each of the five headings at the top of the box leads to a selection of options that vary slightly depending on the selection.

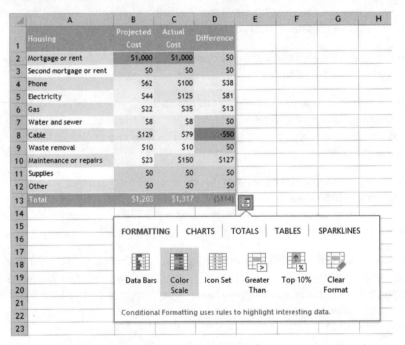

Figure 13-1 The Quick Analysis tool consolidates five common options in one place and offers live previews of their effects.

To use the Quick Analysis tool, choose a category and then move your mouse pointer over any of the options available beneath the headings. When you let the pointer hover over an option, the selection changes to preview the effect of that option. If you like what you see, click to apply the selected option; otherwise, move the mouse pointer to another option (or click a different category).

The following list briefly describes each of your options and what you should and shouldn't expect from each one using Quick Analysis. We provide in-depth details about these analytical options in the remainder of this chapter.

- **Formatting**   The options available here depend on whether your selection contains only text or whether it also includes numbers. For all-text ranges, the options allow you to identify duplicates, unique values, or entries that include a specific text string. If you've included even a single number, you'll see the choices shown earlier in Figure 13-1, which allow you to add data bars, color scales, and icons or highlight specific values.

- **Charts**   Excel offers a selection of one-click charts based on the type of selection you make. The list of available chart types is determined by whether you've chosen a single column of values or multiple columns with labels. The preview chart appears above the Quick Analysis tool, as shown in this example, based on a selection that includes a column of labels and a column of data.

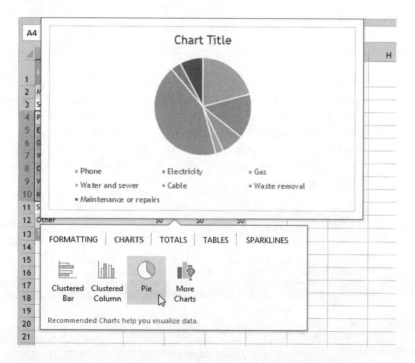

- **Totals**   Assuming you've selected a range that includes numbers, you can add automatically calculated totals in the row beneath your selection, or in the column to its right. For numbers, the list of options scrolls to the right, with row-wise choices listed first, followed by their column-wise equivalents.

	A	B	C	D	E	F	G	H
1	Housing	Projected Cost	Actual Cost	Difference				
2	Mortgage or rent	$1,000	$1,000	$0				
3	Second mortgage or rent	$0	$0	$0				
4	Phone	$62	$100	$38				
5	Electricity	$44	$125	$81				
6	Gas	$22	$35	$13				
7	Water and sewer	$8	$8	$0				
8	Cable	$129	$79	-$50				
9	Waste removal	$10	$10	$0				
10	Maintenance or repairs	$23	$150	$127				
11	Supplies	$0	$0	$0				
12	Other	$0	$0	$0				
13	Sum	$1,298	$1,507	$209				
14								
15								
16								
17								
18								
19								
20								
21								
22								

FORMATTING | CHARTS | TOTALS | TABLES | SPARKLINES

◄ Sum | Average | Count | % Total | Running Total | Sum ►

Formulas automatically calculate totals for you.

- **Tables** This category is a bit of a catch-all; it includes regular tables and PivotTables (we cover the former in much more detail shortly, and the latter in Chapter 14, "Excel inside out"). What you see beneath the Tables heading will always include the Table option and, depending on the arrangement of data, one or more buttons allowing you to preview various PivotTable layouts. Note that in this example, because the Excel window extends to the bottom of the screen, the Quick Analysis tool appears above its launcher.

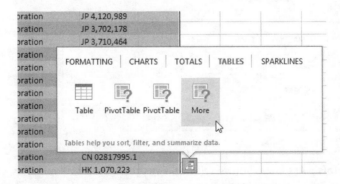

- **Sparklines**   These clever little analytical elements are mini-graphs that appear in a single cell to summarize the trend in a row of data. They're most useful when you want an at-a-glance comparison of a series of numbers in multiple dimensions. We'll discuss sparklines in more detail shortly.

The Quick Analysis tool offers a useful starting point, but it's far from perfect. For anything but the simplest tasks, you'll need to fine-tune the settings and formatting for tables and charts.

Using tables to organize and analyze data

You can create a simple database just by entering data into rows, with or without headings to indicate what's in each column. For example, you can enter a list of names in column A and then, in column B, enter a phone number alongside each name. As long as that list remains short and simple enough to scan quickly, you don't need to do anything more.

But lists have a way of growing, and even moderately long lists can benefit from sorting, searching, filtering, outlining, and summarizing. When you turn a range into a table, Excel provides several tools that simplify the way you work with even long, detail-rich collections of data.

Microsoft introduced the concept of tables (not to be confused with data tables, which are a rarely used relic of Excel's distant past) in Excel 2007. Tables are roughly equivalent to the feature known as *lists* in Excel 2003, but with more sophisticated formatting options. If you open a worksheet originally created in Excel 2003 that contains one or more lists, you'll need to manually convert those lists to tables.

The quickest way to turn a range into a table is to click Table in the Tables group on the Quick Analysis tool, which applies the default table format to the current selection or region immediately. If you want more control over the process, select the range (or select any cell within the range if the list is in a self-contained region), and then click Table in the Tables group on the Insert tab. (You can also use the keyboard shortcut Ctrl+T or Ctrl+L.) You'll see the Create Table dialog box shown in Figure 13-2.

Had we instead clicked Format As Table, in the Styles group on the Home tab, we would have been required to select a table style before seeing the Format As Table dialog box (which is identical to the Create Table dialog box shown in Figure 13-2). Using either keyboard shortcut applies the default table style. (We discuss table styles in much greater detail in the next section, "Formatting tables with table styles.")

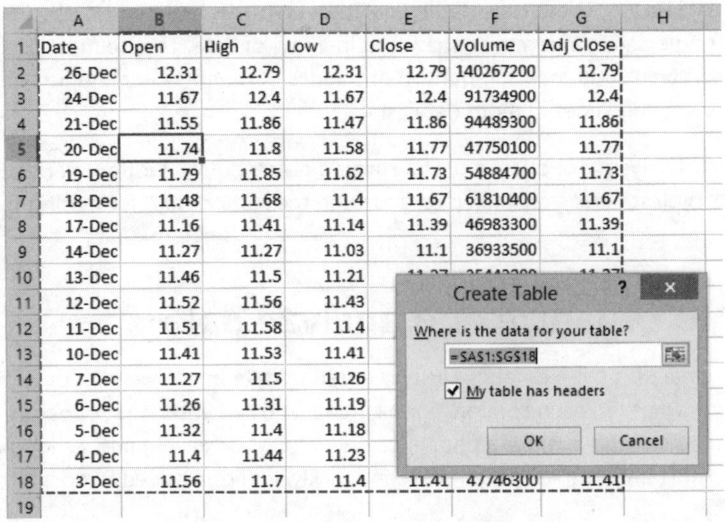

	A	B	C	D	E	F	G	H
1	Date	Open	High	Low	Close	Volume	Adj Close	
2	26-Dec	12.31	12.79	12.31	12.79	140267200	12.79	
3	24-Dec	11.67	12.4	11.67	12.4	91734900	12.4	
4	21-Dec	11.55	11.86	11.47	11.86	94489300	11.86	
5	20-Dec	11.74	11.8	11.58	11.77	47750100	11.77	
6	19-Dec	11.79	11.85	11.62	11.73	54884700	11.73	
7	18-Dec	11.48	11.68	11.4	11.67	61810400	11.67	
8	17-Dec	11.16	11.41	11.14	11.39	46983300	11.39	
9	14-Dec	11.27	11.27	11.03	11.1	36933500	11.1	
10	13-Dec	11.46	11.5	11.21				
11	12-Dec	11.52	11.56	11.43				
12	11-Dec	11.51	11.58	11.4				
13	10-Dec	11.41	11.53	11.41				
14	7-Dec	11.27	11.5	11.26				
15	6-Dec	11.26	11.31	11.19				
16	5-Dec	11.32	11.4	11.18				
17	4-Dec	11.4	11.44	11.23				
18	3-Dec	11.56	11.7	11.4	11.41	47746300	11.41	
19								

Create Table   ?   ×

Where is the data for your table?

=$A$1:$G$18

☑ My table has headers

OK   Cancel

Figure 13-2 Even though we selected only a single cell, Excel expands the selection to include the entire data-containing region, as defined by blank rows and columns.

If the selected range contains a header row with labels for each column, you should select the My Table Has Headers check box. (For the most part, Excel correctly detects the presence of headers, but it can be confused by some configurations, so check this setting before you proceed.) Clicking OK applies the default table style to the range and makes a few other changes. The end result looks like this:

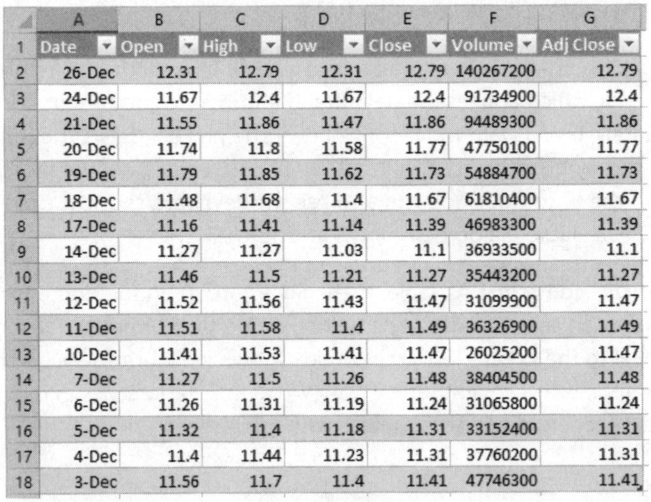

	A	B	C	D	E	F	G
1	Date ▼	Open ▼	High ▼	Low ▼	Close ▼	Volume ▼	Adj Close ▼
2	26-Dec	12.31	12.79	12.31	12.79	140267200	12.79
3	24-Dec	11.67	12.4	11.67	12.4	91734900	12.4
4	21-Dec	11.55	11.86	11.47	11.86	94489300	11.86
5	20-Dec	11.74	11.8	11.58	11.77	47750100	11.77
6	19-Dec	11.79	11.85	11.62	11.73	54884700	11.73
7	18-Dec	11.48	11.68	11.4	11.67	61810400	11.67
8	17-Dec	11.16	11.41	11.14	11.39	46983300	11.39
9	14-Dec	11.27	11.27	11.03	11.1	36933500	11.1
10	13-Dec	11.46	11.5	11.21	11.27	35443200	11.27
11	12-Dec	11.52	11.56	11.43	11.47	31099900	11.47
12	11-Dec	11.51	11.58	11.4	11.49	36326900	11.49
13	10-Dec	11.41	11.53	11.41	11.47	26025200	11.47
14	7-Dec	11.27	11.5	11.26	11.48	38404500	11.48
15	6-Dec	11.26	11.31	11.19	11.24	31065800	11.24
16	5-Dec	11.32	11.4	11.18	11.31	33152400	11.31
17	4-Dec	11.4	11.44	11.23	11.31	37760200	11.31
18	3-Dec	11.56	11.7	11.4	11.41	47746300	11.41

Defining a range as a table makes the following changes, some of which are not immediately apparent. (We explain these changes in more detail shortly.)

- Column widths expand as needed to display header text in full. If column headers are not included, Excel adds generic headers—Column1, Column2, and so on.

- A down arrow appears to the right of each column heading, allowing quick sort and filter operations.

- When any cell or range within the table is selected, a Design tab with customization options appears on the ribbon, under the Table Tools heading.

- A default name is assigned to the table; you can change the name to a more descriptive one by using the Table Name box in the Properties group on the Table Tools Design tab.

- Any cell addresses used in formulas you add within the table are automatically converted to structured references. (For an explanation of how structured references work, see "Adding formulas and totals to a table," later in this chapter.)

- A triangular handle in the lower-right corner of the table allows you to quickly add rows or columns to the table, preserving formatting and copying formulas automatically.

Tables offer a tremendously versatile way to work with large and small amounts of data. In fact, as we explain in Chapter 14, a table can serve as the source of data for a PivotTable report. You can also export a table to a SharePoint list or to a PivotDiagram in Visio (a member of the Office family we don't discuss in this book), using the Export command in the External Table Data group on the Table Tools Design tab.

After you convert a range into a table, you can fine-tune its appearance with custom formatting, expand its size in either direction, and add totals.

What if you change your mind and want to remove the table features, turning the data back into a plain ol' range? Easily done: Click to select any cell within the table and then click Convert To Range, in the Tools group on the Table Tools Design tab. Or right-click any cell in the table and then click Table, Convert To Range on the shortcut menu. This option removes the special treatment of header rows and converts formulas back to ordinary cell references. Any special formatting (such as banded rows) remains in place and must be changed manually unless you remove the formatting first, using the Clear option at the bottom of the Table Styles gallery on the Design tab.

INSIDE OUT   Don't lose track of headings when you scroll

One of the hidden advantages of creating a table from a range is a small but significant improvement in scrolling. If your list is long enough that scrolling through the list causes the Header row to scroll up and off the screen, Excel has an elegant fix. The headings from the table replace the column headings in the worksheet frame, complete with the arrow that allows you to sort and filter, as shown here.

	Date ▾	Open ▾	High ▾	Low ▾	Close ▾	Volume ▾	Adj Close ▾	H
10	13-Dec	11.46	11.5	11.21	11.27	35443200	11.27	
11	12-Dec	11.52	11.56	11.43	11.47	31099900	11.47	
12	11-Dec	11.51	11.58	11.4	11.49	36326900	11.49	
13	10-Dec	11.41	11.53	11.41	11.47	26025200	11.47	
14	7-Dec	11.27	11.5	11.26	11.48	38404500	11.48	

The effect is similar to what happens if you freeze the top row of the table, but it requires no effort from you beyond creating the table in the first place.

Formatting tables with table styles

Table styles apply formatting—colors, fonts, borders, and shading—to the region that makes up a table. Excel offers a selection of 60 options in the Table Styles gallery (plus a None option that removes table formatting). These options are divided into Light, Medium, and Dark groups that correspond to the intensity of the colors used. You can choose from the entire list in either of two ways:

- Click Format As Table in the Styles group on the Home tab. If the current range or region has not already been defined as a table, this option displays the Format As Table dialog box after you make a selection.

- Click the arrow to the right of the Table Styles gallery (or below the Quick Styles button) in the Table Styles group on the Table Tools Design tab.

Figure 13-3 shows the Table Styles gallery in operation. As with other Office galleries, allowing the mouse pointer to rest over an option in the gallery previews the formatting in the table. (It also shows the name of the style in a ScreenTip.)

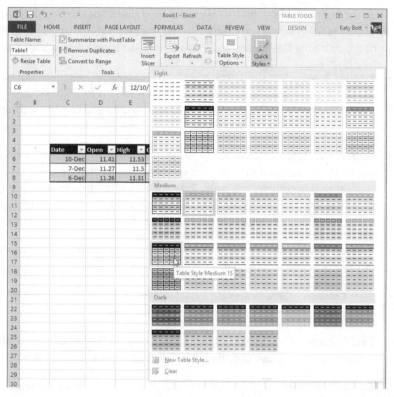

Figure 13-3 Colors and fonts associated with each of these built-in table styles adjust to match the current theme.

The colors and fonts associated with a style vary depending on the theme used for the current worksheet. If you change the theme, any existing table formats change to pick up the color schemes and fonts from the new theme.

For more on how themes allow you to apply consistent formatting, even in different Office programs, see "Using Office themes" in Chapter 5, "Working with graphics and pictures."

If you've applied manual formatting to fonts, font colors, cell shading, and so on within a table region, your formatting is preserved when you apply a table style. To clear any manual formatting and use only the formatting specified in the table style, right-click the style in the Table Styles gallery, and then click Apply And Clear Formatting.

Many of the built-in table styles include formatting that adds shading to alternate rows, which makes reading across wide tables easier. The seven check boxes in the Table Style Options group on the Design tab allow you to fine-tune the following format settings:

- **Header Row**   Clear this check box to hide all column headings. Doing so also hides the down arrow used to access sort and filter options for each column. Note that Excel remembers the name assigned to any column and continues to use it in structured references within formulas.

- **Total Row**   Select this check box to add a row beneath the table, with options to automatically subtotal the contents of one or more columns. If the table contains more than one column, the word *Total* appears in the first column. If you expand the table, this row remains at the bottom of the new range. You can customize the formulas beneath each column by using a drop-down list, as we explain shortly.

- **Banded Rows**   Apply different background colors to alternating rows to make reading across a wide table easier.

- **First Column**   Click to apply special formatting to the first column in the table. Use this option to highlight labels that identify each row.

- **Last Column**   Click to apply special formatting to the last column in the table. This option is especially useful if the last column contains totals for each row.

- **Banded Columns**   Apply different background colors to alternating columns.

- **Filter Button**   Remove the arrow to the right of a column heading that allows you to filter, sort, or search using the contents of that column.

In effect, these check boxes allow you to provide very specific customizations to the current table style. When you combine these options with the 60 entries in the built-in Table Styles gallery, each of whose color palette and font can in turn be reset using any of 21 built-in themes, you have literally thousands of possible looks to choose from. That's not enough? Then build your own table style by clicking the New Table Style link at the bottom of the Table Styles gallery. Doing so brings up the New Table Style dialog box, where you can set the properties for each part of the table individually.

Starting from scratch to create a custom table style is difficult and potentially confusing. In our experience, you'll find it much simpler to duplicate an existing table style and then modify the style you copied. In the Table Styles gallery, right-click the style you want to use as your starting point, and then click Duplicate. That opens the Modify Table Style dialog box shown next.

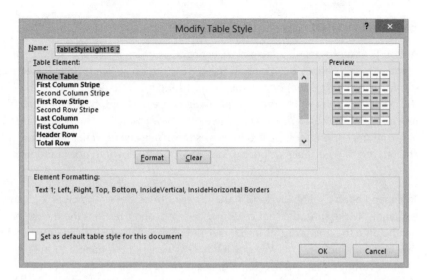

In the Name box, replace the default name with a descriptive name. Then select individual table elements from the list in the center of the dialog box and adjust their definition as needed. Click the Format button to change font style (bold, italic, and so on), cell borders, and shading. The four stripe options allow you to set how many rows are in each stripe that makes up a band. The default is 1, which means that shading alternates from one row to the next. If you choose 2 for First Row Stripe and Second Row Stripe, each band of shading is applied to two rows at a time.

Custom styles appear at the top of the Table Styles gallery. If you right-click on a saved custom table style, you'll notice that Modify and Delete options are available on the menu; you can't modify or delete any of the predefined table styles.

TROUBLESHOOTING

Fonts and colors in custom table styles behave unexpectedly in Excel

Although the Format Cells dialog box for each table element includes a Font tab, most of the options on that tab are unavailable. You can change the font style and color, but the actual font and font size are determined by the current theme. To apply a table font that is not part of the current theme, you must select the entire table and apply the font formatting manually. In addition, if you choose a background or fill color from the selections on the Fill tab, these colors change when you change the theme. To apply a specific color to part of the table and ensure that the color remains unchanged when the theme changes, you must use the More Colors option and define that color manually.

Expanding (or shrinking) a table

Although you can define a table by selecting a range of any size, the most common and useful scenario defines a table using the current region, which is demarcated by blank cells (or the worksheet's edge) on the top, bottom, and sides. To add a row to the table, click in the cell in the lower-right corner of the table range (if your table has a Total row, use the row above it), and then press Tab. Excel adds a new row using the colors, fonts, and shading from the current table style and moves the active cell to the first column in the newly created row. If your table includes a Total row, it shifts down to accommodate the new row as well.

To expand a table manually, look in the lower-right corner of the table for a small triangular handle. Make sure that that cell is not selected, and then aim the mouse pointer at the handle until the pointer turns into a two-sided diagonal arrow. Drag down to add rows to the table, shifting the Total row down if necessary. Drag the handle to the right to add one or more columns (each new column gets a generic heading that you can change later when you're ready to enter data).

You can also drag the table sizing handle up or to the left to remove rows or columns from the defined table range. Any data currently contained in those cells remains, but loses its table formatting.

> **CAUTION**❗
>
> If your table contains a Total row and you move the sizing handle up to remove rows that currently contain data, you create a circular reference. To avoid this, first delete (or move) the contents of any cells that you plan to remove from the table range.

You can add a reference to any table by using its name, as defined in the Table Name box in the Properties group on the Design tab. The range defined by this name automatically expands when you add rows or columns to the table. (It does not, however, include the Header and Total rows.) If you use the current table as the basis for a PivotTable, any new rows or columns you create are automatically available for use in the PivotTable. Likewise, when you use data from rows or columns in a table to define data series, labels, or other elements in a chart, those elements are automatically updated when you expand the table.

Adding totals and formulas to a table

When you create a table, Excel allows you to perform a few tricks with formulas that aren't available within a normal range. The most obvious is the Total row, which you can use to quickly add summaries of table data. As we explained earlier in this chapter, you can manually enable the Total row by selecting its check box in the Table Styles Options group on the Design tab.

Figure 13-4 shows the Total row for a table containing a month's worth of stock prices. Note that Excel automatically added a formula that totals the rightmost column in the table.

	A	B	C	D
1	Date	Open	Close	Volume
2	26-Dec	12.31	12.79	140,267,200
3	24-Dec	11.67	12.4	91,734,900
4	21-Dec	11.55	11.86	94,489,300
5	20-Dec	11.74	11.77	47,750,100
6	19-Dec	11.79	11.73	54,884,700
7	18-Dec	11.48	11.67	61,810,400
8	17-Dec	11.16	11.39	46,983,300
9	14-Dec	11.27	11.1	36,933,500
10	13-Dec	11.46	11.27	35,443,200
11	12-Dec	11.52	11.47	31,099,900
12	11-Dec	11.51	11.49	36,326,900
13	10-Dec	11.41	11.47	26,025,200
14	7-Dec	11.27	11.48	38,404,500
15	6-Dec	11.26	11.24	31,065,800
16	5-Dec	11.32	11.31	33,152,400
17	4-Dec	11.4	11.31	37,760,200
18	3-Dec	11.56	11.41	47,746,300
19	Total			891,877,800

Figure 13-4 Excel uses its own internal logic to decide which columns are summarized in the Total row. You can add or change these formulas with a few clicks.

Although the result is functionally the same as if you had clicked the AutoSum button, the formula itself uses the SUBTOTAL function. You can change the results for an existing formula by selecting the cell and clicking the arrow just to its right. In this example, we're about to change the current formula, which shows the total share volume for the month, to one that shows the average volume per day:

D19			f_x	=SUBTOTAL(109,[Volume])		
	Date	Open	Close	Volume	E	F
16	5-Dec	11.32	11.31	33,152,400		
17	4-Dec	11.4	11.31	37,760,200		
18	3-Dec	11.56	11.41	47,746,300		
19	Total			891,877,800		
20				None		
21				Average		
22				Count		
				Count Numbers		
23				Max		
24				Min		
				Sum		
25				StdDev		
				Var		
26				More Functions...		

In a Total row, you can add a summary formula to any cell. Click that cell to reveal an arrow that you can click to display a drop-down list of available formulas.

What if you want to create a calculated column that displays totals, averages, or other summaries on a per-row basis? Excel can do that automatically. In the previous example, click any cell in any column to the right of the table range and begin entering a formula. In this worksheet, the Open price for each day is in column B and the Close price is in column C, with Volume in column D. So we can click in E2, type an equal sign, click C2, type a minus sign (-), and click B2. As soon as we press Enter, Excel creates a new column using the current table format and copies the formula we just typed to every cell in that column.

INSIDE OUT   Take control of calculated columns

If you create a formula to the right of the current table and you don't want it to be copied to other cells in the column, use the options on the AutoCorrect menu to immediately undo the calculated column. To prevent Excel from automatically copying calculated formulas to the rest of a column, click File, click Options, and then click AutoCorrect Options on the Proofing tab. On the AutoFormat As You Type tab, under the Automatically As You Work heading, clear Fill Formulas In Tables To Create Calculated Columns.

The new column includes a generic heading that you'll probably want to replace with a descriptive heading, and you might also want to insert a formula in the Total row, but Excel does all the work of creating the calculated column, as shown in Figure 13-5.

E2	▾	:	✕	✓	*f*ₓ	=[@Close]-[@Open]		

	A	B	C	D	E	F
1	Date ▾	Open ▾	Close ▾	Volume ▾	Change ▾	
2	26-Dec	12.31	12.79	140,267,200	0.48	
3	24-Dec	11.67	12.4	91,734,900	0.73	
4	21-Dec	11.55	11.86	94,489,300	0.31	
5	20-Dec	11.74	11.77	47,750,100	0.03	
6	19-Dec	11.79	11.73	54,884,700	-0.06	
7	18-Dec	11.48	11.67	61,810,400	0.19	

Figure 13-5 If you add a calculated cell to the right of an existing table, Excel copies the formula to the entire column using structured references.

If you look carefully at the formula bar in Figure 13-5, you'll see that the formula Excel creates includes some unusual cell references. These are called *structured references,* which are designed to make it easy to automatically copy formulas as you add new rows. They're created automatically when you click to select cell references for use in a formula; you can choose to use standard references instead by simply typing the cell address. Brackets indicate a column heading name and an @ sign indicates the current row. The # sign is used with one of four keywords to refer to specific parts of the table: #All, #Data, #Headers, or #Totals.

Sorting and filtering data

In this section we discuss how to create order out of even the most chaotic worksheet data. You can enter or import that data in any order or even at random. Once it's arranged in rows and columns, you can rearrange it as needed. You can sort by numbers, text, or dates. You can also reduce clutter by filtering a list to show only data that matches conditions you define. These options work on simple data ranges and on tables.

Sorting a range, region, or table

You can sort a range, region, or table by using values from one or more columns. That's true regardless of the data type. In a membership roster, for example, you can sort the list in alphabetical order using the Last Name column, or by date, oldest to youngest, using the Birthday column, or by number if you're using the Donations column to track progress in a fundraising drive.

To sort the current region, click a single cell in the column you want to sort by and then click Sort & Filter in the Editing group on the Home tab. The choices at the top of the list vary to reflect the data type. For text, Sort A To Z and Sort Z To A are available, as shown here. For dates, the choice is Sort Oldest To Newest and Sort Newest To Oldest. For numbers, the choices are Sort Smallest To Largest and Sort Largest To Smallest.

If you prefer to sort the current column with a single click, use the commands in the Sort & Filter group on the Data tab, or pin the Sort A To Z and Sort Z To A buttons to the Quick Access Toolbar.

To sort by multiple columns, click Sort on the Data tab; or click Sort & Filter on the Home Tab and then click Custom Sort; or right-click a cell in the table or range, click Sort, and then click Custom Sort.

Any of those roads take you to the Sort dialog box, shown in Figure 13-6. In operation, it's pretty straightforward and easy to figure out. You build a list of sort levels, each based on a column, and then define the sort order for each level.

Figure 13-6 Create as many custom Sort By conditions as you need to arrange your list. Use the up and down arrow buttons to change their order.

INSIDE OUT Create a custom column to preserve original sort order

Is the original order of your data important? If so, then make sure you can return to that order easily. For off-the-cuff tasks, you can simply copy a range to a new worksheet, sort and filter as needed, and then delete the copy when you're done. To ensure that you can always return to the original order of a range or table, even if it's sorted accidentally, add a new column (with a descriptive heading like Original_Order) and fill it with numbers that indicate the current order—starting with 1 for the first row and increasing by 1 for each additional row. With this column in place, you can always re-sort the table or range by this column to display its original state.

Excel sorts dates, times, and numbers exactly as you would expect, depending on the sort order you select—Newest To Oldest, Smallest To Largest, and so on. The rules for text are slightly more complicated. For A to Z (ascending) sorts, numbers come first, then most punctuation characters, and then letters in ascending (A–Z) order. The sort is not case-sensitive, so capital letters and lowercase letters are considered the same for sorting purposes. Apostrophes and hyphens are typically ignored except when two strings of text are otherwise identical; in that case, the one that contains the additional punctuation follows the one without. The precise order for punctuation places the space character first, then uses the same numbering as the Unicode character set to determine the order of additional nonalphabetic characters.

You can also sort by a custom series, such as the January through December and Sunday through Monday series that are defined in Excel by default. For more details, see "Entering and sorting data with custom series" in Chapter 14.

Filtering data in a table

As a list gets longer and longer, it becomes more difficult to see patterns associated with subsets of that data. That's when filtering the list becomes useful, hiding rows except those that match criteria you specify. If you're analyzing data from a dozen schools, stores, or customers, each with a unique identifier in a common column, you can filter the worksheet to show only the names you select from that column. You can filter on numbers and dates as well. For example, to create a filtered list of products that are out of stock (or nearly so), you can include only rows where the value in the QtyOnHand column is below 3.

If the number of choices in a column is limited, or if you know exactly which names or values you want to include, you have two options.

The first option uses a feature called *slicers*, whose capabilities have been expanded in Excel 2013 to work with ordinary tables as well as PivotTables. A slicer is essentially a floating list, built on the fly, that lists all the unique items in a column. By clicking items in the slicer, you instantly filter the table to show matching rows.

To add a slicer to a worksheet, click to select a cell within a table and then click Slicer in the Filters group on the Insert tab. Select the name of the column you want to "slice," and click OK. The result is a list like the one shown here, which scrolls if necessary so that you can see and click items to use as a filter.

Ctrl+click to select or clear multiple items from the filter list. Click the Clear Filter button in the upper-right corner of the slicer (or press Alt+C) to clear your selections and display the lists sans filter.

When you click a slicer box, Excel displays a context-sensitive Slicer Tools Options tab on the ribbon, where you can adjust the name displayed in the slicer's title bar, change the height and width of individual buttons, and display buttons in multiple columns. (Similar controls allow you to adjust the height of the slicer box itself, but it's easier to drag the borders of the slicer to change its height or width.)

And you're not limited to a single slicer. If you use two or more slicers together, they cooperate neatly. In Figure 13-7, for example, we've filtered the list using three company names. Doing so caused the Country Code slicer to display matching values at the top of the slicer, where we are free to click (or Ctrl+click) to filter the list further.

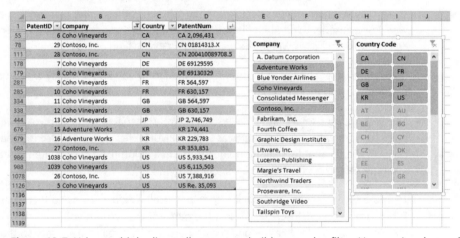

Figure 13-7 Using multiple slicers allows you to build a complex filter. Here, we've changed the button height in the Company slicer and arranged the second slicer into two columns.

The second option, which works with or without slicers, is to filter the contents of one or more columns directly. Click the arrow to the right of the column heading and pick from the list at the bottom of the menu, as shown in Figure 13-8.

The values in this list are drawn from the contents of the current column. Clear the Select All check box at the top of the list to clear all items, after which you can select a few specific items from the list. Click Select All again to reselect all items. When you have a mix of manually selected and cleared check boxes, the Select All box is a solid square as in Figure 13-8.

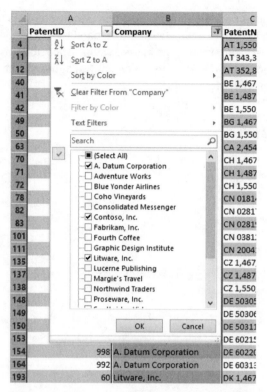

Figure 13-8 To create a completely custom filter, select items in the list at the bottom of this menu, which contains all values found in that column.

If the list of items is too long to be easily manageable, use the search box on the menu to restrict the list of items to those that match whatever you type. The text you enter doesn't have to be a complete word or phrase, and the search results show any match regardless of whether it's at the beginning, middle, or end of a cell's contents. Thus, entering *dat* returns A. Datum Corporation and Consolidated Messenger.

CAUTION

> The option to filter by selecting from a list is limited to the first 10,000 items in a list. In the case of a particularly long list in which a single column has many unique values, you see a warning message beneath the list that reads Not All Items Showing. Try using the search box to reduce the number of unique items, or choose a different filtering method.

For dates that range over a long period of time, Excel automatically collapses the choices in the filter list, allowing you to choose entire years or to expand the list to include months or even days within a year. Here, for example, we started with a list of stock prices that includes data from every trading day for 25 years. By typing **Jan** in the search box, we filtered the list to show only the dates from January.

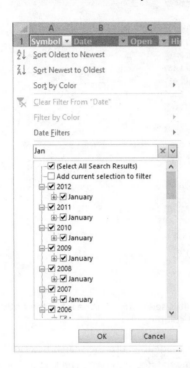

If our goal is just to compare data from the month of January for the past five years, we can click Select All Search Results to clear the current list, then manually include 2012, 2011, and so on. Or we can manually choose certain years. When the selection is complete, select Add Current Selection To Filter, and click OK.

In addition to item-by-item filtering, you can create a custom filter for any column to show or hide rows in the list according to the criteria you specify. The exact set of options depends on the data type. The menu option above the search box reads Text Filters, Number Filters, or Date Filters, depending on the contents of the current column.

Options on the Text Filters menu all lead to the Custom AutoFilter dialog box, where you can define one or two criteria for your filter. You can base criteria on the exact cell contents (Equals, Does Not Equal) or on what the cell begins with or contains. The following example finds all rows where the contents of the Vendor column begin with B, C, D, or E.

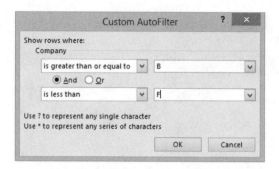

For a column that contains numbers, most of the options on the Number Filters menu lead to the same Custom AutoFilter dialog box. The menu contains three additional choices that work only with numbers. The Above Average and Below Average options work as expected, instantly filtering the list to show only those items that are above or below the arithmetic mean. The other choice, Top Ten, is misleadingly named. It opens the Top 10 AutoFilter dialog box, with Top 10 Items selected by default. However, you can select any number between 1 and 500; you can choose to show the Top or Bottom entries that match that value; and you can change Items to Percent. In this example, we've filtered the list to show only those records with values in the bottom 20 percent.

The options on the Date Filters menu are probably the most extensive. You can quickly define a range of dates, choose relative dates (Yesterday, This Quarter), or create a custom filter. Figure 13-9 provides one example of the full range of options, where we've used check boxes to narrow the list to the three most recent years and then used the Date Filters menu to specify that we want only dates from Quarter 1 in those years.

If you choose the Custom Filter option, the dialog box resembles the one available for text and numbers, with the small but crucial difference that it includes calendar controls to use when you are picking dates.

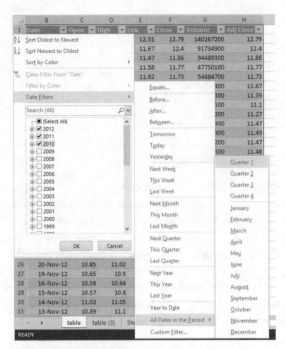

Figure 13-9 Use the Date Filters menu to choose from this extensive list of AutoFilter options when the current column contains mostly dates.

Using conditional formatting to highlight cells based on their content

Tables filled with data can be overwhelming and difficult to understand without lengthy explanations. Are there ways to highlight trends and patterns and identify anomalies while still maintaining a full view of the data in a table? Indeed there are.

You can help your audience (and yourself) make more sense of data by using conditional formatting to highlight values that meet criteria you define. We introduced this feature briefly at the beginning of this chapter, in the discussion of the Quick Analysis tool. In this section, we explain how to take full advantage of it.

The idea behind conditional formatting is simple: You want to be able to look at a table or a range of data and quickly see any values that demand your immediate attention or spot trends that might not be apparent from the raw data. Is a particular value greater than or less than a specific amount? Is it in the top (or bottom) of all values in the range? Does it contain a specific word or string of text or fall within a range of dates?

After you define those conditions, Excel can apply automatic formatting that identifies matching values: displaying the bottom 20 percent of values in red, for example, with the top 20 percent in green; or using a color scale that moves from red to yellow to green as the values in the selection go from low to high; or adding data bars that provide a visual representation of the relative size of values in a cell.

The easiest way to get started is to use the Formatting section of the Quick Analysis tool.

Select a range of data—an entire table, a column or row containing totals, or a subset of data representing groups whose performance you want to examine more closely. Then press Ctrl+Q to open the Quick Analysis tool. The options available depend on whether your selection includes numbers or text. Figure 13-1, at the beginning of this chapter, shows the options available when you select numbers. Figure 13-10 shows what you see if your selection includes only text (in this case, the contents of the Company column).

	PatentID ▼	Company ▼	Country ▼	PatentNum ▼
1125	1222	Blue Yonder Airlines	US	US Re. 34,96512
1126	5	Coho Vineyards	US	US Re. 35,093
1127	1223	Blue Yonder Airlines	US	US Re. 35,15812
1128	511	Southridge Video	US	US Re. 35,910
1129	1041	The Phone Company	US	US Re. 37,222
1130	199	Proseware, Inc.	US	US Re. 40,1778
1131	200	Proseware, Inc.	US	US Re. 40,178
1132	201	Proseware, Inc.	US	US Re. 40,179
1133	202	Proseware, Inc.	US	US Re. 40,180
1134	314	Proseware, Inc.	VN	VN 6,782
1135	315	Proseware, Inc.	VN	VN 6,783
1136				
1137				
1138				
1139				
1140				
1141				
1142				
1143				
1144				
1145				

FORMATTING | CHARTS | TOTALS | TABLES | SPARKLINES

Text Contains | Duplicate Values | Unique Values | Equal To | Clear Format

Conditional Formatting uses rules to highlight interesting data.

Figure 13-10 The Formatting options in the Quick Analysis tool offer these choices when your selection includes only text.

If you click Duplicate Values, Excel applies a red background to all values in the selection that are repeated at least once. Click Unique Values to perform the inverse operation, applying similar formatting to any cell whose contents are not repeated elsewhere in the list.

The Text Contains and Equal To options require some explanation. The effect of clicking either button depends on the contents of the current cell within the selection. (You can move the current cell within the selection using Tab and Shift+Tab.) If the current cell contains "Contoso," click Text Contains to apply a red background to any cell containing that word: Contoso, Contoso Inc., Contoso Pharmaceuticals, and so on. Click Equal To and Excel will highlight only cells that are a perfect match for the current cell.

The options in the Quick Analysis tool for a selection that contains numbers rather than text allow you to add data bars, icons, or colored shading to a selection of data, features we explore in the remainder of this section.

Any conditional formatting you apply using the Quick Analysis tool uses default settings. For greater control over the conditions and appearance of the formatting, you can create conditional formatting rules directly.

To get started, select a range of data and then click Conditional Formatting in the Styles group on the Home tab. That displays the Conditional Formatting menu:

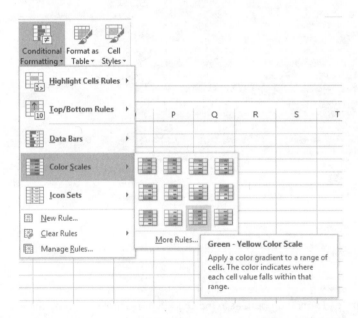

Each of the five main choices on this menu provides access to a range of preset rules. The More Rules option at the bottom of each of the submenus allows you to create custom choices that vary from the preset configurations. The following list describes what you'll find in each of the five main choices:

- **Highlight Cells Rules** Each of the seven preset options opens a dialog box that lets you construct a formula using a comparison operator (greater than, less than, equal to, and so on) along with a value or cell reference to compare with each cell's contents. Excel fills in values using its internal algorithms; you can change those values or point to a cell reference. The list on the right allows you to choose the formatting to be applied to cells matching your specified conditions.

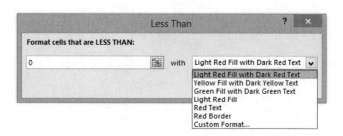

- **Top/Bottom Rules**   The input dialog box that opens when you select any of the choices on this menu also allows you to create a rule on the fly. Don't be misled by the number 10 in the Top 10% and similar options. You can change that value or percentage to a different number if you prefer.

- **Data Bars**   This option adds a small bar (a longer bar equals a higher value) to each selected data cell, using a solid or gradient color. These bars show up as a live preview in the selected data so you can see the effect before you make it final. In the example shown in Figure 13-11, we've already created a customized data bar; choosing an option from the Solid Fill list changes the color without changing other settings. Note the ScreenTip, which explains, tersely, what the thumbnail represents.

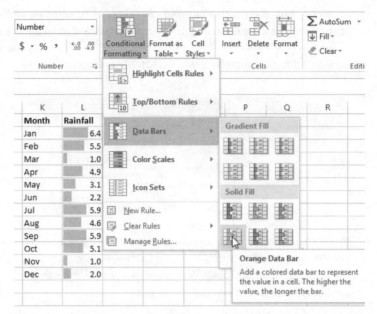

Figure 13-11 Adding a data bar to a range (the Rainfall column, in this example) adds a colored bar to visually represent the data in the selection.

- **Color Scales** This option applies colored cell backgrounds to the selected range using two or three colors in a range that is defined by the data itself. The Green-Yellow-Red option, for example, uses green for the lowest values, red for the highest, and yellow for everything in between. The actual number of shades used is much more than two or three, with more intense shades representing the extremes of higher and lower values.

- **Icon Sets** This is the most visually diverse (and potentially cringe-inducing) of all the preset conditional formatting options. You can choose from arrows, circles and other shapes, flags, and rating scales made up of stars and bars and immediately recognizable symbols like the ones shown here.

	A	B	
1	North	✓	112
2	East	✗	88
3	Northeast	!	100
4	South	✗	72
5	Southeast	✓	121
6	West	!	98
7	Southwes	✓	107

You can combine multiple rules in the same selection, highlighting values in the top 20 percent in bold green text on a light green background, with values in the bottom 20 percent displayed in bold red italics on a light red background, for example.

If none of the preset options match your needs, you can create custom rules from scratch. In some cases, you might start with a preset rule (from the Quick Analysis tool or from the Conditional Formatting menu) and then, after applying it to the selection, modify the rule.

Click More Rules at the bottom of any of the Conditional Formatting menu options to display the New Formatting Rule dialog box. The example shown in Figure 13-12 adjusts the default rules for data bars so that the largest bar in the selection doesn't cover up the number it represents.

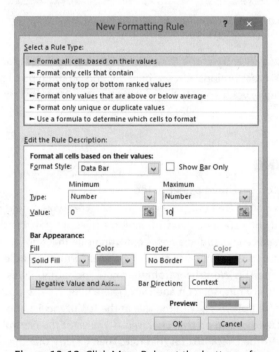

Figure 13-12 Click More Rules at the bottom of a conditional formatting option to build a rule from scratch. Changing the Minimum and Maximum values here adjusts the length of data bars to avoid covering the value.

If you've already defined rules and want to adjust them, click Conditional Formatting (in the Styles group on the Home tab) and then click Manage Rules. That opens the Conditional Formatting Rules Manager dialog box, shown in Figure 13-13. Select This Worksheet to see all rules for the current sheet.

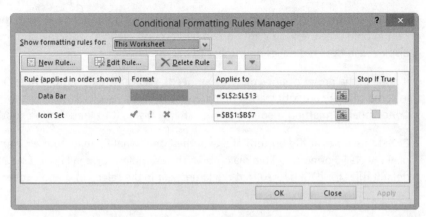

Figure 13-13 You can edit any existing rule from this dialog box. Use the Stop If True option if you want to apply conditional formats in a precise hierarchy.

To edit an existing rule, select its entry in the Conditional Formatting Rules Manager dialog box and click Edit Rule. The exact options you see here depend on the type of rule you originally created. For example, you can hide the underlying value and show only an icon or data bar.

TROUBLESHOOTING

Conditional formats don't behave as expected

If the formats you see in a table aren't displayed as you expected, you should check several possible causes. If you experimented with multiple rules, it's possible that you left an old set of rules in place and added a new, conflicting rule that applies to the same data. To check for this possibility, open the Conditional Formatting Rules Manager dialog box and choose This Worksheet from the Show Formatting Rules For list. If you see an old, unnecessary rule, select it and click Delete Rule. It's also possible you have a conflict between multiple rules, with the rule at the top of the list applying one set of formatting that is then overruled by a later rule. If you want the first rule to take primacy, select the Stop If True check box for that rule. Then be sure that the Applies To range for each rule is correct. When you add, move, or copy cells or formatting, the conditional formats don't always follow in the way you might expect. Finally, check the numbers used as triggers within each rule. Excel applies some default settings when you create the rule. If your data has changed since then, you might need to tweak the rules accordingly.

If you experiment a little too much with conditional formatting rules and want to get a fresh start, click Clear Rules on the Conditional Formatting menu. You can erase the rules from a selection, an entire sheet, a table, or a PivotTable.

Using sparklines to visualize trends within a range

If you think of sparklines as tiny charts that fit in a single cell, you won't be too far from the truth. This feature, introduced in Excel 2010, enables you to visualize a data series in a single cell. The following example shows quarterly results over a period of several years, with a sparkline at the end of each row that shows the up and down gyrations over each year.

The easiest way to apply sparklines to a range of data is to select the range and then open the Quick Analysis tool, as shown here.

	Qtr1	Qtr2	Qtr3	Qtr4	
2001	4447	4230	3339	4112	
2002	4393	4947	4387	4280	
2003	3774	3269	3852	4311	
2004	4337	4401	4731	3231	
2005	4990	4054	3783	4788	
2006	4664	4172	3233	3281	
2007	4427	3335	4446	4948	
2008	3772	3001	4968	4548	
2009	5400	4295	5674	5353	
2010	4730	4255	5285	5719	
2011	4728	5574	4418	5284	
2012	6820	6015	6378	6664	
2013	7201	6689	6518	6978	

FORMATTING | CHARTS | TOTALS | TABLES | SPARKLINES

Line   Column   Win/Loss

Sparklines are mini charts placed in single cells.

Sparklines come in three varieties: Line and Column work almost exactly like their full-size chart counterparts, while Win/Loss shows an up or down marker depending on whether the associated data is positive (win) or negative (loss).

To add a sparkline for a selection other than the full data range, click Line, Column, or Win/Loss from the Sparklines group on the Insert tab. If you made a selection first, the Data Range box is filled in with that range; you just need to select the cell where you want the sparkline to appear.

To change an existing sparkline, use the Design tab under the Sparkline Tools heading (it's only visible when you select one or more cells containing a sparkline). Figure 13-14 shows the commands available on this tab.

Figure 13-14 As with a full-size chart, you can use commands on this specialized tab to change the style of a sparkline, add data markers, and edit the source data.

Most of the options on the Design tab are self-explanatory. One that deserves special attention is the Axis command, which allows you to customize how each axis in the mini-chart is treated. Normally, each sparkline is treated as an independent series, with values charted using only the data in its source data range. If you want Excel to chart multiple sparklines using the same range of values, click Axis, and then change the selections under Vertical Axis Minimum Value Options and Vertical Axis Maximum Value Options to Same For All Sparklines.

Turning data into charts

The process of building a chart in Excel is literally a two-step operation. Step one: select some data. Step two: choose a chart type. Everything beyond that is a matter of refinement, making the resulting chart more visually appealing and understandable, with titles and labels and color gradients and other tweaks.

In this whirlwind tour of the charting features in Excel, we focus on the nuts and bolts of actually building a chart. If you're looking for detailed explanations of the concepts behind turning information into graphics, we highly recommend starting with Edward Tufte's seminal work on the subject (see *www.edwardtufte.com*). And because space is limited in this chapter, we can only dive just below the surface in showing you the many options available when you create and customize Excel charts. For a much more complete picture, we recommend *Microsoft Excel 2013 Inside Out*, by our colleagues Mark Dodge and Craig Stinson (Microsoft Press, 2013).

With that disclaimer out of the way, we ask you to look at the simple line chart shown in Figure 13-15, which illustrates the most common chart elements.

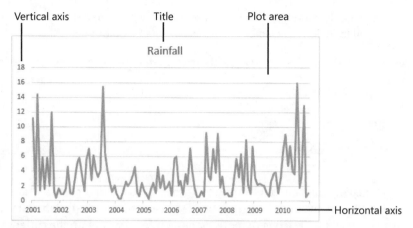

Figure 13-15 This simple line chart includes several basic elements—a chart title, a plot area (with gridlines), and two axes—horizontal and vertical.

With a little more data and a few more clicks, we could make this chart much more compli-cated, although that would defeat its purpose. The following list describes the main chart elements available to you in Excel:

- **Data series and plot area**   Each series of data appears within the plot area, repre-sented as a line, column, bar, or pie slice, depending on the chart type. You can use a unique color in the plot area to make it stand out from the chart background. Three-dimensional charts have a wall, a floor, and rotation options as well.

- **Axes and gridlines**   Column, bar, and line charts typically plot data along two axes. Figure 13-15, for example, shows time along the horizontal axis and rainfall (mea-sured in inches) along the vertical axis. A depth axis is available for 3-D charts. Grid-lines help you compare the values in a data series to the values on an axis.

- **Titles**   If you choose to use a chart title, you can overlay the title on the chart itself or allow the title to sit above the chart. In addition, you can add a title to any axis to help explain the data plotted along that axis. Figure 13-15, for example, might be easier to understand at a glance if the vertical axis had "Monthly rainfall (inches)" as a title.

- **Legend**   This optional element functions as a key when a chart contains multiple data series; it typically provides labels next to the color or shape used for the corre-sponding data series.

- **Labels**   You can add labels to axes to indicate what each step along the axis repre-sents. On the horizontal axis shown in Figure 13-15, we removed the labels for the 12 data points (January through December) within each year and instead used labels to identify entire years. You can also add data labels to a data series in the plot area itself to indicate the actual values represented by plot points.

All of the tools you need to create a chart are in the Charts section of the Insert tab, shown here.

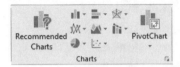

There's nothing subtle about the way this group of commands pushes a signature feature of Excel 2013. Click the oversize Recommended Charts button on the left and you get exactly what you would expect: one or more suggestions on how to turn the current selection or region into a chart. (If you know the exact type of chart you want to use, you can click its icon from the set of eight options in the middle of the command group.)

Figure 13-16 shows one set of recommendations. The choices you see on the dialog box's Recommended Charts tab use your real data and display an accurate representation of what you'll get if you click OK. The exact number and type of suggestions on this tab depend on the type of data you select and how it's arranged.

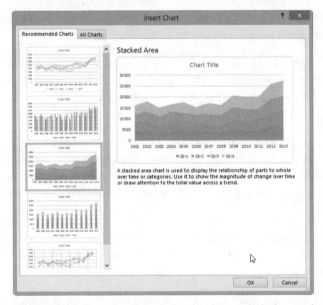

Figure 13-16 The selections on the Recommended Charts tab represent live previews of the current data, so you can flip through the suggestions and choose the one that best tells your story.

If none of the recommendations suits your fancy, click the All Charts tab to choose from the full range of chart types, as shown here.

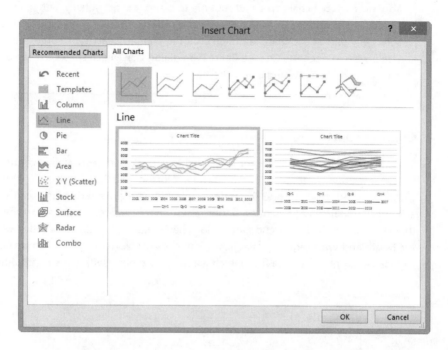

Choose a chart type from the column on the left and then one of the subtypes from the thumbnails along the top of the preview pane on the right. The resulting thumbnails use your live data, and you can get a closer look at any chart by letting your mouse hover over the thumbnail until it zooms.

Choosing the right chart type

How do you know which type of chart is right for your data? Recommendations go a long way, and Excel's algorithms can be spookily accurate. But, as mentioned earlier, building a chart involves equal parts art and science, and there's nothing like your own eye (and perhaps feedback from colleagues) to help you determine whether the chart you've chosen is the right one for the story you're trying to tell.

In this section, we look at the main chart types with an eye to helping you choose the right one.

> ### Note
>
> You must select a chart type and subtype to create a chart initially, but you can switch to a different subtype or even choose a completely different chart type later. Click to select any part of the chart, and then click the Change Chart Type command on the Design tab to open the Change Chart Type dialog box, which shows the same All Charts tab you see when creating a new chart.

Column charts

Column charts are tailor-made for side-by-side comparisons, especially over time. Available subtypes include clustered columns, stacked columns, and 100% stacked columns, with and without 3-D effects. Figure 13-17, for example, shows a clustered column chart that offers a simple comparison of revenues in four regions over four years. It's easy to see at a glance that revenues in the North and East regions have been flat or down slightly over time, while the South and West regions have grown impressively. Note that the recommended chart includes a placeholder for a title, which we need to replace with a meaningful description.

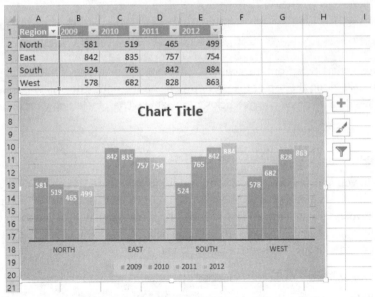

Figure 13-17 Column charts make it possible to compare data points side by side. This clustered column chart shows trends over time for four regions.

Chapter 13

INSIDE OUT   Swap the axes to tell a different story

Sometimes all you need is a slightly different angle to see a completely different picture. Clicking the Switch Row/Column button, in the Data group on the Design tab, is a particularly effective way of looking at column charts from a different perspective. The command name is misleading: what it really does is swap the data series associated with the horizontal and vertical axes. The column chart shown earlier in Figure 13-17, for example, looks at four regions over time, emphasizing the trend for each region. If you click Switch Row/Column, the data series that make up the clustered columns are swapped, and you get the revised chart shown here:

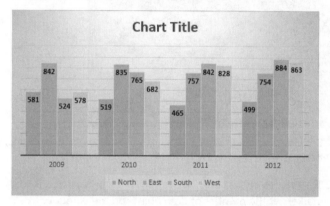

At first glance, the chart looks similar to the earlier arrangement. But the story it tells is different, emphasizing differences over time, with one region dominating in the first year, but with a much narrower gap between the leaders just three years later. Which arrangement you choose depends on which story you want to communicate.

The other main variation in this chart type is the stacked column chart, which combines data from different series into a single column that emphasizes the relationship of individual items to the total. If your data series includes several similar totals and you want to emphasize a percentage change in one or more individual components, use a 100% stacked chart.

For column charts, most of the 3-D subtypes apply visual effects only. The exception is the 3-D Column subtype, which uses the horizontal axis and the depth axis to compare series and categories equally, with values on the vertical axis.

Line charts

Use a line chart when you want to plot data over time (or along ordered categories) to show trends on a continuous scale: revenues by quarter, economic growth by year or decade, rainfall or high and low temperature by month, and so on. The horizontal axis should be divided into equal units, with no gaps. Figure 13-18, for example, shows a month's worth of daily high and low temperatures plotted on a line graph.

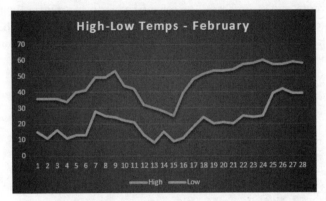

Figure 13-18 Because this line graph has 28 separate data points on each line, we've chosen not to use data markers.

Each of the 2-D subtypes in the Line Chart category includes options to show lines with or without data markers. If the number of data points on the category axis is relatively small, let Excel automatically add markers to show the exact location of each point. That makes it easier to find the value associated with each entry on the horizontal axis. You can customize the color and shape of each marker, as we explain later in this chapter.

INSIDE OUT   Add data labels selectively

Adding data labels to every point in a series can sometimes lead to information overload. The alternative is to add data labels to specific data points. Click to select the data series, and you'll see a selection marker over every point in the series. Click any individual data point to select just that point. Now you can show or hide the label for that point alone. Use the options on the Data Labels menu, under Add Chart Element on the Design tab, to choose a position for the label, or drag it manually.

Pie charts

If the data you want to plot is in a single row or column, it just might fit in a pie chart. Each pie chart consists of a single data series. Each data point is a slice proportional in size to the other items in the series, adding up to 100 percent. Pie charts work best when you have a small number of data points, six or seven at most, and no slice is too close to 0. (Negative numbers aren't allowed in a pie chart.)

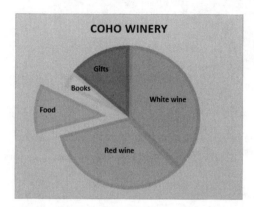

You can emphasize one or more slices of a pie chart by "exploding" it from the rest of the chart, as we've done here. Select a slice and drag it away from the pie. (This option is especially dramatic if you've chosen a 3-D chart type.) If you select the entire series—in other words, every slice of the pie—and drag out, you'll end up with an exploded pie chart. This option is most relevant when you want to talk about each data point separately in order of size.

Two of the advanced pie chart subtypes are surprisingly useful when you want to tell a story within a story. It's also a good way to create a readable chart when you have a dozen or more data points. The Pie Of Pie and Bar Of Pie subtypes let you combine two or more slices into a single slice called Other, with those data points plotted in a second pie or bar chart. Figure 13-19 shows the Bar Of Pie chart subtype.

The options for the second chart are well hidden. Right-click the bar portion of the chart and then choose Format Data Series. In the Format Data Series pane on the right, use the Split Series By options to define which pieces of the original pie are broken out into the second chart. Use the sliders under the Gap Width and Second Plot Size headings to adjust the distance between the two charts and change their size relative to each other.

Doughnut charts are similar to pie charts but can contain multiple data series, with one series inside the "doughnut hole" of the next. Excel's Help system notes that doughnut charts are "not easy to read" and suggests stacked column or stacked bar charts as alternatives.

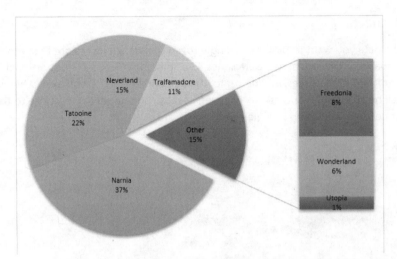

Figure 13-19 You define which values go in the bar chart on the right by setting a condition—in this example, the three smallest values in the list.

Bar charts

A bar chart is, in its simplest form, a column chart turned on its side, with the values on the horizontal axis and categories on the vertical axis. Bar charts are ideal for differentiating winners and losers—or at least those who are in the lead for now. Bar charts work equally well for presenting results of speed tests and for pointing out who's in front in a fundraising competition. In Figure 13-20, for example, we could have just as easily plotted this data as a column chart, but the long school names would have been awkward to position along the horizontal axis and look more natural and readable here.

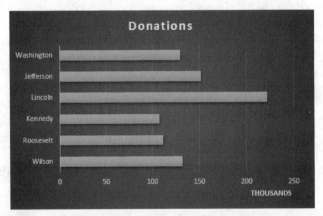

Figure 13-20 Bar charts work especially well when the category names are long, as in this example. The horizontal arrangement makes the current leader easy to identify.

Area charts

Area charts show the magnitude of change in a data set over time and thus offer a good way to show changes in the relative contributions of different parts of a group. In their plainest form, 2-D and 3-D area charts are like line charts, except that the value between the data point and the next lowest point on another series (or the lowest point on the axis) is filled in with color.

A stacked area chart like the one shown in Figure 13-21 adds all the values together so that the highest point on the chart for each point on the horizontal axis represents the total for that point.

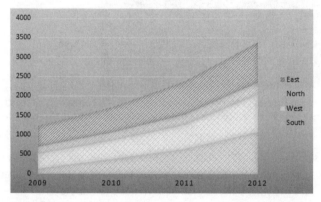

Figure 13-21 Use a stacked area chart to pile each data series on top of the one before it and show its contribution to the total.

Scatter (X, Y) charts

Scatter charts (also known as X, Y charts) are fascinating, versatile, and often misunderstood. A scatter chart is made up of two numeric data series, plotted in pairs on the horizontal and vertical axes (which are also known respectively as the x-axis and y-axis, thus explaining the origin of the name). You can use a scatter chart in place of a line chart when data points on the horizontal axis aren't linear; the visual result is similar, but without the distortion caused by irregular spacing of data points. One common use of a scatter chart is to identify clusters of similar data in a nonlinear set. In Figure 13-22, for example, we've created this chart type by plotting survey data for 15 companies, with customer satisfaction ratings on the vertical axis and price on the horizontal axis.

You'll notice in this scatter chart that we deliberately hid the values on both axes. The numbers themselves can be on any scale you create. It's the position of the data in this chart that matters most. The data point for Wingtip Toys represents the best value, while the one for Wide World Importers is the worst.

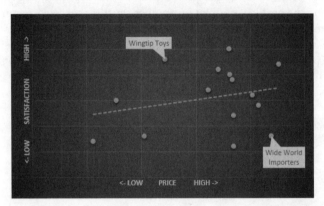

Figure 13-22 Each dot represents a pair of survey results for a company's products. The dashed trendline shows that higher prices generally mean greater satisfaction, but the two data labels identify noteworthy exceptions.

Bubble charts resemble scatter (X, Y) charts with an extra dimension that turns plot points into bubbles of varying sizes. As in a scatter chart, the values in the x and y series plot the location of each data point. The third value determines the bubble size.

Other chart types

The last two tiny icons in the Charts group on the Insert tab cover a hodgepodge of chart types that are useful for specialized purposes. One icon covers Stock, Surface, and Radar charts; the other lets you create a Combo chart.

Analyzing trends in the markets for stocks, bonds, and other securities was once one of the most popular uses for Excel charts. It's less important today, with the widespread availability of online services that can create these charts for you. But if you have a set of data that includes historical stock prices, this chart type is made for you. The four available layout options enable you to plot the movement of stock prices on a daily basis, using a single line to indicate high, low, and closing prices. Opening prices and trading volume are optional data series.

Building a stock chart requires that you arrange your data in a specific order. If you try to create a stock chart using an incorrect arrangement of data, you're greeted with a helpful message like the one shown here. (The exact content of the message changes based on the chart subtype you've selected.)

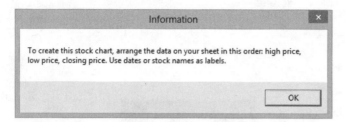

Surface charts are made up of two data series containing numeric data and resemble a topographic map. If you can envision a rubber sheet stretched over a 3-D column chart, you have a pretty good idea of what a 3-D surface chart looks like.

Radar charts plot data in a circular arrangement, where one set of numeric values starts at the center of the chart and a second set of ordered values (typically time) is plotted around the outside of the circle.

Changing a chart's layout or design

After you create a chart, you can change its fundamental organization, layout, and location at any time. You can also tweak the style and appearance of individual chart elements. In previous versions of Excel, these tasks required visits to myriad dialog boxes. In Excel 2013, selecting a chart exposes two custom tabs that appear under the Chart Tools heading.

On the left side of the Design tab is an Add Chart Element menu, which displays options that are specifically designed for the type of chart you've selected. You might want to add labels showing the exact numbers associated with each bar, for example. To do so, click Data Labels. As Figure 13-23 shows, allowing the mouse pointer to hover over an individual option previews the effect of that option on the live chart. Click to apply the change.

Other items on the Design tab allow you to quickly change the layout of a chart, keeping its basic organization but showing, hiding, and rearranging elements such as chart titles and axis titles. The Change Colors menu lets you choose from a selection of ready-made color palettes, some bold and others muted. You can also adjust colors and fonts automatically using thumbnails in the Chart Styles group. All of these options allow you to point and preview their effects in the live chart. If you don't like the effect, move the pointer away to preserve your existing chart choices.

Chapter 13

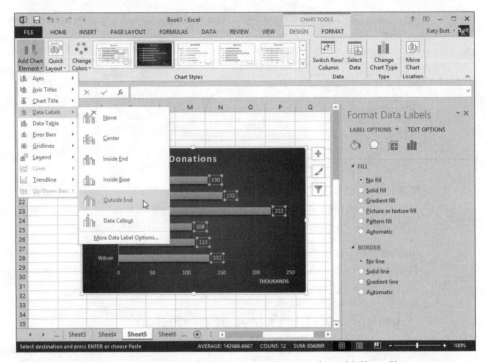

Figure 13-23 Let the mouse pointer hover over any item on the Add Chart Element menu to preview its effects on the graph. Here, you can see the data labels at the end of each bar.

For alternative access to the same controls, click anywhere within the chart to reveal three buttons at the right. Clicking any button reveals additional options, such as the Chart Elements menu shown here.

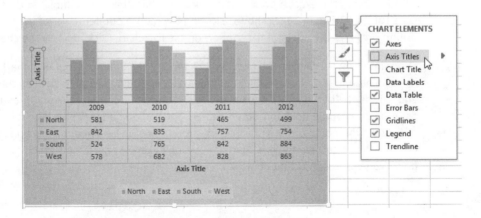

Selecting a check box adds an element to the chart; clearing a check box removes it from the chart. Allow the mouse pointer to hover over the name of an element to preview its appearance. Click the arrow to the right of any item to see a submenu with additional choices. Note that this menu is identical in function, if not appearance, to the Add Chart Element menu on the Design tab.

Likewise, the choices available when you click the second button mirror the options you can choose from the Chart Styles group and the Change Colors menu, respectively, on the Design tab.

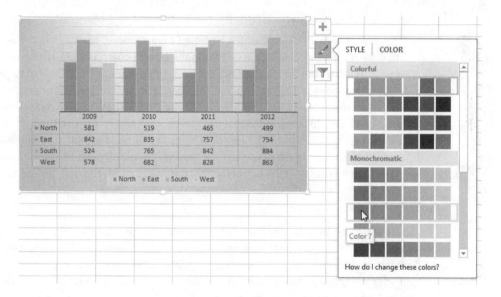

The third and final button has the same effect as the Select Data button on the Design tab, allowing you to adjust the values and names of data series that appear in the chart.

These options work well for most charts, but there are times when you might want to fine-tune the appearance or position of a particular chart element. When that type of situation arises, you have four choices:

- Click the Add Chart Element menu on the Design tab, select an element, and then click the More *element type* Options menu choice below the ready-made choices.

- Click the Chart Elements button (the first one to the right of the chart, identified by a plus sign), click the arrow to the right of the element you want to adjust, and then click More Options at the bottom of the submenu.

- Click the Format tab and choose an element from the list at the top of the Current Selection group; then click Format Selection.

- If the element is visible in the chart, double-click it.

Regardless of which method you select, the tools you need appear in task-specific panes on the right side of the worksheet.

INSIDE OUT   Use the arrow keys to cycle through individual chart elements

If you're more comfortable with a keyboard than a mouse, you can use the arrow keys to cycle through all available elements in the current chart. Double-click anywhere inside the chart borders (but away from axes, titles, legends, and the like) to select the Chart Area, which is the first entry in the Chart Elements list in the Current Selection group on the Format tab. Now use the Up and Down Arrow keys to move through the list, to the plot area, individual data series, axes, and so on. Use the Left and Right Arrow keys to move through individual items in a series, a legend, or another element made up of multiple data points. If the legend is selected, press the Right Arrow key to select the first entry in the list, and keep pressing to move through the entire legend.

There are, quite literally, thousands of individual options available to you when you begin poking around at a granular level with individual chart elements. The pane containing formatting options is typically divided into tabs. The Format Legend pane, for example, includes the Legend Options tab (shown here) and a Text Options tab; both are in turn divided into three subgroups of settings.

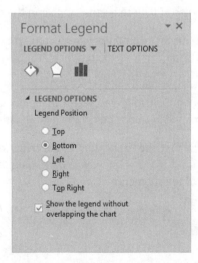

Many of the commands in the formatting panes lead to collapsible menus that present common formatting options. The Format Axis Title pane, for example, shows three options you'll find repeated in the corresponding formatting panes for other elements. From left to right, these are Fill (shown in Figure 13-24), Effects, and Size & Properties.

Figure 13-24 Click one of the three small icons below Title Options to change the set of options shown in this formatting pane.

A surprising range of options is available if you dig deep enough. For example, a graph whose values are expressed in large numbers—thousands or millions—might benefit from having the values shown in a truncated form on the axis, so that 244,778,845 appears between the tick marks for 200 and 250. The Format Axis pane, shown next, lets you do exactly that, setting a value-based axis to show numbers in hundreds, thousands, millions, billions, trillions, or even a logarithmic scale.

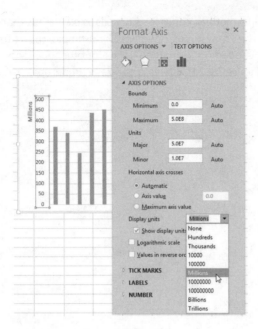

The process of building a chart doesn't have to be linear. After you get a few basic design decisions out of the way, you can revisit and refine the chart's layout, formatting, and style options as needed, in any order, trying out alternatives until you're satisfied.

If the iterative process turns out a collection of settings you're especially pleased with, or if you want to share your handiwork with other people, you can save the current settings as a chart template for reuse. Right-click the chart area, choose Save As Template from the shortcut menu, and give the template a descriptive name. To apply all those settings to a new chart with one pass, click Change Chart Type on the Design tab, choose the Templates category from the All Charts tab, and pick the thumbnail for your saved template.

One final option allows you to change the location of a chart. Click Move Chart (the right-most command on the Design tab) to see the dialog box shown here. You can position the chart on its own sheet or as an object that floats on a worksheet—typically the same one containing your source data.

INSIDE OUT   Change a chart's location to suit the task at hand

It's perfectly acceptable to move a chart to make it easier to work with. As you change the data in a table, for example, you might want to see your changes reflected in real time in a linked chart. In that scenario, move the chart to the current worksheet and position the chart object alongside the data you're entering or editing. When you've polished the chart to perfection, move it to its own chart sheet and give the sheet a descriptive name. That makes finding the chart easier so you can use it in a Word document or a PowerPoint presentation later.

Linking worksheet data to chart elements

The elements that make up a chart are, in most cases, linked directly to data within a worksheet. Series names typically come from the label attached to the column or row that provides the data series values. Axis labels and legends are also derived from source data. If you change any of the data points in the source data, the corresponding chart element is updated immediately.

You can view and edit the source data for a chart by clicking anywhere in the chart and then clicking Select Data, in the Data group on the Design tab. Figure 13-25 shows this dialog box for a chart whose data source consists of four rows (each treated as a separate data series) and four columns (each treated as a separate category).

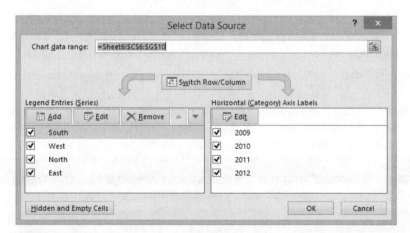

Figure 13-25 You can edit the source data for any series or rearrange the order of series and categories in this dialog box.

Chapter 13

In this example, the source data (as identified in the Chart Data Range box) is a single con-tiguous range. If your chart consists of selected rows or columns from a larger range or table, you'll see each range listed separately, with commas separating the multiple ranges.

The labels above the two main boxes in the Select Data Source dialog box do not change with the chart type, which can lead to some confusing results. For example, in a pie chart, the values in the Horizontal (Category) Axis Labels box define each slice of the pie and are used for the legend, while the values in the Legend Entries (Series) box contain the values that are plotted in the chart and are *not* in the legend.

When you open the Select Data Source dialog box, it positions itself so that the upper-left corner of the chart's data range is visible.

To edit an individual data series, select it in the Legend Entries (Series) list and then click the Edit button. The Edit Series dialog box, shown here, shows you which cell is being picked up as the series name and which range defines the data series. In both cases, you can see the current values to the right of the Collapse Dialog button and the equal sign.

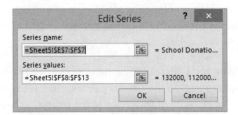

> **Note**
>
> If the series you select is part of a scatter (X, Y) chart, the Edit Series dialog box con-tains separate boxes for Series X Values and Series Y Values.

The Add button opens the same Edit Series dialog box, with no data source selected. Click to fill in the Series Name and Series Values boxes with valid ranges and then click OK to add the new series to your chart. The Remove button completely removes the selected data series from the chart. Use the Move Up and Move Down arrows (to the right of the Remove button) to change the order of the selected data series in the list. (You cannot change the order of categories here—do that by using the Axis Options tab in the Format Axis task pane.)

With a chart that is embedded on the same sheet as the source data, you can edit chart data directly, using color-coded handles that surround the corresponding source data. If you click to select the entire chart, selection handles appear around all values listed in the Chart Data Range box. If you click to select a data series in the chart, the handles appear around the source cells and ranges associated with that series. Figure 13-26, for example, shows the result when we select the fourth and final series in a clustered column chart.

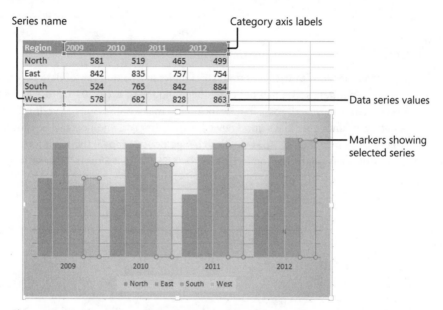

Figure 13-26 The color-coded selection boxes show the series name and values and category axis labels.

The red box indicates the data series names, the blue box indicates the series values (points to be plotted in the chart), and the purple box identifies category axis labels.

If you use a table as the source data for your chart, adding a new row or column automatically extends the corresponding series in the linked chart. If your data source is a simple range, you have to add new data manually. To do so, enter your data first, including the column or row heading, and then click the chart to expose the color-coded handles. Drag the corner of the range containing the series values so that it includes your new row or column, and then drag the series name or category axis label, as needed, to include the newly added cell.

If you find it easier to use the Clipboard, you can add a new row or column to your data source (or select an existing range that isn't currently part of the chart), copy it to the Clipboard, and then click to select the chart and paste the Clipboard contents. Be sure to include the cell that includes the series name or category axis label, if appropriate.

You can also use the sizing handles to reduce the number of series or data points. For example, if you have a column chart that includes 12 months' worth of results but you want to show only the last three months, drag the corresponding selections in the data source to make them smaller, using just the data you want to include.

INSIDE OUT   No more data limits

Previous versions of Excel imposed strict limits on the number of data points you could include per data series and per chart. Beginning with Excel 2010, those limits were completely removed. You can now include as many data points as your PC's memory can accommodate. That's good news for scientists and engineers who want to visualize very large sets of data. However, this change doesn't repeal the most fundamental principle of turning information into graphics: KISS (Keep It Simple, Stupid).

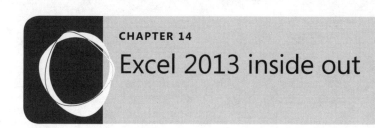

I N THIS CHAPTER, we look at Excel's more advanced features, including the one that separates a real Excel power user from a mere poser: PivotTable reports. We explain how to start with a simple list and summarize it from multiple angles using these versatile reports.

For formatting fanatics, we offer a collection of expert techniques to help you save and reuse custom number formats and cell styles. If you're trying to extract the useful parts of big blobs of imported text, you'll appreciate our instructions on how to transform and manipulate text with the help of the Clipboard and some arcane but extremely useful functions.

At the end of this chapter, we share some of our favorite Excel tweaks, including how to create online surveys using Excel and SkyDrive and how to automatically enter custom lists into a worksheet. We also show you how to prevent data-entry errors.

We start with some tricks that can save you time and effort every time you open Excel.

Customizing the default new workbook

When you create a new workbook, its contents and formatting follow one of two groups of saved settings. The first group of settings is applied if you create a blank workbook without using a template—by starting a new instance of Excel or choosing Blank Workbook from the New pane in Backstage view, for example. For a blank workbook, Excel uses default workbook settings that define the number of worksheets, the default font and font size, and so on. To customize these defaults, open the Excel Options dialog box and adjust the options under the When Creating New Workbooks heading on the General tab, as shown next.

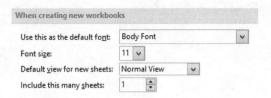

The most useful options here are the ability to change the default number of worksheets and the option to change the default font size. In the Use This As The Default Font box, you'll see that Excel uses Body Font as the default selection. Although you can choose a specific font, we recommend keeping this setting, which allows you to change fonts on the fly by applying a different theme.

You can also create a new workbook using content, graphics, and formatting saved in a template. When you press Ctrl+N, Excel creates a new workbook using the default template and ignores the settings we just looked at.

You can replace this default workbook template with a custom design that includes graphics, title pages, copyright notices, macros, and other elements (including cell contents and formatting) that you would normally need to add manually.

Before you begin customizing your default template, you may need to create the special folder Excel uses for this purpose. In File Explorer (Windows 8) or Windows Explorer (Windows 7), type the following address (including the percent signs): %AppData%\Microsoft\ Excel. That opens a folder within the roaming profile for your user account. If the XLStart folder does not exist, click New Folder to create it, being sure to replace the suggested name with XLStart.

Next, open Excel and add any text, graphics, formulas, and formatting you want to include in every new workbook based on your template. When you finish, click File, click Save As, click Computer, and then click Browse (or use the keyboard shortcut F12) to open the Save As dialog box.

Choose one of the following template formats from the Save As Type list.

- **Excel Template**   This is the default format for Excel 2007, 2010, and 2013. Choose it if you know that all your colleagues are able to open and edit workbooks saved in this format.

- **Excel Macro-Enabled Template**   Choose this option if your default workbook contains macros or if you expect to create macros in new workbooks you create later.

- **Excel 97-2003 Template**   Use this format if you want all new workbooks to be readable without modification by colleagues who are using older versions of Excel.

Note that any features that are specific to Excel 2007 or later versions will not be saved in this format.

In the File Name box, enter **Book** (with no file extension and no number on the end of the file name).

Don't click Save yet! When you choose any of the template formats, Excel proposes saving your new template in the Custom Office Templates subfolder in your user profile. That's fine for templates you want to choose from when you click New in Backstage view and then click the Personal tab. But the default workbook template must be saved in the XLStart folder.

Navigate to the folder you just created: %AppData%\Microsoft\Excel\XLStart. After selecting that location, click Save.

Close the template and press Ctrl+N to confirm that the changes you made are included in new workbooks.

Using PivotTables

The very concept of a PivotTable report (often called simply a PivotTable) can be daunting if you've never worked with one. But once you discover how quickly and effectively you can use a PivotTable to summarize even the most enormous table, we predict you'll be hooked.

PivotTables allow you to filter, summarize, and group data just by dragging fields around on the screen and picking from lists. One of the most interesting options allows you to move rows to columns (and vice versa); this capability, formally known as *pivoting*, is what gives the feature its name.

In this section, we explain how to create a PivotTable, how to customize its layout, and how to create compelling and visually attractive reports.

Creating a PivotTable

Every PivotTable starts with a data source. Although that source can be external, the most common scenario (and the one we discuss in this book) uses source data stored in a range or table on an Excel worksheet. The source data must be organized in columns, with each row containing a separate set of data points. The table must not contain any summaries or subtotals.

The order of rows and columns in the data source doesn't matter, although sorting the data to match your default report type can help you skip some PivotTable customization steps. Headings aren't required either, although we strongly recommend using descriptive headings—trying to create a PivotTable using generic headings (Column1, Column2, and so on) is a painful process.

Excel 2013 uses the same technique it uses for charts to recommend specific PivotTable layouts. To begin, click a single cell in the source data range or table (or select the entire range) and then click Recommended PivotTables, in the Tables group on the Insert tab. The resulting dialog box contains a selection of thumbnails on the left (scroll to see the full list) with a closer view of the currently selected thumbnail on the right.

Figure 14-1 shows the Recommended PivotTables dialog box for a large collection of data (13 columns in 1256 rows) on significant earthquakes, downloaded from the U.S. Geological Survey Real-time Feeds & Data page at *http://earthquake.usgs.gov*.

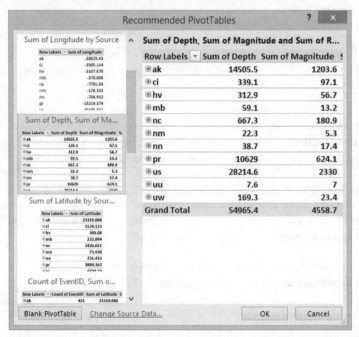

Figure 14-1 Choose a thumbnail from the scrolling list on the left to see a detailed view of the layout on the right.

If the layout you need isn't available, choose one that's close. In the previous example, we chose a layout with Sum Of Depth and Sum Of Magnitude as PivotTable columns. We actually want to see averages, not totals, for those two values. Fortunately, that change is easy to make after the PivotTable is in position.

If you prefer to create a PivotTable from scratch, click a single cell in the source data range or table (or select the entire range) and then click PivotTable in the Tables group on the Insert tab. That opens the Create PivotTable dialog box shown in Figure 14-2.

Figure 14-2 The default options shown here position your PivotTable on a new worksheet within the same workbook.

The first pair of options allows you to change the data source if necessary. The options at the bottom of the dialog box allow you to select a specific location for the PivotTable. For most circumstances, we recommend choosing the default options. Keeping a PivotTable on its own page offers the most flexibility and minimizes the likelihood that it will inadvertently interfere with the contents of an existing worksheet.

If you use a recommended PivotTable, you'll switch to the newly created sheet and see a layout like the one shown in Figure 14-3. On the right side is the PivotTable Fields list pane, whose contents mirror the headings in your source data table or range. Below that list are four boxes containing the fields used in the current PivotTable layout. Two new tabs are visible at the end of the ribbon, under the PivotTable Tools heading. (If you created a Pivot-Table from scratch, none of the fields will be selected.)

Our data set contains columns for the date and time of each event, the depth and magnitude, and the location (in Latitude and Longitude columns and in a Source column that includes a geographic code).

As you click to select fields in the list in the top of the pane, Excel adds each selected field to one of the four sections in the bottom of the pane. The program makes its best guess as to which field goes where, although you can override the default section assignment for any field by dragging it to a different box. Excel also assigns a default calculation type to the value fields.

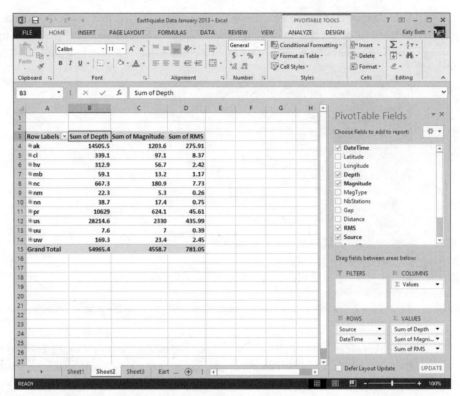

Figure 14-3 To create a PivotTable layout, select fields from the list on the right and add each one as row or column labels, values, or filters.

The default name for each field in the Values list reflects the type of calculation: "Sum of MagType," "Average of Depth," and so on. You can choose a different calculation in place of the default one. So, from a list of individual sales in a data table, you could choose the Sales_Amount field and click Count to calculate how many transactions each sales person had during a comparable period. Or choose Sum or Average to calculate the total sales amount or the average sale per transaction, respectively. Each calculation would give you a different insight into the data.

You can accept the defaults or tweak these settings.

Customizing a PivotTable layout

In this example, we want to see the average depth and magnitude of earthquakes, summarized by location as indicated by a two-letter code in the Source column. We also want to remove the RMS field, which was part of the recommended layout but isn't relevant to the report we're creating.

To start, we clear the check box next to the RMS entry in the PivotTable Fields list. Then we click the arrow to the right of the Sum Of Depth field in the Values box in the lower-right corner of the PivotTable Fields pane and click Value Field Settings, which opens the dialog box of the same name. We change the Summarize Value Field By setting to Average, and in the Custom Name box we shorten the suggested name to "Avg Depth." The results are shown here.

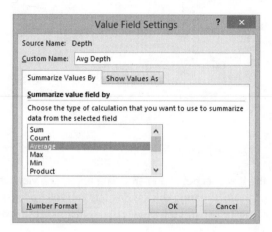

INSIDE OUT   Customize the PivotTable Fields pane

In the upper-right corner of the PivotTable Fields pane is a small gear icon with an arrow to its right. Clicking that icon reveals a menu of five alternative arrangements of the two sections. You can arrange fields and the four areas side by side, or show only one section while hiding the other. For most simple PivotTables, the default layout is good enough. Consider changing the layout if you have a complex data source with many fields.

At this point, we can click the Number Format button to display the Format Cells dialog box, with only the Number tab available. We can apply any number or date format, set the number of decimal places, and specify whether we want to use a thousands separator. This dialog box is available for value fields only.

We repeat this process for the Sum Of Magnitude field and add one more column to the fields list, dragging Source into the Values box, where it appears as Count Of Source. After changing its name to the more descriptive "# of Incidents," we end up with a PivotTable that looks like the one shown here.

	A	B	C	D
1				
2				
3	Source	# of Incidents	Avg Depth	Avg Magnitude
4	⊞ ak	415	35	2.90
5	⊞ ci	34	11	2.86
6	⊞ hv	20	16	2.84
7	⊞ mb	5	12	2.64
8	⊞ nc	63	11	2.87
9	⊞ nm	2	11	2.65
10	⊞ nn	6	8	2.90
11	⊞ pr	203	52	3.07
12	⊞ us	513	55	4.54
13	⊞ uu	2	4	3.50
14	⊞ uw	8	28	2.93
15	Grand Total	1271	43	3.59

If you add multiple fields in the Rows section, you can create an outline view of your data that can be expanded and collapsed. Creating this outline lets you roll up large amounts of data into easy-to-digest subtotals or expand the details under any of those levels.

In the next example, we started with a table containing more than 30,000 data points from weather measurements taken in the Denver, Colorado, area over a 25-year period. The Rows box contains two fields, one for Station Name and the second for Date. Initially, clicking the plus sign to the left of the entry for a station name (Boulder, for example) shows detailed data for every measurement on every individual date recorded at that station. By right-clicking a date and choosing Group, we can use the dialog box shown in Figure 14-4 to summarize the data by year and month.

After you've arranged fields on the PivotTable page, you're ready to tweak the display so that it's even more readable. If you don't like the default sort order for rows, for example, you can change it. Right-click a row label or a data point in any column that contains a field from the Values box and click Sort to rearrange the data in ascending or descending order by that column's values.

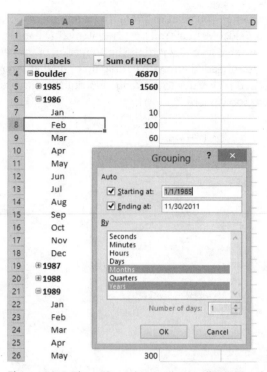

Figure 14-4 These Grouping settings collapse the detailed data into yearly and monthly subtotals. Use the +/– buttons to the left of each heading to expand or collapse the data beneath that heading.

Right-click a row label and then click More Sort Options if you want the option to sort by a different field.

Chapter 14

This option is especially useful when you want to arrange data in a specific order that defies being expressed as a formula. Select Manual (You Can Drag Items To Rearrange Them) in the Sort dialog box for the row label field. Point to the bottom edge of the cell containing any row label until you see a four-headed arrow, then drag up or down to move it. You can also right-click any row label and click Move to rearrange individual items in that column using menu options like those shown here.

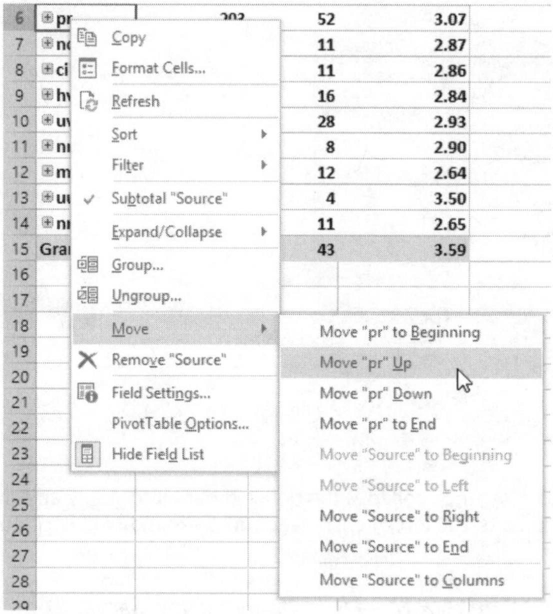

TROUBLESHOOTING

When you refresh the PivotTable, you lose your custom sort order

For row and column labels, the default settings have the AutoSort option enabled. That means you can manually move rows and columns, but as soon as you refresh the Pivot-Table, the sort order pops back to its normal settings. Disabling this behavior requires that you find a well-hidden setting and change it. Right-click the field you want to manually reorder, click Sort, and then click More Sort Options. Click the More Options button (we warned you it was deeply buried), and then clear the check box under AutoSort.

Filtering a PivotTable

You can filter data in a PivotTable in a variety of ways. The most formal is to drag a field from the PivotTable Fields list to the Filters section below it. The resulting filter appears above the PivotTable itself. Choosing an entry from the Report Filters list allows you to reuse the current data arrangement showing only entries you chose from that field. To see the list unfiltered, choose All Items from that list.

To filter a PivotTable on an ad hoc basis, use the field header. (If this drop-down list isn't visible, click the Field Headers button in the Show group on the Analyze tab for the Pivot-Table.) The filter options are very similar to those we described for ordinary tables and ranges. (See "Filtering data in a table" in Chapter 13, "Analyzing data with tables and charts.") You can show or hide specific entries in a list of values or labels or use the search box to find entries that match the text, numbers, or dates you supply.

To quickly filter a list using values in the first column, click or Ctrl+click to select the item or items you want to show or hide, right-click and click Filter, and then click either Keep Only Selected Items or Hide Selected Items.

Changing the format of a PivotTable

The Design tab contains a full range of options for customizing the look and feel of a Pivot-Table report. It's visible at the right side of the ribbon, under the PivotTable Tools heading, whenever the active cell is in a PivotTable.

The options in the Layout group allow you to quickly show or hide subtotals and grand totals. You can show subtotals at the top or bottom of a group and calculate grand totals for rows or columns or both.

The Report Layout command offers three alternatives for arranging the rows in your report, as shown here:

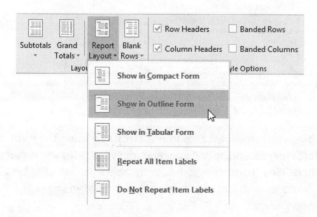

- **Compact Form**   This display option has the least amount of clutter. Multiple levels under a main heading are indented.

- **Outline Form**   Each row label gets its own field header. Each main grouping is in its own row, with secondary groupings in new rows beneath it in a column to the right of the previous level. Subtotals can appear at the top or bottom of each group.

- **Tabular Form**   All data is in a grid, with no indenting. Secondary levels of grouping begin in additional columns to the right of the main heading. In this format, subtotals appear only at the bottom of each group, even if you choose the Show All Subtotals At Top Of Group option.

Figure 14-5 shows examples for each option.

Compact Form

	A	B	C
1			
2			
3	Sum of HPCP	Column Labels ▾	
4	Row Labels ▾	Boulder	Colorado Springs
5	⊟1995		
6	Qtr1	320	72
7	Qtr2	1860	1511
8	Qtr3	490	498
9	Qtr4	160	4
10	⊟1996		
11	Qtr1	230	69
12	Qtr2	710	340

Outline Form

	A	B	C	D
1				
2				
3	Sum of HPCP		Station_Name ▾	
4	Years	▾ Date ▾	Boulder	Colorado Springs
5	⊟1995			
6		Qtr1	320	72
7		Qtr2	1860	1511
8		Qtr3	490	498
9		Qtr4	160	4
10	⊟1996			
11		Qtr1	230	69
12		Qtr2	710	340

Tabular Form

	A	B	C	D
1				
2				
3	Sum of HPCP		Station_Name ▾	
4	Years	▾ Date ▾	Boulder	Colorado Springs
5	⊟1995	Qtr1	320	72
6		Qtr2	1860	1511
7		Qtr3	490	498
8		Qtr4	160	4
9	⊟1996	Qtr1	230	69
10		Qtr2	710	340

Figure 14-5 Three views of the same PivotTable, displayed using different report formats.

As with ordinary tables, you can apply styles to PivotTables by using the PivotTable Styles gallery. The procedures for creating, modifying, and applying styles are identical, so we won't repeat them here. (See "Formatting tables with table styles" in Chapter 13.) The gallery is much larger, however, with 84 default styles to choose from instead of the 60 selections in the Table Styles gallery.

You'll see the reason for the difference when you customize one of the ready-made styles by right-clicking its thumbnail in the PivotTable Styles list and clicking Duplicate. In the Modify PivotTable Style dialog box, you'll find 25 individual options for a PivotTable style; that's nearly double the number of options for a regular table style, reflecting the need for separate formats to cover subtotals and grand totals, header cells, subheadings, and other features found only in PivotTables.

Manipulating text with functions

Data can come from the strangest of places. If you're lucky, you can parse the data at the same time you add it to your worksheet. But in other cases, imported data lands in your worksheet as long strings of text instead of neatly divided chunks of data.

In this section, we introduce you to some functions specifically designed to help you break text strings into smaller pieces and assemble pieces of text into bigger ones.

For a refresher course on this category of functions, see "Text functions" in Chapter 12, "Inside Excel 2013."

You can combine text by using no functions at all with the & operator. If column A is filled with first names and column B with matching last names, you can use the formula =A1&" "&A2 (note the space inside the quotation marks) to combine each pair into a full name in column C, with first and last name separated by a space. You can also use the CONCATENATE function, which combines two or more pieces of text into a single text string. The arguments for this function are separated by commas and can contain literal text (enclosed in quotation marks), cell references, and CHAR functions such as CHAR(10), which inserts a line break at the current location. (The single argument for the CHAR function is an ASCII code, which specifies the character to be inserted by the function; in this case, 10 is the ASCII code for a carriage return character.)

If you have a column of data that is arranged in a predictable fashion, you can extract data from it by using any of three functions: LEFT, MID, and RIGHT. =LEFT(text,num_chars) grabs a specific number of characters from the left side of a text value. If cell A1 contains the string LMSA10042, the formula =LEFT(A1,3) returns LMS. The RIGHT function has a similar syntax, taking characters from the end of the specified text. Use the MID function to return a specific number of characters starting from a specific position. In the previous example, =MID(A1,3,4) takes four characters, starting from the third character in the string: SA10.

In some cases you have to combine multiple functions to accomplish a goal. Here's how you can find the location of a specific string in a cell and then extract all or part of that string. For this example, we want to search for the string "SA10". We can use either of two functions. FIND and SEARCH perform similar jobs, with one difference: FIND is case sensitive and SEARCH is not. To search for the position in a string of text where the characters

SA10 begin, use =SEARCH("SA10",A1). The result is 3 in our example. Now combine that with the MID function and you can extract 6 characters from the point where that string begins:

=MID(A1, SEARCH("SA10",A1),6)

The LEN function returns the length of a text string. In our previous example, we can use =LEN(A1) to determine the length of the text in cell A1, which is 9 characters.

INSIDE OUT   Convert formulas to values with minimal hassle

After using formulas to split or combine data into the exact arrangement you want, you might prefer to get rid of the original data and keep just the transformed cells. But you can't delete the original cells as long as the text-manipulation formulas are in place, because doing so will turn your carefully constructed results into error messages. The solution is to select the cells containing the formulas and press Ctrl+C to copy their contents to the Clipboard. Then, without changing the selection, press Alt, E, S, V, which opens the Paste Special dialog box with the Values option selected. Press Enter to replace the formulas with their results. You can now safely remove the original cells.

Advanced worksheet formatting

A couple of chapters back, we went through the most useful of Excel's formatting options (for a refresher, see "Formatting cells and ranges" in Chapter 12). In this section, we dig into some lesser-known but useful formatting tools and techniques. You're most likely to find them in one of two places: on the Home tab or in the Format Cells dialog box. (It's worth mentioning again that you can summon this dialog box with the keyboard shortcut Ctrl+1, which every Excel user should memorize.)

On the Home tab, the Borders button is almost lost (and perhaps just a little out of place) among the more familiar options in the Fonts group. Click it to open the menu shown in Figure 14-6.

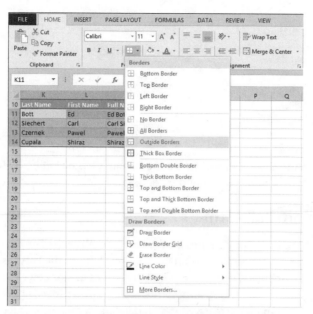

Figure 14-6 You can apply the simplest borders using the choices on the Borders menu. For more intricate projects, try drawing the borders instead.

Whatever option you click on the Borders menu applies to the current selection. Click All Borders, for example, to add black gridlines around and between all cells. This effect works best on small ranges. The Top And Double Bottom Border option is traditionally used to set off the Grand Totals row on a financial worksheet. Click No Border to remove all borders from the current range.

If you want to vary the thickness or color of the borders, use the options under Draw Borders to point and click your way through the process. The Line Color menu lets you choose colors from the current theme, and the Line Style menu gives you a dozen border styles, including dots, dashes, thin lines, and thick lines. The More Borders option at the bottom of the menu opens the Border tab in the Format Cells dialog box, which adds one extra line weight and the option to add diagonal lines through a cell.

The Alignment group on the Home tab contains another, equally well-hidden button, just left of Wrap Text. Aim the mouse pointer at it and you'll see a ScreenTip that identifies it as Orientation. Click to display the options shown next.

Chapter 14

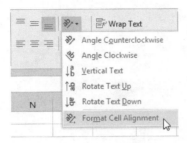

That last option leads to the Alignment tab of the Format Cells dialog box, which offers finer-grain control at angles besides 45 and 90 degrees.

Creating custom cell formats

In our discussion of the built-in categories on the Number tab of the Format Cells dialog box (see "Formatting cells and ranges" in Chapter 12), we left out the very last one: Custom. If none of the ready-made date, decimal, or number formats are exactly what you need for a particular range, you can create a custom format here. You can specify how positive and negative numbers are formatted, create your own date and time formats, and control the number of decimal places and significant digits that appear for each value.

> # INSIDE OUT Reuse custom number formats
>
> Excel saves custom number formats on a per-workbook basis, which allows you to use them on any worksheet in that workbook. To copy a custom number format to another workbook by using the Clipboard, first select a cell containing the custom format in the current worksheet and copy it to the Clipboard; then, in the new workbook, click Paste, Paste Special on the Home tab (or press Ctrl+Alt+V) and choose Formats. To make a custom number format available for all workbooks you create, add it to the default workbook template. (See "Customizing the default new workbook," earlier in this chapter.)

You needn't start with a blank slate when creating custom formats. Select the Custom category to display a long list of ready-made formats, including some you won't find in other categories. In general, it's easier to start with a format that's close to the one you want than to start from scratch. The Type box includes the codes for the format you previously chose in one of the other categories. In Figure 14-7, for example, we started in the Currency category, changed the currency symbol to the British pound, and then flipped to the Custom tab to review and edit the code for that format.

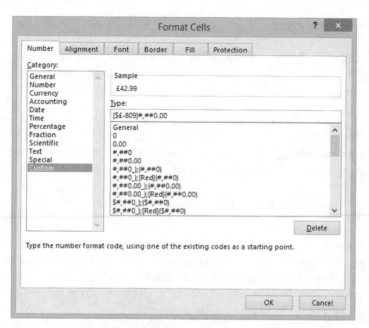

Figure 14-7 Edit the contents of the Type box to add a custom format. The list below it contains all available custom formats. Note the Sample box, which previews the custom format.

Custom formats use codes that define how to display digits, decimal places, dates, times, and currency symbols.

Each custom format can include up to four groups of these codes, separated by semicolons. The four groups define, in order, the display formats for positive numbers, negative numbers, zero values, and text. If you enter only one section, that format applies to all numbers you enter. If you enter two sections, the first set of codes applies to positive numbers and zero values and the second to negative numbers. If you want to skip a format option (specifying formats only for positive numbers and zero values, for example), insert a semicolon for each skipped section.

To specify a color for any section, enclose the name of one of the following eight permitted colors in brackets: black, green, white, blue, magenta, yellow, cyan, red. The color must be the first format code in the section. Thus, [Blue]#,##0;[Red]#,##0;[Black]0 displays positive values as blue, negative values as red, and zero values as black.

The remaining codes available for custom formats divide neatly into four categories.

Number format codes

- **0** Digit placeholder. Displays zero if the number has fewer digits than placeholders. The format 0.00 displays 2.30 if you enter 2.3. For numbers that are less than 1, it includes a 0 to the left of the decimal point.

- **#** Significant digit placeholder. Using the format #.## displays all significant (non-zero) digits to the left of the decimal point and rounds to two digits on the right of the decimal point. Thus, if you enter 0.42, this format displays .42 in the cell, with nothing to the left of the decimal point.

- **?** Align decimals. This digit placeholder works like the # placeholder but aligns decimal points.

Two punctuation marks are useful in custom number formats. Use a period to indicate the position of the decimal point. The comma has two roles. Used with placeholders on either side, it displays the thousands separator: #,###. Adding one or more commas after a custom format scales the number by 1,000 for each comma; to round large numbers (like 42,420,000) by a factor of 1 million, enter this format:

#0.0,," million"

As we explain a bit later, the text in quotation marks appears alongside the result. Thus, this format displays *42.4 million* in the cell, but the value is still stored as a number for calculation.

Date/Time format codes

A custom date or time format allows you to create special date formats that aren't included in any of Excel's ready-made selections. You can combine years, months, and days in any order and keep track of elapsed time as well for recording timesheets in Excel format.

- **d, dd, m, mm** Day or month in numeric format. The two-digit varieties add leading zeros (mm/dd/yy looks like 05/01/11).

- **ddd, mmm, dddd, mmmm** Day or month in text format. Use ddd or mmm for abbreviations such as Mon or Sep; use dddd and mmmm for the fully spelled out day of the week or month.

- **mmmmm** Displays the first letter of the month. Most useful in chart axes where you can easily differentiate between January, June, and July, or between March and May, by position.

- **yy, yyyy**   Year, in two-digit or four-digit format

- **h, hh, m, mm, s, ss**   Hours, minutes, or seconds. Use a two-digit format to add a leading zero when necessary. To display time with extra precision, add a decimal point and extra digits: h:mm:ss.00.

- **[h], [m], [s]**   Show elapsed time (rather than time of day) in hours, minutes, or seconds. Use this type of format when you're performing calculations using times. On a worksheet where you enter start and finish times for a worker's shift, this format allows you to show the total time for payroll calculations.

- **A/P, AM/PM**   Show the AM/PM indicator. If you omit this code, Excel uses the 24-hour time format: 18:15 instead of 6:15 PM.

Text format codes

To display text in a cell that contains numbers, Excel includes a selection of special format codes. Use this type of format to add a word or phrase, such as *YTD* to indicate year-to-date totals or *shortage* after a negative number. You must enclose the text in quotation marks. The format changes the displayed results but does not alter the contents of the cell. As a result, formulas that reference that cell continue to work.

Remember to add a space inside the quotation marks to separate the text from the numeric value, as in this example:

$0.00" Profit";[Red] $0.00" Loss"

A positive value appears in the default text color, like so: *$150.00 Profit*. Negative values appear in red, with the word *Loss* appended.

You can add the space character, a plus or minus sign, an apostrophe, open and close parentheses, and any of the following special characters without enclosing them in double quotation marks:

$ / : ^ ! & ~ { } = < >

In addition, you can use any currency sign, including the dollar sign ($). To enter alternative symbols, use the Symbol command on the Insert tab, or hold down the Alt key in combination with numeric codes from the numeric keypad: ¢ (Alt+0162), £ (Alt+0163), € (Alt+0128), and ¥ (Alt+0165), for example.

A handful of additional formatting codes apply special treatment to text. Use an asterisk (*) followed by a character to fill the cell with that character. Use *- in the third position of a custom format to replace zero values with a line of hyphens, for example.

An underscore (_) followed by a character adds a space the width of that character. Several built-in formats use this code with open and close parentheses to ensure that positive and negative values line up properly.

Use a backslash (\) to display the character that immediately follows the backslash.

The at sign (@) is used only in the fourth (text) section in a custom format and controls the formatting of any text you enter. If you include a text section without the @ character, Excel hides any text in the cell.

Conditions

You can also use conditions as part of custom number formats. Conditions use comparison operators and are contained in brackets as part of a format definition. To see an example, click the Special category, click the Phone Number format, and then click Custom to display the following code:

[<=9999999]###-####;(###) ###-####

If you enter a number of seven or fewer digits in a cell that uses this format, Excel treats it as a local phone number and adds a hyphen where the prefix appears. If you enter a number with eight or more digits, the final seven digits are formatted as a local phone number, and everything preceding that value is enclosed in parentheses.

Creating custom cell styles

If you regularly apply special formatting to cells and ranges, you can avoid the need to repeat the formatting steps by creating a custom cell style. Excel includes a categorized selection of cell styles as part of a default installation, which you can view by clicking Cell Styles on the Home tab to display the Cell Styles gallery. Any custom styles you create appear in a new group at the top of the list, as shown next.

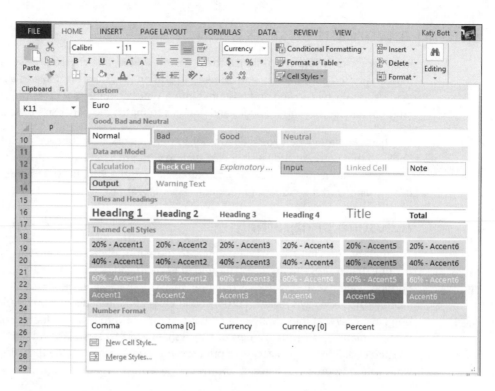

A custom style can include any or all of six formats. In the example shown here, we clicked New Cell Style to begin creating a simple cell style that applies the Currency format using the Euro symbol to the active cell or range. Because we cleared the other check boxes before saving the style, other existing formatting—including alignment, fonts, borders, and fill colors—is unchanged.

Printing a worksheet

Most Excel workbooks are designed to be viewed, edited, and shared on a screen rather than on printed pages. When you do need to add an Excel chart or table to a report, you'll get best results by copying and pasting it into a Word document, where you have a full range of tools for setting up pages and margins to match the paper size in your printer.

But there are times when you indeed want to print a worksheet (or even an entire workbook) so that you can study it offline or share it with others in a meeting. For those occasions, you need to do some extra work before clicking the Print button to ensure that your free-flowing worksheet doesn't break at awkward locations.

Adjusting print settings

The print features in Excel 2013 are similar to those introduced in Excel 2010, with only minor visual improvements. If you upgraded from an earlier version of Office, you'll find printing-related features radically different, thanks to Backstage view. Excel 2013 also includes the Page Layout view (introduced in Excel 2007) that allows you to edit your workbook in a view that mimics the printed page, complete with headers, footers, and margins. If you're planning to print just part of a worksheet, start by selecting that portion; then click File and click Print to gain access to print settings and a preview pane that shows exactly what your output will look like, as shown in Figure 14-8.

INSIDE OUT   Pick the right shortcuts for printing

If you regularly print worksheets, you might want to add a shortcut to the Quick Access Toolbar. Click the arrow to the right of the toolbar, and you'll see two shortcuts available from the Customize Quick Access Toolbar menu. Which should you choose? We don't recommend the Quick Print button. Although the name is tempting, the result might be an unwelcome surprise. Unless you have specifically defined a print area, Quick Print sends the entire current worksheet to the default printer, beginning with cell A1 and extending down and to the right, to the furthest area that contains data or formatting. The better choice is the Print Preview And Print button, which takes you to Print in Backstage view. There, you can double-check all settings, look at the preview to ensure it's laid out the way you want, and click Print when you're ready. Yes, that's one extra click, but it can save you half a ream of wasted paper over time, not to mention avoiding the need to reprint the job the right way. Oh, and regardless of what's on the Quick Access Toolbar, you can always press Ctrl+P to jump straight to the Print pane in Backstage view.

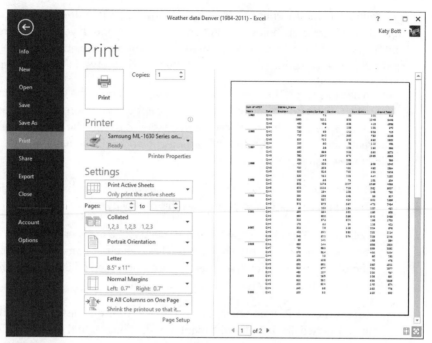

Figure 14-8 You can handle virtually all print setup options in Backstage view. You can't, however, edit worksheet contents, change headers and footers, or adjust page breaks.

INSIDE OUT   Make a printout fit in a specific number of pages

If you want your printed worksheet to fit in a specific number of pages, Excel can calculate the scaling percentage for you. In the Print pane in Backstage view, click the current scaling option (the last box under Settings) and then click Custom Scaling Options. On the Page tab of the Page Setup dialog box, click Fit To. Pick two numbers—one for the number of pages wide, the other for the number of pages tall—if you know exactly how many pages you want to use. (Leave one number blank if you don't want Excel to automatically scale in that dimension.) Click OK to save your settings, check the preview to verify that your worksheet's print settings are correct, and then click Print.

The controls under the Print and Printer headings are pretty self-explanatory. Be sure the right printer is selected, adjust the number of copies to print if you need more than one, and then click the big Print button. The six choices under the Settings heading (seven if the selected printer can print on both sides of the paper) deserve a little more explanation:

- **What to print**   The preset options allow you to print the current selection, print the active sheets (select multiple tabs if you want to print more than one), or print the entire workbook. If the selection is in a table, you'll see the option to print the current table. You can also specify starting and ending page numbers, as shown in the preview pane.

- **Duplexing**   Options to print on both sides of the sheet (and, if so, which way to flip the paper) appear if your printer has this capability.

- **Collated?**   This option applies only if you select a number larger than 1 in the Copies box to the right of the Print button. The default option prints multiple copies in complete sets, one after the other. Choose Uncollated if you want to print all copies of page 1, then all copies of page 2, and so on.

- **Orientation**   Portrait orientation is the best choice for lists and summary pages that are formatted like a Word document. Annual budgets and other financial reports that tend to be wide, with long row labels and grand total columns or notes, are typically more readable when you switch to landscape orientation.

- **Paper size**   The default size is dictated by your country setting; in the U.S., that's Letter (8.5"x11"). You can choose from a fairly long list of preset sizes, including the European A4 standard, or click More Paper Sizes to choose from a potentially longer list.

- **Margins**   The default Normal setting adds 0.75" at the top and bottom and 0.7" on either side, with an extra 0.3" for a page footer and header. You can choose from Wide and Narrow options to add or tighten white space around the printed content on the page. If none of those settings are exactly right, click Custom Margins to tweak all four sides, adjust the depth of the Header and Footer areas, and center the content on the page, as shown next.

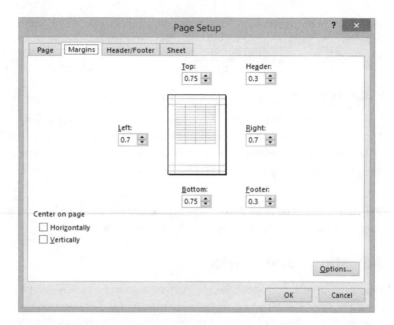

- **Scaling**   Normally, Excel applies no scaling, printing your worksheet at 100 percent of the sizes specified for fonts, graphic objects, row widths, and column heights. You can adjust the scaling to force your printout to fit on a single page, or to shrink the printout so that all rows or columns fit on the page. These options work best for printouts that are just a little bit too large. If you scale the size too small, you'll end up with a printout that saves paper but can be read only with a magnifying glass.

Defining a print area

For worksheets that you update and print out regularly, you can define a print area that includes just the portions you want to print. You might choose to exclude the assumptions and data sections of your budget worksheet, for example, and print just the summary sections as handouts at your executive briefings.

Start by selecting the print range. If you select a noncontiguous range, be aware that each section prints on a separate page. On the Page Layout tab, in the Page Setup group, click Print Area and then click Set Print Area. Excel creates a named range called Print_Area on the current worksheet. You can accomplish the same outcome manually by making a selection, clicking in the Name box, and then typing Print_Area as the range name. (Don't forget the underscore.)

Chapter 14

Each worksheet gets its own Print_Area range. If you select Print Entire Workbook in the Print Settings section in Backstage view, you can preview or print the defined print area on all worksheets in the current workbook.

> **CAUTION !**
>
> When you define a print area, Excel saves its exact location as a named range. If you add rows or columns to the print area later, the named range is *not* updated. You need to clear and then redefine the print area to include the newly created data.

To delete the named Print_Area range on the current sheet and start over, click the Clear Print Area option on the Print Area menu on the Page Layout tab.

Adjusting page breaks

When you print a worksheet, Excel automatically (and mechanically) inserts page breaks at the point where each page runs out of printable area. For large, complex worksheets that span multiple pages, you can and should position page breaks by hand. The easiest way to do this is to click the Page Break Preview button (in the Workbook Views group on the View tab). Excel displays dashed blue lines to indicate its automatic page breaks, with over-size page numbers to show the order in which pages will be printed.

In Page Break Preview, dashed lines indicate automatic page breaks inserted by Excel; solid lines represent manual page breaks. To adjust page breaks in this view, point to the thick line between two pages and drag it in any direction. To adjust the print area, drag the solid lines on any edge of the print area; cells that are not in the print area appear gray. Figure 14-9 shows one worksheet after some manual adjustments.

Page Break Preview works best if you start at the top of the worksheet and work in the order it will print—normally from top to bottom and left to right, unless you used the Page Setup dialog box to specify a different order. Move page breaks up or to the left only; moving them down or to the right can cause unpredictable results if you drag past the size of the page as defined by the paper size.

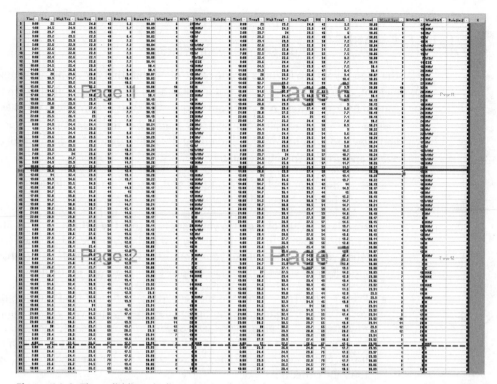

Figure 14-9 The solid lines indicate manual page breaks. The dashed lines (on the far right of the worksheet and below pages 2 and 7) were set automatically by Excel.

You can also add page breaks manually. Select the cell below and to the right of the cell that you want to print in the lower-right corner of a particular page. Click Breaks (in the Page Setup group on the Page Layout tab), and then click Insert Page Break. To add a horizontal page break, select any cell in column A; to add a vertical page break, select any cell in row 1. To remove the page break, select the same cell, go back to the Breaks command, and click Remove Page Break.

To remove all manual page breaks from the current worksheet, click Reset All Page Breaks on the Breaks menu.

Chapter 14

INSIDE OUT   Add extras to your printout

The Page Layout tab includes a wide range of options that allow you to change the margins, orientation, paper size, and other settings that overlap with those in the Print pane in Backstage view. A handful are unique. The most likely options you'll want to change here are potentially confusing. For example, in the Sheet Options group, you'll find View and Print options for Gridlines and Headings, which let you control the on-screen and printed settings separately:

- **Gridlines**   For final printed output, gridlines are normally hidden. Consider using borders to set off data areas.

- **Headings**   Most of the time you want to accept the default setting, with the Print box cleared, to hide distracting row and column headings. The exception is when you want to print out your worksheet so you can study its structure. Showing headings allows you to quickly locate cell addresses for editing.

- **Print Titles**   This option is in the Page Setup section of the Page Layout tab. If your worksheet data spans multiple pages, specify that you want column and row labels to appear on every page of your printout. Identify the headings in the Rows To Repeat At Top Of Each Page and Columns To Repeat At Left Of Each Page boxes. Note the syntax for the row and column addresses shown here, as well as the Page Order box.

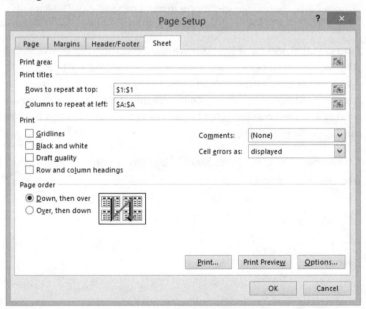

Our favorite Excel tweaks and tips

This section offers a grab bag of interesting tips and techniques that go well beyond the basics but can improve your productivity tremendously.

Navigating with the Go To dialog box

Most of the time, you use scroll bars and keyboard shortcuts to navigate through a workbook. You can use the Name box to jump to named ranges, tables, and charts in the current workbook. A well-hidden Excel feature called the Go To dialog box gives you a list that includes the same options as the Name box as well as a history of cells and ranges you've selected recently. To open this dialog box, click Find & Select (in the Editing group on the Home tab) and then click Go To, or use either of the keyboard shortcuts, F5 or Ctrl+G. The Go To dialog box, shown in Figure 14-10, contains a list of recent destinations.

Figure 14-10 Use the Go To dialog box to jump to a named range or to the cell or range that was selected before the last Go To operation.

In most cases, it's easier to use the Name box to move between named ranges. So why use the Go To dialog box? One advantage is that it keeps track of recent cell addresses you enter directly in the Reference box as well as the most recent cell or range. If you jump to a table from the Go To dialog box, you can jump back to your previous selection by using the Go To dialog box again. (This history is available only during the current session. If you close and reopen the workbook, opening the Go To dialog box shows only named ranges and objects.)

The Go To Special dialog box, available from the Find & Select menu or by clicking the Special button in the Go To dialog box, offers a range of esoteric but occasionally useful options, as shown next.

Make a selection first (or select a single cell within a table to use the entire table as the target). Then open the Go To Special dialog box, select a category, and click OK. This option is most useful when you want to edit, format, or otherwise work with a group of cells that have common characteristics. For example, you can click Blanks to find all blank cells in a range and replace their contents with an error-checking formula or a default value. You can also find only cells that contain constants or formulas (with options to refine the latter selection to show only formulas that produce numbers, text, logical results, or errors).

One especially useful expert trick you can perform with this dialog box is to copy data from a range that includes one or more hidden columns or rows. Normally, copying the current selection also copies hidden cells, which can lead to unexpected results. Select the range you want to copy, open the Go To Special dialog box, choose Visible Cells Only, and click OK. When you paste the Clipboard contents into the destination cells, you'll see exactly what you copied and nothing extra.

Entering and sorting data with custom series

Previously, we explained how to automatically fill a range with a series of numbers or dates or with a repeated block of text values. You can also fill in dates using months or days of the week (in full or abbreviated) and then sort on those dates, with Jan and Feb coming before Mar and Apr instead of being sorted alphabetically: Apr, Feb, Jan, Mar. (If you need a refresher course, see "Entering and filling in data and series" in Chapter 12.)

You can add your own custom lists to the collection, specifying the members of the list and their sort order. You can create a list from any text-based values: department names, budget categories, countries, geographical regions, and suppliers, to name just a few examples. Custom lists are stored in the Windows registry and are available for filling in data by row or column and for sorting data in any workbook. You can add as many custom lists as you need, entering them directly or copying them from an existing worksheet.

You can view and edit existing custom lists or create new ones by using an obscure dialog box. Click File, click Options, select the Advanced tab, and scroll nearly to the bottom. Under the General heading, click Edit Custom Lists. That opens the Custom Lists dialog box shown in Figure 14-11.

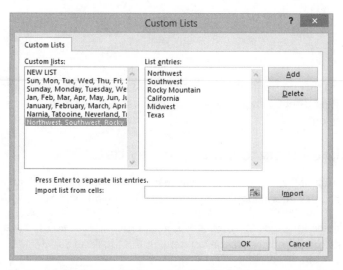

Figure 14-11 For short lists, click in the List Entries box and type entries in order, pressing Enter at the end of each one. Use the Import button to copy longer lists from a worksheet range.

To create a custom list that includes only a few items, select New List at the top of the Custom Lists box on the left and then type the list directly in the List Entries box, pressing Enter after each entry. Click Add when you're finished. To remove an existing list, select its entry in the Custom Lists box and click Delete.

To create a custom list from a worksheet range, first make sure the range is arranged in the exact order you want to use for your new custom list. Then click New List, click in the Import List From Cells box, select the range in the worksheet, and click Import.

To fill in a custom data series, type any entry from the list in a cell and use the fill handle in the lower-right corner to fill the range you select with the remainder of the list. To sort using a custom list, follow the procedure in "Sorting a range, region, or table," in Chapter 13. In the Sort dialog box, select Custom List from the drop-down Order list, choose the custom list you want to use, and click OK. The following example sorts a table by values in the Region column, using our custom list of regions as the sort order.

Chapter 14

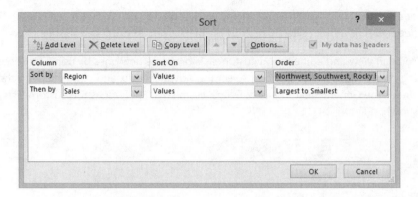

It's worth noting that the contents of your custom list appear twice in the drop-down list under Order. The first entry shows the list contents in the order created. The second shows them in reverse order.

Using online forms to collect survey data

The online version of Excel includes one new feature that solves a longstanding problem: how to collect survey information from customers, club members, or colleagues.

To create an online form, you start by signing in to your SkyDrive account in a web browser. Click the Create menu and choose the last item on this list, Excel Survey.

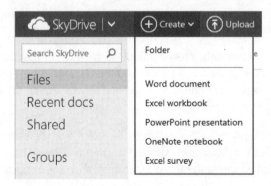

After giving the survey a name, you create questions using a fill-in-the-blanks webpage. Answers for each question can be in a format of your choosing: Yes/No, Text, Number, Date, Time, or Choice, in which case you define a list of options for respondents to choose.

After you finish the survey, you save it and create a link that you can share with other people via email, a blog post, or social media. Survey respondents see a web form like the one shown next.

Each time a respondent fills in the survey form, their answers are captured in the Excel spreadsheet you created. Each question gets its own column heading, and each set of responses gets its own row. You can easily tabulate the results by opening the survey spreadsheet from SkyDrive and creating a PivotTable.

Note that the survey capability, at least at this time, does not include the ability to limit an individual's ability to respond multiple times. So while it's good for capturing feedback from a friendly audience, it's susceptible to ballot-box stuffing. Don't use this type of survey for any sort of popularity contest unless you're prepared to deal with that possibility!

Generating random numbers

When you're building a worksheet, it sometimes helps to be able to plug in sample data to verify that your formulas work properly with a wide range of input values. You could just type some numbers into the cells, but it's easier to let Excel fill in some realistic data for you. The secret is to use either of the following two functions:

- =RAND() uses no parameters and returns a random number between 0 and 1, carried to 14 decimal places

- =RANDBETWEEN(bottom,top) requires two parameters, which can be constants or cell references; it returns whole numbers that are greater than or equal to *bottom* and less than or equal to *top*.

Using either of these functions can require a little ingenuity and a combination of other functions. If you're building a worksheet to analyze sales at a restaurant or retail store, you might want a large collection of data to simulate a series of typical sales. If the minimum transaction is $25.00 and the maximum is $150.00, neither function alone will work. RAND returns results that are well outside the range you're looking for, while RANDBETWEEN returns only whole numbers instead of the dollars-and-cents data you need. The solution? Combine the two functions in a single formula you can use in the range containing sales amounts:

=RANDBETWEEN(25,150)+ROUND(RAND(),2)

The first function generates a random whole number between 25 and 150, inclusive. The second function generates a number between 0 and 1 and rounds it to two decimal places. The combination equals a perfect mix of dollars and cents.

Using data validation to control data entry

Some worksheets are designed for repeated use, with specific cells designated for data input and others used for formulas that transform those data points into meaningful results. The danger of such a design, of course, is that you (or someone using a worksheet you designed) might accidentally enter inappropriate data in an input cell. The result can be summed up in four words: "Garbage in, garbage out."

The cure is to assign a data-validation rule to one or more of those input cells so that they accept only the proper type of data or values in a specific range. Using validation rules, you can restrict entries to those that match a list of approved items (budget categories or department names, for example) and even attach a drop-down list from which items are picked. That strategy eliminates the possibility that someone will misspell an entry and inadvertently mess up a report based on that data.

Each data-validation rule is made up of three parts that correspond neatly to the tabs of the Data Validation dialog box. The Settings tab defines the criteria for valid input data; the Input Message tab allows you to create an optional message that provides helpful information when the cell is selected; and the Error Alert tab specifies what a user sees when she tries to enter invalid data.

To get started, first select the cell or range for which you want to restrict data entry, click Data Validation (in the Data Tools group on the Data tab), and define your rule using the options on the Settings tab. Figure 14-12 shows this dialog box after we filled in the validation criteria Excel will use when deciding whether to accept or reject specific input values. Choose a value from the Allow list to restrict data entry to a specific data type and then use additional criteria to define acceptable values.

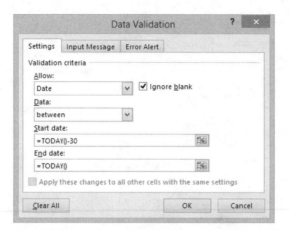

Figure 14-12 The validation criteria defined here use formulas to restrict allowed input to dates that are between the current date and 30 days ago. Any other input will be rejected.

The exact choices available on the Settings tab vary depending on the data type you select from the Allow list. For most data types, you select an operator from the Data list (Between, Less Than Or Equal To, and so on) and then fill in values or formulas that the input data is compared with. In this example, we chose Date as the data type and Between as the operator, adding formulas in the Start Date and End Date boxes that reject any date that is in the future or is more than 30 days earlier than the current date.

The following list summarizes what you can do with each of the options available when you click Allow:

- **Any Value** Ironically, this default setting does not allow any restrictions on allowed input data. Its purpose is to allow you to display pop-up help text by filling in the boxes on the Input Message tab.

- **Whole Number** This data type requires numeric input and rejects any value that contains a decimal point, even if the decimal point is followed by a 0.

- **Decimal** This setting allows any numeric input, with or without a decimal point, provided it meets the other criteria you establish.

- **List** When you choose this option from the Allow list, any values entered in the input cells must match an item in the list. For a short list, click in the Source box and enter the items directly, separated by commas, as shown next. (Note that list items are case sensitive; if you include *Yes* as a term, it is allowed only with an initial capital *Y*.) Alternatively, you can click the Collapse Dialog button to the right of the Source box and enter the address or name of a range that contains the list of allowed values. If you want users to be able to pick from a list containing these values, select the In-Cell Dropdown check box.

- **Date** When this option is selected, Excel will accept input only in a recognizable date format. You must choose an operator and a date or range against which to compare input cells. To allow any date but disallow text or numeric input, choose Greater Than Or Equal To from the Data list and enter 1/1/1900 in the Start Date box.

- **Time** Your choices here are similar to those provided by the Date option, except that the values entered for Start Time or End Time or both must be in a recognizable time format. If you choose Less Than Or Equal To from the Data list and enter 18:00 in the End Time box, Excel will accept 3:32 PM or 14:32:21 but will reject 8:00 PM.

- **Text Length** Use this option with comments fields to prevent long-winded entries or to insist on a minimum number of characters.

- **Custom** When you choose this option, you must enter a formula that returns a logical TRUE or FALSE. This option is most useful when the current input cell is part of a calculation and you want to allow or restrict input based on that calculation. Thus, if you have a formula in cell E5 that sums the values of the four cells above it, you can choose Custom from the Allow list and then enter =E$5 < 100 as the validation criteria for E1 through E4. You can enter any value under 100 in any of those four cells, but if the running total exceeds 100, your input will be rejected.

Use the Input Message tab of the Data Validation dialog box to define a helpful message that appears when you select a cell. The message appears in a pop-up window, with a title in bold and the input message text beneath it. The text you enter here helps prevent confusion by making it clear exactly what type of input is allowed.

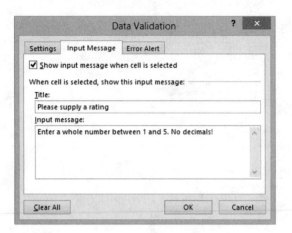

And here's what that input message looks like in a worksheet window.

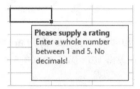

Finally, use the Error Alert tab to specify what should happen when you (or someone else using a worksheet you created) enters invalid data. You can replace the generic and unhelpful error message with one that offers advice on how to correct the input. If the data type is wrong or the value is outside a permitted range, you can refuse to accept the input at all. For values that are outside the normal range, you can display an error alert that forces you to double-check the value to be sure your finger didn't slip and add an extra zero, converting $40 into $400.

On the Error Alert tab, choose one of three options from the Style box:

- **Stop** produces a dialog box with a red X and Retry/Cancel/Help buttons; the user cannot save the invalid entry.

- **Warning** displays a dialog box that lets you accept the data despite the warning.

- **Information** displays a message but accepts the data as soon as you click OK.

As with the Input Message tab, you need to enter a title and text. In both cases, the Title box accepts up to 32 characters, and the message can be up to 255 characters. Here's an error alert message under construction:

And here's what the Warning dialog box looks like when it's triggered by an attempt to enter an invalid value. Note that the text you enter in the Title box appears in the title bar.

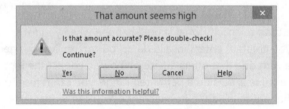

To remove data validation rules, open the Data Validation dialog box, and click Clear All.

TROUBLESHOOTING

Your worksheet contains invalid data

Data-validation rules prevent users from typing invalid data. Unfortunately, users can enter data that fails the validation criteria by pasting it from the Clipboard or by entering a formula that results in invalid data. In addition, data validation rules are not applied retroactively to existing cell contents.

To find cells containing invalid data on the current worksheet, click Data Validation (in the Data Tools group on the Data tab) and then click Circle Invalid Data. Excel draws a bright red oval around any value that fails a validation rule. Edit those cells so that they pass validation and then try again. To remove the red ovals, choose Clear Validation Circles from the same menu.

PART 5

Outlook

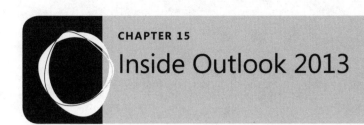
O UTLOOK made its first appearance in Office back before the turn of the century—in 1997, to be precise—as a unified solution for managing email, calendars, and contacts. The program itself has evolved tremendously since then, as has the online world around it.

Today, you're likely to use multiple devices as you move through the week—desktop and portable PCs, smartphones, tablets—and it's crucial that your messages, contacts, and schedule roam effortlessly from one device to the next, without fear that you'll miss an appointment or a must-read email as you make those transitions.

You're also likely to have multiple email accounts—one with your Internet service provider, another at work, and additional accounts on free services like Outlook.com (formerly Hotmail) and Gmail. With its rich feature set and extensive customization options, Outlook 2013 is an essential tool for helping you bring those details into one place and keep them in sync.

Outlook is included with every Office 365 subscription plan, even Home Premium. In fact, the only Office 2013 edition that doesn't include Outlook is the single-PC version of Office Home and Student 2013. If you've never used Outlook before, we encourage you to read through these three chapters to learn the many things it can do for you. And if Outlook is the first program you open in the morning and the last one you use at night, we have tips that can help you get the most from it.

What you can (and can't) do with Outlook

What distinguishes Outlook from other email programs? The biggest difference is the fact that its contents include so much more than just email messages. The key to mastering Outlook is understanding what's in each item type and how to make different item types work together. (If you're a compulsive organizer, skip ahead in this chapter to "Using and managing folders" to learn how to file and store items using folders.)

Later in this section, we introduce each of the major item types in Outlook and describe the diversity of ways you can master each one. But before we get to that list, it's useful to look at Outlook's main program window.

Supported account types in Outlook 2013

Your Outlook profile can consist of a single account, or its contents can be drawn from multiple accounts. Which type of account you use dictates what type of items you can store and sync between devices.

We cover the mechanics of connecting accounts to Outlook later in this chapter. The following is an explanation of what you get with each account type.

- **Exchange (including Office 365)** This is Microsoft's flagship business email program. You'll find it on corporate servers and as a paid-for product from online service providers, including Microsoft's Exchange Online service, which is a part of the business editions of Office 365. Outlook and Exchange were designed specifically to work together, so it's not surprising that this combination is the richest of all, feature-wise. An Exchange account allows you to send and receive email, store your calendar and contacts, access a company address book and shared folders, and even connect to RSS feeds. All the data in an Exchange account can be synchronized between devices so that your local data store is available even when you're offline.

- **Outlook.com (Hotmail, Windows Live Mail, MSN Mail)** Microsoft's free consumer email service has had many names and many interfaces through the years. The current incarnation is, in our estimation, the best and most polished in years. Whether you have an account in the new Outlook.com domain or an older account from Hotmail.com or Live.com, you use the new web-based Outlook interface, which stores email messages, calendar items, and contact information. Links are available to SkyDrive and Skype as well. All your data syncs between devices and between Outlook profiles that include this account type using the Exchange ActiveSync service, which enjoys almost universal support on the hardware you're likely to use.

- **Gmail/Google Apps** This package is Google's competitive answer to Microsoft's Outlook.com/Exchange combo. Gmail is free for consumers and small businesses; Google Apps is a subscription-based product. Both offer email with an online address book, calendar, online storage, and productivity apps designed primarily for use within a web browser. Getting Outlook and Gmail to work together takes some work, as we discuss later in this chapter.

- **IMAP mail accounts** Internet Message Access Protocol (IMAP) is a well-established Internet mail standard. On an IMAP server, your incoming messages stay on the server and are synchronized with a local copy. IMAP supports synchronization of email messages you send and receive (including folders you use to organize messages) between client programs like Outlook and the servers where the primary copies are stored. IMAP servers provide email only, although they may include links to online calendars and contacts.

- **POP and SMTP accounts**   The ancient but still popular POP email standard (it stands for Post Office Protocol) is typically used as a store-and-forward server for incoming email. A server using Simple Mail Transfer Protocol (SMTP) typically runs alongside a POP server to handle outgoing messages. POP messages are typically downloaded from the server and then deleted, with no option to synchronize. Neither type of server is well suited to the modern era where mail is centrally stored and synched between devices; we discuss some effective POP-sync workarounds in "Connecting accounts to Outlook" later in this chapter.

- **Social network accounts**   Previous versions of Outlook supported an optional add-in that allowed you to make connections to social networks. Outlook 2013 adds that capability as a standard feature. In theory, any social network can be connected to Outlook. As we write this, Facebook and LinkedIn are fully supported, allowing you to pick up contact information and shared items from those services directly from Outlook itself. We discuss these connections in more detail in "Connecting to social networks" later in this chapter.

It's also possible that your workplace or a mail provider uses a different corporate email server or protocol. For those cases, ask your corporate IT department or the service provider's help desk for details on how to connect and what capabilities are supported.

In its default view, Outlook displays the contents of your connected mail accounts in the classic three-column arrangement, with the Folder pane on the left, a message list in the center, and the contents of the selected message visible on the right, as shown in Figure 15-1. Four big, bold, touch-friendly targets along the bottom of the program window suggest (correctly) that you can click or tap to view and manage calendar items, contact information for people, and tasks.

INSIDE OUT   Save precious space with compact navigation

The default navigation bar extends across the entire bottom of the Outlook program window, eliminating space for content in the center pane and in any docked panes on the right. To reclaim some of that space, right-click the ellipsis (the three dots at the right of navigation links), and then click Navigation Options on the shortcut menu. In the Navigation Options dialog box, select the Compact Navigation check box and click OK. With that option selected, the four navigation links appear as small (but still touch-friendly) icons along the bottom of the pane on the left, leaving more room for your content in the other panes.

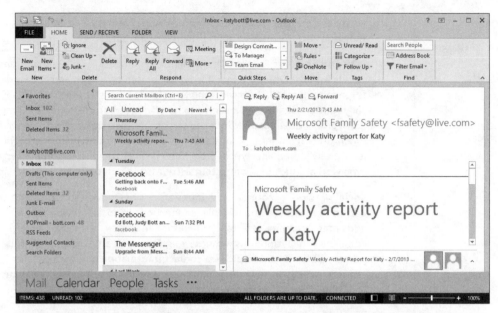

Figure 15-1 This is the classic three-pane Outlook interface, where you click a folder on the left, choose a message from the middle, and view the message contents on the right.

These four links aren't static shortcuts, either. A new feature in Office 2013, called "peeks," allows you to take a quick peek (thus the name) at upcoming appointments, find contacts in the People folder, and see your current task list. All you need to do is aim the mouse pointer at Calendar, People, or Tasks and wait a fraction of a second. Figure 15-2 shows a peek at the calendar for a not-so-busy day.

You can navigate through the calendar by month and click any day to see your appointments and meetings for that date. When you peek at People view, you can search for a contact by entering a name or keyword. You can create a new task by typing in the box at the top of the Tasks peek. And you can open any item you find within a peek, just by clicking it.

So what can't you do from a peek? You can't create a new appointment or contact record using a peek, nor can you edit an item you see in the peek window.

To work with the full range of options for each item type, click its link to switch views.

When you change the view to a different item type, the ribbon changes significantly. Commands on the Home tab are unique to the selected item type, with the contents of some commands on the Folder and View tabs also changing context. When you open an individual item, its window includes yet another arrangement of tabs with commands to help you work with that item.

Click to dock as a pane

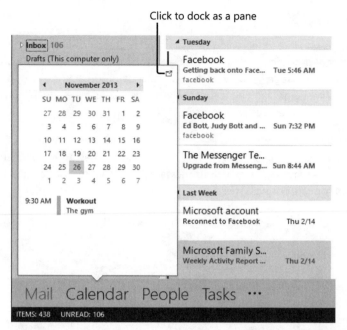

Figure 15-2 Aim the mouse pointer at the Calendar link to pop up this "peek," where you can navigate through the months and click a day to see its scheduled appointments and meetings.

INSIDE OUT   Create a new item from any view

The leftmost commands on the Home tab for every Outlook view allow you to click and begin creating a new item of the type associated with that view. From Mail view, you can click the New Email command; from Calendar view, you get New Appointment and New Meeting; and so on. But what if you're in Tasks view and you want to create a new contact item? Click New Items, and choose from its menu, which includes options for the five most common item types. If this is a regular scenario, learn the keyboard shortcuts for creating a new item of each type:

- **Email message**   Ctrl+Shift+M

- **Appointment**   Ctrl+Shift+A

- **Meeting**   Ctrl+Shift+Q

- **Contact**   Ctrl+Shift+C

- **Task**   Ctrl+Shift+K

In the remainder of this section, we look more closely at each item type.

Email messages

Most of the time, you'll read incoming messages in the Reading pane, which sits by default to the right of the message list. (If you're using a tablet in portrait mode, the Reading pane appears below the message list by default.) For most common actions—responding to the sender, filing the message, tagging it for follow-up, or deleting it—you'll find commands on the Home tab (shown previously in Figure 15-1) to be sufficient.

In Office 2013, you can even reply to messages (or forward them) within the Reading pane. Clicking the Reply, Reply All, or Forward link at the top of a message immediately replaces the contents of the pane with a new draft message. A custom ribbon tab gives you all the tools you need for composing a message.

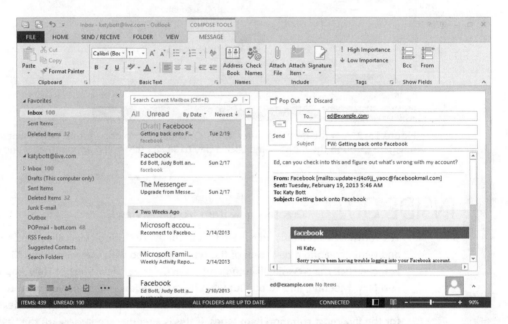

The [Draft] indicator in the message list indicates that you're composing a new message. Use the Pop Out link at the top of the Reading pane to open the draft in its own window.

We cover the mechanics of creating a message, attaching files, and sending it to one or more recipients in more detail in "Creating, sending, and receiving messages" later in this chapter.

For details on how to change the arrangement of the Outlook program window, see "Personalizing the Outlook interface" in Chapter 17, "Outlook 2013 inside out." We describe how to use the People pane, which appears below every message, in "Connecting to social networks" later in this chapter.

Appointments and meetings

Appointments are items in your Outlook calendar that have a start and end time but don't involve scheduling and coordination with other people or resources. If you select the All Day Event check box, the Start Time and End Time boxes are unavailable and the appointment is listed as an event at the top of the calendar for that day.

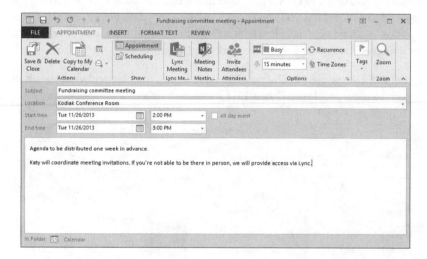

In Outlook's specialized definition, a meeting is an appointment that includes invitations to other attendees (sent by email) and, in some organizations, scheduling resources such as conference rooms that have their own shared calendar. You can turn any appointment into a meeting by clicking the Invite Attendees button.

INSIDE OUT   Meeting requests work with outsiders, too

Outlook's tools for managing meetings work best on corporate networks, where coworkers can use the Scheduling Assistant to pick a time that's most likely to work with everyone's schedule. But even families and one-person shops can use meeting requests to good advantage. Invitees who use a mail client that recognizes meeting invitations (including Outlook, Outlook.com, and Gmail) can accept the meeting request, which automatically adds the meeting to their own calendar and sends a response to the meeting organizer. If any invitee needs to make a change to the meeting schedule, they can send an update to the organizer, avoiding scheduling snafus. The key to using meeting requests under these circumstances is for all parties involved to get in the habit of sending responses to meeting requests so that everyone's calendar is properly updated.

For more about how to create and manage appointments and meetings, see "Managing your calendar" in Chapter 16, "Organizing Outlook information."

Contacts

An Outlook contact item can be as simple as the name and email address of a casual acquaintance, or it can contain the equivalent of a full dossier on a working partner or a key customer. Contacts you create are stored in your data file for the associated account; in Outlook 2013, you can also link contact items so that a single view shows details from your local address book and a social network like LinkedIn.

By default, People view in Outlook 2013 allows you to enter and view details in a clean and streamlined contact form. Figure 15-3 shows this view of a contact item.

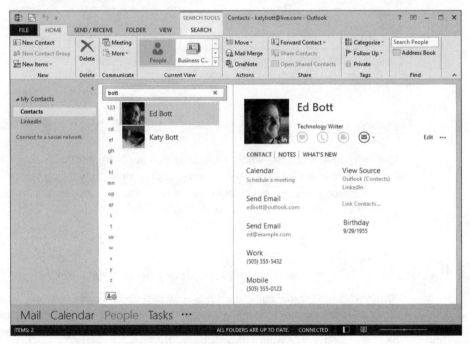

Figure 15-3 Typing in the search box filters the list of available contacts, with details for the selected contact visible in the pane at the right.

You can create contacts directly from incoming mail and also share contacts with other people. It pays to organize large groups of contacts, although the shoebox approach also works, thanks to very effective search tools. Outlook typically displays multiple folders in the Folder pane, each associated with a different mail account or social network. In addition, you can create contact groups so that you can easily bring together a filtered list of contacts who are related in some way—coworkers, classmates, or customers.

For more on how to create and manage contact items, see "Organizing your contacts" in Chapter 16. For more on how to view contacts in an address book when creating an email message, see "Using the Outlook address books," also in Chapter 16.

Tasks

If your productivity depends on to-do lists, you'll use task items frequently. You might never need to open Tasks view, however, because all these items are available as a peek, and you can dock the Tasks pane to the right of mail and calendar folders so that your commitments are easy to see at a glance.

A task, such as the one shown here, can have start dates and due dates, and you can attach reminders to each item as well. As with other Outlook items, you can include a full range of formatting and objects in the notes section, below the header. In the task shown here, we've used both brightly colored bold text and a bulleted list in the notes section.

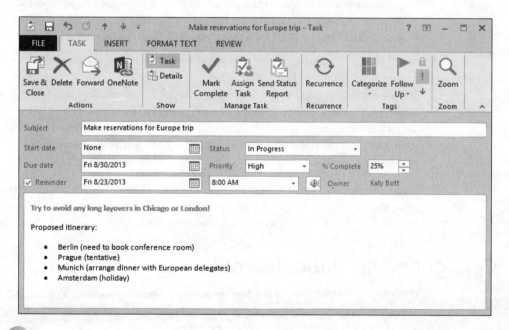

For more on how to attach alarms and deadlines to tasks, see "Setting follow-up flags and reminders" in Chapter 17.

Notes and Journal entries

Two deprecated item types survive in Outlook 2013 and are still available if you search hard enough.

Items in the Notes folder are unlike any other Outlook item type. Clicking the New Note button on the Home tab (or using the Ctrl+Shift+N shortcut) opens an editing window that resembles the yellow sticky notes that are ubiquitous in offices. You can type or paste text into a note (including hyperlinks, which are clickable), but you can't format that text directly, nor can you paste any nontext object, such as a picture, into a note.

INSIDE OUT Better options for note-takers

If you like the small, free-form nature of items in the Outlook Notes folder, you have a much more interesting alternative in OneNote, which allows you to save more types of content on notes. You can open the Send To OneNote tool with the keyboard shortcut Windows logo key+N and then press N to open a new Quick Note, where you can type or paste anything you want. If the idea of sticky notes appeals to you, we encourage you to read Chapter 21, "Inside OneNote 2013," for a proper introduction.

The Journal folder and its associated content type are relics of bygone Outlook versions, where items of this type tried to maintain connections between related items. This functionality is delivered better and more conveniently in modern Outlook versions using search tools, the Activities page, and the People pane. The Journal stays around for compatibility reasons, but it's disabled by default, and there are few shortcuts to open it.

If you accidentally click the Journal folder in the Folders list, you might see an error message. We strongly recommend that you dismiss that message and follow our suggestions in "Connecting to social networks" later in this chapter, instead of using the Journal.

Configuring an Outlook profile

When you start Outlook for the first time after a clean installation of Office 2013, you're prompted to run a startup wizard. The wizard's job is to configure your Outlook profile, which contains two crucial types of information:

- Settings for one or more email accounts—including server names, logon details, email address, and the display name that recipients see on messages you send.

- Where to store local copies of your email, contacts, appointments, and other Outlook items on your PC. Outlook 2013 stores data in local files that use one of two formats.

For Exchange, Outlook.com (Hotmail), and IMAP accounts, which keep a local copy of your data synchronized with a server, Outlook uses an offline Outlook data file, with the file name extension .ost. For POP accounts, which are not synchronized with a server, the Outlook Data File uses the file name extension .pst.

We offer our advice on best practices for working with .pst and .ost data files in "Managing Outlook data files and folders" later in this chapter.

After you finish that startup wizard, you have a single profile that uses the default name, Outlook. For most people, that one profile is sufficient, and they never have to manage that profile or create a new one. If you routinely created multiple profiles with previous Outlook versions, you might find that an architectural change first included in Outlook 2010 makes those extra steps unnecessary. The most important change is the ability to include multiple Exchange email accounts in a single profile—previously, you had to create a new profile for each Exchange account (although you could add other types of email accounts to the same profile).

There are still scenarios where maintaining separate Outlook profiles is necessary, despite the hassle it involves. For example, you might want to maintain a strict separation between one important work email account and your personal email. If those accounts are combined in a single profile, you risk inadvertently sending a personal message from your work account, or vice versa.

To manage existing profiles or create a new one, make sure Outlook is closed, and then open Mail from Control Panel. Outlook adds this icon to the User Accounts And Family Safety group as part of Office setup. If you're using a 32-bit version of Office 2013 with 64-bit Windows, a "(32-bit)" label is appended to the name of the Control Panel icon.

The Mail Setup dialog box is shown in Figure 15-4.

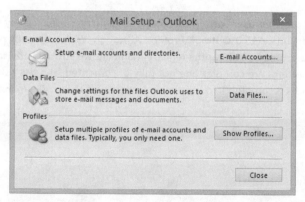

Figure 15-4 The top two choices in this dialog box apply to the default Outlook profile. Click Show Profiles to add, change, or delete a profile.

Clicking E-Mail Accounts or Data Files allows you to change those settings for the default profile. Click Show Profiles to display the profile manager shown here.

Click Add to kick off a wizard that is virtually identical to the Outlook startup wizard, allowing you to build your new profile by filling in the blanks. The Remove button deletes all settings for the selected profile—irrevocably and immediately. Click Properties to change email account and data file settings for the selected profile without opening Outlook. Click Copy to duplicate the selected profile so that you can experiment with settings while maintaining your option to roll back to the original settings.

CAUTION!

Profiles are stored on a per-user basis in the Windows registry, under the key HKCU\Software\Microsoft\Office\15.0\Outlook\Profiles. Although it's theoretically possible to make changes to a profile by editing the registry manually, we strongly advise against it. The individual settings are complex and not fully documented, and the risk of unexpected consequences is too high in our opinion. Instead, use the profile manager from Control Panel.

INSIDE OUT   Make it easy to switch between profiles

You cannot switch to a different profile from within Outlook. If you maintain two or more Outlook profiles that you use regularly, you can configure Outlook so that you have the opportunity to select a profile each time you start up. In the profile manager, under the heading When Starting Microsoft Outlook, Use This Profile, select Prompt For A Profile To Be Used. Click OK, and then restart Outlook to open the Choose Profile dialog box, shown here, where you can select from the Profile Name list or even create a new profile on the fly.

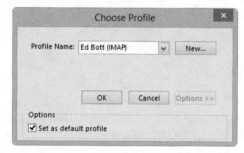

To set the selected profile as the default, click Set As Default Profile at the bottom of the dialog box before clicking OK. If this check box is hidden, click the Options button at the right to reveal the Options section.

Connecting accounts to Outlook

Outlook's prime directive is to manage your email, fetching and processing incoming messages and making sure that messages you compose and send go to their intended recipients. You're prompted to set up the first account by the Outlook startup wizard, which allows you to set up additional accounts at the same time.

After that initial setup, you can add new mail accounts, reconfigure or remove existing accounts, or connect to social networks from Backstage view. Click File, and then click Info to display options similar to those shown in Figure 15-5. (The exact choices available on the Account Settings menu depend on the type of email account selected in the list directly under Account Information. We discuss these differences in more detail in the following sections.)

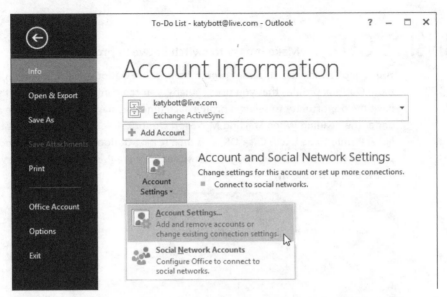

Figure 15-5 Options on the Account Settings menu reflect the current account type. Options for an Exchange account are significantly different from those shown here.

The simplest way to set up a new account is to click Add Account and then enter your display name, your email address, and your password on the Auto Account Setup page of the Add Account dialog box. Configuration is automatic with Office 365 or any other Microsoft Exchange server that has been configured to use the Autodiscover service. For POP and IMAP accounts and for well-known web-based mail services, Outlook first tries to make an encrypted connection, and if that fails, it asks for your approval to try an unencrypted connection.

> **Note**
>
> For technical details about the Autodiscover service in Exchange 2013 and Exchange 2010 SP2, see the TechNet article at *w7io.com/12101*.

If the automatic configuration fails, you see an error message. If you know the server names and any other nonstandard settings, such as alternate port numbers, you can configure the account manually. Click Back to start over, and then select the Manual Setup Or Additional Server Types option. Or, in the dialog box that displays the error message, select Manually Configure Server Settings, and then click Retry.

To change the settings for an existing email account, click Account Settings on the Account Settings menu (and no, that's not a typo—the duplicate menu options are by design), select its entry in the accounts list, and then click Change.

Figure 15-6 shows an Outlook profile that contains three accounts. The white check mark in a black circle denotes the default email account, which is used to send newly created messages unless you specify an alternate account. Replies are always sent using the account through which the original message was received, although you can choose a different account if you prefer.

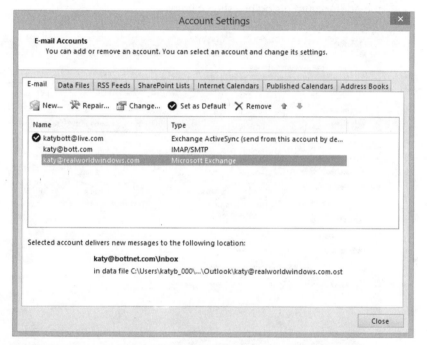

Figure 15-6 The check mark to the left of the top account here means it is used by default for new messages. Click Change to edit settings for an existing account.

Using Internet-standard mail servers

Many traditional Internet service providers and web-hosting companies offer subscribers and customers access to email servers that use well-established, even venerated, email standards. The most common is the combination of POP or IMAP for receiving messages and Simple Mail Transfer Protocol (SMTP) for sending messages.

Some ISPs and hosting companies provide IMAP and POP services on the same server; in that case, Outlook's automatic account configuration might choose IMAP when you wanted

POP, or vice versa. You can't change the account type after initially configuring an account; instead, follow these steps:

1. From Backstage view, on the Info tab, click Add Account. (Alternatively, you can open the Account Settings dialog box and click New. Either option leads to the Add Account dialog box.)

2. Choose Manual Setup Or Additional Server Types and click Next.

3. In the Choose Service dialog box, select Pop Or IMAP and click Next. That leads to the Add Account dialog box shown here.

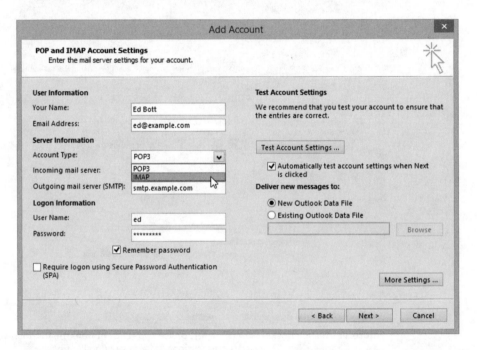

4. From the Account Type drop-down list, choose POP3 or IMAP, and then complete the account configuration.

Most of the information you enter here is straightforward. The User Information block defines what recipients will see in the From field in messages you send from this account. The Logon Information block contains your user credentials. (Clear the Remember Password box if you are willing to tolerate the inconvenience of entering your password each time you open Outlook in exchange for a bit of extra security.)

Clicking Next tests your connection settings to ensure that they work correctly with your server. The More Settings button in the lower-right corner offers access to a collection of settings that can fix some of the following types of email glitches:

- To change the name that identifies the account in the E-Mail Accounts list, click the General tab and enter a name in the Mail Account box. By default, Outlook initially fills this field with the email address for an account, but you might want to replace that with a descriptive account name.

- If your SMTP server requires that you log on before being allowed to send mail, select the appropriate options (and, if necessary, enter a set of credentials) on the Outgoing Server tab.

- For IMAP accounts only, use the Sent Items and Deleted Items sections on the Advanced tab to control where these items are stored. You can choose folders on the server side or folders in your local Outlook data file. (Note that choosing the latter option means that these two types of items will not sync to other devices and will be lost if your data file is deleted or corrupted.)

- For POP accounts only, use the Delivery section on the Advanced tab to specify whether messages should remain on the server or be deleted as soon as they are downloaded.

- If your Internet service provider or network blocks traffic on some network ports, you might need to specify alternative ports to send or receive email. This might happen if your ISP insists that you use its SMTP servers for outgoing messages and blocks traffic on the standard SMTP port 25. If the administrator of your SMTP server has defined an alternate port for either incoming or outgoing messages, you can fill in the correct port numbers on the Advanced tab.

Chapter 15

INSIDE OUT   Set up secure POP, IMAP, and SMTP accounts

The default specification for Internet-standard email accounts allows them to send and receive mail "in the clear," with no encryption. If your service provider or hosting company supports secure options for connecting to this type of server, we strongly recommend you avail yourself of this opportunity. For POP connections, you can click a check box to enable SSL. For IMAP and SMTP connections, you have a choice of SSL, TLS, or Auto. Use whichever option your mail provider allows. In most cases, you'll also need to specify TCP ports for secure traffic. The Internet-standard ports are as follows: POP3 over SSL/TLS, 995; IMAP over SSL, 993. SMTP over SSL does not use a standard port number, although many providers use 465. If in doubt, check with your provider.

Options on the Advanced tab vary slightly between IMAP and POP accounts, as shown in Figure 15-7.

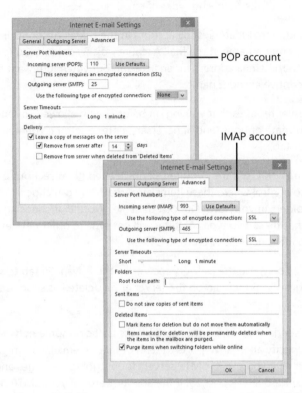

Figure 15-7 The most common reason to access these Advanced settings for POP and IMAP accounts is to enable secure connections and specify nonstandard TCP ports.

Configuring Office 365 and Exchange accounts

If one or more of your email accounts is on a server running Microsoft Exchange, it's almost certain that your account is for business. That's the case with Office 365 Small Business and Enterprise accounts, which support the Exchange Autodiscover service. For this type of account, all you need to do is enter your name, your email address, and your password in the Add Account dialog box. The configuration steps after that are automatic.

If you're using an Exchange account provided by your company or a third-party provider, chances are good it too supports Exchange Autodiscover. If you encounter sign-in prob-lems, a server administrator can provide you with the detailed instructions to connect to that account and begin synchronizing its contents with a local Outlook data file.

By default, new Exchange accounts are set up in Cached Exchange Mode, which allows you to keep a local copy of your mail, calendar, and other items. On Office 365, messages older than 12 months are kept on the server and not synced locally. You can adjust this setting in either direction by opening the Account Settings dialog box from Backstage view, selecting your Exchange account, and clicking Change. On the Server Settings page, shown here, move the slider left to minimize the amount of mail you sync, with available settings of 1 month (minimum), 3 months, or 6 months. If you have ample disk space and bandwidth and want more of your mail stored locally for faster searching, move the slider to the right, to 24 months or All.

INSIDE OUT   Let someone else run your Exchange server

Microsoft Exchange Server has earned a reputation over the years as complex and suitable only for use in large enterprise settings. That intimidating image is softening with the steady growth of hosted Exchange services, which allow businesses of any size (even single-person shops) to connect to Exchange servers over the Internet, paying a monthly fee to a service provider that handles the headaches of server administration and backup. You can purchase a hosted Exchange account directly from Microsoft as part of Office 365 (*office365.com*). You can also try third-party partners such as Apptix (*apptix.com*) and Intermedia (*intermedia.net*).

Setting up an Outlook.com (Hotmail) account

In previous Outlook versions, connecting to a Hotmail account required that you download and install the Outlook Hotmail Connector. Today, Hotmail has a new name, Outlook.com, as well as a new user interface (and a slew of new features) in its free web-based version. In Outlook 2013, accounts in the Outlook.com, Hotmail.com, and Live.com domains connect automatically using Exchange ActiveSync, with no manual configuration or add-in required.

You can synchronize contacts, calendars, rules, and safe/blocked senders lists from your Outlook.com account to Outlook.

You'll find a rich set of features available in the web-based Outlook.com client. For example, you can set up "sweep" rules for newsletters and other frequent mailings so that you keep only the most recent ones. These rules are stored on the Outlook.com server and work on all messages, independently of rules you set up in Outlook. Outlook.com accounts also offer the capability to create aliases that you can use independently of your main account and discard when no longer needed. That's a handy option when you need to interact with another person or company but don't trust them with your real email address.

Getting Gmail and Google Apps to play nicely with Outlook

Microsoft is not the only big company with a free web-based email service. If you set up a new email account using an address (and its associated password) from Google's Gmail (*gmail.com*), Outlook automatically configures the correct account settings, using IMAP for Gmail.

That leaves your Google calendar and contacts in limbo on the server, unconnected to Outlook. If Gmail used Exchange ActiveSync (EAS), that wouldn't be a problem, but as of early 2013 Google has dropped support for that protocol except for customers of its paid Google Apps service. And even then Google's implementation of EAS works only on mobile devices and not in Outlook.

If you're a Google Apps customer, you'll need to use an add-in to enable the Google-to-Outlook connection. As of this writing, Google hasn't updated its own sync tool for Outlook 2013, and we haven't spent enough time with third-party utilities (of which there are several) to recommend one.

And even on the email side, working with Google's mail servers in Outlook can be less than satisfying. Google's labels don't map perfectly to Outlook folders, for example. If you're a fan of the Google way, you'll need to spend most of your time in a browser window to experience its full set of features.

If you prefer Outlook and you're keeping your Gmail address only because it's free and widely used in your circle of friends, consider forwarding your incoming Gmail messages to an Outlook.com or Exchange account.

Connecting to social networks

You might have used the Outlook Social Connector with Outlook 2010, where it was available as an optional add-in. This add-in is installed by default in Outlook 2013.

Adding one or more social network accounts to your Outlook profile allows you to do two things. First, you can use your list of connections as an address book for email and messaging (and, in theory, other types of sharing as well). Second, you can see related activities and items in context with email and contacts.

As of this writing, Outlook supports connections to Facebook and LinkedIn, as well as to SharePoint sites in your organization and on Office 365. To make a persistent connection to one or more of these services, click Info in Backstage view, click Account Settings, and click Social Network Accounts. That opens a dialog box where you can enter and save the credentials for those accounts so that Outlook can retrieve information from the connected services.

Figure 15-8 shows this dialog box after we've already connected a couple of services. Clicking the check box next to Facebook opens a form where we can enter that service's user name and password.

Figure 15-8 Enter your credentials here and Outlook will log on to Facebook or other services automatically, retrieving contact information (including profile pictures) for your friends and professional connections.

Note that LinkedIn allows Outlook to save contact information locally so that you can find phone numbers and email addresses for connections you've made by choosing the LinkedIn folder in People view. Facebook doesn't allow you to save contacts and updates locally.

At the bottom of every email message and contact item is a resizable pane whose purpose is to display information about the person (or persons) associated with that item. The People pane displays contact information about each person, including his or her picture, if it's available. In a series of tabs to the right of the picture are lists of email messages, calendar items, file attachments, and updates from social networks where you're connected with that person. Each link is a live link to the item, so if you receive an email message from Ed Bott, you can quickly scroll through his recent social activity and review your email history before replying to his message.

Managing Outlook data files and folders

Every Outlook profile contains at least one Outlook data file. In some configurations, that one file might be enough to handle all your Outlook data; more complicated profiles with multiple email accounts might have their data stored in several files, some of which are local copies of your mailbox on a server. Each data file appears as a separate node in the Folder pane, with a list of default folders beneath it, in a hierarchy that you can expand or collapse with a click of the arrow to the left of the file or folder icon. You can add folders and subfolders within any of those nodes.

Managing data files

Outlook generally does a good job of insulating you from the need to manage how and where your data files are stored. But on those rare occasions when you need to troubleshoot problems with a data file or export information, you need to know a few technical and logistic details.

For starters, as we explained earlier in this chapter, Outlook stores your data using two different file formats. When you use File Explorer (Windows Explorer on Windows 7), both formats are identified in the Type column as Outlook Data File. The only way to tell which file is local (with a .pst file name extension) as opposed to offline (.ost) is to look at the file name extension or the file icon, both of which are visible in the file's properties. An offline file has a double-headed blue arrow beneath it, as shown here, indicating that it's a synchronized or cached copy of content that is stored on a server.

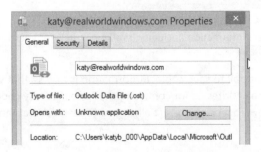

It's crucial to understand the difference between these two file types if you want to avoid the heartbreak of lost data.

Offline (.ost) files represent copies of your real data, which resides on a server. As a result, the local copies are considered dispensable. They're stored in a hidden folder within your local profile, and they are not backed up with personal data files. If you need to recover a backup, you simply add the account to your profile and let it sync again. It might take a few minutes, but your data is safe and sound in the cloud.

By contrast, local (.pst) files contain email messages, calendar appointments, contacts, and other Outlook items that are not synchronized anywhere else. By default, Outlook keeps files of this type in your user profile, in a folder called Outlook Files. This type of file is included with Windows backups by default, and if you have a consistent data backup plan, you can recover a deleted or damaged local data file by restoring it from your backup.

When you set up a new profile using a POP/SMTP email account. Outlook creates a new, primary data file (what used to be called a Personal Folders file). Archiving a mailbox creates a .pst file that is not associated with an email account, and you can manually create a .pst file at any time, an option that is most useful if you want to manually archive Outlook data or copy a subset of a data file for use on another PC.

To see all data files in use in your current profile, click File, and on the Info tab in Backstage view click Account Settings (on the Account Settings menu). Click the Data Files tab to reveal a list like the one shown in Figure 15-9.

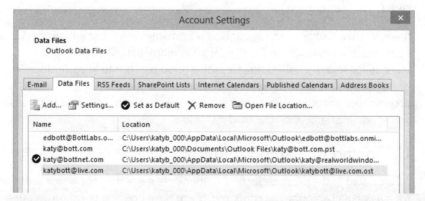

Figure 15-9 In general, each account you set up creates its own data file, either a local file or an offline copy. You can view the full list here.

Chapter 15

CAUTION !

For IMAP accounts in particular, you run the risk of losing all your non-email data in the event of a system crash or a reconfiguration. The email messages in your offline data file are synchronized copies of those stored on the server, but calendar items, contacts, and tasks are stored in that file only and are not synchronized or backed up. You'll be able to spot the telltale warning signs if you look in Calendar, People, or Tasks view and see "(This computer only)" at the end of an item in the Folder pane.

The solution is to avoid this configuration and make sure all items, not just email, are being stored in folders that are regularly backed up. Consider using a free Outlook.com account as the first one in your profile; even if you never use that address for email, you can use it to manage contacts and calendar items. Then set up the IMAP server as a second account and use it as your primary email address. In this configuration, all of your settings are being synced properly, and you don't risk losing any important information.

Why would you want to work directly with an Outlook data file in Windows Explorer or File Explorer? That option comes in handy if you're copying a .pst file for use on another PC or backing up an important data file. Select an entry from the list on the Data Files tab, and then click Open File Location to display that file in File Explorer. An even faster route is to right-click the name of the account in the Folder pane (in Mail or Folder List view) and then click Open File Location.

If you've used Outlook long enough, you probably remember a time when 2 GB was a hard-and-fast limitation on file size for an Outlook data file. Thankfully, that has not been an issue for several versions now. It's still a good practice to keep Outlook files down to manageable sizes for the sake of performance and maintenance, but if you're willing to accept those potential risks, Outlook allows you to fill up a data file that's as large as your server administrator and your hard disk allow.

Using and managing folders

As we noted in the previous section, Outlook creates a data file with a set of default folders for every email account you configure. If you have one and only one account, regardless of what type it is, the local or offline data file includes folders for all supported Outlook data types. If you add a second POP or IMAP account, that account gets a separate data file with a set of folders limited to mail items.

The default Mail view shows only mail folders. Want to see the full set of folders? Click the ellipsis (three dots) to the right of the links in the navigation bar and click Folders. Figure

15-10 shows the full set of folders for a profile that has two accounts: an Outlook.com account, set up first, and a POP account that was configured as an additional account.

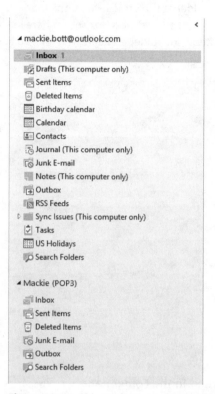

Figure 15-10 This profile is configured for two mail accounts, each with its own set of folders. Note that the second account has only mail-related folders.

The Outlook.com account is synchronized to an offline data file (.ost). The POP account is saved in a local data file (.pst) in the current user's Documents folder. Had we created these accounts in reverse, the set of folders included with the POP account would have included local-only folders for Calendar, Contacts, and so on.

Outlook 2013 groups the most important choices at the top and bottom of the folder list for each data file. At the top are up to four email folders; at the bottom is a single link where you can create Search Folders (which we discuss in more detail in "Mastering Outlook search" in Chapter 16).

On an Exchange or Outlook.com account, those folders are synchronized from matching folders on the server. Technically, the only mail folder you need for a POP account is Inbox, which is where Outlook delivers messages. The other mail-related folders—Sent Items and Deleted Items, for example—are created locally to handle your outgoing and deleted messages, junk mail, and so on.

You can add new folders and subfolders to any location in the Folder pane, with the exception of the Calendar. To create a new folder in the Inbox, right-click the Inbox icon and click New Folder. To create a new top-level folder at the same level as the Inbox, right-click the icon for the data file itself. The Create New Folder dialog box shown here lets you add a descriptive name, specify the type of items the folder contains, and choose a location.

TROUBLESHOOTING

Folders for an IMAP account aren't in the Folder pane

When you add an IMAP account (including Gmail) to an Outlook profile, you might see only an Inbox folder under its heading in the Folder pane, and trying to send or delete a message results in an error complaining that the Sent Items or Deleted Items folder doesn't exist. This can happen if the account is new and those folders have not been created on the server yet. The simplest workaround is to use a web-based interface to create and send a message and to delete at least one message. That creates the necessary folders. Then return to Outlook, right-click the account icon in the Folder pane, and choose IMAP Folders. Click Query to display a list of all available folders, which should now include the previously missing special folders, available for you to subscribe to.

You can also choose *not* to synchronize a specific folder, by selecting the folder and clicking Unsubscribe. That option leaves messages on the server but tells Outlook not to create a local copy. This option is especially useful for archive folders, which can grow quite large and are, by design, intended for long-term storage.

The assortment of default folders under each account name is different depending on the account type. In addition, any third-party services you add to Outlook (including social networks) might add their own folders for storing contacts and news feeds.

You can copy, move, rename, or delete any folder you create; to do so, use the commands in the Actions group on the Folder tab. You cannot move or delete default folders (deleting the Inbox would make it impossible for new messages to be delivered).

Creating, sending, and receiving messages

When you create a new email message or reply to an existing one, Outlook opens a message window like the one shown here.

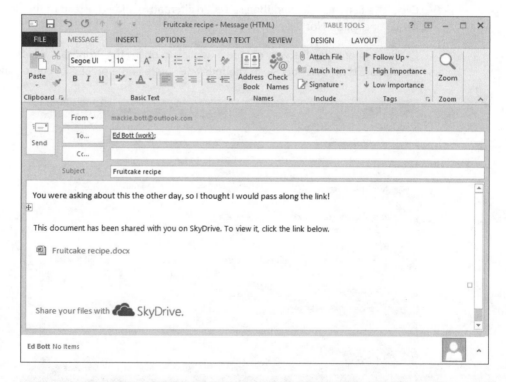

We assume that you've sent and received enough email messages that you can figure out the basics of composing, addressing, and sending a message or reply. In this section, we concentrate on some interesting and useful email options that you're less likely to discover without a determined search.

For starters, there's the Bcc box, which is essential when you want to send a copy of a message to someone without alerting the other recipients. The Bcc box is normally hidden; to make it available, click the Options tab and then click Bcc (in the Show Fields group).

A group of esoteric settings at the far right side of the Options tab (in the More Options group) allow for some interesting treatment of messages you send.

Click Save Sent Item To, and then select an alternative folder (instead of the default Sent Items) or click Do Not Save.

Clicking either Delay Delivery or Direct Replies To opens the Properties dialog box shown in Figure 15-11, which is specific to the message you're in the process of composing.

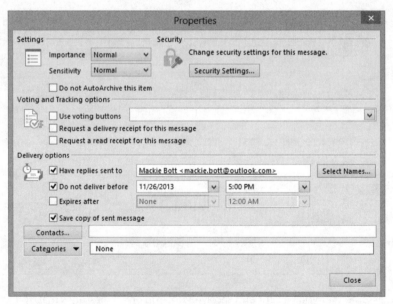

Figure 15-11 The top two settings in the Delivery Options area allow you to specify an alternative Reply To address and delay delivery until a specified date and time.

To delay delivery of your message, select the Do Not Deliver Before check box and enter the date and time when you want the message delivered. Note that your computer must be on (not sleeping or hibernating), and Outlook must be running for the message to be sent. If your computer is off or you've closed Outlook, the message will be sent at the first available opportunity after the specified date and time.

The Have Replies Sent To option allows you to specify an email address that is used when recipients click the Reply button after reading your message. If you're sending out a new press release or sales promotion from your everyday email account, you might want replies to be shunted to a special sales or press alias. That allows a team of people to receive those replies and respond to them promptly, without cluttering your Inbox.

For more on how to avoid errors when addressing email messages, see "Managing Auto-Complete lists" in Chapter 17.

Choosing the right message format

When you compose a new message, Outlook offers three format choices that dictate how the message appears to recipients. These options are available in the Format group on the Format Text tab.

By default, Outlook sends new messages in HTML format, which allows you to use fonts, text formatting, tables, rules, and graphics in much the way you would create a webpage. If you're sending messages from an account on a Microsoft Exchange server to other recipients who have mailboxes on the same Exchange server, your message is sent in Rich Text format, which enables some advanced features that apply only to Exchange users. This format also allows a broad range of text and graphic formatting options.

The Plain Text format strips away all formatting and leaves behind only text. If you've added bold or italic formatting for emphasis, it will be lost. Recipients will see your message using their default font. Any graphics embedded in the message body are stripped out as well (pictures and documents attached to a message as files are handled properly).

When you reply to a message, Outlook tries to match the format of the message you received. So if a correspondent sends you a message in Plain Text format, your reply will be in Plain Text format as well.

For more details than most Outlook users would ever want to know about message formats, see the TechNet article "Content Conversion," at *w7io.com/12179*.

Chapter 15

Receiving and synchronizing messages

If you have a fast, always-on broadband connection, sending and receiving email probably isn't something you think about often. Outlook automatically connects to your outgoing mail server and sends messages as soon as you click the Send button. It retrieves messages from POP and IMAP servers every 30 minutes when you're online. It synchronizes mail, calendar, and contact folders in Microsoft Exchange and Outlook.com (Hotmail) accounts as new items arrive, using the Exchange ActiveSync protocol.

You might choose to adjust these settings if you use a POP or IMAP account and you want notification of new mail more often than every 30 minutes. You also might choose to tweak settings here if you're traveling and have limited Internet access. If your Internet access plan charges by the minute and/or by the byte, you can modify your settings to minimize the amount of data exchange and temporarily suspend send/receive operations for nonessential accounts.

You'll find options for sending, receiving, and synchronizing everything in your Outlook profile on the Send/Receive tab, which is just to the right of the Home tab in every Outlook view, as shown here.

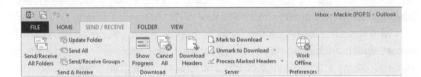

The commands in the Send & Receive group work with all accounts. Send/Receive All Folders connects to each POP, IMAP, and Outlook.com (Hotmail) account, one after the other, without regard to the schedule defined for those accounts. It sends any messages in the Outbox and picks up any newly arrived messages from the server. (For POP and IMAP accounts only, this command is also on the Home tab, at the far right.) The keyboard shortcut for Send/Receive All Folders is F9.

The Send/Receive Groups menu allows you to perform a send/receive operation for a single account. It's also where you can define global settings for automatic send/receive/synchronize operations and where you can set up groups. Click Define Send/Receive Groups to display the dialog box shown in Figure 15-12.

Normally, Outlook shows a progress dialog box as the send/receive operation is under way. If you want to check the results of the most recent send/receive operation, click Show Progress to display this dialog box. The Errors tab displays any messages that indicate a failure to connect or to receive or send messages.

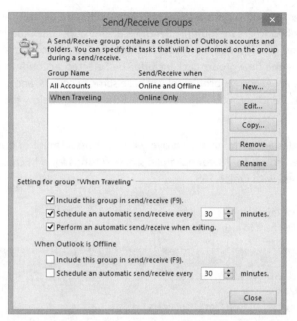

Figure 15-12 This custom Send/Receive group is configured to avoid trying to make a connection when you click the Work Offline command.

INSIDE OUT   Understanding Outlook's unconventional keyboard shortcuts

Despite the fact that it's been a full-fledged member of the Office family since 1997, Outlook has never fit in with its Office-mates when it comes to keyboard shortcuts. In Word, Excel, and the other Office programs, for example, Ctrl+F allows you to search the current document, worksheet, or presentation. In Outlook, that keyboard shortcut forwards the current message, and you need to remember that F4 opens the Find dialog box to search within the contents of an email message. Ctrl+Z is Undo in Outlook, just as in other Office programs, but Ctrl+Y isn't Redo—instead, it opens the Go To Folder dialog box. Outlook's approach to keyboard shortcuts is so quirky, in fact, that we recommend not bothering with them at all. If you're a keyboard diehard, you can find all of Outlook's oddball shortcuts in a single (very long) page, available via Outlook Help or online at *w7io.com/12178*.

By default, Outlook creates a single All Accounts group with separate settings for online and offline use. The Schedule An Automatic Send/Receive Every *nn* Minutes option is set to an initial default of 30 minutes. To change this automatic send/receive interval for all POP and IMAP accounts, enter a different value here. To apply different default settings for different accounts, you need to create multiple Send/Receive groups. Click the New button to create a new group and give it a name of your choosing. For each account whose settings you want to control via the new group, click Include The Selected Account In This Group. Then click Edit for the All Accounts profile, select those same accounts, and clear the check box. You can now select each group in turn and adjust the settings below the group list, as needed.

The Edit button provides access to an almost overwhelming assortment of options, which differ by account type. Figure 15-13, for example, shows settings for a Microsoft Exchange Online account included with Office 365.

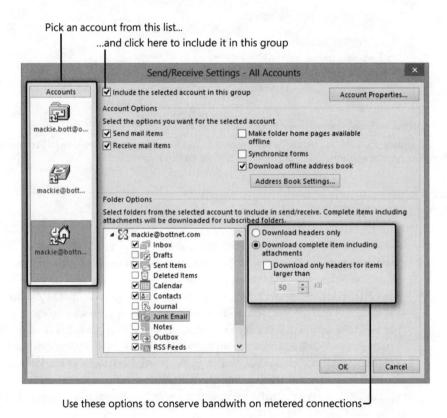

Pick an account from this list...

...and click here to include it in this group

Use these options to conserve bandwith on metered connections

Figure 15-13 Click an account in the list on the left to see its options on the right. If Internet access is expensive or very slow, consider downloading only message headers.

Settings for other types of accounts vary depending on the account type. POP accounts, for example, handle email, and that's all. A POP server is designed to receive incoming email addressed to you and hold it for your pickup. It isn't equipped to keep track of contacts or your calendar or to store messages in folders. Normally, when you connect to a POP server, any waiting messages are downloaded to your Outlook Inbox and then deleted from the server.

For a POP server, as with any account, you can choose to download headers only for the Inbox folder, or to download full messages that are smaller than a specified size and download only headers for messages above that size. (Use the check box under the Download Complete Item Including Attachments option.) For messages with large attachments that could eat into your data usage limit on a metered connection, the first setting tells Outlook to download headers only and leave the attachment on the server for now. That saves you from wasting time or money downloading a large file attachment on a slow, expensive connection.

After you download headers to your account, you can go through and mark the ones you want to download in full, leaving the others unmarked. To accomplish this task, use the Mark To Download and Process Marked Headers commands on the Send/Receive tab.

IMAP accounts are also intended for email only. The key difference from POP accounts is that messages are stored on the server, organized in folders you create. When you connect with Outlook, you synchronize a local copy. Configuring an IMAP account requires a visit to two different locations. The first is the IMAP Folders dialog box, where you can specify which server folders are synchronized with your local copy. Right-click the top-level icon for the IMAP account in the Folder pane and click IMAP Folders on the shortcut menu.

From the Send/Receive Settings dialog box, select the IMAP account and look at its settings on the right. To manage bandwidth by downloading headers instead of full messages, click Receive Mail Items and choose either Download Headers For Subscribed Folders or Use The Custom Behavior Defined Below. The latter option makes the Folder Options section available for defining which folders you want downloaded as headers only.

Synchronizing with an Outlook.com account requires no special settings. The only available setting in the Folder Options section allows you to download headers only for messages in your Inbox.

Organizing Outlook information

O UTLOOK can store an astonishing amount of data on your behalf. But all that information—email messages, contact details, reminders of upcoming appointments—is just wasted disk space if you can't reliably find it when you need it.

In this chapter, we explore your strategies for arranging, filing, and finding Outlook items. We start with basic organizational techniques for calendar items and contacts. We spend the greatest part of this chapter on Outlook's superb search tools; master them, and you can quickly find what you're looking for—even when your filing system is the digital equivalent of a shoebox. We also explain the intricacies of views, which allow you to sort, filter, and arrange the contents of a folder so that you can scan its contents quickly and efficiently.

Finally, we help you make the most of a pair of Outlook features that let you file and process incoming email messages automatically (or with minimal effort). Rules do the work for you; Quick Steps allow you to save a sequence of actions and apply those saved actions to one or more items with a single click.

Managing your calendar

An Outlook calendar can do things that a traditional printed calendar can't. Outlook allows you to keep multiple calendars—so you can keep personal and work-related events firmly separated but combine the two when you're viewing your schedule. You can add follow-up flags and reminders to an appointment, keep perfect track of appointments that recur weekly or monthly, and schedule meetings with coworkers.

If you work in a company that uses Microsoft Exchange, calendaring is a core function of your work environment. You probably have Outlook open at all times, and your calendar and shared calendars for your colleagues are never more than a few clicks away. If you don't use Exchange, you can get equivalent calendar features from Outlook.com.

When you're away from the office, at home or on the road, you can synchronize your calendar (or calendars) with a smartphone or a portable device so that any appointment you enter or change in one place shows up in the other. In general, the work of synchronization is handled by the server—typically using Exchange ActiveSync. If you use Exchange or Outlook.com as a hub, the device never needs to communicate directly with Outlook.

For more details on how to get Outlook to nag you (in a good way) about what's coming up on your calendar, see "Setting follow-up flags and reminders" in Chapter 17, "Outlook 2013 inside out."

Calendar view shows you all meetings, appointments, and all-day events for the selected calendar (or calendars). The Date Navigator control (identical to the one found in the To-Do Bar in other views) sits at the top of the Folder pane, with a list of available calendars just below it. Figure 16-1 shows a single calendar open, with Month view on display.

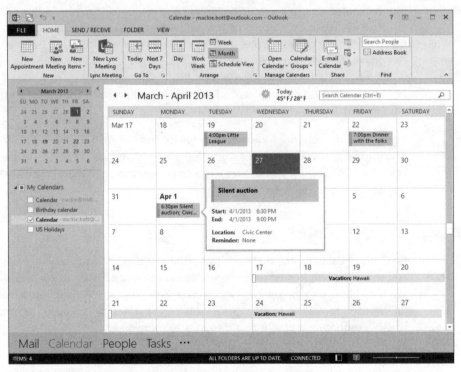

Figure 16-1 Moving the mouse pointer over a calendar item in a monthly view displays a pop-up window with additional details.

Double-click any item to open it for editing. Double-click a date to create a new all-day event on that date and open it for editing. Right-click any date to display a list of different types of calendar items and gain access to additional calendar options.

The Arrange group on the Home tab contains single-click shortcuts that allow you to zoom in on your calendar and see more details. Day, Week, and Month are straightforward, but the other two selections deserve some extra discussion.

- Click Work Week to show a week's worth of events, with all working hours visible and your days off hidden. By default, this view is set for 8:00 A.M. to 5:00 P.M., Monday through Friday. If your hours or workdays are different, you can adjust these settings on the Calendar tab of the Outlook Options dialog box.

- Schedule View gives you a day-by-day view of your calendar that works by scrolling from left to right. It's most useful when you're comparing your calendar with someone else's in search of free time for a meeting or a lunch date. Try selecting Work Week first, and then click Schedule View to scroll through your work commitments for the current week.

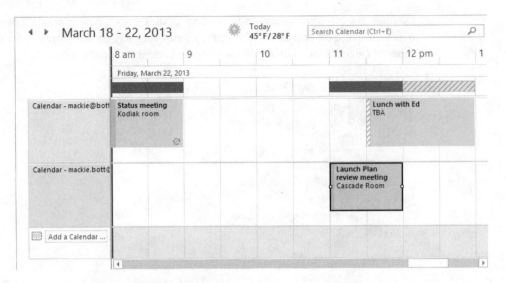

In Day or Week view, where appointments and meetings are presented in columns, pressing Home takes you to the beginning of the selected workday, and End jumps to the end of the workday (based on your work week settings). Press Ctrl+Home or Ctrl+End to jump to the beginning or end of the day—normally midnight. In any Calendar view, press Alt+Page Down or Alt+Page Up to move to the next or previous month, respectively.

INSIDE OUT   Create your own custom group of days

Sometimes you might want to see a group of days that doesn't easily fit into one of the ready-made views. Perhaps you want to see your schedule for the next Friday, Saturday, and Sunday so that you can schedule a long weekend without shirking any work responsibilities. To do that, click the first date in the Date Navigator at the top of the Folder pane on the left, and then use Shift+click to select multiple adjacent dates or Ctrl+click to select multiple noncontiguous dates. The contents pane displays items for those dates only, as shown here.

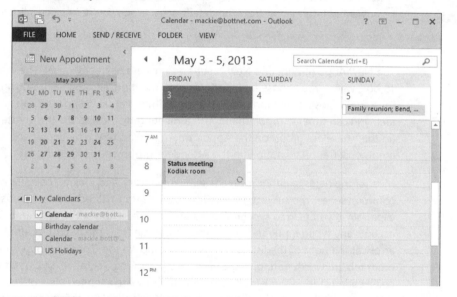

Creating and editing appointments and meetings

To create a new item from scratch in Calendar view, click the New Appointment or New Meeting command on the Home tab. If the date you want to use is visible in Day or Week view, you can double-click a time to begin creating a new item with that date and start time filled in. Drag to select a time interval, and then right-click to open a form with a non-default end time. To begin creating an all-day event, double-click in the colored bar just between the date heading and the top of your hour-by-hour calendar.

INSIDE OUT   Turn an email message into an appointment

If you receive an email for which the follow-up action involves scheduling an appointment on your calendar, you can skip the Clipboard and allow Outlook to fill in the Subject field and add details. Drag the message from the message list and drop it on the Calendar link at the bottom of the Outlook window. That opens a new appointment item using the subject and body text of the message. Pick the correct date and time (the default is for the next available block of time today). You'll probably want to change the subject of the new appointment, and you might also want to trim unwanted information from the details pane. When you're satisfied, click Save & Close.

The New Appointment and New Meeting forms are nearly identical. The difference is the To box, where you choose attendees for your meeting, and the Send button, which replaces the Save & Close command used with appointments that go on your calendar alone. In fact, you can turn an appointment into a meeting by clicking the Invite Attendees button (in the Attendees group on the Appointment tab); to turn a meeting back into an appointment, click Cancel Invitation (in the Attendees group on the Meeting tab).

Most of the fields in either form are self-explanatory, and making best use of them involves common sense. The subject, for example, can be up to 255 characters, but shorter is better, especially if you plan to synchronize calendar items with your smartphone. The Location list accepts any typed input and allows you to choose from the last 10 locations by clicking the arrow at the right of the list. The Show As settings in the Options group on the Appointment tab are worth noting. You can choose Busy, Free, Tentative, or Out Of Office to add a color-coded strip to the left of each item. If you share a limited view of your calendar with other people, they can check times when you're available without seeing details of your schedule.

For meeting invitations where you and your fellow attendees are using Office 365 or Microsoft Exchange, the server handles the work of coordinating who has accepted and who has declined and who has yet to respond. If you're using other mail servers, it's important to send a response so that the meeting organizer doesn't have to manually follow up with you. When you click Accept, Tentative, or Decline, you can choose whether to send a response immediately or to edit the response first. After you send the response, Outlook updates your calendar and moves the meeting request to the Deleted Items folder.

And what if the recipient isn't using Outlook? You still might be able to coordinate your meeting, depending on the calendar system he or she uses. Outlook.com (Hotmail) handles meeting requests properly. Gmail accounts that have been connected to a Google calendar offer a similar Yes/Maybe/No option. In both cases, the meeting organizer gets a proper response and the appointment is updated accordingly.

To understand the intricacies (and possible pitfalls) posed by cross-country and international travel, see "Juggling multiple time zones" in Chapter 17.

Learn Outlook's date and time shortcuts

You can enter dates in any format that Outlook is able to recognize; in the date box alongside Start Time or End Time, for example, type *aug 9* or *8/9* (U.S. style) to enter the date August 9, with the current year assumed. When you open a new item, Outlook fills in dates from the currently selected day, regardless of which view (Day, Week, Month) you're using. To add a couple of days, a week, or a few months to that date, click in either date box and type *2 days*, *1 week*, or *3 months*. When you move to a new field, Outlook automatically adjusts the date by the amount you specified.

You can also use abbreviations for days of the week (*mon*, *thu*, or *thurs*) and date-related words and phrases (*today, tomorrow, two weeks from yesterday*), with or without the names of holidays (*Thanksgiving, three days after Christmas, Friday before New Year's Eve*).

A few shortcuts are also available for entering times. If you simply type a number without using a colon, Outlook converts it to a time. It usually guesses correctly at A.M. and P.M. designations, defaulting to times in your workday if possible. You can override these settings by providing hints: *1015p* becomes 10:15 P.M., and *5a* is 5:00 A.M.

Setting up recurring appointments and events

Any appointment, meeting, or all-day event can be defined as a recurring item that repeats on a schedule you specify. Begin by right-clicking a date or choosing New Items from the Home tab, and then clicking More Items. Then select one of the three choices that begin with New Recurring.

As an alternative, you can open a new or existing item and click the Recurrence command (in the Options group on the home tab for that item, labeled Meeting or Appointment or Event) and specify the details of the schedule using the dialog box shown next.

Chapter 16

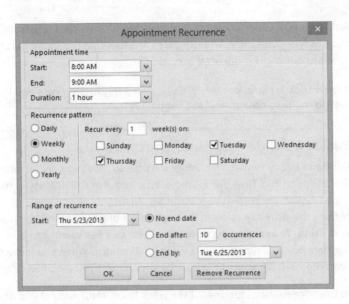

Enter a Start and End time and then select options from the Recurrence Pattern section to define the schedule. If you have a meeting that occurs at the same time on the same days every week, select Weekly and click the scheduled days: Tuesday and Thursday, for example. The Range Of Recurrence section allows you to define a series that ends on a specified date or after a certain number of occurrences.

When you double-click an item on your calendar that is part of a recurring series, Outlook asks whether you want to edit the individual occurrence or the series. Choose the former option if you just want to cancel next Tuesday's meeting; use the latter option to change the schedule to Wednesday and Friday.

Arranging multiple calendars

How many individual calendars are available when you switch to Calendar view? In the Folder pane, under the My Calendars heading, you'll find separate calendars for any accounts that connect to Office 365, Exchange Server, or Outlook.com. If the first account you set up used a legacy mail protocol (POP or IMAP) you'll have a "this computer only" Outlook calendar in a local data file (.pst). You can also open shared calendars from other users, if they've given you permission.

INSIDE OUT   Add holidays to your default calendar

Items on the Holiday calendar are specific to your country and are not included as part of your default calendar. To add items from the Holiday calendar to your current calendar, open Outlook's Options dialog box and click the Calendar tab. Under the Calendar Options heading, click Add Holidays, select your region, and click OK.

Outlook includes several tools to help you arrange multiple calendars on the screen, side by side or overlaid in a single display. When you click the check box to the left of two available calendars in the Folder pane, Outlook displays the calendars side by side.

The side-by-side calendars scroll up, down, and from side to side in unison. If you click a single date or drag to select a range of dates, those dates are displayed in both places. Likewise, any commands in the Arrange group apply to both calendars simultaneously.

INSIDE OUT   Change a calendar's background color

In Outlook, each calendar is color-coded, with the color band in the Folder pane matching the background color for the corresponding calendar. If you find that one of these automatically applied colors makes the calendar hard to read, it's easy enough to change the color. Open the calendar, right-click any empty date or time, click Color, and then choose one of nine pastel alternatives. This option can be especially helpful when you're overlaying two calendars and you want a more obvious visual contrast between items from the different calendars.

Side-by-side displays are fine for a quick comparison, but if you really want a unified display, click the View tab and then click Overlay (in the Arrangement group). Figure 16-2 shows two calendars—one from an Office 365 account, the other from Outlook.com—with the latter displayed as an overlay.

Figure 16-2 Click Overlay (in the Arrangement group on the View tab) to virtually merge two calendars in a single view.

CAUTION !

> When you select or open a meeting or an appointment from a calendar that is not your default calendar, you see a Copy To My Calendar command on the Appointment or Meeting tab. That option does exactly what it says—copying all details from the original item to a new item in your default calendar. It does not create a link between the two items, however. If the original item is in a calendar under someone else's control, you run the risk that he or she will change the date, time, location, or other important details in the original item, leaving you with an incorrect, outdated item. In general, you should copy items to your calendar only when you control both the source and the destination calendars. If you do copy an appointment from another calendar, we recommend that you make a note in the new copy that includes the source of the appointment details, the date it was copied, and (if possible) a link to the original calendar item.

To close a calendar, clear its check box in the Folder pane. Note that you must have at least one calendar open in Calendar view. If you try to clear the check box for the only calendar on display, Outlook will helpfully select the check box for another one on your behalf.

Organizing your contacts

Your Outlook profile has at least one Contacts folder, probably several. Each Office 365, Exchange, or Outlook.com (Hotmail) account includes its own Contacts folder, and connections to social media services like LinkedIn also appear as folders in Contacts view. If you use a POP or IMAP server as your first Outlook account, a Contacts folder is included in a local data file (.pst).

Collectively, your Contacts folders play three roles in Outlook: an address book for email messages and online conversations; a repository of detailed contact information (addresses and job titles, for example) for use with documents like mailings; and a hub for reviewing a contact's activities, including email threads and updates from social networks.

When you switch to People view, Outlook displays three panes. On the left is the Folder pane with a link for every available Contacts folder. The middle pane shows a list of items in the selected folder, and the Reading pane (on the right, by default) shows the contents of the selected item. Figure 16-3 provides an example.

Figure 16-3 The Reading pane in People view provides a clean, uncluttered display of information about the current contact. Note the Edit button in the upper right.

Click Edit (in the upper-right corner of the contact record) to switch from view-only mode and edit fields that are available for you to change. In your Contacts folder, you can change a name or phone number, add work details, and enter separate home and work addresses. To add a new item in a category, like a mobile phone number or a secondary email address, click the plus sign to the left of the category name. In some cases, this presents you with a list of available fields, as shown here.

Be sure to click Save to store your changes in the Contacts folder.

You can't edit fields that are drawn from third-party sources. If you connect to a business associate on LinkedIn, any fields that are drawn from that associate's LinkedIn profile will be displayed as they appear in that person's profile. The contents of those linked fields will change only if the person who owns that profile updates his or her information.

You don't have to switch to People view to see details about a contact. Every address in every email message and every name in a meeting invitation is a live link that provides access to that person's *contact card*. Let the mouse pointer rest over the name, and an abbreviated contact card pops up, like this one. (You can also right-click to show the mini-contact card along with a menu of other options.)

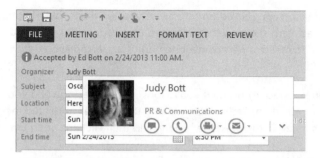

The first three icons in the row of four contact options at the bottom of the card are enabled only if that person is available on a connected messaging system, like Lync.

To see the full contact card, which has additional details such as phone numbers, click the down arrow at the right of the mini-card. Figure 16-4 shows an example of this expanded card. To keep the full contact card from disappearing as soon as you move the mouse pointer, click the pushpin icon in its upper-right corner. That keeps the item visible until you close it.

Figure 16-4 This expanded contact card displays full details, including notes and social updates, for a contact. Note the five tabs for a contact from an Exchange server. Each View Source link leads to a profile page on a connected social network.

If the person whose name you clicked isn't in one of your Contacts folders already, you get an abbreviated contact card showing the name and email address as it appears in the message address header. To create a new contact item for that person and add it to your Contacts folder, click Add.

The Send Email icon is especially useful if you're looking at a message and you want to start a completely new conversation. Rather than reply to the original, unrelated message, right-click your recipient's name in the message header, and then click the Send Email icon.

Viewing and editing contacts in Business Card view

The sleek contact card form we've been concentrating on up to this point is new in Outlook 2013. If you create a new contact, or if you open a contact in Business Card view (click Business Card in the Current View group on the Home tab), you see the version of the form used to add and edit contacts in early Outlook versions.

Figure 16-5 shows the full Business Card version of a contact, with all fields available for editing.

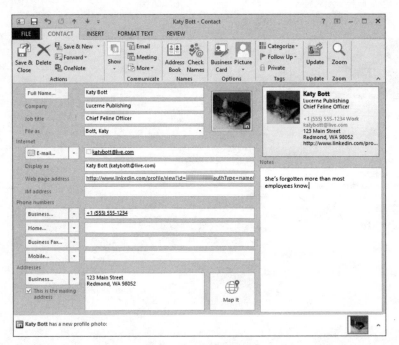

Figure 16-5 The Business Card view includes a few more options than the regular contact card shown in People view, including the Display As and File As options.

Business Card view also gives you access to a couple of fields you won't find in the more modern People view, with its contact card format. This allows you to control how items appear in the contacts list.

When browsing through contacts, you might notice that the name displayed is not necessarily the same as the sort order. That's because the name shown here is taken from the Name field (labeled as Full Name in Business Card view). The sort order is determined by the Display As field; by default, this is Last Name, First Name. If you want to change this order for new cards you create, open the Options dialog box (click File, then click Options) and display the People tab, as shown here.

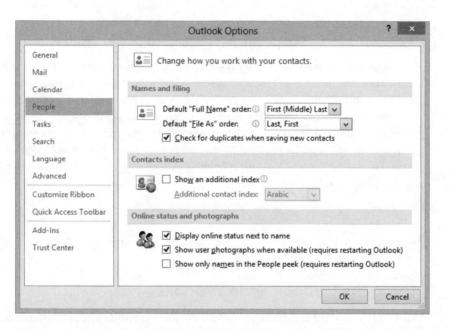

The settings you assign here dictate how these fields are filled in for new contact items. They don't change existing items. At any time, you can override the current settings in the Names And Filing section by editing the contact's File As entry in Business Card view.

For a more compact view of a Contacts folder that contains many items, switch to List view, where the Full Name and File As fields have their own columns.

Searching for contacts

If a Contacts folder contains more than a dozen items, it's often easier to search than to browse. The Search Contacts box at the top of the contacts list lets you instantly filter the contents of the current folder. (Press Ctrl+E to move the insertion point directly to this box so you can begin typing.) This is a word-wheel search that responds immediately (or nearly so) as you type. Contacts appear in the list if any part of any field in that item matches the text you type in the search box. So, typing *ris* locates your friend J*ris* Kalz and anyone whose address is on Har*ris*on Street.

INSIDE OUT   Search through all Contacts folders at once

The Search Contacts box is the fastest way to find someone if you know which Contacts folder contains the details you want to use. But what if you're not sure which folder the person's contact details are located in? Or what if you created a contact record for a business associate and that person's LinkedIn profile is also available in a Contacts folder? For those occasions, click in the Search People box (in the Find group at the right side of the Home tab in any view), enter part of the person or company name you're looking for, and then press Enter. Click a name from the results list to open the full contact card for that person.

For more on how to use search features throughout Outlook, see "Mastering Outlook search" later in this chapter.

Using the Outlook address books

The most important thing to know about the Outlook Address Book is that it doesn't exist. Oh, it looks real enough, and you can get to it from just about anywhere in Outlook. In each of the main Outlook views (Mail, Calendar, People, Tasks), you'll find an Address Book button in the Find group on the Home tab. You can also open the Address Book with its Outlook keyboard shortcut, Ctrl+Shift+B (to memorize this one, just think of *B* for Address *Book*).

You'll find that same Address Book button in the Names group on the Message tab when you create a new email message, in the Names group on the Contact tab when you create a new contact item, and in the Attendees group on the Meeting tab in a meeting request. In any new message window, you can click To, Cc, or Bcc to display the Address Book as well.

So with all those ways to open a window whose name is indeed Address Book, why do we insist that the Address Book doesn't exist? Because its contents come from elsewhere, and the Address Book is just a tiny shell that provides an alternative means of getting to those names, addresses, and other details. If you think of it as "the Address Book view of your Contacts folders," you're getting closer to understanding how it works.

When you open the Address Book from a new message window, Outlook opens a dialog box like the one shown in Figure 16-6. That's a search box in the top left, with a drop-down list of Address Book data sources to its right. A table-style view of the currently selected data source is displayed in the large contents pane. Select any name and click To, Cc, or Bcc to add it to the list of recipients for the message you're creating.

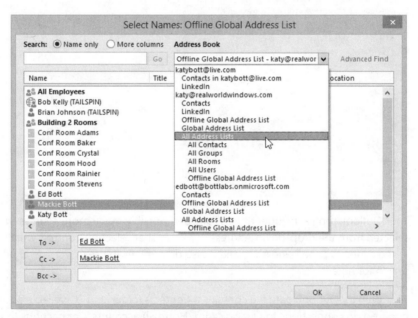

Figure 16-6 Filter the Address Book contents if necessary using the search box on the left, or change its data source by picking a different entry from the Address Book list.

The Address Book search box behaves oddly and inconsistently. When the Name Only option is selected, whatever you type in the search box is treated as if it were an index word, and Outlook jumps to the nearest entry that matches what you typed. If you type *Damien,* but there's no one by that name in your Address Book, the selection jumps to the first name after that entry alphabetically—in this case, probably *Dan* or *Dana* or *David.* All other names remain in the Address Book window, and you can scroll up or down at will.

On the other hand, when you select More Columns, Outlook clears the contents pane immediately and awaits your instructions. Type a search term, and then click Go to filter the list to entries that contain any word that *begins with* your search term.

If you open the Address Book from the main Outlook window, you lose the address field buttons at the bottom but gain some interesting opportunities to tweak the Address Book. For example, click Tools and then Options to reveal this dialog box, where you can use the option at the bottom to make sure you see the right names and email addresses when you open the Address Book.

Your Outlook profile includes at least one and possibly many more sources, which can be selected from the drop-down Address Book list. That selection controls what's displayed in the contents pane beneath it, and it also determines the search scope of anything you search for here.

Your primary Outlook data file contains a Contacts folder that is available as an address book. So do connections to Outlook.com (Hotmail) accounts. Connections to a Microsoft Exchange server give you access to that server's global address list and to your private address list. If you use the Outlook Social Connector to add a service like LinkedIn to your profile, the LinkedIn address book shows as a data source here as well.

INSIDE OUT   Customizing the contents of the Address Book list

If you find that one or more of the entries in your Address Book list is irrelevant—if you never use the Contacts folder for an old Hotmail account where you still receive messages, for example—you can remove it from the Address Book list using one of two well-hidden settings.

The first option: Right-click any folder under the My Contacts heading in People view and then click Properties. Click the Outlook Address Book tab and clear the Show This Folder As An E-Mail Address Book option.

The second, less obvious option is to use the Address Books tab of the Account Settings dialog box. (Click File to go to Backstage view, and in the Info pane click Account Settings and then Account Settings.) Select Outlook Address Book from the list and click Change. That opens the Microsoft Outlook Address Book dialog box shown here and moves you into the very elite circle of people who have actually seen this very obscure dialog box.

If this seems like the long way around, you're right—except that this dialog box offers an option you won't find elsewhere. Use the Show Names By option at the bottom to change the filing order. For a personal or family address book you might prefer the default First Last order, but for a work account you'll probably prefer the File As option, which lets you scroll through the Address Book by last name.

Filtering and filing email messages automatically

Left to its own devices, email has a way of taking over your Inbox and then taking over your life. If you receive 200 emails a day and you spend 10 seconds just scanning each one (forget about thoughtfully reading them), you've lost a half-hour each day. Gaining back control requires that you develop a system for processing your email, and your secret weapons are a pair of Outlook features that we explain in detail in this section.

- **Quick Steps** are customizable shortcuts that enable you to perform a series of actions with one click, such as moving an incoming message to a folder or replying to a message with boilerplate text and then archiving the message immediately.

- **Rules** let you define actions that happen automatically when you receive or send a message, based on conditions you specify. You can use rules to automatically file incoming messages from mailing lists into folders, for example, or forward messages to a coworker based on keywords in the subject or message body.

In both cases, a small investment of up-front effort provides a large payoff later, allowing you to sweep away clutter quickly so you can spend your time dealing with the messages that really matter.

Configuring Quick Steps

Quick Steps appeared for the first time in Outlook 2010, and they work essentially the same way in Outlook 2013. Think of each Quick Step as a shortcut that allows you to perform multiple actions by clicking a button. With the help of a Quick Step, for example, you can reply to an incoming message, flag the message for follow-up in a week, and then move it to a designated folder, all with one click. Creating a Quick Step requires no programming skill. Quick Steps work with email messages only, in any folder.

A default installation of Outlook includes an assortment of Quick Step shortcuts (in the Quick Steps group on the Home tab) to get you started. In addition, you'll find a half-dozen ready-made options (and one Custom choice) on the New Quick Step shortcut menu shown next.

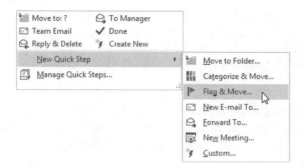

Most of these default Quick Steps are only partially constructed and require some additional setup on your part. If you click Flag & Move, for example, you see a First Time Setup dialog box like the one shown in Figure 16-7. Replace the generic text in the Name box with a more descriptive label and choose options for each of the items in the Actions list, as we've done here, to customize it for your use.

Figure 16-7 This simple Quick Step shortcut moves the currently selected item (or items) to a designated folder and sets a follow-up flag for next week.

TROUBLESHOOTING

Quick Steps you created don't appear on the Home tab

Each Outlook data file has its own collection of Quick Steps. If your profile contains multiple email accounts, the choices available in the Quick Steps group on the Home tab change depending on the account you're working with. If you created a Quick Step for an Office 365 account and you want to use the same actions with your Outlook.com account, you need to create a duplicate Quick Step in the second account.

Chapter 16

Most of the default Quick Step options are easy to figure out from the name. The To Manager and Team Email Quick Steps are most useful if you're connected to a Microsoft Exchange server, in which case Outlook is able to retrieve the necessary information automatically from the global address list; if you use another type of mail server, you can delete these shortcuts or configure them manually.

The most interesting Quick Steps are the ones you build from scratch. You can start with the Create New button in the Quick Steps gallery, or click the Custom option at the bottom of the New Quick Step menu. That brings up the Edit Quick Step dialog box, which is divided into three parts:

- **Name**   This box contains a generic description (My Quick Step initially). Change this to a short, descriptive name. Remember that only the first 15 characters are visible in the Quick Steps gallery on the Home tab, so choose a name accordingly.

- **Actions**   You create the first action by choosing from a drop-down list that contains 25 choices in six categories. Some actions are straightforward: Mark As Read and Create A Task With Text Of Message, for example, do exactly what their names say. Other actions, such as Categorize Message, include additional options. Click Add Action and repeat the previous process for the second action, and so on, until you've built the entire sequence of actions for the Quick Step. (You can include up to 12 actions in a single Quick Step, although we find it difficult to imagine any plausible scenario where you would need that many actions.)

- **Optional**   You can assign numeric shortcuts to up to nine Quick Steps, using Ctrl+Shift in combination with the numbers 1 through 9. You can also add descriptive text that appears in a ScreenTip when you hover the mouse pointer over the Quick Step button.

Figure 16-8 shows a simple Quick Step under construction. Its list of actions starts by creating an appointment from the message text, then marking it read, and finally deleting the message.

Figure 16-8 Starting from a blank Quick Step, build a sequence of actions by choosing from the categorized list shown here.

Quick Steps can be an incredible time-saver if you have a sales or support job that involves "canned" responses to email requests. Choose the Reply action and click Show Options to see the full dialog box shown in Figure 16-9. We've filled in the body of the message in the Text box and also set a follow-up flag for Next Week. In this case, we haven't selected the Automatically Send After 1 Minute Delay option; leaving this check box clear allows us to personalize the message or tweak the boilerplate text to make the reply seem more personal.

Chapter 16

Figure 16-9 Use the Reply action to create one-click responses to routine email requests, optionally adding a shortcut key and ScreenTip.

Outlook Quick Steps don't allow you to connect to other Office programs, so you can't send an email message to OneNote or Word as part of the sequence of actions in a Quick Step.

To edit an existing Quick Step, right-click its button on the Home tab, and then click the Edit command at the top of the shortcut menu. From this same menu, you can also duplicate or delete the Quick Step you're pointing to or open the Manage Quick Steps dialog box.

INSIDE OUT   Organize Quick Steps for easy access

If you use Quick Steps extensively, you'll want to think carefully about how you organize your collection. Each new Quick Step moves to the top position in the Quick Steps group on the Home tab, where buttons appear in columns of three. Depending on the width of the Outlook window, you might see as few as three or as many as a dozen individual Quick Steps on the Home tab itself. The others are in the gallery, available with a click of the More arrow in the lower-right corner of the Quick Steps list. Use the Manage Quick Steps dialog box to change the order of items in the list so that the ones always visible on the Home tab—and thus truly a single click away—are at the top of the list, with names that make it easy to see exactly what each one does. And if you bristle at the thought of having to switch back to the Home tab to get to your Quick Steps gallery, right-click the Quick Steps group label, and then click Add To Quick Access Toolbar. Click the lightning-bolt button to choose a Quick Step without having to use the ribbon.

Using rules to manage messages automatically

Where Quick Steps are manual, rules are fully automatic. Most rules are designed to check incoming messages to see whether they meet specific conditions and, if they do, automatically take a defined action, such as moving those messages to another folder. Rules can also help you file outgoing messages, and you can create "housekeeping" rules to periodically sweep your Inbox or archive folders of clutter.

The most common use of rules is to move low-priority messages out of your Inbox as soon as they arrive, filing them in their own folders (but leaving them marked unread) so you can read them at your convenience. This is a great way to handle newsletters, messages from busy mailing lists, or sales pitches from online vendors.

INSIDE OUT Take advantage of the Unread Mail search folder

If you use rules to sort new, low-priority incoming message into folders, you might only want to monitor your Inbox during the workday, leaving low-priority messages for when you're free to think about things other than work. To gather all your new messages into a single view, use the Unread Mail search folder. (See "Creating and using search folders" later in this chapter for details on how to create it.) Arrange this view by folder, and you can quickly scan what's new by folder. If a particular low-priority folder is full and your time is in short supply, just mark all messages in that folder as read and move on.

The simplest way to create a new rule is to start with an existing message that matches the conditions you want to use. On the Home tab, in the Move group, click Rules. That displays a short menu like the one shown here.

The option to move messages from the sender is always available. If the message was sent to an email address other than the one associated with the current data file, that option is available here. Use that option to quickly create a rule to handle messages sent to a mailing list that you belong to.

If one of the options here will do the trick—if you always want notifications from Facebook to go into your Facebook folder, for example—then click that option and choose a destination folder (or create a new folder) in the Rules And Alerts dialog box. Outlook immediately creates the rule and runs it against the contents of the current folder, moving other messages that match your condition to the folder you just specified.

What if the condition you want to use as the trigger for your rule isn't on the short menu? In that case, click Create Rule, which opens the dialog box shown here. It offers a slightly expanded set of actions and conditions. Choose at least one condition from the top half of the Create Rule dialog box and at least one action from the bottom half, click OK, and you're done.

In this example, we trimmed away unnecessary parts of the subject and then selected the top two check boxes. Now, any message that arrives from Facebook and contains the words *notifications pending* will be automatically moved to its own folder.

For full access to all the capabilities of Outlook's rules engine, click the Advanced Options button at the bottom of the Create Rule dialog box. That opens the Rules Wizard, where you can build your rule by clicking through its four somewhat cluttered pages. On each page, you select from a list of options in the top of the page and view a rule description in the box at the bottom. When a condition or action requires additional details, click the blue link in the description box at the bottom to fill in those details.

First, you select the conditions to check for. The list of more than 30 options here is impressive; for example, if you want to define special treatment for any messages sent by anyone in your organization, you can use the With Specific Words In The Sender's Address condition and specify your company's domain.

Next, you specify the actions to perform, as shown in Figure 16-10.

Chapter 16

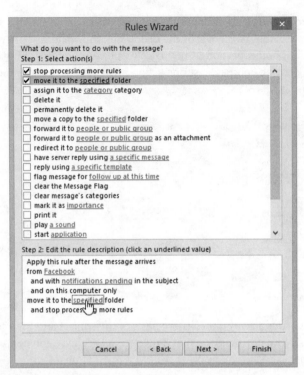

Figure 16-10 For conditions or actions that require input from you, click the "specified" link in the box at the bottom and choose a folder name, enter text or a date range, or provide other necessary details.

On the third page, you specify any exceptions to the rule—for example, you might want to automatically file any messages sent to a particular mailing list unless they're also addressed directly to you.

The wizard's final page allows you to specify a name for the new rule and gives you one last chance to review its conditions before enabling it and, optionally, running it on the contents of the Inbox.

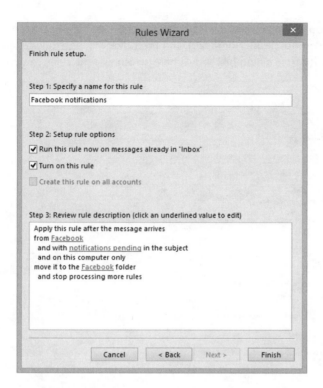

CAUTION

The Permanently Delete It action is a powerful alternative to the more conventional Delete It action. Maybe too powerful, in fact. What's the difference? Delete It moves the targeted messages to the Deleted Items folder; Permanently Delete It bypasses that safety net and removes the selected message or messages completely, with no option of recovery. We strongly recommend against using the Permanently Delete It action with rules that apply to incoming messages because of the risk that you will inadvertently delete an important message. Instead, use this action with cleanup rules that you run manually after making a good backup of your data files.

Chapter 16

To manage rules you've already set up, or to create a new rule based on a template, click Rules (in the Move group on the Home tab), and then click Manage Rules & Alerts. That opens the Rules And Alerts dialog box shown here, which lists the rules you previously created.

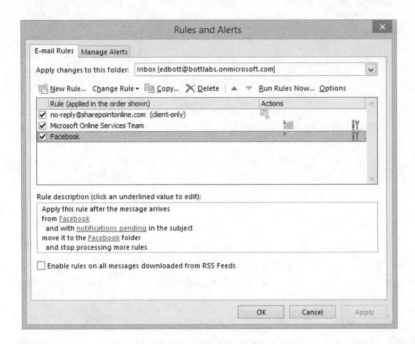

The New Rule button offers a set of templates before proceeding to the full-blown Rules Wizard. Click Change Rule to choose from a group of options for editing the currently selected rule. The Move Up and Move Down arrows (just to the left of Run Rules Now) are so subtle that you might miss them. But these options are extremely important for ensuring that your most important rules run first. If you have created a rule that trumps all others—such as one that flags messages from your manager as High importance if they contain any of the words *urgent, now,* or *important*—you want it to run first, and you don't want the same message to be processed by another, lower-priority rule. For best results, move the primary rule to the top of the list and make sure it includes Stop Processing More Rules as its final action.

Mastering Outlook search

Outlook's search capabilities are, in our estimation, pretty close to magical, living up to the feature's formal name, Instant Search. On even the most modest modern hardware, Outlook should be able to locate a message, a contact name, or an appointment instantly, or very nearly so, even with large Outlook data files.

The secret of this search engine's success is that it works with Windows Search, which is a core feature of Windows 7 and Windows 8. Outlook items are indexed along with documents, pictures, and other files and folders in your user profile. In Windows 8, the search index is unified, but the capabilities to search for Outlook items outside Outlook itself have been removed.

You'll find a search box above the list pane in the Mail, People, and Tasks views and above the contents pane in Calendar view. Click in the search box (or press Ctrl+E) and begin typing to kick off a search. Because this is a word-wheel (or "search as you type") search, the results of your search appear instantly (or at least very quickly), and any matches are highlighted in yellow.

To clear a search and restore the full view of all items in the current folder, click the X to the right of the search box, click Close Search on the Search tab, or just press Esc.

As soon as you click in the search box, Outlook displays the Search tab (under the orange Search Tools heading). After you see the initial results, you can fine-tune your search to change its scope—so that it looks in subfolders of the current folder or in other folders that contain items of the same type, for example—or adding filters so that it returns a reasonable number of results.

The exact options available on the Search tab vary depending on the item type for the current folder. Figure 16-11, for example, shows what you see when you click in the search box with your Mail view open.

Figure 16-11 You can refine any search by using options on the Search tab. Choose an option in the Scope group to expand or narrow which folders and items are searched.

Changing the scope of a search

When you type in the search box, Outlook compares your search string against the contents of the current folder, with one exception: if you're viewing the contents of your Inbox, anything you type in the search box returns results that match messages in the current mailbox, including those in other folders or subfolders.

You can change the scope of your search in either of two ways. Use the commands in the Scope group, at the left of the Search tab, or click the arrow at the right of the search box to display the drop-down list shown here.

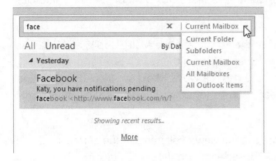

- **Current Folder**   This option is normally selected when you click in the search box— unless you change the default using the steps we describe in this section.

- **Subfolders**   If you've created subfolders within your Inbox, their contents are not normally searched. Click this option to change the current scope so that it includes the current folder and all subfolders, but no other locations.

- **Current Mailbox**   This option is on by default in the Inbox, where Outlook returns search results for any item in any mail folder that matches your request.

- **All Mailboxes**   Use this option if you have multiple mailboxes set up in your profile and you want to find a message from a specific sender, or one that contains specific keywords, regardless of which account it was received in.

- **All Outlook Items**   Use this option when you want to find every Outlook item (messages, meetings, tasks, people, and so on) that contains your search term in any of its main fields (names, addresses, subject, and message body, for example).

If your email arrives via multiple mailboxes and you don't need to keep them separate, you might prefer to set the default search scope to include all folders. You'll find this setting on the Search tab in the Outlook Options dialog box (click File and then click Options). Change the first setting under the Results heading to All Mailboxes to always start with an expanded search.

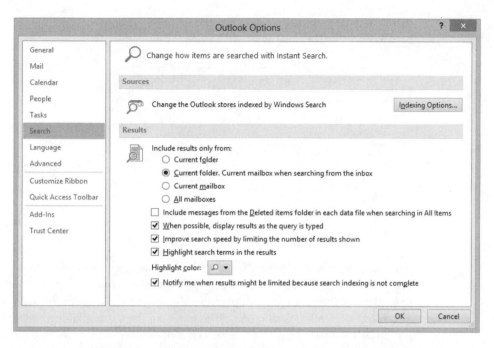

Note that the light gray text in the empty search box always displays your current search scope: for example, Search Current Mailbox (Ctrl+E).

> For more on how to create and configure rules that move incoming messages into folders automatically based on their contents or the sender's name, see "Using rules to manage messages automatically" earlier in this chapter.

Adding criteria to a search

If you simply begin typing in the search box, Outlook returns an item in the results list if your search text matches any of the main fields in that item: sender or recipient name, subject, body, and so on. Partial matches succeed if the search text appears at the beginning of a word in an item, but not if it's in the middle of a word. So, searching for *ed* turns up email messages sent or received by Ed Bott but not those from Pedro Ferreira; it returns those containing the word *editor* in the message body but not those containing *shipped*. If your search term contains two or more words separated by spaces, Outlook treats each word as a separate search term and returns only results that contain all of the terms in your list. To find a phrase, enclose it in quotation marks.

If you want to search only within a specific field, use the options in the Refine group on the Search tab. As we noted earlier, the available options are different depending on the item type you're currently viewing, and they represent a subset of all the properties available for that item type. In some cases you can choose from a drop-down list, such as the Search For Mail By Received Date list, as shown here.

If the exact field you're looking for isn't in the Refine group, click More to see a list of all available search properties. This list also includes the top options that are highlighted in the Refine group. This is not just a duplication of what you can do with the main options on the Refine tab—instead, selecting one of these options adds it as a fill-in-the-blanks field or list just below the search box. This creates a custom search form like the one shown in Figure 16-12, which is ideal for filtering a Contacts folder filled with many items. In this example, we filtered the list to search using any combination of First Name and Last Name.

Figure 16-12 Adding search fields creates the equivalent of a custom search form. This arrangement of fields reappears when you return to this view and click in the search box, even if you restart Outlook.

Search fields you add this way remain in place and are available the next time you search for that item type. You can have separate arrangements of search fields—essentially custom search forms—for each item type.

The techniques we've described so far represent ways to automatically build a search query in the search box by using keywords and criteria that can be combined for extremely fine-grained results. In the next section, we look more closely at the syntax for this powerful feature.

Building search queries with keywords

The Instant Search query syntax isn't particularly difficult to master. Each individual element in a query consists of a keyword that defines which field to search, followed by a colon and (optionally) an operator (an equal sign or greater than/less than sign), followed by criteria that define what to search for. Some keywords use text strings as criteria, others accept dates (or text that represents specific date ranges, such as *next week*), and still others use a simple yes/no syntax. You can combine multiple keyword/criteria pairs to build refined searches that zero in on exactly what you're looking for. This, for example, is a search query that finds all messages in the currently defined search scope that were received in the current month, have one or more file attachments, and contain the word *confirmation* in the message body:

```
hasattachment:yes received:this month contents:=confirmation
```

Note the use of the equal sign, which specifies that the exact text must be used for the comparison; without that equal sign, the result would return any word that begins with that text (both *confirmation* and *confirmations*). In this example, each keyword/criteria combination is separated from its neighbors by a space, which functions the same as the Boolean operator AND. (Outlook is smart enough to ignore the space in *this month* and treat it as the criteria for the *received* keyword.) You can also use OR and NOT as operators, with or without parentheses. The following example returns messages sent in March or April of the current year, from any sender whose name or email address includes a word that starts with Carl or Ed, unless the subject contains the word *confirmation* or *confirmations*.

```
from:(Carl OR Ed) sent:March OR April NOT subject:confirmation
```

For all these Boolean operators, you must use capital letters. If you enter *and, or,* or *not* in lowercase letters, the search engine treats them as normal text.

For date ranges, numbers, or text, you can use the equal sign (=), greater than sign (>), or less than sign (<). Use these operators in combination to specify a range of dates:

```
sent:>=1/1/2013 <3/15/2013
```

In the case of text, a minus sign has the same effect as the NOT operator. So, *–confirmation* returns a match for anything in the current view that doesn't contain *confirmation* in the subject, body, or message header.

You have a surprising amount of flexibility when entering dates as criteria. You can enter a specific date in any format that Outlook recognizes (based on the Windows regional settings). So, in the United States, you can type 29-Sep, 9/29, or Sep 29, and Outlook will recognize that specific date. You can type a day of the week, fully spelled out or abbreviated (*thursday* works, as does *thu* or *thur*); a month, with or without a year, abbreviated or spelled out (*feb* or *February*); or a year (*sent:2013*).

The following date-related words and phrases also work with any keyword that uses dates for its criteria:

- yesterday

- today

- tomorrow

- last week, last month, or last year

- this week, this month, or this year

- next week, next month, or next year

In all, Outlook supports well over 100 search keywords, most of them specific to one or two item types.

We don't have room in this volume to document all the keywords. But you can see (and copy) most of them for yourself by building searches interactively in Outlook and looking at the results in the search box. If you click the Flagged button and then click Has Attachment, for example, you end up with this syntax:

```
followupflag:followup flag hasattachments:yes
```

INSIDE OUT Keep the message, ditch the attachment

In some cases, you might want to keep an email message that contains important information, but do you really need its big, bulky file attachment in your Outlook data file? If you no longer need the attachment, or if you've saved it to a local drive or a shared network folder, you can remove it without disturbing the message. In the Reading pane or the message window, click the attachment to display it in the preview pane, and then use the Remove Attachment command on the Attachment tab; if you want to save a single file or all attachments before removing them, use the Save As or Save All Attachments command. Use this option after searching for all messages that contain attachments and you can quickly cut the size of your Inbox.

Creating and using search folders

Search folders resemble subfolders but are actually virtual folders designed to work specifically with mail folders. Their contents are assembled dynamically from messages in one or more folders that match conditions you specify. Search folders work on the contents of a single data file only and are saved with that data file.

The Search Folders link for an Outlook data file appears in the Folder pane at the bottom of the folder hierarchy for that file. Initially, the Search Folders node is empty. On the Folder tab, click New Search Folder to display the dialog box shown here.

The New Search Folder dialog box contains 13 default options that you can use to create useful search folders, as well as an option to create a custom search folder. If you use rules to automatically sort incoming messages into folders according to their sender or their content, for example, you can and should use the Unread Mail search folder to see all unread messages in a single view, grouped by folder.

INSIDE OUT   Make a search folder a favorite

You can add search folders to the Favorites list at the top of the Folder pane in Mail view. That's an excellent spot for the Unread Mail search folder. It's also a good location for custom search folders, such as those that show you all mail you received today or this week, or all messages that are flagged for follow-up and are due (or overdue) today.

These ready-made search folders offer limited customization options. If you click Mail From Specific People, for example, you're prompted to choose one or more names from your Address Book (you can also enter a domain name or an email address manually in the From box). For a more comprehensive set of tools for creating a finely tuned search folder, click Create A Custom Search Folder at the bottom of the list in the New Search Folder dialog box, and then click Choose. That opens the Custom Search Folder dialog box shown here.

Give the search folder a short, descriptive name, click Browse to select which folders to search, and then click Criteria to open the Search Folder Criteria dialog box, where you can select criteria using form fields. On the Messages tab, for example, the Time box allows you to choose Sent or Received and then choose from a list that includes Yesterday, Today, In The Last 7 Days, Last Week, This Week, Last Month, and This Month. These dates are always relative to the current date, so a search folder that uses Sent In The Last 7 Days as one of its search criteria always shows exactly one week's worth of email, up to and including the current day. Use this search folder in combination with the search box to quickly find a recent message that contains a particular word or phrase.

INSIDE OUT   Don't overlook simple Find and Filter options for email

You don't need to dive into search tools to perform some simple search tasks. In the message list, you can right-click any item and choose Find Related, which displays a menu of two choices: Messages In This Conversation and Messages From Sender. (The same options are also available if you open a message in its own window; use the Related menu in the Editing group on the Home tab.) You can also refine which items are shown in the current email folder by using the Filter Email menu, in the Find group on the Home tab. Choices here allow you to show messages that meet a certain condition and hide all others. For example, you can choose Unread to filter out messages you've already opened or previewed, or refine the list by date—Today, Yesterday, This Week, and so on.

Outlook 2013 inside out

I F YOU'VE made it this far, congratulations. Outlook isn't just an email program for you—it's an essential work/life management tool. In this chapter, we explain how to personalize Outlook's interface so that you see more of what's important to you at a glance. That means putting favorite mail folders at the top of the Folder pane and pinning details about your favorite contacts to a list on the To-Do Bar, just beneath the at-a-glance view of your calendar.

We also dive into the nuances of follow-up flags, which can be assigned to email messages and to contacts, and reminders you can set for calendar items and tasks. Using this feature correctly means you're less likely to forget important tasks and more likely to have a satisfyingly complete to-do list at the end of the workday.

In our experience, Outlook power users also tend to amass larger-than-average mail collections. If that's you, we recommend you read through our explanation of Outlook's archive and cleanup options.

And finally, we end this part of the book with our absolute favorite tweaks and tips.

Personalizing the Outlook interface

As you've discovered by now, Outlook is essentially four programs in one, and if you use all its capabilities you'll find yourself switching between views frequently. The tweaks and techniques we describe in this section allow you to avoid time-consuming trips to folder lists and menus.

Docking your calendar, contacts, or tasks in the To-Do Bar

Right-click any of the four headings at the bottom of the main Outlook window to display a shortcut menu. By using the top choice on that menu, you can open the selected view in a new window, allowing you to arrange windows side by side so that you can browse your entire calendar while still seeing all of your mail folders. The Options command is a convenient one-click shortcut to the tab for that view in the Outlook Options dialog box.

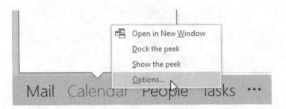

The second option on the shortcut menu for the Calendar, People, and Tasks links allows you to keep an abbreviated view of those items in sight as you browse your mail. In Mail view, for example, click Dock The Peek for Calendar and then for People to create a layout like the one shown in Figure 17-1.

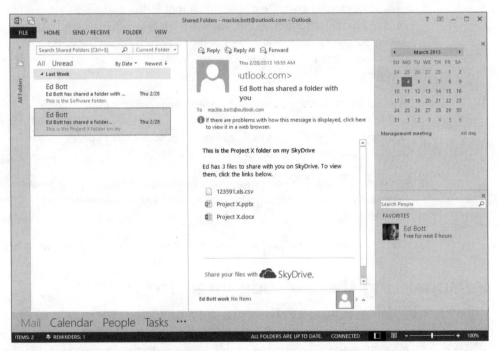

Figure 17-1 Docking the Calendar and People peeks in Mail view gives you quick access to your calendar and your favorite contacts.

These docked arrangements are independent for each view. You can dock the People and Tasks peeks to the Calendar view, for example. In this example, note that we've also cleared some distractions by minimizing the Folder pane on the left and closing the ribbon.

Collectively, the area in which these docked views appear is called the To-Do Bar. You can close any docked portion by clicking the X in its upper-right corner, or hide the entire thing by clicking Off on the To-Do Bar menu (in the Layout group on the View tab).

INSIDE OUT   Put your favorite people on Outlook's "front page"

For most effective use of the People peek, be sure to add your regular contacts as favorites. Right-click any name—in an email message, in People view, or in search results—and click Add To Favorites. From a contact card, click the ellipsis (three dots) in the upper-right corner to find and click the Add To Favorites option. From that point forward, you'll see that person's name and picture in the People peek. If you dock People to your Mail screen, you can keep details about your favorite contacts close, making it easy to call or send mail with just a click or two.

Customizing the Folder pane

In all views, the Folder pane is visible by default on the left side of the Outlook window. In Mail view it contains a list of every data file in the current profile, with a list of folders and subfolders for each that can be expanded or collapsed. The single biggest improvement you can make in the Folder pane in Mail view is to pin the folders you use most often to the Favorites group at the top of the pane. You can drag a folder from the list to the Favorites area and drop it in position, or right-click a folder and click Show In Favorites.

Notice that if you include two identically named folders from different accounts (Inbox, in this example), Outlook helpfully tags each one with the account name, in light gray.

On PCs with a small display size, you can minimize the Folder pane to a slim strip on the left by clicking the arrow in the upper-right corner of the pane. (You can also use the Minimized option on the Folder Pane menu on the View tab.) This gives you more room for working with the contents of the current folder.

When the Folder pane is minimized, an All Folders link appears in all views, in bold letters running sideways up the pane; in Mail view only, you see the first few choices from the Favorites section above All Folders. Click All Folders to display a pop-out view of the Folder pane so you can change folders. After you make a selection, the list disappears again.

To completely hide the Folder pane, click the View tab and select Off from the Folder Pane menu (in the Layout group). Note that any adjustments you make using the Folder Pane menu apply in all views.

To restore the pane to its full width, click the Expand arrow at the upper-right corner of the minimized pane, or use the Folder Pane menu on the View tab.

Using the Reading pane

The Reading pane allows you to click an individual item and preview its contents without having to open that item in its own window. Although it's most obviously useful for reading and replying to email messages, you can use this pane in other views as well, and any customizations you make (whether to show or hide the pane and whether to position it at the bottom or the right of the contents pane) are saved for each view independently.

If you're using Outlook on a portable or desktop PC with a typical widescreen display, the Reading pane works best on the right. Showing the Reading pane on the bottom works best when using Outlook on a tablet in portrait mode.

Clicking Options on the Reading Pane menu (in the Layout group on the View tab) opens the dialog box shown here, where you can control whether and when new messages are marked as read after you view them in the Reading pane.

Creating and saving custom views

Each folder in Outlook has a standard view that defines the arrangement and format of items and the layout of navigation elements. From any folder, you can click the View tab to choose a different predefined view, tweak the currently applied view, or create and save a custom view.

In previous editions of Outlook, custom views represented an essential way to organize your data—in fact, many of the options we talk about here were on the Organize menu in previous editions. In Outlook 2013, you can accomplish most of those same organizational goals much more directly by using Instant Search tools and filters.

We think that most Outlook users will choose a standard view for each folder and then stick with it rather than invest a great deal of time creating and managing custom views. If you need a fresh view of your Contacts folder, you can change the sorting and grouping of data temporarily—to group your Contacts folder by company, for example, so you can see how many of your contacts work at each one. If you find yourself using that view regularly, you can save it as a custom view.

INSIDE OUT   Be more productive with multiple Outlook windows

If you regularly use two or more Outlook views—Mail and Calendar, for example—consider keeping each view open in a separate window. In the Folder pane, right-click any folder or view icon, and then click Open In New Window. For these secondary windows, such as those for the Contacts or Tasks view, you can make the most economical use of space by hiding the Folder pane and collapsing the ribbon. This configuration also allows you to arrange windows side by side. That arrangement makes it easy to see openings and conflicts on your calendar as you reply to email messages from clients or customers. It also allows you to drag contacts or email items into your calendar to create appointments.

The view options we discuss in this section work with all Outlook item types. In most cases, you'll find the options on the View tab, where the exact choices vary by folder. If you click Change View, you see a list of all the predefined views for folders of the current item type. Figure 17-2 shows this menu for the Calendar, where you can choose one of four predefined views. In this example, we've switched from the default Calendar view to List view.

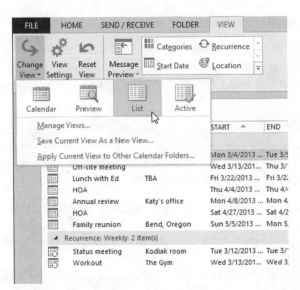

Figure 17-2 In List view, you can see more items than in the conventional Daily/Weekly/Monthly Calendar views. Use the Search box to filter the list.

In List view, items are normally grouped. In this example, the default grouping is by the Recurrence Pattern field, which divides appointments into those that occur once and those that recur at regular intervals. To change the grouping—for example, to see all appointments by location, right-click a list heading and click Group By This Field, as shown here.

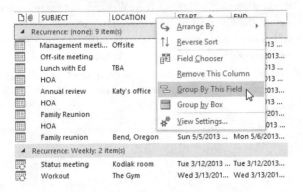

You can group by multiple fields, with groupings shown by field names in the Group By box above the list. Right-click a field name in the Group By box and click Don't Group By This Field to remove it from the grouping settings.

To save your custom view settings so you can reuse them later, click Change View (in the Current View group on the View tab) and then click Save Current View As A New View, which adds it to the menu of defined views.

For views of Mail folders, the predefined views are Compact, Single, and Preview, which define how many lines are used in the message list. Use the Arrange By options (in the Arrangement group on the View tab) to change the sort order. The Show In Groups option is available for all item types, but only in table views such as the three message views used to display email.

To restore the default sort/group orders, click Reset View (in the Current View group on the View tab).

Viewing email conversations

One setting on the View tab in Mail folders deserves some special discussion. If the Show As Conversations check box (in the Messages group) is selected, Outlook automatically pulls together messages and replies (even, in some cases, when those messages are in other folders, such as Sent Items) and displays them in a threaded view, with the most recent message at the top. Any conversation that includes even a single unread message has a bold heading in the message list, as shown next.

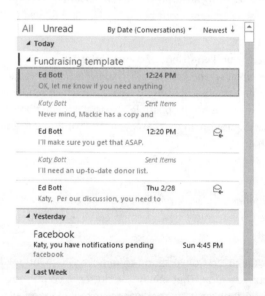

Conversation view in Outlook 2013 is greatly simplified compared with its confusing presentation in Outlook 2010, where the feature debuted. Even so, the initial view can be confusing if you're used to a purely chronological order for your Inbox. If you don't like Conversation view, you can turn it off by clearing the Show As Conversations check box.

Chapter 17

TROUBLESHOOTING

Some of your conversations are broken

Conversation view (introduced in Outlook 2010 and available in Outlook 2013 as well) is based on properties that are defined as part of an Internet standard. The behavior differs in Outlook depending on what email server (or service) delivered a particular message to your Inbox. Here's a quick summary:

For Internet Mail (POP and IMAP), Outlook attempts to build a Conversation-ID property based on the SMTP Message-ID property. If the References field contains a message ID (indicating that the message is a reply in a thread), this property is based on the first message ID in the References field. Most PC-based mail clients support this behavior; however, some webmail clients mangle the References field and thus cause Outlook to treat replies as new threads.

With Exchange Server 2007 and earlier, Outlook behaves as prior versions of Outlook would have, using the PR-Conversation-Topic property to group the mail (this property is most often equivalent to the subject). In this configuration, you will likely see conversations grouped by subject only.

A server running Exchange Server 2010 or 2013 looks at the Message-ID, References, and In-Reply-To properties to set or fix an appropriate Conversation-ID on incoming messages. If Outlook sees that a conversation is being tracked and tagged in this way, it uses that information.

If you see unusual or apparently broken strings of conversations in your Inbox, the most likely cause is a quirky email server somewhere in the chain of messages. It might take some advanced testing and troubleshooting to figure out which sender is to blame, and fixing the problem might not be possible, especially if you don't have direct control over that server's configuration. In that case, your best option is to turn off conversation tracking for that view.

If you occasionally feel overwhelmed by work-related email, we can suggest two good reasons to persevere through the Conversation view learning curve. Both of them are in the Delete group on the Home tab.

Click Clean Up, and then click Clean Up Conversation to remove what Outlook identifies as redundant messages in a conversation. That minimizes clutter in your Inbox, but it also runs the risk of deleting an important message that was mistakenly tagged as redundant. To lessen that risk, you can adjust the Conversation Clean Up options (click File, then click Options, and look about halfway down the Mail tab).

Conversation Clean Up

Cleaned-up items will go to this folder: [   ]   Browse...
Messages moved by Clean Up will go to their account's Deleted Items.
- [ ] When cleaning sub-folders, recreate the folder hierarchy in the destination folder
- [ ] Don't move unread messages
- [x] Don't move categorized messages
- [x] Don't move flagged messages
- [x] Don't move digitally-signed messages
- [x] When a reply modifies a message, don't move the original

If you prefer to be able to recover cleaned-up messages, click the Browse button and select a backup folder where you want the cleaned-up messages to be preserved.

Setting follow-up flags and reminders

Many Outlook items are ephemeral: read, delete, move on. Others, though, demand follow-up at some future date. To ensure that attention is paid when it's due, click Follow Up, which is available in the Tags group on the Home tab for an email message or a contact item. (For tasks, the Follow Up options get their own group on the Home tab, and calendar items don't need flags; instead they use start and end times as well as reminders.)

Clicking Follow Up allows you to add an item to the To-Do list at the top of Tasks view. For some account types, you can optionally set an item's Due Date field using any of the half-dozen options at the top of the menu, as shown here. (For messages and contacts in an Outlook.com/Hotmail or Gmail account, these options are not available.)

Choosing Today or Tomorrow has an obvious effect on the Due Date field. If you choose This Week or Next Week, Outlook sets the Due Date field to the last day of your work week—Friday, unless you change this default.

TROUBLESHOOTING

In Gmail and Outlook.com, the Follow Up menu shows only a single choice

Outlook displays the full range of Flag options on messages from an account on a Microsoft Exchange server, including Office 365, or from a POP account. But these options are not available on Outlook.com (Hotmail) accounts, or on any IMAP account, including those on Google's Gmail service. For messages associated with these account types, Outlook supports only the most basic form of flagging: click Flag Message from the Follow Up menu to add the item to your To-Do list, and click Clear Flag to remove the item from that list. The Mark Complete option is unavailable, as are the date-related options in the Follow Up group on the Task List tab. Fortunately, there is a workaround. Move or copy the message from the folder in the data file associated with your IMAP account to an Outlook data file associated with a supported account type. The same email message, stored in this alternative location, supports all Flag options.

A flag consists of four properties, including a Reminder date and time. You can see (and change) any of these four settings in the Custom dialog box. If you click the Custom option on the Follow Up menu, Outlook opens this dialog box without changing any settings. If you click Add Reminder, Outlook opens the Custom dialog box and selects the Reminder check box, if necessary. Reminders are tremendously useful if you want Outlook to nag you when an item is due (or overdue) for follow-up. You can also change the text that appears in the Reminders window. Figure 17-3 shows a to-do item under construction.

Figure 17-3 Click the Reminder check box and set the exact date and time when you want Outlook to nag you about the current flagged item.

The four properties of a flag that you can edit are as follows:

- **Flag To** The default text is *Follow up*, and for most items this will probably work fine. Choose one of the other options in this list or enter your own text if you want a more detailed description of why you flagged an item. This text appears at the beginning of the InfoBar at the top of any flagged item and at the top of the Reminders window for the selected item. For a flagged contact item, you might choose Call or Send Email as the Flag To text.

- **Start Date**   Outlook fills in this field by using a default value if you choose one of the ready-made options on the Follow Up menu. Use this field for a rudimentary form of project management. If you estimate that a project will take two weeks, you can fill in a start date based on the due date. If you make use of this field, add Tasks to the To-Do Bar and click the Arrange By heading in the Task list to change the grouping to Start Date or back to Due Date.

- **Due Date**   This field is filled in automatically when you choose Today, Tomorrow, This Week, or Next Week. As with the other date-related fields in this dialog box, you can use a calendar control to pick a date. In the Custom dialog box, click the arrow to the right of the Due Date field to display the date picker. Use the Today button to fill in today's date, or click None to remove the due date.

- **Reminder**   When you select this check box, you can enter an exact date and time when you want Outlook to pop up a Reminders window with a link to your flagged item and play an accompanying sound. For the date field, click the down arrow and use the familiar date picker. For the time field, you can pick from the drop-down list, with intervals at round half-hour increments (10:00 AM, 5:30 PM), or you can type an exact time (4:55 PM).

INSIDE OUT   What makes Calendar reminders different?

The Reminders window shows flagged items and upcoming appointments and meetings. Reminders for calendar items work differently than their counterparts on flagged messages, contacts, and tasks. To set a reminder directly for any calendar item, use the drop-down Reminder list in the Options group on the Appointment or Meeting tab. Unlike flagged items, for which you can specify the exact time when you want Outlook to pop up a reminder, calendar items only allow reminders that are relative to the start time of the meeting or appointment. You can choose a reminder time from this list—15 Minutes, 3 Days, or 1 Week, for example. You can type your own values in this list as well, provided that you use the proper relative format. So, you can enter 45 Minutes or 5 Days, even though neither option is on the default menu, but you can't use a specific date and time for the reminder on a calendar item. If you try to enter a specific date or time, Outlook simply ignores your input.

Chapter 17

When Outlook is running, it keeps track of reminders you set previously. If Outlook is running when the reminder time rolls around, it opens a Reminders window. (If your PC is turned off or Outlook is not running at the specified time, you see the missed reminders the next time you start Outlook.)

When you see a reminder, you can click Dismiss to clear the reminder for that item and ensure that you don't see it again; click Dismiss All to do the same with every item in the Reminders window. If you want to deal with a reminder later, select the item, pick a time from the list at the bottom of the dialog box, and then click the Snooze button.

The absolute fastest way to flag an email message for follow-up is to click the flag icon at the right of its entry in the message list. By default, this has the same effect as clicking Today on the Follow Up menu. To change this default for messages on an Exchange server or in a local data file associated with a POP account, right-click the Follow Up icon in the message list, then click Set Quick Click, and choose an alternative from the list in the Set Quick Click dialog box.

If you use OneNote, don't overlook that program's strong connections to Outlook, including the ability to link OneNote pages and paragraphs to Outlook tasks. We explain this feature in full in "Using OneNote with Outlook" in Chapter 23, "OneNote 2013 inside out."

Importing, exporting, and archiving Outlook data

There are all sorts of reasons to copy Outlook items. You might want to share a few items (messages or contacts) between different accounts, or make backup copies of important messages or mailboxes, or archive old messages to reduce the size of your local data file.

You can, of course, move items between different folders in the same account by dragging them from one folder to another. You can also drag items to move them into a folder in an Exchange store or .pst file.

You can also drag any Outlook item into a folder in File Explorer to save it as an individual item that you can open later in Outlook. Use this technique to share individual items between different Outlook profiles (even on different PCs). Drag a group of messages or contacts to a folder on a USB key, for example, and you can open that same folder on another PC and drag the saved items directly into an Outlook folder on that computer. (Be sure to keep different types of items separate. In File Explorer, all items you save this way are identified generically as having the file type Outlook Item.)

To copy a large number of messages, contacts, appointments, or tasks to or from Outlook, use the Import And Export Wizard. The path to this utility is simpler than in previous Outlook versions. Click File, then click Open & Export, as shown next.

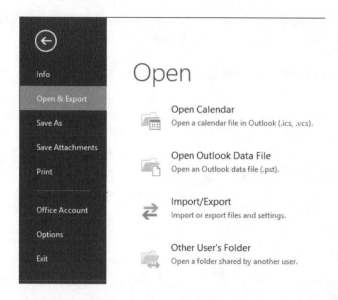

Most of the options on this menu are about opening files. The Import/Export option is the only one that works in the opposite direction as well. Click it to open the Import And Export Wizard, shown here.

Three of the options shown here (one export, two import) are used with Outlook's collection of RSS feeds, a rarely used feature and one we don't cover in this book. Another two options deal with the standard Contact and Calendar formats we discuss later in this chapter (see "Sharing contact and calendar items").

Chapter 17

That leaves the two generic options, Export To A File and Import From Another Program Or File, which we describe in more detail in the balance of this section.

Importing and exporting Outlook items

Unlike previous versions, Outlook 2013 supports only two file types for data transfer: Select Import From Another Program Or File or Export To A File and then click Next to see this limited set of choices.

Comma Separated Values, a standard database format, is usually the best choice when transferring data to a program other than Outlook. Choose Outlook Data File (.pst) if you want to open the file directly in Outlook (in the same profile or in a different Outlook profile, even on a different PC). We explain why this format is so useful in the example that follows.

Click Next to move to the next step of the wizard, where you select the folder or folders from which you plan to export data. The exact options available here depend on the output file type you previously selected. Using a CSV file, you can choose entire folders (including subfolders), but you can't make your selection any more granular. Because we're exporting to a .pst file, however, we have the option to export only a portion of the folder's contents by clicking the Filter button and filling in criteria using the Filter dialog box. Figure 17-4 shows the settings we used to export only contact items where the Company field includes *Lucerne*.

Click Next, and then choose a location for the exported items. The default location is the Outlook Files subfolder in your Documents folder. The default file name is Backup.pst. You can change that name to something more descriptive. If the file name you specify already exists, the items you export are added to the file. Click Finish to complete the export.

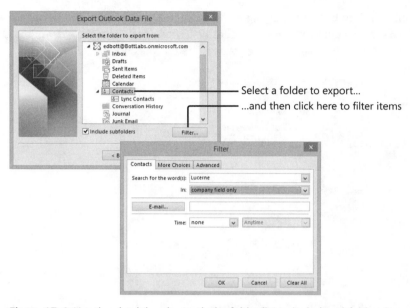

Select a folder to export...

...and then click here to filter items

Figure 17-4 Use the check box beneath the folder list to include subfolders in your export. Click Filter to refine the list of what gets exported—by company name in this example.

INSIDE OUT   How effective is Outlook's password protection?

If you choose Outlook Data File (.pst) as the export file type, you're offered the option to create a password with which to protect the file. This option provides only a basic level of security, mostly intended to prevent a casual snoop from peeking at the contents of the file. A determined data thief would have no problem blowing past that password by using one of the many password-cracking tools available on the Internet. So add a password if you feel like it, but don't expect it to offer real protection for sensitive data. If you can't remember the password for an Outlook data file, we recommend NirSoft's free PstPassword utility to help recover it. Details are at *w7io.com/12305*.

To import saved data from a file into Outlook, you go through a similar process. Select Import From Another Program Or File and then click Next to display the same meager list of two supported file types. Note that you cannot use Outlook to import data into an Outlook.com or IMAP account.

Click Next to browse for the file and choose how you want to handle duplicates. Then click Next to fine-tune your import. Figure 17-5 shows the Contacts folder in the Outlook data file we created earlier, which contains a filtered collection of contact items.

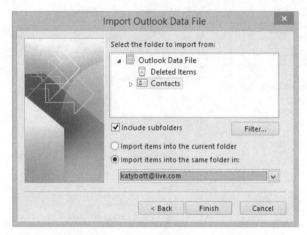

Figure 17-5 Importing information from a .pst file is a straightforward process. Pick the folder to import from, select a destination folder, and then click Finish.

Had we chosen to import a comma-separated values file, we would have had to deal with one additional step: mapping the values in the original file to the fields in the destination folder. If the source data comes from Outlook, this mapping should be perfect. If the source data is from another program, you'll need to drag field names out of the From pane and drop them onto field names in the To pane to set up the correct mapping.

INSIDE OUT   When in doubt, use a temporary folder for imports

Importing large amounts of information incorrectly can make a complete mess of an Outlook folder. If you have even the slightest doubt about the import process, try importing your data to a temporary folder as an intermediate step. Start by creating a new, empty folder to contain the type of items you're importing (on the Folder tab, click New Folder). Then go through the import process, selecting your new, empty folder as the destination. After the import is complete, inspect the folder's contents carefully. If you're satisfied that things went well, you have two choices: you can drag the items out of the temporary folder and move them into their permanent destination, or you can run the import operation again, and this time select the actual destination folder. In either case, when the import is complete, you can safely delete the temporary folder.

Cleaning up your mailbox

Without regular pruning, Outlook data files have a way of growing to gargantuan proportions. Keeping a data file lean improves performance and also makes it easier to perform backups and other maintenance tasks.

Outlook 2013 provides a helpful assortment of tools you can use to clean up a single folder or an entire data file manually. For quick access to this toolkit, click File, select a mailbox from the list beneath the Account Information heading, and then click Cleanup Tools on the Info tab to display the menu shown in Figure 17-6.

Figure 17-6 To manage the size of your Outlook mailbox, start by selecting an account, and then click Cleanup Tools.

Note that if you're connected to an Exchange server and your server administrator has restricted the size of your mailbox, you'll see a bar beneath the Mailbox Cleanup heading (to the right of the Cleanup Tools button) that shows how much of your quota is in use and how much remains available.

Click Mailbox Cleanup to open the dialog box shown in Figure 17-7, which provides centralized access to information about the contents of the currently selected mailbox as well as a variety of management tools.

CAUTION!

If you configure your Outlook profile with multiple email accounts, be sure you select the right account before opening the Mailbox Cleanup dialog box. The options shown here apply to that account only. If you use the AutoArchive option, you can move or permanently delete data in that file. When in doubt, double-check!

Chapter 17

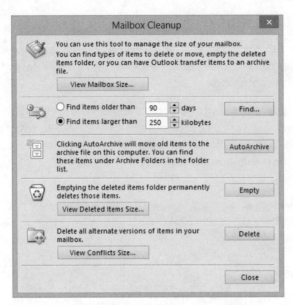

Figure 17-7 Use the options shown here to gather information about the contents of the current mailbox and manually archive or delete items.

The Mailbox Cleanup tools are divided into five groups, each with at least one button:

- **Mailbox size**   Click to open the Folder Size dialog box, which gives you a bird's-eye view of how much space each folder is occupying in the current data file. For Microsoft Exchange accounts, this dialog box includes a second tab (Server Data) that lets you see how much of your server quota is in use.

- **Find**   Choose either of the Find Items options and select settings to archive items based on their age or size. Then click Find to open the Advanced Find dialog box with those settings entered on the Advanced tab, and click Find Now to run the search.

- **AutoArchive**   Clicking this button immediately begins moving and deleting items from the current account, based on your AutoArchive settings, which we describe in more detail later in this section.

- **Deleted Items folder**   Click View Deleted Items Size to see just how much space is being used by items you previously sent to the trash, or click Empty to immediately and permanently remove the contents of the Deleted Items folder.

- **Conflicts**   This section is available only with Microsoft Exchange accounts. (It's not available for other account types.) It shows the size of the Conflicts folder, which contains items that the server was unable to synchronize properly. To view the items in this folder, switch to Folder List view and look under the Sync Issues folder.

Archiving Outlook data

An Outlook archive file is an Outlook data file (with a .pst extension) that is created specifically to store items you want to move out of the file associated with an email account. By default, when you use one of Outlook's archive options, it creates a file named Archive.pst and stores it in the Outlook Files subfolder of your Documents folder. (You can change the name and location of this file when you create it.) When you perform an archive operation, Outlook opens the archive data file and displays it in the Folder pane, where it gets its own Archives node. It remains open until you explicitly close it by right-clicking the Archives heading in the Folder pane and clicking Close "Archives" on the shortcut menu.

You can run archives automatically or manually, using default settings or fine-tuning settings to determine exactly which items are archived.

If you prefer not to be bothered by manual maintenance tasks, you can have Outlook do the work of archiving old items for you automatically on a schedule you determine. Auto-Archive settings are fully customizable on a per-folder basis. You can use default settings for all folders or customize settings for each one individually. Select any folder in the Folder pane and then click AutoArchive Settings (in the Properties group on the Folder tab) to display the dialog box shown in Figure 17-8. In this example, the title bar shows that the settings in question will apply to the Investment Newsletters folder.

Figure 17-8 Use the bottom set of options in this dialog box to fine-tune what Outlook does with that folder's contents when you use the AutoArchive feature.

CAUTION

"Permanently delete" means just that. If you set this option for a folder, its contents will be vaporized when you run AutoArchive. The only way to recover those deleted messages is from a backup copy of the Outlook data file. Use this option on folders that you know for certain contain only nonessential messages.

Setting custom AutoArchive options is especially useful for folders containing messages that you don't need to archive, such as daily email updates from a newspaper or sales pitches from online merchants. For those folders, consider setting the Permanently Delete Old Items option.

By default, the global AutoArchive options clean out items older than six months. If you want to be more or less aggressive than that with your archiving strategy, you can change this setting for all folders in one operation. Start by selecting Archive Items In This Folder Using The Default Settings, and then click the Default Archive Settings button to display the dialog box shown next.

Note that all options here appear dimmed and are unavailable unless you select the Run AutoArchive Every *nn* Days check box. After you do that, you can change the settings under the During AutoArchive heading and then click Apply These Settings To All Folders Now. When that operation is complete, you can leave the Run AutoArchive Every *nn* Days option selected (choosing a different interval if necessary), or clear it and click OK. To perform a manual AutoArchive operation using the current settings, click Archive on the Cleanup Tools menu, select Archive All Folders According To Their AutoArchive Settings, and click OK.

To archive a single folder, click Archive (the last option on the Cleanup Tools menu). Doing so opens the dialog box shown next.

Select a folder from the list, choose a date to use as the cutoff point, and select an archive file as the destination. If the file you choose doesn't exist, Outlook creates it; if the file exists, your archived items are added to that file's contents.

This archiving option works with a single folder and all of its subfolders—you can't cherry-pick multiple folders or subfolders for archiving (although you can archive all folders in a single data file by clicking the top-level folder). Items from the selected folder go to the same location in the archive folder and are deleted from the original file.

INSIDE OUT   For safety's sake, copy (don't move) important items

You can't move system folders, such as the Inbox, and you shouldn't move folders that you intend to keep using. For example, you might have created a subfolder under your Inbox that contains all incoming orders, using a rule to move incoming orders to this folder. A month or two into the new year, you want to archive last year's orders. But your Orders folder already contains some email from this year that shouldn't be moved. The alternative? Don't use the Archive tools. Instead, copy the Orders folder to your archive file, and check to be sure all the messages survived the trip. Then use Instant Search to clean up each copy. In the newly added folder in your archive data file, type **Received:this year** in the search box to find all messages in that folder that are from the current year and don't yet belong in the archives. Delete them. In the Orders folder, do the same thing, except with **Received:last year**.

Chapter 17

When you click OK, the Archive dialog box closes, and you might be momentarily lulled into thinking that nothing's happening. Look closer, and you'll see that Outlook is busy doing your bidding. For starters, look just to the left of the zoom controls in the status bar, where a small message advises you of the progress of your archiving operations, with a bright red X you can click to cancel the archiving. In the Folder pane, you'll see the Archives folder. Click to open that file, and you can see its contents change as items are moved from the original data file into their corresponding archive folders and subfolders.

Our favorite Outlook tweaks and tips

In this section, we include some of our favorite little tweaks for Outlook, ones that don't fit anywhere else but are too good and useful not to mention.

Dealing with duplicate contacts

Having multiple contact items for a single person, each in a different folder and synced with its own account, is inevitable if your mail setup includes multiple accounts. For those cases, you can link the contacts so that their consolidated information appears on the contact card regardless of which linked entry you select.

Outlook does this automatically for contacts in social networks, as long as they have the same email address. You can manually combine items into a single linked card by clicking Link Contacts on the contact card and searching for contacts with similar names.

If you try to add a new contact in a folder and use the same File As name as an existing contact, Outlook intervenes and offers to merge information from the new contact into the existing contact. This works especially well when you get a message from a friend who has updated her email address. Right-click the address in the message header, and click Add To Outlook Contacts. If a contact item with the same File As name already exists, you see a dialog box like the one shown here:

INSIDE OUT   How to merge two contacts into one

As we note in this section, Outlook intercedes if you try to create a new item with the same name as an existing contact. But how do you force this detection if you accidentally create multiple contact items for the same person under slightly different names? The technique is a little tricky.

1. Start by switching to Folder view. In the row of icons below the Folder pane, click the ellipsis (three dots), and click Folders. Find the Outlook data file that contains the items you're working with and click to display its Contacts folder.

2. Scroll or search to find the contact items you're trying to merge, and make sure the Full Name field (the Name box at the top of the contact card) is identical for both contacts.

3. Click to select the contact item whose email address you want to see as the first one in the merged contact. Press Delete. (Don't worry, this is only a temporary step.)

4. Finally, select the Deleted Items folder for the data file you're working with, click the freshly deleted contact item, and press Ctrl+C to copy it to the Clipboard. Return to the Contacts folder, and press Ctrl+V to create a new item from the contents of the Clipboard.

Outlook will offer to merge the two items. If you approve, click Update. This process is surprisingly effective, and it even combines the contents from the Notes field in both items so that you don't lose any important information you inadvertently kept in two places.

Adding and editing email signatures

A signature can add crucial contact details, branding, or a whimsical touch to any message. Typing your name, title, and phone number at the end of every message is a tedious process, and you risk making an embarrassing error if you do this often enough. A much better option is to create and save one or more signatures, any of which can be associated with new messages or replies sent from a specific email account. A signature can include formatted text, hyperlinks, graphics, and HTML markup.

To create a new signature, click the New Email command or open an existing message window. From the Include group on the Message tab, click Signature and then click Signatures. That opens the Signatures And Stationery dialog box. Click New, and give your signature a name (you can change it later). Click in the Edit Signature box, and then enter the text you want to use for your signature, using the formatting tools to adjust fonts and font sizes, change alignment, and insert graphics and hyperlinks. (You can also paste formatted text and graphics into this box.)

Although the built-in signature editor offers a reasonable set of tools, it lacks some capabilities, including the capability to insert tables, horizontal rules, and clip art. All of these capabilities are present in the Outlook email message editor. If you want any of these items to be part of a signature, start with a blank message and use it to create a signature from scratch in the empty message window. You can also start with a signature you created manually in a previous message.

After you've formatted the signature to your satisfaction, select the signature block in the message editor and copy it to the Clipboard. Then open the Signatures And Stationery dialog box and paste your work into the Edit Signature box. Figure 17-9 shows a signature we created using a horizontal rule to set it off from the message text. The clip art is in one cell of a table (with hidden borders), with contact information in a cell to its right. A signature this complex cannot be created directly in the Edit Signature box.

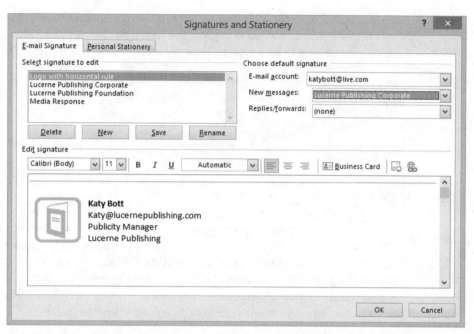

Figure 17-9 Use different signatures for different types of email. This signature, composed in a message window, includes a rule, some clip art, and a hidden table.

To insert a signature from your collection into a message you're composing, click Signature, and then choose the name of the saved signature. To switch to a different signature, right-click the signature block in the message body and choose an alternative from the list of saved signatures.

Juggling multiple time zones

When you create or edit an appointment or a meeting, you have the option to specify a time zone for both the Start Time and End Time fields. This feature was introduced in Outlook 2007, and it solves a longstanding headache caused when you and Outlook travel across the country or around the world.

What's the problem? Consider this scenario. You're leaving Los Angeles on Sunday and flying to Sydney, Australia. Your flight leaves at 10:30 P.M., and you arrive Down Under at 7:20 A.M. on Tuesday. You have a handful of meetings during the day on Tuesday. When you enter times, Outlook assumes that the time you specify is in the current time zone. So, when you change time zones on your portable PC, the times displayed in Outlook change as well. If you were in Los Angeles and entered details for an appointment on Tuesday at 10 A.M., changing the time zone on your PC would change the starting time of that appointment—making you late by 18 hours.

The solution is to click the Time Zones command on the Appointment or Meeting tab and then select the correct time zone for both the start time and end time. That allows your Sydney appointment to be displayed correctly when you change the time on your PC.

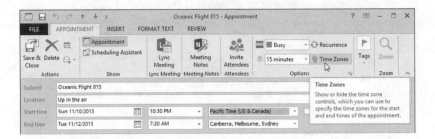

Having multiple time zones in your Outlook calendar solves that problem but causes another one, as you have to continually guess about which time zone you're currently showing. To add a label to the time list on the left of the Calendar window, open the Outlook Options dialog box, click the Calendar tab, and enter descriptive text in the Label box. You can also choose to show an additional time zone in the calendar. That's useful if you're traveling, and also if you work with people in different parts of the world.

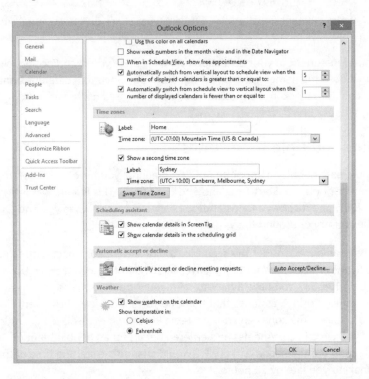

Seeing both time zones allows you to tell at a glance whether you're trying to call a business in Moscow at midnight or Hong Kong at 3:00 A.M., when no one's there to take the call. Figure 17-10 shows the Calendar with two time zones listed to the left of current appointments.

Figure 17-10 If your travels will take you across two or more time zones, add a second time zone to the Calendar view to avoid having to make on-the-fly conversions.

Managing Auto-Complete lists

If you've used Outlook for any length of time, you've probably seen its Auto-Complete feature at work. You've also probably had at least one Auto-Complete fail, in which a message you meant for one person went to someone completely different, whose name just happens to start with the same letters.

When you click and start typing in an address field for a new email message, a list of suggested names and email addresses appears below the field. You can click to accept one of these Auto-Complete suggestions.

Auto-Complete causes problems when you inadvertently select an incorrect address that was saved as a potential shortcut for you, or when a frequent correspondent changes email addresses, making your saved Auto-Complete entry for his or her name incorrect.

Fixing a single incorrect Auto-Complete entry is easy: start typing until you see the incorrect entry and then click the X at the end of the list item. That deletes it immediately.

In Outlook 2007 and earlier, the Auto-Complete list was saved in a file on your PC, with the file name extension .nk2. In Outlook 2010 and 2013, these entries are saved in your Outlook data file (or, for Microsoft Exchange Server accounts, in your mailbox on the server, which allows the same list to appear on any computer where you use Outlook with that account).

To clear the Auto-Complete list and start over, open the Options dialog box (File, Options), click the Mail tab, and click Empty Auto-Complete List, under the Send Messages heading. To stop Outlook from suggesting names in this way, clear the Use Auto-Complete List To Suggest Names When Typing In The To, Cc, And Bcc Lines check box in the same location.

Changing default fonts for new email messages

When you create, reply to, or forward an email message formatted using HTML, any text you enter uses the default font of 11-point Calibri. You can change this look by assigning a theme to your Outlook messages, or you can choose specific fonts, font sizes, font colors, and formatting such as bold or italic. You can also choose different settings for messages you create and for replies and forwards.

You'll find the necessary settings in the Outlook Options dialog box, on the Mail tab. Click the Stationery And Fonts button to bring up the Signatures And Stationery dialog box, shown in Figure 17-11.

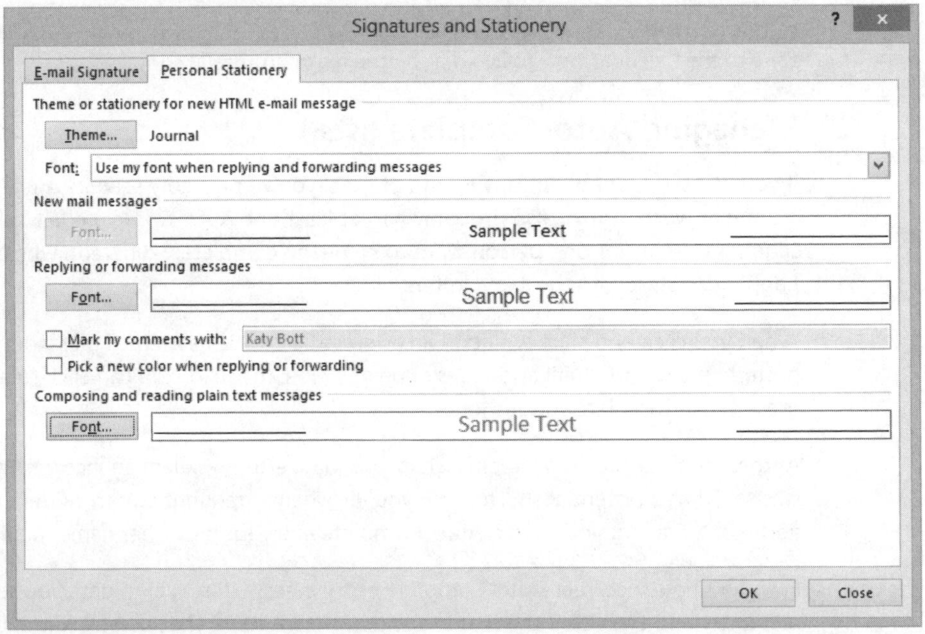

Figure 17-11 If you don't like Outlook's default typeface selections for outgoing HTML-formatted messages, you can change them here.

If you click Theme, you can choose one of the Office-wide themes, which includes body and heading fonts as well as background images, colors, and horizontal rules (but not custom bullet characters). If you prefer your own fonts, you can choose Always Use My Fonts in the Theme Or Stationery For New HTML E-Mail Message section (or use no theme). If you don't use a theme, click the Font button beneath New Mail Messages and Replying Or Forwarding Messages to choose fonts, sizes, and colors for each of those settings.

INSIDE OUT   Choose the right font for your outgoing messages

It's worth making an effort to choose fonts that your recipients can view. If you choose an obscure font, your outgoing messages will look just fine on your PC, but there's no telling what your recipients will see—their PCs will substitute another font when necessary that might or might not have the same visual appeal of your choice.

The best solution is to use any of the fonts in Microsoft's ClearType Font Collection, the six font families designed for and included with all versions of Windows since Windows Vista. (For more details, see *w7io.com/12303*.) The list includes all weights of Constantia, Corbel, Calibri, Cambria, Candara, and Consolas. (We think Candara is especially attractive for email.) If you encounter a friend or coworker who can't see these fonts correctly, they're probably using an old version of Windows and don't have a modern version of Office installed. Suggest that they install one of the free Office viewer programs for Office 2007 or later, all of which include these font families.

Sharing contact and calendar items

You've entered contact information in Outlook, and you want to send it to someone else, without a lot of tedious cut-and-paste work.

You're in luck. Outlook allows you to share contacts with anyone, as Outlook items or in Internet-standard formats specifically designed for data interchange.

Both of these standard formats consist of simple text files, with a syntax that any compatible program can decode. For sharing contact items, Outlook uses the vCard format, which creates a file with the .vcf file name extension. (For more details about the vCard format in Outlook, see the Microsoft Knowledge Base article at *w7io.com/290840*.) For calendar items, Outlook uses the standard iCalendar format.

Why would you want to send someone else an item from your Contacts folder? The most common situation, we suspect, is sending your personal or work-related contact information to someone else via email, just as you would hand them your business card if you were to meet at a trade show. You can also forward another contact's details—if you want an associate to follow up with a prospect you met at a trade show, for example.

To send contact information via email, start in the Contacts folder by selecting one or more items. Then click Forward Contact (in the Share group on the Home tab). You have two options:

- **As A Business Card** The resulting email message contains an embedded image of the card (in JPEG format) and a file attachment in the standard vCard format, with a .vcf file name extension. You can edit the message subject or text before sending. If you receive one of these messages in Outlook, you can right-click the business card image and click Add To Outlook Contacts. Or, as an alternative, double-click to open the item in an Outlook Contact window, where you can add your own notes or edit existing fields before clicking Save & Close.

- **As An Outlook Contact** The resulting email message contains a blank body and an attachment that contains the full Outlook item, with a .msg file name extension. (This is the same format you would get if you dragged the item into File Explorer in Windows.) As long as the recipient has Outlook installed, he or she can double-click to open the contact, make any changes or additions, and then click Save & Close.

To share details of appointments in your Outlook Calendar, the procedure is similar to what you do with a contact. Click the arrow to the right of the Forward command (in the Actions group on the Appointment tab) and then click Forward or Forward As iCalendar. (For meeting requests, you should have the meeting organizer add the recipient to the meeting rather than forward someone else's meeting request details.)

Both options send the item as an attachment to an email message. The Forward command sends your appointment in Outlook item format (with a .msg file name extension). If the recipient has Outlook installed, she can double-click the attachment (or open it in the Reading pane) and then click Copy To My Calendar. Use the Forward As iCalendar option whenever you are not certain whether the recipient has Outlook installed.

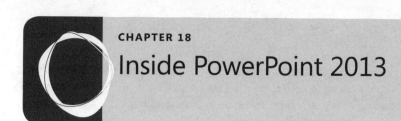

CHAPTER 18

Inside PowerPoint 2013

Easy to use, hard to master. That's been the story of PowerPoint since its earliest days. Anyone can create a simple slide show. How hard is it, after all, to double-click the PowerPoint icon and then click and type inside a box that tells you to do just that? But creating an engaging presentation that doesn't lull your audience to sleep takes more than mere pointing, clicking, and typing.

In PowerPoint 2013, slides are still the basic building blocks of a presentation. You can still add bullet points, charts, tables, and pictures. You're still presented with the familiar boxes labeled "Click to add text." What's different is the inclusion of more ways to work with rich media, including online media. You can edit photos, video, and audio within PowerPoint. PowerPoint 2013 also includes new options for sharing your presentation with a wider audience, whether via SkyDrive or with a live presentation over the Internet.

Add it all up, and you'll see that the features in PowerPoint 2013 make it possible for occasional PowerPoint users to go beyond basic slide shows. PowerPoint has evolved into a versatile communication tool that works for a broad range of uses: sharing family vacation photos, creating polished reports for the classroom, or preparing sales and marketing presentations for a business of any size.

In this chapter, we'll whiz through the essential tasks of building a presentation, adding interesting graphical elements to your slides, and customizing the overall design. In the chapters that follow, we'll tackle the tasks of delivering your presentation—in person or over a network.

What's in a PowerPoint presentation?

A PowerPoint presentation comprises a collection of *slides*, where each slide is a screenful of information. A slide can contain text, graphics, tables, videos, animations, charts, and links—in short, anything that can be presented in two dimensions within the confines of a computer screen.

The best PowerPoint presentations include just enough detail to get your point across and the right balance of visual interest to hold someone's attention for the duration. An effective strategy for developing a compelling presentation is to start with a slide (or two), create a rough outline and a basic design, preview and save regularly as you flesh out your ideas, and add audio and video elements as the final step.

Figure 18-1 shows a slide in Normal view, the view you use most for developing presentations. In this view, you see each slide individually, with the current slide filling the main part of the window. The Notes pane below the slide allows you to add speaker notes, and the Navigation pane shows a thumbnail of each slide in the current presentation.

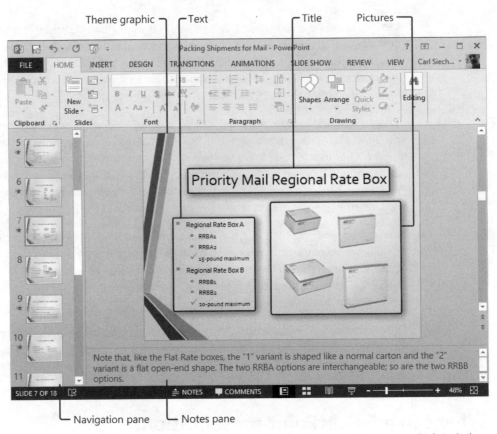

Figure 18-1 This slide, shown in Normal view, uses the Two Content slide layout, which includes an area for the title and two blocks for text or other elements.

Working in an appropriate view

Although most of your design work is done in Normal view, PowerPoint has several other views better suited to particular tasks. You can switch between the most frequently used views by clicking icons in the status bar at the bottom of the PowerPoint window, as shown in Figure 18-2.

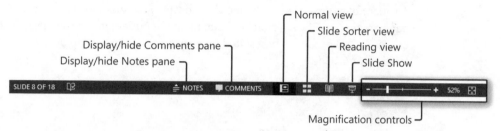

Figure 18-2 Common view options are available at the lower-right corner of the window. Additional view options appear on the View and Slide Show tabs.

You can switch to Normal, Slide Sorter, or Reading view by using tools in the Presentation Views group on the View tab, as shown in Figure 18-3. This group of tools also includes a Notes Page view and is alongside the Master Views group you can use to create new slide layouts.

Figure 18-3 The View tab offers options not available in the status bar, including Notes Page view and access to master slide views.

The sections that follow provide more detail about each view.

Normal view

Normal view, shown earlier in Figure 18-1, is the most common view for working with each slide and its individual elements. In Normal view, which is the only view that gives you access to the full set of tools for working with text and placeholder objects on individual slides, you can edit text, manage placeholders, and set animations and transitions.

In Normal view, the Navigation pane appears at the left. Click a thumbnail in the Navigation pane to jump to a particular slide. Drag slides within this pane to reorder them, or right-click and use shortcut menu commands to copy, delete, and duplicate slides.

Chapter 18

Drag the border between the panes to change the relative size of the Navigation pane. Likewise, you can drag the border to resize the Notes pane at the bottom of the screen, which you show or hide by clicking Notes in the Show group on the View tab or by clicking the Notes icon in the status bar.

Outline view

A variant of Normal view is Outline view, in which the thumbnail images of the Navigation pane are replaced by a hierarchical outline of the presentation's slide text, as shown in Figure 18-4. Outline view is best suited for viewing and editing slide titles and one set of bulleted text per slide.

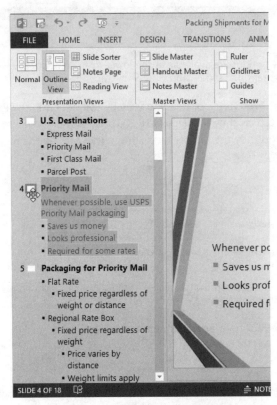

Figure 18-4 Dragging slides in the Navigation pane in Outline view reorders them. If you move the text of one slide directly into the middle of another slide, PowerPoint adjusts the outline hierarchy.

In Outline view, you can manipulate the slide and bullet hierarchy without cutting and pasting text across multiple slides and placeholders. Edit your text directly in the outline pane; edits to the currently displayed slide appear in the slide as you type.

As in Normal view, you can change the order of slides in Outline view. To move a slide, select the small slide icon to the left of any slide title. When the pointer changes to a four-headed arrow, drag it to the new location in the outline hierarchy. By pointing to the left end of slide text, you can use the same dragging technique to move text from one slide to another. Dragging text to the left or right promotes or demotes the text in the outline hierarchy.

INSIDE OUT   Formatting text using Outline view

When working with Outline view, you can select multiple bulleted lines at the same time by holding down the Ctrl key as you click to select slide titles or bullets. Use tools on the Home tab to apply custom formatting to all the items in your selection. You can't reorder noncontiguous bullets in this way, but it does make quick work of what would otherwise be a series of repetitive formatting operations.

INSIDE OUT   Maximize your editing space by hiding panes

One of the downsides to working with Outline view is the size of the pane on the left, which in its default configuration is just too narrow for serious work. You can drag the divider bar to the right to give yourself some more space. However, when you're making large-scale text edits, you might prefer to hide the Slide pane and allow the outline to use the full PowerPoint window. To do that, hold down Ctrl and Shift and click the Slide Sorter view button on the status bar. Hold down Ctrl and Shift and click the Normal view button on the status bar to hide the Navigation pane and the Notes pane and show just the Slide pane, with full access to all editing tools.

Slide Sorter view

When you need to work with more slides than you can see in the thumbnails in the Navigation pane in Normal view, switch to Slide Sorter view, shown in Figure 18-5. In this view, you work with entire slides rather than with the individual placeholders. Because Slide Sorter view lets you see so many of the slides in your presentation, it makes quick work of rearranging slides by dragging and dropping.

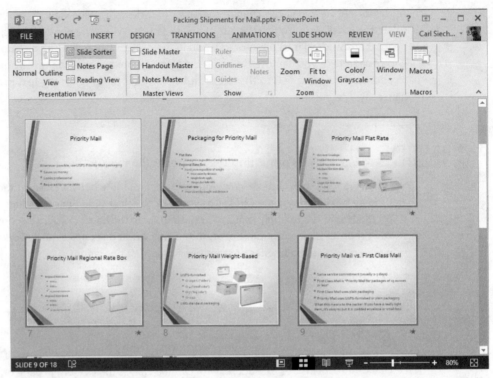

Figure 18-5 Use the Zoom slider to change the size of thumbnails in Slide Sorter view and increase or decrease the number of slides you can see at one time.

In Slide Sorter view, you can duplicate one or more slides by selecting them and pressing Ctrl+D. The duplicated slides appear immediately after the last slide in your selection; the new slides are selected so that you can drag them to a new location if necessary. You can also apply transitions to multiple slides (contiguous or otherwise) or to all slides in the presentation.

To return to Normal view, double-click the thumbnail of the slide you want to edit.

Reading view

Reading view, shown in Figure 18-6, is like Slide Show view (described later in this chapter), with one difference: it displays your slides within the confines of a window rather than filling the screen. This view lets you see how your slide show looks while you work with other programs alongside the presentation, such as a supporting document in Word. Reading view is literally read-only: you can't make any changes to text or content.

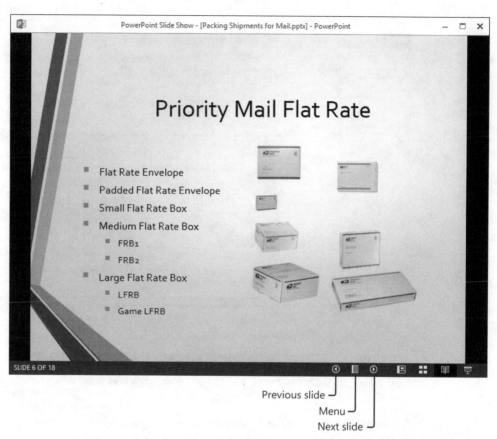

Figure 18-6 In Reading view, you see each slide, absent speaker notes and thumbnails for other slides.

Advance through your presentation by using the Next and Previous buttons in the status bar. Press Escape to return to your previous view.

Notes Page view

In Normal view, you can display a small pane just below the slide where you can enter and review presentation notes. Some people use this as a place to keep their presentation script, whereas others use it to store agenda topics or key points they want to be sure to mention. If you're creating a training presentation, this is also a good place for additional details that are simply too long to place directly on the slide.

As shown in Figure 18-7, Notes Page view gives you a larger area to type and format your speaker notes or presentation handouts. This view lets you see exactly how much text fits on a printed page. However, the only text editing you can do in this view is to your notes; you can't make changes to your slides.

Chapter 18

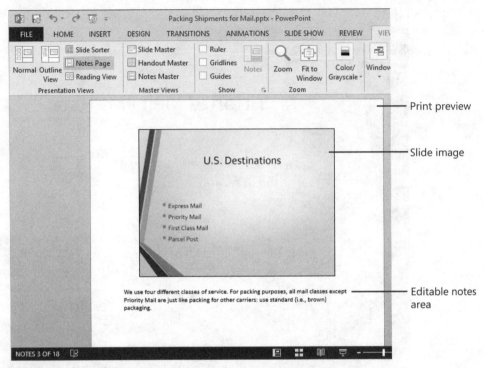

Figure 18-7 In Notes Page view, you can edit your notes and preview how the page looks when printed.

For more information about formatting and printing handouts, see "Creating notes and handouts" in Chapter 19, "Polishing and delivering a presentation."

About master views

In addition to the presentation views described in the preceding sections, the View tab is also home to the Master Views tools. Master views contain all of the behind-the-scenes layout and formatting for the slides in a presentation. This is where the positioning of placeholders is defined, as well as the formatting characteristics of the text contained in each. This is also where you can define objects—such as a company logo—that appear on every slide. PowerPoint uses three types of masters: slide, handout, and notes.

- **Slide Master** The slide master contains master slide templates for each of the slide layouts in your presentation. (For more information, see "Using slide layouts" later in this chapter.) In Slide Master view, you can rearrange placeholders, insert additional graphics, modify the formatting of text, and insert content placeholders.

Use the large slide master thumbnail at the top of the Navigation pane to modify the placeholder layout for the entire presentation—adding elements that you want to be in the same position and with the same formatting on every slide. Items that appear on a slide because they are part of the slide master can't accidentally be moved during regular slide editing. Thumbnails below the large one at the top are for individual slide layouts.

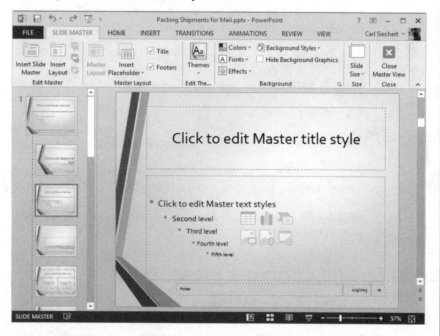

- **Handout Master**   The handout master defines the layout of handouts you print to accompany your presentation. Using the Handout Master tab, you can specify how many slides print on each page, the page orientation, and which header and footer elements should print. While in Handout Master view, use the Insert tab to add elements (for example, a company logo) to print on each page.

- **Notes Master**   In the Notes Master view, you can change the appearance of Notes Page view on your screen and in printouts. For example, you can modify the size of slide images to allow more or less room for your notes.

For information about customizing these masters, see "Laying the groundwork for an expert presentation" in Chapter 20, "PowerPoint 2013 inside out."

Slide Show view

The last view we discuss—and perhaps the most important one—is nowhere to be found on the View tab. Rather, Slide Show view has a tab of its own, where you'll find tools for starting, configuring, and controlling a slide show. This is the view to use when you deliver your presentation in front of an audience. In Slide Show view, your slides fill the entire screen and all accoutrements such as the ribbon, status bar, and panes are hidden. You get the full effect of all animations, transitions, and timings. In Slide Show view, as with Reading view, you can't edit your presentation.

To invoke Slide Show view, do any of the following:

- Click the Slide Show button on the status bar.

- Press F5.

- On the Slide Show tab, click From Beginning.

Click anywhere to advance to the next slide or trigger the next animation. To return to the last-used editing view, click past the last slide in the presentation or press Esc.

For more information about navigating in Slide Show view, see "Delivering a live presentation" in Chapter 19.

Creating and editing a presentation

You start creating or modifying a presentation from Backstage view in PowerPoint. There, you'll find options for creating a new, blank presentation, for creating one based on a template or a theme, and for opening an existing presentation file. For details, see "Where (and how) Office stores files" and "Using templates to streamline document creation" in Chapter 6, "Managing Office files."

Each "page" in a presentation is represented by a slide. Alone, slides can be used to communicate single ideas: a flyer for a garage sale or school play or a company organization chart. By assembling multiple slides and adding transitions and effects, you create a presentation that can be delivered in person or run independently at a trade show kiosk. (Collectively, the slides in a presentation are sometimes called a *deck*.)

To add a slide that uses the default layout, click New Slide in the Slides group on the Home tab, or press Ctrl+M; to choose a slide layout, click the arrow beneath the New Slide tool and pick from a menu of predefined slide layouts. (We describe layouts in more detail in the next section.) There's no limit to the number of slides you can add to a presentation.

Anything you place on a slide is linked to a content placeholder, which is a movable box with dotted borders. Unlike in Word, you can't just click and begin typing at a blank spot on the slide. To add text to a slide, you must use a slide layout with a content placeholder (or you can add a placeholder to an existing slide layout); click in the placeholder and *then* begin typing. To add a table, chart, graphic, or other nontext object, you have to click an icon in the center of the placeholder. (Alternatively, you can use commands on the Insert tab, as described later in this chapter.) A placeholder behaves like other objects: when you select one, additional tabs appear on the ribbon depending on the content type. You can resize a placeholder by dragging a selection handle on any side or corner, or move it by dragging the border.

Because PowerPoint is designed with the idea that most slides are shared on the screen with other users—and that printouts simply position those slides on a piece of paper—there aren't any margins.

Using slide layouts

When you add a new slide to a presentation, it's displayed with its own set of placeholders. Which placeholders you see depends on the slide layout you choose. The first slide in a new presentation typically uses the Title Slide layout, with placeholders for a title and subtitle. To create a slide with a different layout, click the arrow under New Slide to display a gallery of slide layouts, as shown in Figure 18-8. You can also change the layout of an existing slide; click Layout (also in the Slides group on the Home tab) to display a similar gallery, sans the three commands at the bottom.

The type of content you plan to use on a slide dictates which layout you should choose. For example, if your presentation is intended to compare and contrast two products or topics, you might use the Comparison layout for a slide showing pictures of each, arranged side by side. Follow that with a pair of slides using the Content With Caption layout, with a picture and details (in bullet format) about each item.

Slide layouts are interchangeable. That is, even if you change the layout after you add text, PowerPoint preserves your text within the context of the new layout.

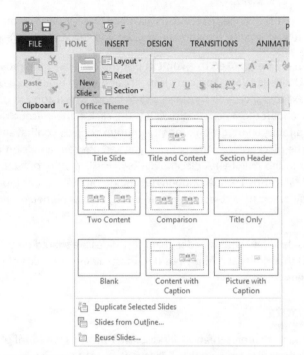

Figure 18-8 Slide layouts determine the location and arrangement of placeholders on a slide. They also reflect the current theme, whose name is shown in bold at the top of the menu.

PowerPoint includes nine standard slide layouts:

- **Title Slide**   This layout offers two placeholders: one for the title of the presentation and one for a subtitle. Use this layout to create an opening slide for your presentation or to signify the start of a new topic or idea.

- **Title And Content**   This layout is the default when you insert a new slide after a title slide and is one of the most commonly used. It offers two placeholders: one for the title of the slide and one for content. Use this layout when you need to communicate a single idea using a chart or a table, or if you want to build a standard slide with bullet points.

- **Section Header**   The Section Header layout has two text placeholders: one for the section title and one for the section subtitle. Use this layout as a low-key alternative to the Title Slide layout when transitioning between presentation topics or introducing new ideas.

- **Two Content**   This layout is similar to the Title And Content layout, but it has a placeholder for the slide title and two placeholders for content. A common use for this layout puts text alongside a graphic or media clip.

- **Comparison**   The Comparison layout looks a lot like the Two Content layout. The difference is that this layout contains placeholders for headings above each of the content placeholders. Use this layout to show how one idea compares with another: before and after, A versus B, and so on.

- **Title Only**   This layout displays just one placeholder for a slide title. Like the Section Header layout, this layout is good to use when a presentation transitions from one topic to another. Another use for this layout is to have full control over content placement, because it gives you nearly a full slide to add your placeholders to.

- **Blank**   This layout doesn't contain any placeholders. Use the options on the Insert tab to populate the slide with the types of placeholders you want, in the exact position you prefer. Use this layout when you need complete control over where placeholders appear on your slide. .

- **Content With Caption**   The Content With Caption layout gives you three placeholders to work with: one for the slide title, one for slide text, and one very large placeholder for content of your choice. Use this layout when the inserted content (a chart or table, for example) should be the main focus of the slide, but it needs a title and a few words (a sentence or two at most) for context or introduction.

- **Picture With Caption**   This layout gives you three placeholders: one for the slide title, one for slide text, and a large one for a graphic. Use this layout when you have a single image that communicates the main idea of the slide.

Some PowerPoint templates include additional slide layouts, and you can create your own custom layouts. Note also that the position of the placeholders for a particular layout might vary based on the presentation theme.

For information about creating your own custom layouts, see "Laying the groundwork for an expert presentation" in Chapter 20.

Creating a presentation from an outline

If you've already typed your presentation outline in another program, such as Word, you can import that text into a PowerPoint file and automatically create slides. You need to be sure that your outline (in Word) has the proper styles applied so that PowerPoint knows how to format the text you're importing. Figure 18-9 shows a formatted outline in Word.

For information about working in Outline view and setting heading levels in Word, see "Using outlines to plan, organize, and edit documents" in Chapter 10, "Working with complex documents."

Chapter 18

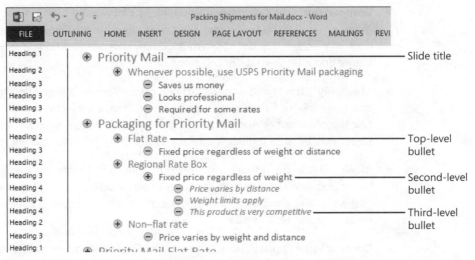

Figure 18-9 Use heading styles in Word to control text location on your PowerPoint slides. Each Heading 1 entry becomes a slide title, with subheadings becoming bullets.

To convert a Word outline to a PowerPoint presentation, select All Outlines as the file type in the Open dialog box in PowerPoint. When you open a Word outline, PowerPoint looks for heading styles. For example, text formatted with the Heading 1 style becomes the title of a new slide in PowerPoint. Figure 18-10 shows the outline in Figure 18-9 converted to a PowerPoint slide.

With your text in place, you can use the Design tab to apply a theme and quickly enhance how your presentation looks visually.

For more information about themes in Office 2013, see "Using Office themes" in Chapter 5, "Working with graphics and pictures."

INSIDE OUT   Use outline text to add slides to an existing presentation

Just as you can start a presentation from a Word outline, you can also use a Word outline to add slides to an existing presentation. This is useful when you've already selected a design in PowerPoint and just need to fill in the text.

Start by selecting the slide that will appear before the newly inserted slides. Then, on the Home tab, click the arrow beneath the New Slide tool, click Slides From Outline, and pick the Word file containing your outline text.

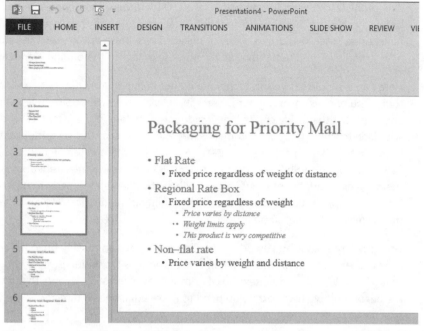

Figure 18-10 Although the initial formatting is plain, opening a Word outline in PowerPoint captures all the text with little effort.

Editing presentation text

Presentations consist of many different elements, but the most common is the basic "Click to add text" variety. But what if you need to add a "Confidential" warning with an embargo date at the top of each slide or type your company's tagline just above each slide's title? In either of these cases, you need to add text in a nonstandard location, outside the familiar boundaries of default layout types. This requires the creation of a text placeholder.

On the Insert tab, click Text Box (in the Text group), and then click the slide where you want the text box to be located. The exact location doesn't matter because you can always move it later. The text box you insert becomes another placeholder on your slide.

For more information about working with text in PowerPoint, including formatting text, inserting symbols and special characters, checking spelling, and more, see Chapter 4, "Entering, editing, and formatting text."

One of the fastest ways to edit text is to use Outline view. Modifying slide text in the outline is quicker than adding or removing individual text boxes on the slide itself. In this small pane, press Enter to add new slides or bullet points, press Tab to move the current line to a new, lower level, and use Shift+Tab to promote bullets in the outline hierarchy.

Here's an example where this technique comes in handy. You start with a slide listing five topics you plan to cover in your presentation, each as a bullet point in a text placeholder, and you want to quickly create a new slide for each item in the list. Start by clicking the slide icon to the left of your summary slide, and then press Ctrl+D to duplicate that slide. In the Outline pane, position the insertion point anywhere in the first bullet point on the new slide and press Shift+Tab to turn that bullet into a slide title. Repeat that process for the remaining four bullet points. You now have five new slides ready to fill in. (As one final bit of cleanup, be sure to delete the slide containing the duplicated—and now redundant—title from your original summary slide.)

Using the Enter and Tab keys in the Outline pane, you can quickly build the framework for your entire presentation this way. Remember that this technique is most effective for slides that use a title and a single text box. For more advanced slide layouts that include graphics, media, or multiple text boxes, you need to make adjustments directly on the slide in Normal view.

INSIDE OUT Copy a group of slides quickly

If you're building a presentation that uses a specific sequence of slide layouts for each of a group of topics, you can streamline the presentation-building process by duplicating those slides for each group. Start by creating the slides for the first group. Then, in the Navigation pane, select all the slides in the group, click the arrow beneath the New Slide tool on the Home tab, and click Duplicate Selected Slides. Repeat these steps for each topic.

Basic guidelines for effective presentations

Once you start placing objects on your slides, it's easy to get carried away. How do you know when enough is enough? That depends on what you're creating. The cardinal rule is to be sure that the end result works for your intended audience. The images, colors, and fonts you use for a school presentation might be inappropriate for a corporate boardroom, for example. Beyond that one overarching rule, it's possible to work with some more general guidelines.

When working with text, bigger is typically better. This is especially true for presentations for which a projector will be used. In this case, you want to ensure that the person sitting in the back row doesn't have to squint. Look at the text sizes for bullet points in one of the built-in themes, and you'll see that they're much bigger than body text in a standard Word document.

Unfortunately, as text size increases, the amount of space on the slide decreases. As a rule, keep slides focused and to the point to minimize the amount of text required. If you plan to present your slide show live, you should use short, bulleted text points that help the listener follow along; as the speaker, you can fill in the gaps and avoid the dreaded "Oh no, he's reading his slides" effect. If your presentation will run unattended at a trade show or on the web, you need to be more creative. If the text is too long, consider breaking it up by inserting a video or recorded narration. When in doubt, split the text across two slides with some graphics to add visual interest. Your audience will appreciate the effort.

Starting with an outline allows you to define each slide's main point and see how it fits in the overall theme of your presentation before you get into your design work. Outlines can also help you organize text so that each slide contributes to a consistent flow, with a similar number of bullets per slide and the same basic structure and tone.

If you simply don't know where to start, you can get a little push from the templates Microsoft offers online. One of our favorites is "Duarte's Five Rules." (To locate this template, click File, click New, type **five rules** in the search box, and click the Start Searching button.) Not only is this a highly engaging, self-running presentation, it offers useful tips on how you can create great presentations yourself. As a bonus, it shows some pretty terrific animation effects that will inspire both novice and advanced users.

Chapter 18

Using slide sections

Dividing your presentation into sections allows you to group related sets of slides into logical categories. This feature, which was introduced in PowerPoint 2010, is useful when you're working with large presentation decks or when you're collaborating with another person and each of you is responsible for a specific set of slides. You can also use sections as you begin a new presentation to organize the larger ideas that you want to communicate.

Sections can be defined in either Slide Sorter view or Normal view. Select the slide you want to use as the first one in your new section. On the Home tab, in the Slides group, click Section, and then click Add Section. (You can also right-click the first slide in a new section and choose Add Section from the shortcut menu.) With the new section created, click Section, Rename Section, and give the set of slides that follow a meaningful description. Figure 18-11 shows several sections in Slide Sorter view.

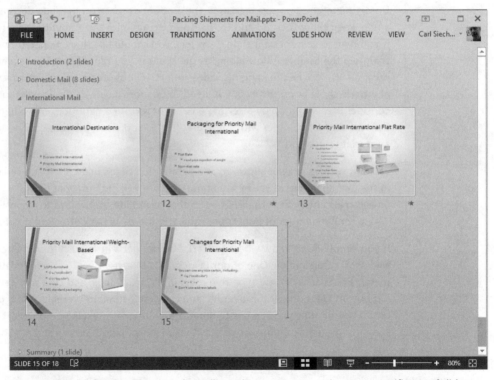

Figure 18-11 Defined sections can be collapsed to narrow your view to a specific set of slides.

Using other commands on the Section menu (in the Slides group on the Home tab) and on the shortcut menu that appears when you right-click a section name (shown next), you can move an entire section of slides up or down in the presentation. You can also delete all slides that belong to a section.

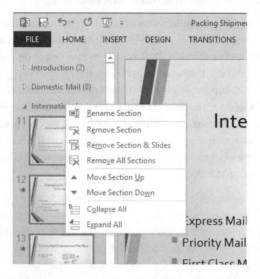

Setting page orientation and size

A slide's orientation can be either portrait or landscape. Because most computer monitors and projectors use landscape orientation, that's the default in PowerPoint. Presentations on tablets, phones, and the rare portrait monitor benefit from an orientation change. On the Design tab, click Slide Size, Custom Slide Size. Figure 18-12 shows the dialog box that appears.

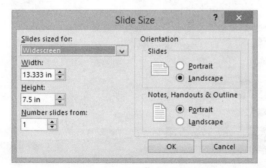

Figure 18-12 The orientation you select affects all slides within the same presentation.

INSIDE OUT Create a slide show that mixes orientations

Although your selection in the Slide Size dialog box sets the orientation for an entire presentation, there is a workaround in case you need to show a few slides in a different orientation from those in the rest of the deck. The trick is to *link* two slide shows, each created using a different orientation. Create an object on a slide in the first presentation that you can click while in Slide Show view. With that object selected, click Action on the Insert tab. On either tab (Mouse Click or Mouse Over), choose Other PowerPoint Presentation from the Hyperlink To menu. On the last slide of the second presentation, create a similar object with an action that returns to the first presentation, at the slide immediately following the one where you left. (For details about action settings, see "Inserting action buttons" in Chapter 20.)

So that your presentation fills the screen, you want to select the aspect ratio that matches the screen on which you'll present. Traditionally, presentations have used a 4:3 aspect ratio, which was designed to display well using an 800×600 resolution on an old-school SVGA computer monitor or projector, or a standard-definition TV. Recent years have seen a dramatic shift to widescreen displays, on which the aspect ratio is typically 16:9 (for a 1080p or 1080i HDTV with a native resolution of 1920×1080) or 16:10 (for computer monitors with a native resolution of 1920×1200).

To make this crucial change, click Slide Size on the Design tab. In the Slide Size dialog box, shown earlier in Figure 18-12, select an option from the Slides Sized For list, shown next.

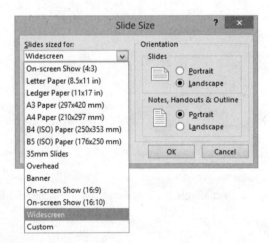

In this same dialog box, you can adjust the orientation of your slides, notes, and handouts or define a specific width and height.

CAUTION !

> Adjusting a presentation's aspect ratio after content has been added can wreak havoc. For example, images that looked fine at a 4:3 aspect ratio appear squashed when you switch to 16:9. If possible, determine your final presentation format before graphics and other media are placed on your slides. Otherwise, allow yourself time to modify these items after a new aspect ratio is applied.

Saving and sharing a presentation

Before you share your presentation, you must save it. Use the default PowerPoint Presentation format (with a file name extension of .pptx) for presentations that you might edit later. That's the standard XML-based format for use with PowerPoint 2013, PowerPoint 2010, and PowerPoint 2007.

To share a presentation in a format that retains full fidelity with your views in PowerPoint yet can't be modified in any way, save the file in PowerPoint Show format (with a file name extension of .ppsx). Opening a file of this type runs the presentation in Slide Show view.

If you need to share your presentation with someone who doesn't have a copy of Power-Point, you have a couple of options:

- The recipient can install PowerPoint Viewer, a free program that works with Windows XP and later versions and can be downloaded from *w7io.com/11803*. This program allows users to view (but not modify) PowerPoint presentations stored as a presentation or a show.

- Save your presentation as a PDF document, which can be opened on any computer running any operating system by using Adobe Reader or a compatible program. While this provides a satisfactory solution for static slides, PDF does not support animations, transitions, and other effects.

To save a file in presentation or show format, click File to open Backstage view, and then click Save or Save As. You can also use that method to save your presentation as a PDF, but a quicker path is to click File, Export, and then click Create PDF/XPS.

The Share pane in Backstage view offers several more ways to share a presentation stored on SkyDrive. For more information, see "What happens when you sign in with an Office account?" in Chapter 7, "Connecting Office 2013 to SkyDrive and other online services."

Another way to share a presentation is to present it online rather than sharing a file. For more information, see "Delivering a live presentation online" in Chapter 20.

In PowerPoint 2013, you also have the option of saving your presentation as a video that you can burn to a DVD or upload to the web, or in a smaller, portable format. You'll find these options in the Export pane in Backstage view. For more information, see "Turning your presentation into a video" in Chapter 20.

Supported file formats in PowerPoint 2013

In addition to the standard PowerPoint Presentation (.pptx) format, PowerPoint can open, edit, and save files in several other formats.

PowerPoint 2013 can open and save documents in any of these formats:

- **PowerPoint Presentation**   The default format for PowerPoint has several variants developed over the years: XML-based .pptx (PowerPoint 2007 and later), .ppt (PowerPoint 97, PowerPoint 2000, PowerPoint 2002, and PowerPoint 2003), and macro-enabled .pptm. Only the latter type can contain VBA macro code.

- **PowerPoint Show**   This format automatically opens as a slide show. Three variants are supported: .ppsx (PowerPoint 2007 and later), .ppsm (macro-enabled), and .pps (earlier PowerPoint versions).

- **PowerPoint XML Presentation**   This Office 2003 format (.xml) uses XML tags that correspond to an XML schema, making it useful for some custom data interchange applications.

- **PowerPoint Template**   Supported template formats are .potx (PowerPoint 2007 and later), .pot (earlier PowerPoint versions), and .potm (macro-enabled). For information about using templates, see "Using templates to streamline document creation" in Chapter 6.

- **Office Theme**   An Office theme file (.thmx) incorporates a set of colors, fonts, and effects that you can use to apply a consistent look to Word documents, Excel workbooks, and PowerPoint presentations.

- **PowerPoint Add-In**   The macro-enabled .ppam format is for a presentation designed to be run as a supplemental program; the .ppa format is for versions earlier than PowerPoint 2007.

- **OpenDocument Presentation**   The XML-based .odp format is used by the OpenOffice.org office suite.

- **PowerPoint Picture Presentation**   In this format, which also uses a .pptx file name extension, each slide in a presentation is saved as a picture instead of an editable layout.

- **Outline/RTF**   The .rtf format preserves presentation text in a standard word-processing format.

PowerPoint 2013 can open (but not save) documents in these formats:

- **Web Page**   The .htm, .html, .mht, and .mhtl formats open a webpage as a presentation.

- **Outline**   You can open a presentation using the text in a standard word-processing document in any of several formats, including those used by Word (.doc, .docx, .docm), WordPerfect (.wpd, .doc), and Microsoft Works (.wps), as well as rich text format (.rtf) and plain text (.txt) files.

PowerPoint 2013 can save (but not open) documents in any of these formats:

- **PDF**   Portable Document Format (.pdf) lets you create documents that can be viewed on nearly any computer. For details about working with PDF files, see "Exporting files and data to alternative formats" in Chapter 6.

- **XPS Document**   The seldom-used .xps format provides an alternative to PDF. XPS documents can be viewed with the built-in Reader app in Windows 8, with XPS Viewer in Windows 7 or Windows 8, or with an add-in viewer for other platforms.

- **Video**   You can save your presentation in Windows Media Video (.wmv) or MPEG-4 (.mp4) video formats. For more information about saving your presentation as a video file, see "Turning your presentation into a video" in Chapter 20.

- **Graphics**   Save your slides in any of these standard graphics formats: GIF Graphics Interchange Format (.gif), JPEG File Interchange Format (.jpg), PNG Portable Network Graphics Format (.png), TIFF Tag Image File Format (.tif), Device Independent Bitmap (.bmp), Windows Metafile (.wmf), or Enhanced Windows Metafile (.emf).

Adding graphics, video, and audio

Graphic images and video clips can help you communicate complex ideas in a simple manner. Sometimes, one well-placed image or clip can tell your entire story, with no bullet points necessary.

In PowerPoint, as with other Office programs, you can insert various graphical object types, including pictures, online pictures, shapes, SmartArt, charts, screenshots, and WordArt text effects. This content works the same here as it does elsewhere.

For information about inserting and working with each of these standard graphical object types, see Chapter 5, "Working with graphics and pictures."

As in other Office programs, you can insert nontext content using tools on the Insert tab. But PowerPoint has something the other programs don't have—layouts. In fact, many of the layouts contain a placeholder for "content." This generic term is used because content can mean any one of six options: Table, Chart, SmartArt, Picture, Online Picture, or Video. Figure 18-13 shows the content options displayed inside a content placeholder.

Figure 18-13 Click an icon in a placeholder to insert a table, chart, SmartArt graphic, picture, online picture, or video, or click anywhere else inside the placeholder to insert text.

To insert one of these content types, click the associated icon. Clicking any one of the six content icons is akin to clicking the same option on the Insert tab, only quicker. In any layout with a content placeholder, you can instead insert text by clicking inside the place-holder, away from the content icons.

Working with objects

For the most part, you work with graphical objects—tables, pictures, online pictures, screenshots, shapes, SmartArt, charts, and so on—in PowerPoint in exactly the same way you do in other Office programs.

For example, you can use the Selection pane to select, name, reorder, and hide objects. (To display the Selection pane, press Alt+F10 or, on the Home tab, in the Editing group, click Select, Selection Pane.) For more information about the Selection pane, see "Selecting graphics and pictures" in Chapter 5.

And you can use the same tools to add interest to your images. You can crop, remove back-grounds, enhance or correct colors, add artistic effects and borders, and more. For details, see "Making your pictures look great" in Chapter 5.

For aligning objects with other slide elements, use the Align tool on the Format tab that appears when you select an object. For more information, see "Positioning objects" in Chapter 5.

PowerPoint provides a few alignment tools unlike those available in other Office programs:

- **On-screen grid**   The grid overlays vertical and horizontal dotted lines in Normal view. This way, when you move objects, there's no guesswork as to whether they're lined up with any other object on the slide. To display the grid, click the View tab and select Gridlines (in the Show group). To set the grid spacing, click the dialog box launcher in the lower-right corner of the Show group on the View tab to open Grid And Guides, shown next. (The dotted lines forming the grid maintain their one-inch spacing, but the dots that make up the lines adjust to the spacing you set here.)

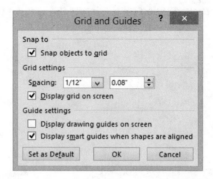

- **Snap To**   When you select Snap Objects To Grid in Grid And Guides, objects snap to the closest intersection of the grid as you move them.

- **Smart guides**   If the last box in Grid And Guides is selected, smart guides pop up when you move one object within close proximity of another. This is PowerPoint's way of telling you that the object you're moving is aligned (left, right, or center) with another object already on the slide.

Working with video

Video clips can greatly enhance a presentation, and they're easy to insert. You can embed a video clip in a presentation, which eliminates the need to send or store additional files with your presentation. But doing so increases your overall presentation's file size, which can lead to performance issues. Another option is to link to a video stored in an accessible location (like the Internet or your hard drive).

Inserting video

To place a video on a slide, click the Insert Video icon in a placeholder, or click Video in the Media group on the Insert tab. Either way, you then must choose between:

- **Video stored on your computer**   If you clicked the placeholder icon, click Browse next to From A File. If you clicked Video on the Insert tab (shown next), click Video On My PC.

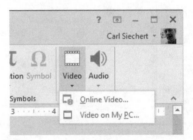

An Insert Video dialog box, similar to the familiar File Open dialog box, then appears. Navigate to and select the video file you want to use, and then decide whether you want to embed the file in your PowerPoint presentation (click Insert) or insert a link to the file (click the arrow by Insert and choose Link To File). Linking to a file produces a smaller PowerPoint presentation file, but the video file must remain in the same folder to avoid breaking the link.

- **Video stored online**   From the Video tool, click Online Video. This takes you to the Insert Video dialog box shown next, in which you choose the source of the video—the same dialog box you get if you simply click the placeholder icon. With the exception of videos from SkyDrive, PowerPoint does not embed online video files in your presentation file. Therefore, you must have a network connection available whenever you present your show.

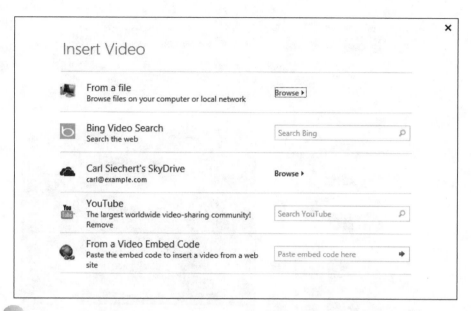

This dialog box is essentially the same as the Insert Video dialog box in Word. For more information about using it, see "Inserting video" in Chapter 11, "Word 2013 inside out."

Note that different types of video enjoy varying degrees of support in PowerPoint. For example, with Windows Media Video (.wmv) files, you have a full range of available formatting and editing options, as described in the next section. But with Flash files (including videos from YouTube), you lose some key features. For starters, you can't use special effects and fade or trim options on a Flash file. Additionally, you don't have the ability to compress your file size with embedded Flash files as you can with embedded files using video formats such as Windows Media Video or QuickTime.

Playing video

When you point to a video on a slide in either Normal view or Slide Show view, a media controls panel appears below the inserted video. With this panel, shown in Figure 18-14, you can play or pause your video, jump to a specific section, and adjust the volume. If you prefer to not show the media controls during a presentation (for example, when a video is set to play automatically), you can remove this panel from Slide Show view by clearing the Show Media Controls check box in the Set Up group on the Slide Show tab.

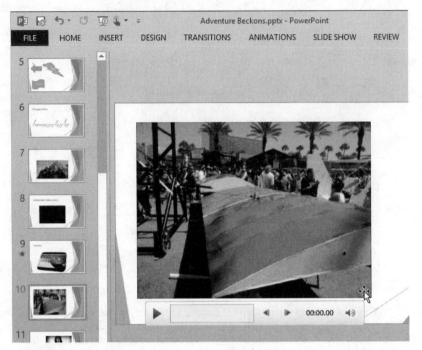

Figure 18-14 The media playback controls below the video image appear when you point to or select the video.

The media controls do not appear with all video types. For example, an online video from YouTube shows nothing. To play one of these videos, select it and click Play on the Playback tab under Video Tools, or right-click the video and choose Preview. YouTube's playback controls then appear; click them to play, pause, control volume, and choose other options.

Click outside the video to stop playback.

Editing video

In addition to playing video, PowerPoint offers the ability for you to edit videos that have been embedded in or linked to your presentation. This feature becomes useful when you have access to a video that has dead space at the beginning or end or is simply too long for your presentation's needs. For these instances, select the video and then click Trim Video (in the Editing group on the Playback tab under Video Tools).

Figure 18-15 shows a 4-minute video that has been trimmed to just 16 seconds by shaving time off both the beginning and end of the embedded video.

Figure 18-15 Set your video start and stop times by entering times directly in the boxes or by dragging the start and stop points on the timeline.

The Playback tab under Video Tools offers several options for controlling how your video appears during your presentation, including fade in and fade out options, playback looping and rewind, and the ability to play the video in full-screen mode. There's also an option that allows you to hide your video in Slide Show view when it isn't playing. Use this option when the video playback is triggered by an automatic animation; otherwise you have no way of accessing the video during your presentation.

Another option on this tab allows you to add bookmarks, which are points in your video and audio files that you save for easy access later. Bookmarks allow you to jump to specific audio or video segments within a larger media file and also to start animation effects based on the bookmarked position. To bookmark one or more areas of a video while the video is playing (in Normal view), click Add Bookmark on the Video Tools Playback tab as soon as you reach a spot you want to bookmark.

Bookmarks are noted by small circles that appear on the media controls panel. To remove a saved bookmark, click it once, and then click Remove Bookmark on the Video Tools Playback tab.

For more information on setting animation effects, see "Enlivening a presentation with animations" in Chapter 19.

Chapter 18

Compressing your file

The more graphics and other media you add to your presentation, the larger it gets. That's especially true if you add high-quality video clips. Large files are difficult to share with others via email, and they're a potential hassle for anyone using a slow Internet connection. For presentations that have audio or video clips, use the Compress Media option in the Info pane in Backstage view, shown in Figure 18-16.

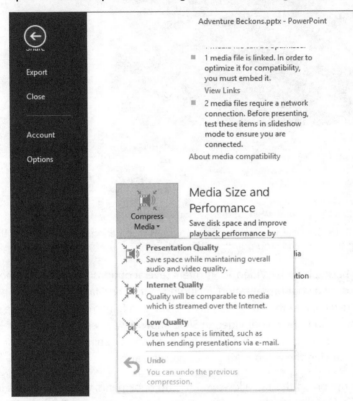

Figure 18-16 Choose compression settings to minimize file size and make it suitable for distribution. This option appears only for presentations that contain audio or video clips.

For more information about sharing your presentation, see "Delivering a live presentation online" in Chapter 20.

Tools on the Format tab under Video Tools offer a variety of effects similar to those available for pictures. (For more information about those tools, see "Making your pictures look great" in Chapter 5.) With these tools, you can:

- Adjust brightness and contrast. Click Corrections.

- Apply color effects. Click Color.

- Replace the video still preview image with another image of your choice. Click Poster Frame.

- Apply frames and borders, shadows, reflections, 3-D perspective views, and various other effects. Click Video Styles to select from a gallery of quick styles, or click other tools in the Video Styles group to roll your own.

- Crop or resize your video frame. Use tools in the Size group, or use the Video Shape tool in the Video Styles group to crop to a shape.

Working with audio

Like video, audio clips can be embedded in a presentation. Playing your company's commercial jingle or sharing a clip from an interview can add impact to a presentation. Using recorded audio as narration enables a presentation to run unattended at a kiosk.

Inserting audio

In PowerPoint, you can insert audio from any of three sources, each of which is represented by a command on the Audio menu (in the Media group on the Insert tab):

- **Online Audio**   Choose this option to search for and insert royalty-free sound clips from Office.com.

- **Audio On My PC**   Choose this option to include audio from a file stored on your computer. In the Insert Audio dialog box, navigate to and select the file. Then click Insert to embed the file into your presentation, or click the arrow next to Insert and click Link To File to insert a link to the file. The first option results in a larger PowerPoint presentation file, but because everything is in a single file, you don't need to keep track of the location of each linked file.

- **Record Audio**   If your computer has a microphone, you can record your own audio. When you click Insert, Audio, Record Audio, a dialog box appears:

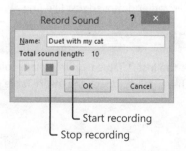

Provide a name for your audio clip (the name, which can be up to 24 characters long, appears in the Selection pane) and then use the controls to record, stop, and play back your recording. If you're not satisfied with the result, click Cancel and try again. Click OK when you're done.

Another way to add audio to your presentation is to record narration. For details, see "Recording narration" in Chapter 19.

Editing audio

Regardless of which audio type you insert on a slide, PowerPoint uses a small speaker icon to represent the audio clip. You select this icon when you want to play back or edit the audio clip. When you do so, the media controls panel appears below the icon, and Format and Playback tabs appear under Audio Tools on the ribbon.

The Format tab might cause some initial puzzlement, as it has tools—such as Remove Background, Color, and Artistic Effects—that seem more suited to pictures than sounds. Indeed they are. Use tools on the Format tab to modify the appearance of the speaker icon. Your first edit might be to substitute a picture for the icon; do that by clicking Change Picture (in the Adjust group).

You'll find options for editing the actual audio on the Playback tab, and you'll see that they are quite similar to the options available for editing video. Just as with video, when you're working with audio, you can add or remove bookmarks, trim audio start and stop points, set fade in and fade out locations, hide the audio during the slide show (just be sure the audio plays on an automatic animation), and loop or rewind the clip.

Working with tables

Even if you eschew video, audio, and fancy graphics in your presentations in favor of text, you'll find that there's more to PowerPoint than bulleted lists. Some types of data are best presented in tabular form, and PowerPoint has the tools for creating attractive tables with ease.

Unlike tables in Word, which are generally inserted in-line with text, tables in PowerPoint are free-floating objects that can be resized and moved just like images.

Inserting a table

To add a table to a slide, you can click the Insert Table icon in a placeholder or, on the Insert tab, click Table, Insert Table. Either method opens the Insert Table dialog box shown in Figure 18-17.

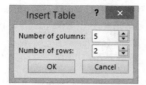

Figure 18-17 In PowerPoint, a table can have as many as 50 columns and 50 rows.

But a more visual method exists: on the Insert tab, click Tables and then point to the grid that appears. As you move the pointer, PowerPoint displays a live preview of the table as it will appear on your slide. Click on the square that represents the number of columns and rows you want. When you use this method, PowerPoint inserts the table in place of the next unused content holder. If none exist, PowerPoint places the table in a seemingly random location, but you can drag the resulting table to the position you want.

If your table is going to have an irregular layout, you can draw it. On the Insert tab, click Table, Draw Table. With the mouse pointer now adopting a pencil shape, drag on the slide to define the table's outer bounds. To complete the table, on the Design tab under Table Tools, click Draw Table. The pencil-shaped mouse pointer reappears, and you can draw cell borders within the table.

TROUBLESHOOTING

Attempting to draw cell borders creates a new table

Getting the hang of drawing cell borders takes a bit of practice. You might find in your early attempts that after clicking Draw Table on the Design tab, when you try to draw a line you end up with a new table nested inside the original table. The trick is to select the table, click Draw Table on the Design tab, and then start drawing your first column or row divider *just outside* the outer edge of the selected table. You'll know you've got it right when a dotted straight line appears instead of a dotted rectangle.

After you insert a table, simply click in each cell and type to enter table data.

Modifying a table

When you select a table, two new tabs appear on the ribbon under Table Tools: Design and Layout.

Tools on the Design tab are devoted to controlling the color and appearance of table cells and borders. The Effects tool lets you embellish with reflections, shadows, and 3-D effects.

The Layout tab, shown next, is the place to go when you need to add or remove cells, columns, or rows; resize the table or cells; and control the layout of text in the table.

Some of the key features on this tab:

- Click Select to select the column or row containing the insertion point or current selection, or to select the entire table. (You can also select directly with a mouse. Move the pointer above a column and when the mouse pointer changes to a small black arrow, click to select the column. A similar arrow at the left end of a row selects the row. Drag to extend the selection to multiple columns or rows. To select the entire table, click the outer border.)

- Use tools in the Rows & Columns group to delete or insert a column or row.

- Tools in the Merge group merge selected cells into a single cell or split each selected cell into multiple cells.

- Tools in the Cell Size group let you specify the dimensions of selected cells, of course. The tools on the right—Distribute Rows and Distribute Columns—set all selected rows or columns to the same size.

- The six tools on the left side of the Alignment group, along with the Cell Margins tool on the right, set the location of text within each selected cell: left, centered horizontally, or right; and top, centered vertically, or bottom.

- The Text Direction tool, also in the Alignment group, sets the layout of text in the selected cells. As alternatives to normal horizontal text, you can rotate text so that it reads top to bottom or bottom to top, or you can set text to stack vertically.

Customizing your presentation's design

Up to this point, our discussion has centered on getting content into your PowerPoint presentation. Now we look beyond slide layouts at design-related features. Design is often the first thing people try to work with in PowerPoint, but it really should be the last. Ideally, you want to get the core of your message down first. The design changes you make will affect much of what you've already entered, but they shouldn't cause you to rework your message. In short, the design should fit your message, not the other way around.

Formatting text

Formatting PowerPoint text isn't any different from formatting text in a program like Word. You select the text and then use the formatting options on the Home tab or the Mini toolbar. PowerPoint allows you to format all or just selected pieces of text within a text box.

To format all the text inside an individual placeholder, click once inside the placeholder, and then press Esc. This selects the placeholder as an object. Now, any formatting changes you make affect all the text inside the selected placeholder. Pressing Esc one more time removes the placeholder selection altogether.

For more information about formatting text, see "Applying text formatting" in Chapter 4.

Adding footers

A footer with slide numbers can help keep you and your audience oriented to where you are in the presentation. Footers can also include the date and time and other custom text that you set.

To customize the footer for the current slide or for all slides, click Header & Footer on the Insert tab (in the Text group). Use the Header And Footer dialog box, shown in Figure 18-18, to set your preferences. Click Apply to add your settings to the current slide or Apply To All to add your settings to all slides in the presentation. Selecting Don't Show On Title Slide suppresses the footer on any slide formatted with the Title Slide layout.

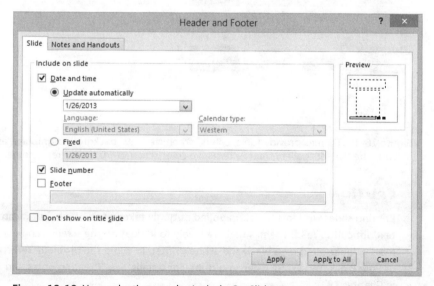

Figure 18-18 Your selections under Include On Slide appear as tiny black boxes in the Preview box.

You can drag individual footer elements to change their location. To change the location on all slides, you need to edit the slide master. For information about customizing these masters, see "Laying the groundwork for an expert presentation" in Chapter 20.

Applying themes

Applying a theme can save you considerable design time. As in other Office programs, themes store related sets of fonts, colors, and graphic effects that affect all slides in a presentation. In PowerPoint, themes also bring along background colors and graphic images as well as customized slide layouts.

In PowerPoint, you find themes on the Design tab. The Themes gallery is shown in Figure 18-19.

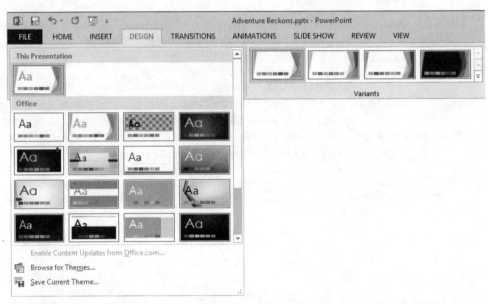

Figure 18-19 Themes provide fonts, colors, graphic effects, background graphics, and slide layouts. The Variants gallery offers alternative color schemes for the current theme.

CAUTION

Printing slides with lots of color applied not only takes a ton of ink, but it can make the text difficult to read. Themes that are lovely to look at on the screen can be a muddy mess when printed on a black-and-white printer. To avoid the problem, select Grayscale or Pure Black And White when you print. For details, see "Creating notes and handouts" in Chapter 19.

When you hover your mouse pointer over a theme, you'll see the familiar Live Preview functionality, and you have the option to customize and save themes here that become available in your other Office programs. Themes bring a consistent visual look to all of the slides in your PowerPoint deck.

For more information about themes, see "Using Office themes" in Chapter 5.

Adding backgrounds

For more control over the color and design of your slides, you can set your own background, which fills the entire slide area with colors, clip art, pictures, or patterns. One potential benefit of defining your own background is that, unlike a theme, it can be applied to a specific slide and doesn't affect all slides in the presentation.

You customize the background using the Format Background pane, shown in Figure 18-20. To display it, on the Design tab click Format Background (in the Customize group).

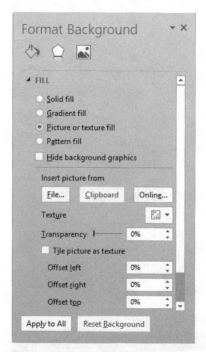

Figure 18-20 Use the Format Background pane to specify the type of background you want to create: solid or gradient fill, picture or texture fill, or a pattern.

When you insert an image file, it appears immediately on the current slide. Use that preview to customize the offset. This helps you place the image in the most appropriate location based on the slide content. Then, for a watermark effect, use the Transparency slider.

Chapter 18

You can make further adjustments to color, brightness, and contrast on the Picture tab in the Format Background pane. (For more information on picture corrections, picture color, and artistic effects, see "Making your pictures look great" in Chapter 5.)

Changes you make in Format Background apply only to the current slide. To use the same custom background on all slides in the presentation, click Apply To All. Note that when a custom background is applied to all slides, you lose the Reset Background option. To remove the background from all slides, reapply the original theme.

CHAPTER 19

Polishing and delivering a presentation

N ANY OF YOUR AUDIENCES, it's likely that you'll have a mix of verbal and visual learners, and you want to present to both learning types. That's why you include a blend of text and media in your slides. But even with pictures and graphics, your presentation can still look static. Adding movement to your presentations in the form of content animation and slide transitions can make them much more interesting.

In this chapter, we show how you can build on existing presentations to add a level of interactivity through animations and transitions. Then we look at the steps for planning, rehearsing, and delivering a live presentation. A welcome improvement in PowerPoint 2013 is an enhanced Presenter view, which provides cheat sheets and other tools you can use while you deliver a live presentation.

We wrap up with a discussion of delivering your slides and notes on paper.

Enlivening a presentation with animations

You've created a presentation, carefully refining the message. You even found a few graphics and a design theme that work well with your content. So, what's the problem? All the information is there, but that's it. It's just there. It's boring.

What your presentation lacks you can make up for with a little creativity and some content animation. For example, is it necessary to fill a slide that lists security protocols just with text? Does your audience need to remember all 100 words, or can you summarize it in one really big, animated word supplemented with some audio narration? If you have a bulleted list, does your audience need to see the whole list at the same time, or can you show just one item at a time?

Think outside the box. With animation, you don't need a separate slide each time you want to show something on the screen. You can control which objects appear when and for how long. Objects can have multiple animations assigned to them, each with its own trigger and timing.

Need some inspiration?

Animation is best experienced and not read about; you'll learn more by doing and seeing than by reading. For a little inspiration, check out some of the templates and sample presentations at Office.com. Click File, New. In the Search box in the New pane in
Backstage view, type **animations** and click the Start Searching icon. You can narrow the
search results by clicking Animation and other relevant terms under Category. (Another
good example of effective animation is the Five Rules presentation that we mentioned
in Chapter 18, "Inside PowerPoint 2013." You can find it by searching for **five rules**.)

The presentations you find here were developed to inspire you with some well-placed
animation, slide transitions, and other effects. After you open one of these presentations, watch it in Slide Show view so you can get the full experience. Then switch to
Normal view. Many of the presentations include in the Notes pane complete descriptions and instructions for creating the effects. Armed with that information, the
descriptions in this chapter, and a bit of imagination, you'll be able to create your own
dynamic presentations.

Adding animation

When you're ready to add your own animations, use Normal view and the Animations tab,
which is shown in Figure 19-1.

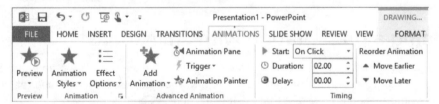

Figure 19-1 From the Animations tab, you can add, remove, and customize animation effects
and timing.

Note that you create and edit animation effects in Normal view, but they're ordinarily seen
only in Slide Show view. However, the Animations tab includes a Preview option that lets
you see the animation in action while you're working in Normal view.

For more information about working in Normal view, see "Working in an appropriate view"
in Chapter 18. For more information about working in Slide Show view, see "Delivering a live
presentation" later in this chapter.

There are several types of animations you can apply to selected objects by using the Add Animation option on the Animations tab, including entrance, emphasis, exit, and motion paths:

- **Entrance** controls how an object first appears on a slide.

- **Emphasis** sets animation on an object already on a slide.

- **Exit** defines how an object leaves a slide.

- **Motion paths** are the most customizable and allow you to define a specific direction or path that an animated object follows. This effect works well for nonstandard motions, such as along a curve.

Using each animation effect or a combination, you can bring life to your slide's objects. You can use animation to stack objects, minimize the amount of text your audience reads at any given time, catch your audience's attention, or mimic a video (as the Five Rules template does). For example, you could use an entrance effect to bring text onto a slide, an emphasis effect to change the color of the text, and then an exit effect to remove it to make room for the next set of text items you'll talk about.

When you click Add Animation, the Animation gallery, shown in Figure 19-2, shows you many available animations.

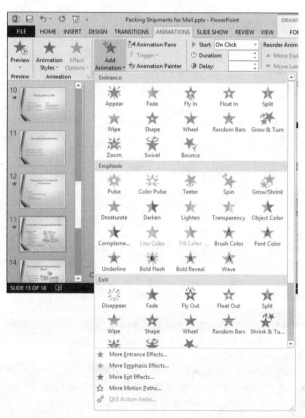

Figure 19-2 Set a selected object's animation effect from the Animation gallery. You can assign multiple animations to an object.

The Animation gallery shows a good selection of animations—but those are just the most commonly used ones. To see all available animations, click one of the More commands below the gallery. The resulting dialog box lists all available animations for the selected type. If you move the dialog box to the side and then select an effect, you can see a preview of the effect on the selected object on the slide.

Layering animation effects

Let's walk through an example to see how animation works. Figure 19-3 shows a slide ready for animation.

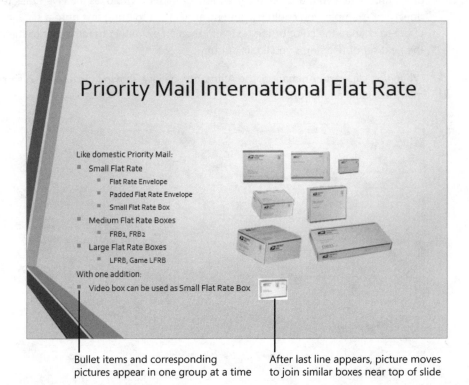

Bullet items and corresponding pictures appear in one group at a time

After last line appears, picture moves to join similar boxes near top of slide

Figure 19-3 Instead of overwhelming viewers with a slide filled with text and pictures, we can better hold their attention by introducing a few elements at a time.

On this slide, we use animation to control how and when each object appears on the screen and then move a picture to a different part of the screen to drive home a point.

The first animation is easy. Select the text box with the bulleted list, click Add Animation on the Animations tab, and select an entrance effect. For this example, we use Zoom. Next we'll add the Fly In entrance effect to each of the four groups of pictures.

To make each cluster of related pictures fly in together (that is, the Small Flat Rate packages in the first row, the Medium Flat Rate Boxes in the second row, and so on), we grouped them. (For more information, see "Grouping objects" in Chapter 5, "Working with graphics and pictures.") However, it's not necessary to do so; you could instead select multiple objects and then add an animation to the selected objects. (To select multiple objects, hold Ctrl as you click each one, or drag around the objects to "lasso" them.) By grouping the objects, we can work on them as a single object; applying animation to multiple selected objects simultaneously results in separate animated objects. Which method you choose depends on how you want individual animation effects to interact.

Note that most animations, like Fly In, have their own set of effect options. For example, the default for Fly In is to move up from the bottom of the slide, but you can set an option to fly in from any direction. After you apply an animation, you can see its available options by clicking Effect Options on the Animations tab. The options vary depending on the animation type, but they often include an animation direction. In the case of a text box, you also get the option of animating all the text at once, as one object, or as a paragraph. Because we want each item in our bulleted list to appear separately, we use the default option, By Paragraph.

INSIDE OUT   Animate a SmartArt object

After you apply an entrance effect to a SmartArt object, you can use the Effect Options menu on the Animations tab to specify whether the object is built all at once or with each element "one by one." Apply the One By One setting to see each bullet or level displayed separately, one at a time.

Next we apply a motion path to the picture near the bottom of the screen so that, after it appears, it will move up to take its place with the first group of pictures. Select the picture, click Add Animation and then, under Motion Paths, click Turns. Set the effect options to Up (so that the picture will move right and then up), and then drag the outline of the motion path so that the start and end points are in the right places, as shown in Figure 19-4.

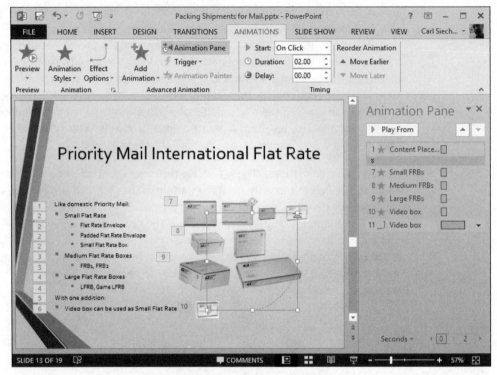

Figure 19-4 The motion path, selected in the slide and in the Animation pane, shows the path the picture will take when it moves to the upper right.

To display the Animation pane, shown in Figure 19-4, click Animation Pane (in the Advanced Animation group on the Animations tab). With the Animation pane, you can reorder your animations, preview them, and modify their timing and effect options. Numbers in the Animation pane correspond to numbers displayed next to the animated object on the slide. You can click a number in either place to highlight the corresponding number in the other, making it easy to find a particular animation in the list or on the slide.

INSIDE OUT   Assign names to objects

If you see a list of generic names in the Animation pane, open the Selection pane (click the Home tab, and in the Editing group click Select, Selection Pane), and rename your slide objects. For more information on renaming objects using the Selection pane, see "Working with multiple graphics and pictures" in Chapter 5.

You'll probably find that you need to switch back and forth between the Animations tab and the Animation pane to get your animations working just the way you'd like.

If you decide to use a different animation for an object you've already animated, click Animation Styles (in the Animation group), not the Add Animation tool. Using Add Animation (in the Advanced Animation group)—the same tool you use to apply an animation originally—applies another animation effect to the same object.

To remove an animation effect, select the animation in the Animation pane, click the arrow next to the animation, and choose Remove from the menu. Other commands on the menu, shown next, duplicate tools on the Animations tab—specifically, the tools in the Timing group and the Effect Options tool.

Setting animation order and timing

If you add animations in the order you want them to occur, you don't need to reorder them. In our example, the order is almost correct. Our first step in the previous section was to add a single animation to the text in the content placeholder. Although the By Paragraph effect option causes each bullet point to display separately, we want to intersperse the appearance of graphics between the appearance of each bulleted item. Changing the order is easy, using either the Animations tab or the Animation pane. After expanding the display of the content placeholder in the Animation pane, we can simply select an item and then click the up or down arrow in the upper-right corner of the pane to change the order. (You can use the Move Earlier and Move Later options on the Animations tab to achieve the same effect.) With just a few clicks, the pictures of the Small Flat Rate packages now appear immediately after the pictures' descriptive text appears on screen. Likewise with the Medium Flat Rate Boxes and Large Flat Rate Boxes.

By default, each newly added animation is set to appear "on click." But for some animations, it's nice if they simply happen. For instance, for our pairs of related bulleted items and pictures, we don't want to have to click to make each picture appear. Instead, we can time the pictures so that they enter the slide automatically after the bulleted item appears.

On the Animations tab, you work with options in the Timing group, shown in Figure 19-5, to control animation timing. To have selected animations occur automatically, one after another, click the arrow next to the Start option and choose After Previous. Choosing With Previous displays all selected animations on the slide concurrently.

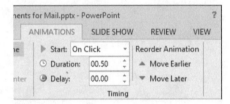

Figure 19-5 Use the Start, Duration, and Delay options on the Animations tab to control when an animation begins and how long it lasts.

The Duration option in the Timing group affects the selected animation and is separate from slide timings. The default duration for most entrance effects is half a second. If your text and other objects with entrance effects show up too quickly and don't match the pace of your presentation or the slide's background narration, you can increase the duration.

One final option related to animation timing is delay. In the Delay box, specify (in seconds) how long the animation should wait before appearing on the slide. A delay is helpful if the narration needs time before the next object appears or if you don't want the presentation to feel rushed.

To learn more about setting slide timings, see "Planning and rehearsing a presentation" later in this chapter.

In Slide Show view, animations follow either your mouse click or the animation timings that you define. For animations that are set to advance on a mouse click, you can also use the keyboard shortcuts you use to advance to the next slide. For example, pressing Enter triggers the next animation or slide, whichever comes first.

For a list of keyboard shortcuts used in Slide Show view, see "Navigating in Slide Show view" later in this chapter.

Duplicating animations with Animation Painter

As you start working with animations, it becomes clear fairly quickly that a lot of customization can be assigned to just one object. Once you animate one object precisely the way you want it—with the right effects, options, and timing—re-creating those steps on a similar object can be time-consuming. Fortunately, PowerPoint includes Animation Painter for copying animation effects applied to one object to another. It works on animations the same way Format Painter works on formatting.

To use this feature, select an object with an animation assigned, click Animation Painter on the Animations tab, and then click the object you want to copy the animation to.

Animation Painter works well when you're developing complex animations or with objects that contain several animation properties.

INSIDE OUT   Copy animation settings to multiple objects

When you click Animation Painter, it stays active until you click an object. If you need to copy animation from one object to multiple objects, you can keep Animation Painter active until you finish copying.

After you select the object that holds the animation settings you want to copy, double-click the Animation Painter option. Now you can apply the animation settings to as many objects as you need to. When you finish, just click Animation Painter once or press Esc.

Triggering an animation effect

For the most part, animations start based on other animations. One follows another, two start at the same time, or they wait for a cue from the presenter. Another way to get an animation effect to start is through a trigger. Separate from the Start option, triggers can be used to display other, hidden objects when the presenter clicks a specific object or reaches a bookmark in a video.

As an example, you can hide a video when it's not playing. Using a trigger, you can then set the video's animation trigger to play when another object (such as a picture or a text box) on the slide is clicked. To accomplish this, insert and select the video. On the Animations tab, click Trigger, On Click Of, and then click the name of the object you'll click to trigger the video to appear and play.

INSIDE OUT   Overlay text on a video with animation

You can use text boxes with animation triggers to overlay text on top of a playing video at defined bookmarks. This works well to create a closed-captioning effect or to highlight specific areas of a video.

To start, create bookmarks for your video at the points when text should appear. Then create a text box, apply entrance and exit animation, and apply a trigger to display the text box at a specified bookmark. As soon as the playing video reaches the bookmark, the text box animation is triggered. If you want to overlay multiple boxes, be sure to set an exit animation or define a duration for each text box. Otherwise, you end up with text boxes running over the top of one another.

Setting additional effect options

Each animation has various settings and effects that control how the animation appears. To preview and select these options, select an animation in the Animation pane, and then click Effect Options on the Animations tab. A gallery of effects appears, and as you point to each one, a live preview demonstrates the effect.

However, these galleries don't include all the available effect options. To see additional settings, click the dialog box launcher in the lower-right corner of the Animation group on the Animations tab. Alternatively, click the arrow next to any effect in the Animation pane and choose Effect Options from the menu. Either way, a dialog box with two or three tabs (depending on what type of object is selected) opens. In this dialog box, you can get more specific with your effect timing, appearance, and sounds.

For example, most animations are set to occur evenly and smoothly. But if you want the motion speed to vary as the object moves or you want the object to "bounce" when it reaches its goal, for example, you can set options on the Effect tab, as shown in Figure 19-6. Options under Enhancements let you accompany animations with sound and perform an action after the animation completes. Options here include dimming (changing the color) or hiding the object in order to emphasize items that follow. This can be effective when you're showing a bulleted list and want previous bullets to disappear as each new bullet is displayed.

Figure 19-6 The effect options dialog box is different for each type of animation effect.

The Timing tab in the effect options dialog box offers Repeat and Rewind options in addition to options comparable to those in the Timing group and with the Trigger tool on the Animations tab. Under the Repeat option, you can select (or type) a specific number of times for the animation to occur, including keeping it going until you click or until the end of the slide is reached. This effect works well if you're animating a ball rolling up or down a hill, but it's often more annoying than effective when you display an object on the screen over and over again.

If you select Rewind When Done Playing, the object returns to its original size and location after an animation is complete. For example, if you use an emphasis animation to increase the size of text, setting it to rewind restores the text to its original size.

CAUTION !

> When you start customizing animation effects, it's easy to select the wrong type of animation in the Animation pane because they all look alike. You could end up setting the rewind option on a text's entrance effect, which, instead of rewinding the emphasis animation, takes the text off the slide altogether. Pay attention to the colored bar next to each animation. Green bars indicate entrance effects, yellow bars indicate emphasis effects, red bars indicate exit effects, and aqua bars indicate motion path effects.

Using transitions between slides

Animations affect individual objects on a slide; transitions affect how the slides themselves enter the screen in Slide Show view. Like animations, transitions have enough tools, options, and variations to merit their own tab, which is shown in Figure 19-7.

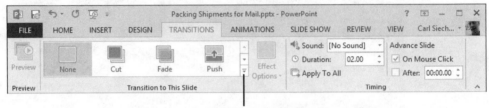

Click to display Transitions gallery

Figure 19-7 Use the Transitions tab to apply and customize transition effects for selected slides. To apply the same transition to all slides in your deck, click the Apply To All option.

You can assign a transition to any displayed slide by choosing a transition from the gallery shown in Figure 19-8. To display the gallery, click the More button in the lower-right corner of the gallery subset shown on the ribbon.

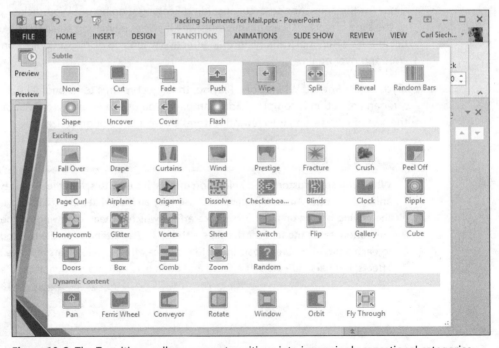

Figure 19-8 The Transitions gallery groups transitions into increasingly sensational categories.

Transitions are grouped into three categories:

- **Subtle** transitions typically slide in from a set direction; they are quick and barely noticeable by the audience. Use a subtle transition to create a smooth flow from one slide to the next.

- **Exciting** transitions are generally more noticeable to the audience than a subtle transition. Use an exciting transition to make a more dramatic statement between slides.

- **Dynamic Content** transitions are designed to make your slides look like they are moving through space as one slide leaves and another enters.

Once you select a transition, you'll see a preview in both Normal and Slide Sorter views. If you miss it, click the Preview option on the Transitions tab to see it again. Each transition holds a set of customizable properties that include speed, duration, sound, and—in many cases—direction, shape, and format.

For instance, when you apply the Honeycomb transition, you can modify the default 4.4 seconds that it takes to move from the current slide to the next, but not much else. But when you apply the Shred transition, you can also choose the type of shredding effect you want to see by clicking Effect Options on the Transitions tab.

When you apply a transition, it affects only the transition to the currently displayed slide (Normal view) or selected slide (Slide Sorter view). You can select multiple slides before you apply your transition settings to affect more than one slide. Press Ctrl as you click to select noncontiguous slides, or press Shift and click to select contiguous slides. You can select multiple slides in Normal view, although you might find this easier in Slide Sorter view.

You can use the Timing options on the Transitions tab to define whether a transition occurs automatically after a set length of time or only when the presenter chooses to advance the slide (On Mouse Click).

> **Note**
>
> The timing you enter here is independent of the duration you enter on the Animations tab. If the total of the timings you set for animation effects is greater than the slide duration you enter on the Transitions tab, the animation timings take precedence.

To remove a transition already assigned to a slide, choose None at the top of the Transitions gallery.

For more information about working in Normal or Slide Sorter view, see "Working in an appropriate view" in Chapter 18.

Planning and rehearsing a presentation

Preceding every great presentation is usually a lot of practice. The first thing you need to determine is what your primary method of delivery will be. Will this be a self-running presentation set up for individual viewers or for a booth at a conference? Will you be delivering it live before an audience? Will you print your slides? Will your presentation use a combination of these options?

You have other things to consider as well: How long will the presentation be? How long should each slide remain on the screen? Will you include audio narration?

Instead of guessing how long each slide should remain on the screen, you can use the Rehearse Timings option on the Slide Show tab to make a practice run through the presentation. As you watch and listen to the presentation in Slide Show view, PowerPoint records the time. Each time you click to move to the next slide, the time the last slide was on the screen is recorded, and that slide's timing is set.

For a presentation that runs automatically, it's a good idea to have someone unfamiliar with the content use rehearsal mode. This way, you can get a true picture of how long someone new to the presentation needs to become familiar with the message on each slide. To start rehearsal mode, click Rehearse Timings on the Slide Show tab. This switches your presentation into Slide Show view and displays the Recording toolbar, shown in Figure 19-9.

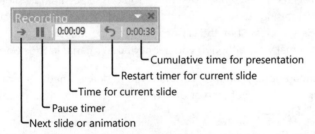

Cumulative time for presentation
Restart timer for current slide
Time for current slide
Pause timer
Next slide or animation

Figure 19-9 Use the Recording toolbar to see how long each slide in your presentation is on the screen. When you finish, you can save or discard the slide timings.

Once you start the rehearsal, go ahead and practice your presentation aloud or have someone else review the content for you. This gives you a good idea of the pacing to use and ensures that each slide is displayed for the right amount of time.

While working in rehearsal mode, you can also pause at any time to make notes, collect your thoughts, or answer your phone. Click Resume Recording in the dialog box that appears after you pause to start again right where you left off. One great benefit to rehearsal is that you get an overall idea of just how long your presentation will last.

You can end rehearsal mode at any time by pressing Esc. It also ends when you reach the last slide in your presentation. In either case, you're given the option of saving the timings recorded in rehearsal mode as the actual timing for each slide.

Recording narration

The Record Slide Show tool on the Slide Show tab allows you to set the timing for each slide and animation—like rehearsing timings—and you have the additional options of recording narration and laser pointer gestures at the same time.

Record Slide Show offers two choices: you can start the recording from the first slide or from the currently selected slide. (If you don't start recording from the beginning—or if you don't record all the way to the end—PowerPoint retains any timings you've previously recorded for the remaining slides.) Either way, you first need to decide exactly what you will record, as shown in Figure 19-10.

Figure 19-10 When you choose to record a slide show, you can record slide and animation timings, narrations and laser pointer movements, or both.

Once the recording starts, you use the Recording toolbar shown earlier in Figure 19-9 as you would when you're running a rehearsal.

When you record audio narration for a self-running presentation (one that runs without a live presenter), the audio adds depth, making the presentation feel more interactive. In addition, recording narration eliminates the need to add a separate audio file to each slide from the Insert tab. (For information about inserting and editing audio on a slide, see "Working with audio" in Chapter 18.)

Enabling the narration option also records your mouse actions when you enable it as a laser pointer, which is helpful if you plan to point to specific areas on a slide, like the high point on a chart. (For more information about this feature, see "Turning your mouse into a laser pointer" later in this chapter.) After you record your slide show, the new slide timings are applied to each slide. You can see them in Slide Sorter view just below each slide thumbnail, or in the Timing group on the Transitions tab.

Note that when you add narration through the Record Slide Show option, a small speaker icon is added to each slide, which indicates that audio narration has been recorded for the slide. In Normal view, you can click that icon to hear or edit the audio. However, the icon does not appear in Slide Show view because the Hide During Show option is enabled by default; you can find this option in the Audio Options group on the Playback tab under Audio Tools.

Setting presentation options

There's one last detail to attend to before the lights go down: On the Slide Show tab, click Set Up Slide Show to display the dialog box shown in Figure 19-11. Settings in this dialog box specify how the presentation will be delivered.

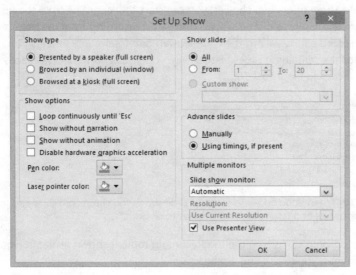

Figure 19-11 Set up your slide show by working through each of the five groups—Show Type, Show Options, Show Slides, Advance Slides, and Multiple Monitors—to define how you'll use this presentation.

Each time you get ready to present, use the Set Up Show dialog box to customize how your presentation will appear. You can make the following settings:

- The three options under Show Type determine the availability of other options in the Set Up Show dialog box. Presented By A Speaker (Full Screen) provides the most options, including Presenter view (if you are using more than one monitor) and the ability to change the annotation pen color. If you select Browsed By An Individual (Window), you lose both of these options. Choosing Browsed At A Kiosk (Full Screen) disables Presenter view and makes the slide show set to loop continuously until you press the Esc key.

- Under Show Options, you specify how the show plays. When Loop Continuously Until 'Esc' is selected, your slide show starts over when it reaches the last slide instead of fading to a blank slide. This works well for presentations set to run at trade shows or at the front desk to greet customers as they walk into your office. Another good use of this feature is a presentation for a school science fair project. It cycles through the slide deck until someone tells it to stop.

If you have recorded narration or applied animations, the next two check boxes allow you to disable those features when Slide Show view is activated. Pen Color sets the default pen color for annotations. (This color can be changed during the presentation from the shortcut menu in Slide Show view.) Laser Pointer Color sets the color of your laser pointer when it's activated during a presentation. For more information, see "Turning your mouse into a laser pointer" later in this chapter.

- Under Show Slides, you can specify a range of slides that play during the presentation. This option comes in handy when you need to present just a portion of your entire deck. This is a good place to denote a range of slides that make up just one or two sections. Keep in mind, though, that the range of slides must be continuous. Finally, if you have custom shows set up, you can choose the custom show you need to play here. For information about custom shows, see "Creating custom slide shows" in Chapter 20, "PowerPoint 2013 inside out."

- Under Advance Slides, you have the option to use slide timings or not. Slide timings are set manually on the Transitions tab or automatically by using the Rehearse Timings or Record Slide Show tools. By selecting Manually, you override all slide timings. This way, the presentation animations and slides advance only on the presenter's cue. For more information on setting slide timings, see "Planning and rehearsing a presentation" earlier in this chapter.

- Under Multiple Monitors, you specify whether you want to use Presenter view and, if you do, on which monitor Slide Show view should be displayed. With Presenter view, you can show your presentation with speaker notes on a different monitor. For details, see "Working with Presenter view" later in this chapter.

CAUTION

Before you begin your presentation, check to be sure that the aspect ratio on your computer matches that of the projector. If they don't match, you can run into display issues or your slides might be cropped. You can use the aspect ratio in the Slide Size dialog box to correct this at presentation time, although you should try to verify this setting well before you arrive for your presentation. For more information about setting the aspect ratio, see "Setting page orientation and size" in Chapter 18.

Delivering a live presentation

The animations are in; transitions are set. It's time to actually present this slide show in front of a live audience. The traditional method is to use Slide Show view, in which your presentation fills the screen. You can begin a slide show in Slide Show view using any of these methods:

- On the Slide Show tab, in the Start Slide Show group, click From Beginning.

- Press F5.

- Click Slide Show in the status bar. Note that this method starts the show from the current slide.

The following sections provide additional details on presenting in Slide Show view.

If you have multiple monitors (or a monitor and a projector), you'll want to take advantage of Presenter view, which displays the presentation on one monitor, and a "behind the scenes" view on another. For details, see "Working with Presenter view" later in this chapter.

Navigating in Slide Show view

When working in Slide Show view (unless you've chosen to use timings), you control how your slides progress. Ideally, your slides have been created in a logical first, next, last order, but sometimes delivery isn't always as succinct. What are your options? Table 19-1 shows the keyboard shortcuts you can use while delivering a slide show.

TABLE 19-1 Shortcut keys for controlling a slide show

Action	Shortcut key
Go to the next slide or animation	N, Enter, Page Down, Right Arrow, Down Arrow, or Spacebar (also: left mouse click)
Go to the previous slide or animation	P, Page Up, Left Arrow, Up Arrow, Backspace
Go to a specific slide	*number*, Enter
Display a blank, black screen	B or Period
Display a blank, white screen	W or Comma
Display the All Slides dialog box	Ctrl+S
End the slide show	Esc

If you need to navigate to a specific slide in Slide Show view, but you don't know the slide number, press Ctrl+S to bring up the All Slides dialog box, shown in Figure 19-12.

Figure 19-12 From the All Slides dialog box, you can select the slide to display by using the presentation's slide titles.

A shortcut menu dedicated to Slide Show view, shown in Figure 19-13, appears when you right-click during a presentation. Its commands allow you to navigate to a specific slide, show a black or white screen, or end the show from any slide, among other options.

Figure 19-13 The shortcut menu that appears in Slide Show view has commands for changing the mouse pointer into a laser pointer, pen, or highlighter, and for hiding the pointer altogether.

As an alternative to interrupting your show with large menus and dialog boxes, if you move your mouse pointer to the lower-left corner of the screen, a toolbar appears. Its options are similar to those for tablet and touch screen users, as described in the following sidebar, "Using Slide Show view on a tablet."

Using Slide Show view on a tablet

If you use Office with a tablet computer, you've undoubtedly discovered that, in most ways, it works the same way it does on a traditional laptop or desktop PC. You've learned to mentally translate "click" whenever you see it in this book or elsewhere to "tap." You probably make a similar translation from "right-click" to "tap and hold." And indeed, that process continues to serve you well as you work with a tablet.

However, some of the methods that work so well for presenting on a traditional PC become unwieldy on a tablet with no keyboard or mouse. And for that reason, Power-Point has some additional methods for running a presentation with a touch screen.

To move to the next slide or animation, simply swipe to the left. To move to the previous slide or animation, swipe to the right. For other options, tap anywhere to display a tappable toolbar, shown next.

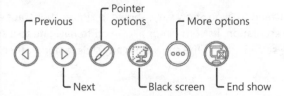

Tapping Pointer Options lets you select a laser pointer, pen, highlighter, or eraser. Drag with your finger to annotate a slide. With the laser pointer, you can tap the screen to keep the pointer in one spot.

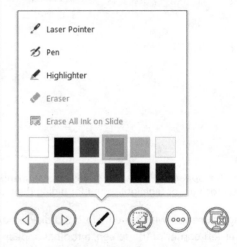

Tapping More Options displays a menu comparable to the shortcut menu that mouse users see, albeit with larger finger-friendly spacing.

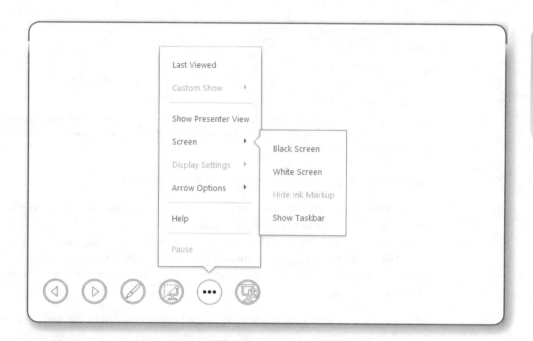

Adding annotations during a slide show

During your presentation, you can create on-screen annotations, which are useful for high-lighting certain areas of the presentation without altering the content. Annotations turn your mouse pointer into one of three shapes: an arrow, a pen, or a highlighter.

While using Slide Show view, right-click any slide to display the shortcut menu. From there, click Pointer Options, and choose the type of annotation you want. You can also set the ink color and specify whether your pointer is hidden or visible while you're presenting (choose Pointer Options, Arrow Options). Note that you can change the default pen color of your slide show in the Set Up Show dialog box. After selecting Pen or Highlighter, just drag with the left mouse button to draw on your slide.

Note that when you use the mouse pointer in this fashion, you can no longer click to advance to the next slide or animation. You have three choices: click the Next button on the toolbar, use any of the numerous keyboard shortcuts for displaying the next slide, or return to the shortcut menu and choose Pen or Highlighter again to deselect it.

When you reach the end of the presentation (or press Esc to stop), you have the option of saving the annotations or discarding them, as shown in Figure 19-14.

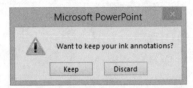

Figure 19-14 Saved annotations are converted into drawing objects and saved on each slide. Once annotations are saved, you can work with them the same way you work with shapes you add in Normal view.

Turning your mouse into a laser pointer

Traditionally, the PowerPoint presenter's toolkit includes a laser pointer for directing viewers' attention to key points in the presentation. PowerPoint now has the ability to change your mouse pointer into something that resembles a laser pointer—and the light it sheds is probably a lot less jiggly. This option works in both Slide Show view and Reading view, and it allows you to point out something on a slide without drawing on the slide or annotating it.

You need to drive with two hands to show the laser pointer; hold Ctrl and click (and hold) the left mouse button. Once you release the mouse button, your mouse pointer returns to normal. Although this feature works well and does cause your mouse pointer to mimic a laser pointer, it can be cumbersome because it forces you to use the keyboard and the mouse together. (With a touch screen, you simply drag your finger to show a moving laser pointer, or tap to display a stationery dot. Tap again to hide it.)

By default, the laser pointer color is red. This can be changed in the Set Up Show dialog box, which you reach by clicking the Set Up Slide Show option on the Slide Show tab.

Zooming in for a closer view

When the folks in the back can't read your slide or when you want to focus attention on a particular part of a slide, use the Zoom command. From the shortcut menu, shown earlier in Figure 19-13, click Zoom In. Move the mouse to place the highlighted box over the area you want to zoom in on, and click. You can move the zoom window around using the arrow keys. Right-click to zoom out, or press Page Down to zoom out and move to the next slide or animation.

Working with Presenter view

Consider this scenario: You're standing in front of a large audience getting ready to make your presentation when suddenly you can't remember exactly what you were going to say. What if you forget to mention an important point? And what are all those shortcut key combinations for moving through a presentation? It's a lot to remember.

This is where Presenter view can help. When Presenter view is enabled, you can show your audience the presentation in Slide Show view (on the projector or a second monitor) while you see your slides and notes on your screen, with quick access to annotation tools and slide-show shortcuts. This way, you can refer to your notes while presenting, but the audience never knows the difference—all they see is Slide Show view. To start, you need to connect your computer to a second monitor. A new feature of PowerPoint 2013 automatically sets up the second monitor, extending your desktop to that monitor. When you're ready to go, enable the Use Presenter View option on the Slide Show tab and select the presentation monitor from the Monitor list, as shown in Figure 19-15.

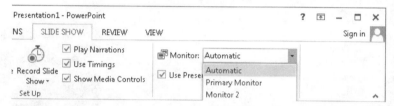

Figure 19-15 Be sure to select the monitor you're sending the presentation to in the box above the check mark; in most cases Automatic makes the correct choice for you.

> **Note**
>
> It's not entirely accurate to state that Presenter view *requires* a second monitor. Presenter view works just fine on a single monitor, but aside from rehearsing a presentation or making an online presentation (for details, see "Delivering a live presentation online" in Chapter 20), there's little to be gained without a second monitor. If you have only one monitor, press Alt+F5 to invoke Presenter view.

Then, when you start your slide show, your presentation is displayed in Slide Show view on the presentation monitor (the one you selected in the drop-down list). Back on your screen, you see Presenter view, which is shown in Figure 19-16.

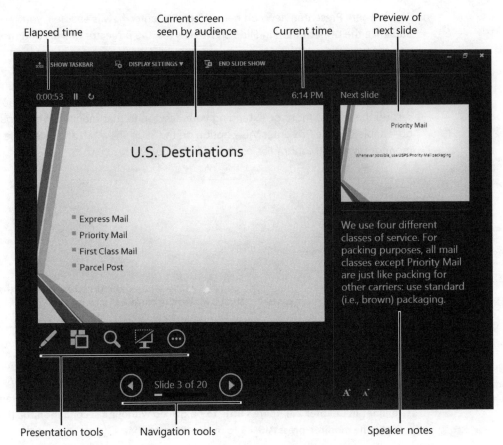

Figure 19-16 Presenter view offers a behind-the-scenes look at your slides and speaker notes and access to slide-show tools.

The large slide that dominates the window is the same slide your audience sees on the presentation screen, so you know exactly what they're seeing. (Almost. Slide transitions and animations don't appear in Presenter view. Instead, while the transition or animation plays, you see a message to that effect.) The smaller slide in the upper-right corner shows the next slide or animation—so you know what's coming. Below that are the notes that accompany the current slide. You can drag the divider line between each of these three panes to adjust their size. Use the icons in the lower-left corner of the notes pane to adjust the size of the notes text.

Just below the large slide is a set of control buttons. Use the arrows to move to the next or previous slide in the presentation. You can also move to the next slide or animation by clicking either slide image, or by using any of the keyboard shortcuts shown earlier in

Table 19-1. If you forget those shortcuts, click More Options (the button with three dots inside a circle) and click Help or, more simply, press F1.

The other presentation tools provide easier access to features we described earlier:

- Pen and laser pointer tools

- See all slides

- Zoom into the slide

- Black or unblack the slide show

- More options

You can keep an eye on your presentation time with clocks above the large slide. Tools to the right of the elapsed time let you pause or reset that timer.

Creating notes and handouts

PowerPoint, of course, is designed around presentations that are displayed on a monitor or projector. But you'll sometimes want to print your presentation so that audiences can take a copy with them for further review.

As with other Office programs, to print you click File to open Backstage view, and then click Print. You can print each slide on a separate page or squeeze as many as nine slides on each sheet of paper. Click the second button under Settings to display the layout options shown in Figure 19-17.

The options are separated into two categories: Print Layout and Handouts. The options under Print Layout are generally for the presenter's use. The Notes Pages option prints an image of a slide and the speaker notes for that slide. The Handouts options, as the name suggests, apply to audience handouts. They show just the slides, with blank lines for note taking in some layouts.

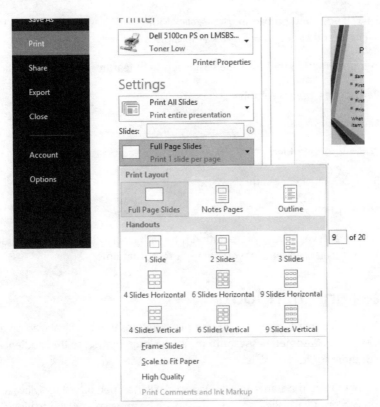

Figure 19-17 From this menu, you can also add a border around each printed slide by selecting Frame Slides.

Printing notes

Although the speaker notes are intended for the presenter, that doesn't mean you can't print the notes pages for your audience. You can add a lot of formatted content to the speaker notes area, including graphics. To print notes pages, from the menu shown in Figure 19-17, select Notes Pages.

To learn how to customize your notes page, see "Customizing other masters" in Chapter 20.

Printing handouts

When you print notes pages, you have only one option. But nine different print layout options are available for handouts. Printed handouts are designed mostly as takeaways for your audience, and the layouts provide varying numbers of slide thumbnails per page.

Figure 19-18 shows the 3 Slides handout layout.

Figure 19-18 The 3 Slides layout also prints a series of blank lines next to each slide thumbnail, providing a handy place for your audience to record handwritten notes during your presentation.

To print handouts, from the menu shown in Figure 19-17, select one of the layouts under Handouts.

Setting color options

Most presentations contain a lot of color. Color is used not only in graphics, but also in the background color from applied design themes. The problem is that you don't always want to print using that much ink—particularly on a color printer that consumes expensive ink. You can lower your print costs and make your handouts more legible by not printing in color. To do that, choose an option from the last button under Settings.

To conserve your color ink, change the print setting to Grayscale or Pure Black And White. Figure 19-19 shows a comparison of the same slide printed in color (it's printed in this book with only black ink, but you can see which colored elements print), grayscale, and pure black and white. Printing in Grayscale changes theme elements to shades of gray and removes slide backgrounds. Printing in Pure Black And White removes all theme elements and prints slide text in black on a plain, white background.

> **Note**
>
> If the selected printer does not print color, the preview image on the Print tab appears in grayscale even when Color is selected. However, all theme elements and backgrounds are included—much like the "color" image shown in Figure 19-19.

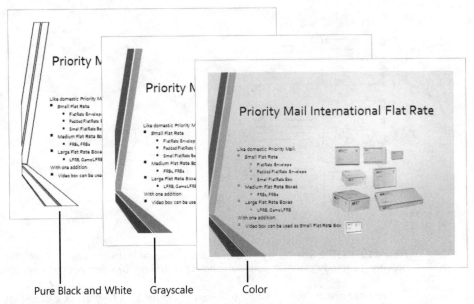

Pure Black and White   Grayscale   Color

Figure 19-19 Use the Grayscale and Pure Black And White print options to print without showing all of the presentation's design and theme colors and elements.

INSIDE OUT   Customize color mapping

Some color combinations that look great on a color monitor lack contrast—and therefore legibility—when they're reduced to grayscale or black and white. With a bit of tinkering, you can control how individual colors and objects print when you are not printing in color. To do that, start on the View tab, and in the Color/Grayscale group, click Grayscale or Black And White. That displays a preview image, but unlike the preview on the Print tab in Backstage view, this one is fully editable. A new tab also appears (either Grayscale or Black And White, matching the option you click), as shown next. You can click an object on a slide and then click the way you want that object to print when you select Grayscale or Pure Black And White on the Print tab.

Editing the handout header and footer

In the same Header And Footer dialog box that you use to set the footer for each slide (for details, see "Adding footers" in Chapter 18), a second tab controls the header and footer for your handout pages. You can access the dialog box from the Insert tab or by clicking Edit Header & Footer on the Print tab in Backstage view. Figure 19-20 shows the Notes And Handouts tab in the Header And Footer dialog box.

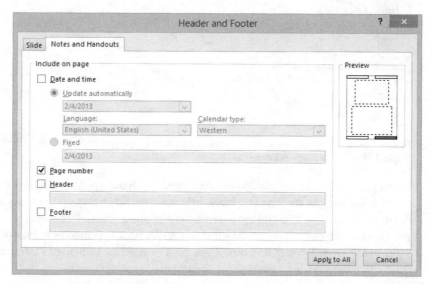

Figure 19-20 Use the Header And Footer dialog box to specify a custom header or footer for each of your printed notes and handout pages.

Unlike settings on the dialog box's Slide tab, the settings you define here are applied to all pages in the printout. You can also add a header to your handouts—a feature that's not available for slides.

Editing handouts in Word

Although the print layouts for handouts work in most instances, they don't allow much customization. You might be able to create handout masters to meet your needs, but a quicker option is to use Microsoft Word. When you export handouts to Word, you have access to all its features, including more control over creating custom headers and footers based on sections. To send your handouts to Word, click the File tab, click Export, and then click Create Handouts. Click the large Create Handouts button that appears, and then choose your preferred page layout from the Send To Microsoft Word dialog box, shown in Figure 19-21.

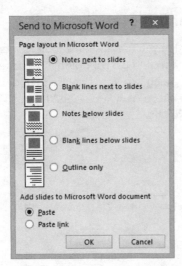

Figure 19-21 When you send your handouts to Word, you get options that differ from the printed handout layouts in PowerPoint.

When you click OK in this dialog box, your selected layout opens as a new document in Word. Note that the changes you make in Word have no impact on the slides in Power-Point. By default, the two files are independent of one another. This means you can't edit your speaker notes in Word and see those changes back in PowerPoint. However, in the Send To Microsoft Word dialog box, if you select Paste Link instead of Paste, you create a connection between your PowerPoint file and the Word document.

CAUTION

Be careful with the Paste Link option. It creates a one-way link between the slides in PowerPoint and the slide images in Word. If you make a change to a slide in Power-Point, the next time you open the Word handout file, you're prompted to update the links, and the slide images are updated. However, if you edit speaker notes in either file, no changes are shared between the two files. You should create a link between Power-Point and Word only for handouts that contain the slide images and not the speaker notes.

For information about creating headers and footers in Word, see "Adding headers, footers, and page numbers" in Chapter 9, "Inside Word 2013." For information about using sections in Word, see "Formatting columns and sections" in Chapter 10, "Working with complex documents."

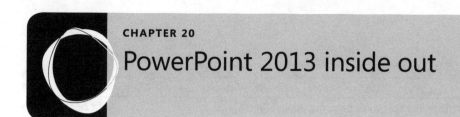

MICROSOFT POWERPOINT 2013 is a program that you can use to make professional-looking presentations without a lot of effort or experience. Using just the techniques we covered in the previous chapters, you can create presentations that effectively communicate your ideas. Yet there's much more to PowerPoint; in fact, it has spawned a new job title in some companies: Presentation Development Specialist.

In this chapter, we look at ways to save and reuse your work in PowerPoint, including themes, slides, and layouts. We also look at some features usually reserved for the experts, like working with master views and creating custom slide shows. We begin the chapter by describing one of the coolest new features in PowerPoint 2013, the ability to broadcast a presentation over the Internet without requiring any special software on viewers' computers. We also cover other methods for sharing your presentations.

Whether you develop presentations professionally or are an occasional PowerPoint user, we think you'll find these features interesting and useful.

Sharing a presentation with others

In the previous chapter, we explained how to deliver a live presentation. But that generally works best when you're in the same room at the same time with your audience. In the following sections, we describe three different methods for sharing a presentation without the constraints of proximity and shared schedules. Which one you use depends on many factors, including the location and technical acumen of the people you want to share with and whether you want them to be able to retain, reuse, and edit your presentation. Table 20-1 summarizes the key differences to help you decide which method is best for you.

TABLE 20-1 Methods for sharing a PowerPoint presentation

	Online presentation	Video	CD package
Viewer requirements	Web browser; availability at presentation time	Media player	PowerPoint or PowerPoint Viewer
Retains full fidelity	Good	Better	Best
Can be played back any time	Optional	Yes	Yes
Can be edited by viewer	Optional	No	Yes

Delivering a live presentation online

With the high cost of travel, more and more people are forgoing face-to-face meetings in favor of working remotely, sometimes with teams located around the world. Many families have members who are scattered far and wide as well. As a result, the need for easier communication is increasing every year.

PowerPoint 2013 addresses this need with its online presentation feature, which lets you share presentations with coworkers, family, or friends over an Internet connection. As the presenter, all you need is PowerPoint 2013 and a Microsoft account (formerly known as a Windows Live ID). PowerPoint uses the Office Presentation Service, a free service from Microsoft. The people you broadcast to view your presentation in their web browser, so they don't need PowerPoint to see your presentation.

For example, you can create a photo album of a recent trip and then send a link via email to your grandmother. All she needs to do is click the link, and your slide show is displayed on her computer in her web browser. You can share the photos while talking to her on the phone about the trip. You can, of course, use a similar approach when making presentations to other audiences; they, too, will appreciate the simplicity.

When you're ready to share your presentation, click File to open Backstage view, and then click Share, Present Online. If a menu appears at the top of the page, click Office Presentation Service. Then click the Present Online button, as shown in Figure 20-1. (As an alternative to Backstage view, click the Slide Show tab. In the Start Slide Show group, click Present Online, and then click Office Presentation Service. In the dialog box that appears, click Connect.)

If your network includes a Lync server, you might see an option to present online using Lync. For more information about Microsoft Lync, see "Screen sharing and whiteboarding" in Chapter 25, "Inside Lync 2013."

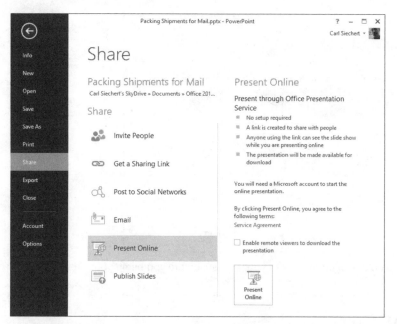

Figure 20-1 Decide whether you want viewers to be able to download your presentation file and set the check box accordingly.

> **Note**
>
> At this point, you might see a warning about media in your presentation. Some video and audio files are incompatible with some viewers, and some are simply too large for efficient Internet transmission. The dialog box has a link to the Optimize Media tool, which can reduce the size and improve transmission speed.

After you click Present Online, PowerPoint connects to the presentation service and then displays a dialog box with a link that you can share with others. (See Figure 20-2.) This link is valid only while you are presenting in Slide Show or Presenter view. During that time, anyone who receives the link, either directly from you or from another person, can view your broadcast.

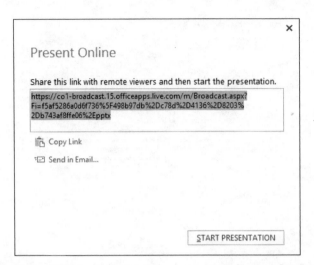

Figure 20-2 Send the link to your viewers before you begin your presentation.

INSIDE OUT   Use a URL-shortening service

A long, gnarly link doesn't present a problem when you send it via email or as an instant message, because recipients just need to click it. In some situations, your audience members must type the URL—perhaps because you're providing the link by phone or because you're presenting to a group and you want everyone to view and download the presentation on their own portable computers. In these cases, use a URL-shortening service such as *snurl.com* or bit.ly to trim the link to one that you can easily transmit verbally.

The next step is to click Start Presentation in the Present Online dialog box. The Present Online tab appears on the ribbon, as shown in Figure 20-3. (In certain configurations, clicking Start Presentation starts the presentation in Slide Show view. You can suspend the presentation and view the Present Online tab by pressing Esc.)

Figure 20-3 Options on the Present Online tab are similar to those on the Slide Show tab.

When you're ready to begin broadcasting your presentation, click From Beginning or From Current Slide on the Present Online tab. At that point, the slide appears in your viewers' browsers. Until you start the broadcast, people who have clicked the link see "Waiting for the presentation to begin…" in their browser. You can use either Slide Show or Presenter view to run your show. (For information about Presenter view, see "Working with Presenter view" in Chapter 19, "Polishing and delivering a presentation.")

> **Note**
>
> **To use Presenter view when you have only one monitor connected to your computer, press Alt+F5.**

When you broadcast, you lose some presentation features that are available when you use traditional presentation methods such as a projector or a second monitor. Although you see the full-featured presentation on your screen, your viewers' experience differs in the following ways:

- All transitions are shown as Fade transitions.

- You cannot add annotations or highlighting while broadcasting. (Furthermore, although the laser pointer and zoom functions are available for selection during an online presentation, online viewers won't see your pointer and zoom actions. These features work only when presenting through Lync.)

- If you click a link on a slide that opens a website, your viewers don't see the website; their browser continues to show whatever slide is displayed in PowerPoint.

While you're broadcasting, your viewers see only the display from Slide Show view. You can press Esc to exit Slide Show view and go back to Normal view, but your viewers continue to see the last slide that was displayed in Slide Show view. They see this slide until you pick another slide to display or end the broadcast.

When you begin an online presentation, you have the option of allowing viewers to download your presentation. (See Figure 20-1.) Choosing that option enables other features for viewers: in addition to saving the presentation file locally, they can view slide thumbnails, view speaker notes, and view slides at their own pace by clicking icons at the bottom of the Web App window. At any time, they can return to your location in the presentation by clicking Follow Presenter. These features are available because the online presentation uses PowerPoint Web App.

Turning your presentation into a video

Delivering a presentation online doesn't work if your audience isn't available at the time you want to give the presentation. And unless you have a concurrent connection via phone, Skype, Lync, or a similar audio service, your viewers can't hear you speak during your presentation.

You can overcome those limitations by saving your presentation as a video, complete with recorded narration. The resulting video is saved in your choice of MPEG-4 (.mp4) or Windows Media Video (.wmv) format and plays with the media player programs included with Windows or with most third-party players. You can burn the resulting file to a DVD, upload it to YouTube or another video-sharing site, or send it via email.

Unlike the online presentation feature, a video can incorporate all recorded timings, narrations, annotations, and laser-pointer movements. All transitions play normally, as do embedded audio and video. Because it's a movie, however, you lose any interactive capabilities, such as jumping directly to a particular slide, displaying hidden slides on request, and so on.

To create a video, click File to open Backstage view. In the Export pane, click Create A Video. As shown in Figure 20-4, your options are few.

Figure 20-4 Before you click Create Video, expand the two menus above the button and set your output options.

On the first menu, you set the size of your video output, choosing between small, medium, and large. In the second, choose whether to include any assigned slide timings or recorded narration in the final video. After you make your selections, click Create Video.

Creating a CD presentation package

Now we examine a third method for sharing a presentation: packaging for CD. With this option, you can save multiple presentations to one location (physical media such as a CD or a shared network location, for example) to share with others. PowerPoint creates a menu of presentations as part of the package, making it easy to select one for viewing. Saving files to a CD package also provides a portable backup of your work; presentations on the CD are saved as standard PowerPoint files. In addition, fonts are embedded and all linked files are included in the package. A CD package works well for sharing with coworkers, turning in a final project to your instructor, or sharing a photo album with family members.

Like the other methods, this one has its own drawbacks. Because the package contains standard PowerPoint files, package recipients must have PowerPoint or the PowerPoint Viewer (a free program that can be downloaded from Microsoft) installed on their computers. The computers, of course, must be capable of running PowerPoint. Although this feature is intended for distributing final presentations, for some reason you cannot create a package from a presentation that has been marked as final.

> **Note**
>
> In some previous versions of PowerPoint, you could select an option that included a copy of the viewer program with the CD package. This option is not available in PowerPoint 2013. However, the package's menu screen includes a prominent link to the download site for the viewer.

To create a CD package, click File, Export, Package Presentation For CD, and then click Package For CD. This opens the Package For CD dialog box, shown in Figure 20-5.

The open presentation appears as one of the files to be copied to the package. Click Add to select additional presentations or other files. You can add files of any type to a CD package. Each file you include gets a link on the menu that PowerPoint creates for the CD package.

The name you specify is used as the volume name if you copy the files to a CD, so it has a maximum length of 16 characters. (This limitation applies even if you save the package to a folder.) The name also appears as the title in the package menu. If you save the package to a folder, PowerPoint proposes to use the CD name as the folder name, although you can override this suggestion.

Chapter 20

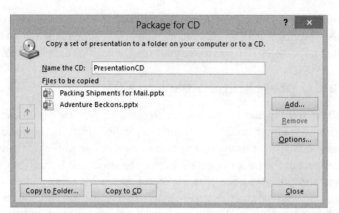

Figure 20-5 Here you can add or remove presentations to include in the package. Use the arrow buttons to determine the order in which the presentations appear on the menu that PowerPoint generates.

Click Options to specify whether linked files and embedded fonts should be included in the package. The Options dialog box, shown in Figure 20-6, also includes options to require a password to view or edit the presentations in the package.

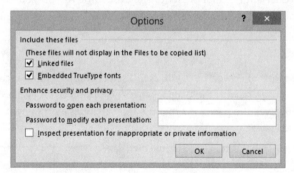

Figure 20-6 By default, linked files and embedded fonts are included, and no password protection is applied.

With your options set, click OK to return to the Package For CD dialog box. Insert a blank CD in your writable drive and click Copy To CD. If you'd rather save the package to a hard drive or network drive, click Copy To Folder. PowerPoint copies the requested files and also creates a menu similar to the one shown in Figure 20-7. If AutoRun is enabled on the computer when you insert the CD, the menu appears automatically. If AutoRun is disabled or if you saved the package to a folder, you can display the menu by opening the CD or folder in File Explorer, opening the PresentationPackage subfolder, and double-clicking the file named PresentationPackage.html.

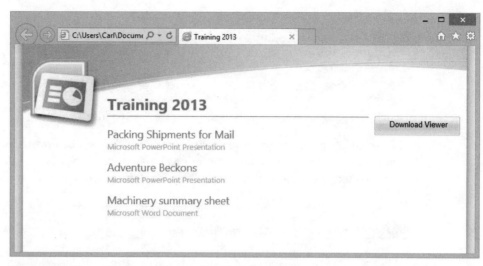

Figure 20-7 The menu is actually a webpage with a link to each presentation or other file included in the package.

Working collaboratively on a presentation

One of the biggest challenges of working with a team is to find a day and time when all team members can meet. If everyone can't meet, you're left to rely on meeting minutes and email comments to get the latest status update. In PowerPoint 2013, you can track team members' suggestions with the Comments feature and then bring two presentations together for comparison as a method of collaborating.

Another way to work collaboratively is for multiple authors to work on a single PowerPoint presentation file simultaneously. For details, see "Editing a shared document in real time" in Chapter 7, "Connecting Office 2013 to SkyDrive and other online services."

Using comments

The commenting feature in PowerPoint is limited compared with the review and change-tracking capabilities in Microsoft Word. Nonetheless, you can attach comments to a character, a word, a graphic or other object, or an entire slide. Comments don't actually change a slide's content; it's best to think of them as notes you would write on a paper to remind you or a team member of edits to make at a later date.

You add a comment by clicking New Comment on the Review tab, shown in Figure 20-8.

Figure 20-8 Click Show Comments to show or hide the Comments pane.

The Comments pane, shown in Figure 20-9, appears with a text box where you can type your comment text. The comment is inserted at the insertion point or the selection; if nothing is selected, the comment appears in the upper-left corner of the current slide.

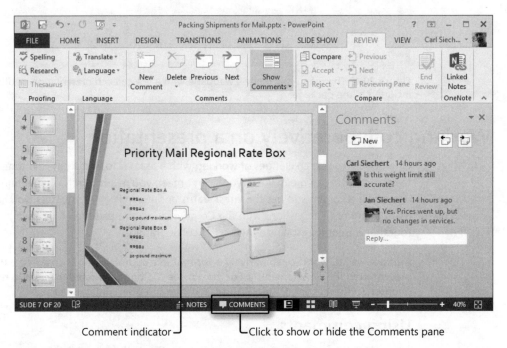

Comment indicator ⌐   ⌐Click to show or hide the Comments pane

Figure 20-9 You can drag a comment indicator to relocate it on the slide.

Comments are indicated by a small balloon icon. To display a comment when the Comments pane isn't open, simply click it. Alternatively, click Next or Previous on the Review tab to cycle through all comments in your presentation.

Although the Review tab includes some of its functionality, the Comments pane is the best place to perform all comment-related tasks: create a new comment, reply to an existing one, edit (click a comment), or delete (point to a comment and click the X that appears). You can open the Comments pane by clicking Show Comments on the Review tab or clicking Comments in the status bar. The Review tab retains one unique capability: click the arrow below Delete to access commands that delete all comments on a slide or in an entire presentation.

TROUBLESHOOTING

Your comments have disappeared

If you know there are comments on a slide, but you don't see the indicators, be sure that Show Markup is enabled. On the Review tab, click the arrow below Show Comments and click Show Markup. Even when Show Markup is turned off, you can click Next or Previous to view each comment.

Merging and comparing presentations

When more than one person works on a version of a presentation, comparing the two versions can be tedious. The Compare tool on the Review tab makes the task a little easier. Click Compare and then select another version to merge with the open presentation. The second presentation is combined with the first presentation, and changes to text and formatting are highlighted in the Revisions pane, shown in Figure 20-10, along with any comments. (You can hide or display the Revisions pane by clicking Reviewing Pane in the Compare group on the Review tab.)

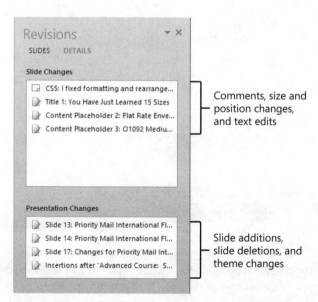

Figure 20-10 Comments are listed by reviewer initials on the Details tab in the Revisions pane.

CAUTION

Using the Compare feature does not create a third file, as the comparable feature in Word does. Instead, the second file's differences are merged into the first file. When you click Save, you overwrite the original file. To preserve an unaltered copy of the destination file, use Save As before you start to save a copy under a different file name.

You'll see revision indicators in the Revisions pane and on the slide. Click any of these indicators to see a description of the revision. To accept the revision, select the check box next to it, as shown in Figure 20-11. Alternatively, click Accept in the Compare group on the Review tab.

When you accept a revision, you haven't yet committed to the change. Until you end the review, you can clear the check box or click Reject to undo your acceptance. Note also that the Compare group on the Review tab, shown earlier in Figure 20-8, has some additional options that are available during a review. By clicking the arrow next to Accept or Reject, you can accept or reject all revisions for the current slide or all revisions for the entire presentation. If you completely trust (or distrust) your reviewers, these options make quick work of the review process. If you want to take a more methodical approach, click Next or Previous to step through each change.

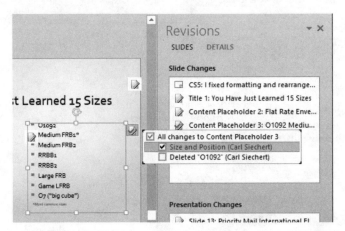

Figure 20-11 Click any revision to see the change in greater detail. The change appears on the slide when you select the check box next to a specific revision.

After you complete your review, click End Review. Doing so stops the review process and closes the Revisions pane, discarding all revisions that you did not accept.

Saving and reusing slides and themes

Carefully crafted slides offer the proper balance of text, graphics, and animation to make a concept come to life. Whether your slides contain business proposals, training material, research, or something else altogether, you might find yourself gravitating toward a certain "look." One way to reduce development time on future presentations is to reuse slides and elements you've created in the past.

Reusing slides

While working on a presentation, you can grab slides from a different presentation with the Reuse Slides pane, shown in Figure 20-12. To open it, on the Home tab, click the arrow below New Slide and click Reuse Slides. In the Reuse Slides pane, click Browse, Browse File to select the presentation that contains the slides you want to use in the current presentation. You can then click thumbnails of the slides in the presentation you selected to insert them in the open presentation.

Figure 20-12 Click a thumbnail to insert it in the open presentation.

When you insert a slide using Reuse Slides, it inherits the theme of the selected slide in the current presentation. If you want the reused slides to retain their original theme, select Keep Source Formatting in the Reuse Slides pane.

Another method of copying slides from one presentation to another is to open both files and then use the Arrange All option (in the Window group on the View tab) to position the two windows side by side. Once the presentations are arranged, select the thumbnails for the slides you want in one presentation and drag them to the other presentation. You can drag slides between Navigation panes in Normal view, or you can use Slide Sorter view. Slides take on the formatting of the target presentation unless you choose Keep Source Formatting from the Paste Options button that appears after you copy the slides.

INSIDE OUT Reuse slides stored in a Slide Library

Companies running Microsoft SharePoint can create a repository for slides to be shared among team members with appropriate permissions. This repository is called a Slide Library. Your network administrator (or someone with Design permissions for Share-Point) needs to set this up. To add slides to the Slide Library, click File, Share, Publish Slides. When you save a presentation to the Slide Library, each slide becomes its own file, making it easier to update and reuse the slides in other presentations.

Saving themes

Office themes are an integral part of PowerPoint—so much so that almost an entire tab (the Design tab) is dedicated to their use. You can also specify a theme when you create a presentation using File, New.

For details, see "Applying themes" and "Creating and editing a presentation" in Chapter 18, "Inside PowerPoint 2013."

Because you can customize themes, they provide an important benefit—branding. Many businesses create their own themes to ensure that the presentations they create match their company image. Typically, this involves choosing a preexisting theme and then modifying the individual elements—fonts, colors, effects, and backgrounds.

After you have a presentation's theme looking the way you want, save the theme so that you can reuse it in other presentations. From the Themes gallery on the Design tab, choose Save Current Theme. Saved themes show up at the top of the Themes gallery and are available in other Office programs as well.

You can also send your themes to coworkers and friends. By default, themes have the extension .thmx and are stored in %AppData%\Microsoft\Templates\Document Themes. (On a Windows computer with default settings, %AppData% expands to C:\Users\ *username*\AppData\Roaming.)

For more information about themes in Office 2013, see "Using Office themes" in Chapter 5, "Working with graphics and pictures." For information about backgrounds, see "Adding backgrounds" in Chapter 18, "Inside PowerPoint 2013."

Creating custom slide shows

Custom shows allow you to present a portion of a larger presentation. For example, you might have a 60-slide presentation for new employees that includes a section of 10 slides about the company's security policy. If you receive a request to teach a short seminar about these policies, you can create a custom show using only the relevant slides.

Based on your needs, you create custom shows by hiding selected slides or by setting up a new presentation order for a specific set of slides. Both techniques are equally easy to use. The difference is that when you hide slides, you don't have the option of changing the order the slides are displayed in. When you create a custom show, you do.

Hiding slides to create dynamic presentations

Hiding slides is a quick way to prevent certain slides from appearing in Slide Show view. When a slide is hidden, it is still visible in any of the editing views (Normal, Slide Sorter, and so on). The only view it isn't displayed in is Slide Show view (and the related Presenter view)—unless you explicitly request it.

The ability to display a hidden slide on command is part of what makes this technique so appealing. Hiding slides works well for content that you think might come up during the course of a presentation. It's the equivalent to being over prepared. For example, if you create a slide show to present a thesis, you need to cite your sources, but those citations need to be available only on request. In this case, you could create a slide that contains your citations, mark it as hidden, and display it only if an instructor asks to see your sources.

To hide a slide, select it. Then, on the Slide Show tab, click Hide Slide in the Set Up group. Alternatively, right-click a slide and choose Hide Slide.

Hidden slides let you anticipate audience questions and then stray a little from your agenda if necessary. In Slide Show view, you can display a hidden slide in any of the following ways:

- Type the slide number, and then press Enter.

- Right-click and choose See All Slides. (Alternatively, click See All Slides on the toolbar in the lower-left corner or in Presenter view.) An array of slide images appears. You can identify a hidden slide because its thumbnail image is dimmed and its number has a slash through it. Click the title of the slide you want to display.

- Press Ctrl+S to display the All Slides dialog box, which includes a list of slide numbers and titles. The slide number of each hidden slide is enclosed in parentheses. Use the arrow keys to make your selection, and then press Enter.

For more information about keyboard shortcuts you can use in Slide Show view, see "Navigating in Slide Show view" in Chapter 19.

> **Note**
>
> Hidden slides print by default. When you print handouts for a presentation that contains hidden slides, you can prevent the hidden slides from printing by clearing the Print Hidden Slides option on the Print menu, shown here.
>
>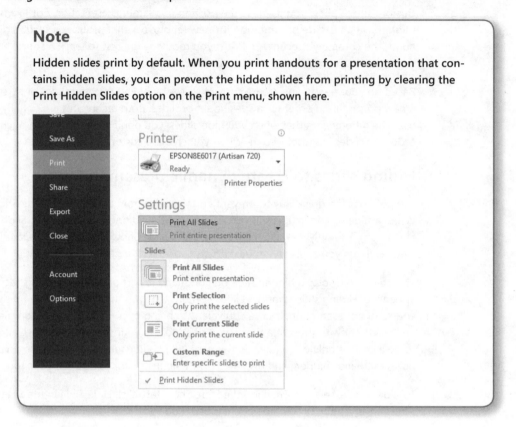

Defining a custom show

A custom show offers more flexibility than hiding slides because you can specify which slides are displayed and in what order. You define a custom show by using the Custom Slide Show, Custom Shows command on the Slide Show tab. This command displays the Custom Shows dialog box, where you click New to create a custom show. Custom shows are based only on the open presentation and are set up in the Define Custom Show dialog box, shown in Figure 20-13.

Custom slide shows are listed under the Custom Slide Show option on the Slide Show tab. Choosing a custom show launches the presentation in Slide Show view. To edit a custom show or to delete one, you need to go back to the Custom Shows dialog box.

Custom shows are also listed in the Set Up Show dialog box (opened from the Slide Show tab). When you select a custom show in that dialog box, the custom show becomes the default show when the slide show is presented.

Figure 20-13 In the Define Custom Show dialog box, select slides from the open presentation to appear in the custom show.

INSIDE OUT   Identifying slides by adding hidden titles

In the Define Custom Show dialog box, any slide without a title is listed only by slide number. In a large presentation, this makes identifying the content on some of your slides difficult if not impossible. To fix this, add a title to untitled slides by applying a simple layout, such as Title And Content. (If a slide already uses a layout that includes an unused title placeholder, you don't need to change the layout.) Add a title in the title placeholder, and then drag the title off the slide area. The titles don't show up in your presentation, but they give you the background information you need to identify slides in the Define Custom Show dialog box.

CAUTION!

When you run a custom show, slides that you didn't include from the complete presentation are not available in Slide Show view. To retain access to slides you might need to refer to, hide the slides instead.

Laying the groundwork for an expert presentation

Like a professionally decorated room, great presentations give the audience a sense of flow, with harmonious touches that help connect the content on each slide to the greater whole of the presentation. A consistent look and feel from slide to slide helps to maintain the flow. This consistency is controlled by masters (slide masters, handout masters, and notes masters). You can access each from the Master Views group on the View tab.

Customizing the slide master

Slide masters control the layout and formatting of slides in your presentation and are therefore a critical component in achieving a consistent appearance. By editing the slide master, you define the default settings for every slide in the presentation—including the background, colors, fonts, effects, and placeholder sizes and positions. Figure 20-14 shows a typical Slide Master view.

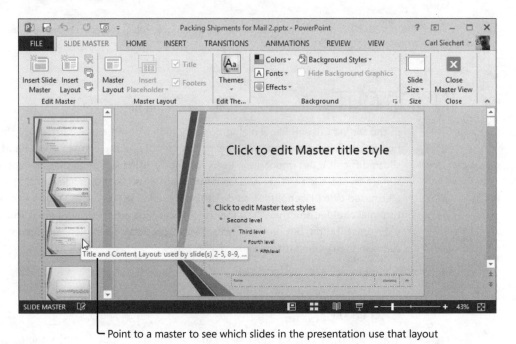

Point to a master to see which slides in the presentation use that layout

Figure 20-14 The top master in Slide Master view is the slide master, which holds the design elements for the entire presentation. The indented masters define formatting and design elements for each of the theme's available layouts.

On a slide master, you can add your company logo or a picture of your school mascot. When you create your slides, the image appears in the same location on each slide.

As you can see in Figure 20-14, the Slide Master tab appears when you click Slide Master on the View tab. Use this tab to work with theme settings and to add or remove slide masters or slide layouts. The other tabs (such as Insert, for inserting a logo or another graphic, and Home, for applying text formatting) remain available.

Slide masters can save you time because changes you make on them affect all slides you add later. Of course, you can overwrite these design settings in Normal view; on the slide master you're merely setting the presentation defaults.

Under the slide master, the indented thumbnails show layout variants based on the theme and other characteristics of the slide master. For example, an image you add to the slide master appears on all slides in the presentation, whereas an image you add to a slide layout appears only when that layout is applied to a slide.

CAUTION!

If you're thinking about modifying the slide master, do so before you create your presentation slides to ensure that every slide matches the slide master settings. If you edit the slide masters after you've done some editing in the presentation, the new master slide settings might not carry over. Whether the revised slide master settings prevail depends on several conditions that, practically speaking, make it somewhat unpredictable. If you find that your slides aren't using newly applied master slide formats, try using the Reset Slide option on the Home tab in Normal view.

To avoid this problem and make creating presentations easier in the future, make your changes to the slide master and layouts, and then save the presentation as a template.

INSIDE OUT   Use more than one theme in a single presentation

When you apply a design theme to a presentation, it affects all slides. It's the best and worst thing about PowerPoint. What if you want to use two design themes in the same presentation? (Despite the desire for consistency within a presentation, this is not an uncommon requirement. For example, it's useful when you have several topics in your presentation and you want to differentiate each topic, perhaps with a colored bar down the side or "tab" indicators along the top of each slide.)

You can do this with slide masters. Simply add a second slide master to your presentation in Slide Master view. (On the Slide Master tab, click Insert Slide Master.) Apply a different theme to each slide master, or make other changes. Then, in Normal view, apply the layout with the theme you want by choosing it from the gallery that appears when you click New Slide or Slide Layout in the Slides group on the Home tab.

Creating a custom layout

Each theme has its own set of layouts. You often end up picking a layout that provides the closest match for what you need and then move things around a bit. Your time might be better spent customizing layouts with placeholders where they'll be used most often.

To create a custom layout, in Slide Master view, click Insert Layout on the Slide Master tab. A basic layout with a title placeholder (and little else) appears. Add placeholders by clicking Insert Placeholder on the Slide Master tab to display the gallery of placeholder types shown in Figure 20-15. Select a placeholder, and then drag on the layout to position it.

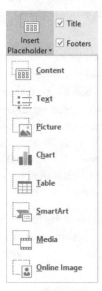

Figure 20-15 Add placeholders to custom slide layouts so you can easily insert content when you create a presentation. Clear Title and Footers to omit those items from the layout.

Unfortunately, PowerPoint doesn't do a great job of naming layouts you create. The first layout you create is named "Custom Layout." Subsequent layouts are assigned names with numbers in front, like "1_Custom Layout." It's a good idea to give your custom layouts meaningful names while you're still working in Slide Master view. Select a layout thumbnail and click Rename in the Edit Master group on the Slide Master tab. This simple step makes finding the layout you need much easier while you're working in Normal view. If you still have trouble locating your layouts, consider deleting the default layouts you don't use.

INSIDE OUT   Use a customized slide master in other presentations

Customizing a slide master takes work, although not nearly as much work as customizing every slide in a deck. The changes you make apply only to the current presentation. To make a customized slide master available for other presentations, save the presentation as a template. Then, to use your new template, click File, New, Personal, and open a new presentation based on the template you created.

Customizing other masters

When customizing your presentation masters, you'll probably spend most of your time in Slide Master view. But there are two other master views you can work with: Handout Master and Notes Master.

These views, which are used primarily for printed output, offer fewer options for customization. Unlike with slide masters, you can't add content placeholders to either handouts or notes, but you can add items like headers, footers, page numbers, and slide thumbnails. The available options appear on the tab for each type of master. Figure 20-16 shows the options for handout masters; similar options are available for notes.

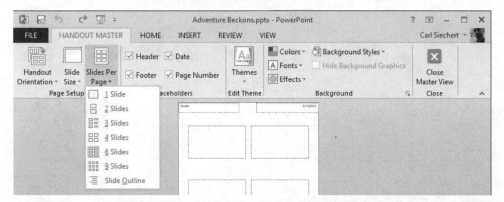

Figure 20-16 On the Handout Master tab, you can specify the orientation for printed handouts and for the slides on each handout.

For details about printing handouts and notes, see "Creating notes and handouts" in Chapter 19.

Our favorite PowerPoint tweaks and tips

Up to this point, we've shown you everything you need to know to create some beautiful presentations. Combine this knowledge with some of the graphics techniques discussed earlier in this book, and you're way ahead of the presentation game. But we're not done yet. On the following pages you'll learn about some additional features in PowerPoint that just might make you go "Wow."

Creating a photo album with PowerPoint

Remember the days when you sat on the living room floor with hundreds of vacation photos in front of you and stuck them, one by one, onto the pages of a bound photo album? Now you can create electronic photo albums that display your pictures much like those old albums did, except they're far easier to share. You can use these electronic albums to document birthday parties and family vacations, but they're not just for personal use. Photo albums also work well to document the progress of a project or to show a sequence of before and after photos.

The Photo Album feature in PowerPoint creates a new presentation that includes the photos you want. Although you can achieve the same results by creating a presentation with File, New, it's quicker and easier with Photo Album. Instead of creating a presentation, inserting a slide for each picture, inserting each picture individually, and then adding titles and captions, the Photo Album feature performs the entire process with a single dialog box, which is shown in Figure 20-17.

Figure 20-17 Use the Photo Album dialog box to select your photos, retouch them as necessary, and define the slide layout.

To create a photo album, follow these steps:

1. On the Insert tab, in the Images group, click Photo Album. The Photo Album dialog box shown in Figure 20-17 appears.

2. Click File/Disk to open the Insert New Pictures dialog box, which is nearly identical to the standard Open dialog box. Select the picture (or pictures) you want, and then click Insert.

INSIDE OUT   Insert pictures the easy way

You can do a couple of things to expedite this step. First, put all the pictures you want to use in a single folder. Second, instead of selecting a single picture file, clicking Insert, and then clicking File/Disk to insert another, select multiple files in the Insert New Pictures dialog box. To do that, click the first picture file, and then Shift+click the last picture file in the sequence to select them all. If the files you want are not contiguous, press Ctrl as you click each file name.

3. Click New Text Box for each text box you want to include. Each text box you insert takes the place of a picture in the layout. You might want one for each picture or one for each slide, for example. (You enter the text for each text box in Normal view after the photo album is created.)

4. Under Album Layout, in the Picture Layout list, select the number of pictures you want on each slide.

   From the Frame Shape list, select the type of frame you want around each picture. (This option isn't available if you choose Fit To Slide as the picture layout.)

   If you want to apply an Office theme, click Browse, select a theme file, and then click Open.

5. Now return to the Pictures In Album list. The numbers identify the slide for each picture or text box. Use the arrow buttons to set the order of pictures and text boxes as you want it.

6. In the Pictures In Album list, select each picture, and then use the tools under the preview image to make corrections to the picture as needed. (More advanced tools are available in Normal view, which appears after the photo album is created. For details, see "Making your pictures look great" in Chapter 5.)

7. If you want to show the name of each picture file below the picture, select Captions Below All Pictures. (This option isn't available if Fit To Slide is selected.)

8. Click Create. Your photo album opens in a new PowerPoint window.

There's nothing special about a presentation created with the Photo Album feature. You can work with the resulting images and text boxes in much the same way you would if you had inserted each individually, you can apply themes, and you can make other changes to your presentation. However, you might find it easier to revisit the Photo Album dialog box to reorder items, adjust the layout, or add more text boxes. To do this, on the Insert tab, click the arrow next to Photo Album, and then click Edit Photo Album.

Inserting hyperlinks

Adding hyperlinks to a presentation gives you and your viewers a quick way to jump to specific slides or websites. You can also use hyperlinks to launch an email message or create a document. For example, if you're creating a slide deck with information about your company's products, you can lead the viewer to more information by embedding links to your company's website or to another slide with additional information. To create a hyperlink, start by selecting the text or object you're linking from, click the Insert tab, and then click Hyperlink.

INSIDE OUT   Create a linked custom show

Inserting a link to a custom show allows you to create dynamic agenda slides on which each agenda item is linked to a custom show. You can also incorporate "one-off" custom shows that you can launch via a hyperlink if topics off the agenda come up during the course of the presentation. For more information about custom shows, see "Defining a custom show" earlier in this chapter.

For more information about inserting hyperlinks, see "Entering hyperlinks" in Chapter 4, "Entering, editing, and formatting text."

Inserting action buttons

Action buttons are shapes with defined hyperlinks that allow you to jump to specific slides in a presentation. In this way, action buttons are similar to hyperlinks—but you can do much more with an action button.

To insert an action button, click the Insert tab, click Shapes (in the Illustrations group), and scroll to the bottom of the Shapes gallery, where you'll find the Action Buttons category.

Click one of these buttons, and then drag to draw it on your slide. The Action Settings dialog box, shown in Figure 20-18, appears.

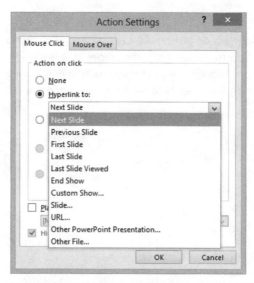

Figure 20-18 This dialog box appears automatically when you insert an action button. You can display it later by selecting the button (or other object) and clicking Action in the Links group on the Insert tab.

On the Mouse Click tab in the Action Settings dialog box, select the action you want to occur when a viewer clicks the button. Similar settings are available on the Mouse Over tab; these actions take place when a viewer hovers the mouse pointer over the button in Slide Show view.

As shown in Figure 20-18, the list below Hyperlink To offers options similar to those in the Insert Hyperlink dialog box. Other options in the Action Settings dialog box allow you to specify a program or macro to run or a sound to play when the button is clicked.

INSIDE OUT   Apply mouse click and mouse over actions to any object

There's nothing magical about the action button shapes. True, when you insert one on a slide the Action Settings dialog box opens automatically, and each button has a predefined action assigned to it. But actions that take place on mouse click or mouse over can be assigned to any object—other shapes, pictures, or text boxes, for example. Simply select an object, and then click Action in the Links group on the Insert tab to assign an action.

You might find it useful to include action buttons in a self-guided presentation because some people might not know how to navigate between slides in PowerPoint. You can add familiar navigation action buttons to the bottom of every slide to help your viewers move to the first and last slides in the deck as well as to the next and previous slides, as shown in Figure 20-19.

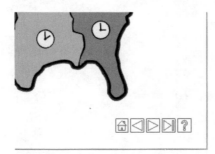

Figure 20-19 Action buttons used for slide navigation are easily spotted in the lower-right corner of each slide. After you create the first set, copy the objects and paste them onto the remaining slides—or better yet, add them to the slide master.

Typically, navigation buttons are best when they have been placed on every slide in the presentation. This can create the feeling of consistency for your audience. It's best to pick a location that doesn't interfere with any object on any of the slides. Then, consider creating and placing the action buttons on the slide master. This way, you can be sure they show up on every slide in the same location.

For information about adding elements to the slide master, see "Customizing the slide master" earlier in this chapter.

INSIDE OUT   Use action settings to create hot spots

A hot spot is an area on an image that is linked to another slide or a website. For example, in a group photo, you might define a hot spot around each person that displays that person's contact information when the hot spot is clicked. You could take it a step further by adding the person's name as a ScreenTip.

As another example, on a map of the United States, you could create a hot spot in each time zone; clicking the hot spot takes the viewer to a slide with information about that region of the country, such as a radio or television broadcast schedule. To do that, follow these steps:

1. Insert a shape. For this example, insert a rectangle that's slightly larger than the Central Time zone.

2. To make the hot spot invisible, use options on the Format tab under Drawing Tools to remove both the fill and outline color.

3. Use Edit Shape, Edit Points on the Format tab to set the shape's points to roughly correspond to the time zone borders, as shown here.

For information about inserting a shape, formatting it, and editing points, see "Adding shapes and text boxes" in Chapter 5.

4. Select the shape, and on the Insert tab, click Action. In the Action Settings dialog box, select Hyperlink To, select Slide, and select the slide about the Central Time zone.

To test your handiwork, open the slide in Slide Show view. You won't be able to see the shape that defines the hot spot area, but when you click it, PowerPoint should jump to the specified slide.

Embedding fonts in a presentation file

An issue we often see is presentation text that looks fine until it's displayed on a different computer. This typically happens when the computers you're using don't have the same sets of fonts. A way to prevent text from looking different on other computers is to embed the fonts a presentation uses into the file.

To embed fonts in your presentation, click File, Options. In the PowerPoint Options dialog box, click the Save tab, and select Embed Fonts In The File, as shown in Figure 20-20. Selecting this option embeds each OpenType and TrueType font that's used in the presentation. (Other font types, such as PostScript and printer fonts, can't be embedded.)

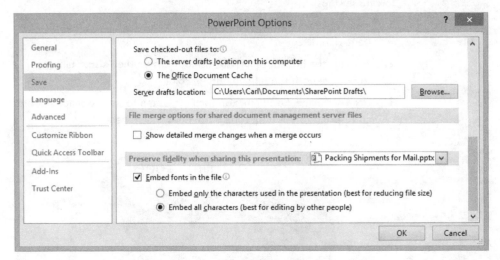

Figure 20-20 Under Embed Fonts In The File, select the first option if the presentation will be viewed on other computers; select the second option if it will be edited on another computer.

CAUTION

Be sure the fonts you plan to embed don't have any license restrictions that might prevent them from being embedded. When embedded, some fonts allow printing and viewing but not editing. Other fonts allow full use when embedded, and still others don't allow embedding at all. To determine whether a particular font can be embedded, open the Fonts folder in Control Panel, right-click the font (an individual font, not a font family), and choose Properties. On the Details tab, check the Font Embeddability property.

Playing music behind your slides

Some presentations—particularly photo montages—don't require narration and can benefit from a musical accompaniment. You can apply music (or other recorded audio) to a series of slides or to an entire presentation. Along with a snappy Office theme, adding music can really enhance an otherwise snooze-inducing photo album of vacation snapshots.

> **CAUTION**
>
> Although digital rights management (DRM) technologies that prevent copying music tracks are largely disappearing in favor of DRM-free formats like MP3, be aware that most recorded music is protected by copyright. A roomful of lawyers (probably with no two of them agreeing) could explain how copyright law applies to music used in PowerPoint presentations, but understand that legal minefields abound, particularly if your presentation will be posted to the Internet or presented in anything resembling a "public performance."

To set up background music, begin by inserting the audio file on the slide where you want the music to start playing. (On the Insert tab, click Audio, Audio On My PC.) After inserting the audio object, select it and click the Playback tab under Audio Tools. In the Audio Styles group, click Play In Background. As shown in Figure 20-21, doing so makes several settings under Audio Options—exactly the settings you need for background music.

Figure 20-21 Selecting Play In Background makes the crucial settings under Audio Options that enable background music.

In Slide Show view, the audio starts playing automatically when you display the slide where you inserted the audio file.

INSIDE OUT   Hide the audio icon

If the icon for the audio object gets in your way while you're editing in Normal view, drag it off the slide into the gray area on the side.

Creating custom bullets

Many of the text placeholders you use in PowerPoint include bullets for bulleted lists. As you can with other Office programs, you use the Bullets option on the Home tab to select bullet shapes and styles. Office has a little-known feature that is particularly useful for bullets in PowerPoint presentations: the ability to import your own images. For example, on a corporate presentation, you might use the company logo as a bullet.

To create your own custom picture bullets, select the lines of text you want to modify and click the arrow next to Bullets in the Paragraph group on the Home tab. Click Bullets And Numbering, the command at the bottom of the Bullets gallery. In the Bullets And Numbering dialog box that appears, click Picture. In the Insert Pictures dialog box, click the picture location, and then select the picture you want.

Click Insert, and your new bullet is applied to the selected text on the slide. Notice that your custom bullet now appears in the Bullets gallery, making it easy to apply to other lists.

For something like a corporate logo that you'll want to use in all business presentations, apply your custom bullet on slide layouts within your slide master that include bulleted lists.

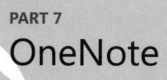

PART 7

OneNote

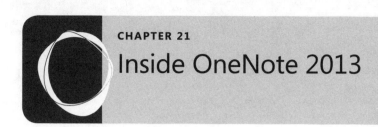

MICROSOFT introduced OneNote more than 10 years ago, and it's finally getting its due. In earlier Office versions, OneNote was included in just a few Office editions, but in Office 2013, OneNote is elevated to marquee status and is part of every edition.

So what is OneNote exactly? The program's metaphor is absolutely accurate: OneNote is a digital replacement for a traditional loose-leaf notebook in which you can save class notes, academic research, meeting minutes, or just about anything else you might be tempted to put on a piece of paper. You can type, write, paste, print, scan, snip, clip, and send just about anything to OneNote, which saves each item on a page in a section of a notebook. You can move the pieces around on the page, format text and resize pictures, and arrange text into tidy outlines and lists.

OneNote notebooks are infinitely expandable. You can add new pages and sections, organize pages and subpages, and create as many new notebooks as you can fit in your default storage location. Personal notebooks are stored on your hard drive; you can share and sync notebooks using SkyDrive, a shared network folder, or a SharePoint site.

What's in a OneNote notebook?

The basic organizational unit of OneNote is the notebook. When you create a new notebook or open a saved one, its icon and name appear in the Notebook pane on the left of the OneNote window, with the hierarchy of sections (and, optionally, section groups) shown in an indented list below the notebook icon and in tabs along the top of the contents pane. Selecting a section displays its contents in the page tabs bar on the right. Selecting a page from that list displays it in the contents pane. To begin adding your own notes, pictures, and web clippings, you can rename the default section and page or start adding new sections and pages of your own.

Figure 21-1 shows an open notebook containing four sections and one section group, with five pages in the open section.

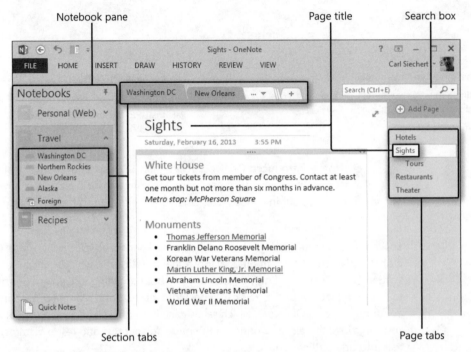

Figure 21-1 Select a notebook, click one of its section tabs (in the Notebook pane or above the contents pane), and then select a page in the current section by using the list on the right.

As your collection of notes grows in size and complexity, you can combine sections into section groups and gather a group of related pages together as subpages. To avoid clutter, you can selectively collapse and expand section groups; similarly, you can collapse subpages under a parent page. You can also create clickable links that open other OneNote pages, Office documents, Outlook items, or webpages.

For more on how to manage section groups and subpages, see "Working with sections and section groups" later in this chapter. You'll find details on how to link pages to one another and to external content in "Using links for quick connections" in Chapter 22, "Tagging, organizing, and finding information."

As a notebook grows in size (and especially when you use multiple notebooks), search becomes essential. Use the search box above the page tabs. For details, see "Smart search strategies" in Chapter 22.

There's no limit on the type of information you can save in a notebook. A partial list of common tasks and activities includes the following:

- Taking notes during classroom lectures and lab sessions

- Organizing online research

- Recording the minutes of a meeting

- Planning a family reunion or vacation

- Creating to-do lists for short-term tasks and long-term goals

- Organizing manuals and warranty information for household appliances

Or anything that strikes your fancy, really.

There's no right or wrong way to build a notebook or to organize its parts. Your personal preferences dictate how you can manage and use notebooks.

Creating and opening OneNote files

One striking difference between OneNote and other Office programs is the absence of a Save button or command. OneNote does indeed store its work in files, but it handles virtually all of the management tasks for those files in the background. Except in rare circumstances, you should never need to directly manipulate OneNote files.

To create a new notebook, click File, New. Click the place where you want the notebook files stored, provide a name for the new notebook, and then click Create Notebook.

If you choose Computer from the list of places, OneNote creates a folder in the OneNote Notebooks subfolder of your user profile's Documents folder by default. You can specify an alternative location by clicking Create In A Different Folder.

The text you enter in the Notebook Name box is used as both the folder name and the display name shown in the Notebook pane. After you create a notebook, you can change its display name at any time without affecting the original folder name. To do so, right-click the notebook name in the Notebook pane and click Properties. That opens a dialog box like the one shown in Figure 21-2, which also allows you to change the location or format of the notebook.

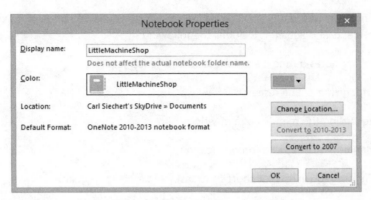

Figure 21-2 Changing the display name of a notebook here does not affect the name of the folder where its files are stored.

So what about the files themselves? Each notebook section is saved in its own file, using the default Microsoft OneNote Section format with a file name extension of .one. If you create a OneNote notebook by clicking File and then New in OneNote 2013, the program creates a tiny file with the name Open Notebook; this file is saved in Microsoft OneNote Table Of Contents format, with a file name extension of .onetoc2.

Strictly speaking, the Open Notebook file isn't needed. If you point OneNote to a folder filled with OneNote section files, it will ask you if you want to open the folder as a notebook. If you click Yes, OneNote creates a new OneNote Table of Contents file, using the folder name as the notebook display name and populating it with all section files contained within the folder.

You don't need to manually save OneNote files. OneNote automatically saves your work every 30 seconds and when you close a notebook or the program itself. If you've just made a large number of changes and you want to force a save instead of waiting for the next automatic save, press Ctrl+S.

The Export menu allows you to export or share notebooks, pages, and sections in a variety of formats, as we explain in "Printing, publishing, and sharing notes" in Chapter 23, "OneNote 2013 inside out."

Choosing the right OneNote file format

When you create a new notebook in OneNote 2013, your files are automatically saved in the OneNote 2010-2013 file format, the format that was introduced with Office 2010. If you intend to share notebooks with people who are still using OneNote 2007, or if you want to preserve the ability to open those files on another computer using the earlier version of OneNote, you need to explicitly choose the alternative format.

To convert a notebook from OneNote 2007 format to OneNote 2010-2013 format (or vice versa), right-click the notebook icon in the Notebook pane and then click Properties. Click Convert To 2010-2013 or Convert To 2007. This conversion applies to the entire contents of a notebook. When you make the conversion, the format you choose becomes the default format for new sections within that notebook.

When you move a section from one notebook to another, OneNote automatically converts the section to the default format of the destination notebook. If you use File Explorer to manually move a section file saved in OneNote 2007 format to a notebook whose default format is OneNote 2010-2013, the older format is preserved, and you see an information bar warning you of potential incompatibilities when you open that section.

If you choose to save a notebook using the older OneNote 2007 file format, the following features are affected:

- The math equations feature is unavailable, and any existing equations are converted to static images.

- Context links (linked notes) and version information are permanently removed.

- Subpages are preserved but can no longer be collapsed in the pages tab list.

- The contents of the Recycle Bin for that notebook are permanently removed.

In addition, you must use OneNote 2010-2013 format to save a notebook in a SkyDrive folder or on a SharePoint site so that you can open and edit the notebook in a web browser using the OneNote Web App.

OneNote 2013 allows you to open a notebook saved in OneNote 2003 format, but that notebook is opened in read-only mode. If you convert a notebook from OneNote 2003 format to either OneNote 2007 or 2010-2013 format, the conversion is permanent and cannot be undone.

Chapter 21

Filling a notebook with text, pictures, clippings, and more

Every time you type, paste, or otherwise insert a new item on a notebook page, OneNote creates a note container for that item. Note containers can hold text, pictures, audio and video clips, handwriting, and clippings from a webpage or from the screen. The initial size of the container matches the size of the object you're creating or inserting; if you click and begin typing, a new note container is created immediately and expands in width and depth to accommodate your input.

Note containers are normally invisible. To see the container, move the mouse pointer over its contents, click to select the contents, or position the insertion point within the container. Figure 21-3 shows a note container, with the pointer positioned over the Move handle at the top. Drag the handle to move the container and its contents to a new position on the page. Click the Move handle to select the entire container so that you can cut, copy, or delete it and its contents. Drag the right edge to make the container wider.

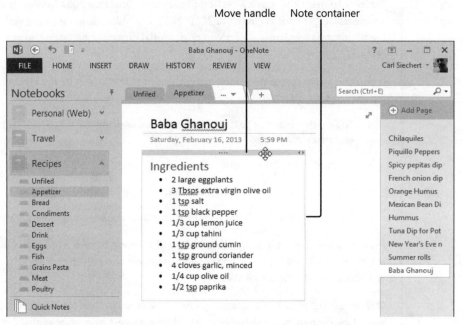

Figure 21-3 Drag the Move handle at the top of a note container to reposition the container and its contents on the page.

INSIDE OUT   Merge or split note containers

If you've typed or pasted text into separate containers on the same page, how do you merge them into a single container? Simple: click the Move handle on the second container to select its entire contents. Then, hold down the Shift key as you drag that container into the first one. When you see the contents of the second container snap into position in the first container, release the Shift key. To split text in a single container into two discrete containers, select the text you want to move into a new container and drag it outside the original container. When you release the mouse button, OneNote creates a new container, which you can then work with independently.

In the remainder of this section, we explain how to work with different types of content that you enter directly or paste from the Clipboard—text, pictures, equations, and ink, for example. But you can also send items directly to OneNote by using the Screen Clipping tool and the Send To options in Outlook and Internet Explorer. When you send a web clipping, a screen clipping, or an Outlook item to OneNote, you see a dialog box like the one shown in Figure 21-4. If you select a notebook section, the item is sent to a new page in that section; you can also select a specific page within a notebook and send the item to that page, where it's placed at the bottom of the page, below any existing content.

Figure 21-4 When you send an item or a clipping from another program to OneNote, you specify the destination page or section here.

For information about the Send To options in Outlook, see "Using OneNote with Outlook" in Chapter 23. For information about the Screen Clipping tool and other Send To options, see "Customizing the OneNote taskbar icon" and "Using quick notes," also in Chapter 23.

Text

Entering text from the keyboard is the simplest way to fill a notebook. Click to position the insertion point on a page and start typing. (You can also paste text into a page, with or without formatting.) The text you enter or paste appears in a single note container.

OneNote supports basic outlining functions for text. Press Enter to create a new paragraph, and then change the outline level for that paragraph by pressing Tab or Shift+Tab to demote or promote it to the appropriate level.

You can move any paragraph up or down or adjust its outline level by dragging it. You can also use keyboard shortcuts: press Alt+Shift and then use the Up or Down Arrow key to move the paragraph up or down in the outline; use Alt+Shift and the Right or Left Arrow key to demote or promote a paragraph in the outline. When you move the mouse pointer over a paragraph, a Move button appears to its left. Move the mouse pointer over the button, and the pointer turns to a four-headed arrow; click to select the entire paragraph and move it up, down, left, or right. In the example shown next, the mouse pointer is to the right of "Reptiles," so the Move button appears to the left of that line.

Mammals
Birds
Reptiles
Amphibians
Fishes
Insects
Miscellaneous Animals

INSIDE OUT   Add a date and time stamp to any text

At the top of every notebook page is a title, and beneath the title is a date/time stamp that shows when you created that notebook page. If you use a notebook page to collect random thoughts over a period of weeks or months, you might want to stamp individual notes with the date and time. Right-click where you want the time stamp to appear. At the bottom of the shortcut menu, click the menu option that lists your name and the current date and time. To insert just the current date, use the keyboard shortcut Alt+Shift+D. To insert the current time, press Alt+Shift+T. To insert both the date and time (without your name), press Alt+Shift+F.

Lists

You can format any text on a OneNote page as a list using bullets or numbering. List formatting applies to the current paragraph or, if multiple paragraphs are selected, to all paragraphs in the selection. If you've used list formatting in Word or PowerPoint, you already understand the basics. OneNote adds a few twists to simple lists.

To choose a bullet character and immediately apply it to the current paragraph or selection, click the arrow next to the Bullets tool (on the Mini toolbar or in the Basic Text group on the Home tab). The selection of characters in the Bullet Library (shown in Figure 21-5) is fixed and cannot be customized.

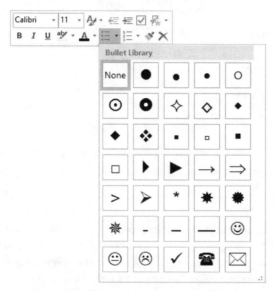

Figure 21-5 Click the arrow next to the Bullets tool on the Mini toolbar (shown here) or on the Home tab to display the Bullet Library.

To format the current paragraph or selection with the most recently used bullet character, click the Bullets tool or press Ctrl+Period. To insert a standard bullet character (a big black dot), type an asterisk followed by a space or tab at the beginning of a paragraph.

Numbered lists work in similar fashion. To begin a simple numbered list, start with a number or letter followed by a period, a closing parenthesis, or a hyphen; then press the Spacebar. The Numbering Library (shown in Figure 21-6) offers an assortment of numbering and outline formats; to display it, click the arrow to the right of the Numbering tool on the Mini toolbar or in the Basic Text group on the Home tab.

Chapter 21

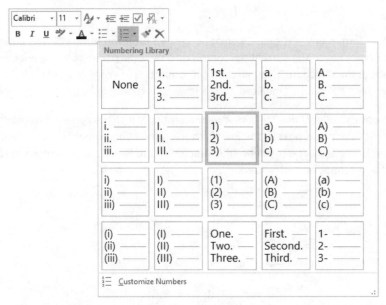

Figure 21-6 Numbering Library choices automatically number multilevel lists appropriately.

As with automatic list formatting in other Office programs, pressing Enter continues the list formatting in the next paragraph. To end automatic formatting, press Enter twice.

Tables

You can add a simple table to any page in OneNote, using its rows and columns to arrange data that doesn't lend itself to paragraphs. OneNote tables offer a basic set of features and formatting options, far simpler than those found in Word or PowerPoint. When the insertion point is within a table, OneNote makes a custom Layout tab available, as shown in Figure 21-7. (The same options are also available if you right-click anywhere within the table.)

To create a table, use either of the following techniques:

- On the Insert tab, click Table. Then click the grid square representing the number of rows and columns you want, or click Insert Table and select the number of rows and columns from a dialog box.

- Easiest of all, type the text you want to appear in the first cell of the first row, and then press Tab. Continue pressing Tab to create new columns, with or without text, and press Enter to begin a new row.

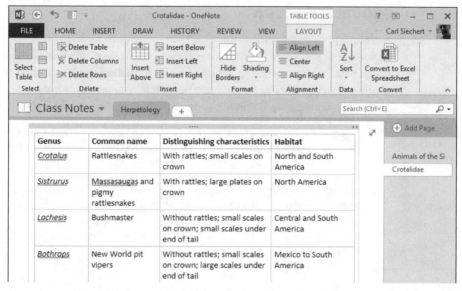

Figure 21-7 The Layout tab under Table Tools allows you to arrange rows, columns, and cells in a OneNote table and align their contents. A new feature in OneNote 2013 lets you sort table rows based on the content of the column containing the insertion point.

If you use OneNote tables regularly, you can save some time by learning a few keyboard shortcuts in addition to the Tab and Enter keys. To create a new column to the left or right of the current column, press Ctrl+Alt+E or Ctrl+Alt+R, respectively. To create a new row below the current one, press Ctrl+Enter. To create a new row above the current one, move the insertion point to the beginning of the row and press Enter. (To insert a row above the first row, click anywhere in that row and then click Insert Above, in the Insert group on the Layout tab.) To begin a new paragraph in the same cell, press Alt+Enter.

Web clippings

OneNote and Internet Explorer work exceptionally well together. As you browse, you can collect snippets of text, images, or entire pages for insertion into a notebook page. The mechanics are simple: make a selection (skip this step if you want to save the entire page) and then click the Send To OneNote button on the Command bar in Internet Explorer. Alternatively, you can right-click a selection or a page and then click Send To OneNote on the shortcut menu. These steps open the Select Location In OneNote dialog box (shown earlier in Figure 21-4), where you can specify a section or page as the destination.

TROUBLESHOOTING

A webpage doesn't look right when you send it to OneNote

Although the process of sending a webpage to OneNote is easy, the results are not always what you'd expect. In particular, heavily formatted webpages often translate poorly onto a OneNote page, with text flowing in an unreadable fashion and tables rearranged haphazardly. If that happens, click Undo and try either of these approaches.

- Select the most important portions of the webpage and try to send them individually to your OneNote page. You'll lose the overall design, but that might not matter if you're mostly concerned with content.

- In Internet Explorer, "print" the page or selection. In the Print dialog box, select Send To OneNote 2013 under Select Printer. Because this method prints the page or selection as an image, you lose the ability to copy or edit text on the resulting item, but you are certain to get an accurate (and readable) representation of the page.

If you use a browser other than Internet Explorer, your best option is to select all or part of a webpage, copy the selection to the Clipboard, and paste the result into OneNote.

Regardless of the method you choose, OneNote adds a link to the source webpage at the end of the item, making it easy to revisit the source when you review your research later.

Pictures

Pictures fit nicely in OneNote pages, either alone or accompanied by text. To add a picture to a OneNote page, you can paste it from the Clipboard or click Pictures on the Insert tab and then choose an image file.

What happens next depends on the destination you select. If you choose an empty page as the paste target, OneNote drops the picture into a note container, resizing the image if necessary to fit the page, with the insertion point positioned just below the picture, awaiting your caption. If you insert another picture, it appears in the current note container at the insertion point. However, if you click an empty space outside a note container, and then insert a picture into a page that already contains at least one item, the pasted picture appears at its original size with no note container. In either case, you can resize the image using handles on the bottom and right sides; use the handle on the lower-right corner to preserve the picture's aspect ratio. To resize any image to the full dimensions of the original file, right-click the picture and then click Restore To Original Size.

For a complete picture of how to work with photos and illustrations in Office 2013, see Chapter 5, "Working with graphics and pictures."

OneNote treats each picture as if it were a paragraph, so you can move it up and down with text (or other pictures) in a note container. You can also paste or move a picture into a table. After you insert the first image and resize it to fit the column width and row height, pictures you paste into other cells are scaled accordingly.

OneNote can recognize text in pictures and use that text for searches; we explain how this works in "Converting printouts and pictures to text" in Chapter 23.

Screen clippings

Other Office programs allow you to copy and paste a screenshot from any open window. OneNote offers a more limited Screen Clipping version of that feature.

For full details on how to use screenshots and screen clippings in Office 2013, see "Capturing and inserting screenshots" in Chapter 5.

As with the other Office programs, you can use the ribbon to kick off the process: click Screen Clipping on the Insert tab to select a portion of any window to automatically copy and paste into OneNote. When you use this option, OneNote temporarily minimizes itself so that you have full access to the rest of the screen; just make sure the window from which you want to clip is visible behind OneNote. Your selection is inserted in the current page at the current insertion point.

Unlike with the other Office programs, you can use the Create Screen Clipping keyboard shortcut, Windows logo key+S, to capture a portion of the screen, even if OneNote isn't running. (If OneNote is open, the OneNote window remains visible on the screen, allowing you to capture a clipping from one page and paste it in another.) After you use this option, OneNote displays a variation of the Select Location In OneNote dialog box, shown in Figure 21-8. You can choose a OneNote section or page or use the Copy To Clipboard button to save your selection and use it in another program.

Figure 21-8 When you use the Create Screen Clipping shortcut (Windows logo key+S) to copy part of a screen, options at the bottom of the Select Location In OneNote dialog box let you paste the image into OneNote or save it to the Clipboard.

Every screen clipping you add to a page is tagged with the date and time it was taken; if the source is a webpage, the tag includes the page name and URL.

Scanned images

If you have a scanner or camera attached to your computer, you can use it for capturing images and inserting them in OneNote pages—a trick that's not available in other Office 2013 programs. To insert an image, click the Insert tab and click Scanned Image (in the Images group). A dialog box appears, as shown next. Select your device and then click Insert or Custom Insert. If you choose Insert, OneNote uses settings from your previous scan. If you choose Custom Insert, another dialog box appears, in which you make new scanner settings or select a picture on a camera. The appearance of this dialog box and the settings available depend on your attached device.

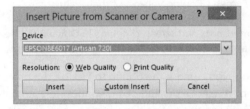

Ink

Your keyboard and mouse aren't the only way to put stuff on a OneNote page. The Draw tab includes a full gallery of pens (shown in Figure 21-9) that you can use to draw, write, and highlight information on a page.

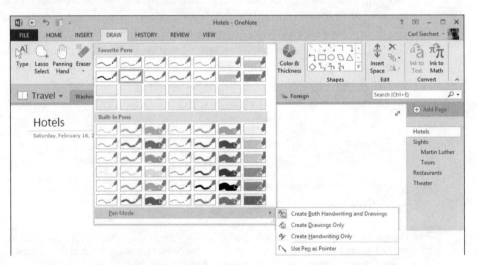

Figure 21-9 Fine-point pens work best for handwriting. The thick markers in the rightmost column are ideal for highlighting text.

If none of the built-in pens are quite right, you can customize pens and highlighters, choosing from a variety of colors and thicknesses.

When you select a pen from the Tools group on the Draw tab, the pointer changes to a colored dot or brush whose color and thickness match the pen you selected. Use the pen to draw or write in an unused area of the page, and your ink is captured in a container, where it moves along with any text or graphics in the container. If you use a highlighter, your markup is treated as a discrete drawing and does not move when you move the text. (To highlight text, use the Highlighter tool in the Basic Text group on the Home tab, as we describe in "Formatting text" later in this chapter.)

To switch from pen mode back to mouse/keyboard interaction, click the Type button at the left of the Draw tab.

If you intend to take handwritten notes or create anything more interesting than stick figures, you'll need a touch-enabled PC or a digitizer and stylus. Although you can add ink using a mouse, the results are rarely satisfactory, especially for handwriting recognition. One noteworthy exception is the set of thick fluorescent-colored highlighters, which work well for marking up printouts.

You can convert handwritten text into typed characters. On a page with handwritten text, click Ink To Text (in the Convert group on the Draw tab). OneNote instantly changes the scrawl into editable text. The handwriting-to-text conversion isn't perfect (although we've seen it correctly interpret scratchings that we had trouble reading ourselves), so be sure to proofread it carefully. If you find an error, right-click it to see and select likely alternatives; click More to see the original handwriting, as shown next.

Equations

Engineers and math majors can use the Equation menu on the Insert tab to create valid, editable math equations in OneNote. The tools are identical to those available in other Office applications. OneNote has the additional capability of converting handwritten mathematical expressions to text. Using the Lasso Select tool on the Draw tab, select the handwriting and then click Ink To Math.

For more information about math-related features, see "Entering mathematical equations" in Chapter 4, "Entering, editing, and formatting text."

Email messages and other Outlook items

If you use Outlook, you'll find a Send To OneNote tool (in the Move group on the Home tab) when you're viewing a mail message in the message list or in a message window. Click that tool to send the entire message to OneNote, with the message header (Subject, From, To, and Sent date) in a table and the text of the message itself just below the header.

If you select an Outlook appointment, meeting, task, or contact, you'll find a Linked *Item* Notes button (where *Item* is the item type) with a slightly different button image. Clicking this button allows you to send relevant details from the current item to a OneNote page with a link back to the original item. (If you've already created the item in OneNote, clicking this button returns you to that page.) A Notes section at the bottom of the item allows you to enter additional text. You can use this feature to keep notes about a meeting or to record details of your history with a contact.

You can also create new linked items in Outlook directly from OneNote. We discuss the tight connections between the two programs in "Using OneNote with Outlook" in Chapter 23.

File attachments

You'll find a File Attachment tool in the Files group on the Insert tab. When you click that tool, select a file from the Choose A File Or A Set Of Files To Insert dialog box, and click Insert, OneNote offers a choice:

- **Attach File**   OneNote embeds the selected file and displays its icon and name on the page. The file attachment is an independent copy, not linked to the original file in any way. Changes you make to the original file are not reflected in the OneNote attachment, and vice versa.

- **Insert Printout**   OneNote embeds the file—as with the first option—*and* inserts a printout of the file as an image.

Attaching a file to a notebook is a good strategy when you want to preserve the file for historical purposes with your notes, or you want to make sure it's always available with the notebook, even if it's deleted from the file system or email message from which it originated. For a document that you want to continue editing, especially with other members of a team, the preferred strategy is to create a link in OneNote to a file stored in a shared network folder or in SkyDrive.

For more details about creating links to files, see "Using links for quick connections" in Chapter 22.

Printouts

When you want to preserve the formatting of an original document or webpage, you can insert it in a notebook as a printout. During setup, OneNote adds a virtual printer to your Devices And Printers folder in Control Panel. When you choose this "printer" as the output from any program (including a web browser or another Office application), OneNote creates an image of the file as it would appear on paper and inserts that printout on a page you select. You can also create a printout from within OneNote; on the Insert tab, click File Printout (in the Files group), and then select the file you want to print.

There's a subtle but significant difference between the two techniques for adding a printout to a OneNote page. If you use the virtual Send To OneNote 2013 printer, your printout appears on the page you select, without any links to the original document. In addition, you can choose which page (or pages) you want to include on the OneNote page. When you click File Printout on the Insert tab and select the same file, OneNote adds the selected file to the current page as an attachment, with a link to the location of the original document. It then opens the associated program in the background, creates the printout, and inserts the printout below the file attachment.

Formatting text

Regardless of its original source, any text on a OneNote page can be formatted using the same tools you use elsewhere in Office. The Basic Text group on the Home tab contains common formatting options, giving you the capability to select a font, change font size and color, and add character attributes such as bold, italic, underline, and strikethrough formatting. You'll also find the Format Painter tool on the Home tab, in the Clipboard group. Most of these options are available on the Mini toolbar as well.

For an overview of common text formatting techniques in Office 2013, see "Applying text formatting" in Chapter 4.

As in Word and PowerPoint, you can apply some character formatting without making a selection first. If the insertion point is in a word, for example, and you press Ctrl+B or Ctrl+I (or click the Bold or Italic tool), your formatting is applied to the entire word. To apply formatting to a phrase or sentence, you have to select the text first. One formatting shortcut you'll find only in OneNote is a toggle to apply or remove strikeout formatting: Ctrl+Hyphen.

The Ctrl+A (Select All) keyboard shortcut works a bit differently in OneNote than it does in the rest of Office. If the insertion point is within a paragraph, pressing Ctrl+A selects the entire paragraph. Press Ctrl+A again to select the entire contents of the current note container, and press the combination once more to select the contents of all note containers on the current page.

If you've used indenting to create an outline, you can select the current paragraph and all its subordinate paragraphs by using the keyboard shortcut Ctrl+Shift+Hyphen.

Similar to Word, OneNote 2013 allows you to select from a small group of ready-made styles to apply to text. The list, shown next, includes six heading styles as well as predefined styles for page titles and some common types of body text.

Styles on this list are applied to all text in the current paragraph, regardless of whether any text is selected. In addition, Word users will appreciate that some common style-related keyboard shortcuts work just as well in OneNote. Use Ctrl+Alt+1 through Ctrl+Alt+6 to apply the Heading 1 through Heading 6 styles, and use Ctrl+Shift+N to quickly convert all formatting for the current paragraph to the built-in Normal style.

There's no keyboard shortcut for the built-in Page Title style, but it's worth noting that Ctrl+Shift+T jumps to the page title and selects all text there. You can apply any text formatting to all or part of a page title; if you are unhappy with the results, reapply the Page Title style.

The bad news about OneNote styles is that the formatting associated with this list cannot be customized, nor can you add your own styles to the list.

INSIDE OUT   Apply highlighting quickly

If you want portions of text on a page to stand out, use Text Highlight Color to apply a fluorescent yellow background (use the drop-down arrow to choose a different color). You can also use either of two keyboard shortcuts to highlight the current selection using the last color you selected: Ctrl+Alt+H or Ctrl+Shift+H. Note that this highlight applies formatting to the text itself and is not the same as the highlighter pen we describe in "Ink" earlier in this chapter. That pen creates a graphic image of the high-lighter ink that can be used over a printout, a picture, or text.

Navigating in OneNote

At the beginning of this chapter, we described the basic organization of OneNote, which consists of pages arranged into sections within notebooks. You don't need us to tell you how to use the basic navigation tools—section tabs along the left and top of the page con-tents, page tabs on the right. In this chapter, we focus on some of the more subtle naviga-tion elements, especially keyboard shortcuts and hidden tricks that you'll value when your collection of notebooks grows too big to simply scan.

The best navigation assistant of all is OneNote's search box, which we discuss in detail in "Smart search strategies" in Chapter 22.

INSIDE OUT   Zoom in for a closer look

Most programs in the Office family include a status bar that offers, among other tools, a slider to zoom in on or out from the current page. OneNote lacks a status bar, but that doesn't mean it's lacking in the zoom department. The Zoom group on the View tab includes a list of preset zoom settings that range from 25% to 200%, or you can type values from 10% through 500%. Alternatively, you can use the Zoom In and Zoom Out tools, which increase or decrease the zoom level in discrete steps. The keyboard equivalents are Ctrl+Alt+Plus Sign/Minus Sign (on the numeric keypad) or Ctrl+Alt+Shift+Plus Sign/Hyphen (to the right of the numbers on the main keyboard).

Chapter 21

Opening and moving between notebooks

Each open notebook has an entry in the Notebook pane. Normally, clicking a section in another notebook replaces the page shown in the contents pane with the most recently opened page in the new section. You can open a second notebook without losing your place in the current one; switch to the View tab and click New Window in the Window group (or press Ctrl+M). If you have OneNote pinned to the taskbar, you can open a new OneNote window by holding Shift as you click the OneNote taskbar icon.

If you prefer keyboard navigation to mouse clicks, here's how to switch to a different open notebook. Press Ctrl+G to move the focus to the first open notebook in the Notebook pane. Press Tab to move down the list of open notebooks (use Shift+Tab to move back up). When you see the selection highlight on the notebook you want to open, press Enter.

Working with sections and section groups

OneNote displays the names of all sections for open notebooks in the Notebook pane. (Click the arrow to the right of the display name to collapse or expand the list of sections for a notebook.) You can also see a list of section tabs for the current notebook along the top of the contents pane. Click a tab to switch immediately to that section. To move quickly between sections in the current notebook, in order, press Ctrl+Tab. (Use Ctrl+Shift+Tab to move through the sections in reverse order.)

The simplest way to create a new section in the current notebook is to click Create A New Section (the plus sign) at the rightmost edge of the section tabs at the top of the contents pane. Alternatively, you can press Ctrl+T. In either case, the new section's default name (New Section 1, for example) is selected so you can start typing immediately to replace it with a descriptive name. To rename a section, double-click its tab and begin typing. Because the displayed section name is the same as the .one file that stores the section content, it has the same limitations as file names in Windows. For example, you can't use certain characters, including these: **< > : " / \ | ? ***.

New sections are automatically added to the bottom of the section tabs list. To change the order of sections, drag tabs up or down in the Notebook pane, or drag left or right at the top of the contents pane. You can also drag sections out of one notebook and into another to move them. Hold down the Ctrl key as you drag a section to make a copy in another notebook. If you prefer using dialog boxes for move and copy operations, right-click the section name and choose Move Or Copy from the shortcut menu. Choose a section from the list of open notebooks, as shown in Figure 21-10, and then click Move or Copy to complete the operation.

You can also combine the contents of two sections using the Merge Into Another Section command on the shortcut menu. Choosing this option has the same effect as moving all pages out of the first section and into the second one and then deleting the first section.

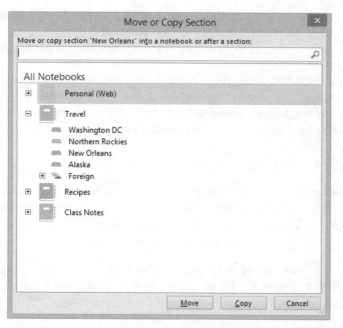

Figure 21-10 To move or copy a section, use this dialog box. You might need to click the plus sign to the left of a notebook name to see its list of sections.

If the number of sections within a notebook starts to become unmanageable, the easy solution is to create one or more section groups. The advantage of section groups is that they can be collapsed and expanded in the Notebook pane. Although you can manually adjust the order of section groups by dragging them in the section tabs list, section groups always appear after sections that are not part of a group, as shown next.

To create a section group, right-click the notebook name and then click New Section Group. Give the new section group a descriptive name and drag sections into it (or create new sections). Note that section groups can be nested within other section groups.

There's nothing magical about section groups. They're actually nothing more than subfolders within the folder that contains the notebook. Creating a section group creates a new subfolder, and moving sections to that section group moves the corresponding OneNote Section files (with the .one file name extension) to that new subfolder.

Working with pages

The techniques for working with pages are similar to those for working with sections. If you right-click any page name in the page tabs bar, you can use options on the shortcut menu to create a new page, delete the selected page, cut or copy the current page to the Clipboard, or paste a page from the Clipboard to the current section.

To move quickly between pages in the current section, use the keyboard shortcuts Ctrl+Page Up and Ctrl+Page Down. To jump to the first or last page in the currently visible set of page tabs, press Alt+Page Up or Alt+Page Down, respectively.

To rename a page, select the page title box and adjust the text there. You cannot directly edit the title text shown on a page tab.

To change the order of pages in a section, drag a page tab up or down in the page tabs bar, or use the keyboard shortcuts Alt+Shift+Up Arrow and Alt+Shift+Down Arrow. To move a page to a different section in the same or another notebook, drag the page to a section tab, either in the Notebook pane or above the contents pane. (Hold down Ctrl while dragging to create a copy and leave the original page intact.) You can also right-click any page and choose Move Or Copy (or press Ctrl+Alt+M) to choose a destination from a dialog box.

Selecting a page involves a few subtle techniques that can be confusing at first. For example, if you click a page tab, the focus shifts to that page, and the insertion point appears on the page at the point where it appeared when you last edited the page. If you're picking up where you left off with a set of meeting minutes or research notes, you can simply start typing. If you click that page icon a second time (or press Ctrl+Shift+A), the entire page is selected, as indicated by a thick border around the page in the contents pane. You're then free to cut or copy the page to the Clipboard or press Delete to send it to the Notebook Recycle Bin.

To create a new, blank page, click Add Page at the top of the page tabs bar or press Ctrl+N. Either way, your page is added at the end of the current list of page tabs. To create a new page just below a specific page, click its page tab and press Ctrl+Alt+N. To add a new page at a specific location using the mouse, move the mouse pointer up and down the page tabs bar. As you do so, you'll see a new-page button alongside the page tabs bar. Point to the button to display an insertion line, as shown next; click the button to add a new page at that location.

Navigating on a page is a straightforward process, with one twist. Although every page has a paper size assigned to it for printing purposes, pages aren't restricted to a fixed size; instead, they expand as needed, in both width and depth, to fit the content you add. If you plan to insert new content above existing content, you can manually add space to a page. On the Insert tab, click Insert Space, and then move the mouse pointer over the page. As you move up or down, the pointer changes to a downward arrow. When you reach the spot where you want to add space, click and drag in the direction you want. Horizontal lines and a large arrow, similar to the one in Figure 21-11, show you the new space you're about to add, with a ghosted image of any existing content appearing in its new position.

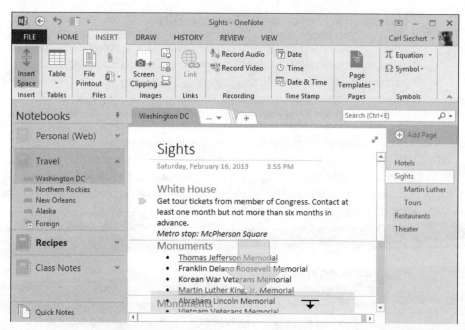

Figure 21-11 Click Insert Space and drag down to add new space above existing content.

You can also use Insert Space to add space at the left side of a page (click in the left margin and drag to the right) or to remove unwanted white space from the bottom or right edge of a page (click and drag up or drag from the right margin to the left).

When editing a page, you can use any of the following shortcuts:

- To scroll up or down in the current page, press Page Up or Page Down.

- To move to the top of the current page, press Ctrl+Home. To move to the bottom of the note container that's lowest on the page, press Ctrl+End.

- To move down the page, from one note container to the next, press Alt+Down Arrow.

You can create subpages that are indented beneath a main page. For notebooks saved in OneNote 2010-2013 format, these subpages are linked to the main page. The group can be collapsed or expanded and can be selected and moved or copied as a group. To create a new subpage below the current page, press Ctrl+Alt+Shift+N.

To increase or decrease the indent level of the current page tab (or a group of adjacent page tabs), click and drag right or left, or right-click and use the shortcut menu options Make Subpage and Promote Subpage. You can also use the keyboard shortcuts Ctrl+Alt+] (right bracket) and Ctrl+Alt+[(left bracket) to increase or decrease the indent.

Using the Notebook Recycle Bin

When you delete a page or section from OneNote, the object doesn't actually disappear for good. Instead, OneNote moves the object to that notebook's Recycle Bin, which is stored in a special folder called OneNote_RecycleBin. This folder is created the first time you delete a page or section—but only for notebooks using the OneNote 2010-2013 file format. If you convert a notebook to OneNote 2007 format, this folder is deleted immediately.

When you delete a section from a notebook, the entire section file is moved to the OneNote_RecycleBin folder. When you delete one or more pages, those pages are moved to the OneNote_DeletedPages file, which is stored in OneNote Section format in the OneNote_RecycleBin folder. To recover deleted pages or sections, click Notebook Recycle Bin on the History tab. In this read-only section group, you'll see all pages and sections you've deleted in the past 60 days. (OneNote automatically deletes items after they linger in the Recycle Bin for 60 days.)

Figure 21-12 shows the Recycle Bin folder for the Travel notebook. It contains two deleted sections (Washington DC and Northern Rockies) and an indeterminate number of pages in the Deleted Pages section. To restore a previously deleted section or page, right-click the section tab or the page tab, click Move Or Copy, and select a destination.

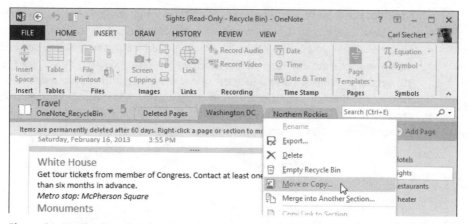

Figure 21-12 The "Read-Only – Recycle Bin" label in the title bar and the information bar at the top of the contents pane serve as reminders that you're working in the Recycle Bin.

For more information about recovering pages, see "Managing page versions" in Chapter 23.

Customizing the look and feel of a notebook page

By default, every new OneNote page starts out with a bland white background and no adornment. You can change the appearance of a page in a variety of ways—some for purely aesthetic reasons and others, such as rule lines, for practical effect. In this section, we discuss the main customizations you can apply to a page.

OneNote 2013 includes an assortment of templates that incorporate many of the customizations we discuss in this section, and you can save your own templates as well. For details, see "Saving and using custom page templates" in Chapter 23.

Page title

The page title box appears at the top of every page in a fixed location, with a date and time stamp below it that (initially, at least) indicates when the page was created. Any text you enter as the title on the page is also used as a label on the page tab.

As far as we've been able to determine, there's no technical limit on the number of characters you can include in a title. From a practical standpoint, however, shorter is better; remember that the main purpose of a title is to provide a label in the page tabs bar.

By default, all page titles are formatted as 20-point Calibri Light. You can change the font, font size, and color of a title. You can also add hyperlinks, tags, and just about any other type of formatting that's applicable to text. This sort of custom formatting might be useful if you intend to print a notebook page or save it as a PDF file for sharing; just remember that the page tab label does not reflect any formatting.

You can't change the position of the date/time stamp just below the page title, nor can you add your own text to it. You can, however, change the date and time. This option is useful if, for example, you create a page in advance of a meeting so that you can keep minutes and want the date and time stamp to reflect the actual starting time. Click the date field to expose a calendar control (like the one shown next) and choose a date. Click the time stamp and then click the clock icon to choose a new time. The Change Page Time dialog box initially displays the current system time; the list of available alternate times is limited to round values, on the hour and half-hour.

For some pages, such as those that include design sketches or diagrams, you might prefer to have no title. Click Hide Page Title (in the Page Setup group on the View tab) to remove the existing title and date/time stamp and hide the page title box.

CAUTION

Don't be misled by the wording of the Hide Page Title button. When you click that button, it permanently deletes the current contents of the page title box and replaces the page tab label with the first recognizable text on the page. If you want to keep the page tab label, copy the page title to the top of the page before "hiding" the title.

We discuss the best way to use the Quick Notes section in "Expert organizational techniques" in Chapter 22.

Page color

The default background color for every notebook page is white. You can adjust this color to one of 16 pastel alternatives using the Page Color tool on the View tab. To remove the background color from a page, click No Color at the bottom of the Page Color menu.

Rule lines

Adding rules or grid lines to a page can help with a variety of note taking and drawing tasks. To add a default set of rule lines (including a vertical red line in the left margin, just like the one on a legal pad or notebook paper), click Rule Lines on the View tab. You can change the default lines by clicking the arrow below Rule Lines and selecting from an assortment of rules and grid sizes in the gallery, shown next.

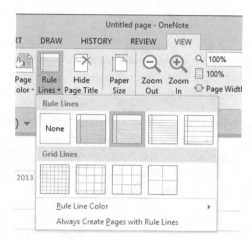

To adjust the color of rule lines from their default light blue to one of 17 alternatives, use the Rule Line Color list on the Rule Lines menu.

You can show or hide rule lines as needed for a specific task. If you're using a tablet to take handwritten notes, for example, you might use rule lines to help keep your notes from creeping up or down the page and then hide them for reviewing later. Likewise, you can use grid lines to initially position images on the page. To toggle the display of rule or grid lines using the keyboard, press Ctrl+Shift+R.

If you prefer to use rule lines for all new pages, choose a set of rule or grid lines and then set it as the default. To accomplish this task, click Always Create Pages With Rule Lines at the bottom of the Rule Lines menu. This has the same effect as selecting Create All New Pages With Rule Lines on the Display tab in the OneNote Options dialog box.

Background image

In addition to background colors, you can choose a single image to use as the background of a page. This option works best with an image that has been specifically created (or edited) for use as a page background. The ideal image has strong elements limited to the top and left margins and soft or faded image elements in the body of the page, where they won't adversely affect readability of the page contents.

For examples of pages that use background images effectively, see "Saving and using custom page templates" in Chapter 23.

To add a background image, first insert the image on the page and position it in the upper-left corner, making certain it is not enclosed in a note container. Then right-click the image and choose Set Picture As Background. To remove a background image, first clear the Set Picture As Background option, click to select the picture, and then press Delete.

Paper size and margins

The Paper Size setting for a default OneNote page is Auto, which means it can expand in any direction with no limits. That's fine if you're planning to use a notebook for strictly digital purposes. However, if you intend to print one or more pages, you'll want to define paper sizes and margins that match the paper and printer you plan to use.

OneNote includes 14 predefined paper sizes as well as a Custom option that allows you to specify your own dimensions. To edit these settings for an existing page, click Paper Size on the View tab. That opens the Paper Size pane on the right side of the page. In Figure 21-13, we've used the Index Card setting to mimic a standard 3-by-5-inch index card; to enhance the effect, we've hidden the page title and added rule lines.

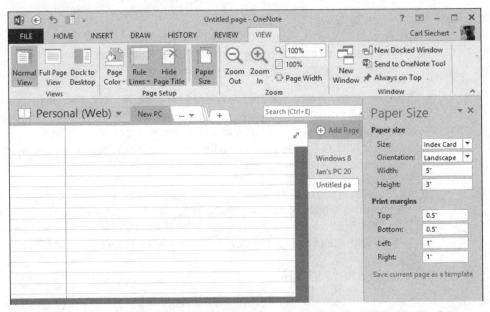

Figure 21-13 These settings allow a OneNote page to mimic a standard 3×5 index card. Save the page as a template to reuse it on new notebook pages.

Personalizing the OneNote interface

You can customize OneNote's user interface by using the same tools available in the other Office 2013 programs, notably the options to fine-tune the ribbon and the Quick Access Toolbar. In particular, the Touch/Mouse Mode toggle (an easy addition to the Quick Access Toolbar) is useful if you use OneNote on a tablet or touch-enabled PC.

> **For step-by-step instructions on how to customize these common Office interface features, see "Personalizing the ribbon" and "Customizing the Quick Access Toolbar," both in Chapter 3, "Using and customizing the Office interface."**

The most useful set of personalization options for OneNote reflect the common desire to hide clutter and maximize the workspace as much as possible. This is particularly important when you're typing class notes or meeting minutes on a notebook or netbook, where screen real estate is severely limited. In that scenario, where access to other pages and sections isn't necessary, the quickest path to a clean workspace is the F11 key, which toggles Full Page view. (There's also a Full Page View button on the View tab and in the upper-right corner of every page.) In Full Page view, section tabs and page tabs are completely hidden, and the ribbon is minimized to a narrow, empty strip. To toggle back to Normal view, press F11 again or click the diagonal arrow in the upper-right corner, as shown in Figure 21-14.

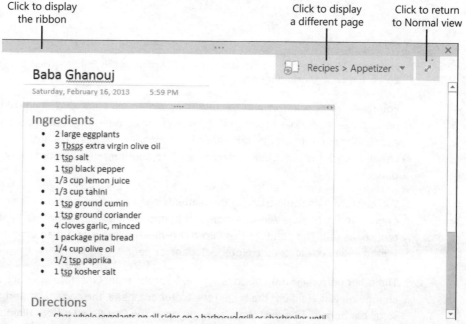

Figure 21-14 In Full Page view, the notebook name and section name appear in the upper-right corner of a window otherwise devoted entirely to the content of a OneNote page.

Chapter 21

The full complement of ribbon tools appears when you click anywhere in the title bar. You navigate in Full Page view by clicking the notebook and section name in the upper-right corner. Doing so opens a new window, shown in Figure 21-15, from which you can jump to a page in any open notebook.

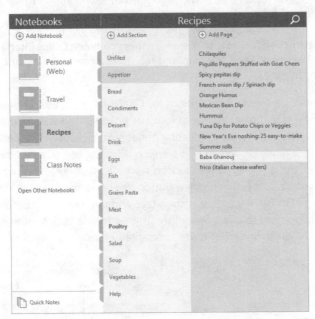

Figure 21-15 Right-click a notebook, section, or page in the Full Page view navigation pane to access the usual shortcut menus.

For a less drastic solution, you can unpin the Notebook pane. Click the pushpin icon to the right of the Notebooks heading. The name of the current notebook supplants the word *Notebooks*. (You can see the difference by comparing Figures 21-9 and 21-11, earlier in this chapter.) Click the notebook name to switch to another notebook or to repin the Notebook pane.

You can also gain some space in the contents pane by adjusting the width of the Notebook pane or the page tabs. Aim the mouse at the border between either element and the contents pane until the pointer turns into a two-headed arrow, and then drag in either direction to widen or narrow the Notebook pane or page tabs bar.

The other personalization options available for the main OneNote interface allow you to change on which side of the screen the Notebook pane, the page tabs, and the vertical scroll bar appear. To adjust these settings, open the OneNote Options dialog box (click File, Options) and click the Display tab, where you'll find three "appear on the left" options:

one each for page tabs, navigation bar (Notebook pane), and vertical scroll bar. When the relevant check box is not selected, the item appears on the right side of the window.

The other significant personalization option involves the OneNote icon in the notification area. We discuss its settings in more detail in "Customizing the OneNote taskbar icon" in Chapter 23.

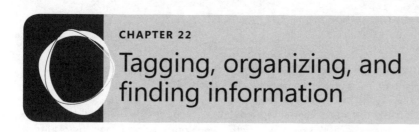

CHAPTER 22

Tagging, organizing, and finding information

T HE MORE you use OneNote, the bigger your collection of pages and sections and notebooks becomes. And as that collection grows in size and diversity, the challenge of finding something you wrote last month or last year becomes ever more daunting. Fortunately, you have a variety of options to help you create order from chaos.

In this chapter we look at the range of tools, techniques, and strategies you can use to stay organized in OneNote. We start with the powerful tags feature, which allows you to assign a label and an icon to a paragraph and then collect similar tags into summary pages and to-do lists. This feature works best when you discard the default tags and create your own.

We then document OneNote's potent but occasionally confusing search capabilities. We also highlight OneNote's many tools for creating links to documents, webpages, and other OneNote pages and sections. That's just one of the strategies you can use to keep from being overwhelmed by a large collection of notebooks.

And finally, we explain how OneNote's automatic backup features work, and recommend a few tweaks to ensure that you'll have the best chance of finding a page or a section if you accidentally delete a page containing irreplaceable information.

Using tags to highlight important notes

You can attach a *tag* to any paragraph (including the page title) on any page in OneNote. Each tag provides a label (To Do, Important, Remember For Later) and, optionally, a small icon that appears to the left of the paragraph as well as custom font colors and highlighting that are applied to the entire tagged paragraph.

Attaching a tag to a paragraph makes spotting action items easier when you're scanning a page—you just look for the colorful icons or highlighting. But the real value of tags, as we explain later in this chapter, becomes apparent when you search for tagged items throughout a notebook (or a group of notebooks) and gather them into a single pane. That step makes it easy to find all the to-do items on your list, every snippet of research you've tagged as important, or ideas you've flagged for discussion with your partner.

Figure 22-1 shows a list containing several tagged items. The page title has been tagged as well. The Tags Summary pane on the right side of the OneNote window shows the results of a search for tagged items in the current notebook.

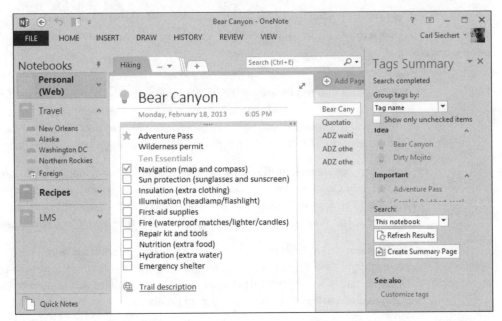

Figure 22-1 The icons to the left of items in this list indicate they've been tagged. The Tags Summary pane on the right includes tags from multiple pages.

> For details about the Tags Summary pane, see "Finding tagged notes" later in this chapter.

You'll find a lengthy list of predefined tags, arranged in an arbitrary order, in the Tags group on the Home tab. Click the arrow below the Tag tool to reveal the entire list.

Applying and removing tags

To apply a tag to a paragraph, click anywhere within the paragraph and then click an entry on the Tags menu. (It doesn't matter whether any text is selected; the tag is applied to the entire paragraph.) You can apply up to nine tags to a single paragraph. For example, you might apply the Critical, To Do, and Project X tags to an item so that it appears in your search results if you look for any of those tags. Remember that images live in note contain- ers as paragraphs, so you can tag an image just as easily as a snippet of text.

INSIDE OUT   Use numeric shortcuts for your favorite tags

If you look to the right of the first nine tags on the Tags menu, you'll notice that each is assigned a numeric shortcut, Ctrl+1 through Ctrl+9. To apply one of these nine tags to the current paragraph, press the keyboard shortcut assigned to it.

Changing the shortcut for a given tag or assigning a shortcut to a tag that currently doesn't have one is simple, if not exactly intuitive: open Customize Tags and use the Move Tag Up and Move Tag Down buttons (indicated by up and down arrows) to move your tags into the correct position. Whichever tag you move to the top of the list is assigned shortcut Ctrl+1, with the tag in the next position getting Ctrl+2, and so on.

You can also access the Tags menu by right-clicking any paragraph and clicking the Tag button on the Mini toolbar. Use the cascading menu to select a specific tag, or click Tag to apply the most recently used tag.

To remove a tag from the current paragraph, click Remove Tag at the bottom of the Tags menu, or use the keyboard shortcut Ctrl+0. You can also right-click the tag icon and click Remove Tag on the shortcut menu.

What happens if you position the insertion point within a tagged paragraph and then click the same tag on the Tags menu? That depends. For most tags, the result is a simple toggle: click once to apply the tag, click again to remove it. But there's a third option for any tag that includes a check-box symbol, such as the default To Do tag. (Because it's at the top of the list, it has the Ctrl+1 keyboard shortcut assigned to it.) If you click the To Do tag or press Ctrl+1, an empty check box appears to the left of the current paragraph. Click that box to add a check mark to it, which indicates the item is completed, as shown here.

☑ Change backup tape

You can distinguish between open and completed tags when using the Find Tags option. For details, see "Finding tagged notes" later in this chapter.

The check box to the left of a tagged item is a toggle that marks the tagged item as open or completed. (The simplest way to mark an item complete is to click the check box, which toggles the check mark.) By contrast, the tag on the Tags menu (and the corresponding keyboard shortcut) are three-way toggles: click once to apply the tag, click again to fill in the check box and mark it as completed, and click once more to remove the tag.

Chapter 22

Customizing tags

The standard list of 29 tags that is included with OneNote is interesting, but it's hardly useful. For starters, it includes some items that cry out for customization, like Project A and Project B, not to mention Discuss With <Person A> and Discuss With <Person B> (both of which actually include the angle brackets). Are you really going to use the Movie To See or Remember For Blog tags? And why would you want to tag something as a Phone Number?

Clearly, this built-in list is strictly for illustrative purposes, to give you an idea of things you can do with tags. If you plan to use OneNote seriously, we recommend that you take a few minutes and personalize the list of tags. Delete tags you'll never use, add custom tags that match your work/study/research habits, and rearrange the order so that the tags you use most often have keyboard shortcuts. If you need only three tags, that's all you should have.

Your starting point is the Customize Tags dialog box, which is accessible from the bottom of the Tags menu. Figure 22-2 shows the Customize Tags dialog box after adding some new tags and changing the order of existing ones.

Figure 22-2 From this dialog box, you can add or remove a tag, modify an existing tag, and change the order of tags in the list.

To eliminate a tag you have no intention of using, select its entry in the list and click the Remove button (just below the Move Tag Up and Move Tag Down buttons at the right).

To add a custom tag to the list, click New Tag. To change the settings for an existing tag, select its entry in the list and click Modify Tag. The resulting dialog box is nearly identical, with the only difference being the name displayed in the title bar. Figure 22-3 shows the generic Project A tag in the process of being modified.

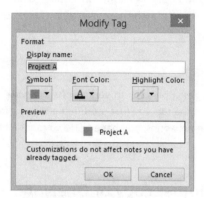

Figure 22-3 When creating or modifying a tag, you can give it a name and specify how tagged paragraphs appear on the page.

Every tag consists of four elements, each of which can be customized here:

- **Display Name**   This is the name that appears on the Tags menu. It can include any combination of letters, numbers, spaces, and punctuation—up to a maximum length of 200 characters.

- **Symbol**   This setting defines the small icon that appears to the left of a tagged item. You can choose from the collection of 138 symbols shown here or click None to create a symbol-free tag. All of the symbols in the group of three columns on the left are check boxes that can be marked as open or completed. You cannot assign a custom icon of your own creation.

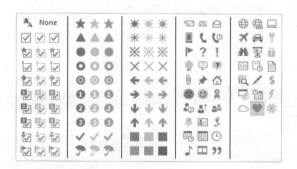

- **Font Color** Use this setting to choose which of 40 colors will be applied to all text in a paragraph when this tag is applied to it. The default setting is Automatic, which retains the color set by selecting a style or applying direct formatting to text.

- **Highlight Color** Use this setting to apply highlight formatting to all text in the tagged paragraph. The 15 color choices match those available via the Text Highlight Color tool on the Home tab.

CAUTION

When you customize a tag, your changes apply only to paragraphs that you tag from that time forward. Existing instances of the tag you just modified are not affected. If you want to sync the old tags with the new ones, you have to do so manually.

Copying custom tags to another copy of OneNote

Any customizations you make to OneNote tags are saved in your user profile. So, if you use more than one computer (a desktop computer in the office and a portable PC on the road, for example), you need to expend some effort to synchronize your customized tags between the two devices. Unfortunately, OneNote does not include an easy tool for transferring these settings from one PC to another. Instead, you have to choose one of three somewhat clunky options.

The first, most obvious, option is to re-create your customized tags manually. If you use only a handful of custom tags, this option might be the simplest. If your list of custom tags is large, the process will probably be too tedious.

An easier alternative is to copy tags one at a time from your existing OneNote notebooks to your uncustomized copy of OneNote. When you see a tag that was created on another PC and isn't yet on the one you're using now, right-click the tag symbol and choose Add To My Tags, as shown next.

INSIDE OUT   Use OneNote to keep a record of your custom tags

How do you compare the custom OneNote tags on your office PCs with the ones on your home PC? Take a picture—or more precisely, take a screen clipping. Click the Tags menu to display its contents, and then press Windows logo key+S. Use the Screen Clipping tool to capture a picture of the list, and save the result in a notebook that you can share with the new PC. If you're willing to spend a little more time and energy, on a shared page make a list of the names of your custom tags, in order, and then apply that tag to each entry in the list. That way, you can use the Add To My Tags command to install the tags on a different computer.

The final and most drastic alternative is to transplant the OneNote preferences file from one computer to another. If the first computer is customized exactly as you like it and the second computer has no special settings you want to keep, this option is appropriate.

Before you try this, be sure you have up-to-date backups for all your OneNote data files just in case something goes wrong. Be sure that OneNote is closed on both computers, and then follow these steps to copy the customized settings from your customized PC to your new PC:

1. On both computers, open the folder %AppData%\Microsoft\OneNote\15.0 in File Explorer (Windows Explorer in Windows 7). Enter this exact address, including the percent signs, and Windows automatically expands it to the correct path within your user profile, based on your user name.

2. On the customized PC, copy the Preferences.dat file to a location that you can access from the new PC—a shared network drive, SkyDrive, or a USB flash drive, for example.

3. On the new PC, replace the current copy of Preferences.dat with the file you copied from your other PC.

4. Reopen OneNote, and check to be sure that your custom tags transferred correctly.

Chapter 22

Using links for quick connections

On any OneNote page, you can create a clickable link that takes you somewhere else. Links can lead to a file (often an Office document, although you can link to other file types as well), to a webpage, or to another location in a OneNote notebook.

Some links are created automatically—when you send a webpage clipping to OneNote, for example, or when you drag the icon for certain types of files from File Explorer and drop it on a page. You can also paste links from the Clipboard and create links manually.

Creating links to webpages or files

When you clip something from a web browser and paste it onto a page, OneNote adds a hyperlink to the source page at the bottom of the note container.

If you prefer, you can create a link to a webpage manually by using the Link dialog box. To make existing text or a graphic into a link, make that selection first; if you plan to add new text for the link, click in an empty place. Then, on the Insert tab, click Link (or press Ctrl+K, or use the Link option on the right-click shortcut menu). As Figure 22-4 shows, the Text To Display box holds the link text, and the Address box contains the link location.

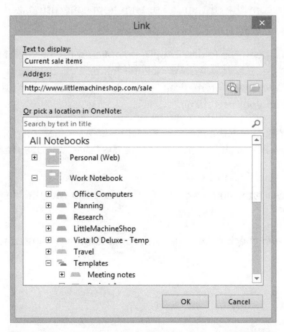

Figure 22-4 The top box is filled in automatically if you select text before creating a link. Use the browser icon to open a browser window, locate a webpage, copy its URL from the Address bar, and then return to the Link dialog box and paste the URL into the Address box.

The folder icon, to the far right of the Address box, opens Link To File, a dialog box similar to the familiar File Open dialog box in which you can select a file from a local or shared folder. Select a file, and OneNote enters the file name into the Text To Display box (you can change it) and the path in the Address box.

For more on how to manage connections between OneNote and documents you create using Word or PowerPoint, see "Linking notes to documents and webpages" in Chapter 23, "Office 2013 inside out."

Creating links to other places in OneNote

Being able to jump back and forth between locations in OneNote can be extremely useful for staying organized, especially when you're picky about where you store particular types of data. For example, say your Business notebook contains two sections: a Suppliers section, with a separate page for your notes about every supplier you do business with, and a Complaints section, where you keep notes about your dealings with dissatisfied customers. If a customer complains about a Tailspin Toys product they bought from your shop, you can keep notes in both places, linking the related discussions so that you can quickly cross-reference the discussions later.

The bottom of the Link dialog box (shown earlier in Figure 22-4) lets you link a snippet of text or a graphic to a OneNote location; just choose a notebook, section group, section, or page from the list of OneNote locations.

If you want to create a link to a specific paragraph, use the Clipboard. Right-click the paragraph, click Copy Link To Paragraph, and then paste that link into another page in the same notebook or in another notebook. You can use this technique to copy a link to a single paragraph, an entire notebook, or anything in between. If you right-click a page tab, for example, you can choose Copy Link To Page, as in Figure 22-5.

Section and section group tabs and the notebook icons in the Notebook pane offer corresponding options on their respective shortcut menus. Paste the copied link on any page, and you can click it to jump directly to the linked paragraph, page, section, section group, or notebook.

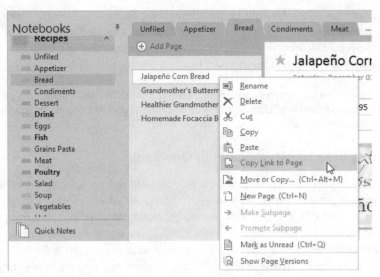

Figure 22-5 Right-click a page tab (as shown here) or a notebook, section, or paragraph to copy a link that can be pasted onto another page.

Editing and removing links

To remove a link completely, regardless of what location it points to, just delete the text or graphic containing the link. If you want to leave the text or graphic intact, right-click the link and choose Remove Link from the shortcut menu.

To change the display text or address of a link, right-click and choose Edit Link. That opens the Link dialog box, where you can change a file location or web address or point to an alternative notebook, section, or page.

We don't recommend editing links to OneNote destinations. If you choose the Edit Link command for a link that points to a paragraph elsewhere in OneNote, you'll see a complex URL that starts with onenote: and contains a long string of alphanumeric characters (known as a globally unique identifier, or GUID) in a strange syntax. Editing that syntax isn't for the faint of heart; you're better off deleting the current link and creating a new one instead.

INSIDE OUT   Build an instant notebook with wiki links

OneNote supports the same link-creating syntax used in several popular wiki packages. If you enter a pair of left brackets followed by some text and a pair of right brackets, OneNote turns the bracketed text into a link as soon as you type the second right bracket. If the link text matches the name of an existing page or section in the current notebook, the link points to that location. If no existing page or section has that name, OneNote creates a new page in the current section. You can use this technique with a brand new notebook to build a Table of Contents page and fill the notebook with new blank pages with relevant titles, all ready for you to fill in. Enter a page name in wiki syntax format, press Enter, and repeat.

Smart search strategies

By design, OneNote encourages (or at least enables) a bit of disorganization. The program's breezy, casual, loosely structured format allows you to add thoughts, save snippets as you work, and create new pages as needed without having to worry too much about where those pages go. You can overcome this seeming chaos by using OneNote's many search tools. In this section, we explain how to search for text on a page and how to find words and phrases within a section or section group, within a notebook, or across every open notebook. We also demonstrate how to pull together tagged items into a collection that you can sort, filter, and click to review.

The search feature in OneNote is extremely fast, and search results appear as you type in the search box.

If you use Windows 7, pages and sections from OneNote appear in the search results when you use the search box on the Start menu, but you'll get much better results by searching from within OneNote. (With Windows 8, the system search feature examines OneNote notebooks only if you use the Windows Store version of OneNote. For more information, see "Using the immersive Windows Store app" in Chapter 23.)

Chapter 22

Searching on a page

To find a word or phrase on a page, press Ctrl+F, and then begin entering search terms in the search box just above the current page, to the far right of the section tabs. Every match is highlighted on the page itself. To the left of the search box is a yellow results list that displays the number of matches; click the up and down arrows to scroll through search results on the page (or use the keyboard shortcuts F3 and Shift+F3).

When you search on a page, OneNote treats each word you enter as a distinct search term, meaning that it finds all occurrences of every search word. If you want to search for a phrase, enclose it in quotation marks. Figure 22-6 shows a keyword search that includes results for two words.

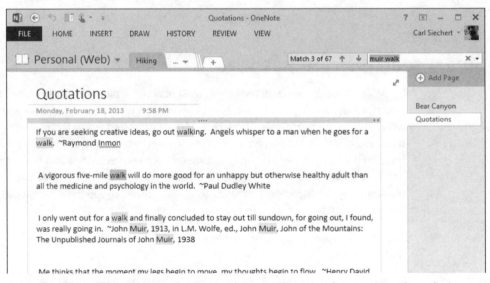

Figure 22-6 Press Ctrl+F and type in the search box to the right of the section tabs to find text on the current page.

Searching by section or notebook

To expand your search so that it includes more than the current page, click in the search box (or press Ctrl+E to position the insertion point there) and begin entering search terms. As you type, results appear instantly in a list just below the search box. Figure 22-7 shows the results when we begin typing *wal*.

Some salient characteristics of OneNote's search are worth noting, especially if you're accustomed to using search in other contexts. For starters, search works only on open notebooks. If you can't see a notebook in the Notebook pane, you can't search its contents.

Search results are grouped, with the pages or sections you've used most recently at the top; followed by results containing the search term in a page, section, or notebook name; and then by results where the search term appears in the body of a page. At the bottom of the list are pages from the recycle bins for all open notebooks. These groupings cannot be modified.

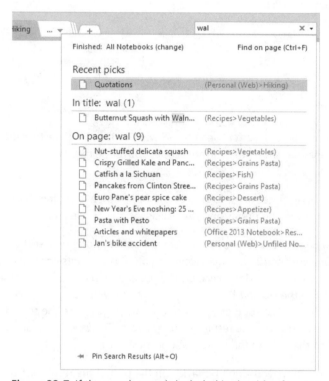

Figure 22-7 If the search term is included in the title of a page, section, section group, or notebook, that match is highlighted in this results list. All pages that include the term are listed under On Page.

Search terms are not case-sensitive. You can enter terms using any mix of uppercase and lowercase letters, and the results will be the same. OneNote treats each word as a distinct search term and treats each space as a logical AND. (In other words, all terms must be present on a page to produce a match.) Enclose your search term in quotation marks to search for a phrase, and place OR (in capital letters) between two terms to return pages and sections that include either term.

If the results aren't what you expected, you can change the scope of the search, increasing or decreasing the amount of ground that OneNote covers while looking for your search terms. If you haven't yet begun your search, click the arrow at the right of the search box to display the list shown here.

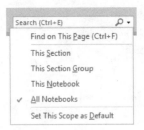

If you're viewing results for a current search and want to expand or restrict the scope of the search, click the link that shows the current scope, above the results list, and then choose a new search scope.

The default scope is All Notebooks. To choose a more restrictive setting as the default, choose the search scope you prefer, and then click Set This Scope As Default.

When you click a page in the results list, the corresponding notebook, section, or page appears in the OneNote contents pane, allowing you to preview its contents. The results list remains visible if you look but don't click on the page, so you can select another entry from the results list (or use the Up and Down Arrow keys to move through the list) and continue previewing search results. As soon as you click within a page or use the scroll bars to go beyond the preview, however, the results list disappears. (To close the results list immediately, click the X to the right of the search box or press Esc.)

That now-you-see-it-now-you-don't behavior on the part of the results list can be annoying if you have a lengthy list of search results that you want to examine in detail. The solution? Click the Pin Search Results link at the bottom of the results list (or press the keyboard shortcut Alt+O). Doing so opens an alternative view of the search results in a pane on the right side of the OneNote program window. Figure 22-8 shows the Search Results pane in action.

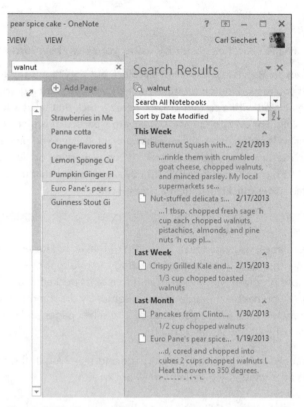

Figure 22-8 The Search Results pane remains visible while you click through its results.

The text at the top of the Search Results pane shows the current search term. From this pane, you can do the following:

- **Change the search scope**   You can restrict the scope by section, by section group, or by notebook.

- **Change the sort field**   Instead of the default sort, which shows results in reverse order by the date they were last modified, you can choose to sort by section or by title, in alphabetical order.

- **Change sort order**   Click the button to the right of the sort field to toggle between ascending and descending order for the results list.

One thing you can't do with the Search Results pane is change the search term. For that, you have to enter a new search term in the search box (which is pushed to the left by the appearance of the Search Results pane) and then click Pin Search Results at the bottom of that new results list.

INSIDE OUT   Make searches easier by using your own keywords

Tags are a useful way to associate a note with a project, but they're not the only trick available to you. If you're working on multiple projects and you want a quick way to locate all pages associated with a certain project, here's a trick that takes advantage of OneNote's search skills. For every page associated with a particular project, embed a unique keyword or code associated only with that project. Be sure you pick a term that you are unlikely to ever use in any other context. (If you're working on your company's annual report for 2013, try a code like ARX2013.) By searching for that unique marker, you can find related pages quickly with just a simple search.

As you can with other panes, you can adjust the width of the Search Results pane by dragging its inner edge in either direction. You can also drag the title to move the pane to the left side of the OneNote program window, or drag it free of its docked position so that it floats over the page. (If you have a multiple-monitor setup, try dragging the Search Results pane to your secondary monitor, where you can use it to select pages and view them on your primary monitor without any visual distractions.)

You can switch between searching on the current page and searching in the currently defined search scope at any time by pressing Ctrl+F or Ctrl+E.

Reviewing recently modified pages

Another of OneNote's useful search tricks is the ability to find the pages you've worked on in recent days, weeks, or months. You do this with Recent Edits, on the History tab. Figure 22-9 shows the contents of a single notebook filtered to show only pages that were changed in the past seven days.

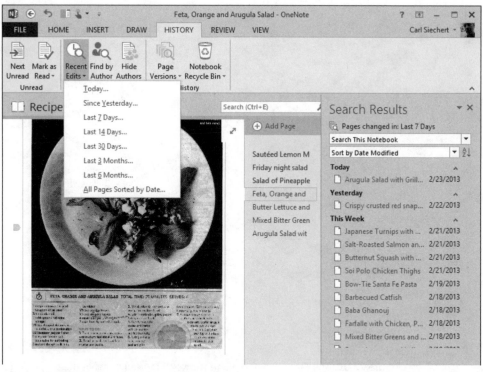

Figure 22-9 Recent Edits displays its results in the Search Results pane, where you can change the scope and adjust the sort field and sort order.

Finding tagged notes

If you use tags to mark individual paragraphs for follow-up, then you need to know how to find those tagged items when you need them. Your starting point is the Find Tags button, in the Tags group on the Home tab. Clicking this button shows or hides the Tags Summary pane, shown in Figure 22-10.

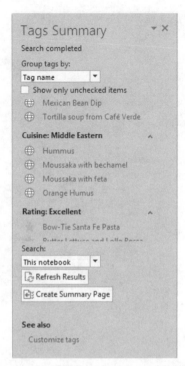

Figure 22-10 The Tags Summary pane shows all tagged items in the scope you've selected.

In essence, the Find Tags button acts as a saved search that finds all tagged items. The Tags Summary pane offers some options to filter and group its search results; it doesn't offer any way to restrict the summary to only those tags you select, although you can collapse and expand the display of individual tags in the results list. From top to bottom, here's what you can do with the Tags Summary pane:

- **Group Tags By**   By default, the results in the Tags Summary pane are grouped by tag name. Use this list to change the grouping to display the results by date, section, page title, or by the note text.

- **Show Only Unchecked Items**   Selecting this option filters the list to show only those items that have a check box (such as the built-in To Do tag) and where you haven't clicked the check box to mark an item as completed.

- **Search**   These options filter the search scope (to the current section or notebook, for example) and also offer date-based options, such as Today's Notes or Last Week's Notes.

- **Refresh Results**   The Tags Summary pane remains visible as you work, but its contents don't update automatically. If you're working through your list of tagged items, click this button occasionally so that the list reflects your changes.

- **Create Summary Page**   This option allows you to create a new page in the current section containing all the tagged items that are visible in the Tags Summary pane. Use the expand/collapse arrows to the right of each heading in the list of tagged items to control whether the items under that heading appear on the summary page. On the summary page, point to a tag and click the OneNote icon that emerges to jump to the page where the original tagged item appears. Right-click the OneNote icon for additional options.

CAUTION!

When you use the Create Summary Page button, items on the resulting page are copies of the originals and include links to the original items. They are not, however, synchronized with those items. If you click the check box next to an item on the summary page to mark it as complete, the original tagged item remains unchecked. Likewise, any notes you add to an original item are not reflected on a summary page you created earlier.

Expert organizational techniques

Some people file using meticulously labeled folders. Others use a shoebox. In OneNote, the shoebox is called Quick Notes, and it resides at the bottom of the Notebook pane.

When you first set up OneNote, the program creates a section called Quick Notes and saves it in the OneNote Notebooks folder in the Documents folder of your user profile. Initially, the Quick Notes link at the bottom of the Notebook pane points to this section. (If you upgrade over an earlier OneNote version, you might find Unfiled Notes, the predecessor to Quick Notes, located in a notebook called Personal or as a section in your default notebooks folder.)

INSIDE OUT   Point Quick Notes to an alternate section

The Quick Notes shortcut doesn't have to point to a section by that name. You can point the Quick Notes shortcut to any section in any notebook and use it as a one-click way to jump to that location. To make the change, click File, Options, Save & Backup, and then modify the Quick Notes Section location.

The primary purpose of Quick Notes is to give you a single destination for screen clippings, printouts, and stuff you collect while browsing webpages or working in Outlook. Rather than specify a destination for each item, you can send them to a new page in Quick Notes. That lets you surf, clip, and print without interruption and then sift through your Quick Notes section later, at your leisure.

You can customize the destination for all of these Send To options. To do so, click File, click Options, and then adjust the settings on the Send To OneNote tab. By default, each option in this list is initially set to Always Ask Where To Send. Figure 22-11 shows the results after we adjusted some settings.

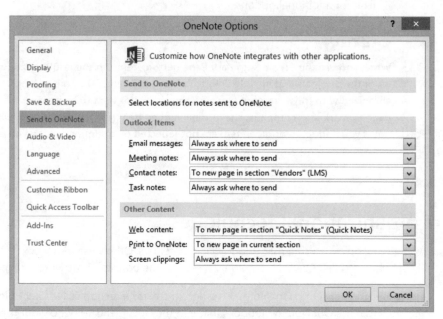

Figure 22-11 Use this dialog box to set default locations for common Send To interactions between other programs and OneNote.

Several of the settings in this dialog box can be set automatically from Select Location In OneNote—the dialog box that appears when you send web clippings, screen clippings, and certain other content to OneNote.

For details on inserting web clippings and screen clippings, see "Filling a notebook with text, pictures, clippings, and more" in Chapter 21, "Inside OneNote 2013." For instructions on how to create links between Outlook items and OneNote, see "Using OneNote with Outlook" in Chapter 23, "OneNote 2013 inside out."

Backing up and recovering notebooks

By default, OneNote is configured to automatically create weekly backups of every open notebook and to keep the two most recent backup sets for each notebook in a local folder, regardless of the actual location of the notebook itself. You can change the frequency and the number of saved backups, as well as the location of the backup folder. (And yes, the hidden Recycle Bin section for each notebook is backed up as well.) To view the current settings and change them if necessary, click File, and then click Options. Figure 22-12 shows the Save & Backup tab in the OneNote Options dialog box.

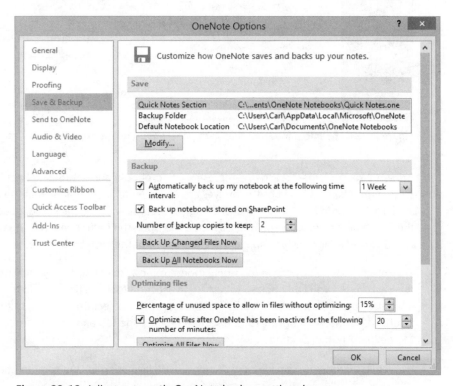

Figure 22-12 Adjust automatic OneNote backup settings here.

If you're paranoid about losing data, you can change the value for Automatically Back Up My Notebook At The Following Time Interval on a scale that ranges from 1 minute to 6 weeks. To disable backup copies completely, clear this check box. You can also set the Number Of Backup Copies To Keep to a value between 0 and 99,999. (You'll need a very large hard drive for the latter setting.)

Backup files are saved in a folder deeply buried in your local user profile (the %LocalAppData% folder). Fortunately, you don't have to dig to recover a saved backup. Click File, and in the Info pane (shown in Figure 22-13) click the Open Backups button.

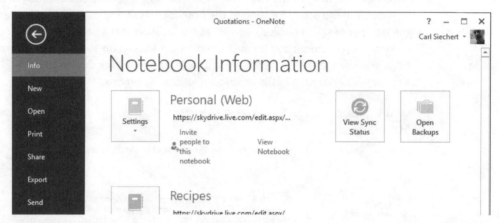

Figure 22-13 The Info pane—not the Open pane, as you might expect—is the entry point to file recovery.

Browse through folders (each one represents a notebook) and subfolders (sections and section groups). The backups themselves are in OneNote Section files, with the extension .one. Each backup has the name of the original section, with the backup date appended to the file name. Select a section and click Open to open the section in a new quasi-notebook called Open Sections, which appears at the bottom of the Notebook pane.

The selected section opens in read-only mode. You can select and copy information from the backup, but you can't edit it. To restore the section (or specific pages in the section) to a regular notebook with full editing capabilities, drag the section or pages to the desired location. Alternatively, right-click the section tab or page tab and choose Move Or Copy or Merge Into Another Section.

For details about moving pages and sections, see "Navigating in OneNote" in Chapter 21.

When you close OneNote, the sections in Open Sections close, and unlike your other open notebooks, they don't reopen when you next start OneNote.

If you or a coworker changed part of a page you've been working on, you might be able to recover all or part of the earlier version. See our discussion in "Sharing and synchronizing notebooks" in Chapter 23.

INSIDE OUT   You might have more backups than you think

The default backup settings in OneNote allow you to recover from accidental deletions for up to two weeks. But what if you discover that the page you desperately need right now went missing last month? Look to the File History feature in Windows 8 or the Previous Versions feature in Windows 7 to locate older backup copies. With Windows 8, open your My Documents folder in File Explorer, select the OneNote Notebooks folder, and then click History in the Open group on the Home tab. With Windows 7, open your My Documents folder in Windows Explorer, right-click the OneNote Notebooks folder, and click Restore Previous Versions. Depending on your Windows settings, you might have days' or weeks' worth of previous versions to restore. Ironically, you can even find previous versions of the backups in your Backup folder (%LocalAppData%\Microsoft\OneNote\15.0\Backup). If you use an alternative backup strategy, such as a Windows server or a network storage device, be sure to check those backup copies as well.

Chapter 22

MORE THAN any other member of the Office family, OneNote inspires fierce loyalty among people who use it regularly. In this, our final OneNote chapter, we dive deep into the features and capabilities that make people so passionate about this program—including a few features you might never discover on your own.

We start by exploring the tight connections between OneNote and Outlook. By using these two programs together, you can create a flexible, expandable system to help you manage contacts, tasks, meetings, and other items outside the rigid confines of the Outlook Notes box. We also explain how to link OneNote pages to Word documents and slides in Power-Point presentations so that you can keep OneNote's free-form notes and discussions in sync with the more formal output from those programs.

Although it's tempting to think of OneNote as a tool for keeping your personal affairs organized, you needn't limit yourself. In this chapter, we explain how you can share a notebook with other people—or with yourself—on multiple PCs. The synchronization process is as close to magical as it gets. We also cover more traditional options for sharing the contents of a notebook by sending pages (or entire sections) to a printer or publishing them to alternative file formats or blogs.

And finally, we end this chapter with a grab bag of advanced features, including instructions on how to incorporate audio and video recordings into a notebook. Our list of favorite OneNote tweaks includes customizations for the OneNote taskbar icon, information about an even more tablet-friendly version of OneNote, and details about custom page templates.

Using OneNote with Outlook

The more you use Outlook, the more likely you are to be frustrated by the limited text box it offers for capturing notes about a contact or a task. And don't get us started about the difficulty of keeping minutes and tracking follow-up tasks from the box at the bottom of a meeting item in an Outlook calendar.

The solution? For contacts, appointments, and meetings, link a OneNote page to the corresponding Outlook item. A button on the Outlook ribbon makes it easy to create the linked page initially, after which you can click a link in either program to move from the item to the OneNote page and vice versa. You can send any task to a OneNote page or, conversely, turn any paragraph on a OneNote page into an Outlook task, complete with a little red flag that allows you to mark the task complete.

But we start with the simplest and most useful connection of all: sending an email message from Outlook to OneNote.

Sending email messages to OneNote

Some email messages are worth saving outside your email store. For a frustration-free vacation, you probably want to save emailed confirmations of hotel reservations and etickets for plane or train travel. When you purchase software online, the publisher might send license information and product keys that you'll want to keep at hand if you need to reinstall and reactivate the software at a later date. If your research project at school or work includes any interviews conducted via email, you'll want to save that correspondence along with your other notes.

You can send an entire email (with attachments) to a OneNote page with a single click. You can use this technique for simple archiving of important email messages, or you can add those messages to a OneNote page and add notes or other details. In Outlook, you can find a Send To OneNote button (labeled OneNote and located in the Move group on the Home tab) when you're viewing a mail message, either in the message list or in a message window. Click that button, choose a destination in OneNote, and your message appears on the page you selected, as shown in Figure 23-1.

As this example illustrates, the saved message includes essential information from the email header, as well as attachments and the entire message body. No link exists between the original message and the saved copy. Changes you make in Outlook (including deleting the message) do not affect the saved copy of the message in OneNote; likewise, when you edit the saved message in OneNote, the original message in Outlook is untouched.

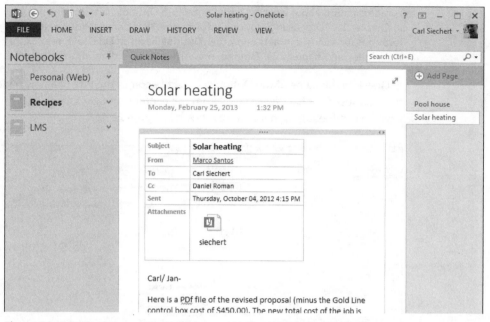

Figure 23-1 Outlook messages that you send to OneNote include attachments.

Linking Outlook contacts to OneNote pages

Each entry in your Outlook Contacts folder represents a relationship. You're most likely to open that contact item when you want to make a phone call, send an email message, address an envelope, or perform some other action associated with the person or company whose details are saved there. The relatively small Notes box in a contact item is good for adding little details about a contact ("Met at tradeshow in Scranton, Jan 2009"), but it's a terrible place for keeping detailed records of your interactions with someone. For that, OneNote is a much better choice.

With minimal effort, you can tie an Outlook item and a OneNote page together so that jumping from one location to the other takes a single click. Changes you make in each place are completely independent; the link is simply a navigational aid.

From any Outlook contact item, click the OneNote button. (The ScreenTip identifies this button as Linked Contact Notes. You'll find it in the Actions group on the Home tab, in slightly different locations depending on whether you're viewing a single contact or a selection from the folder view.) If there's no matching page, OneNote creates a new page in the default location for new contact notes or asks you to select a section for the new page. If the linked page already exists, clicking this button opens it and allows you to add new notes or review notes you entered previously. You cannot create a new set of linked contact notes on an existing OneNote page; instead, create a new page and then copy or move the notes from that other page to the newly created page.

For information about working with contacts in Outlook, see "Organizing your contacts" in Chapter 16, "Organizing Outlook information." For details about customizing the default locations for saving contacts and other Outlook items in OneNote, see "Expert organizational techniques" in Chapter 22, "Tagging, organizing, and finding information."

In OneNote the name of the Outlook contact becomes the title of a new page in the section you specify. A handful of fields from the contents of the Outlook item are added in a new table at the top of that page, as shown in Figure 23-2.

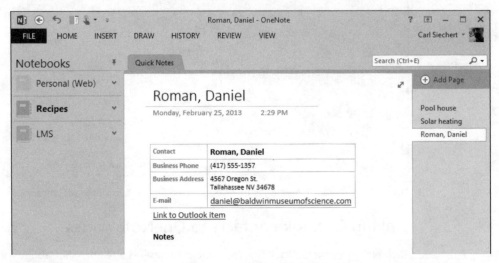

Figure 23-2 If the details you need about a contact aren't in this default set, click Link To Outlook Item and see the full contact item in Outlook.

INSIDE OUT   Link an entire Contacts folder to OneNote

When you select multiple items in an Outlook Contacts folder, clicking the OneNote button creates a new page for each selected contact that does not already have a linked page. It then opens or switches to OneNote and shows you the linked page for the last contact you clicked in the current selection. If you like the idea of linked contact notes and want to dive right in, open the Contacts folder, press Ctrl+A to select all items, and then click OneNote on the Home tab. When Outlook finishes, you have a single section filled with linked pages, one for each item in your Contacts folder. A big advantage of this strategy is that your entire Contacts folder is available from the search box in OneNote, and you can link other OneNote pages or sections to the page for each contact. The biggest gotcha: you have to remember to manually add or delete the associated OneNote pages each time you add or delete a contact.

Connecting appointments and meetings to OneNote

With Outlook appointments and meetings, you can copy the details of a meeting into a notes page, where you can add comments. A link on the OneNote page makes it easy to jump back to the Outlook item.

Adding details from an appointment or a meeting item to a page is simple. Create a new page, or click to position the insertion point on an existing page. Then, in the Meetings group on the Home tab, click Meeting Details. That opens a list showing all appointments on your calendar that are scheduled to start today.

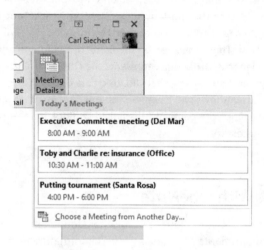

The assumption here is that you're preparing to take notes for a meeting that's about to begin—but you can easily jump to meetings for another day. When you click an entry in the meetings list, a small table appears on the current OneNote page, containing the subject, date, time, location, and attendees for the meeting, as drawn from your calendar. In the middle of the meeting details is a hyperlink labeled Link To Outlook Item; clicking it jumps to the linked appointment or meeting item in Outlook. Click under the Notes heading to begin adding your own comments.

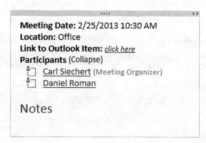

You can also link a meeting to a OneNote page by starting in Outlook. Select the meeting or appointment item in your calendar, and then click Meeting Notes. You'll find this command on the Meeting or Appointment tab.

INSIDE OUT Create a custom shortcut to linked Outlook items

When you use the OneNote button to create linked notes for an Outlook contact, appointment, or meeting, the resulting page contains a Link To Outlook Item shortcut. What isn't immediately obvious is that the modest-looking, text-only hyperlink works outside OneNote as well. Right-click the shortcut in OneNote, and click Copy Link. If you paste the copied text into a text editor, you can see the format of the link. It starts with **onenote:outlook?folder=**. That's followed by the name of the folder, typically Contacts or Calendar, and a lengthy GUID that represents the Outlook item. Don't be misled by the unfamiliar syntax; you can use that URL to create a new shortcut in a folder or on the desktop, and Windows will have no problem opening it. In fact, saving that shortcut opens both the OneNote page and the linked Outlook item—opening either or both programs if necessary.

Using Outlook tasks with OneNote

As far as OneNote is concerned, tasks are different from other Outlook items. In the case of contacts, meetings, and appointments, the idea is to send information from Outlook to OneNote. With tasks, the flow of information moves both ways. You can link an existing task to a OneNote page, just as you can with those other types of items. Unlike with those other item types, however, the process also works in reverse. Using the options on the Outlook Tasks menu in OneNote, you can create a new Outlook task linked to the current paragraph in OneNote. From that point onward, you can jump directly from a OneNote page to a linked Outlook task and back again.

If an item on your task list represents a complex project, you might want to create a single task in Outlook to serve as your launching point. You can then break the big project into multiple milestones and add a list of those milestones to a OneNote page, with each item on that list linked to a separate Outlook task, each with its own start and due dates.

Here's an example: Suppose you're in charge of delivering the company's annual report this year. You might start with a single task called Annual Report, with a start date and due date that represent the timeline of the entire project. Figure 23-3 shows this task.

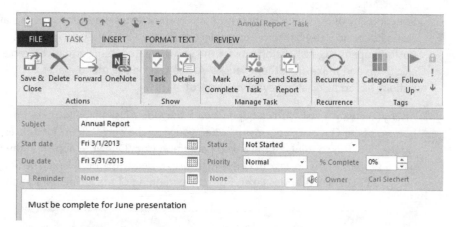

Figure 23-3 Click the OneNote button to create a new linked page in OneNote with a page title there that matches the Subject field here.

After saving the task, click the OneNote button in the Actions group on the Home tab. Select a OneNote section, and OneNote opens to show a new page whose title is the same as the text in the Subject field of your task. Nothing else is copied to OneNote from that task—no body text, no start or due dates, no status or priority indicators.

On the newly created page, enter the individual milestones or subtasks you want to track as part of the overall project. Then, for each one, click the Outlook Tasks button (in the Tags group on OneNote's Home tab) and choose one of the six available flags. Figure 23-4 shows the page after we've created two tasks and while we're in the process of creating a third.

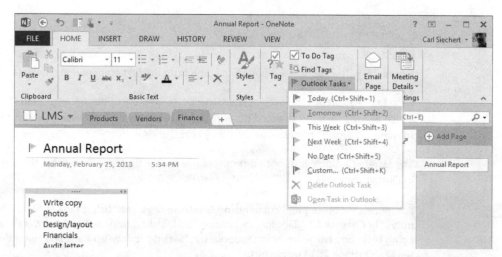

Figure 23-4 The first five options on this menu create and save an Outlook task immediately. The Custom option opens a dialog box where you can choose start and due dates.

Selecting any of the first five options on this menu creates a new task with a start date and due date (or no date) based on your selection on the Outlook Tasks menu. The sixth option, Custom, opens the Task dialog box for the newly created item so that you can assign specific dates and make any other changes. As the text on the menu makes clear, each of these options has an associated keyboard shortcut.

After you create a task, you can open it with the Open Task In Outlook command at the bottom of the Outlook Tasks menu. When you view the new task in Outlook, as shown in Figure 23-5, the contents of the linked paragraph from OneNote appear in the body of the new task, with a Link To Task In OneNote shortcut below the body text. The Subject is limited to 255 characters and is taken from the beginning of the linked paragraph.

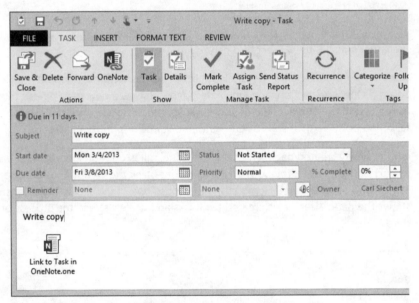

Figure 23-5 The Subject and body text come from the text you enter in OneNote.

Each task you create this way gets a flag icon to the left of the paragraph in OneNote, which in turn links the selected paragraph to the newly created task. You can click the flag to mark the task complete—in OneNote and Outlook.

The Delete Outlook Task option removes the follow-up flag and deletes the linked task item in Outlook.

For more about using and customizing OneNote tags, see "Using tags to highlight important notes" in Chapter 22, "Tagging, organizing, and finding information." For details about managing tasks and to-do items in Outlook, see "Setting follow-up flags and reminders" in Chapter 17, "Outlook 2013 inside out."

TROUBLESHOOTING

The subject of a linked task doesn't match the note

The commands on the Outlook Tasks menu in OneNote are programmed to pick up text from your OneNote paragraph and use that text for the Subject field of any task they create in Outlook. If you select a picture or other nontext item on a OneNote page and then click an option on the Outlook Tasks menu, you can still create a linked task, but the body contains only the link back to the OneNote page, and the Subject reads "[Click the OneNote link in task body for details]." You can and should edit the Subject of the new Outlook task so that it contains descriptive text.

Sending a OneNote page via email

You can send a OneNote page to an email recipient by clicking E-Mail Page on the Home tab in OneNote (or pressing Ctrl+Shift+E). Doing so sends the entire contents of the page, including the title and date/time stamp, to a new message window in Outlook, with the page title as the Subject line. Add a recipient, edit as you see fit, and then click Send.

By default, every page you send this way includes a faint tagline at the end, advertising OneNote. If you prefer a personalized message (or none at all), open the OneNote Options dialog box, click Advanced, and change the text in the Add The Following Signature... box, under Email Sent From OneNote. (Clear this option to disable the taglines completely.) This dialog box also lets you specify whether you want the email message to include a copy of the page in OneNote format and how you want to handle embedded files on the page.

Linking notes to documents and webpages

In the previous chapter, we explained how to insert a link to a file or a webpage into a OneNote page. (See "Using links for quick connections" in Chapter 22.) That labor-intensive process is suitable for creating one-off links, but it gets tedious and distracting if you're juggling multiple sources. For intensive, heads-down research projects, switch to Linked Notes view and let OneNote automatically create links to the documents or webpages you view as you work in OneNote.

Using Linked Notes takes a little bit of practice; before you begin tinkering with this feature, be sure you have a clear understanding of its requirements and limitations:

- A page containing linked notes must be in a section that is saved in OneNote 2010-2013 format. If you see the words *Compatibility Mode* in the OneNote title bar, you cannot use Linked Notes with the current page.

- Linked notes are automatically created and attached to paragraphs in your OneNote page.

- Linked notes work only with webpages viewed in Internet Explorer, documents opened in Word (any format), presentations opened in PowerPoint, and other OneNote pages.

- You can create linked notes only to documents and presentations that have been saved.

In Linked Notes view, the OneNote window has a simplified user interface similar to Full Page view (for details, see "Personalizing the OneNote interface" in Chapter 21, "Inside OneNote 2013"), but with fewer tabs on the ribbon. Unlike Full Page view, in Linked Notes view the window is docked to one edge of the screen. A Linked Notes icon appears in the upper-right corner of the page.

To begin adding linked notes to the current page, click Dock To Desktop on the View tab (in the Views group) or on the Quick Access Toolbar, or use its keyboard shortcut, Ctrl+Alt+D. You can also begin entering linked notes by clicking the Linked Notes command on the Review tab in Word, PowerPoint, or OneNote, or by clicking OneNote Linked Notes on the toolbar in Internet Explorer. (If you don't want to display the Command bar in Internet Explorer, press Alt to display the menu bar, and then press T, K to open the Tools menu and choose OneNote Linked Notes.) If you have previously saved any linked notes using that document, presentation, or webpage, OneNote opens the page containing the linked notes and docks it to the side of the screen. If this is the first time you've used Linked Notes with this document, presentation, or page, you're prompted to select a location for your notes. You can select a specific page or choose an existing section and allow OneNote to create a new page for your notes.

INSIDE OUT Choose the position of the docked OneNote window

By default, the OneNote window snaps to the right side of the primary monitor. If you prefer it on another edge (including top and bottom), or if you have multiple monitors and prefer that it be docked on a different display, drag the title bar to move the docked window to the new position. When you reach the edge of any display, the window automatically snaps into the correct position. To change the width of the docked window (or its height if you docked it to the top or bottom of the display), drag its inside edge. The docked window can use up to half of the available display.

With the docked window in place, you're ready to begin taking notes. Open a webpage or document in any of the four supported programs, and then click in the OneNote window and begin typing your notes. As soon as you type the first character, OneNote adds a link to the page or document to that paragraph. The link appears as a small program icon to the left of the paragraph. If you point to the icon, as shown in Figure 23-6, a ScreenTip shows a thumbnail image or a snippet of text from the linked page or document.

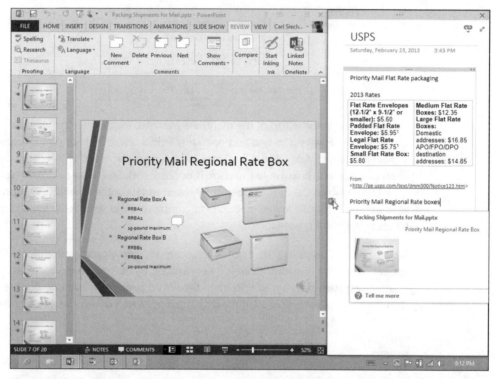

Figure 23-6 The icon to the left of any paragraph indicates that the note is linked to a webpage, a document, or another OneNote page.

If you select some text in a document or page and then begin to type a new paragraph in OneNote, the linked note uses your selection as the text associated with that link.

Continue this way, clicking in Internet Explorer, Word, PowerPoint, or a separate (undocked) OneNote window and then entering your comments in a new paragraph that automatically acquires a link to the location you selected. To stop taking notes, undock the OneNote window by clicking the title bar and then clicking Normal View on the Views tab, or press Ctrl+Alt+D.

As we noted earlier, you can identify a page that contains linked notes by the icon in its upper-right corner. If the OneNote window is docked, clicking this icon leads to a menu like the one shown next.

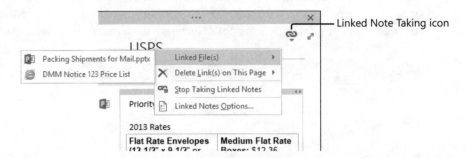

Linked Note Taking icon

The two options at the top of the menu are available even when the window is undocked. Choices here allow you to find and open any linked documents or pages or delete links to a specific document or page. Click Stop Taking Linked Notes to temporarily disable the creation of automatic links while the page is docked; click Start Taking Linked Notes to resume. Click Linked Notes Options to open the Advanced tab of the OneNote Options dialog box, where you can disable linked-note taking completely and remove all linked notes from all pages in the current notebook.

On a page that contains linked notes, the program icon indicating that a link is present appears when the insertion point is in a linked paragraph or when you move the mouse pointer over such a paragraph. To open the linked page or document, double-click the link icon. To manage the link itself, right-click the icon, which opens the menu shown next.

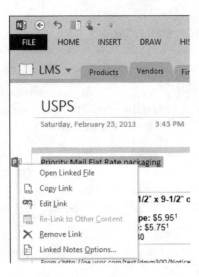

You can use the second and fifth options on this menu to copy a link and paste it into another paragraph on the same page or to remove a link. Both options are available even when the page is undocked and linked-note taking is disabled. A Repair Link option appears if linked-note taking is enabled and then only if OneNote detects that the current link leads to a document or page that is unavailable (because it has been moved or deleted, for example). The Re-Link To Other Content option is also available only when linked-note taking is enabled. To use this option, click the webpage, Word document, PowerPoint presentation, or OneNote page you want to set as the new link for the current paragraph, and then immediately right-click the link you want to change.

Sharing and synchronizing notebooks

When you work with a notebook stored on your PC—in your personal profile—you and you alone can work with it. But if you save a notebook to a location that is accessible from your local network or over the Internet (SkyDrive is an ideal platform), you can access its contents remotely from multiple PCs (your desktop PC at the office and a notebook PC, for example). You can also share that notebook with other people if they have access to the location where the remote copy is stored.

And you don't have to be online to collaborate. OneNote keeps a local copy of each shared notebook, allowing you to work with the most recently synchronized version even when you're disconnected from the network. When you reconnect, all of your changes and any changes made by other users are merged so that the shared copy on the network and your local copy are once again identical.

The unusual nature of the OneNote data file format is tailor-made for fast synchronization in the background. Each note container and each page are treated as separate objects, which means that two or more people can add or change notes on the same page at the same time with a minimal risk of collision. In fact, if you open a page in a shared notebook on an active network connection at the same time that a coworker has that page open, you can see her changes appear on the page seconds after she enters them.

If you're creating a new notebook, you can enable shared access from the start by saving it on SkyDrive or on a SharePoint server. On the New tab in Backstage view, select one of these locations, give the notebook a name, and then click Create Notebook. OneNote creates the notebook and then asks if you'd like to share it with other people. Click Invite People to go to the Share pane in Backstage view. (If you choose not to share your notebook initially, you can always go to the Share pane later.)

To share an existing notebook that's stored on a local drive, you first need to move it to a shared location. To do that, in Backstage view, click Share. There you can select a new, shared location and then click Move Notebook.

Chapter 23

INSIDE OUT How often does OneNote sync with a shared notebook?

OneNote has no Save button. Any additions, deletions, or changes you make to a page or section are saved immediately to the local, cached copy of your notebook. This is true even with a notebook that is saved on your PC and not shared with anyone else. (You can view and change the cache location in the OneNote Options dialog box, at the bottom of the Save & Backup tab.) The cached copy of each notebook section is synchronized at regular intervals with the main copy. How regular? That depends on the location of the main copy. For local files, replication takes place every 5 seconds. For notebooks stored on a local network and accessed via UNC shares (*server_name*\ *share_name*), the interval is 30 seconds. Notebooks shared from SkyDrive, SkyDrive Pro, or a SharePoint library sync instantaneously while you or another person sharing the notebook are editing. When the editing stops, the sync interval reverts to 30 seconds. (You can also force synchronization at any time, as we explain later in this section.)

Once you have a notebook in a shared location, whether it was created there or moved there, you can share it by clicking File, Share. In the Share pane (Figure 23-7), click Invite People and enter the requested information on the right side of the screen. After entering email addresses of the people with whom you want to share, select a permission level (Can Edit or Can View), add a message if you like, and then click Share.

The message that invitees receive contains a link that they can use to open the notebook. If you choose Require User To Sign In Before Accessing Document, the recipient must sign in using a Microsoft account to successfully open the link. The Microsoft account might be associated with a different email address than the one to which the message was sent. Without that option in place, the link in the email message can be used by anyone. And sometimes that's a good thing. If you're more interested in widely sharing a notebook than in ensuring its security, you can generate sharing links that you can distribute as you see fit. Anyone with a link can view or edit the shared notebook, depending on the type of link you distribute. To generate such links, click Get A Sharing Link in the Share pane in Backstage view. Click either or both Create Link buttons and then copy the resulting links.

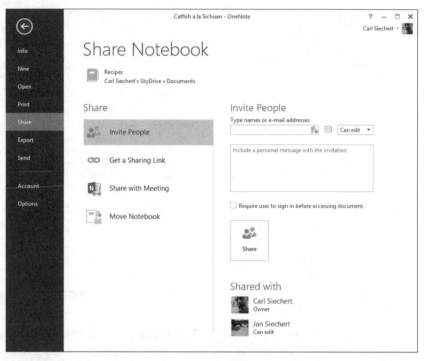

Figure 23-7 Click the icon to the right of the address box to select from your Contacts list. Click the icon inside the address box to validate the names you entered (like Check Names in Outlook).

To stop sharing a remote notebook, return to the Share pane and click Get A Sharing Link. For each person under Shared With who should no longer have access, right-click the name and choose Remove User. (You can also switch their permission between Can View and Can Edit.) For each link under Shared Links, right-click and choose Disable Link.

On notebooks in remote locations, you might occasionally notice an icon by the notebook name. That's the Sync Status icon, which displays one of two status messages: green spinning arrows when the notebook is in the process of syncing, and a red circle with an *X* to indicate that the remote notebook is not available online.

When you click the Sync Status icon or right-click a notebook name and choose Notebook Sync Status, you see the Shared Notebook Synchronization dialog box shown in Figure 23-8.

Chapter 23

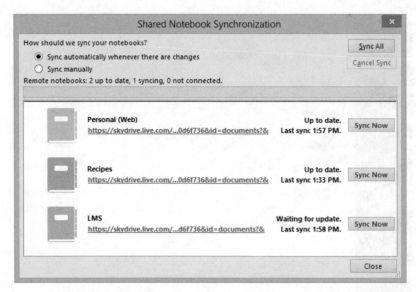

Figure 23-8 By default, all remote notebooks are synchronized automatically. To allow only manual syncing, choose Sync Manually.

Normally, OneNote detects when you're connected to a remote notebook and automatically synchronizes its contents at regular intervals. If you make changes while you're disconnected from the network, those changes are synced as soon as you reconnect, with no manual intervention required. The Sync Manually option allows you to suspend replication even when you're connected to the network, an option you might choose if you want to avoid unnecessary network traffic or distractions from changes made by other users of the shared notebook. To sync manually, use any of the following techniques:

- To manually sync changes for a single notebook, right-click its icon in the Notebook pane and click Sync This Notebook Now (or click to select any section within the notebook and then press Shift+F9). Alternatively, open the Shared Notebook Synchronization dialog box and click Sync Now by the notebook's name.

- To manually sync changes in all remote notebooks, click Sync All in the Shared Notebook Synchronization dialog box, or press F9.

INSIDE OUT   Keeping prying eyes away from your notebooks

Do some parts of a shared notebook contain sensitive information? You can restrict access to those sections by protecting them with a password. This option is available by right-clicking any section tab and choosing Password Protect This Section. In the Password Protection pane, you can set or remove a password for the current section. After you do that, anyone who wants to view that section (including you!) can do so only after entering the password you create. By default, sections are locked automatically after 10 minutes of inactivity—you can adjust this setting by clicking Password Options at the bottom of the Password Protection pane. Note that the contents of password-protected sections are not available via search unless they are currently unlocked.

Any changes made to a shared notebook are tagged with the author's name and initials, as well as the date and time when the change was made. When changes made by someone else are synced to your copy of a shared notebook, the names of changed pages and sections are highlighted in bold. Options in the Unread and Authors groups on the History tab let you filter the list of recent edits and search for changes by a specific person. If you don't want to be distracted by the tags and highlighting alongside changed items, click Hide Authors to suppress them. Click Hide Authors again to resume the display of author information.

Printing, publishing, and sharing notes

Short of sharing an entire notebook, as described in the preceding section, OneNote offers other ways to disseminate your notebook content, whether you're talking about a single page, two or three sections, or an entire notebook.

If you want the other person to be able to see your notes directly in OneNote, you can save a page or a section as a file (in OneNote 2010-2013 or OneNote 2007 format) and send the saved file as an email attachment. The other person needs to have OneNote installed to open the file locally; as an alternative, they can upload the .one file to their own SkyDrive folder and open it using the OneNote Web App.

For a discussion of how Office Web Apps and SkyDrive work together, see Chapter 7, "Connecting Office 2013 to SkyDrive and other online services." To learn more about OneNote file formats, see "Creating and opening OneNote files" in Chapter 21.

Chapter 23

If remaining true to the OneNote format is not a priority, you have many more options available, including exporting all or part of a notebook to alternative file formats and printing your notebook to distribute in physical form.

In this regard, at least, OneNote retains its idiosyncratic character. Most of the Office programs have a Save As pane in Backstage view for these tasks. Lacking any form of a Save command, OneNote instead employs the Export pane for saving to other file formats. Equally out of step, OneNote places commands comparable to those found in the Share pane in other programs (send by email, post to a blog, and so on) in its Send pane.

Options on the Send pane work only with the current page:

- **Email Page**   Inserts its contents into an email message.

- **Send As Attachment**   Sends the page as an email attachment in two formats: OneNote .one section *and* as a single-file webpage (.mht).

- **Send As PDF**   Sends the page as an attachment to an email message in Adobe Portable Document Format.

- **Send To Word**   Opens the page contents (or the current selection) in a new Word document for editing.

- **Send To Blog**   Opens the page (or the current selection) in Word as a blog post. (For more information, see "Using Word to create and edit blog posts" in Chapter 11, "Word 2013 inside out.")

The format choices available when you select either Page or Section under Export Current in the Export pane in Backstage view (see Figure 23-9) are identical. If you click Notebook, your options shrink to include only PDF and XPS formats as well as an oddball format not found elsewhere. The OneNote Package format (with a .onepkg file name extension) can be used to transfer an entire notebook from one PC to another. Although you can also accomplish this goal by copying a folder full of section files, the OneNote Package format has the advantage of residing in a single file. To import a file in this format into OneNote, click File, then click Open. Set the file type to OneNote Single File Package, select the saved file, and click Open.

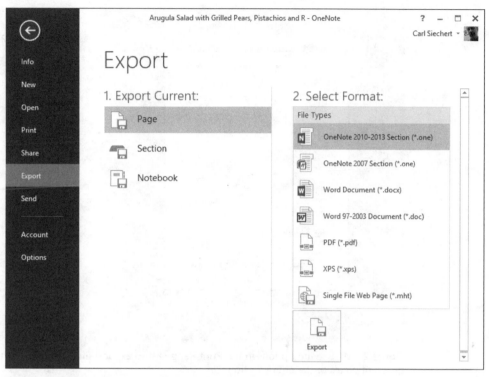

Figure 23-9 Export options for a page and a section are the same.

The Print tab in Backstage view offers a downright Spartan set of options for sending all or part of a OneNote section to hard copy. The top choice is Print, which opens the Print dialog box and allows you to select a printer and choose which part of the current section to print. The second option, Print Preview, opens the dialog box shown in Figure 23-10, which provides a thumbnail view of your printed output and allows a number of self-explanatory options.

If you Ctrl+click to select multiple pages first, you can choose to print only those pages. However, the option to print a selection of pages from the current section is not available when you choose Print Preview.

Chapter 23

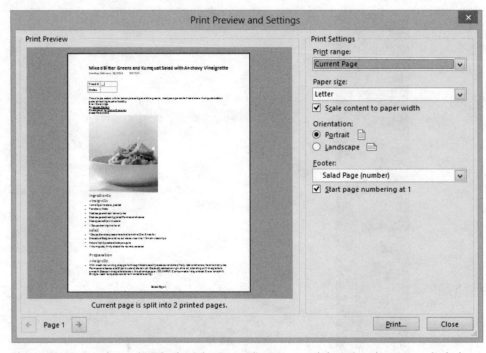

Figure 23-10 Use the options in the Print Range list to expand the printed output to include a group of pages or the entire section.

Recording audio and video

If you're using OneNote to record the minutes of a meeting, why not literally record the proceedings? OneNote pages aren't just for text and pictures—they can also hold audio and video notes, which in turn are synchronized with the notes you type. Later, when you review your notes, you can add context and fill in any missing pieces by listening to the original remarks. If your PC is equipped with a webcam or other video input source, you can embed video clips (and the accompanying audio track) in a page.

To record an audio or video note, be sure your microphone is properly set up in Windows. Then click Record Audio (or Record Video) on the Insert tab. That opens the Recording tab under Audio & Video, shown in Figure 23-11.

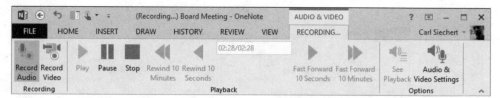

Figure 23-11 You can pause or stop a recording at any time from the Recording tab. The audio or video file itself is embedded in the page, with a time stamp to indicate when it was recorded.

The recording process begins immediately. OneNote adds an embedded icon to the current page, with a date and time stamp beneath it to indicate when the recording began. You can now begin adding notes on that page.

To stop recording temporarily, click Pause. To stop recording and save the file, click Stop. After you click Stop and save an audio or video file, you can no longer add to that file. If you remain on the same page and click Record Audio or Record Video again, OneNote adds a new recording, with its own date/time stamp. Each recording is independent and can be played back separately.

After you begin a recording, you can type or write notes on the same page that contains the recorded file. OneNote adds a synchronization marker—indicated by a small Play button—at the beginning of each paragraph. Those small markers (visible only when the insertion point is in a paragraph or the mouse pointer passes over a paragraph) are key to effectively using OneNote with audio and video.

You can play back your recording in either of two ways:

- To listen to the complete recording, click Play on the Playback tab under Audio & Video, or double-click the file icon that represents the recording. If the See Playback option is selected, as the recording plays each section during which you entered notes, OneNote highlights the corresponding notes, using the synchronization markers it created during the original recording.

- To play back a selection that corresponds to a specific section within your notes, click in the paragraph and then click the Play button to its left.

Figure 23-12 shows playback in progress. Note that the Playback controls allow you to skip forward or back, 10 seconds or 10 minutes at a time. (Use the keyboard shortcuts Ctrl+Alt+Y and Ctrl+Alt+U to move 10 seconds backward and forward, respectively.)

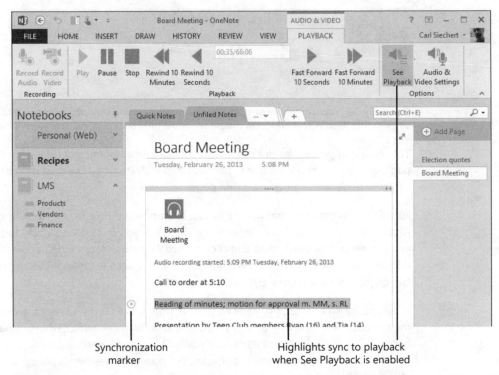

Figure 23-12 Clicking a synchronization marker lets you instantly replay what was recorded when you created the accompanying note.

You can revise or add to your notes during playback without affecting the synchronization markers. (The noteworthy exception, of course, is that deleting a paragraph deletes the synchronization marker as well.)

To play the file in the default external player for that file type, right-click the file icon and click Open Original. To save a copy of the recording in its default format, right-click the file icon and click Save As.

The default format for OneNote audio recordings is Windows Media Audio Voice 9, which records in mono, at a relatively low quality that is adequate for voice recordings; for video, OneNote uses Windows Media Video 9 format (Windows Media Video 8 if you're using Windows 7), at a quality rate determined by your hardware. You can change either of these default settings by clicking Audio & Video Settings on the Playback or Recording tab, which opens the OneNote Options dialog box to the Audio & Video tab, as shown next.

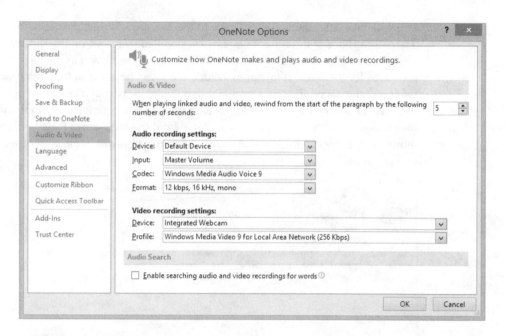

As with all such options, you have to make a tradeoff between recording quality and file size. If your goal is to capture details of a professor's notes on a whiteboard or to record a musical performance in stereo, you'll want to choose a higher-quality video profile and/or audio codec.

Our favorite OneNote tweaks and tips

If you've made it all the way through to the end of our three OneNote chapters, congratulations. You now have a solid grounding in how the program works and how you can integrate OneNote into your workflow. The tips and tweaks included in this section are intended for advanced users like you.

Managing page versions

For every notebook that uses the OneNote 2010-2013 format, OneNote adds a pair of features designed to help you recover quickly and easily if you accidentally delete valuable needed content: Page Versions and the Notebook Recycle Bin. (These features are not available for notebooks that are saved using the older OneNote 2007 format.)

For information about the Recycle Bin, see "Using the Notebook Recycle Bin" in Chapter 21.

OneNote takes snapshots of every page that is changed by multiple users. You can see alternate versions of the current page by clicking Page Versions on the History tab. Previous versions then appear as additional pages below the current page in the page tabs bar. The page tabs for these new (old) pages include the saved date and author name, and a note at the top of the page serves as a reminder that you're looking at an older version. Click that reminder to replace the newest version with this page, or click Page Versions again to hide the previous versions. Other options available from the drop-down Page Versions menu, shown next, allow you to delete all previous versions of pages in the current section, in the section group, or in the notebook.

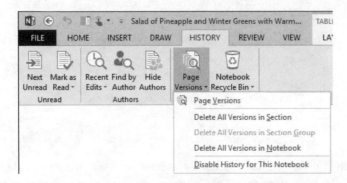

If you'd prefer not to save any previous versions of a page or deleted pages or sections for an individual notebook, click the arrow at the bottom of either the Page Versions or the Notebook Recycle Bin command in the History group and then click Disable History For This Notebook.

Customizing the OneNote taskbar icon

By default, OneNote adds a Send To OneNote Tool icon in the notification area at the right side of the taskbar. The program that displays the icon (Onenotem.exe) runs at startup so that it's available even when OneNote is not running. The icon is normally hidden; to make it visible full time, click the arrow to the left of the notification area and drag the icon into place with other visible icons in this region. Right-click this icon to display a menu like the one shown next.

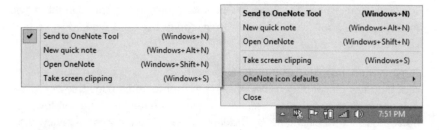

Using the right-click shortcut menu, you can choose any of the four options shown. A simple (left) click on the OneNote icon performs the default action, which is indicated in bold on the menu. To change the default action, click OneNote Icon Defaults and select a different option. Your current choice is indicated by a check mark. You have four options:

- **Send To OneNote Tool** opens a window with options for capturing a screen or a selection and sending it to OneNote, or creating a new quick note (described next).

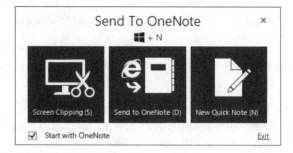

- **New Quick Note** opens a new quick note window, as described in the next section.

- **Open OneNote**, not surprisingly, opens or switches to OneNote.

- **Take Screen Clipping** captures an image of the screen and pastes it in a OneNote page. For more information, see "Screen clippings" in Chapter 21.

To remove the OneNote icon temporarily, click Close. To prevent it from restarting, open the OneNote Options dialog box, click the Display tab, and clear Place OneNote Icon In The Notification Area Of The Taskbar.

Using quick notes

At one time or another, everyone has the need to jot down a thought without interrupting other work. That need is met by quick notes. A quick note is a small OneNote window with few adornments other than an *X*-style close button. Enter your notes and either leave the window open or close it. The new quick note is saved in the Quick Notes section.

Chapter 23

To create a quick note, the Send To OneNote Tool icon (described in the previous section) must be in the notification area. Click that icon or use the keyboard shortcut Windows logo key+N, N to create the new quick note.

To pin a quick note so that it floats above other programs as you work, click the title bar, click the View tab, and then click Always On Top. To add a page title or move your new quick note page to a different section, switch to the full OneNote window with its full ribbon and navigation elements by clicking Full Page View, also on the View tab (or press F11). You cannot return to the simplified Quick Note view from the full OneNote program window.

Converting printouts and pictures to text

When you send a file to OneNote using the Send To OneNote 2013 virtual printer, the program uses its built-in optical character recognition (OCR) features to capture and save any text included as part of that printout. The converted text is also added to the OneNote index, which allows you to locate that printout later using the OneNote search box. The same conversion occurs with screen clippings, pictures, and scanned images you insert.

To copy the converted text to another document, right-click the printout or picture and click Copy Text From This Page Of The Printout, Copy Text From All Pages Of The Printout, or Copy Text From Picture.

Text recognition uses CPU resources; if you're using OneNote on a low-powered PC, you might want to disable this option completely. From the bottom of the Advanced tab in the OneNote Options dialog box, select Disable Text Recognition In Pictures.

To disable text recognition for a specific printout, right-click the printout, click Make Text In Image Searchable, and then click Disabled.

Saving and using custom page templates

As we noted previously, you can change fonts, add or hide rule lines, change background colors and graphics, and add boilerplate text to a OneNote page. (All of these formatting options are discussed in "Customizing the look and feel of a notebook page" in Chapter 21). If you want to reuse a set of such customizations, you can save the result as a page template, which then is available for use in the same or any other notebook.

OneNote includes a selection of ready-made templates that you can use with or without additional personalization. To see the full collection, click Page Templates on the Insert tab. Doing so opens the Templates pane, shown next.

The ready-made templates are divided into five default categories, which can be expanded or collapsed using the arrows to the right of the category name. Click any template name to create a new page using the template.

The two options at the bottom of the Templates pane are worth mastering. Under Always Use A Specific Template, you can select any template to use whenever you create a new page in the current section. If you use the section to take class notes or minutes for a regularly scheduled meeting, using a custom template makes it easier to capture required information in a standard format. If you've customized the current page, click Save Current Page As A Template to add it to the list. If this is the first custom template you've saved, OneNote creates a new My Templates group at the top of the pane. All custom templates appear in this list.

Using the immersive Windows Store app

If you use Windows 8, you'll find a couple of shortcomings in OneNote 2013. First, of course, it's not a Windows 8–style full-screen app. Instead, like the other Office 2013 programs (and, perhaps, like many of your other favorite programs), OneNote runs in a window on the desktop. Second, the unified search that is accessible via the Search charm in Windows 8 does not include any of your OneNote notebooks.

Chapter 23

Microsoft offers a free solution in the form of a OneNote app you can obtain through the Store app in Windows 8. In the Windows Store, find and install OneNote. The app is fully compatible with your existing OneNote notebooks, and it adds search capability through the built-in search in Windows. In addition, it takes advantage of other Windows 8 features, such as the Share charm. (In other Windows Store apps—for example, Maps, News, or Internet Explorer—click Share to send the current item to a OneNote page. Similarly, from OneNote, click Share to send a OneNote page to another app or to a Mail recipient.)

The app is missing many of the features and capabilities of OneNote 2013, and it has a new interface (see Figure 23-13) that might give you new appreciation for the maligned ribbon. But you might find it a worthy complement to the full-featured version; give it a try. We find that it's a useful app for reading notes that are best created in the desktop version of OneNote.

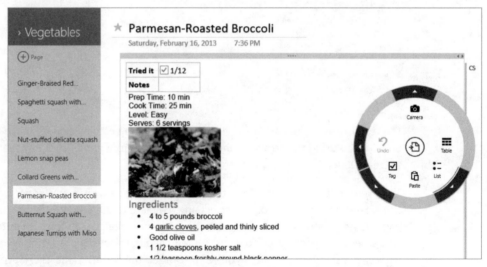

Figure 23-13 Instead of a ribbon, the OneNote app offers commands through a context-sensitive wheel.

PART 8

Other Office programs

Inside Publisher 2013

I N THE FINAL PART of this book, we take a whirlwind tour of three programs that are not part of the core Microsoft Office experience. Publisher and Access have traditionally been included only with the more expensive business-oriented Office editions. These programs enjoy a much larger audience now that they're included in Office 365 Home Premium in addition to the Small Business Premium, Midsize Business, and Enterprise editions of Office 365. They continue to be a part of Office Professional 2013 as well. The other program we cover in this part—newcomer Lync—requires a connection to Lync Server and is therefore included only in the business editions of Office.

- Publisher—the subject of this chapter—is a desktop publishing program. With it, you can create professional-looking brochures, calendars, cards, certificates, posters, flyers, and the like. It offers design and layout features unavailable in Word or other Office programs and produces output suitable for reproduction by a commercial printing company as well as from a desktop printer.

- Lync is a communications program that lets you connect with others via instant messaging, audio and video calls, and online meetings. For more information, see Chapter 25, "Inside Lync 2013."

- Access is a database program that enables storage and retrieval of all manner of information. In addition to traditional desktop databases, Access 2013 supports a new type of shared database, an Access web app. For more information, see Chapter 26, "Inside Access 2013."

Because these programs lie a bit outside the Office mainstream, our coverage is briefer than it is for Word, Excel, Outlook, PowerPoint, and OneNote. Nonetheless, we think you'll find enough details here to get you started with these unfamiliar programs—and perhaps entice you to explore further on your own.

Publisher vs. Word

In recent years, Word has added numerous features for creating compelling printed documents, including greater support of pictures and other graphics, the ability to add typographic embellishments, and themes. Despite those capabilities, Word's strength continues to be the text-centric document, whether it's a brief letter or a book-length manuscript. Publisher, on the other hand, is a better choice for publications in which graphic elements dominate, text may be positioned differently on each page, or pages need to be laid out in a nonstandard way for printing or folding.

Among the differences between Publisher and Word:

- With Publisher, you can create pages up to 240 inches square. (That's 20 *feet*—billboard size.) The maximum page size in Word is 22 inches by 22 inches.

- Publisher allows you to flow text from one text box to another, on the same page or another page. This works well for brochures and newsletters, for example, where an article begins on one page and is continued on another. For more information, see "Inserting text" later in this chapter.

- Publisher has more options for handling pictures. For example, you can work with a batch of photos by putting them in the scratch area. You can quickly swap two pictures, and you can easily apply a picture to the background of a page. For more information, see "Inserting graphics" later in this chapter.

- With Publisher, you can save a publication so that each page is a photo that you can send to a photo printing company. Use this feature to print high-quality photo albums, for example.

- Publisher can also save publications in a form that most commercial printers can use. For more information, see "Printing a publication" later in this chapter.

You'll find plenty of other differences between Publisher and Word in capabilities and in implementation. Let's dive in and take a look.

Supported file formats in Publisher 2013

Publisher uses a proprietary file format (.pub) that can't be opened in other Office programs, including Word. You can see Publisher's favored formats by clicking File, Export, Change File Type, as shown next.

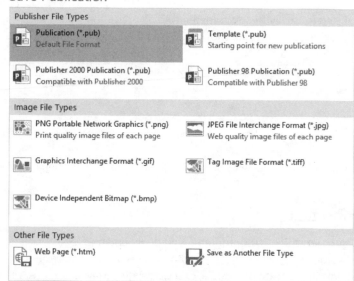

As you can see, the supported file formats—most of which can be used for import as well as export—fall into one of three categories:

- **Publisher files**   This is the native format for Publisher, which naturally supports all Publisher features. The variants shown here—all with the .pub extension—are merely for interchange with earlier versions of Publisher.

- **Image files**   You can save your publication as an image for use in other applications.

- **Other files**   Publisher works with various word-processing files as well as webpages. The degree of fidelity between Publisher and a word processor can vary greatly depending on the complexity of the publication.

Chapter 2

Creating a publication

Like the other Office 2013 programs, Publisher opens by default to a Start screen filled with templates along with links to your recent publications. If neither of those options suits you, use search to find additional templates, or click Open Other Publications to search your storage locations. Ideally, you find a template that resembles the publication you envision.

Your next step is usually to add something to a publication. Your base of operations for this group of tasks is the Insert tab, shown in Figure 24-1.

Figure 24-1 We discuss elements of the Text, Illustrations, and Building Blocks groups in the sections that follow.

Inserting text

With most other Office 2013 programs, you begin entering text by clicking where you want it to go—somewhere on a page in Word or in a cell in Excel, for example. In Publisher, you can type only into a text box, a table, or a shape. (In certain situations, you can simply click and type—but only because Publisher automatically creates a text box to contain your typing. This occurs, for example, if you click on a completely blank page.) Text boxes are somewhat akin to content placeholders in PowerPoint, except you must create them yourself.

To insert text then, your first step is to create a text box. To do that, click Draw Text Box in the Text group on the Insert tab. (Because of its importance, Draw Text Box also appears in the Objects group on the Home tab.) Click on the page where you want the text box, and then drag to size it. As you drag, alignment guides appear so you can easily align the text with other objects on the page or with fixed ruler measurements.

You can then enter text in the text box. The usual assortment of tools for formatting text (font, size, color, bold, and so on) and paragraphs (alignment, indents, line spacing, and so on) appear on the Home tab. Clicking Styles opens a gallery of styles, each of which applies a collection of text and paragraph settings to selected text, similar to styles you use in Word or Excel.

To create a new style, click New Style at the bottom of the Styles menu. At first glance, the settings for defining a style in Publisher are similar to those in Word. But as you explore each setting by clicking the buttons on the right side of the New Style dialog box, shown in Figure 24-2, you'll discover a few options not available in Word.

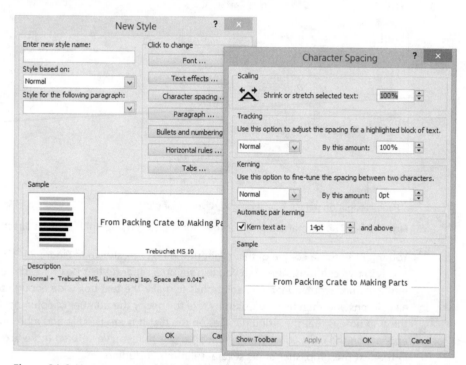

Figure 24-2 You can use sophisticated typographic features in Publisher styles.

Other tools for controlling the appearance of text appear on the Format tab under Text Box Tools, as shown in Figure 24-3. Here you can specify the number of columns within the text box and set internal margins.

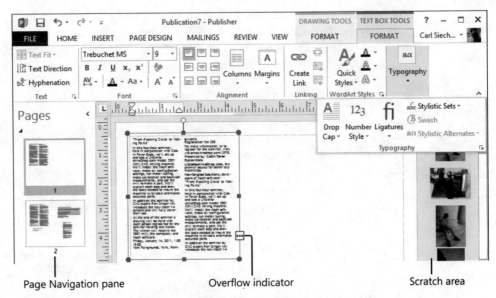

Page Navigation pane   Overflow indicator   Scratch area

Figure 24-3 The Format tab includes tools for applying typographic settings directly.

You might notice a couple of things about the text box shown in Figure 24-3. First, the text is in two columns. Although you can set up a separate text box for each column in a multicolumn layout, a far easier solution is to make the text box wide enough to include all columns and then use the Columns tool to specify the number of columns. The second thing to note is that the sizing handles on the text box are filled in and a boxed ellipsis (...) appears on the right edge. These are indications that you've entered more text than will fit in the text box. Publisher offers several solutions, including:

- **Autofit** Click Text Fit on the Format tab under Text Box Tools or right-click the text box and choose Format Text Box.

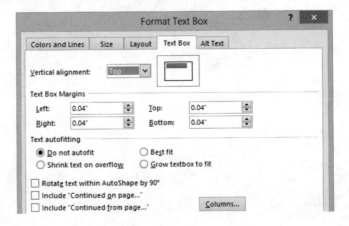

In either place, your options include:

- ○ **Best Fit**   Publisher increases or decreases the text size to fill the box without overflowing.

- ○ **Shrink Text On Overflow**   Publisher reduces the text size so that all text fits.

- ○ **Grow Text Box to Fit**   Publisher increases the size of the box so that all text fits.

- ○ **Do Not Autofit**   Publisher leaves it to you to solve the problem.

Note also the two Include check boxes, which come into play if you use the next solution...

- ● **Linked text boxes**   With this simple yet powerful feature, text flows from one text box to another (and another and another, if needed), on the same page or on another page. To flow text, create a new text box. Click the ellipsis overflow indicator (see Figure 24-3), and then click in the new text box, where the text that doesn't fit in the first box continues. The ellipsis changes to an arrow, which you can click to jump to the next text box. Tools in the Linking group on the Format tab under Text Box Tools help you to manage linked boxes and navigate between them.

INSIDE OUT   Enter frequently used company text and logos with Business Information

If you create publications for a company or other organization, you undoubtedly enter much of the same information in every publication: company name, address, logo, and so on. You can automatically insert any of that information, fully formatted, by clicking Business Information in the Text group on the Insert tab. Fields at the top of the menu that appears enter the information as plain text; options near the bottom insert formatted text. To edit the information, click Business Information, Edit Business Information. (Alternatively, you can view and edit it in the Info pane in Backstage view.) When you make changes, you can optionally apply the new information to all occurrences already in the publication. You can maintain multiple sets of business information as well.

Inserting graphics

For the most part, in Publisher you insert and format pictures and other graphics in the same way you do in other Office 2013 programs. (For details, see Chapter 5, "Working with graphics and pictures.") Not surprisingly, Publisher has some additional tricks for working with pictures.

Most notable is the *scratch area*, an area outside the page where you can store thumbnails of images you might want to use in your publication. (As shown earlier in Figure 24-3, the scratch area initially appears on the right side of the window, but you can place scratch items anywhere in the colored area outside the page.) When you use Pictures or Online Pictures on the Insert tab and then select more than one picture before clicking Insert, Publisher places them in the scratch area. You can also drag pictures from the publication or from File Explorer to the scratch area. Items remain in the same place in the scratch area as you navigate between pages, making it easy to insert scratch-area pictures anywhere in the publication. To insert one of these pictures, simply drag it onto the page.

INSIDE OUT   Getting one-button access to all your picture sources

Somewhat confusingly, Publisher has two Pictures tools that work slightly differently. The Pictures tool on the Insert tab lets you browse for pictures on your computer, and the nearby Online Pictures tool lets you browse various online sources. The Pictures tool on the Format tab under Picture Tools, however, opens a dialog box that provides links to all your picture sources, local and online. The Format tab appears if you select a picture placeholder in your publication or a picture (either in the publication or in the scratch area).

In Publisher, you can format multiple pictures simultaneously. Hold down Ctrl as you click each picture to select it; you can select pictures in the publication and in the scratch area. Effects you choose (shadows, reflections, color effects, and so on) are then applied to all selected pictures.

Another nifty trick is the ability to swap two pictures—either two pictures in a publication, or one in a publication and one in the scratch area. To make the swap, select two pictures and then click Swap on the Format tab under Picture Tools. The two pictures change locations and each picture assumes the size and position of the other. And there's an easier method: Select one picture you want to swap and point to the center of the picture until an icon with a mountain appears, as shown next. Drag the icon to the picture you want to replace, and when a pink border appears around the picture, release the mouse button. Instant swap.

A picture that fills a page can make a dramatic background, and in Publisher it's easy to set up. See Figure 24-4.

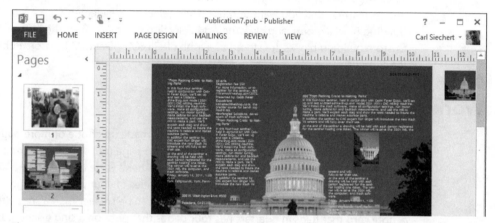

Figure 24-4 To use a picture as a page background, right-click it and choose Apply To Background. To remove a background picture, on the Page Design tab click Background, No Background.

Inserting building blocks

Earlier we mentioned Business Information, a way to quickly insert chunks of oft-used text. The formatted Business Information chunks are stored as *building blocks*, reusable content blocks such as headings, calendars, advertisements, and borders. You can use the building blocks included with Publisher as is, modify them, or create your own.

To insert a building block, click Insert and then click one of the four tools in the Building Blocks group:

- **Page Parts**   Building blocks in this category include preformatted headings, pull quotes, reply forms, sidebars, stories, and tables of contents.

- **Calendars**   Monthly calendars for any month are available in a variety of formats. Insert multiple calendars to create calendar pages with the previous and next month as well as the current month, or to create a full-year calendar.

- **Borders & Accents**   Bars, boxes, frames, and other items can direct focus and add visual interest.

- **Advertisements**   This category includes some complete advertisements along with coupons and other elements you might want to use in an ad of your own design.

Clicking any of these tools displays a gallery of building blocks from which to choose, plus a command at the bottom to open a library with even more building blocks you can use.

To create your own building block, first create it in Publisher, including all the text, pictures, and formatting that you want to reuse. Then select all the elements, click a tool in the Building Blocks group, and click the Add Selection command near the bottom of the menu. Custom building blocks are stored as a .pbb file in %AppData%\Microsoft\Publisher Building Blocks.

Working with pages

Like Word documents, Publisher publications are made up of one or more pages. It's important to understand the difference between a page (put another way, the content) and a sheet (the paper output from a printer). In Publisher a page can be up to 240" × 240"; the maximum sheet size is determined by the capabilities of your printer. A page can be larger than a sheet (it prints across several sheets), or it can be smaller than a sheet (for example, a note card that folds in quarters has four pages that print on a single sheet). Just to add to the confusion, sheet size is sometimes referred to as paper size; in Publisher *sheet* and *paper* are synonymous, and neither has the same meaning as *page*.

You navigate between pages in Publisher with the Page Navigation pane (shown earlier in Figure 24-3). If the pane is not visible, click the View tab and select Page Navigation.

Adding or deleting a page

To add one or more pages to your publication, click the arrow below Page on the Insert tab. Three options appear:

- Click Insert Blank Page to insert a blank page after the current page. The keyboard shortcut Ctrl+Shift+N does the same thing.

- Click Insert Duplicate Page to insert a copy of the current page (or press Ctrl+Shift+U).

- Click Insert Page to open a dialog box with additional options, shown next. In addition to the insertion types available with the other commands, this one lets you insert multiple pages at once, and lets you create pages with a text box.

To change the order of pages, select one or more page thumbnails in the Page Navigation pane and drag them to the new location.

You might find it useful to give each page a name, which you do by clicking Rename in the Pages group on the Page Design tab. You might be disappointed with the implementation, however: the name you assign appears only when you hover the mouse pointer over the page thumbnail.

To delete one or more pages from your publication, select the pages in the Page Navigation pane. Then click Delete in the Pages group on the Page Design tab.

Formatting a page

When you start a publication from a template, you can generally concentrate on the content of your publication and not worry about the page layout, as that is part of the template. If you're creating a new publication based on a blank page, or if you're not satisfied with the template's layout, you'll need to dive into the settings described in the following sections.

Size, margins, and orientation

To change the page size, the page margins, or the orientation, click the Page Design tab, where you'll find tools for each of these settings. Click a tool and choose an option from the menu that descends.

For books and booklets with a bound edge, click Margins, Custom Margins. On the Margin Guides tab in the Layout Guides dialog box, select Two-Page Master. Left and right margins change to inside and outside margins; the inside margin is used on the binding edge of each page. Note that changing the margins does not move any existing objects on a page; it merely moves the margin guides, to which you can align text boxes and other objects.

If you need to make more significant changes to the layout, click the Page Setup dialog box launcher (the arrow in the lower-right corner of the Page Setup group on the Page Design tab) to display the dialog box shown in Figure 24-5. Here you can set the page size (and, by extension, the orientation) and margins—and also change the layout.

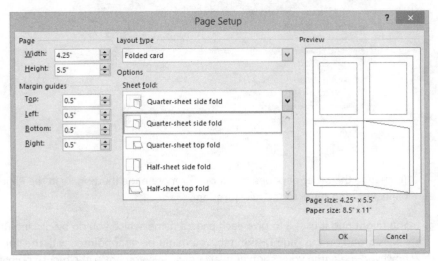

Figure 24-5 Selecting a different option under Layout Type triggers different types of settings to appear under Options.

Layout guides

To enable accurate alignment of various objects in your publication, you can use layout guides. Guides don't show up when you print your document, and their appearance as dotted lines on the screen is optional, as determined by settings on the View tab. You might see layout guides only when you're moving or sizing an object.

Publisher uses several types of layout guides:

- **Margin guides** set the white space around the edges of a page. Setting margins as described in the preceding section moves the margin guides. Margin guides apply to all pages based on the same master page. (For more information about master pages, see "Master pages" later in this chapter.) Margin guides appear as blue dotted lines if Guides is selected on the View tab.

- **Grid (column and row) guides** set the number of columns you want between the left and right margins, and the number of rows you want between the top and bottom margins. Publisher divides the space evenly, and optionally inserts space between the columns or rows. To set up these guides, on the Page Design tab click Guides, Grid And Baseline Guides. In the Layout Guides dialog box, click the Grid

Guides tab. Guides you select here appear only on currently selected pages. Grid guides appear as blue dotted lines if Guides is selected on the View tab.

- **Baseline guides** are used to align text in different columns. (The *baseline* is the imaginary line on which the bottom of most characters rests; characters with *descenders*, such as *g, j,* and *p,* extend below the baseline.) On the Baseline Guides tab of the Layout Guides dialog box, you set the line spacing to match that of the paragraph you want to align with. If necessary, enter an offset—the amount of extra white space between the top margin guide and the first baseline guide. Baseline guides appear as green dotted lines if Baselines is selected on the View tab.

- **Ruler guides** allow a less structured approach than the other types of layout guides. You can place ruler guides—straight horizontal or vertical lines—anywhere on a page to help with alignment. To add ruler guides to a page, click Guides on the Page Design tab. A gallery of preconfigured ruler guide sets appears, as shown in Figure 24-6. You can select one of these options or click Add Horizontal Ruler Guide or Add Vertical Ruler Guide to add a single guide to the page. Unlike the other types of layout guides, you can drag ruler guides on the page to move them. Ruler guides appear as black dotted lines if Guides is selected on the View tab.

Figure 24-6 The Ruler Guides command opens a dialog box in which you can set ruler guides using numeric measurement values.

Note that all the layout guides are simply that: guides. When you insert or resize a text box, picture, or other object, it snaps into alignment as it nears each guide. But nothing prevents you from placing objects anywhere you want, even outside the margin guides.

Headers and footers

To add headers and footers to your publication pages, click a tool in the Header & Footer group on the Insert tab. Headers and footers apply to all pages that use the same master page. (Master pages are the topic of the section that follows.) For that reason, clicking Header or Footer takes you to Master Page view, with a text box awaiting your input. Enter anything you like in the text box, resize it, or move it to fit your design. On the Master Page tab, click Show Header/Footer to jump into either text box.

Using master pages

Much like slide masters in PowerPoint, a master page in Publisher is a base page that contains elements common to all publication pages based on the master. We've already mentioned some page design elements that are stored as part of a master page: margins, headers, and footers. In addition, you can place other common elements, such as layout guides, page borders, watermarks, logos, or anything else that should go in the same place on each page.

To work with master pages, click Master Page in the Views group on the View tab. The master page for the current page appears in the main window. Several clues alert you to the fact that you're in Master Page view: the ribbon includes a Master Page tab (shown in Figure 24-7), the Page Navigation pane shows only master pages, and the background of the main content pane is a yellowish color instead of its usual gray.

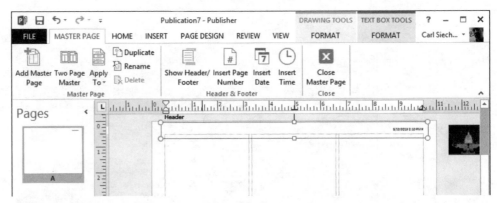

Figure 24-7 Switching to Master Page view also switches to the Master Page tab on the ribbon, but all other ribbon commands remain available so you can add content to the master.

Your publication might require several master pages. You might want to use a different layout for the cover or first page, for example. To create a new master page, click Add Master Page on the Master Page tab. Publisher then asks you to provide a name and description for the new master page. The "name" must be brief: a single character, which appears below the master page thumbnail in the Page Navigation pane. By default, Publisher uses a letter to identify each master page, which differentiates them from the numbers used for publication page identifiers.

After you create a master page, you might want to apply it to existing pages in your publication. To do so, click Apply To on the Master Page tab. Your choices are to apply the selected master to all pages, to the currently selected pages, or to pages you specify by number in the dialog box that appears when you click Apply Master Page, shown next.

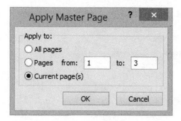

To return to Normal view, click Close Master Page on the Master Page tab or Normal on the View tab.

You can also apply a master page from Normal view. Select the page (or pages) that should use a different master page and then click Master Pages on the Page Design tab. To apply a specific master page when you add a new page to your publication, on the Insert tab click Page, Insert Page. If your publication has more than one master page, the Insert Page dialog box includes a Master Page selection box.

Applying themes

Publisher doesn't fully implement the themes feature included in Word, Excel, PowerPoint, or Outlook. (For details about this feature, see "Using Office themes" in Chapter 5.) Although it doesn't have themes, it does have *schemes*, which provide much of the functionality of Office themes.

Specifically, Publisher has color schemes (palettes of complementary colors) and font schemes (pairs of complementary typefaces, one for headings and one for body text). Applying a color scheme or font scheme can instantly change the appearance of your entire publication with just a few clicks.

To apply a color scheme, click the Page Design tab and then click the More button in the lower-right corner of the color chips in the Schemes group. As you point to different color schemes, a live preview shows you precisely how the current page will change if you click that scheme. Use the same technique to apply a font scheme: on the Page Design tab click Fonts, point to different schemes to see a live preview, and then click to apply a scheme.

> **Note**
>
> Color schemes and font schemes are similar to, but not the same as, theme colors and theme fonts in the main Office programs (Word, Excel, PowerPoint, and Outlook). Therefore, you won't be able to find your favorite Office theme colors and fonts in Publisher, and vice versa. Likewise, you can create your own custom color schemes and font schemes, but the custom schemes you create in Publisher don't appear in the other Office themes. You can, however, match Publisher schemes to Office themes; you just have to do it twice.

Merging data

Publisher is not just for printing pretty static pages—although it does that very well. In this section we introduce two powerful features that you might want to explore further: catalog pages and mailings.

Catalog pages

With catalog pages you pull data from a database to create—you guessed it—a catalog, such as a product catalog. Having a data-driven catalog allows you to set up a single catalog page, which Publisher then fills repeatedly with data from your database. This is far easier than meticulously laying out each page in your catalog. Your publication can still include other pages, such as a cover, introductory pages, and so on, allowing you to have a mix of custom pages and generated pages.

To create catalog pages, begin by clicking Catalog Pages, in the Pages group on the Insert tab. Notice in the Page Navigation pane that the thumbnail for your new page appears as a stack of pages. Click the Format tab under Catalog Tools (shown in Figure 24-8) to set up the merge data.

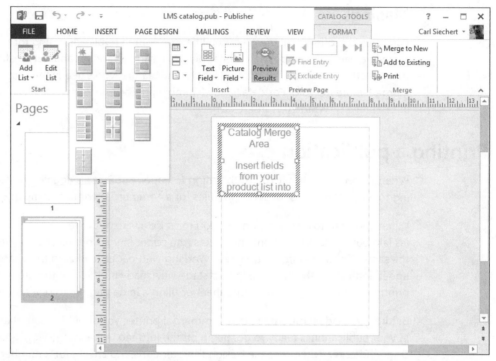

Figure 24-8 A gallery in the Layout group on the Format tab under Catalog Tools offers several predefined page layouts; other tools in the Layout group let you define your own.

To complete the merge, work your way across the Format tab from left to right.

1. Click Add List in the Start group to select your data source. A wide variety of data sources is supported, ranging from Outlook contacts to Excel spreadsheets to all manner of database files to ODBC connections.

2. In the Layout group, select a layout for the page.

3. Using tools in the Insert group, insert text fields and picture fields from the database into the merge area on the page. You can also enter fixed information, borders, and other objects using tools on the Insert tab.

4. Use tools in the Preview Page group to view data in place.

5. Use tools in the Merge group to send your catalog pages to another publication or to the printer.

Mailings

Publisher also offers mail merge capabilities for printed publications and for publications sent via email. This can be useful for applying mailing addresses and personalized greetings to newsletters, or simply for printing labels. The feature works nearly the same as the mail merge feature in Word. For details, see "Combining documents and data with mail merge" in Chapter 11, "Word 2013 inside out."

Printing a publication

When it's time to commit your publication to paper, Publisher is equally comfortable printing to a desktop printer or preparing files for a commercial printing company.

When you print to a desktop printer, you must be aware of the relationship between pages (as laid out in the publication) and sheets (the paper in your printer), as they're not always the same. (For more information, see "Working with pages" earlier in this chapter.) Options under Settings on the Print tab in Backstage view lead you through the process, whether it's printing multiple pages on a single sheet or tiling a large page onto several sheets.

Before you send an output file to a commercial printer, you should ensure that everything in your publication is ready to go. Begin on the Info tab in Backstage view, and click Run Design Checker. This opens the Design Checker pane and checks for a number of possible errors. To see just what Design Checker is looking for, click Design Checker Options at the bottom of the Design Checker pane. A dialog box like the one shown next appears.

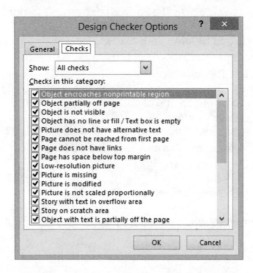

With the design check out of the way, click File, Export. Then, under Pack And Go, click one of these options:

- **Save For Photo Printing**   This option is intended for printing photo albums and similar publications that you send to a commercial photo printer. Publisher saves each page in the publication as a high-quality image file in either .jpg or .tif format.

- **Save For A Commercial Printer**   With this option, shown in Figure 24-9, you select a print quality, specify which files to include (most printers nowadays prefer PDF over .pub files), and then click Pack And Go Wizard. The wizard assists you in copying the files to removable media for delivery to the printer.

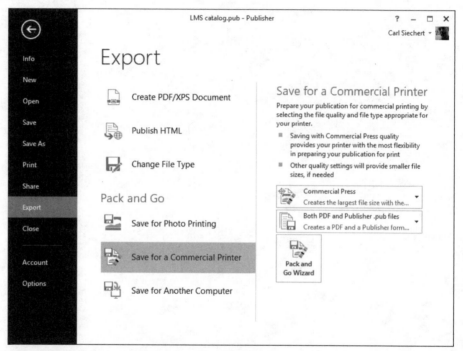

Figure 24-9 Options for printing a publication at a commercial printer are on the Export tab.

A post on the Publisher team blog explains more about preparing files for a commercial printer; view it at *w7io.com/32401*.

W HEN PEOPLE in an organization communicate with each other, they're likely to be more productive and have fewer misunderstandings. That's the basic premise behind Lync, an unusual member of the Office family specifically designed to help people talk with one another.

Lync isn't new to Office, although previous versions went by a decidedly more prosaic name: Office Communicator. To get the most out of the program, you need to connect to a Lync server, which is why earlier versions of the program were originally available only in enterprise editions of Office.

So why do we cover Lync in this book? Because Lync Online, a hosted version of the Lync server software, is now included as a standard feature in business editions of Office 365. That means small businesses and individuals have access to these powerful communication tools that were previously available only to enterprise Office installations.

If you work in a large enterprise, your system administrators have probably customized Lync to work with your company. In this chapter, we focus primarily on how Lync works with Office 365 in small and medium businesses.

> ## Note
>
> At the time we wrote this chapter, Microsoft had announced its plans to integrate Lync with Skype, the popular consumer communications program it purchased in 2012. When that integration is complete (which should have already happened by the time you read this), you'll be able to use Lync to connect to any Skype account, and vice versa. We were, alas, unable to test or document any of these tantalizing new capabilities.

What is Lync?

In appearance and operation, Lync is unlike any other member of the Office 2013 family. It has no ribbon, it doesn't create data files, and it's almost impossible to use alone.

Like OneNote, Lync comes in two versions: one designed for the Windows 7 desktop, the other for Windows 8. (We explain where to find the Windows 8 apps in "Working with Office 365 business plans" in Chapter 8, "Using Office 2013 with an Office 365 subscription.")

When you install Office 2013 Professional Plus with your Office 365 business subscription, the desktop version of Lync 2013 is included automatically. The first time you run it, you're prompted to sign in with the user name and password assigned to your Lync account. (That's normally the same set of credentials you use to sign in to Office, but check with your administrator to be sure.) If you've ever used an instant-messaging (IM) program, the resulting program window, shown in Figure 25-1, will no doubt look familiar.

Figure 25-1 The Lync program window is made up of elements that should be familiar if you've ever used an instant-messaging program.

Most of the information on that screen is also available in the Windows 8–only Lync app, where you can tell your contacts whether you're available to talk or whether you'd prefer not to be disturbed. You can also see your list of Lync contacts, including those you've designated as Favorites.

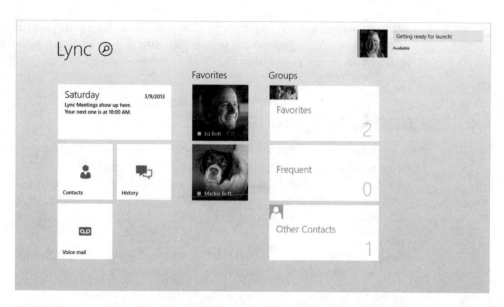

You can build your Lync contacts list from your company directory, or you can add contacts manually using the search tools in the desktop and Windows 8 versions of the Lync client. For each contact on that list, you have a variety of communication options, ranging from simple, text-based one-on-one chats to video conferences involving entire committees.

In broadest terms, your options with Lync include the following:

- **Instant messaging and presence**   From Outlook or Lync (the programs are well connected), you can quickly chat with a contact. Presence information lets you see at a glance a contact's photo and location and whether she is available.

- **Telephony**   You can make voice calls to other Lync or Skype users. If your organization has enabled Lync-to-phone features, you can also place calls to and receive calls from any phone number.

- **Videoconferencing and web meetings**   From Lync or Outlook, you can plan, moderate, and participate in meetings that include audio and video. Invitees from outside your organization can participate in meetings using their web browser, even if they're not Office 365 or Lync Online subscribers.

- **Screen sharing**   During any messaging session or meeting, you can share your entire screen or a single app window with other participants.

- **Whiteboarding**   Participants in an online brainstorming session can share notes using a virtual whiteboard.

Although our focus in this chapter is on Lync in Windows 8, it's worth noting that Lync apps are available on other desktop and mobile platforms as well. So, for example, you can use Lync on your mobile phone (Windows Phone, iPhone, or Android) and continue the conversation on the go.

Configuring Lync options

As we noted earlier, Lync's user interface is different from other Office programs. It's so different, in fact, that you might miss its main menu, which is hidden beneath an oh-so-tiny gear icon in the Lync desktop app. Click to reveal it, as shown here.

Use the options at the top of the File menu to sign out or to change your sign-in address. Clicking Close might not have the effect you intended. Although the program window disappears from view, the program icon remains on the taskbar and the Lync icon appears in the notification area. That's actually intended behavior. Lync works best when you allow it to run in the background so that other people can reach you. If you want the program to end, click Exit.

INSIDE OUT   Make the Lync menu available full time

If you find the hidden Lync menu bothersome, there's an easy fix. Click the gear icon to reveal the menu, and then click Show Menu Bar, the last choice on the list. With that option selected, the four menu options appear at the top of the main Lync program window, just above your status.

The Tools menu includes an Always On Top option, which is useful if you are engaged in ongoing messaging sessions and don't want to keep tracking down the Lync window behind the program you're currently working with. Click Options to take you to the dense, multitabbed dialog box shown in Figure 25-2.

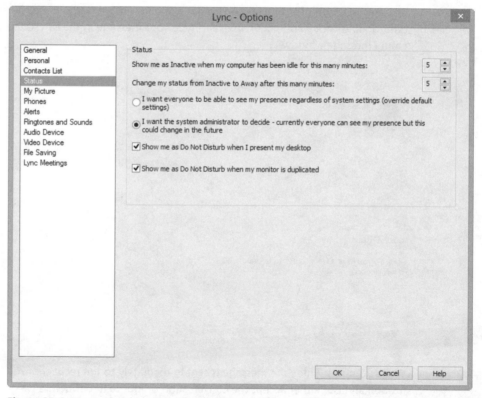

Figure 25-2 It's worth taking a quick pass through all the tabs in this dialog box to ensure that your Lync setup matches your preferences.

From this dialog box, you can configure whether Lync starts up automatically when you sign in to Windows. You can also assign a picture to your Lync account, enter phone numbers where contacts can reach you, and define the ringtones you hear when you receive incoming Lync calls or messages.

The Windows 8 Lync app offers a smaller feature set and a correspondingly smaller set of options. You can find those options when the app is running by using the Settings charm (Windows logo key+I).

Using audio and video with Lync requires that you have the appropriate hardware installed and configured. You can check and, if necessary, adjust your configuration using the Audio Device and Video Device tabs in the Lync Options dialog box.

Instant messaging and presence

The simplest form of interaction on Lync is a text instant message. To get started, open Lync, double-click a contact's name, and type your message in the box at the bottom of the empty message window.

When you press Enter, the message is sent immediately to the recipient, who sees a notification and can either accept the conversation or ignore it. But before we get to those options, let's look more closely at that simple message window. It contains a surprising amount of information as well as multiple entry points to Lync's more advanced features.

For starters, note the strip of information across the top of the window. The green bar to the left of the contact's photo means she's set her Lync status to Available—a message that's confirmed by the text to the right of the photo. That status also confirms that she has video capabilities.

Look closely at the five buttons at the bottom of the window as well. Only the first one is illuminated, indicating that we're carrying on a text conversation. The remaining four buttons offer options to expand the conversation with capabilities we discuss later in this chapter.

By default, Lync allows you to carry on multiple conversations in a single tabbed window, like the one shown in Figure 25-3.

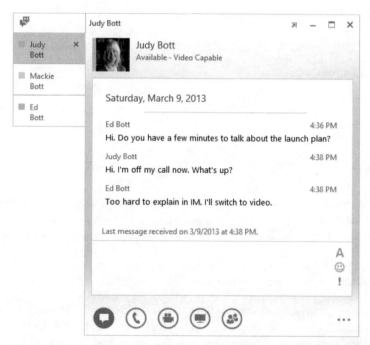

Figure 25-3 The tabs on the left side of this window allow you to switch effortlessly between multiple simultaneous conversations.

Note that each tab also indicates the current status of the other party in the conversation: green for Available, yellow for Away, red for In A Conference Call. By default, Lync switches your status to Inactive if there's no keyboard or mouse activity for five minutes, and to Away after another five minutes with no physical input. If you're participating in a Lync call, anyone checking your status will see a red block and a note that you're in a call.

Those color codes and status messages define your *presence*. The green/red/yellow blocks make it easy for other people to see at a glance whether you're available or not.

You can manually define your status anytime. The easiest way is to open the Lync program window and use the drop-down list just below your name.

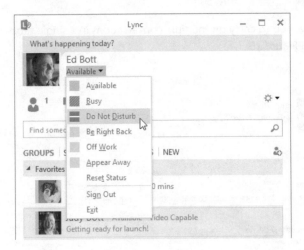

Any of the choices you make here will override automatic settings from the program. The Do Not Disturb option allows you to suppress most incoming calls—a handy choice when you're on a tight deadline and don't want well-meaning colleagues to interrupt you.

Other choices include a yellow Off Work status, as well as a sneaky Appear Away choice—which you can use as a kinder, gentler alternative to Do Not Disturb.

The text above your name allows you to enter a short message that your contacts will see when they check your status in Lync. Click "What's happening today?" to enter a personalized message here. You can enter a whimsical or inspirational message, or you can use the space to expand your status: "I'll be in a training session all day."

You can also carry on an instant-messaging conversation using the Windows 8 Lync app. The display is dramatically different from what you see in the desktop app, as shown in Figure 25-4.

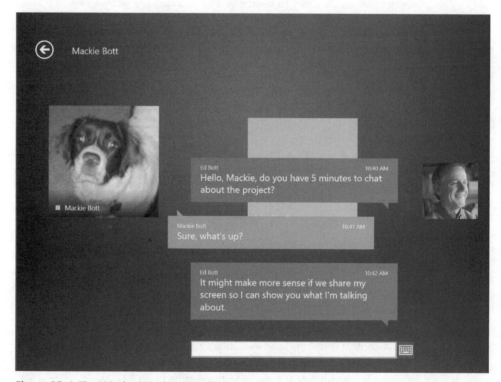

Figure 25-4 The Windows 8 Lync app displays instant-messaging chats in a bigger, bolder window, with fewer distractions than its desktop counterpart.

IM chats aren't restricted to two parties. You can add participants by clicking or tapping the rightmost button on the bottom of the desktop Lync program, or by swiping up from the bottom of the Windows 8 app and tapping Participants. In either case, you'll see an Invite More People button whose function is self-evident.

Telephony and videoconferencing

Sometimes simple text messages aren't enough to explain a complex problem. For those occasions, Lync's ability to handle voice and video are invaluable.

You can start an audio call from scratch by clicking the second button at the bottom of a contact card. Or turn an IM session into a voice call using the same button. When you use this option, you see a simple window like the one shown next.

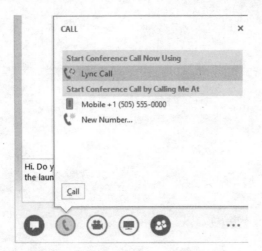

If the contact is on Lync and available, Lync Call is the only option. That's a direct line of communication from one Lync client to another, using the Lync protocols to transmit and receive voice and video. If you're in the middle of an IM session and you want to switch to a mobile device or a land line, you can provide that number directly to the other parties in the conversation, who can then dial in to continue the call.

Clicking the third button at the bottom of a contact card or chat window adds video capabilities to the call. Lync supports full high-definition video, making it possible to have a face-to-face conversation with a colleague or family member, even if you're thousands of miles away.

A video call can occupy the same small pane as a chat window. Your chat partner always gets the lion's share of the screen, with your own video in a thumbnail display in the lower corner.

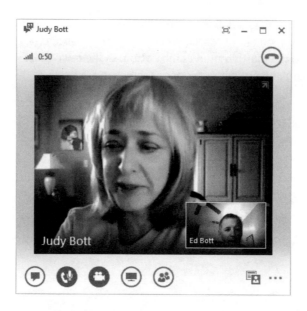

In both the desktop and Windows 8 versions of Lync, you can expand a call to occupy the full screen. For multiparty video calls, you have the option to keep the text (IM) windows open as well. That allows you to continue private conversations with other callers while a larger meeting is going on.

In the upper-left corner, a network icon provides an indication of the network signal strength and the elapsed time for the current call. The large red icon in the upper-right corner of the call window does exactly what you would expect—when your session is over, click that icon to hang up and end the call.

Screen sharing and whiteboarding

Lync's most interesting options are the collaborative tools it offers for two or more people to view or work on a document simultaneously. In a one-on-one session, you and a colleague can collaborate on a document, passing control back and forth as you work your way through it.

For larger meetings, you can use Lync to deliver a PowerPoint presentation, where attendees can follow along (and even skip ahead, if you allow them to do so). The most interesting option of all is the Lync whiteboard, which allows you to type or sketch on a virtual whiteboard—ideal for brainstorming sessions.

For formal occasions, you can schedule a Lync meeting from Outlook and invite attendees from within your organization or outside. Or you can turn any chat or Lync call into a meeting instantly, by clicking the fourth button at the bottom of the call or chat window. That opens the set of meeting and presentation options shown in Figure 25-5.

Figure 25-5 Use the first two options to share a program or your entire desktop.

Whichever option you select as the presenter appears to attendees in what Lync calls the *stage*. The presenter sees a status bar at the top of the screen, with a one-click Stop Presenting button, which is also available in the Lync program window. Attendees see the stage in its own window. Figure 25-6, for example, shows a Lync call (audio only) in which one party is sharing (technically, "presenting") a Word document.

As an attendee, you can click the Request Control button to ask the presenter for permission to work directly with whatever is being shared at the moment. A few other options on this screen are worth calling out as well:

- Click or tap the blue icon at the upper right of the stage to toggle the shared content between Actual Size and Fit To Window modes. This option is essential if the attendee's display is of a lower resolution than the presenter's.

- Click or tap the faint Pop Out indicator in the display of participants' pictures (or videos, if you've enabled that option) to move that element out of the way so you can see the entire shared item.

Chapter 25

- Click or tap the Full Screen icon, just to the left of the Minimize/Maximize/Close buttons) to expand the stage so that it occupies the full screen.

Actual Size/
Fit To Window

Full Screen

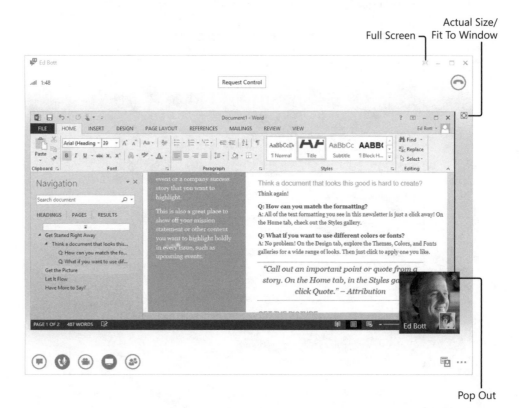

Pop Out

Figure 25-6 As an attendee in a Lync meeting, you can see the shared content on the stage and adjust its display using the controls shown here.

Note that if you use the Windows 8 Lync app, some desktop sharing options are not available. In particular, you are unable to take control of a shared screen and you can't use the whiteboard.

If you choose the Desktop option, every party in the meeting can see your entire desktop, including any email, File Explorer windows, or instant messages that might appear during the session. This option is most valuable if you're using Lync as a support or training tool, with one party helping the other solve a problem or learn how to use a program or feature. It's usually inappropriate for larger, more formal meetings.

Chapter 25

Clicking Program opens a list of all running programs that can be shared via Lync. Select the one you want to share and click Present, and your attendees will see only that program on the stage.

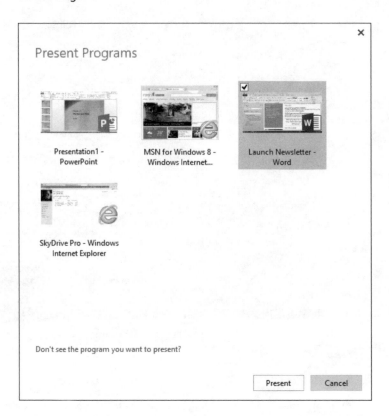

Choosing the PowerPoint option allows you to deliver a presentation to your audience, giving them access to features that aren't available if you simply share a PowerPoint window. If the meeting organizer designates you as a presenter rather than an attendee, you can change the display to show thumbnails and notes. You can even skip to other slides in the presentation without affecting the display seen by attendees.

This option is most useful if two or more people are cooperating on a presentation to a larger group. While your colleague is working through the first portion of the presentation, you can jump ahead to your portion and be ready to take over as presenter when the time comes. Figure 25-7 shows your private view.

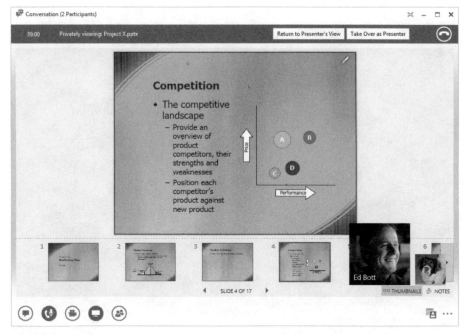

Figure 25-7 When you're designated a presenter rather than an attendee, you can skip ahead in a PowerPoint slide deck without interrupting the current presenter.

For more information about sharing a PowerPoint presentation, see "Delivering a live presentation online" in Chapter 20, "PowerPoint 2013 inside out."

The Whiteboard option looks exactly as you would expect it to look, turning the stage into a blank canvas with a white background on which meeting participants can type (or sketch, if you have a pen handy).

Finally, the Poll option is useful in large meetings where the presenter wants to ask a question and get immediate feedback. Attendees can vote, but the organizer chooses whether to make the results visible.

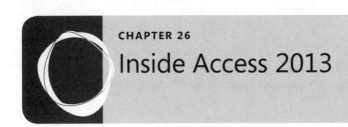

T HE DATABASE management program Microsoft Access is now in its tenth version. Access 2013 traces its lineage back to the first version in 1992. That version was developed as an alternative to the database management system (DBMS) programs of that era, which relied on lots of programming code. Access, by contrast, had a graphical interface that made it much easier for developers and even nonprogrammers to manipulate table structures, lay out forms and reports, and create queries—all without using a line of code. Yet it was—and is today—a powerful relational database management system that works with many types of data sources in addition to Access databases.

Although Access is easy to use by DBMS standards, it remains the toughest nut to crack among the Office programs. In this book, Access gets admittedly short shrift—partly because it's not one of the core Office programs that nearly everyone has to use at one time or another, and partly because it really can't be adequately covered even in a sec-tion the size of those we devote to Office mainstays like Word and Excel. Instead, we offer a brief introduction that shows you some of its capabilities and how to get started with Access. But there's much more to learn. Depending on the depth of your interest, you might want to explore Microsoft Press offerings ranging from *Access 2013 Plain & Simple* through *Microsoft Access 2013 Step by Step* to *Microsoft Access 2013 Inside Out*.

Uses of a database management system

A database is a collection of records that are organized for a particular purpose. You can create a database as a list or table in Word, as a table in Excel, or in various other ways, including a box of index cards. Most of those methods become unmanageable with more than a handful of records. A true relational database management system like Access, how-ever, can quickly handle enormous quantities of data while minimizing data input require-ments (for example, by picking up existing customer information and applying it to a new order) and enabling output in myriad forms (including searches, queries, reports, charts, and documents such as invoices, to name a few).

By default, the Start screen (and the New pane in Backstage view) shows 12 templates. Besides the two blank templates for building a database from scratch, you'll find two each for five different applications:

- **Asset Tracking** Track values, locations, and other information about equipment and other business assets.

- **Contacts** Manage contact data for customers, vendors, and other business relations.

- **Issue Tracking** Record issues related to your business, connect them to customers, assign them to employees, and track their resolution.

- **Project Management** Organize projects into a series of interdependent tasks and assign them to employees.

- **Task Management** Create tasks, assign them to employees, and oversee their progress.

Why two each? The templates that include the word *desktop* in their name create traditional Access databases that are stored on your computer or on your network. The others create a type of database that's new with Access 2013, an *Access web app*. Access apps store data in the cloud, which makes the information available from any location via a web browser. You can share the app with others, and in addition to the web interface, you have the full power of the desktop application for performing queries, creating reports, and so on.

Figure 26-1 shows a database created with the Desktop Contacts template, which you can compare with the web app created with the Contacts template, shown in Figure 26-2.

Databases created by each of those default templates can be modified to suit your needs. Of course, many more templates are available by searching from Backstage view. Whether you need to manage an event by keeping track of attendees, schedules, payments, mailings, and name badges; operate a sports league, with schedules, scores, player stats, and standings; perform financial recordkeeping, including payables, receivables, invoicing, checkbooks, and inventory; or manage personal databases, such as investment tracking, recipes, or contacts, you can find a template or build a database.

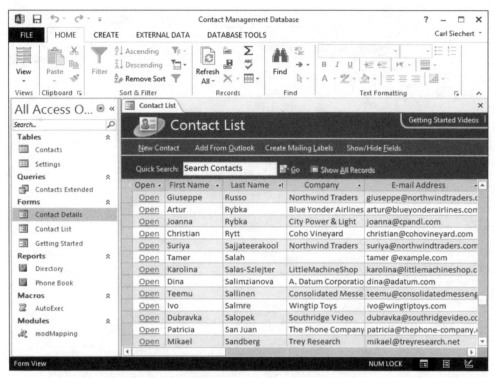

Figure 26-1 With its ribbon, Navigation pane, status bar, and Office theme, a desktop database displaying a form appears much like other Office applications.

For more information about each of the Access database types, see "Using Access web apps" and "Using desktop databases" later in this chapter.

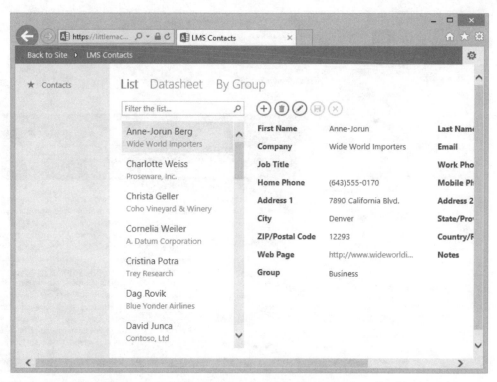

Figure 26-2 You create and modify an Access web app in the desktop application, but when you go to use the data, the app opens in a web browser, as shown here.

Database basics

A database in Access comprises several types of *objects*. (An object is essentially something that has a name.) You can display the different types of objects—and display the objects themselves—by clicking in the Navigation pane, as shown earlier in Figure 26-1. These are the main objects in an Access database:

- **Tables** A table stores data. Each table holds information about a particular subject, such as vendors or orders. A table has *records* (analogous to rows in a spreadsheet) and *fields* (columns). Each field holds a specific type of data, such as text, numbers, dates, pictures, or hyperlinks.

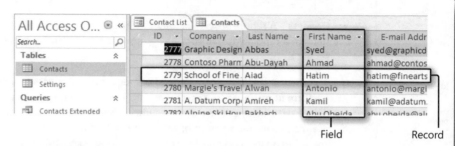

Field   Record

Each record in a table stores information about one instance of the table's subject, such as a vendor or a single order. Each field in a record holds one piece of information, such as company name or order number.

Much of the power of Access (compared with tables in Excel, for example) comes from table *relationships*—that is, linking via related values. For example, you might have a vendors table that lists your company's vendors and their contact information, a products table that lists each of the products you purchase and their cost, and an orders table that lists each purchase order. You can then create relationships by using a common field. For example, you could join vendors to orders by matching the vendor ID number in a vendors table and an orders table. Using a product ID, you can join products to the orders table.

Keeping data in separate related tables helps to enforce consistency. For example, when you create a new purchase order, you select a vendor from the vendors table instead of re-creating (possibly differently) the information for each order. Separate related tables enhance efficiency in another way too: you end up with smaller tables. This saves on disk space and, more important, provides faster access to your data.

- **Queries** A query provides a custom view or performs another action on data from one or more tables. You can use queries to view, add, delete, or change data based on criteria you specify. Queries can also calculate or summarize data. Often, you use a query to populate a form or a report. Underlying each query is an SQL (Structured Query Language) statement, but graphical tools in Access let you create queries without writing any code.

- **Forms** A form provides a visual layout of your data, somewhat like a dialog box. You can use a form for data input and for data display. Form data can come from multiple tables and queries. You can design forms that run a macro or a procedure based on certain events, such as when data changes or when you click a button.

Chapter 26

- **Reports** A report provides a way to format, calculate, and summarize selected data. In a report you can sort and group your data. You can view a report on-screen or print it.

- **Macros** A macro is a sequence of one or more actions that you want Access to perform in response to a certain event. You can use macros to add, change, or delete data, or to validate data accuracy whenever the value changes. You can use macros to open a form or other object—perhaps as a result of selecting or changing an item on another form. Macros can execute queries, open tables, print reports, or even run another macro.

- **Modules** Like a macro, a module contains sequences of actions for Access to perform—but they're written in Visual Basic for Applications (VBA). (We noted earlier that you can perform extensive database operations in Access without writing a line of code. But that doesn't mean you *can't* use programming code in your database; quite the contrary.) Modules provide additional functionality not supported by macros (such as error trapping, support for additional commands, and functions that can be called from anywhere). You can convert a macro to VBA code and then build upon it.

Using Access web apps

The big new feature in Access 2013 is *Access web apps* or, more simply, apps. An Access web app is a database that you create in Access, and then use as an app in a web browser, similar to the other Office Web Apps. Your database objects and data are stored on your Office 365 site or on a SharePoint 2013 server as a SQL Server or Windows Azure SQL database. You can share the database within your organization.

> **Note**
>
> To build Access web apps, you need Access 2013 and an Office 365 plan that includes Access services (primarily business editions such as Small Business Premium, Midsize Business, or Enterprise E3) or SharePoint Server 2013. To use an app created by someone else, you need a web browser and an account with access to the Office 365 site or a SharePoint server.

Creating an app

To create an Access web app, you start by selecting a template on the New pane in Back-stage view. In general, templates that don't contain the word *desktop* in their name are for web apps, but you'll know for sure when you click the template and see the description, as shown in Figure 26-3.

Figure 26-3 Templates for Access web apps ask you to provide an app name and select a location before you can proceed.

In other Office applications, you create a new file by clicking File, New, selecting a template, and then clicking Create. You don't provide a file name until you save the file. In Access, by contrast, you enter an app name (or a file name, if you're creating a desktop database) before you click Create. And for web apps (but not desktop databases), you must also select a location from the Available Locations box. Making a selection here sets the proper path under Web Location as well. Selecting an option that includes the words *Personal Apps* or *SkyDrive* creates an app that is available only to you, not to others who use your Office 365 site.

TROUBLESHOOTING

The Available Locations box is missing

You must be signed in to an account that has access to an Office 365 site or SharePoint 2013 Server site that has Access services enabled. If you have such an account, you can sign in by clicking your name in the upper-right corner of any Office program or by going to the Account pane in Backstage view. If your account isn't shown under Connected Services on the Account tab, click Add Services and sign in. For more information, see "What happens when you sign in with an Office account?" in Chapter 7, "Connecting Office 2013 to SkyDrive and other online services."

Adding tables

Whether you start with the Custom Web App template (to create a "blank" database) or a template that produces a working app straightaway, at some point you'll likely need to add one or more tables. To do that, click Table in the Create group on the Home tab, as shown in Figure 26-4.

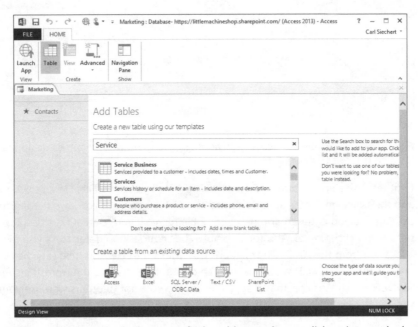

Figure 26-4 Type a search term to find a table template or click an icon at the bottom to create a table from an existing data source.

Creating and customizing views

A view (analogous to a form in a desktop database) is a way of displaying data. By default, each web app includes at least two views—List and Datasheet. (You can see an example of List view for a Contacts database in Figure 26-2 earlier in this chapter.) To create additional views or modify existing views, click a table name in the left pane and then click the view name. (If the view you want to modify doesn't appear, click Navigation Pane on the Home tab and then double-click the name of the form.) Figure 26-5 illustrates your next steps.

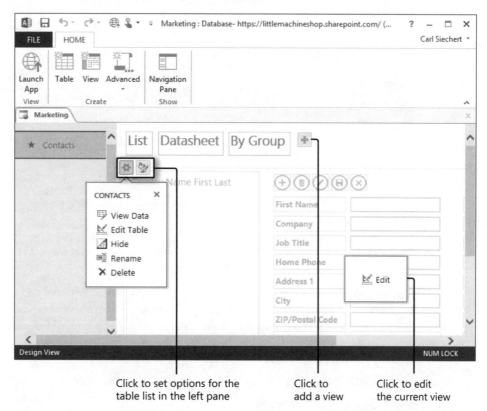

Click to set options for the   Click to   Click to edit
table list in the left pane   add a view   the current view

Figure 26-5 Change the layout of a view by clicking Edit and then dragging items.

When you open a view for editing, you can drag items to move them. Tools on the Design tab under View let you add other items (including fields from any table in the database) and format items in the view. Other icons let you set custom actions for the view.

Adding data

When you create an app and then add and modify its tables, views, queries, and macros, you work in the Access 2013 desktop program. But when it comes time to populate your app with data, you open it in a browser. (One exception: if you create a table from an existing data source—one of the options shown earlier in Figure 26-4—that process brings in all the data from the data source. Data sources can include Excel worksheets, Access databases, delimited text files, and ODBC data sources.) To open the app in a browser, on the Home tab or on the Quick Access Toolbar, click Launch App.

To add a record, click a table name, click a view, and then click Add (the circled plus sign icon). To add multiple records, click a blank record in Datasheet view and then paste data copied from a spreadsheet or other data source. See Figure 26-6.

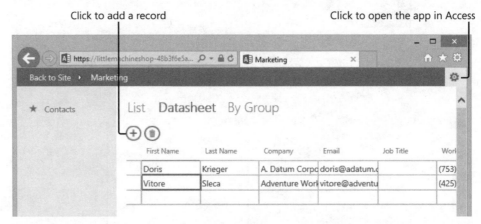

Figure 26-6 Datasheet view shows data in tabular form, which makes it easy to enter multiple records.

Running an app in a browser is the normal operational mode. Whether adding or deleting records, searching for data, or running queries, you (and others who have access to the stored app) do it in the browser. To make changes to the app itself (rather than its data), return to Access 2013. You do that by clicking the gear icon in the upper-right corner and clicking Customize In Access.

Using desktop databases

If you've used any previous version of Access, you've probably used what is now called a *desktop database* (to differentiate the other database type in Access 2013, the app). A desktop database doesn't necessarily reside on your local hard drive. Rather, the term refers to a database in Access database format (.accdb file) or the older .mdb format, which also can be stored in a shared network location.

Compared to Access web apps, desktop databases enable more powerful query options, more flexibility in forms and reports, and the ability to link data to external sources.

To create a desktop database, on the New pane in Backstage view look for a template that includes the word *desktop* in its name. Click it, provide a file name (and, optionally, change the location for the file), and then click Create. Figure 26-7 shows a database created with the Desktop Issue Tracking template.

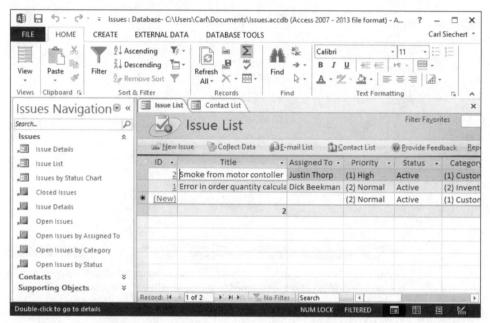

Figure 26-7 The Navigation pane on the left can be set up as a menu of forms and queries.

Adding a table

To add a table, click the Create tab and click Table. You then add fields by clicking Click To Add. As shown in Figure 26-8, this opens a menu of data types. You can rename a field by double-clicking its name at the top of the column. The Properties, Formatting, and Field Validation groups on the Fields tab under Table Tools allow you to control the values and appearance of data in that field.

For more information about tables, including creating table relationships, setting table properties, more details about adding fields, and setting field properties, see "Introduction to tables" on the Office website at *w7io.com/32601*.

More Fields

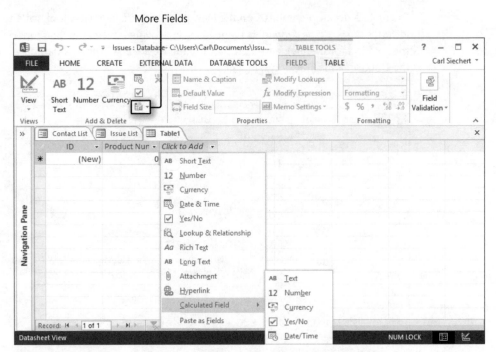

Figure 26-8 You can also add fields by clicking tools in the Add & Delete group. The More Fields button offers many more field types than the list shown here under Click To Add.

Adding data

You can add data to a table in several ways. For adding individual records, you can work with forms designed for data entry. You can type directly into a table in Datasheet view. You can copy data from other programs such as Word documents (this works best if the data is in a table in Word) or an Excel worksheet; switch the table to Datasheet view and then paste.

Using tools on the External Data tab, shown in Figure 26-9, you can import data from other data sources or you can link to the data. When you import the data into Access, the information is copied into Access tables, and no connection to the original data source is maintained. With a link, Access uses the information in its original location.

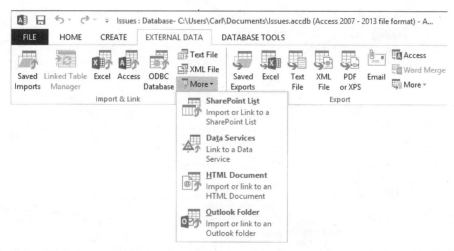

Figure 26-9 Access can import from and link to data sources shown on the External Data tab.

Two articles on the Office website provide additional details. See "Import data into an Access database" (*w7io.com/32602*) and "Link to SQL Server data" (*w7io.com/32603*).

Using queries

To this point we've talked primarily about getting information into a database. A query is one of the key methods for retrieving data that you need. The simplest type of query, a select query, is a tool for finding specific data by filtering on criteria you specify. Queries can also be used to make calculations or to summarize data. Other types of queries can add, change, or delete data—or even create a new table populated with query results.

Queries typically pull data from multiple tables, filter it to show only the information you want, and then display the results in a form or report. You can create a query by clicking tools in the Queries group on the Create tab. Clicking Query Design opens the query in Design view, as shown in Figure 26-10.

For more information, see "Introduction to queries" on the Office website at *w7io.com/32605*.

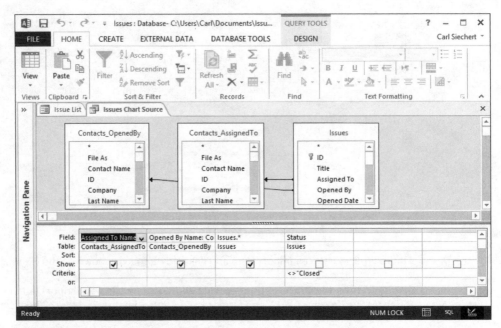

Figure 26-10 This query draws information from three tables. To see the code underlying the query, click SQL on the status bar.

Working with forms

An Access window, with a crowded ribbon, the Navigation pane filled with cryptic object names, and data in dense tabular form, can be overwhelming—and counterproductive. (It's certainly not the most egregious example, but Figure 26-7 earlier in this chapter gives a taste of this visual overload.) A form can present information in a much more useful way, making it easy to view, add, or edit data. More important, a form can retrieve data from multiple tables, display query results, and much more. Figure 26-11 shows an example of a form that shows details for a single issue.

You create a form using tools in the Forms group on the Create tab. You use Design view, shown in Figure 26-12, to lay out a form.

For more information, see "Create an Access form" on the Office website at *w7io.com/32604*.

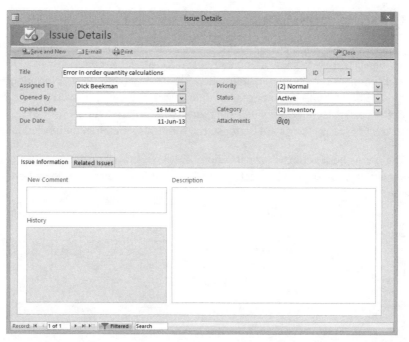

Figure 26-11 This simple form draws data from a Contacts table and an Issues table.

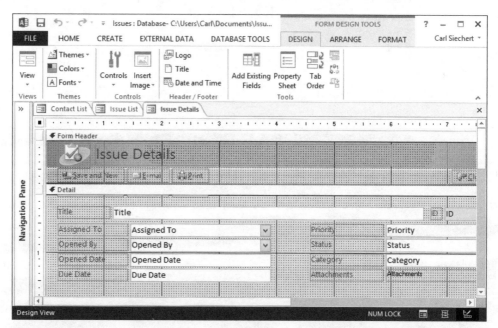

Figure 26-12 The same form shown in Figure 26-11 looks like this in Design view.

Creating reports

Reports provide another way to present information in an Access database. Whereas forms are typically used to show a single item, reports are more commonly used to sort, group, and summarize multiple data items. Reports are often designed for printing, which can provide an archival snapshot of your data as well as serving other reporting needs. Because of the flexible layout capabilities of reports, you can use a report for tasks such as printing labels. But many reports are better suited for display and aren't intended for printing at all.

The phone book report shown in Figure 26-13 works well on-screen—where the names serve as hyperlinks to a Contact Details form with more information—or on paper.

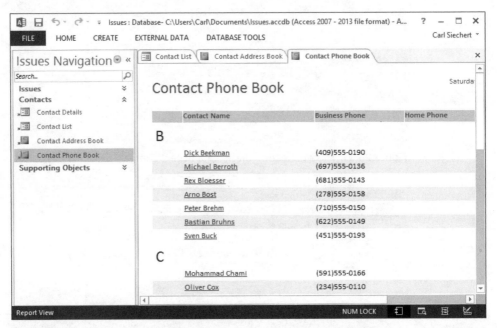

Figure 26-13 This attractively formatted report sorts contacts by name and groups them by the first letter.

For more information, see "Introduction to reports in Access" on the Office website at *w7io.com/32606*.

Automating with macros and modules

The real power of Access is realized by automating the use of all the objects we've mentioned—tables, queries, forms, and reports—through the use of macros and modules. Programming Access quickly enters the realm of software developers. At the risk of scaring you off altogether, we offer a glimpse of the macros in the Issues Tracking database. (See Figure 26-14).

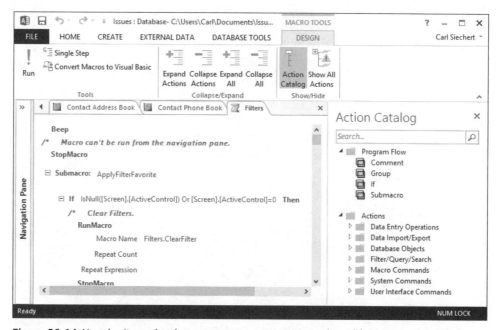

Figure 26-14 You don't need to be a programmer to create and modify macros—but it helps.

After you master macros, you can take the next step toward becoming a programming guru: convert them to Visual Basic. Modules use the Visual Basic for Applications (VBA) programming language, and Access includes an integrated development environment for working with VBA code. All that is beyond the scope of this book, of course, so we leave you with links to more information on the Office website.

Have we piqued your interest? Check out "Create a macro that runs when you open a database" (*w7io.com/32607*) and "Add data macros in a desktop database" (*w7io.com/32608*).

Index of troubleshooting topics

Index

Symbols and numbers

$ (dollar sign), 393, 475
2-D effects in charts, 445
2-D line charts (Excel), 442
3-D effects in charts, 441, 443, 445
32-bit editions, 27, 38
64-bit editions, 27, 38
& (ampersand), 374, 377, 469
' (apostrophe), 396, 422
* (asterisk), 371, 377
@ (at sign), 476
\ (backslash), 476
^ (caret), 233, 371, 377
: (colon), 361, 365, 375, 565
= (equal sign), 373, 377, 565
/ (forward slash), 371, 377
>= (greater than or equal to sign), 373, 377
> (greater than sign), 373, 377, 565
<= (less than or equal to sign), 373, 377
< (less than sign), 373, 377, 565
– (minus sign), 371, 377, 565
<> (not equal to sign), 373, 377
% (percent sign), 371, 377
+ (plus sign), 371, 377
" (quotation marks), 385, 475, 745
; (semicolon), 365
_ (underscore), 476

A

absolute cell references, 363, 375–377
.accdb file extension, 360
.accde file extension, 360
Accept button (Review tab), 307
accepting revisions, 680
Access
    about, 20, 787, 823–825
    database basics, 826–828
    subscription edition, 9
    templates supported, 824
    troubleshooting, 830
Accessibility Checker, 314

Access Options dialog box, 6–7
Access web apps
    about, 824, 828
    adding data, 831–832
    adding tables, 830
    creating, 826, 829
    creating views, 831
    customizing views, 831
    modifying, 826
Accounting format, 393
Account option (Backstage view)
    about, 54
    activating Office installation, 36–37
    Add A Service menu, 187
    Office Background option, 47
    signing in to Office, 183
    User Information heading, 187
    viewing account details, 185–187
accounts. *See* Microsoft accounts
Account Settings dialog box
    Address Books tab, 549
    Data Files tab, 519
    keeping local copies setting, 515
    New option, 512
ACOSH worksheet function, 387
ACOS worksheet function, 387
action buttons, 692–695
actions
    Quick Step, 552–554
    rule-based, 557–560
Action Settings dialog box, 693–695
Activate dialog box, 403
activating Office
    process overview, 36–38
    subscription plans, 23–24
    trial editions, 36–37
    volume-license editions, 38
ActiveX controls, 172, 174
Add Account dialog box, 510, 512–513
Add A Digital Signature command, 316
Add A Service menu
    Images & Videos submenu, 187
    Sharing submenu, 187

About the authors

Ed Bott is an award-winning author and technology journalist who has been researching and writing about technology, in print and on the Internet, for more than two decades, with no intention of stopping anytime soon. He has written more than 25 books, all on Windows and Office. His books have been translated into dozens of languages and distributed worldwide. You can read Ed's latest opinions and hands-on advice at The Ed Bott Report on ZDNet (*www.zdnet.com/blog/bott*) and on his personal site at *edbott.com*. Ed and his wife, Judy, live in northern New Mexico, with a pair of very lucky pets, Mackie and Lucy, who were adopted with the help of English Springer Rescue America (*springerrescue.org*). They and their much-missed feline friend Katy make cameo appearances in this book.

Carl Siechert began his writing career at age eight as editor of the *Mesita Road News*, a neighborhood newsletter that reached a peak worldwide circulation of 43 during its eight-year run. Following several years as an estimator and production manager in a commercial printing business, Carl returned to writing with the formation of Siechert & Wood Professional Documentation, a Pasadena, California, firm that specializes in writing and producing product documentation for the personal computer industry. Carl is a coauthor of more than 20 books, covering operating systems from MS-DOS 3.0 to Windows 7 and productivity applications from Microsoft Works 3 to Office 2013. In a convergence of new and old technology, Carl's company now operates a popular website for hobby machinists, *littlemachineshop.com*. Carl hiked the Pacific Crest Trail from Mexico to Canada in 1977 and would rather be hiking right now. He and his wife, Jan, live in Southern California.

Microsoft

How To Download Your eBook

To download your eBook, go to

http://aka.ms/PressEbook

and follow the instructions.

Please note: You will be asked to create a free online account and enter the access code below.

Your access code:

LZZMJZN

Microsoft Office Inside Out: 2013 Edition

Your PDF eBook allows you to:

- Search the full text
- Print
- Copy and paste

Best yet, you will be notified about free updates to your eBook.

If you ever lose your eBook file, you can download it again just by logging in to your account.

Need help? Please contact:
msinput@microsoft.com